Springer Proceedings in Business and Economics

Springer Proceedings in Business and Economics brings the most current research presented at conferences and workshops to a global readership. The series features volumes (in electronic and print formats) of selected contributions from conferences in all areas of economics, business, management, and finance. In addition to an overall evaluation by the publisher of the topical interest, scientific quality, and timeliness of each volume, each contribution is refereed to standards comparable to those of leading journals, resulting in authoritative contributions to the respective fields. Springer's production and distribution infrastructure ensures rapid publication and wide circulation of the latest developments in the most compelling and promising areas of research today.

The editorial development of volumes may be managed using Springer Nature's innovative EquinOCS, a proven online conference proceedings submission, management and review system. This system is designed to ensure an efficient timeline for your publication, making Springer Proceedings in Business and Economics the premier series to publish your workshop or conference volume.

This book series is indexed in SCOPUS.

Paula von Wachenfeldt • Lorenzo Cantoni
Nadzeya Sabatini • Teresa Sádaba
Editors

Fashion Communication in the Digital Age

Proceedings of the FACTUM 25 Conference, Stockholm, Sweden, 2025

Springer

Editors
Paula von Wachenfeldt
Fashion Studies, Department of Media Studies
Stockholm University
Stockholm, Sweden

Lorenzo Cantoni
Institute of Digital Technologies for Communication
USI – Università della Svizzera italiana
Lugano, Switzerland

Nadzeya Sabatini
Gdansk University of Technology and USI – Università della Svizzera italiana
Lugano, Switzerland

Teresa Sádaba
ISEM Universidad de Navarra
Madrid, Spain

ISSN 2198-7246 ISSN 2198-7254 (electronic)
Springer Proceedings in Business and Economics
ISBN 978-3-031-99480-7 ISBN 978-3-031-99481-4 (eBook)
https://doi.org/10.1007/978-3-031-99481-4

This work was supported by Stockholm University.

This Springer imprint is published by the registered company Springer Nature Switzerland AG
The registered company address is: Gewerbestrasse 11, 6330 Cham, Switzerland

Preface

We are very happy to see the FACTUM Conference "Fashion communication: Between tradition and future digital developments" reaching its fourth edition.

Back in 2019, when the FACTUM Conference series was started in Ascona (Switzerland), it was just a trial, to explore the relevance *for* and interest *by* the academic community in the Fashion communication domain; we can now declare very confidently that it has been a quite successful bet!

FACTUM has become a reference point in its field, and the three volumes published so far have collected a major attention. If we just consider the latest one, published in open access in August 2023, it has been accessed, as of March 2025, more than 335 thousand times…

Since its very beginning, FACTUM aimed at promoting theoretical and empirical interdisciplinary work on how various communication practices impact both the fashion industry and societal fashion-related practices and values. In particular, it aims at:

- establishing and consolidating an international and interdisciplinary network of scholars in the field of fashion communication;
- sharing methodological approaches;
- expanding the dialogue between communications studies and fashion-related disciplines;
- encouraging junior researchers to pursue their scientific interests in the field.

This volume demonstrates very well that we have *walked the talk*, offering a very broad smorgasbord of research, gathering studies by researchers from all over the world at different stages of their career and tackling fashion communication from a number of different perspectives.

This volume includes 22 full papers and 10 research notes. Full papers have been further clustered according to four main thematic sections:

- Heritage and archiving;
- Communication strategy;
- Digital Fashion, artificial intelligence and emerging technologies;

- Sustainability, social and political issues.

It is worth noticing the emergence of two streams: the (generative) Artificial Intelligence theme, which is covered extensively in the dedicated section and even beyond that; and the Heritage and archiving topic has attracted a growing attention.

In addition to full papers and research notes, emerging track and books presentations, as well as three keynote speakers enrich the program of FACTUM25:

- Patrizia Calefato, from Università degli studi di Bari Aldo Moro (Italy), on *Fashion and the Body in the Datafication Age*
- Sophie Kurkdjian, from the American University of Paris (France), on *Fashion and Geopolitics—A Question of Image and Communication*
- Jennie Rosén, from the Swedish Fashion Council (Sweden), on *Swedish Fashion Council and Fashion Transformation*

We would like to thank all contributors, as well as all reviewers, who have helped to ensure the high quality of this volume. We extend our gratitude also to Paulina Rydén, PhD candidate from Stockholm University, as well as Charlotte Stachel and Mirjam-Sarah Lepp, PhD candidates from USI—Università della Svizzera italiana for their invaluable support all throughout the organizational process

We hope that this Proceedings volume will contribute to a better and deeper understanding of Fashion Communication and to further advancements in this emerging and fascinating research field.

Your FACTUM25 Conference Chairs

Stockholm, Sweden — Paula von Wachenfeldt
Lugano, Switzerland — Lorenzo Cantoni
Lugano, Switzerland — Nadzeya Sabatini
Madrid, Spain — Teresa Sádaba

FACTUM25 Program Committee

- Romana Andò, Sapienza University of Rome, Italy
- Nathaniel Dafydd Beard, Kingston University, UK
- Francesca Bonetti, HEC Montreal, Canada
- Simonetta Buffo, Università Cattolica del Sacro Cuore, Italy
- Dorrit Bøilerehauge, Aarhus University, Denmark
- Alessia Grassi, University of Leeds, UK
- Olga Karamalak, National Research University Higher School of Economics, Russia
- Ethan Lascity, Southern Methodist University, USA
- Katharina Lobinger, Università della Svizzera italiana (USI), Switzerland
- Isabella Maggioni, ESCP Business School, France
- Veronica Neri, University of Pisa, Italy
- Tekila Harley Nobile, Università della Svizzera italiana (USI), Switzerland
- Alice Noris, University of Applied Sciences and Arts of Southern Switzerland (SUPSI), Switzerland
- Michela Ornati, University of Applied Sciences and Arts of Southern Switzerland (SUPSI), Switzerland
- Marco Pedroni, University of Ferrara, Italy
- Fanke Peng, University of South Australia, Australia
- Magdalena Petersson McIntyre, Lund University, Sweden
- Anna Picco-Schwendener, Università della Svizzera italiana (USI), Switzerland
- Cristina Sánchez Blanco, University of Navarra, Spain
- Katharina Sand, Università della Svizzera italiana (USI), Switzerland
- Simona Segre, University of Bologna, Italy
- Synne Skjulstad, Kristiania University College, Norway
- Satomi Sugiyama, Franklin University Switzerland, Switzerland
- Marta Torregrosa, University of Navarra, Spain
- Alessandro Tosi, University of Pisa, Italy
- Ana Uribe Sandoval, Erasmus University Rotterdam, Netherlands
- Cecilia Winterhalter, Accademia Costume e Moda Rome, Italy
- Julia Wolny, EADA Business School, Barcelona, Spain

Contents

Communication Strategy

Digital Fashion, Artificial Intelligence and Emerging Technologies

Sustainability, Social and Political Issues

Contributors

Gabriela Ambás Universidad Panamericana, Mexico City, Mexico

Dimple Bahl National Institute of Fashion Technology, New Delhi, India

Lavina Nimba Bhaskar National Institute of Fashion Technology, New Delhi, India

Ana C. Broega Minho University, Textile Engineering Department, Guimarães, Portugal

Daniela Calva-Cabrera Universidad Nacional de Loja, Loja, Ecuador

Isabella Campagnol Istituto Marangoni, Milano, Italy

Lorenzo Cantoni USI - Università della Svizzera italiana, Lugano, Switzerland

Carlos Checa ISEM Fashion Business School, Madrid, Spain

Catarina Costa Minho University, Textile Engineering Department, Guimarães, Portugal

Karen Cross Robert Gordon University, Aberdeen, Scotland, UK

Maria Ida De Ioanni Université Paris Nanterre, Nanterre, France

Filippo Maria Disperati Università degli Studi della Campania "Luigi Vanvitelli", Caserta, Italy

Sandra Bravo Durán Princeton University, Princeton, NJ, USA

Evgeniia Filippova Faculty of Creative Industries, National Research University Higher School of Economics, Moscow, Russia

Nicoletta Fornara USI – Università della Svizzera italiana, Lugano, Switzerland

Paula Gargoles Universidad Panamericana, Mexico City, Mexico

Universidad de Navarra, Pamplona, Spain

Sara Greco USI – Università della Svizzera italiana, Lugano, Switzerland

Isabel Garcia Hiljding UDIT Universidad, Madrid, Spain

Olga Karamalak HSE University, Moscow, Russia

Myles Ethan Lascity Southern Methodist University, Dallas, TX, USA

Pietro Lattao USI - Università della Svizzera italiana, Lugano, Switzerland

Marie Ledendal Lund University, Helsingborg, Sweden

YeSeung Lee University of Westminster, Harrow, UK

Tatiana León-Alberca Universidad Nacional de Educación, Cañar, Ecuador

Mirjam-Sarah Lepp Università della Svizzera italiana, Lugano, Switzerland

Vittorio Linfante Alma Mater Studiorum - Università di Bologna, Bologna, Italy

Alejandra Valerio Matos Instituto Tecnológico Santo Domingo, Santo Domingo, Dominican Republic

Magdalena Petersson McIntyre Section for Fashion Studies, Lund University, Lund, Sweden

T. Muhammed Ashraf National Institute of Fashion Technology, Kannur, India

Aoife Murray Central Saint Martins, London, UK

Haze Ng The Hong Kong Polytechnic University, Hung Hom, Kowloon, Hong Kong

Laura Mejía Ocampo Universidad de Bogotá, Bogotá, Colombia

Rafael Almeida de Oliveira Università degli Studi di Napoli Federico II, Napoli, Italy

Michela Ornati University of Applied Sciences and Arts of Southern Switzerland – SUPSI, Manno, Switzerland

USI – Università della Svizzera italiana, Lugano, Switzerland

Hsin-Pey Peng Department of Mass Communication, Open University of Kaohsiung, Kaohsiung City, Taiwan (R.O.C.)

Jorge del Río Pérez School of Communication, Universidad de Navarra, Pamplona, Spain

Greta Rizzi Politecnico di Milano, Milan, Italy

Angela Dotor Robayo Universidad de Bogotá, Bogotá, Colombia

Nadzeya Sabatini USI – Università della Svizzera italiana, Lugano, Switzerland

Gdańsk University of Technology, Gdańsk, Poland

Paulo Salgado Minho University, Department of Communication Sciences, Braga, Portugal

Cristina Sánchez-Blanco School of Communication-University of Navarra, Pamplona, Spain

Katharina Sand Parsons Paris, Paris, France

Patricia SanMiguel School of Communication-University of Navarra, Pamplona, Spain

Tatiana Sokolova Faculty of Creative Industries, National Research University Higher School of Economics, Moscow, Russia

Charlotte Stachel USI – Università della Svizzera italiana, Lugano, Switzerland

Josie Steed Robert Gordon University, Aberdeen, Scotland, UK

Tyla Stevenson Massey University, Wellington, New Zealand

Marta Torregrosa School of Communication-University of Navarra, Pamplona, Spain

Angel Torres-Toukoumidis Universidad Politécnica Salesiana, Cuenca, Ecuador

Angelica Vandi Politecnico di Milano, Milan, MI, Italy

Espejo Mendez Maria Veronica USI – Università della Svizzera italiana, Lugano, Switzerland

Ksenia Vertlib HSE University, Moscow, Russia

Elisa Zanola USI – Università della Svizzera italiana, Lugano, Switzerland

Qingyi Zhang The Hong Kong Polytechnic University, Hung Hom, Kowloon, Hong Kong

Dai Zhu USI – Università della Svizzera italiana, Lugano, Switzerland

Heritage and Archiving

Following the Trace in Fashion: From Zhivago Look to Slavic Core

Olga Karamalak and Ksenia Vertlib

Abstract Fashion is closely interconnected with traditional and digital media and the latter is widely known for setting and dissemination trends and making them viral. For example, TikTok set a trend for fur which climaxed in the winter 2023 and will probably stay in fashion longer with posts hashtagged #slaviccore, #slavicgirl, #slavicgirlcore, #slavicbimbo, or #slavicbimbogirl, where women promote the style of being dressed in furs. This cultural trend referring to Slavic people and the nostalgia for the 1990s and early 2000s is worth studying and discussing from semiotic and historical perspectives. An earlier boost in the popularity of fur in the West, initiated by the media, can be witnessed with the US release of *Doctor Zhivago* in 1965. The hashtag #zhivagolook is still circulating on Instagram. This article describes these two cases and interprets them referring to Derrida's concept of "trace" and Schoenberg's concept of "developing variation" based on visual content analysis. We conclude that the current trend can be considered as a fashion reiteration with a recognizable trace, which is varied and thematically regenerated.

Keywords Slavic core · Slavic bimbo · Zhivago look · Trace by Derrida · Index by Pierce · Fur · TikTok · Instagram · Fashion · Media

1 Introduction

Fashion is interconnected with both traditional and digital media: it gets inspiration from the media, for example from visual aspects of cinematography, songs, digital social media in general, and fashion influencers, in particular; conversely, fashion trends are embodied in the media: fashion films, awards ceremonies, fashion magazines, digital social media, etc. Instagram and TikTok have enormous visual potency

O. Karamalak (✉) · K. Vertlib
HSE University, Moscow, Russia
e-mail: okaramalak@hse.ru; kvertlib@hse.ru

P. von Wachenfeldt et al. (eds.), *Fashion Communication in the Digital Age*, Springer Proceedings in Business and Economics,
https://doi.org/10.1007/978-3-031-99481-4_1

in disseminating fashion images which is facilitated and enhanced by hashtags with a number of affordances for spreading digital fashion content (making the post visible, searchable, retrievable, referencing itself, allowing for creating communities, promoting interactions, etc.) [1–3].

Verbally a hashtag should be attractive, memorable, and create viral opportunities. Such digital potency in fashion appears to be the suffix "core," which has substituted the notion of trend or style and can be referred to some fashion aesthetics, for example, Barbiecore inspired by Barbie Doll, normcore meaning casual clothing not to stand out or minimalism, Kidcore—nostalgic fashion of the 90s and others [4]. All these digital fashion trends present fashion aesthetics based on visual categorization and emotional engagement. The term "aesthetics" describes an online community on digital social platforms with preserved visual coherence. López (2023) also argues that millennials, who were born between 1982 and 1994, and Generation Z, who were born between 1995 and 2010, are attracted by nostalgia for the past due to social instability and the uncertainty of the future [5].

It proves the claim by Crepax and Liu (2024) about the considerable affectionate and emotional part of fashion, where aesthetics, including nostalgic aesthetics, are attractive while communicating with possible consumers [6].

Slavic core is one of these digital fashion trends designed to influence online followers emotionally on the visual and sound levels, posting women dressed in slavic outwear, mostly fur coats and hats referring to the 1990s when Russia experienced a boom in fur consumption. The previous western trend for furs initiated by the traditional media was after the release of the film "Doctor Zhivago" in 1965. Nowadays both "Zhivago look" and "Slavic core" or "Slavic bimbo" tags with images can be found on Instagram, TikTok, and other digital visual platforms.

This paper compares these two cases of global media-inspired popularity for fur on the basis of visual content analysis describing people/actors (1), clothes (2), and context surrounding objects (3) with a sampling of 100 video reels and images on TikTok and Instagram retrieved by tags "Slavic core," "Slavic bimbo," "Slavic girl," and 30 images on Instagram retrieved by tags "Zhivago look," "Dr. Zhivago look."

2 Literature Review

Fashion is a multifaceted phenomenon, which serves as a medium which can communicate societal and cultural values influencing consumer behavior and perceptions.

According to Lehnert [7], fashion as a cultural practice allows us to trace symbolic interactions between people and fashion artifacts. Fashion is connected to culture and aesthetic preferences. It is a cultural semiotic system in its broad sense. It can be "read" or interpreted, however, it is not constrained to interpretation only. Fashion practices give free space to construct different meanings like in Pierce's (1958) multiple interpretations [8] or Barthes' (1968) creative semiosis [9]. Lehnert states that fashion is a dynamic process that constantly reproduces itself and not only reflects cultures but mostly promotes them. This dynamic process of fashion is materialized in artifacts and manifests itself in cultural practices [7].

Traditionally, fashion and communication are closely intertwined as, firstly, fashion in its essence has great communicative capacity and, secondly, it is dictated by advertising and marketing as consumers should recognize brands and be informed about current trends [8].

Fashion and cinema coexist and develop together since clothing plays a significant role in character descriptions and personality portrayals in films. Fashion houses contribute with designing clothes and creating unique fashion storytelling, akin to cult films. Examples include Givenchy's little black dress tailor-made for Odry Hepbern in *Breakfast at Tiffany's* or Giorgio Armani's clothing for Richard Gere in *American Gigolo*. Today's fashion films are enhancing the potency of fashion imagery and creating new brand experiences for online shoppers. They do this by combining modern Internet logic with traditional cinematographic language to create new worlds for fashion businesses [10, [11]. Fashion films shift the focus from viewers as buyers and make them an audience [12], implying the aesthetic nature of cinematography in contrast to fashion commercials and online videos in social media.

In the new digital environment, fashion and social media such as Instagram, Twitter, Facebook, and TikTok have become closely interconnected. Fashion trends are communicated directly to people by the means of short videos or posts and get an immediate response from the audience. In this respect, not only are wider audiences aware of new trends, but users can also provide instant feedback and collaborate with influencers. Thus, social media have democratized communication as users can now participate in fashion discourse on a different level. Another distinctive feature of social media in creating trends is the ability to spread and evolve brands quickly and efficiently by the virtue of hashtags, challenges, and viral movements [13]. Similarly, digital social media are gaining popularity due to their accessibility and immediacy, which means that users can get acquainted with the latest trends, styles, and fashion inspirations with a click [14].

TikTok is a digital platform popular mainly with young users, in particular, the representatives of Gen Z and teenagers [15]. TikTok is effective for quick trend creation and their further dissemination, making them viral through short entertaining videos which are liked, shared, and commented on. Trends can be taken up by a large number of users and become viral due to an influencer or a celebrity posting an outfit or fashion style, attracting the attention of millions of users.

Instagram is an image-sharing service which is aimed at instant communication of trends and visual information [16], providing a rapid diffusion of trends. According to Ha et al. (2017), Instagram has reshaped the fashion industry through the hashtag function and consumer-generated content [17]. On this platform fashion trends and values are communicated to people through the posts of fashion bloggers and influencers. Luxury items are sold as lifestyles on Instagram, meaning that the digital platform is utilized by luxury brands to spread the ideas of exclusivity and a wealthy lifestyle [18]. The internet has become a complex tool for "meta-mediation," where people create imaginary worlds which they identify themselves with. Proliferation of closed imaginaries leads to new trends appearing [19, p. 75].

3 Methodology

The research is qualitative in its nature. Its objectives are to describe the trend for fur and aesthetics such as "Zhivago look" and "Slavic core." First, general data about these two aesthetics are gathered with a brief historical overview. Then, sampling is performed: images with the tag of "Slavic core," "Slavic bimbo," "Slavic girl" and "Zhivago look" or "Dr. Zhivago look" are randomly gathered from two platforms, Instagram and TikTok (total 130 images), where people are dressed in fur. The dates for sampling are the following: Dr. Zhivago aesthetic: April 2014–December 2022 and Slavic core aesthetic: November 2023–December 2024. Countries of posts are specified where possible to see the general spread of the trends. Third, subject matter, according to Barrett [20], or visual elements such as people, clothes, and context surrounding objects are described. The analysis discusses how these elements contribute to the general stylistics, the meaning of the expressed aesthetics, and what values are incorporated into them. Identifying and characterizing people, things, locations, or events in an image is a helpful first step in descriptive analysis [21]. By analyzing images and speculating on nonverbal messages different aesthetic values can be outlined and the connection between the trends can be traced. Formal analysis techniques are used: compare and contrast, and interpretation. The semiotic theory of Derrida's trace and Schoenberg's concept of "developing variation" are discussed with regard to these two aesthetics. This content interpretive analysis contributes to research of aesthetics.

4 Results

4.1 The "Zhivago Look" Aesthetic

According to Devan (2018), the term "Zhivago look" first appeared after the premiere of the American movie "Doctor Zhivago" in December 1965 [22]. Based on Boris Pasternak's book, this David Lean-directed movie featured elaborate costumes by Phyllis Dalton [23]. Fashion trends at the time were swiftly impacted by the looks portrayed in the movie, which were distinguished by fur-trimmed coats and hats.

Christian Dior designer Marc Bohan was inspired by the movie and used it in his autumn 1966 collection, which included features reminiscent of the characters' clothing [24]. Later, Yves Saint Laurent in 1976 created an autumn–winter haute couture collection "Opéra—Les Ballets Russes" inspired by the "Zhivago look" and

Russian winter fur outwear [25, 26]. The "Zhivago look" became popular as a result of this influence and can still be found on Instagram with reference to the main actors such as Julie Christie, Omar Sheriff, and Geraldine Chaplin. The "Zhivago look" emerged as a major fashion icon in the late 1960s and beyond, impacting numerous designers and continuing to be discussed decades later.

Julie Christie, who plays Lara, wears a dark fur beret which has become synonymous with the "Zhivago look" and shows practical elegance and femininity. Tonya's white and pink fur outfits emphasize luxury and femininity. The fur-trimmed collars and oversized coats reflected the fashion of that time and served as a cornerstone for the fashion history.

Instagram "Zhivago look" images are personal photos of mostly American or British women, rarely men and children. Sometimes pictures of pets wrapped up in faux fur were posted with the hashtag #Zhivagolook. The prototypical element of all the pictures is a fur hat, sometimes fur-trimmed coats or jackets can be observed.

4.2 The "Slavic Core" Aesthetic

Although the Slavic girls' fashion was initially noticed by TikTokers in 2021, the trend took a fresh turn and climaxed in the winter 2023 with the boost of videos with the hashtags #slaviccore, #slavicgirl, #slavicbimbo, and #russianbimbo to Katya Lel's 1990s track "My Marmeladny." The song has onomatopoeic sounds "mwah-mwah" imitating kisses, and "uh-uh" and "dzhaga-dzaga" imitating sex. This sexually implied content in the song could have triggered sensual stimulus and aroused pleasurable responses in people's senses, which contributed to its virality (the third place on Spotify). This digital social trend, which started outside Russia, triggered fur fashion trend dissemination of faux fur in Russia in physical stores by different fast fashion brands, for instance Love Republic, Lime, Sela, and Oodji, which is evidence of the direct influence of digital social media on purchasing demand.

It should be noted that although "Slavic" refers to all Eastern European countries, Russia is a representative of this trend due to climatic conditions, where wearing fur is in most cases first regarded as a necessity, then gives aesthetic pleasure to the look.

Fashion of the 1990s due to the period of Glasnost and Perestroika changed previous Soviet uniformity and scarcity for capitalist creativity, bright-colored leggings, short skirts, long boots, and fur clothes. Capitalist items dominated the mass market, while the Perestroika creative class opposed both socialism and capitalist homogeneities, as evidenced by haphazard and disorderly flea-market findings [27].

In the 1990s and 2000s, in Russia a fur coat or a fur hat could be referred to as an indispensable garment, it emphasized the high status of a successful lady. Buying a fur coat was considered to be an obligatory thing, though not everyone could afford it [28]. Different shopping tours were organized, for example to Greece or Turkey, to buy numerous fur items [29]. The government tried to control this to prevent massive resale and profiteering. Since not everyone could afford natural fur coats, a fur hat was a minimum [30], people were proud of them and wore them even inside.

Fur hats have many names in the Russian language, which linguistically and cognitively prove the importance of this accessory: either toponymic names like *sibirka* (Siberia—a famous cold region of Russia), *kubanka* (Kuban—part of Russia; kubanka or papakha, originally a headdress of the Kuban Cossacks, usually a black karakul hat [31, 32]. Another name for a fur hat is *boyarka*, named after a title "boyars"—a ruling elite of Eastern Europe, large landowners belonging to the upper stratum of the ruling class [33]; or a proper name, *Barbara* (after Barbara Brylska—a polish actress who wore this kind of hat in the film "The Irony of Fate" of 1975, which is traditionally shown on New Year's Eve).

The "Slavic core" aesthetic shows a beautiful and well-groomed woman who wants to stand out and look impeccable despite the hardships of the 1990s and turbulent events in our time [34]. The term "Slavic bimbo" could have different interpretations. "Bimbo" has changed its meaning: it originates from the Italian word bimbo, which means "a little (baby) boy" or "a young (male) child" (the feminine variant is bimba). This term, which was first used in the United States as early as 1919, was slang for a stupid guy. According to the Oxford English Dictionary, bimbo is often an attractive or glamorous young woman. Later chiefly: a young woman, who is regarded as sexually attractive, but unintelligent or frivolous (usually considered derogatory and offensive). However, nowadays it can have another meaning of looking beautiful but being intelligent at the same time. The idea itself has been reinterpreted by contemporary influencers, who assert that it is possible to be successful, intelligent, and attractive at the same time [35].

A fur coat and a large fur hat known as a *boyarka* are two important components of the attire of a "typical Slavic woman" of either vintage natural fur or modern faux fur. The images highlight high-heeled boots, short skirts, fancy bags, sunglasses bearing luxury brand logos, and extravagant gold jewelry that the women are wearing. Other objects include bouquets of flowers, guns, cigarettes, a bottle of champagne or vodka, caviar, Red Square as a background, snowy streets, snowy scenery with mountains, or some attributes of the 1990s such as a carpet on the wall—all prototypical features of a Slavic image. The gangster themes emphasize the 1990s. The images in the reels are staged to attract the attention of online users, to get a response—a comment or to encourage a similar video reel or image posting. The trend's aesthetic is influenced by the fashion of wealthy Eastern European women of the 1990s and 2000s. The movement #SlavicGirl is a contrast to the trend of "quiet luxury." Modern "Slavic bimbos" are dressed mostly in faux fur or vintage fur coats. The trend is associated with conscious consumption in fashion or sustainability both environmental and ethical. The make-up is bright and standing out, usually the cheeks are pinky blushed and women are wearing red lipstick, which was considered fashionable and sex appealing among slavic women.

The spread of "Slavic core" is obvious with Russia and Poland pioneering this trend. However, the results of the investigation on Instagram and TikTok have shown that this trend is ubiquitous and worldwide (See Fig. 1).

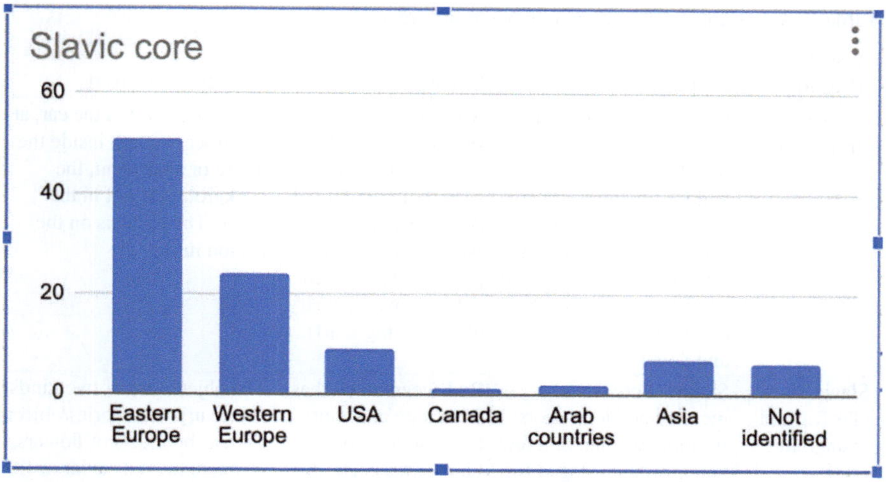

Fig. 1 Slavic core distribution

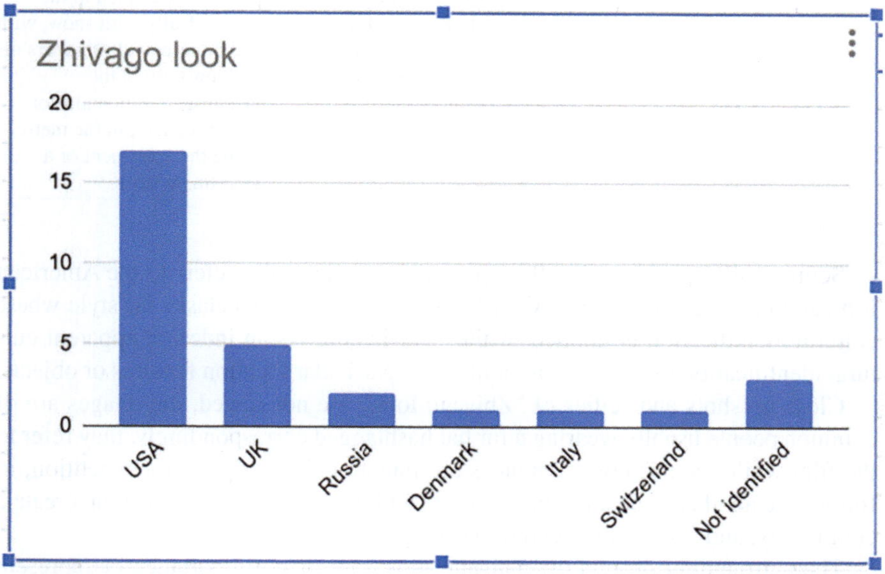

Fig. 2 Zhivago look distribution

Unlike "Slavic core," "Zhivago look" is less widespread and distributed primarily in the USA and UK, which is illustrated by the bar chart below (see Fig. 2). It can be explained by the fact that the movie "Doctor Zhivago," from which this term originates, was created 60 years ago and might be less popular now.

Below is the comparative table of two trends which describes people, clothes, and surrounding objects as a context (see Table 1).

Table 1 A descriptive subject matter table of two trends

Aesthetic (Platform)	People	Clothes	Objects as a context
Zhivago look (Instagram).	Close-up shots or selfies. Middle-aged women mostly from the USA and UK, pictures are not staged, from real life. Besides women there are pictures of a middle-aged American man, Russian children and pets (cats and dogs).	A fur hat is in each shot and it is in the center of attention as a symbol of the trend. A fur coat can be rarely observed, some accessories are used (bags, gloves, jewelry, glasses, a big scarf).	The images are in the car, at the grocery store, inside the house or apartment, the background is not in the focus. The focus is on the person in fur.
Slavic core (TikTok and Instagram).	Staged shots, mostly medium and long shots. A young woman or a few young women staged for reels or a picture (from different mostly east European countries).	Red accent in clothes. Both long and short faux fur coats or vintage fur coats. A scarf on the head or a fur hat, long high-heeled boots (white in most cases), short skirts, big sunglasses, jewelry, luxury bags, mittens, or gloves.	The objects are of two kinds: (1) luxury accessories/objects such as bouquets of flowers, champagne, red caviar or (2) reminiscence of the 1990s: a carpet on the wall, cigarettes or alcohol drinks and guns. The reels are taken in the street, ideally with snow, with Red Square or skyscrapers of Moscow City in the background, mountains or winter scenery, in the metro, inside the apartment or a department store.

Semiotically speaking, Dr. Zhivago aesthetic indexically refers to the American film, and in most cases to Julie Christie, in particular, with a classy fur style where cultural identification is implied, while "Slavic core" is an index of apparent cultural identification to Slavic community with particular location features or objects.

Close-up shots and selfies of "Zhivago look" are not staged, the images are of common people usually wearing a fur hat hashtagged correspondingly, they refer to the film while "Slavic core's" images are intentionally designed for repetition, to follow one another in posting these images with the desire to be in fashion, create a community, and spread this trend of wearing fur.

The surrounding objects of "Zhivago look" are of no importance or represent common everyday reality while in "Slavic core" aesthetic surrounding objects create different stylistics: low (criminal of the 1990s), high (luxury) and in both cases cultural (showing prototypical landmarks of Moscow, winter scenery, or other objects associated with Slavic culture).

5 Discussion

The survey reveals that fashion for fur can be referred to as a "long run secular trend spanning decades and centuries" [36, p. 116]. The two cases have shown that the trend for fur is inspired by traditional and digital social media.

The "Zhivago look" triggered by the 1965 Hollywood film "Dr Zhivago" can still be traced on Instagram. Despite being a western trend, it refers implicitly to a Russian identity showcasing this style of wearing fur garments, fur hats, in particular. A fur hat symbolizes this trend and serves as an index, according to Pierce's semiotic theory since there is a direct relationship between the trend "Zhivago look" and a fur hat which makes this style recognizable. Mostly worn by middle-aged American and European women, it has a lady-like feminine stylistics. This trend is disseminated on Instagram since the target audience is older than on TikTok, whose users are less familiar with the "Zhivago look."

"Slavic core" brought about mainly by TikTok is a reiteration of the previous trend with a different target audience, Zoomers, and different stylistics of the trend which is twofold. First, it shows low gangster-like stylistics of the 1990s. Modern generations are characterized by a nostalgic mood which explains the connection to the 1990s in reels. Second, it is stylistically high-luxury and chic "nouveau riche Russian." The latter is transmitted mainly on Instagram since this platform is directed to promoting luxury lifestyles or a "dream formula," an ideal image to strive for. According to Featherstone (2007), "consumer culture uses images, signs, and symbolic goods which summon up dreams, desires, and fantasies which suggest romantic authenticity and emotional fulfillment" [37, p. 56].

We consider "Slavic core" not as a totally new trend but as a thematically different trend for fur traced in the "Zhivago look," which maintains its main essence since similar fur items are worn with a similar design. According to Derrida's philosophical and literary deconstructionist concept, a trace is the correlation of the enigmatic relationship of outside and inside and the present to something else in the past that can be difficult to capture [38]. Trace in fashion, according to Gill (2016), can be interpreted as follows: behind the present design or a finished fashion product there are a lot of practices and concealed elements or background elements which influence the emergence of the garment [39, pp., 320, 321]. In fashion, the obvious value of the trace is the interpretive act of tracing elements of meaning, for example to establish and decode notions of conventional clothing design and use. Trace in the context of this research is an unseen interpretive element of the present phenomenon, such as "Slavic core," which can be constructed on the basis of past similar trends, not only of the 1990s but also earlier, such as the "Zhivago look." The cultural and identity background is the same—Slavic and/or Russian winter clothing style.

Moreover, from a semiotic perspective, Derrida argues that meaning is not fully present, it is constructed through relationships. Meanings of the fashion trends are not stable either. Fashion trends are open for reinterpretation and the meaning can shift: fashion for fur items inspired by the film is reinterpreted nowadays with different meanings where a Slavic bimbo can be, on the one hand, a frivolous and silly girl of the 1990s, or, on the other hand, a luxury and intelligent lady.

Schoenberg's concept of "developing variations" in music has a similar semiotic idea that everything created in the present is an altered past. He confirms constant transformations and the absence of fixed forms. Fashion is also known for developing variations based on past experiences: trend cycles and fashion reiteration [36, 40, 41]. In the case of "Slavic core," its connection to the past "Zhivago look" is not obvious or not seen directly, that is why we refer to it as a "trace."

In both trends there are several common values: a luxury seasonal style, Slavic identity, nostalgia, and sustainability. Fur garments add attraction, femininity, and luxury accent and refer to both winter weather conditions and Eastern European people's culture of wearing fur. Both trends are affective since they rely on nostalgic feelings of pleasure and recognition: "Slavic Core" refers to the 1990s while "Zhivago Look" refers to the film's characters. The use of faux fur or vintage fur proves the importance of fashion sustainability value.

6 Conclusion

The relationship between media and fashion plays a pivotal role in shaping trends, consumer behavior, and brand interactions. The survey describes the two trends "Zhivago look" and "Slavic core" originated from the media. It confirms their affective and nostalgic influence on consumers, reference to Slavic identity, and fashion sustainability proliferation. "Slavic core" points not only to the 1990s with the boom on fur but also some traces of "Zhivago look" can be followed. Semiotically, both trends act as indices since there is a connection between signifiers ("Zhivago look" and "Slavic core") and signified (fur garments). Slavic core is a reiteration of fur trends in fashion cycles with variable changes in design and different nostalgic references. It has become viral due to its visual attractiveness, nostalgia, affectionate part, and incorporation of luxury life.

This descriptive research contributes to better understanding of social media influence on fashion, exemplified with the "Slavic core" digital movement in fashion which has become viral among online users and consumers creating demand for fur.

References

1. Cantoni, L., Tardini, S., Inversini, A., & Marchiori, E. (2009). From paradigmatic to syntagmatic communities: A socio-semiotic approach to the evolution pattern of online travel communities. In W. Höpken, U. Gretzel, & R. Law (Eds.), *Information and communication technologies in tourism*. Springer. https://doi.org/10.1007/978-3-21193971-0_2
2. Karamalak, O., Kalbaska, N., & Cantoni, L. (2021). What do hashtags afford in digital fashion communication? An exploratory study on Gucci-related hashtags on Twitter and Instagram. *Semiotica, 243*(1), 325–351.

3. Karamalak, O., & Cantoni, L. (2021). Rallying hashtags as a tool for societal change in fashion. In T. Sádaba, N. Kalbaska, F. Cominelli, L. Cantoni, & M. Torregrosa Puig (Eds.), *Fashion communication. FACTUM 2021*. Springer. https://doi.org/10.1007/978-3-030-81321-5_18
4. Spellings, S. (2022). *Core is the new chic*. Vogue. Retrieved December 12, 2024, from https://www.vogue.com/article/core-fashion-explained
5. López, L. M. (2023). The Dark Academia aesthetic: Nostalgia for the past in social networks. *The International Journal of Creative Media Research, 10*. https://doi.org/10.33008/IJCMR.2023.08
6. Crepax, R., & Liu, M. (2024). Affective fashion trends: Aesthetic and digital affects from nostalgia to AR. *Fashion Theory*, 1–27. https://doi.org/10.1080/1362704X.2024.2389595
7. Lehnert, G. (2013). *Mode: Theorie, Geschichte und Ästhetik einer kulturellen Praxis*. Degruyter. https://doi.org/10.1515/transcript.9783839421956
8. Peirce, C. S. (1958). In A. Burks (Ed.), *The collected papers* (Vol. 7 & 8). Harvard University Press.
9. Barthes, R. (1968). *Elements of semiology*. Hill and Wang.
10. Kalbaska, N., Sádaba, T., & Cantoni, L. (2018). Fashion communication: Between tradition and digital transformation. *Studies in Communication Sciences, 18*(2), 269–285. https://doi.org/10.24434/j.scoms.2018.02.005
11. Buffo, S. (2017). Brand narration and fashion films. *Journalism and Mass Communication, 7*(6), 292–304.
12. Khan, N. (2012). Cutting the fashion body: Why the fashion image is no longer still. *Fashion Theory, 16*(2), 235–249.
13. Boero, M. (2023, November). Sociosemiotics of fashion: Theory, trends, and communication tools. In *5th international conference on language, linguistics, and literature (COLALITE 2023)* (pp. 4–17). Atlantis Press.
14. Kaur, B. (2023). Influence of social media on fashion trends. *Dogo Rangsang Research Journal UGC Care Group I Journal, 13*(6), 43–47.
15. Su, Y., Baker, B. J., Doyle, J. P., & Yan, M. (2020). Fan engagement in 15 seconds: Athletes' relationship marketing during a pandemic via TikTok. *International Journal of Sport Communication, 13*(3), 436–446.
16. Ferrara, E., Interdonato, R., & Tagarelli, A. (2014, September). Online popularity and topical interests through the lens of Instagram. In *Proceedings of the 25th ACM conference on hypertext and social media* (pp. 24–34).
17. Ha, Y. I., Kwon, S., Cha, M., & Joo, J. (2017, May). Fashion conversation data on Instagram. In *Proceedings of the international AAAI conference on web and social media* (Vol. 11, No. 1, pp. 418–427).
18. Khan, S. W., & Raza, S. (2024). Luxury brands and social media: Drivers and outcomes of consumer engagement on Instagram. *IRAPA International Journal of Business Studies, 1*(1), 01–17.
19. Neri, V. (2019). Imaginaries, fashion and the Internet. Towards a new ethics paradigm. In N. Kalbaska, T. Sádaba, F. Cominelli, & L. Cantoni (Eds.), *Fashion communication. FACTUM 2019* (pp. 66–78). Springer.
20. Barrett, T. (2005). *Criticizing photographs: An introduction to understanding images*. McGraw-Hill.
21. Schroeder, J. E. (2006). Critical visual analysis. In *Handbook of qualitative research methods in marketing*. Edward Elgar Publishing.
22. Devan. (2018, January 9). 1965's Doctor Zhivago's impact on fashion. The Courtauld. Documenting Fashion. A Dress History Blog. https://sites.courtauld.ac.uk/documentingfashion/2018/01/09/5186/
23. Leese, E. (1991). *Costume design in the movies: An illustrated guide to the work of 157 great designers*. Courier Corporation.
24. Butchart, A. (2016). *The fashion of film: How cinema has inspired fashion*. Hachette UK.
25. Martin, R. H., & Koda, H. (1995). *Haute Couture: [exhibition held at] The Metropolitan Museum of Art, New York, [December 7, 1995-March 24, 1996]*. Metropolitan Museum of Art.

26. Rees-Roberts, N. (2016). All about Yves: Saint Laurent and the Warhol effect. *Journal of European Popular Culture, 7*(2), 143–162.
27. Bartlett, D. (2022). Objects, people, politics: From perestroika to the post-Soviet era. *Fashion Theory, 26*(4), 525–544. https://doi.org/10.1080/1362704X.2022.2055918
28. Vainshtein, O. (2000). Fashioning women: The dressmaker as cultural producer in Soviet Russia. *Para-sites: A Casebook Against Cynical Reason, 7*, 195.
29. Grigorakis, A. (2019). From open markets to Russian products stores to "big business": Economics and ethics. In *Pontic Greek communities of Thessaloniki after the Soviet experience*.
30. Worster, M., Lawrence, S., & Lugg, S. (1986). Weather, war and furry hats: School pupils' perceptions of the USSR. *Teaching Geography, 11*(4), 152–154.
31. Haga, L. P. (2016). Coming to terms with Europe: Konstantin Simonov and Oles' Honchar's literary conquest of East Central Europe at the end of World War II. *Socialist Internationalism in the Cold War: Exploring the Second World*, 19–48.
32. Zakharova, O. (2020). Diplomatic counterculture as a tool of the Soviet Foreign Policy. *Krakowskie Studia Małopolskie, 3*, 7–21.
33. Crummey, R. O. (2014). *Aristocrats and servitors: The boyar elite in Russia, 1613–1689* (Vol. 866). Princeton University Press.
34. Negoda, V. (2023, December 7). Osoznannost', Katja Lel' i shuby — otkuda vzjalsja slavic core i pro chto on [Conscious Consumption, Katja Lel' and fur coats - Where Slavic core comes from and what it means]. Momenty [Moments]. Retrieved December 10, 2024, from https://momenty.org/style/23730
35. Zhernakova, V. (2024, January 17). DG Home Lifestyle. Slavic Bimbo core: pochemu ves' internet pomeshalsja na stile slavjanok (i prichem tut Katja Lel'). [Slavic Bimbo core: why is the Internet mad on Slavic style?]. Retrieved December 10, 2024, from https://dg-home.ru/life/slavic-bimbo-core_b1139925/?srsltid=AfmBOoo8l29WrrA5qXxgCcfAH90bL-hLY3m2PM_LIkMYbOQYEuny04gh
36. Sproles, G. B. (1981). Analyzing fashion life cycles—Principles and perspectives. *Journal of Marketing, 45*(4), 116–124.
37. Featherstone, M. (2007). *Consumer culture and postmodernism* (2nd ed.). SAGE.
38. Derrida, J. (1976). In G. C. Spivak & transl. (Eds.), *Of grammatology*. John Hopkins University Press.
39. Gill, A. (2015). Jacques Derrida: Fashion under Erasure Alison. In A. Rocamora & A. Smelik (Eds.), *Thinking through fashion: A guide to key theorists*. Bloomsbury Publishing.
40. Acerbi, A., Ghirlanda, S., & Enquist, M. (2012). The logic of fashion cycles. *PLoS One, 7*(3), e32541.
41. Carman, J. M. (2024). The fate of fashion cycles in our modern society. In *Fashion marketing* (pp. 125–136). Routledge.

From Rituals to Runways: Theorizing the Folkloric Turn in Contemporary Fashion Through Simone Rocha's "Lughnasadh"

Aoife Murray

Abstract This paper argues that there has been a recent "folkloric turn" in contemporary fashion, by analyzing Irish designer Simone Rocha's AW23 collection "Lughnasadh." Drawing on a theoretical framework informed by Walter Benjamin's ideas on time, this work of applied theory decodes the material and symbolic expressions of Irish heritage and identity that can be seen on the runway in 2023. This paper posits that the contemporary folkloric turn is a response to the increased globalization and secularization of Western culture in an era of digital capitalism, which produces an aesthetic interest in the "traditional" beliefs, customs, and histories of a given community. While folklore's commercialization raises questions of authenticity, this paper argues that its presence in fashion offers an alternative way of engaging with "fashion time" that fosters sustainability and deeper engagement with cultural heritage.

Keywords Folklore · Simone Rocha · Time · Fashion runway · Cultural heritage

1 Introduction

Models walk to a haunting soundtrack of traditional folk music, with red bows dripping down their cheeks and straw-like raffia stuffed under their skirts. The audience lines a cavernous room that is in shadow, leaving a conspicuous dark space in the center of the red carpet as the ritual unfolds. This ritual is the Autumn/Winter 2023 collection of Irish designer Simone Rocha, called "Lughnasadh" after the Celtic harvest festival. The collection materializes an encounter with the folk culture of the island of Ireland—the crafts, myths, and rituals both Christian and Pagan, ancient and modern. Further examples of Irish designers working with folk culture that season include Robyn Lynch and Roísín Pierce, who showed traditional Irish craft techniques on-schedule in London and Paris, respectively. Indeed, referencing folk

A. Murray (✉)
Central Saint Martins, London, UK

P. von Wachenfeldt et al. (eds.), *Fashion Communication in the Digital Age*, Springer Proceedings in Business and Economics,
https://doi.org/10.1007/978-3-031-99481-4_2

heritage was such a prominent fixture across the 2023 season of shows that it made headlines, highlighting brands like Paolina Russo and Chopova Lowena who imbued their collections with folk culture [1, 2]. The turn, or return, to a nation's heritage and folk culture can also be seen in the work of off-schedule brands and designers. In 2020s' Ireland, an entire generation of creatives has been reconnecting with ancient and traditional symbols, crafts, and stories that had previously been absorbed into the tourism lexicon or forgotten in the island's race into the future [3]. Since 2022, symbols like the Claddagh ring, St. Brigid's cross, and harp have been reproduced on modern sporting-style scarves and sweaters by independent designer Megan Nolan Walsh; printmaker and textile artist Aoife Cawley; knit- and sportswear label Pellador FC, to name a few. The Design and Craft Council of Ireland hosted the second annual Irish Design Week in November 2023, programmed around the question "Is folklore the future?". The program of events reflected the longstanding engagement with folklore that has shaped Irish culture and marked this as a particularly fecund time to analyze fashion's contribution to the island's contemporary cultural outpouring. Building on the existing scholarship on the history of Irish textiles and fashion up to the early twenty-first century [4–6], and drawing from scholarship on folkloric turns in Irish literature and Irish studies, this paper will analyze Irish identity, culture, and folklore through its materialization in contemporary fashion and explore the wider folkloric turn of which it is part. The writing of Walter Benjamin (1892–1940) is the key theoretical framework for this research and has informed my understanding of what a folkloric turn is: the return, whether intentional or not, of the past in an encounter with the present.

1.1 Methodology

Fashion theorist Francesca Granata's method of "applied theory" in studying the carnivalesque and grotesque in fashion at the turn of the millennium has been instrumental in this paper. Granata's approach "places the objects and images in dialogue with a theoretical framework," which in this case is derived from fashion studies, literary studies, critical theory, folklore studies, and visual culture [7]. After the methodology described by Granata, which builds upon the work of Caroline Evans (2003), I have engaged primarily with the "contextualization of the garments through runway photography" [7] to theorize the folkloric turn in fashion today. The fashion show is an ephemeral spectacle, but one that leaves behind residue in the form of digital media: runway photography, video recordings, and show notes are now commonly shared digitally and publicly by brands. To highlight the resonances between contemporary fashion and the folklore of Ireland, I support my primary sources with folk sources from Dúchas.ie—a digitization project of the National Folklore Collection (NFC) of Ireland. Placing the study of Simone Rocha's AW23 runway presentation within a broader theoretical framework is the key to "applied theory"—as Granata describes, "the theories enable a greater understanding of the garments and performances discussed, while in turn the work discussed opens up new possibilities for theories of fashion." [7].

2 Theoretical Framework

The models of time that emerge from Benjamin's writings on modernity are often cited by fashion theorists: time as a tiger's leap [8], as a labyrinth [9], and as "fragmented memory images" [10]. Benjamin himself presents fashion as a force that structures time, in its "technological development" and its "aesthetic component" [8]. In his 1936 text, *The Work of Art in the Age of Mechanical Reproduction,* Benjamin examines the effects of mechanical reproduction on the aura and authenticity of art [11]. He further discusses the spectral and phantasmagoric elements of capitalist culture in a 1935 essay, proffering the idea of "wish images" that are produced by the shift from old means of production to new ones and contain "the resolute effort to distance oneself from all that is antiquated—which includes, however, the recent past." [12]. In the 2020s, the recent past seems incredibly dense thanks to the advent and advances of internet and mobile technology, and the increased speeds at which information and products circulate in the global fashion system. This is a much-progressed form of "spatiotemporal compression," in which the acceleration of life under capitalism collapses spatial barriers as well as temporal ones [13]. Dialectic, labyrinthine, and fragmented—within these models of time, the folk haunts the present while also surviving it. From neolithic agriculture to modern industrialism, from paganism to Christianity, through colonialism to capitalism and the current digital information age—the folk culture of Ireland has been adopted and absorbed into each new system and its organization of space, time, and people. While the invocation of folklore within the system of fashion is undoubtedly an act of commercializing heritage and culture, the act carries a revelatory potential.

2.1 Folk, Folklore, Folkloric: Defining the Term

The term "folkloric turn," attributed to the historians Guy Beiner and David Hopkin, indicates a turn to folk sources as legitimate subjects for historical analysis, similar to the cultural turn's positioning of culture [14]. Using folkloric sources and methodologies opens up another way of thinking about history that enables us to see "the detail and the whole at the same time" and to "escape the established unities of time and space" [14]. Hopkin's use of the term also highlights the importance of analyzing "ritual, gesture, clothing, and material culture" [14], which coalesce in the fashion runway presentation. According to UNESCO, "folklore (or traditional and popular culture) is the totality of tradition-based creations of a cultural community" and is made up of intangible and tangible elements including, "among others, language, literature, music, dance, games, mythology, rituals, customs, handicrafts, architecture, and other arts." [15]. Ireland has a strong tradition of folklore, particularly in literature, music, and sports. The late-nineteenth and early-twentieth century saw a concerted effort to foster and strengthen these traditions—The National Folklore Collection (NFC) of Ireland comprises material collected since roughly 1930 [16]. The NFC's impetus to record and document traditions and folklore came "at a point in time when the Irish language was in serious decline," yet before urbanization and industrialization could significantly erode "older cultural patterns and practices" [16]. This highlights the pattern of folklore's return to prominence in social consciousness at times of cultural, economic, and political shift—times of uncertainty and change that pose a potential threat to the preservation or continuation of cultural traditions.

The twenty-first century thus far has been characterized by such uncertainty. Writer and editor Shumon Basar articulates this in his series of articles on "Lorecore," a term denoting "An era, belonging to digital capitalism, characterized by people's existential need to storify themselves at the very moment global narratives collapse in an unprecedented manner." [17]. This echoes Eric Hobsbawm's influential thesis on "the invention of tradition," which argues that artificial commemorations replaced long-held customs in the wake of secularization [18]. In the face of narrative collapse and environmental crisis, folklore provides a conceptual spyglass through which to view the present and to imagine new futures through the lens of the past. The stories that connected us to our place in the world, that made sense of the land and seasons we live in, are under more and more strain, creating an urgent desire to replace them—and it seems like we can only, or more readily, access those stories through consuming fashion or fashion content. This calls into question the identity-making weight that folklore, as a cultural expression, is conventionally afforded. Are designers like Rocha working within the phenomenon of nostalgia, repeating elements of folklore that are removed from their context, their meaning diluted in the capitalist fashion system's process of commodification? Or are they infusing this system with a sort of folk methodology, massaging the conventions of fashion to make space for newly imagined futures?

2.2 *From Rituals to Runways: The Folk in Irish Fashion*

Folklore is tightly woven throughout fashion and dress histories of Ireland from the Golden Age in the sixth century. Historians have found that from color symbolism to hand craft techniques, the clothing produced and worn by generations of Irish people carries narrative and symbolic weight at a personal/local and a social/national level [5, 6]. Historian and folklorist Síle de Cléir highlights the high-quality fabrics and crafts produced in Ireland, whether in the home or the industrial factory, which created a culture in which "folk and fashionable dress were not regarded as mutually exclusive" [5]. The fluidity between homespun and industrially produced fashion and dress, between the folk and commercial, echoes the fluid movement of folk motifs and forms between oral and literary sources in early and modern Irish literature—in each case illuminating the symbolic meaning and value of both [19]. This fluidity can be traced particularly clearly around the Irish Literary Revival of the 1890s–1920s, when traditional crafts and garments became weighted with narratives of identity and nationalistic fervor in an Irish inflection of the aesthetics of the British Arts and Crafts movement. This period of modernization saw historical and folkloric sources return as major influences on culture and championed an idealized, anti-industrial figure of the "medieval craftsman-artist as an alternative to capitalism's alienated factory laborer" [20]. However, researchers have found a contradiction between its ideology and material reality, namely between "the purity of crafts and the joy of labor in a market economy," which similarly haunts the folkloric turn in fashion today [20]. Indeed, Benjamin was critical of fashion given its culpability in capitalism [8]. If the folkloric turn today is to morph into something more reformist than revivalist, it necessitates a departure from the norms of the fashion industry.

2.3 *Considering Authenticity*

Folklore—like fashion—combines the mundane and routine with the ceremonial and the ritual, offering a paradigm through which to explore questions of identity, culture, and commerce that arise in fashion studies. The fashion runway presentation is a commercial event that carries potent communicative power, especially when designers reference cultural heritage. The fashion show is also "directly linked to the rise of mass production in the wake of industrialization" [21]. It is ironic that Irish folk culture is appearing in fashion shows now, as these are the very things that the NFC once identified as a threat to it. However, the fashion show and the folk ritual do share key characteristics: each is an embodied spectacle and momentary performance freighted with meaning, occurring at a special time and place and sometimes limited to certain members of the community [22, 23]. The folk culture that is revived or interpreted as a commodity of fashion, and thus mediatized for digital platforms and fashion content, suggests that the contemporary folkloric turn in fashion is inherently concerned with questions of authenticity and genuineness, which are complicated in the era of digital culture that turns primarily on images shared online, en masse, and in an increasingly ephemeral way [13, 22]. The folkloric turn indicates a desire for narratives to connect us to time and place, but the very act of narrativizing folk culture complicates its claim to authenticity.

Folklorist Regina Bendix's reflexive analysis of the field of folk studies in the 1990s was particularly concerned with authenticity's "deceptive promises of transcendence" in folklore studies [24]. In her later work, she argues that amid globalization people turned more and more to "material possessions and individual experiences," in particular tourism, to "satisfy their craving for authenticity—that is, for a however-brief experience of the inaccessibly remote…" [25]. The fashion show is an experience of the "inaccessibly remote" (the creative concept, the craftsmanship, the glamor of exclusivity) brought within one's grasp, the clothing and accessories serving as tokens or souvenirs [25]. The narration of such encounters is of particular importance, in fashion and in tourism alike, as it "recovers" the ephemeral moment and enables "its communicative restaging and its ever-new mental savoring." [25]. Today, fashion shows are digitally live-streamed and shared via images or video near-simultaneously so that the momentary experience stretched across time and space [13]. Both tourism and fashion emerge as modes of narrativization and thus commoditization of heritage and culture—including folklore.

While art may have lost its cultish aura in the linked processes of secularization and industrialization, in fashion we still find a cultish aura that gathers around the designer as an artist-craftsperson figure. The prevalence of blockbuster museum exhibitions dedicated to a sole designer illustrates this: since 2011, major art institutions like the Victoria and Albert Museum in London and the Metropolitan Museum of New York have staged exhibitions dedicated to Karl Lagerfeld, Coco Chanel, Christian Dior, and Alexander McQueen. Simone Rocha, well established after more than a decade in business and numerous accolades, has amassed a cultish aura in art spaces as well as fashion: Rocha's work was exhibited at MoMu, Antwerp (November 2023 to February 2024) alongside the work of artist Louise Bourgeois and choreographer Anne Teresa De Keersmaeker. This follows a 2022 group show, "girls girls girls," curated by Rocha herself, in Lismore Castle Arts, Ireland. The enshrining of fashion and its designers in spaces like the museum or art gallery proposes an intriguing development of Benjamin's observations on art in modernity—but whether it is a reversal of it, or if art is succumbing to the commodity fetish, remains to be seen.

3 Simone Rocha's "Lughnasadh"

The daughter of Chinese-Irish designer John Rocha, Simone Rocha attended the National College of Art and Design, Dublin, before studying MA Fashion at Central Saint Martins, London with a London Fashion Week debut in 2010. Even in her education, the designer was guided by a sense of Ireland: so much so that tutor Louise Wilson demanded she "stop with all the Irish references." [26]. Rocha did not, regularly alighting upon them alongside recurring material motifs like pearls, bows, tulle, and voluminous silhouettes that have become closely associated with the brand. Since Rocha's graduate collection, inspired by mourning dress in the West of Ireland and Irish photographer Perry Ogden's work with Irish Travellers, Ireland's tangible and intangible history has remained a reference alongside themes of femininity and masculinity. Rocha's brand works on a system of polysemic, symbolic signs that carry dual cultural specificity—signs of Irishness that require a familiarity with its cultural heritage as well as the conventions of her own design language. For example, to the uninitiated, a pearl might just be a pearl, but in Rocha's system of codes it becomes an emblem of femininity, of life and death, and even of Irishness. Indeed, this is supported by historical research: in Irish fashion and dress from the sixth to ninth centuries, embellishments included pearls which were surprisingly sourced from local rivers [6].

Surveying the brand's digitally archived collections, from SS15 through to AW23, four stand out as particularly clear gestures to Irish folklore, thus marking them aesthetic precursors to the "Lughnasadh" collection [27]. SS20 was inspired by the straw-adorned Wren Boys—a rural St. Stephen's Day tradition still practiced areas of Ireland today. AW20 references a play from the Irish Literary Revival, connecting themes of birth and grief with the sea, and traditional materials like Aran knit with lurex. The AW22 collection materialized the Children of Lir, a tragic legend of three children transformed into swans, through patent shoes that resemble wet beaks, feathery appliqués, and folds of white fabric bursting forth from tailoring to resemble wings. The same story had served as the narrative of the SS15 collection, illustrating the designer's long-held interest in Irish folktales. This repetition yields satisfyingly different iterations of garments and outfits that retain a recognizable Simone Rocha look, reminiscent of the repetition of motifs and structural fluidity that define folk tales in orality and literature. The 53-look AW23 collection can be read as a narrative overview of both the brand history and a retelling of Ireland's cultural history. The show notes lack conventional syntax, instead running on in a series of phrases that whisper of earthiness, ritual, and materials under duress, "Stuffed roses, pressed ribbon, trapped lace," to convey the themes that form Rocha's "twisted lullaby": love, absence, return, and the tension between the pagan and irrational, the Christian and sensible [28]. The collection draws on the harvest festival Lughnasadh, as well as rituals for romantic relationships and protection: "Peeling the apple in the mirror to reveal your future love. The blood daubed on children's foreheads for protection from otherworldly beings and bad luck." [28].

Folklorist Máire MacNeill's 1962 study of the festival draws upon the entirety of the NFC's collection and establishes the origins, practices, and variations of Lughnasadh throughout history. The festival falls in August, to mark the end of summer and the beginning of the harvest. Named after the ancient Celtic deity Lugh, god of crafts and skills, MacNeill states that the customs of the festival included the cutting of the first corn; a "ritual dance-play" and other plays representing Lugh; the installation of a carved stone head; multiple celebrations and a feast of the harvested food, bilberries, and a sacrificed bull [29]. These ritual traditions were carried on through to modern Ireland but, like many of the pagan rituals that marked the passing of seasons, were given a narrative gloss by Christianity, eventually becoming cultural traditions quite divorced from their spiritual roots. For example, in the early 2000s I, an urban dweller, made corn dollies with my Catholic primary school class as a seasonal craft activity—not an act of pagan worship. The co-existence of the pagan past and Christian modernity in Irish folk culture can be seen on a material level in the collection particularly through the tailored separates, bishop sleeves, oversized lace tunics, and beaded collars in Looks 13–25, which are aesthetically reminiscent of a Eucharistic Congress. From Look 25, a black tulle dress stuffed with raffia, the presentation progresses the folkloric references to Lughnasadh through more extended use of hay and raffia, as well as spliced-together dresses that echo Rocha's continued exploration of contrasts and symbioses throughout her entire body of work—like "fragmented memory images" [10]. Rocha's AW23 collection draws upon the rich narrative of this folk festival as well as other folkloric sources, deftly materializing a range of ritual traditions in a collection that is also encoded with the lexicon of her brand.

3.1 Materializing Folklore: Raffia

Raffia is the key material in the "Lughnasadh" collection. Chosen for its aesthetic similarity to harvested hay, it is woven into sashes, bags, and dresses as well as the plaits and twists that are stuffed under the designer's signature transparent tulle gowns. Dúchas holds a manuscript that describes a straw plait, or the "cailleach," that is made when the harvest is complete (Fig. 1). This echoes in the AW23 collection as plaited straw garlands in Look 10, 24, and 39. Raffia is bundled up like harvested straw and stuffed into tulle skirts and puff sleeves, even trailing off models' fingers (Fig. 2). The plaited construction of Look 50 (Fig. 3) and Look 52 aesthetically recalls corn dollies traditionally made after the harvest—the example in Dúchas is even tied with a red bow (Fig. 4). The use of raffia or other straw-like materials in fashion has long been a sign of paganism or folklore—for example, Sarah Burton showed "a very pagan-looking 'corn dolly' dress" for her first collection as Creative Director of Alexander McQueen in 2010 [30]. This differs from the

Fig. 1 Murphy. M (no date) Garland Sunday, (Lúnasa): Harvest; cutting the Cailleach, Dromintee, Slieve Gullion. "The Photographic Collection, H046.25.00001" by Dúchas © National Folklore Collection, UCD is licensed under CC BY-NC 4.0

Fig. 2 Look 53 Simone Rocha AW23. Photo courtesy of firstVIEW

use of raffia by, for example, Italian behemoth Prada, whose woven raffia bags are intended not to reference folk rituals, but to evoke a sense of summertime. This highlights the arbitrariness of meaning attached to the fashion object, as well as illuminating the shared elements of folk cultures across borders. Raffia, when used in fashion to symbolize folk rituals or customs, comes to bear spatiotemporal significance.

The act of harvesting falls at the turn of the seasons and gave structure to agrarian calendars, but Rocha's use of it in AW23 marks the turn of the seasons in "fashion time," which is "characterized by ephemerality as opposed to the stability and immortality traditionally claimed by other cultural forms." [7]. Folk culture stakes a relatively strong claim to this stability and immortality, at least in the Irish context, given its continuity throughout various historical shifts and breaks: as an Irish literary critic pointed out, "Irish traditions are at their most vital when they have been proclaimed about to die." [31]. The AW23 raffia pieces are not for sale as part of the main collection, instead existing as pieces just for the show or editorials. In this way, they are the most allegorical pieces of the collection—akin to folk ritual artifacts held by museums or archives, more valuable for their symbolic meaning than their material use. However, folk rituals are not necessarily centered around a specific, singular object but rather a totem that can exist in multiple copies. Indeed, "Lack of identifiable authorship, multiple existence over time and space, variation of the

Fig. 3 Look 50 Simone Rocha AW23. Photo courtesy of firstVIEW

Fig. 4 Barron N (2002) Corn dollie: harvest knot. "The Photographic Collection, H046.06.00002" by Dúchas © National Folklore Collection, UCD is licensed under CC BY-NC 4.0

items," all conventionally function as the "ways of testing folklore's authenticity." [24]. This at first seems incompatible with fashion, particularly with a brand like Simone Rocha that has such distinct codes from which to identify authorship, but the communicative and symbolic power of a brand enables more participation using copies or tributes that ascribe to their codes.

Rocha's choice of Lughnasadh, a seasonal ritual observed in August, as the guiding reference for a collection released to stores throughout August and September indicates either a serendipitous or a conscious rethinking of fashion time as an organizing force. At least conceptually, the AW23 collection reconnects the timing of the fashion industry calendar to an older and more rooted sense of seasonal time. This collection encourages us to see time, and the ways in which the recent and distant past returns to the present, through its design. The continuation of formal elements and preoccupation with folk culture in Rocha's body of work, raffia being an example with particularly weighty symbolism, aligns the AW23 collection particularly closely to a changing version of fashion time: one that is moving closer to the cyclical time of natural seasons and denaturalizing the rapid pace of the industry. Rocha's "Lughnasadh" is a fashion runway show that is really a restaging of a ritual, one that plaits together the folklore of Ireland as well as that of the Simone Rocha brand.

4 Conclusion

The contemporary folkloric turn, illustrated in part by Simone Rocha's "Lughnasadh," reveals a renewed engagement with cultural heritage and temporality within fashion. If, as Benjamin posits, "Fashion prescribes the ritual according to which the commodity fetish demands to be worshipped" [12], then the folkloric also bears the potential to prescribe a new ritual for fashion—one that centers hand crafts and more natural rhythms of time, as well as compelling narratives that offer something beyond the purely commercial. Rocha's highly symbolic AW23 collection does to some extent adopt folkloric crafts, motifs, and narratives into the commodity fetishism of fashion, but by the same process it enables alternative ways of viewing fashion time, production, and consumption. A brand that cyclically returns to the same narratives and motifs to explore them afresh invites consumers to participate in a prolonged relationship, and to treasure the old as much as the new. However, the newness of the fabrics themselves is inescapable—the folkloric turn in fashion can only denaturalize the capitalist system if it continues to move beyond the aesthetic and narrative into the material production of fashion, opening the system up to new imagined futures where newness is redefined. A 2018 report from FashionSEEDS highlights potential avenues for this, encompassing four macro areas in sustainable fashion practice: environment, economy, social, and culture [32]. The report explores the idea of cultural heritage sustainability, which requires fashion brands, educators, and communicators to engage with it on a local level—working with artisans and knowledge-holders to integrate folk methods into modern design without altering the very authenticity that makes them so appealing to us today.

Abandoning fashion's contrived seasons in favor of a more intuitive schedule can allow time for ethical and more sustainable production and provide heightened aesthetic and narrative experiences that feel more akin to a folk ritual than a commercial event. In fashion, where "dreams are the motor that drive a capitalist economy as much as iron, steel, and microchips" [9], the folkloric turn presents a vehicle with which to return to true seasonal scheduling, to a calendar dictated by and in harmony with both the natural and social world rather than the capitalistic one.

References

1. Cartner-Morley, J. (2023, February 19). Patchwork and pearls: London fashion week embraces folk heritage. *The Guardian*. https://www.theguardian.com/fashion/2023/feb/19/patchwork-and-pearls-london-fashion-week-embraces-folk-heritage
2. Oostermeijer, M. (2023, August 23). Neo-Paganism is casting its spell over fashion. *i-D*. https://i-d.co/article/neo-pagan-witchcraft-fashion-trend/
3. Magliocco, S. (2023, July 21). Why young Irish designers are embracing Irish symbols. *RTÉ*. https://www.rte.ie/lifestyle/fashion/2023/0721/1395830-why-young-irish-designers-are-embracing-traditional-irish-symbols/
4. De Cléir, S. (2010). Ireland. In *Berg encyclopedia*. https://doi.org/10.2752/BEWDF/EDch8052
5. De Cléir, S. (2011). Creativity in the margins: Identity and locality in Ireland's fashion journey. *Fashion Theory, 15*(2), 201–224. https://doi.org/10.2752/175174111X12954359478726
6. Mahon, B. (2000). *Rich & rare: The story of Irish dress*. Mercier Press.
7. Granata, F. (2016). Fitting sources—Tailoring methods: A case study of Martin Margiela and the temporalities of fashion. In H. Jenss (Ed.), *Fashion studies: Research methods, sites, and practices* (pp. 142–159). Bloomsbury Publishing Plc. Available from: ProQuest Ebook Central. Accessed: 10 November 2023.
8. Geczy, A., & Karaminas, V. (2015). Walter Benjamin: Fashion, modernity and the city street. In A. Rocamora (Ed.), *Thinking through fashion: A guide to key theorists* (pp. 81–96). I. B. Tauris & Company, Limited. Available from: ProQuest Ebook Central. Accessed: 11 November 2023.
9. Evans, C. (2023[2003]). Fashion at the edge: Spectacle, modernity and deathliness. Yale University Press.
10. O'Neill, A. (2005). Cuttings and pastings. In C. Breward & C. Evans (Eds.), *Fashion and modernity*. Berg.
11. Benjamin, W. (1936/2008). *The work of art in the age of mechanical reproduction* (Transl. J. A. Underwood). Penguin Books—Great Ideas.
12. Benjamin, W. (1935/2002). Paris, the capital of the nineteenth century. In E. Jephcott, H. Eiland, et al. (transl.), and H. Eiland, & M. W. Jennings (Eds.), *Walter Benjamin: Selected writings, Vol. 3, 1935–1938* (pp. 32–49). The Belknap Press of Harvard University Press.
13. Rocamora, A. (2013). New fashion times: Fashion and digital media. In *The handbook of fashion studies*. Bloomsbury.
14. Hopkin, D. (2012). Introduction: Folklore and the historian. In *Voices of the people in nineteenth-century France* (pp. 1–31). Cambridge University Press.
15. UNESCO. (1989). Recommendation on the Safeguarding of Traditional Culture and Folklore. Retrieved September 24, 2023, from https://www.unesco.org/en/legal-affairs/recommendation-safeguarding-traditional-culture-and-folklore
16. UCD History of the National Folklore Collection. https://www.ucd.ie/irishfolklore/en/about/historyofnfc/, last accessed 2025/02/07.
17. Basar, S. (2022). *The laws of lorecore*. Zora Zine. https://zine.zora.co/the-laws-of-lorecore-shumon-basar

18. Beiner, G. (2014). Probing the boundaries of Irish memory: From postmemory to prememory and back. *Irish Historical Studies, 39*(154), 296–307. http://www.jstor.org/stable/43654775
19. Covington, S. (2018). Towards a new "folkloric turn" in the literature of early modern Ireland. *Literature Compass, 15*, 11. https://doi.org/10.1111/lic3.12497
20. Kreilkamp, V. (2016). *The arts and crafts movement: Making it Irish*. McMullen Museum of Art, Boston College.
21. Evans, C. (2001). The enchanted spectacle. *Fashion Theory, 5*(3), 271–310. https://doi.org/10.2752/136270401778960865
22. Halliday, R. (2020). *The fashion show goes live: Exclusive and mediatized performance*. Bloomsbury Visual Arts. Available from: ProQuest Ebook Central.
23. UNESCO: Social practices, rituals, and festive events. https://ich.unesco.org/en/social-practices-rituals-and-00055, last accessed 2023/11/18.
24. Bendix, R. (1997). *In search of authenticity: The formation of folklore studies*. University of Wisconsin Press.
25. Bendix, R. (2018). *Culture and value: Tourism, heritage and property*. IU Press.
26. Horyn, C. (2019, February 7). Queen of the new weird. *The Cut*. https://www.thecut.com/2019/02/simone-rocha-is-the-queen-of-the-new-weird.html
27. Simone Rocha. https://simonerocha.com/blogs/collections, last accessed 2025/02/11.
28. Simone Rocha Autumn/Winter 2023., https://simonerocha.com/blogs/collections/autumn-winter-2023, last accessed 2025/02/11.
29. MacNeill, M. (1962). *The festival of Lughnasadh: A study of the survival of the celtic festival of the beginning of harvest*. Oxford University Press.
30. Fox, I. (2010, October 5). Alexander McQueen protégé Sarah Burton steals the show in Paris. *The Guardian*. https://www.theguardian.com/lifeandstyle/2010/oct/05/alexander-mcqueen-sarah-burton
31. Killeen, J. (2014). *The emergence of Irish gothic fiction: History, origins, theories*. Edinburgh University Press. http://www.jstor.org/stable/10.3366/j.ctt9qdrh2.4
32. Williams, D., et al. (2019). *Education and research: Benchmarking report*. POLIMI.

Harris Tweed Hebrides: Producing, Promoting, and Protecting Harris Tweed® in the Twenty-First Century

Karen Cross and Josie Steed

Abstract This paper on Harris Tweed® today discusses projects with Scottish textile manufacturer Harris Tweed Hebrides (HTH) that focused on reducing the seasonality of their all-wool product, exploring new markets, and digital and sustainable innovations within their communication, design, and production processes. The partnership project was between HTH and Robert Gordon University where they collaborated on a 2-year Knowledge Transfer Partnership (KTP) and funded research project, to address the needs of the industry in producing, promoting, and protecting Harris Tweed® in the twenty-first century. Reflecting on the projects, the authors detail the new practices instigated within the context of the changes that have taken place in the Harris Tweed® industry since Judith Ennew's chapter 'Harris Tweed: construction, retention, and representation of a cottage industry' in Esther Goody's (ed.) *From Craft to Industry* (1982) book. While a timespan of over 40 years has passed, elements of Ennew's media constructed Hebridean Myth continue to play a role in the communication and marketing of Harris Tweed®; however, digital and immersive interventions provide opportunity for modernisation of both the brand's processes and consumer perceptions about Harris Tweed®.

Keywords Harris Tweed · Design innovation · Knowledge transfer · Sustainable textiles

1 Introduction

Harris Tweed® is recognised as a traditional textile product with 'cult status' [1, p. 118]. Historically, it evolved from crofting practices for individual use to an industry of tweed production in the mid-1800s [2]. The Harris Tweed Association

K. Cross · J. Steed (✉)
Robert Gordon University, Aberdeen, Scotland, UK
e-mail: lncs@springer.com

P. von Wachenfeldt et al. (eds.), *Fashion Communication in the Digital Age*, Springer Proceedings in Business and Economics,
https://doi.org/10.1007/978-3-031-99481-4_3

was established in 1909 as a protective body for the cloth and in 1964, the Hunter Judgement reinforced the requirement that all stages of production had to take place in the Outer Hebrides of Scotland. From peak production in the 1960s, a decline in exports to North America in the 1980s [3] saw this iconic industry almost collapse entirely. Much work went into rescuing and modernising production of the cloth, while protecting its unique heritage and craft status. The Harris Tweed Association was redeveloped as part of the 1993 Harris Tweed Act of Parliament [4], resulting in today's Harris Tweed Authority (HTA). The Act provides strict regulations governing what constitutes genuine Harris Tweed®, and the HTA certifies every length of cloth, stamping it with the distinctive and internationally recognised Orb mark (see Fig. 1) to communicate provenance and authenticity. This hand-done procedure, involving a hot iron and wax transfer, remains a low-tech but affordable regimen; although forays into technology-based traceability have been trialled [5], these currently come at too high a cost for the industry to adopt. Production of Harris Tweed® is industrialised at the spinning, dyeing, and finishing stages, with these operations presently taking place at three mills located in Scotland's Outer Hebrides. Weaving, however, remains a home-based artisan craft, conducted on non-powered tappet looms, making Harris Tweed® the only hand-woven cloth produced in commercial quantities. The intrinsic relationship between the three parties including the HTA, the mills and self-employed weavers, is key to the success and survival of the Harris Tweed® industry, where without one the other would be unable to carry on.

The largest of the three mills is Harris Tweed Hebrides (HTH), which commenced operations in 2008, reviving a derelict mill based in Shawbost on the Island of Lewis and Harris. It is one of Scotland's few remaining vertical mills, encompassing the entire textile process from receiving the raw wool, through the dyeing, carding, spinning, and warping procedures, to finishing the woven cloth. In its 15 years of operation, HTH has provided valuable employment for this remote island community and has invested to update the mill with new dyehouse equipment

Fig. 1 The Harris Tweed Orb logo

and staff facilities. In 2021, a 2-year KTP, part-funded by the Arts and Humanities Research Council (AHRC) began to explore innovative ways to address seasonality issues of their woven woollen product, explore new market opportunities, and initiate sustainable innovations within their design and production processes. KTPs are designed to support UK businesses to undertake a strategic innovation project which a business would be unable to achieve on their own [6]. Through partnership with a university, a business gains access to academic expertise and resources and a recent graduate (referred to within the KTP structure as the Associate) who is employed for the duration of the project to carry out the work. The majority of KTPs tend to be in the science and engineering fields with only a few that are design-led and fewer still within the fashion and textile design sector [7].

2 Sustaining Employment and Sustainable Practice: The Harris Tweed Hebrides Mill

> Because weavers are the pivot of the advertising of Harris Tweed, it is often forgotten that the mills employ a sizeable work force, which is engaged in the other operations of textile production [2, p. 191].

Today HTH provides employment for approximately seventy mill workers. The mill carries out all the preparatory processes of fibre dyeing, spinning, and warping prior to the loom beams being sent across the isles to home weavers. Once woven the fabric is returned to the mill for all finishing processes, quality checking and final inspection by the HTA to authenticate the fabric as Harris Tweed® before it leaves the mill. During the KTP project, several new initiatives at the mill were implemented to improve production and their sustainability credentials. These comprised certification, development of a natural collection, purchase of a computer-aided design (CAD) system, and a focus on reducing the seasonality of the product offer.

2.1 Certification

To prove its production of authentic Harris Tweed®, the company utilises the HTA certification trademark 'the Orb Mark' [2, p. 173] for its finished cloth. The HTA holds an extensive portfolio of registered trademarks worldwide, which are actively protected. One of the KTP project's objectives was to research and apply for a worldwide industry recognised certification that focused on sustainability, recognising 'heightened consumer awareness of fashion's contribution to the climate crisis' [8, p. 11]. An application to OEKO-TEX® for their Standard 100 award was identified as the most appropriate, as their criteria for certification confirm 'the human-ecological safety of textile products from all stages of production (raw materials and fibres, yarns, fabrics, ready-to-use end products) along the textile value chain'

Fig. 2 Communicating sustainable standards on the HTH website

(OEKO-TEX®, 2022). Applying for this certification did require significant time and effort, highlighting the benefit of placing the Associate within the business, thus increasing their capacity to resource this process. The application was successful, and the company now has an additional certification recognised internationally that communicates assurances to their customers (both business-to-business and end-user) that their textile production is safe, environmentally friendly and manufactured in a socially responsible manner (see Fig. 2). Increasingly, certifications are acknowledged as a means to communicate certain standards to ethically- and sustainability-focused fashion consumers, described as a 'crucial environmental cue' by Lee, Bae, and Kim [9].

2.2 *Development of a Natural Collection*

> … extensive knowledge of the use of natural materials for dyes was not common… commercially manufactured, purchased dyes were often used [2, p. 179].

The least sustainable process in the HTH mill is fibre dyeing where both acid and reactive synthetic dyes are used to colour wool. These require vast quantities of water during the process of chemically binding the dye pigments to the wool fibre. Each yarn is a blend of between two and nine fibre colours, creating the unique mélange shades synonymous with Harris Tweed® fabric. Alternatives to synthetic dyes are gaining interest within textile research [10]; natural dyes could potentially replace the harmful processes used in synthetic dyeing. However, natural dyeing has not yet advanced to the scale required within an industry setting that requires consistent batch dyeing. The island location of HTH production also limits access to the wide variety of natural materials required for natural dyeing. To address this, a new natural collection using undyed wool to reduce chemical use was developed and trialled for the commercial market. This required the Associate to invest significant time in sourcing supplies of suitable natural colours of wool that complied with the requirements of the Harris Tweed Act (1993). Weave structures and a selection of natural wool colours inspired by the local environment were combined to produce a small range of undyed patterns that would offer customers a sustainable fabric option whilst also supporting HTH's image and marketing strategy together with their sustainable development ambitions. This was not only a new product development for the company but also the first large-scale initiative of this kind in the contemporary Harris Tweed® industry (Harris Tweed® was, of course, traditionally made using undyed and naturally dyed fibres before the introduction of chemical dyes). The initiative provides a new sustainable product option for HTH's customers. One of the biggest production challenges when reproducing a natural collection after an initial run is colour consistency. As with all natural materials there is no way to guarantee replication of the same shade with each new delivery of wool fibre. This does present a unique opportunity for the customer to purchase a one-of-a-kind or limited-edition design, enhancing the exclusivity of this expensive wool product and cementing its luxury credentials [11]. While an undyed product offering is unlikely to replace the traditional colourful Harris Tweed® fabrics, the Natural range does align with neutral colour trends and end-consumer environmental concerns; customer demand will continue to inform the direction of this and other future designs. The Natural collection was launched in 2023 alongside the company's annual Autumn/Winter collection and has been communicated across its marketing platforms (see Figs. 3 and 4).

Fig. 3 The Natural collection communicated on HTH's Instagram feed

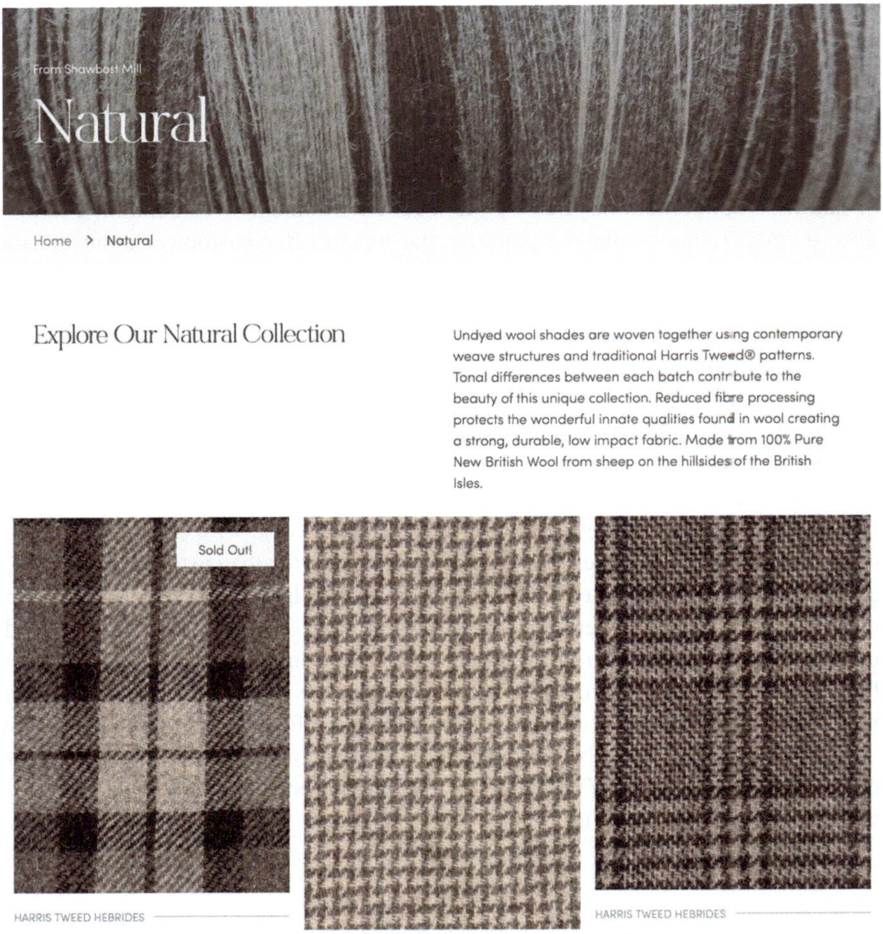

Fig. 4 The Natural collection communicated on HTH's website

2.3 *Computer-Aided Design (CAD) System*

CAD can be used to provide a sustainable alternative to physical sampling, reducing textile waste and communicating quick design options for customers. Prior to the KTP project, HTH did not have in-house digital expertise. Rather, all sampling had to be carried out manually; dyeing, spinning, warping, and hand weaving each new sample as part of a 'blanket' or 'range' of tweed patterns. A key remit of the KTP project was to research viable CAD options for the company, to secure its purchase and implement it operationally. The preferred CAD system was successfully installed, although this was not a smooth process, requiring several trials and much patience, especially to get accurate colour representation (a very important consideration as Harris Tweed® is renowned for its rich colours). Once installed, key staff were trained which has reduced sampling, use of resources and textile waste, and

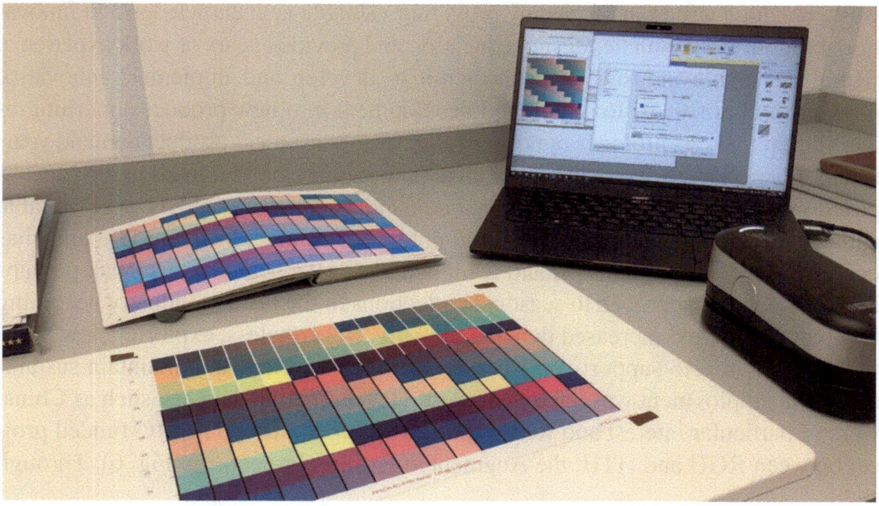

Fig. 5 Computer-Aided Design (CAD) at Harris Tweed Hebrides

saved time in terms of manpower, as well as allowing the company to respond to customer requests more efficiently. The introduction of a CAD system also supports the continued high quality of Harris Tweed®; providing an image of new and existing designs with current paperwork as it progresses through each stage of production allows for a smaller margin of error. This visual aid enables both mill employees and weavers to see how the final product will look, the colours it contains, where they appear in the design, and the overall weave structure. This information is then universally understood across the business, which is provided alongside technical information (see Fig. 5). In addition, this digitisation of the design process is facilitating the storage of design knowledge that was largely held within the minds of specific individuals, safeguarding and preserving this knowledge for future generations.

2.4 Seasonality

> As demand is seasonal, there is little certainty of continuity of employment. Workers are subject to being laid off work, with no definite security about being re-employed. They also endure short-time working and week-about arrangements (working on alternate weeks) with consequent reductions in income [2, p. 193].

Deriving from what was originally a cottage industry, the scale of Harris Tweed® production poses sustainable benefits in terms of its small batch production, British wool-based, localised supply chain, and rural employment provision (aligning with United Nations Sustainable Development Goals 8, Decent Work and Economic Growth, and 12, Responsible Consumption and Production). The HTH mill is one of the largest private employers on the Island, providing work for people across the Outer Hebrides. The graduate designer (the Associate) employed during the KTP was embedded within the company providing valuable new knowledge and innovation, brought from both her design education and previous years of work experience within the textile industry, with the remit to develop and implement innovative products and practices. Research and development into new product opportunities in different markets provides opportunity to create seasonless product demand year-round. Harris Tweed® is traditionally an autumn/winter fabric, which in the past has posed problems, where due to seasonal demand, production periods were variable and consistent employment for all could not be maintained. In recent years this has become less of a problem, demand is high, and sales appear less seasonal, perhaps in part due to the approach to seasonal collections in the fashion industry becoming less regimented and increased demand globally. Nevertheless, exploring new product opportunities to support year-round consistent workload and maintain sustainable rural employment was a focus of the KTP. Alternative markets, such as China, were of particular interest and were explored through a second AHRC-funded project between RGU and HTH, the Augmented Fashion Project (see Fig. 6). Through

Fig. 6 The augmented fashion project

Augmented Fashion, the use of immersive technologies such as Augmented Reality (AR) and Virtual Reality (VR) was piloted for HTH with both UK and Chinese consumers (see [12]). Although HTH's existing marketing activities successfully communicate their brand values to a traditional and mature customer base, new markets such as the Chinese consumer are seeking excitement and innovation and are discovering brands and products on a range of different digital platforms. Initial investigations found that younger consumers did not view the HTH brand as being relevant to them, regarding it as for a mature, traditional, and wealthy customer. The use of immersive technologies within the project was successful in facilitating engagement with younger and more diverse audiences and led to a change in perceptions about the brand. Test users of the immersive technology content described the brand as more fashion-forward, and for a younger target consumer, desirable outcomes for a heritage brand seeking to engage with new audiences and markets.

2.5 Sustaining Employment, Communicating Craft: The Home Weaver

> Although the weaver is portrayed as an independent producer in the advertising literature, he is in effect an employee of the mill... Like employees directly employed by the mills in spinning, warping, and finishing, the weaver depends upon the mills for a cash income [2, p. 188].

Today, since the introduction of the Griffith double width loom in 1993, there are still hand weavers in the Outer Hebrides that weave independently from mills on the traditional single width Hattersley loom. Those who weave on the double width mostly, but not exclusively, weave for mills, however, as defined by the Harris Tweed® Act of Parliament all cloth must be woven at the weavers' homes in the Outer Hebrides, regardless of whether they are self-employed or employed by a mill. Warp beams and weft threads are delivered to the home weavers by the mill, and the woven cloth is transported back to the mill for finishing and certification. Ennew described how the home weavers within the Harris Tweed® industry retain 'certain cottage-industry elements' [2, p. 169]. Today, some weavers still choose this job to support their lifestyle as crofters or to support other part-time work; for others, it is their full-time job. In each scenario, the weavers bring years of experience and knowledge to the role. It is well known that many Scottish islands face problems with depopulation and an ageing demographic; this is also reflected in registered Harris Tweed® weavers. The HTH mill works with around one hundred and twenty home weavers who carry out all their required weaving on double width non-powered tappet Griffith looms. Most looms today are privately owned, with some rentals available through projects such as the community wind farms across the island located in Tolsta, Harris, Shawbost, and Lochs. The craft of weaving, together with loom maintenance skills are passed from weaver to weaver on the island. Mills work closely with the HTA to provide training opportunities with a buddy system used to share knowledge between new and experienced weavers. This

Fig. 7 Video profile of a Harris Tweed® home weaver

system is a testament to the community ethos and neighbourly reality of island life. As part of the Augmented Fashion Project, video profiles of home weavers were created and embedded within the virtual reality showroom, along with 360-degree photographic images of their loom sheds, providing potential consumers with an insider view of how the cloth is created. For Harris Tweed®, there is a tension between communicating the cottage-industry credentials of the home weaver as an artisan craftsperson, and conveying the industrialised levels of quality, certification and production that are demanded by their business-to-business customers today. Ennew linked the development of marketing techniques for Harris Tweed® with the 'complex of ideological constructions which combine to form the Hebridean part of the Celtic Myth' [2, p. 199], and while the work of the Augmented Fashion Project sought to engage with more contemporary consumers, the wild and natural tropes of the Hebridean landscape were still part of the content, albeit with a less romanticised and more realistic view of the home weavers today (Fig. 7).

3 Conclusion

This paper highlights the revival and ongoing success of Harris Tweed®, an authentic and artisan product with a strong sustainability ethos at a time when environmental and ethical concerns are subject to the focus of government legislation and consumer concerns. The Harris Tweed Hebrides mill has proven to be open to both environmental and technological innovations, embracing the key project outcomes that included the implementation of a CAD system, the development of an undyed Natural collection and gaining environmental certification. These outcomes update the brand's design and production processes, provide an element of preservation, and provide newness for the customer. In addition, exploring more futuristic communication methods via virtual and augmented reality evidence the brand's willingness to experiment and its commitment to engaging with new audiences, an important consideration for any traditional or heritage brand. Thus, this research provides an important example for other traditional textile brands seeking to secure their place in an era of fast and disposable fashion products. It highlights the value of investing in new talent, new product, and new technologies. Digital development is fast paced; it is important that traditional brands are not left behind, and instead are supported to embrace and capitalise upon these new technologies. Further research into the intersection of traditional textile brands and digital developments, in terms of communication, production, and sustainability are encouraged, given that this was a small-scale, interpretive study involving one brand. Nevertheless, the benefits of knowledge exchange and collaboration through initiatives such as KTPs and funded research projects are evident, in that they stimulate new ideas and afford opportunity for innovation, especially important in this traditional and heritage textile sector, '...ensuring that Harris Tweed is not simply a survivor of folk skills and craft which have been passed down from generation to generation' [2, p. 182] but that it continues to thrive for generations to come.

Acknowledgments This work was supported by Innovate UK under Grant number KTP012168 and the Arts and Humanities Research Council award reference AH/T011483/1.

References

1. Young, C., & Martin, A. (2017). *Tartan and Tweed.* Frances Lincoln.
2. Ennew, J. (1982). Harris Tweed: Construction, retention and representation of a cottage industry. In E. N. Goody (Ed.), *From craft to industry, the ethnography of proto-industrial cloth production* (pp. 166–199).
3. Harris Tweed Hebrides/Heriot Watt University (HTH/HWU). (2015). *Context workshops people process impact.* Heriot Watt University.
4. Platman, L. (2011). *Harris Tweed from land to street.* Frances Lincoln.
5. Innovation in Textiles (2021). Harris Tweed partners with Fibre Trace. Retrieved January 11, 2023, from https://www.innovationintextiles.com/harris-tweed-partners-with-fibretrace/
6. UK Government. (2022). Knowledge transfer partnerships: What they are and how to apply. Retrieved January 11, 2023, from https://www.gov.uk/guidance/knowledge-transfer-partnerships-what-they-are-and-how-to-apply
7. Coulter J. (2013). Interdisciplinarity: creativity in collaborative research approaches to enhance knowledge transfer. Retrieved January 11, 2023, from https://pure.ulster.ac.uk/ws/portalfiles/portal/11303508/COULTER_Interdisciplinarity_in_knowledge_Transfer.pdf/
8. McKinsey and Company. (2023). The State of Fashion 2023. Retrieved January 11, 2023, from https://www.mckinsey.com/industries/retail/our-insights/state-of-fashion
9. Lee, E. J., Bae, J., & Kim, K. H. (2020). The effect of sustainable certification reputation on consumer behaviour in the fashion industry: Focusing on the mechanism of congruence. *Journal of Global Fashion Marketing, 11*, 137–153. https://doi.org/10.1080/20932685.2020.1726198
10. Casciani, D., & Chen, M. (2023). Conveying natural dyes in the fashion industry through a design-driven innovation. In I. Cantista et al. (Eds.), *Fashion for the common good* (pp. 46–64).
11. Upshaw, D., Amyx, D., & Hardy, M. (2017). The nature of exclusivity. *Journal of Marketing Development and Competitiveness, 11*(2), 46–63.
12. Cross, K., Mesjar, L., Steed, J., & Jiang, Y. (2023). Immersive innovations for the communication of heritage, handcraft and sustainability. *International Journal of Fashion Design, Technology and Education*, 1–11. https://doi.org/10.1080/17543266.2023.2277264

Contemporary Archives for the Memory and Legacy of Brands Shaping "Colombian Luxury": A Review of MH's Digital Archive

Laura Mejía-Ocampo and Angela Dotor-Robayo

Abstract This article is the result of a research on fashion archives as tools for building legacies and identity in Colombian fashion brands. For this study, the digital archive of Mario Hernández was analyzed as it is one of the most relevant brands in the country whose tradition and construction of luxury is rooted in national manufacturing and artisanal textile techniques.

To effectively analyze the archive, a semiotic interpretive methodology was applied with the aim of examining and interpreting images and short videos from an advertising analysis perspective, specifically that of Jacques Fontanille. In the case of this research the mentioned approach led to findings related to categories such as woman, luxury, body and identity, which are connected to the elite and politically charged environment of the country.

Keywords Fashion archive · Instagram · Identity · Luxury · Heritage

1 Introduction

This article presents a study on how fashion archives have come to be valued by brands, textile companies, and academies due to their ability to preserve the environment, culture, memory, and tradition through images while also serving marketing and communication purposes, as seen in the archives constructed in digital repositories and social media networks.

Understanding the identity of brands through their repositories allows for a discussion of luxury as a cultural concept, constructed through the archives established in Colombian fashion. This has been a key focus and point of inquiry in this research. With the aim of understanding the strategies involved in both the construction and

L. Mejía-Ocampo (✉) · A. Dotor-Robayo
Universidad de Bogotá Jorge Tadeo Lozano, Bogotá, Colombia
e-mail: laura.mejiaoc@utadeo.edu.co; angela.dotorr@utadeo.edu.co

P. von Wachenfeldt et al. (eds.), *Fashion Communication in the Digital Age*,
Springer Proceedings in Business and Economics,
https://doi.org/10.1007/978-3-031-99481-4_4

preservation of identity and heritage for Colombian brands, which in turn contribute to the national identity of fashion, this study delves into the role of fashion archives.

In this regard, a study on the role of fashion archives in Colombia can be understood. While contemporary and digital archives on social media networks currently serve a communicative and exploratory purpose, their accessibility to the public, due to the available digital tools, makes them relevant and instrumental in the interpretation of luxury concepts, their associations, symbols, and signs through metaphors from everyday life.

High-impact global brands such as Salvatore Ferragamo, Giorgio Armani, Versace, Gian Franco Ferré, and Loro Piana have demonstrated the effectiveness of fashion archives in preserving and communicating their heritage using various digital tools. Understanding brand identity and luxury as a cultural concept constructed through the media established in Colombian fashion has been a driving force and area of inquiry for this research. In this way, the study aims to comprehend the strategies for constructing and preserving both the identity and heritage of Colombian brands, which further contribute to the development of the national fashion identity.

In Colombia, several brands have managed to consolidate themselves in the local market due to the quality of their products, customer loyalty, and the history they have built over time. It is identified that these brands lack specialized fashion repositories or archives that catalog and preserve their iconic products, which could be useful for design processes based on tangible and intangible heritage, as well as for marketing strategies that create brand value and narratives that tell the brand's legacy and craftsmanship. However, it has been noted that some brands, such as Mario Hernández, Zephir, and Olga Piedrahita, use digital tools particularly social media platforms like Instagram to gather and communicate creative aspects and their legacy.

Finally, this study aims to analyze the images posted as content on the Instagram platform, using Jacques Fontanille's methodology to determine how these brands are constructing a sort of archive and the meanings they generate through these visual contents and discourses.

2 The Archive, Memory, and Heritage

In recent years, brands, companies, and even prestigious universities have begun to explore methods and approaches to document, catalog, and organize objects and images that form part of what is known as an archive. These can be physical or digital, produced and preserved by organizations, companies, or public entities. An archive may consist of a collection of documents, a space, or a collection of information connected by common attributes [1]. While the term "archive" is easy to define and associate with a technical and practical task, as a concept it has evolved due to new reflections on the importance of the archive itself, the agents who manage its contents, the contexts in which this process takes place, and the symbolic value of the objects and images selected and organized within these media. As

Mauricio Puentes-Cala mentions, citing other authors, the archive is "a set of testimonies, traces, symbols, images, or sounds, organized with unity" [2].

Jacques Derrida developed a concept of the archive that, in addition to clarifying its rationale, identifies premises that provoke reflections on memory, the future, and the power of those who configure and organize the archives. In his famous essay *Archive Fever: A Freudian Impression*, the author defines the archive by identifying several key elements, such as "arkheion," a Greek term that refers to the house or residence of senior magistrates (the Archons), who are responsible for safeguarding what is deposited and have the capacity to interpret the archives [3]. Moreover, he asserts that "The archive is situated in the origin and structural rupture of so-called memory" [3]. In this sense, both physical and digital fashion archives of brands could be linked to the construction of the cultural memory of the brand, which can be connected to the reflection and visibility of metaphors and social discourses from daily life. These relate directly to the context, presenting portraits and photographs that showcase the everyday life of traditional elites, which, in turn, are influenced by international trends.

Regarding memory, it is the raw material of archives. When it is appropriated and reconstructed through a felt recollection, it materializes and externalizes by being recorded in documents or other mediums, which later become part of an archival process [2]. Memory can be individual or collective, which allows archives and documents to serve as historical sources or objects of study. Mauricio Puentes states that "both the document and the archive are institutionalized forms of memory, mnemonic technologies that materialize and communicate the experiences of a past time, and thus constitute a specialization of the traces of the past." In this regard, through fashion archives, we can recognize social constructions of bodies, genders, their relationships, and their social contexts, which in this case self-define as luxury and elite.

Memory is related to heritage, which is understood as a set of both immaterial and material assets valued as elements of a historical inheritance. According to Puentes-Cala, citing Gramsci, "heritage is, like memory, an artifact within a social system that can be modified and reinvented according to the hegemonic-cultural criteria and interests of power structures and in accordance with the conventions and worldviews of social groups". When memory is externalized, socialized, and acquires cultural value, it transforms into a patrimonial manifestation. From this perspective, understanding and making visible objects and products as cultural objects that generate collective Colombian memory becomes important for the historical tracking of both the brand and the country's culture.

Archives are also public spaces where, traditionally, only historians have had access to consider what memory presents as fact [1]. Without archives, there is no memory, and it is these archives that ensure that historical understanding is not lost or forgotten; they validate experiences, perceptions, narratives, and stories [4]. However, the vast undocumented and unstudied space of fashion and dressing memory is a topic of discussion, as is the role of historians in this field. It may also be important to question whether it is only historians and government organizations with traditional practices who can generate open memory and archives. We might ask: Can these digital repositories of material culture of brands be relevant and faithful to a historical moment in the field or localized culture? Or can they be only the memory and legacy of the brand itself?

What is certain is that the relationship between culture and context, as proposed by Fontanille [5], demonstrates that bodies and fashion reveal “ways of life” that express contemporary styles, which undoubtedly unveil social modes, moments, and hierarchies of culture in terms of texts or signs, as suggested by Lotman [6]. In this way, these stories captured through total looks become visible in certain Colombian brands as they studied here. While they may not possess a physical archive, they have chosen to showcase iconic pieces that reflect a local identity, intangible heritage tied to the use of artisanal techniques, and business know-how that has developed over time. These are presented to the public through audiovisual content that constructs narratives about the brand, its vision of luxury, and the story and trajectory of the brand. All of this is curated on an open, widely used platform like Instagram.

3 Cataloging Archives and Opening to the Digital World

Resources related to the fashion system have prompted three main areas of intervention in the archive, according to Canella: the heritage of a brand or designer preserved in archives or libraries; the production or manufacturing processes in product and apparel areas; and images from magazines, advertisements, or audiovisual productions. Pierce categorizes archives into four types: corporate fashion archives, heritage fashion archives, academic fashion archives, and online digital fashion archives. Thanks to this variety, these archives can contain everything from textile samples to garments, accessories, sketches, technical sheets, and fashion films [7].

As mentioned, the archive catalogs and preserves artifacts, documents, or images, but also collects symbols created due to the context in which it is built and the intention of the archivist. In the fashion system, this is even more complex due to the quantity and variety of elements that may form part of the archive, as well as the diversity of individuals who may consult and freely enjoy its documents. Moreover, archives have become increasingly important in the fashion system, as they allow companies, brands, and institutions to preserve their own legacy, which can be accessed by both internal and external parties to produce or reproduce a product or implement marketing and advertising strategies [8]. This is the case for global luxury brands such as Dior, Armani, Versace, and Ferragamo, among others, which have dedicated human and financial resources to create their own archives, in many cases in digital formats. For example, the pioneering Gian Franco Ferré Foundation created a platform in 2008 with the goal of preserving and cataloging everything that constitutes the designer’s creative career, making thousands of images available to the public for free [7]. Similarly, Armani focused its archival practices on digitizing iconic pieces, which were then transferred to a platform developed specifically to catalog and access these images. These can be consulted in a dedicated area with computers at their Museum in Milan. On the other hand, Ferragamo has created a section on its museum website where users can take a virtual tour of their archive.

Digital platforms have allowed archives to move from being almost fixed, isolated, and closed spaces to being positioned in a broader, more international sphere, reaching diverse users and democratizing access. The arrival of the 4.0 revolution brought new digital techniques, which are being explored and used in the digital transformation of many entities, including those focused on the arts and culture. New technologies also invite reflection on future forms, techniques, and tools for cataloging and preservation. Additionally, access to platforms like Instagram has enabled institutions, archives, and museums to engage different types of users, making them part of the documentation process due to their open and participatory nature. As Jensen states, "The archives have the opportunity to place themselves in the mediation junction between communication, self-presentation, and memory and offer history and eternity to the volatile photo practices as a part of their strategy" ([9], p. 311). In the case of Mario Hernández, the brand does not have a physical space designated as an archive; however, Instagram has facilitated communication and marketing strategies, which have established a dynamic of communicating the brand's trajectory while showcasing its legacy, iconic products, and new products that somehow reflect Colombian identity. This is evidenced in photography campaigns and the type of content that showcases the artisanal production process behind each collection and the connection to the MH brand, its visual identity, and branding.

Another vital aspect of building archives is the act of consigning. Referring to Derrida, the act of consigning not only involves depositing or assigning documents to be preserved but also gathering signs systematically, where elements are articulated as a unit. As mentioned in the previous section, opening the archive to the public is key, as its purpose is to communicate and serve as a knowledge space where people and historians can explore the past. Casareto, cited by Puentes-Cala, states that "there is no archive without an outside". If this does not happen, the archive becomes a mere storage space or a collection of documents and images, a fixed, immovable place relegated to obscurity. Thus, archives present themselves as dynamic elements, products of intentions that influence what is archived and that bind the entire collection of elements [1]. Jensen mentions that hashtags on Instagram can be used to catalog and systematize content. In this aspect, based on the analysis of posts from the MH account, hashtags can be more specific in terms of what is being cataloged and organized as a contemporary style or mode. However, from the observer's perspective, these modes, styles, and bodies can be understood as cultural and sociological categories, transforming these consigned elements into structuring and organizing components.

4 Identity Through Mastery of Technique

Craftsmanship, evidenced in products, materials, inputs, and primarily in the manual manufacturing technique, is a characteristic element of luxury fashion brands. Accessories and garments from this market are associated with the know-how, saper fare, and savoir-faire of artisans, masters who, through a diversity of techniques, bring certain representative pieces of a fashion house to life.

Craftsmanship, according to Ramón Rivas, is a cultural heritage through which a people can identify themselves, feel represented, and pass a particular technique from generation to generation [10, p. 80]. In the case of globally recognized fashion houses like Louis Vuitton, Gucci, Hermès, Ferragamo, and others, their iconic products, as handcrafted works, represent a heritage through which they identify themselves as a brand, and in some way, they inherit a know-how that transcends generations of producers and consumers. This is the case with Bottega Veneta's *intrecciato* leather weaving technique used in high-end leather accessory production, Chanel's bouclé tweed weaving by Lesage, Ferragamo's leather craftsmanship for shoes, the handcrafting of the Hermès Kelly Bag, and the bamboo handle carving of Gucci bags.

Rivas also quotes Hoelscher in his article, who mentions that today, heritage constitutes elements associated with identity and refers to the contemporary uses of the past for a variety of strategic goals, whether economic or particularly relevant for constructing identities. In the context of luxury brands, designers, in their creative processes, take elements from their identity to rethink silhouettes, narratives, and proposals that, while drawing from contemporary influences, continue to construct identity. One of the purposes of the archive is to preserve the *savoir-faire*, the *know-how*, the *saper fare* of a brand, which can be "consulted" and transferred by being exposed digitally and analogously in image or video formats that communicate the techniques traditionally carried out by artisans. Preserving heritage, as it is referred to by many luxury brands, has been a concern for different fashion houses in Europe in recent years, as they possess a wealth of production techniques, materials, styles, and a narrative that has transcended time and certain population contexts. This is often done alongside global marketing and branding strategies that communicate artisanal processes and techniques through various channels such as Instagram and YouTube [11].

Digital environments have allowed fashion archive audiences to become more diverse, in line with the different types of archives that can be created. These agents, who make up this audience, can include students, academics, designers, and producers, among others. This has led to a sort of democratization of archives, allowing for the preservation of the material they contain and the transfer of the mentioned heritage. Documents and archives play a role that transcends borders, in the sense that they are built according to the purposes and needs of social groups and organizations. They are multifunctional, meaning they can be interpreted in various ways, assigning different values and uses to their nature, depending on the context in which they are constructed.

In the case of designer Mario Hernández, Instagram has been a space that not only exposes new products but also shares photos and short videos that reveal the industrial and artisanal processes behind some pieces, the iconographic elements implemented in the designs, and the aesthetics that permeate the creative development of the brand. At the same time, by incorporating elements of Colombian culture into the designs, the brand generates memory, heritage, and an identity associated with "local luxury." It is noteworthy, according to the analysis conducted, that this production and communication model is borrowed from the luxury established by the previously mentioned European brands.

It is evident that part of the creative and productive legacy of the company lies in the reinterpretation of elements associated with Colombian identity. One such example is the "sombrero aguadeño," an iconic symbol of Colombian culture. Not only is it notable for the over 150-year tradition of its unique and collective weaving technique from the region of Aguadas, Caldas, but it is also recognized for its use of the endemic Iraca fiber. This hat has become a symbol of Colombian identity, especially among the traditional and conservative political class, who wear it as part of their political image. Recent Colombian presidents have also used it to complement their wardrobe, linking it to national heritage.

Similarly, the *ruana* from the Cundiboyacense highlands, associated with the indigenous and rural culture of the country's central region, has become a symbol of national identity. It is crafted from the finest wool fibers, providing a connection to artisan luxury. Alongside this, the *carriel paisa* (a traditional leather saddle bag from the region of Valle de Aburrá) serves as a symbol of coffee culture and the rural heritage. The brand has reimagined this item in high-end leather designs, combining traditional craftsmanship with contemporary attributes and the brand's signature graphics, like the monarch butterfly. These items are distributed through a digital archive consisting of photos and reels. These reels showcase product images, models, Colombian landscapes, and locations, along with texts discussing tradition and luxury. Additionally, reels communicate the manufacturing process, highlighting the human component, from the operators and artisans to the creators and owners of the company. In this way, digital platforms have become a space where heritage, technique, and identity converge, presenting luxury goods not only as symbols of high craftsmanship but also as elements that carry cultural meaning, bridging the past and present.

5 The MH Digital Archive Studied and Method

The nature of contemporary fashion archives is characterized by cross-media integration and a diversity of content, resulting in repositories laden with meanings derived from a brand's intentions and what it seeks to represent and preserve as integral to its identity.

For this interpretation, a semiotic interpretative methodology was employed to analyze images and short videos from the perspective of advertising visual analysis, specifically that of Jacques Fontanille. In this regard, the study, based on Fontanille's semiotic practices, considers the examination of semiotic objects—given that advertisements produce specific forms of signification imbued with values and modes—to understand the rationale and context of these values as objects of inquiry [5]. Complementarily, the visual semiotic analysis method of Jean-Marie Floch was incorporated, which was utilized to describe the "Total Look of Coco Chanel" [12]. This approach provides the possibility to construct relational instruments and resources for analyzing advertising photography, reels, short videos, and the brand's documentary photography, with the aim of visualizing and interpreting the image alongside the advertising messages, resources, objects, scenes, bodily representations, models, poses, attitudes, narratives, and discourse that together configure a particular style and way of life through communication.

Since the objective of this analysis is to understand the concepts associated with identity and luxury, as well as to comprehend the composition of discourses based on both the materiality of the archives and their advertising, the concept of metaphor by Lakoff and Johnson is adopted. This concept engages with discourse analysis based on everyday reality to interpret not only the scene itself but also the potential cultural relationships. Analytical instruments for the study of photographs, videos, and advertisements are constructed through the application of the theories of Fontanille [13] and Floch [12]. See Table 1.

As the research body, a sample of 100 posts from the visual archive of Mario Hernández—deposited on Instagram (@mh_colombia) and spanning the last 2 years (2023–2024)—was selected. The brand Mario Hernández was chosen due to its extensive history of nearly 15 years in the Colombian market, and slightly less internationally, factors that establish it as one of the emblematic Colombian fashion brands. For this reason, the images and reels published on Mario Hernández's Instagram feed initially demonstrate a series of internal practices whereby the brand stages Colombian cultural values and practices in its content to communicate various aspects of the company, ranging from its products to the production process of certain designs.

Table 1 Matrix of analysis. Source: Own elaboration

Factor Analyzed	Physical Dimension
Physical dimension	Distribution of images, statements, spatial arrangements
Discourse and narration	Context, social, or everyday life narratives, advertising messages
Corporeality	Age, pose, gestures, ethnicity, values, roles, and representation of models
Statement analysis	Expressive figures, textual resources, discursive strategies, objectives
Ethos	Lifestyle, practices, and style

6 The Embodiment of Luxury and the Vision of the Colombian Product

Subjecting luxury to a process of embodiment has become highly significant in the development of brand identity. Clearly establishing a corporeal brand deepens experiential expectations and even fosters a form of pedagogy about how to live and experience life from a bodily perspective. In this regard, everyday life situations of individuals—segmented according to the characteristics of their lifestyles—are proposed as models and metaphors for luxury. Initially, the brand delineates people as agents who model the ideals of luxury and identity as proposed by Mario Hernández. In this sense, on the first observation the models promoted adhere to the traditional heterosexual matrix, with advertising presented in a conservative and traditional manner as distinctly feminine and masculine. In the case of femininities, thin, blonde, and fair-skinned corporealities are predominantly utilized; however, naturally stylized brown skin with Latino features is also introduced. Nonetheless, these corporealities remain highly idealized, conforming to the beauty stereotypes of slenderness and youth, and—coupled with sublime poses—tend to evoke impressions of seduction, confidence, and status.

The roles associated with luxury and elitism involve social spaces such as clubs, restaurants, and landscapes like the Bogotá savannah, which illustrate how nature is linked to the enjoyment of club life, thereby presenting this lifestyle as exemplary. In these settings, both men and women, dressed in sophisticated attire, form the communicative framework and spectacle of luxury in Colombia. Similarly, men also slender assuming a more moderated form of masculinity. Their corporeal representations are not overly muscular but are instead constructed through an emphasis on security, style of dress, and the environments in which they are situated—thereby defining a style of man associated with social, business, club, and travel circles. In this regard, Colombia has crafted various luxury imaginaries through fashion and its products; thus, the conception of social clubs, travel, and the broader social sphere as exclusive spaces plays a significant role in how luxury is understood. Moreover, the idea of localization and identity as luxury is regarded as a key differentiator for the Mario Hernández brand. Emphasizing the value of artisanal products—and recognizing artisans as master craftsmen—further enriches the discourse on cultural and natural wealth as a luxury experience.

In this sense, showcasing the work and development of artisans from the production stage engenders a certain refinement in the brand's fashion products and accessories. While Louis Vuitton is renowned worldwide for the mastery of its leather goods—balancing tradition, skill, and modernity—the Colombian brand follows a similar trajectory by incorporating the value of its national craftsmanship, which is also tied to traditional trades, the biodiverse landscapes of Colombia, and the hands that create them. This approach provides a positive appraisal of the artisanal realm.

Even though the strategy might appear to parallel that of Louis Vuitton, it is evident that there exist a localization and differentiation in the discourses and visions that define the brand as intrinsically Colombian. Symbols such as the Aguadeño hat—associated with coffee culture—the "carrieles," Gabo's butterflies, as well as textiles and braids, serve as elements that evoke and reimagine Colombian culture as a space of luxury and sophistication.

7 Conclusions

Although digital network tools are presented as spaces for visibility, brand communication, and transparency as living repositories, they are constructed as public digital memory. Such repositories facilitate cataloging, documentation, and dissemination, enabling not only the tracing and understanding of a brand's history, tradition, and discourse but also serving as a viable and fundamental tool for assessing their impact on audiences. In this context, the role of the contemporary historian and archivist can be enriched by these repositories, which provide a window into the study of material culture through brands. This is achieved without diminishing traditional practices, techniques, and documentation—those that are analogous and specific to well-known archives—while simultaneously broadening the scope of study to include categorization within the social and digital realms (e.g., hashtags, likes, among others).

As observed, archives are spaces for the preservation of memory through documentation, cataloging, and organization. They communicate a distinct know-how that forms the identity of a brand and encapsulates a corporate and creative trajectory that ultimately becomes a legacy. This legacy enables entities to connect consumers, designers, and brand owners with the future while re-signifying the past.

Regarding the construction of legacy and heritage, archives are fundamental for documentation and record-keeping. It is through these readings that one can delve into the identity elements which reveal what brands truly value, build, and communicate. In this study, it becomes apparent that luxury continues to uphold conservative and elite visions that involve traditional gender roles and are linked to beauty stereotypes constructed on appearance, as well as the enduring imprint of coloniality.

A compelling possibility is that identity and artisanal work may, from the outset, constitute the true essence of luxury—although, due to colonial perceptions, this idea is only just beginning to be proposed. International brands have increasingly recognized this as a fundamental value in fashion. The overall look of luxury communicated by the brand is associated with bodies, races, people, places, and products. In this way, the symbolic universe of luxury in Colombia alludes to nature as a space of exclusivity, to stereotypical bodies, to binary constructs, and to the coffee tradition. In line with Derrida's notion of the archive as discourse, the discourse of Colombian fashion has shifted toward the luxury of the artisanal, with Mario Hernández emerging as one of its foremost proponents.

References

1. Barros, A. N. (2016). Archives and the "archive": Dialogue and an agenda of research in organization studies. *iOrganizações & Sociedade, 23/i*(79), 609. https://www.scielo.br/j/osoc/a/gM3PyV7ykgXJdW4LNYdzhHp/#ModalTutorsclass
2. Puentes-Cala, M. (2022). Archivística e historia: Un diálogo por el deber de recordar y el derecho a saber. *E-Ciencias de la Información, 12*(1), 158–187. https://doi.org/10.15517/eci.v12i1.48172
3. Derrida, J., & Prenowitz, E. (1995). Archive fever: A Freudian impression. *Diacritics, 25*(2), 9–63. https://doi.org/10.2307/465144
4. Schwartz, J. M., & Cook, T. (2002). Archives, records, and power: The making of modern memory. *Archival Science, 2*, 1–19. https://doi.org/10.1007/BF02435628
5. Fontanille, J. (2016). Análisis del curso de acción de las prácticas. *Contratexto, 25*(025), 127–152. https://doi.org/10.26439/contratexto2016.n025.655
6. Lotman, I. M. (1998). *La semiosfera I*. I.S.B.N. Retrieved from https://circulosemiotico.files.wordpress.com/2012/10/i-lotman-semiosfera-ii.pdf
7. Canella, M. (2017). Archives for studying the relationship between fashion, society and politics in Italy. *Contemporanea, 20*(4), 699–705. http://www.jstor.org/stable/44809828
8. Andò, R., Briatore, S., & Denaro, G. (2023). Rethinking fashion storytelling through digital archives and immersive museum experiences. In N. Sabatini, T. Sádaba, A. Tosi, V. Neri, & L. Cantoni (Eds.), *Fashion communication in the digital age. FACTUM 2023. Springer proceedings in business and economics*. Springer. https://doi.org/10.1007/978-3-031-38541-4_26
9. Jensen, B. (2013). Instagram as cultural heritage: User participation, historical documentation, and curating in museums and archives through social media. *2013 Digital Heritage International Congress (DigitalHeritage), 2*, 311–314.
10. Rivas, R. D. (2018). La artesanía: Patrimonio e identidad cultural. *Revista De Museología, 9*, 80–96. https://doi.org/10.5377/koot.v0i9.5908
11. Cabigiosu, A. (2020). An overview of the luxury fashion industry. *Digitalization in the Luxury Fashion Industry.*, 9–31. https://doi.org/10.1007/978-3-030-48810-9_2
12. Floch, J. (1967). El total look de Coco Chanel. *Revista de Occidente, 366*, 181–200.
13. Fontanille, J. (2014). *Prácticas semióticas*. Universidad de Lima, Fondo Editorial.

Leveraging Heritage Argumentation Strategies in Luxury Fashion Brands' Storytelling

Elisa Zanola, Charlotte Stachel, and Sara Greco

Abstract The concept of heritage preserves and promotes a brand's storied past to maintain its symbolic appeal in the present and future (Hakala et al., Journal of Product and Brand Management 20:447–456, 2011). Through storytelling techniques, luxury fashion brands draw on their historical narratives to transmit values such as authenticity, continuity, and exclusivity via offline and online channels (Kapferer and Bastien, Digitalization in the luxury fashion industry. Palgrave Macmillan, 2020; Cabigiosu, Digitalization in the luxury fashion industry. Palgrave Macmillan, 2020). A strategic use of heritage not only serves to strengthen brand identity but also provides a competitive advantage by linking creative legacy with cultural heritage and creating an emotional bond with consumers (Visconti, Communicating luxury brands through stories. In Morhart et al. (Eds.) Research handbook on luxury branding (pp. 203–221). Edward Elgar Publishing, 2020; Hakala et al., Journal of Product and Brand Management 20:447-456, 2011; Bernasconi et al., Storytelling empresarial: Relações públicas contador de histórias. Intercom, Sociedade Brasileira de Estudos Interdisciplinares da Comunicação, 2011). This study aims to contribute to a deeper understanding of the role of heritage in the digital communication of luxury fashion brands Gucci and Louis Vuitton. The types of heritage-related arguments and rhetorical strategies the two brands use to create consistent storytelling are analysed by examining their official websites and Instagram accounts. Introducing the locus from internal authority as a new concept in argumentation studies offers a fresh perspective on how brands can leverage their history as a source of credibility.

Keywords Heritage · Storytelling · Argumentation · Digital fashion communication · Locus from internal authority

E. Zanola · C. Stachel (✉) · S. Greco
USI – Università della Svizzera italiana, Lugano, Switzerland
e-mail: elisa.zanola@usi.ch; charlotte.stachel@usi.ch; sara.greco@usi.ch

P. von Wachenfeldt et al. (eds.), *Fashion Communication in the Digital Age*,
Springer Proceedings in Business and Economics,
https://doi.org/10.1007/978-3-031-99481-4_5

1 Introduction

The luxury fashion sector is characterised by its long-established traditions, historical importance, cultural value, and uniqueness, which are linked to its goods [1]. Luxury items distinguish themselves through their attributed authenticity, exclusivity, and quality [2, 3]. To maintain their longstanding reputation as well as the notion of being desirable and sophisticated in a competitive market, luxury fashion brands rely on consistent narratives to convey their identity and values, engage consumers, and invite them into meaningful brand universes [4, 5]. This entails carefully orchestrating language, visuals, and further elements reinforcing the brand's heritage while showcasing its relevance in the contemporary world. Omnichannel strategies create a seamless, cohesive, and brand-focused experience that is essential for effectively transmitting clear messages around brand heritage. Luxury brands' websites and social media accounts are among the main tools for communicating identity and values, ensuring that storied pasts resonate with a digital audience [6].

This study analyses how luxury fashion brands Gucci and Louis Vuitton leverage their heritage through storytelling on their official brand websites and Instagram accounts. It identifies similarities and differences in heritage-related terms (keyword analysis) as well as argumentative strategies (argumentation analysis), and it examines to which extent the storytelling elements, themes, and messaging strategies are aligned across the two platforms (comparative consistency evaluation). Based on the analysis, a new concept emerges in argumentation studies: the locus from internal authority. This represents a novel perspective on analysing how luxury fashion brands leverage heritage in their digital communication.

2 Literature Review

2.1 Heritage in Luxury Fashion Brands

Heritage has become increasingly relevant for fashion brands in the 2000s to enhance their historical narratives [7]. Urde et al. (2007, p. 4) define brand heritage as "a dimension of a brand's identity found in its track record, longevity, core values, use of symbols and particularly in an organisational belief that its history is important" [8]. Pecot and De Barnier (2017) further describe a brand's legacy as a set of symbols and values that express its anchoring to the past and continuity over time, which implies longevity and stability [9]. Fashion heritage can thus be summarised as "the visual, physical, and cognitive legacy of a brand" [10, p. 297]. Further key features of heritage in luxury fashion brands are "the history associated with its founder and its craftsmanship" [11, cited in 12, p. 132]; a connection to a specific territory, which demonstrates craftsmanship and cultural capital [13]; and iconic products, that are continuously reinvented, featuring visual symbols that reflect the tradition and provide consistency [14]. The sum of these visible (products and symbols) and invisible elements (values and history) can create a perception of quality that serves to maintain a brand's credibility, reliability, and authenticity [15, 16]. From a consumer's perspective, luxury brands with a history have a symbolic appeal as they reflect a longstanding reputation, conveying the notion of being valuable and sophisticated [4, 17]. This sense of continuity over time is embodied in brand heritage, which can lead to higher positive sentiments, trust, and customer loyalty [14, 18, 19].

The brands' corporate archives play an essential role in building heritage. These historical collections and spaces represent the brands' essence; they provide knowledge that inspires current design practices and contain assets for marketing and communication efforts [13]. Since the 2000s, fashion exhibitions based on brands' archival content have gained significant popularity. Besides showcasing fashion heritage in museums, luxury fashion brands rely on other channels to transmit their history and legacy to potential consumers [7]. Martin and Vacca (2018) highlight the importance of engagement in the relationship between heritage, archives, and knowledge development in fashion retail. This can take numerous forms, including store design and fashion movies, to create immersive customer experiences [20].

2.2 *Brand Storytelling on Digital Platforms*

Storytelling serves as a vehicle for cultural transmission, education, and entertainment, as this universal technique effectively conveys consistent messages to diverse audiences and excels in digital environments [5, 21, 22]. To communicate brand heritage, storytelling techniques are especially suited, as they build narratives upon a core story related to the brand identity, enriched with core values, products, and visual emblems [14, 23, 24]. It is thus an indispensable strategy for luxury brands, driven by an increased focus on customer experiences and the multiplication of touchpoints between them and their customers [25–27]. The interplay between narrative persuasion and emotional engagement is especially relevant for luxury brand storytelling [23].

Stories surrounding products can enable entertainment and escapism and intensify the symbolic meanings of luxury brands, thus increasing positive brand associations and leading customers to look beyond the brands' commercial aims [5, 28–30].

Visconti (2020) outlines two different storytelling strategies that luxury fashion brands can apply: (1) a *denotative* (literal) *approach* [31], suggesting that stories about the brand itself (e.g. its creator, history, iconic items, endorsements, and universe) should be embraced as opposed to (2) a *connotative* (metaphoric) *approach* [31], which weakens the connection between the narrative and the product by promoting narratives that are not directly related to the brand itself, yet attractive to the luxury brand's clientele [32].

2.3 Argumentation in Digital Fashion Communication

Modern consumers perceive brands not merely as providers of products but as connectors that facilitate meaningful interactions. While websites remain a popular platform for brands to apply different storytelling strategies, this evolution aligns seamlessly with the essence of social media [33]. Instagram stands out as a powerful platform for the luxury fashion industry, with 93% of consumers' engagement with luxury brands occurring on the channel [34, 35].

As consumer attention is increasingly fragmented across numerous digital platforms, the stories told by fashion brands have to be compelling and credible to persuade their recipients [36]. This can be achieved through successful argumentation, which is a discourse-based communication activity ideally "aimed at convincing the addressee of the acceptability of the standpoint by making them see that mutually shared critical standards of reasonableness have been met" [37, p. 6]. Thus, argumentation studies, since their Aristotelian origin, ideally appeal to reasonable persuasion as opposed to manipulation and deception. Within argumentative discussions, arguments are exchanged in support of standpoints [38]. Marsh (2007) highlights the importance of specific rhetorical strategies or argument schemes in advertising and suggests a more nuanced approach to message creation by applying classical rhetorical invention to enhance creativity and effectiveness in copywriting [39]. The author examines how the four causes identified by Aristotle as present in social reality and reasoning processes—namely, efficient, material, final, and formal cause—are often employed to structure advertising messages [39]. The study of specific argument schemes in argumentation studies has a long tradition, often related to the metaphor of the topos or locus (English: place), as the seat or source from which concrete arguments are drawn [38]. Hence, if a bag is advertised based on the argument that "It is made from the best Italian leather", for example, it is based on the locus from material cause, as it is based on the materials of which it is created. Beyond the loci based on the four material causes by Marsh (2017), other loci are listed in the Argumentum Model of Topics (AMT) [38, 39]. In particular, we consider the locus from authority, which draws the acceptability of the standpoint from the authority of an external source (e.g. a testimonial, expert or influencer). This study has revealed the locus from internal authority. To the best of our knowledge, this new locus is unknown in previous literature. It is based on an internal authority relative to the brand, for example, the authority of the founder, or of iconic and traditional pieces.

3 Methodology

This study seeks to uncover how Gucci and Louis Vuitton communicate their heritage narratives. It compares the frequency, context, and way heritage-related terms appear in the brands' Instagram posts and website contents and the related argumentative strategies. Thus, the following research questions are asked:

1. What are the key terms and specific loci that communicate the brands' heritage?
2. To what extent do luxury fashion brands leverage their heritage and create consistent storytelling across their online communication?

Data were collected from the official brand websites (Gucci's *History of Gucci* page and Louis Vuitton's *La Maison* page) and the official Instagram accounts between February and July 2024. The Instagram sample comprised 56 posts from Gucci and 100 posts from Louis Vuitton. The smaller number in Gucci Instagram posts resulted due to the change of its creative director from Alessandro Michele to Sabato De Sarno, which caused all Gucci Instagram posts prior to September 16, 2023, to be deleted. The sample period concluded on March 5, 2024, and the previously stated number of posts published before this date was included. This end date coincided with the closing of Paris Womenswear Fall/Winter 2024–2025 Fashion Week, a pivotal event that gathers significant attention and engagement from both brands and consumers. Thus, it is an opportune moment for brands to reinforce their narratives and storytelling efforts. Only Instagram posts with at least one heritage-related keyword were analysed; reels were not considered.

Keyword analysis and argumentation analysis were applied to answer the first research question. Comparative consistency evaluation was conducted to answer the second research question.

3.1 Keyword Analysis

Through a systematic review of the texts and captions, terms in the semantic field of heritage were identified and categorised, and the frequency and context of these keywords were determined [40]. The keywords were derived from the literature review and iteratively from the analysed texts. The complete list of terms can be seen in Table 1. These keywords served as the basis for the textual examination undertaken in the argumentation analysis.

Table 1 Number of frequently used heritage-related keywords on Gucci and Louis Vuitton websites and in Instagram posts

Keywords	Gucci		Louis Vuitton	
	Website (488 words)	Instagram (1976 words)	Website (1324 words)	Instagram (4566 words)
Archive/archival	7	9	0	1
Code	0	8	0	10
Craftsmanship/artisanal	2	4	5	7
Emblematic	1	8	1	24
Heritage	1	10	2	15
History/historic	1	5	1	5
Icon/iconic	0	16	1	30
Legacy	0	2	0	1
Monogram	2	2	3	16
Savoir-faire	0	0	1	10
Signature	1	10	0	27
Timeless	0	3	0	8
Travel/traveller	1	16	4	13
Trunk/luggage	1	1	10	14
Voyage	0	0	0	7
Total	*17 (3.5%)*	*94 (4.8%)*	*28 (2.1%)*	*188 (4.1%)*

3.2 Argumentation Analysis

Argumentation analysis is a suitable method to "analyse multimodal social media content with a critical outlook. It allows retrieving the standpoint brought forward by the speaker, which arguments are adopted to support it and, finally, how to evaluate their soundness" [36, p. 109]. The AMT model introduced by Rigotti and Greco (2010, 2019) is used to identify recurrent loci in the verbal content. One of the important characteristics of the AMT model is that it posits that each argument is based on combining two interrelated components [38, 41]. The former is a procedural-inferential component based on the locus, constituting the *inferential machinery* that strengthens each argument. The latter is a material-contextual component, which anchors the specific argument in the cultural context that is accepted by the arguers [38]. While we leave the detailed explanation and traditional terminology of the AMT model out (see [38]), for this study, we have used a schematised version of the AMT model. Table 3 includes the names of the loci, while Table 4 shows the inferential principle, which represents the rule governing the inferential machinery of the considered locus. Table 4 also includes the cultural premise, the culturally and contextually anchored general premise on which the argument is based. The cultural premise is then associated with a factual premise, which states how the general cultural principle is instantiated in the case of the specific product considered. Each of these premises reveals the hidden component of each argument. The premises can all be discussed in terms of truth or acceptability for the relevant audience and evaluated. In this way, the AMT model proves a tool to disentangle the different components of an argument and evaluate their strength. Pictures are part of logical arguments and can reinforce them. In a previous study by Zanola (2024), visual components on the brands' websites and Instagram posts were considered for the analysis by combining the AMT model with Groarke's (2017) ART approach to multimodal argumentation [42, 43]. Due to space limitations, they were omitted from this study.

3.3 Comparative Consistency Evaluation

Through a comparative consistency evaluation, the coherence of the heritage narratives within the brands' communication across the two platforms was assessed to determine how carefully the brands tailor their messaging to suit the specific audience and maintain a coherent brand identity across different digital touchpoints.

4 Results

4.1 Keyword Analysis

Websites The *History of Gucci* section on the official Gucci website is structured into various sections within a single page, seamlessly guiding the viewer through the brand's history. Central to the webpage is a timeline charting Gucci's milestones from its inception in the 1920s to the present, featuring iconic products. Within the 488-word text, 17 heritage-related keywords were detected. On the official Louis Vuitton website's *La Maison* section, visitors can find a subsection concerning Heritage, which provides rich textual and visual content that reflects the brand's history and values. Table 1 lists the heritage-related keywords used by the brands and their number.

Within the 1324-word text, 28 heritage-related keywords were identified. Due to the higher total number of words, Louis Vuitton presents a more varied use of heritage-related terms on its website. The most-used words are *trunk/luggage*, which refer to the brand's historical roots in trunk-making. On the Gucci website, the variation of heritage-related terms is more limited: they appear a maximum of twice, except for *archive* and its Italian translation *archivio*, which are the most-used words. This is because Gucci's website emphasises archival content and historical collections, with detailed descriptions and images of historical collections taken from the archive. However, the percentage of heritage-related terms is higher on Gucci's website (3.5%) than on Louis Vuitton's (2.1%).

Instagram Equally to the results from the website analysis, Louis Vuitton demonstrates a more varied use of heritage-related terms on Instagram than Gucci. Gucci's most-used keywords in the Instagram captions are *travel/traveller*, which hints at the brand's history in producing travel goods, and *icon/iconic*. Also in Louis Vuitton's Instagram captions, the most-used keyword is the *icon/iconic*. This term highlights the brands' emphasis on positioning certain products as timeless, historically, and culturally relevant, thus maintaining an iconic status, a critical aspect of luxury brand storytelling. Two examples are Gucci's Jackie bag and Flora Motif and Louis Vuitton's signature Monogram trunks and patterns.

4.2 Argumentation Analysis

Websites The brands' website contents focus on educating the reader about the brand's history and heritage rather than explicitly promoting product purchases. Table 2 shows the number and types of loci that have been found on both brands' websites and Instagram posts.

Due to this descriptive nature of the text, the number of loci identified is relatively low. Gucci's website contains arguments of three different loci (from internal authority, efficient cause, and formal cause). While featuring five loci, Louis Vuitton's website mostly displays the locus from internal authority and final cause (besides formal cause, efficient cause, and external authority). For Gucci, the narrative frequently references the brand's historical significance and the craftsmanship behind its products. In this case, the locus from authority is not external. Notably, the authority is exceptionally internal, as Gucci itself relies on its own history and heritage to represent the authority, justified by its longstanding tradition and past. For Louis Vuitton, the locus from internal authority is reflected in the brand's mention of its historical roots in trunk-making and artisanal skills, which embody historical credibility, tradition, and expertise. In the case of both brands, the locus from internal authority is about the alignment with a tradition that holds intrinsic or internal authority. In some respects, it resembles the locus from efficient cause (i.e., the

Table 2 Number and types of loci identified on the websites and in the Instagram posts of Gucci and Louis Vuitton

	Gucci		Louis Vuitton	
Locus	Website (488 words)	Instagram (1976 words)	Website (1324 words)	Instagram (4566 words)
External authority	0	18	1	31
Internal authority	8	49	9	87
Efficient cause	2	26	1	59
Final cause	0	5	8	8
Formal cause	2	18	2	52
Material cause	0	3	0	17

connection between the producer and the product). Still, it goes beyond the locus from efficient cause by incorporating the element of tradition, which functions as an internal authority. In the case of Gucci, for example, references to Guccio Gucci and the brand's early years are not just historical anecdotes; they serve as authoritative endorsements of current products. The suggestion is that if a product aligns with Gucci's storied tradition, it is automatically endowed with prestige and credibility. This ethos of self-confirmation, where the brand's origin and history act as an internal authority, sets the locus from internal authority apart from other previously identified loci.

In contrast to the locus from internal authority, the locus from efficient cause is about the creation process of the products. It is highlighted on both brands' websites through the detailed descriptions of the craftsmanship, artistry, and skill involved in manufacturing the products. This is evident in both Gucci's and Louis Vuitton's emphasis on their artisans and the processes involved in their workshops, which emphasise the authenticity of the brands, but also in the highlighted concepts of Italian quality for Gucci and French savoir-faire for Louis Vuitton. The locus from formal cause is reflected in both brands' design principles and aesthetic values, as shown in the narratives about the design evolution of specific products like the Gucci loafers or the Louis Vuitton Monogram. The locus from final cause reflects the aims and objectives of the designers, the products, or the documents. Table 3 demonstrates how the AMT model is applied to a sentence from the Gucci website and led to identifying three arguments based on three different loci.

The primary explicit standpoint on both websites is a prescription: "Learn more about the brand's history and heritage", which is related to the brands' intention to educate the viewers about their history and heritage. The commercially oriented standpoint "Buy these products" is less explicit on the website. Instead, it states that the products are desirable and embody the brands' legacy and craftsmanship, thus encouraging viewers to purchase them. The hyperlinks are the manifest expression of this standpoint, as they invite the viewer to visit the e-commerce websites to buy the products. In the brands' Instagram posts, the general standpoint is "Buy these products", which should encourage the audience to make a purchase, besides other calls to action such as "Visit this store" or "Visit this exhibition". For space reasons,

Table 3 Application of the AMT model to a sentence from the Gucci website

Statement	"His [Guccio Gucci's] vision combined exceptional Tuscan materials and craftsmanship with the elegant English aesthetic."	
Issue	Should customers buy Gucci products?	
Standpoint	Yes, customers should buy Gucci products.	
Arguments	1.1 Because they represent Guccio Gucci's vision.	Locus from internal authority
	1.2 Because they are made with exceptional Tuscan materials.	Locus from efficient cause
	1.3 Because they encapsulate the elegant English aesthetic.	Locus from formal cause

Table 4 Reconstruction of an argument from the Gucci website with a locus from internal authority

Inferential principle	If X is an authority in domain D, and product P is guaranteed to be in line with its authority, then P is likely to be a valuable product.
Cultural premise	Historically, the brand Gucci and its founder Guccio Gucci are an authority in the fashion domain.
Factual premise	These products represent Guccio Gucci's vision and are in line with its authority.

the reconstruction of an argument based on the locus from internal authority on the Gucci website has been selected among the different loci to be presented in Table 4.

Instagram In contrast to the brands' website texts, the presence of loci is higher and more varied in their Instagram captions. This is because the total word number is higher on Instagram, and the captions include more direct calls to action. Therefore, the probability of identifying more loci is increased. Both brands predominantly use the locus from internal authority and efficient cause across their Instagram pages, indicating that their arguments rely heavily on their established reputation and their products' inherent quality and craftsmanship. The locus from external authority is present for both brands on Instagram, while it is almost nonexistent on the websites. This is because testimonials, brand ambassadors, and celebrities are almost exclusively used in social media collaborations rather than on websites.

4.3 Comparative Consistency Evaluation

In general, both Gucci and Louis Vuitton strategically utilise their heritage in their online communication, albeit with distinct approaches that mirror their brand identities and market positioning and vary according to the specific platform. The communication strategies chosen by the two brands on the two platforms are largely consistent and cohesive. Louis Vuitton employs a more direct and assertive strategy in leveraging heritage across both online platforms, thus creating an elaborate and multi-faceted argumentative structure and narrative. The brand frequently uses a variety of heritage-related terms and loci to reinforce its craftsmanship, iconic products, and historical connection to the worlds of sport and music. Gucci adopts a more balanced and robust approach to using heritage in its online communication. Through a nuanced use of heritage terms, the brand focuses on archival references and brand history, both on Instagram and on its website, to emphasise the brand's connection to travel. Formal and efficient causes on its website serve as a structured method of explaining how the products are crafted, as well as the significance of the designer and the notion of being made in Italy.

Websites and social media accounts serve different purposes and audiences, which requires distinct communication strategies: On the one hand, websites deliver more substantial narrative content and descriptive explanations. Both Louis Vuitton and Gucci effectively use their websites to provide deeper educational content about their history and craftsmanship, focusing on detailed historical narratives. Although less prominent, the advertising aim remains evident through hyperlinks that direct the reader-customer to the e-commerce web pages. On the other hand, Instagram favours quick, diverse messaging to maintain engagement. The brands' more dynamic and varied Instagram storytelling contrasts with and complements their website content, employing more direct promotional language in the captions to engage and convert consumers. The significantly higher presence of loci in both brands' Instagram posts reflects this. Gucci and Louis Vuitton predominantly use loci from internal authority and efficient cause in their Instagram captions, indicating that their arguments rely significantly on their established reputation and their products' inherent quality and craftsmanship.

5 Discussion

Gucci and Louis Vuitton share many similarities in heritage-infused communication, which are discussed in this section. Both brands often present iconic products (including Louis Vuitton's Monogram and Gucci's Flora motif) to anchor their heritage narratives and guarantee that the current products align with an established tradition. Additionally, both brands are historically associated with the themes of travel and exploration, which is evident in their regular promotion of products like trunks on Instagram. Equally, they emphasise their craftsmanship, frequently referring to trunk-making and artisanal skills. Another similarity between Gucci and Louis Vuitton is that they prominently feature their creative directors, Sabato De Sarno for Gucci and Nicolas Ghesquière and Pharrell Williams for Louis Vuitton, in their storytelling. These directors are shown as the custodians of the brand's heritage, reinterpreting historical elements to create new, contemporary collections. For example, posts may highlight Ghesquière's reinterpretation of classic Louis Vuitton travel trunks in a modern context or De Sarno's archival inspirations for new Gucci collections.

The primary language used in the captions of the Instagram posts of both brands is English. However, French words appear in Louis Vuitton posts, and Italian words are featured in Gucci posts, adding a unique touch to their captions. Terms like *savoir-faire*, referring to French craftsmanship and Paris as the origin of Haute Couture, and *voyage* are only used by Louis Vuitton, connecting the brand with its French origin by using this linguistic choice. Similarly, by embedding Italian terminology such as *archivio* or the hashtag #GucciValigeria into its communication, Gucci aligns itself with the broader narrative of Made in Italy and Italianness, commonly associated with craftsmanship and a distinctive lifestyle. This multilingual approach reflects the global nature of these brands. It hints at a tactic rooted in the brands' desire to be intrinsically linked with the cultural heritage of their country of origin, thus improving their reputation and reinforcing their image [44].

The locus from internal authority used by Gucci and Louis Vuitton extends beyond traditional loci and stands out as a context-specific argumentation strategy related to heritage. Unlike the locus from external authority, which derives authority from external sources such as expert opinion or testimony, the locus from internal authority is deeply embedded within the brand itself, relying on its own history as a source of persuasive argumentation. This new dimension of brand rhetoric is especially pertinent in the luxury fashion industry. The locus from internal authority leverages the brand's historical reputation and significance to construct inherently authoritative arguments, effectively utilising its legacy as a form of self-validation. The cultural premise of this locus can be formulated as: "Historically, the brand Gucci/Louis Vuitton is an authority in the fashion domain". This premise is an expression of the inherent authority that the brands derive from their legacy and deep-rooted tradition in the fashion industry. They create a form of argumentation that is almost religious in its justification: the heritage itself becomes the guarantor of reliability and authenticity, much like it does with religious and other cultural traditions. Suggesting that the products are inherently valuable and trustworthy because they align with a prestigious lineage presents a powerful, yet subtle persuasive strategy. This approach resonates deeply with luxury consumers, who often seek products symbolising historical continuity and cultural significance.

6 Conclusion

This study explored the terms, depth, and consistency with which luxury brands Gucci and Louis Vuitton communicate their heritage across digital platforms. Both brands extensively and strategically leverage their longstanding history and consistently refer to it in their communication via official websites and Instagram posts—yet with varying intensity, focus, and techniques.

Louis Vuitton demonstrates a more assertive and diverse approach on Instagram, presenting a higher number and a more comprehensive range of keywords and loci. This frequent and varied use of loci suggests a more substantial approach to leveraging heritage. Gucci adopts a more balanced focus on archival and iconic elements of the brand, connecting them to new products in a more contemporary manner. It shows a more robust strategy for embedding heritage into its social media narratives with a focus on specific terms, which is also reflected in the descriptive approach on its website. The brands' nuanced sophisticated storytelling across different digital platforms underlines the importance of adapting the brand narratives to the nature of the medium to maintain relevance and engagement in the digital space.

Adopting connotative storytelling strategies and understanding narrative transportation and intertextuality can help luxury brands create engaging stories that stand out in a competitive market [32]. By forming immersive narratives that resonate with consumers' desires for connection and escapism, luxury brands can develop lasting emotional connections with their audience, foster deeper consumer relationships, and ultimately drive brand success. Both brands employ a variety of rhetorical strategies to engage the viewers. In general, the main standpoints are "Learn more about the brand's history and heritage", "Buy Gucci/Louis Vuitton products", and "Visit this store/exhibition". Concerning the use of different loci, both brands predominantly use internal authority and efficient cause, relying on their established reputation and their products' inherent quality and craftsmanship. The presence of the locus from internal authority in both Gucci's and Louis Vuitton's online communications presents a distinctive way to use the concept of heritage to reinforce their brand narratives, leveraging a quasi-religious tradition through argumentation. Identifying this locus is particularly relevant in the luxury sector, where brands can capitalise on their history as a unique selling proposition. Furthermore, the integration of the locus from internal authority into argumentation theory represents a major advancement in understanding how brands can use their heritage not just as a background narrative but as a central component of their persuasive strategy, particularly within the luxury fashion industry.

References

1. Okonkwo, U. (2007). *Luxury fashion branding: Trends, tactics, techniques*. Palgrave Macmillan. https://doi.org/10.1057/9780230590885
2. Montemaggi, M., & Severino, F. (2007). *Heritage marketing: Come aprire lo scrigno e trovare un tesoro*. Franco Angeli.
3. Pine, J. B., & Gilmore, J. H. (2007). *Authenticity: What consumers really want*. Harvard Business School Press.
4. Cabigiosu, A. (2020). *Digitalization in the luxury fashion industry*. Palgrave Macmillan. https://doi.org/10.1007/978-3-030-48810-9
5. Velar, M. (2021). Luxury fashion storytelling: Branding performance on Instagram. In T. Sádaba, N. Kalbaska, F. Cominelli, L. Cantoni, & M. Torregrosa Puig (Eds.), *Fashion communication* (pp. 309–320). Springer. https://doi.org/10.1007/978-3-030-81321-5
6. Portela, C., Sabatini, N., & Cantoni, L. (2021). Omni-channel retailing in the fashion industry: Its definition and implementation. In T. Sádaba, N. Kalbaska, F. Cominelli, L. Cantoni, & M. Torregrosa Puig (Eds.), *Fashion communication* (pp. 3–16). Springer. https://doi.org/10.1007/978-3-030-81321-5
7. Gnoli, S. (2015). Moda. In *Enciclopedia Treccani*.
8. Urde, M., Greyser, S. A., & Balmer, J. M. (2007). Corporate brands with a heritage. *Journal of Brand Management, 15*(1), 4–19. https://doi.org/10.1057/palgrave.bm.2550106
9. Pecot, F., & De Barnier, V. (2017). Brand heritage: The past in the service of brand management. *Recherche et Applications en Marketing (English Edition), 32*(4), 72–90. https://doi.org/10.1177/2051570717699376
10. Muñoz, D., & Díaz, S. (2021). The revival of heritage fashion houses: Brand identity in the digital era. In T. Sádaba, N. Kalbaska, F. Cominelli, L. Cantoni, & M. Torregrosa Puig (Eds.), *Fashion communication* (pp. 295–307). Springer. https://doi.org/10.1007/978-3-030-81321-5
11. Nueno, J. L., & Quelch, J. A. (1998). The mass marketing of luxury. *Business Horizons, 41*(6), 61–69. https://doi.org/10.1016/s0007-6813(98)90023-4
12. Hines, T., & Bruce, M. (2007). *Fashion marketing* (2nd ed.). Butterworth-Heinemann. https://doi.org/10.4324/9780080468174
13. Throsby, D. (1999). Cultural capital. *Journal of Cultural Economics, 23*(1–2), 3–12. https://doi.org/10.1023/A:1007543313370

14. Hakala, U., Lätti, S., & Sandberg, B. (2011). Operationalising brand heritage and cultural heritage. *Journal of Product and Brand Management, 20*(6), 447–456. https://doi.org/10.1108/10610421111166595
15. Fionda, A., & Moore, C. M. (2009). The anatomy of the luxury fashion brand. *Journal of Brand Management, 16*(5–6), 347–363. https://doi.org/10.1057/bm.2008.45
16. Leigh, A. (2006). Trust, inequality and ethnic heterogeneity. *Economic Record, 82*(258), 268–280. https://doi.org/10.1111/j.1475-4932.2006.00339.x
17. Kapferer, J. N., & Bastien, V. (2012). *The luxury strategy: Break the rules of marketing to build luxury brands* (2nd ed.). Kogan Page.
18. Rose, G. M., Merchant, A., Orth, U. R., & Horstmann, F. (2016). Emphasizing brand heritage: Does it work? And how? *Journal of Business Research, 69*(2), 936–943. https://doi.org/10.1016/j.jbusres.2015.06.021
19. Wiedmann, K. P., Hennigs, N., Schmidt, S., & Wüstefeld, T. (2012). The perceived value of brand heritage and brand luxury. In A. Diamantopoulos, W. Fritz, & L. Hildebrandt (Eds.), *Quantitative marketing and marketing management* (pp. 191–210). Gabler Verlag. https://doi.org/10.1007/978-3-8349-3722-3
20. Martin, M., & Vacca, F. (2018). Heritage narratives in the digital era: How digital technologies have improved approaches and tools for fashion know-how, traditions, and memories. *Research Journal of Textile and Apparel, 22*(4), 336–353. https://doi.org/10.1108/RJTA-02-2018-0015
21. Barthes, R. (1964). Rhétorique de l'image. *Communications, 4*, 40–51.
22. Barthes, R. (1975). An introduction to the structural analysis of narrative. *New Literary History, 6*(2), 237–272.
23. Bernasconi, A., Alfeu, A., & Aleixo, D. (2011). *Storytelling empresarial: Relações públicas contador de histórias*. Intercom, Sociedade Brasileira de Estudos Interdisciplinares da Comunicação.
24. Donzé, P. Y., & Wubs, B. (2019). Storytelling and the making of a global luxury fashion brand: Christian Dior. *International Journal of Fashion Studies, 6*(1), 83–102. https://doi.org/10.1386/infs.6.1.83_1
25. Atwal, G., & Williams, A. (2009). Luxury brand marketing: The experience is everything! *Journal of Brand Management, 16*(5), 338–346. https://doi.org/10.1057/bm.2008.48
26. Gerrig, R. J. (1993). *Experiencing narrative worlds: On the psychological activities of reading*. Yale University Press.
27. Heine, K., & Berghaus, B. (2014). Luxury goes digital: How to tackle the digital luxury brand-consumer touchpoints. *Journal of Global Fashion Marketing, 5*(3), 223–234. https://doi.org/10.1080/20932685.2014.907606
28. Lundqvist, A., Liljander, V., Gummerus, J., & van Riel, A. (2013). The impact of storytelling on the consumer brand experience: The case of a firm-originated story. *Journal of Brand Management, 20*(4), 283–297. https://doi.org/10.1057/bm.2012.15
29. Seo, Y., & Buchanan-Oliver, M. (2015). Luxury branding: The industry, trends, and future conceptualisations. *Asia Pacific Journal of Marketing and Logistics, 27*(1), 82–98. https://doi.org/10.1108/APJML-10-2014-0148
30. Wentzel, D., Tomczak, T., & Herrmann, A. (2010). The moderating effect of manipulative intent and cognitive resources on the evaluation of narrative ads. *Psychology & Marketing, 27*(5), 510–530. https://doi.org/10.1002/mar.20341
31. Stern, B. B. (2006). What does brand mean? Historical-analysis method and construct definition. *Journal of the Academy of Marketing Science, 34*(2), 216–223. https://doi.org/10.1177/0092070305284991
32. Visconti, L. M. (2020). Communicating luxury brands through stories. In F. Morhart, S. Czellar, & K. Wilcox (Eds.), *Research handbook on luxury branding* (pp. 203–221). Edward Elgar Publishing. https://doi.org/10.4337/9781786436351
33. Tuten, T. L., & Solomon, M. R. (2018). *Social media marketing* (3rd ed.). SAGE Publications Ltd.

34. Torregrosa, M., Sánchez-Blanco, C., SanMiguel, P., & del Río Pérez, J. (2023). Instagram: Digital behavior in luxury fashion brands. In N. Sabatini, T. Sádaba, A. Tosi, V. Neri, & L. Cantoni (Eds.), *Fashion communication in the digital age* (pp. 14–26). Springer. https://doi.org/10.1007/978-3-031-38541-4
35. Digimind. (2018). 93% of consumer engagement with luxury brands happens on Instagram. Retrieved May 24, 2024, from https://www.digimind.com/en/news/93-of-consumer-engagement-with-luxury-brands-happens-on-instagram#:~:text=Nov%2030%2C%202018-,93%25%20of%20Consumer%20Engagement%20with%20Luxury%20Brands%20Happens%20on%20Instagram,safeguarding%20their%20brand%20against%20controversies
36. SanMiguel, P., Nobile, T. H., Sánchez-Blanco, C., & Sabatini, N. (2024). *Social media in the fashion industry: Fundamentals, strategy and research methods*. Routledge. https://doi.org/10.4324/9781003505495
37. Van Eemeren, F. H., & Snoeck Henkemans, A. F. (2017). *Argumentation: Analysis and evaluation* (2nd ed.). Routledge.
38. Rigotti, E., & Greco, S. (2019). *Inference in argumentation: A topics-based approach to argument schemes*. Springer. https://doi.org/10.1007/978-3-030-04568-5
39. Marsh, C. (2007). Aristotelian causal analysis and creativity in copywriting: Toward a rapprochement between rhetoric and advertising. *Written Communication, 24*(2), 168–187. https://doi.org/10.1177/0741088306298811
40. Baker, P. (2004). Querying keywords: Questions of difference, frequency, and sense in keywords analysis. *Journal of English Linguistics, 32*(4), 346–359. https://doi.org/10.1177/0075424204269894
41. Rigotti, E., & Greco Morasso, S. (2010). Comparing the argumentum model of topics to other contemporary approaches to argument schemes: The procedural and material components. *Argumentation, 24*(4), 489–512. https://doi.org/10.1007/s10503-010-9190-7
42. Zanola, E. (2024). *Leveraging heritage: Exploring diverse strategies in communication and storytelling within the fashion luxury industry*. (Unpublished Master's thesis). USI—Universita della Svizzera italiana.
43. Groarke, L. (2017). *Depicting visual arguments: An "art" approach*. Windsor Studies in Argumentation.
44. Dallabona, A. (2014). Narratives of Italian craftsmanship and the luxury fashion industry: Representations of Italianicity in discourses of production. *Global Fashion Brands: Style, Luxury & History, 1*(1), 215–228. https://doi.org/10.1386/gfb.1.1.215_1

Communicating Sacred Meanings Through Perfumes: From the Bible to Current Times

Pietro Lattao and Lorenzo Cantoni

Abstract Perfumes have been extensively used in religious contexts, stimulating memories, suggesting meanings and promoting inner motions in a vertical movement from human beings to God. The paper re-traces the role of perfumes within the Biblical tradition and within the Christian message, highlighting its role in cultural practices, as well as a signifier of a pure orientation toward Heaven. Such role has been constantly in dialogue with perfumery practices and ingredients, creating a very rich and nuanced olfactory language. The research adopts a qualitative method to explore these dimensions.

While in current times perfumes appear less linked with religion or religious practices, it keeps several active links with them, as highlighted in the second part of the paper, which presents a dialogue with two major experts, exploring how current perfumes and practices have been deeply inspired and influenced by such tradition.

Keywords Perfumes · Cosmetics · Olfactory communication

1 Introduction

The aim of this research is to explore how perfumes, through their symbolic, theological, and cultural significance in the Bible, have functioned as a means of communication, conveying messages of identity, spirituality, and social belonging.

By examining perfumes as a form of non-verbal communication, this research investigates how fragrances shape identity, influence trends, and engage with

P. Lattao (✉)
USI – Università della Svizzera italiana, Lugano, Switzerland
e-mail: pietro.lattao@usi.ch

L. Cantoni
Institute of Digital Technologies for Communication, USI – Università della Svizzera italiana, Lugano, Switzerland

P. von Wachenfeldt et al. (eds.), *Fashion Communication in the Digital Age*, Springer Proceedings in Business and Economics,
https://doi.org/10.1007/978-3-031-99481-4_6

broader cultural narratives. It contributes to the fashion research community by expanding the scope of material culture studies and offering a new perspective on sensory experiences in fashion, encouraging further exploration into the role of scent in the construction of personal and collective identities within the fashion industry.

The sense of smell has been an integral part of human history, transcending mere utility to become a profound means of connection with memory, emotions, and identity. Perfumes are more than just sensory delights, they have also played a pivotal role in cultural expressions and religious practices, as it is exemplified by the Judeo-Christian and Islamic traditions. By examining the symbolic and functional significance of perfumes in the Bible, this study seeks to uncover their historical, theological, and cultural dimensions, tracing their evolution from ancient rites to contemporary consumption trends.

Throughout the centuries, the sense of smell has been a powerful tool that has kept human beings away from danger, allowed us to feed ourselves and enabled the survival of humankind. The sense of smell is in fact connected to the limbic system, which is involved in establishing emotions and forming memories, this is why some smells have such a strong ability to evoke strong feelings and past memories.

According to Lewis [1], "A number of behavioral studies have demonstrated that smells trigger more vivid emotional memories and are better at inducing that feeling of 'being brought back in time' than images," this effect is called "Proust phenomenon," named after the famous French writer Marcel Proust; it refers to an illustrious passage in Proust's novel *In search of lost time*, in which the narrator is eating a madeleine, a French dessert, and is immediately transported back in time by the sensation, the taste, and smell of dessert. This experience brings him back to his childhood and a series of memories associated with it [2].

Perfumes have been a significant aspect of human experience and cultures, serving not only as a means of personal hygiene but also as a crucial component in social interactions as well as in marketing strategies [3]. Several scholars have investigated the use of scents as relational signals in interpersonal communication, emphasizing their symbolic value in expressing intimacy, trust, and affection. Individuals can establish interpersonal relationships and develop emotional connections by utilizing smells' associative ability [3].

Perfumes are therefore a tool for conveying individual and collective messages, capable of expressing personal identities but also cultural heritage shared by several individuals.

In a few words: perfumes have always been a powerful means of communication.

The word "perfume" itself, derived from the Latin *per fumum*—"through smoke," holds a rich history that intertwines with human spirituality. Throughout civilizations, fragrances have served purposes far beyond aesthetics: they have symbolized purification, divine connection, and sacred offerings. Perfumes are then able to convey wealth, cultural identity, and reverence... Perfumes represent a form of non-verbal communication, capable of conveying cultural, identity-related, and emotional meanings. Through their ability to stimulate olfactory memory and influence sensory perceptions, perfumes transmit stories, values, and experiences of different communities, as well as individual expressions and interpersonal connections.

From these perspectives, the research explores how the meaning attributed to perfumes in biblical traditions has influenced the perception, production, and consumption of fragrances in the contemporary context, thus contributing to a wider understanding of the link between religion, culture, and market.

2 Literature Review

In this section, the studies on the olfactory system as well as those on the role of perfumes in the Bible are outlined.

2.1 Smell and Human Brain

The relationship between smell and brain has been the subject of several studies over the years, and there is a growing interest in the connections between olfactory stimuli and brain responses.

Smell is closely linked to emotions, due to the anatomical conformation of the human central nervous system. Compared to other senses, the olfactory system has more connections with the areas of the brain that deal with the management and control of emotions, namely the limbic system and the hypothalamus. As anticipated, the olfactory system is also closely linked to memory [4].

While time leads to forgetting most visual and verbal memories, it does not seem to have an impact on olfactory stimuli, they are resistant to oblivion, thanks to the multisensory characteristics and holistic coding to which they are subjected.

Rachel Herz, a Canadian cognitive psychologist and neuroscientist, also claims that our brain has the ability to recall certain smells with precision, if linked to precise memories of the past, associated in turn with intense emotional experiences [5]. This issue has also been investigated in 2020 from a group of researchers of the University of Stockholm, who focused on the relationship between olfaction and learning, with the aim of understanding whether and how olfactory memory can be effectively trained. Through a series of experiments, they were able to show that olfactory memory can be significantly improved through specific training, more than those of visual memory [6].

Another important aspect is that smells remain alive in people's memories much longer than visual images do [7]. A study by Rockefeller University showed that humans are able to remember about 35% of what they have smelled, but only 15% of what they have tasted, 5% of what they have seen, and 2% of what they have heard [8]. This underlines the central role of perfumes in creating a shared collective memory.

2.2 Perfumes in the Bible

The representation of perfumes in the Bible has been extensively investigated [9, 10].

Cristiano and De Martino [11] analyzed the role of fragrances in the Bible by offering a view related to tradition, history, and the social contexts. Their study shows how perfume—beyond its spiritual functions—played also a relevant cultural and diplomatic role in the Old Testament. The Queen of Sheba's gift of precious aromas to King Solomon, as described in the Books of Kings and Chronicles, exemplifies this: by presenting these gifts, the Queen not only honored Solomon but also reflected the deep-rooted traditions and social customs of her time. This interaction provides a glimpse into the olfactory landscape of the ancient world, revealing how perfumes were integral to trade and cultural exchanges, as well as their role as symbols of wealth and reverence.

This domain is also explored in depth by Thurlkill [12], who analyzes the role of fragrances in the Bible by drawing parallels with the Islamic culture and also emphasizing how the cultural context influenced the perception of fragrance in society.

The representation of fragrance in the Bible has also been studied from the point of view of symbolism. Coniaris [13] analyzed the role of symbols in religion, offering a broad view of the meaning of certain flowers and raw materials, belonging to the world of perfumery. This type of study is certainly fundamental in order to be able to link ancient perfume materials and practices with contemporary ones. This approach, which was further explored by Twomey [14] in his text *On the scent of Mary*, allows us to understand the importance of flowers and perfumes in the perception of saints and figures linked to salient moments in Christianity. This connection has created links that are still very close in-between modernity and antiquity, creating a collective olfactory memory that levelled tastes and preferences regarding perfumes and flowers.

Several studies have been done regarding specific raw materials and their role in the Bible: Mckenna and Hughes [15] investigated the role of incense and the connection between culture, medicine, and spirituality. Understanding the role of raw materials in the context of the territory where they are harvested is crucial to fully grasp the deep link between natural resources and cultural identity. Raw materials are not just economic resources, but represent a heritage that can tell the story, traditions, and evolution of a community. They influence the way people live, work, and interact, becoming fundamental pillars of collective life and culture.

Each territory, with its geographical, climatic, and environmental characteristics, offers unique resources that contribute to define its identity. This deep connection is reflected in the traditions, rituals, and shared values of a community, consolidating a sense of belonging and connection to the land. Deepening this relationship, the importance of considering raw materials as elements embedded in social culture emerges: they not only provide livelihoods, but also shape the cultural landscape, influencing art, architecture, and everyday practices. Awareness of this interconnectedness is fundamental to preserving resources sustainably and respecting the cultural heritage associated with their management and use.

Khair et al. [16] have investigated the personal branding through perfume in the Middle East. In particular, they investigated the role of perfume in self-representation, one's state of mind, and even as an expression of social status. Perfume is thus indicated as a description of the individual but also of the cultural identity of a place or people. However, this research doesn't address these issues in relation to current practices and those found in the Bible, leaving open new perspectives on how the presentation of fragrance in the Bible has influenced the way biblical fragrance are linked to contemporary society.

For example, in the Bible, perfumes are often linked to deep and symbolic meanings, such as purification, consecration, or divine adoration through the use of sacred ointments or incense. However, a direct connection between these contexts and the contemporary world is rarely examined. In the contemporary world, perfumes are often used as a means of self-expression or to create a personal identity, whereas in biblical times they were tangible signs of devotion and connection to the divine. This creates an interesting overlap between ancient stories and modern dynamics of self-presentation.

3 Methodology

This research adopted a qualitative approach to investigate the role of perfumes and raw materials in the Old and New Testament of the Bible and their significance in religious contexts.

The decision to adopt a qualitative approach is rooted in its capacity to offer an in-depth examination of the complex role of perfumes within religious and cultural contexts, particularly in the Biblical and Christian traditions. This approach allows for a nuanced understanding of how perfumes have functioned as symbols of spiritual elevation, memory, and meaning, as well as their ongoing influence on contemporary practices. By engaging with expert perspectives, the qualitative method facilitates a comprehensive exploration of the dynamic interplay between historical religious practices and modern perfumery, aspects that cannot be fully captured through quantitative analysis alone.

The research begins with an analysis of the Bible in order to gain a broader view of the evolution of the role of fragrance. The aim of this initial analysis is to understand and examine the symbolic meanings, ritual uses, and theological implications of fragrances. To complement the biblical analysis, secondary sources were consulted, including papers on biblical theology, cultural anthropology and on the historical use of fragrance in religious traditions.

The analysis of texts on the role of fragrance in contemporary times provided a broader view of the role of fragrance in contemporary spirituality and religion. In order to investigate the role of fragrance in contemporary life, four in-depth interviews were also conducted with members of both the ecclesiastical and perfumery worlds.

Instead of using a predefined list of detailed questions, the interviews were semi-structured, guided by broad thematic prompts. This approach encouraged open-ended responses, allowing interviewees the freedom to elaborate on their perspectives and organically link the various topics. Thematic prompts focused on areas such as the symbolic significance of fragrances in religious texts, their ritual applications, and their influence on contemporary practices. This flexible structure allowed the conversation to adapt to the skills and interests of each participant, fostering a richer and more nuanced understanding of the topic.

With the first interviewee, a priest and prominent member of the Milanese dioceses, we investigated the mystical power of Holy Chrism as a powerful vehicle of immaterial values for the Christian community. The second interviewee is a cloistered nun from a monastery in Varese. She is the head of the restoration department of the monastery, and thanks to her expertise we investigated the role of fragrances in the history of the saints and in particular the role of flowers in Christian iconography. The other two interviewees are renowned perfumes, creator and owners of two niche and artistic perfume brand. With these two experts, who are influential players in the global olfactory landscape, we focused on an analysis of how the narrative of perfumes in the Bible might have influenced the modern market by shaping individual and collective conceptions of raw materials.

Participants' responses were transcribed and analyzed thematically to identify recurring topics and variations in perspectives.

4 Results

4.1 Old Testament

In the Old testaments, cult perfumes play a multifaceted role significant for both the Jewish and the Christian traditions.

The representation of perfumes is strongly linked to symbolic messages. The oils carry meanings that corroborate specific gestures or actions.

In the Genesis (Gen 28, 17–18), in the Hebrew text, when Jacob performs the act of anointing the votive stones after dreaming of angels, the oil is called "Shimen," composed by "Shin" representing fire, but also the Spirit and "Mem" representing the water, but also the Faith. The act of anointing with perfumes becomes an affirmation of commitment and sanctification. Through the sprinkling of perfumes there is a transformation of the stone in the dwelling place of God.

To understand the meaning of these words, we can analyze three Hebrew words that often appear in the Old Testament: wind אוויר (ruah), perfume ריח (reakh), and spirit רוח (ruach). This resonance testifies to a connection between perfumes and the spirit. The wind carries the essence of things, and in that essence, we might find the true nature of things—its "essence."

As an evidence of the symbolic communication value of perfumes in the Old Testament, we might think of the meeting of King Solomon and the Queen of Sheba. The legendary Queen of Sheba, by travelling along what is still known and remembered today as the "incense route," a caravan route that connected the end of the Arabian Peninsula, Oman and Yemen, with the Mediterranean, paid homage to King Solomon by gifting him perfumes and aromas in great quantities (Kgs 10, 10).

This excerpt from the Old Testament highlights how perfumes and resins were not exclusively reserved for a religious use, although they play a crucial role in this domain. These raw materials were, for all intents and purposes, already widespread consumer goods and a highly sought-after luxury good. Throughout the Bible, references to perfume are allegories of the blessings received, which translate into spiritual and material fruitfulness [17].

Perfume becomes the symbol of fraternal union, which is compared to perfumed oil on his head, descending on Aaron's beard and on the collar of his robe (Psalm 133). An image that expresses the richness and copiousness derived from that odorous anointing, the taste for vegetable fats that impregnate the body with holiness just as they anointed Jacob's votive stones [17].

The sharing of perfumes at a banquet was a custom that was probably widespread throughout the Middle East. In the book of Amos, the guests are described as being sprinkled with perfumed oils (Amos 6, 6). Perfumes are therefore associated with images of friendship, wealth, and prosperity.

While thinking of aromas, however, there might be always an ambivalent perspective, since perfumes remain luxury goods and the excess of luxuries can lead to sins. The corrupt woman attracts the young man to her by evoking intoxicating images similar to those linked to getting drunk with wine: "I have perfumed my bed with myrrh, aloé and cinnamon, let us enjoy loving pleasures together" (Proverbs 7, 17–18; [17]).

The Book of Esther was most likely composed between 160 and 150 BC during the persecution under Antiochus IV Epiphanes, to be an educational work commemorating God's victory over paganism. Set during Ahasuerus' reign, it tells the story of Esther, a Jewish lady, Mordecai's granddaughter, who rose to queenship through a year-long ritual of scented treatments, including 6 months with myrrh and 6 months with fragrant cosmetics. This excerpt emphasizes the metaphorical importance of scent in personal care, seduction, and change. Esther's fragrant preparation is described as a metamorphosis that transforms her from mortal to heavenly. The queen's presentation, with her body saturated with oils and enveloped by a balsamic haze, emphasizes purity and transcendence above the earthy. Perfume therefore functions as both a metaphor for divine change and a reflection of societal aspirations of beauty and immortality. Perfumes in the Old Testament play a crucial role also in the understanding of the natural resources and the dynamics of the market. The representation of raw materials and perfumes in the Bible provides a geographical map that shows a clear subdivision of the market based on the natural resources. This phenomenon underlines how, already in ancient times, the production and the commerce of essences were closely connected to the specific characteristics and the social values of the territory they came from.

In Exodus (30, 34–36) God orders Moses to prepare oils. The translation of the biblical texts brings with it some problems of identification. In this case, the Hebrew term for "aromas" is *saamìn*', this term defines both a type of substances and a wider group, especially of vegetable origin that have a pleasant but strong odor. Resins represented precious gifts to pay homage to important people conveying values and reverence, for example in the case of the Queen of Sheba to King Solomon or the Magi to Jesus.

Incense, one of the most mentioned resins in the Bible is burned to honor God after an act of benevolence. That's the case of Noah, who came out of the ark after the universal flood and burned incense in order to make it reach the sky as a means to create the link between heaven and earth. In this context, Noah's act of burning incense can be interpreted as a way to elevate his gratitude and worship to God, offering not only material sacrifices, but also his spiritual devotion. In addition, incense has traditionally represented a sign of purification and holiness. Therefore, its use by Noah could also be interpreted as a sign of his desire to purify himself and his spiritual environment after the experience of the flood, renewing his commitment to God and His commandments.

The spiritual sense of smell uncovers the trace of God, discovering—in absence—the scent of His Presence. We must consider that in many translations of the Bible, the word "perfume" could also be rendered as "Spirit," while in others as "delight." In other words, the spirit of God is symbolically manifested through the image of perfume.

Among the first trees mentioned in the Bible there is the fig tree. According to the biblical narrative, after disobeying God's orders, Adam and Eve realized their nakedness and twisted fig leaves to cover themselves, forming belts. This symbolic gesture highlights the sudden awareness of their vulnerable condition and the need to hide their nakedness [11, 18].

The bond between God and humanity is bilateral: this example demonstrates the representative value of fragrance even from God to humanity. Fragrance brings joy to the soul.

At the end of the Sabbath, known as Havdalah, which means "separation" in Hebrew, especially during the Havdalah ceremony, rabbis recite a prayer. During this prayer, the Besamin is diffused, a mixture of spices or other aromatic plants. According to Jewish tradition, this fragrance helps to find peace and make the soul happy.

The prayer of Havdalah recites:

הארומות מגוון את יוצר אשר אתה,העולם מלך,אלוהים,אתה ברוך (Adonai Eloheinu, elekh ha-olam, bo're minei b'shamin), which means: "Blessed are you, Lord our God, King of the universe, who creates the variety of aromas."

God creates the earth and with the earth its essences. According to a Jewish belief, when God expelled Adam and Eve from the Garden of Eden, Adam took with him a sprig of myrtle: the scent of the holiest garden in religion is enclosed in a sprig of myrtle. Still nowadays in Israel, during the procession for the Feast of Tabernacles that starts from Siloam and ended at the temple, everyone waved branches of myrtle in remembrance of the aroma of God and the call to the sacred garden of Eden, a garden of blessedness without sin.

4.2 New Testament

In the New Testament there is abundant evidence of the role of perfumes as means of communication, capable of conveying messages and being powerful symbolic/metaphorical substances.

In the New Testament it is told that fulfilling the messianic oracles of the prophet Isaiah, who foretold the birth of Jesus, the Magi, wise men from the East, offered to Jesus gold, incense and myrrh. These gifts are rich in allegorical meaning: in particular,

the incense is symbol of divinity and worship. By offering incense to Jesus, the Magi recognize his divine nature and his dignity as the Son of God. This gesture underlines the sacrality of his earthly mission.

Myrrh, known for its aromatic and conservation properties, is also associated with death and burial. This gift prefigures the Passion and death of Jesus on the cross, as well as his burial and resurrection. In the Biblical text, the word Myrrh is written σμύρναν, which also indicates the name to the city of Smyrna, one of the most important cities in Turkey. The Turkish city is named Smyrna because of the flowering presence of trees from which myrrh was extracted.

Perfumes also play a key role in other passages of the Gospels in the form of different substances such as myrrh, aloe, and nard; they fill not only a spiritual and social role, but are also expression of luxury and purity.

In the original Greek text presenting the emblematic figure of Mary of Bethany, it is used the expression "Nardos Pistikès" to describe the type of perfumes used to anoint Jesus. The word "Pistikès" can be translated with the word pure, authentic, underlining the importance of authenticity of perfumes but also the nature of Mary's gesture.

According to Matthew and Marc, Mary poured a precious ointment contained in an alabaster vase on Jesus' head. This episode took place 6 days before Easter, and by doing this Mary heralds the aromatic embalming of Jesus' body after the crucifixion. This episode highlights the anticipatory function of perfumes, already observed in the gifts of the Magi to the newborn Jesus. It also underlines the economic capital of perfumes at that time. Judas, keeper of the communal treasury, criticized the use of the ointment, suggesting that it could have been sold for 300 denarii, the annual salary of an agricultural official, and the proceeds given to the poor. The oil used by Mary was in fact pure spikenard, extracted from the root of a shrub that grows in the mountains of India, and prized by Jews, Greeks, and Romans [11].

Mary of Bethany communicates love and devotion through the use of that perfume: it becomes the vehicle of a profound message, the expression of Christian charity, that is, love for God. Furthermore, this act manifests her conversion and transforms the perfume into a symbolic sacrifice. The anointing with perfumed oil by Mary of Bethany is therefore not just a gesture of generosity, but an expression of absolute love, prefiguring Christ's sacrifice and emphasizing its divine dimension.

The connection between perfume and women is narrated throughout the Bible and has a pivotal role in the narration of the Resurrection. Early on the first day after the Sabbath, Mary Magdalene, Mary of Jacob, and Salome purchased aromatic oils to anoint the body of Jesus. Upon arriving at the tomb at sunrise, they discovered the stone sealing the tomb had been rolled away. Inside, only oil-soaked bandages remained. Death and sin are symbolized by decay and stench, while resurrection and divine renewal emit a pleasing scent. Perfume thus emerges as a metaphor for new life and the victory over death.

The theme of fragrance as a divine sign extends to the Book of Revelation, where a rising cloud of fragrant incense symbolizes the transcendence of death and the promise of eternal life, culminating in a celestial vision of joy and triumph (Revelation 19, 3). This imagery suggests that aromas serve as a medium for divine communication, embodying God's grace, hope, and love, which believers are called to share through their words and deeds.

4.3 Perfumes Between Religion and Everyday Practices

The representation of perfumes in the Bible has shaped the perception of modern perfumery and modern practices both from a theological and from a cultural perspective.

In biblical traditions, perfumes were not merely olfactory elements but powerful communicative tools, symbolizing divine presence, purification, and identity. This sacred association has persisted over time, influencing how fragrances are used today to convey meaning, whether in religious rituals, personal identity, or branding strategies within the perfume industry. The ritualistic use of scented oils in Christian liturgy, as well as the symbolic connection between specific fragrances and spiritual experiences, demonstrates how scent continues to serve as a medium for communication, linking the sacred to the sensory.

In Christian liturgy, perfumes and oils carry spiritual significance and communicative power. The first interviewee, a priest from the Diocese of Milan, explains that the chrism, a perfumed oil made by olive oil and aromatic essences, is named after Christ, with means "the anointed," emphasizing the deep tie to Christian identity. From Baptism, where an individual is anointed with chrism to symbolize their initiation into Christian life, to confirmation and ordination, chrism becomes a tangible sign of grace and presence of God. The chrism is a perfumed representation of unity and identity communicating the belongingness to Christ of his followers [19].

The use of oils and perfumes during the liturgy emphasizes the sensory engagement and the spiritual experience, creating a deeper connection to the sacred and leaving a lasting impression, which symbolizes the enduring presence of God in a believer's life.

For instance, the oil used in the sacrament of the sick serves as a balm for physical and spiritual healing. Its fragrance symbolizes comfort, hope, and divine support in moments of suffering. Similarly, the oil of catechumens, used before Baptism, recalls the anointing of athletes in ancient Greece, representing strength and preparation for the challenges of Christian life. The cyclical presence of this sacred chrism, from baptism to the anointing of the sick, reflects and communicates a believer's lifelong journey. This relationship emphasizes the concept that divine grace is both ever-present and repeating, revealing itself visibly via the ritual use of fragrant oils.

As seen, perfumes in the Bible are crucial in consecration, purification, prayers, and their communication ability between God and believers. The aroma of catechumens' oil may arouse sentiments of comfort, inspiration, and defense, bolstering the sacrament recipients' faith and commitment. Perfumes are able to evoke emotions and memories and to foster connections, whether in religious ceremonies or everyday life thanks to their ability to convey intangible meanings and values through the olfactive sense. The sacred chrism creates a link between the physical and the spiritual world communicating the mystery of grace. From the "oil of gladness" in Isaiah's prophecy to the modern liturgical anointing, perfume remains a universal medium for expressing and communicating mercy, renewal, and the enduring presence of the sacred.

In the Christian tradition, flowers are of great importance—in particular, the rose, which is the quintessential flower in perfumery and has symbolic value spiritually, artistically, and culturally; so much so that it has become a symbol of several saints and is associated with the figure of the Virgin Mary. From the Middle Ages onward, she has been named "the rose without thorns," referring to her sinless conception, or "Rose of roses, flower of flowers," inspiring devotional practices like the Rosary.

The second interviewee, a cloistered nun at the Santa Maria del Monte Monastery in Varese, elaborates on this Marian link, explaining how May, month dedicated to the cult of Mary, is also the month of roses. In perfumery one of the most precious rose used in formulation is in fact the rose of May, a very precious and exquisite type of rose. She notes, "The association of Mary with roses stems from ancient traditions celebrating renewal and fertility." In Christian iconography, the symbolism concerning roses extends to colors, white representing purity, red the passion of Christ, gold: glory and perfection. The thornless rose represents the immaculate conception, while the mystical five-petaled dog rose evokes Christ's wounds.

The rose and its aroma are associated with many saints. Thérèse of Lisieux is an emblematic example of connection to roses, foretold at her death, "I will rain down a cascade of roses," symbolizing divine graces. Similarly, St. Rita of Cascia, the "Saint of Roses," requested a rose in winter, an act reflecting her faith amid adversity. Other saints like St. Rosalia and St. Rose of Lima are honored with roses and lilies, representing virginity, spiritual union, and divine grace.

The interviewed nun highlights this floral mysticism: "The rose's cyclical bloom mirrors human life—its vitality, transience, and eternal renewal through resurrection." Saints' life, linked with roses, becomes a metaphor for spiritual and physical growth. The rose and its perfume becomes a symbol of dualities and contrasts: earthly passion and heavenly perfection, life and death, silence and revelation. The petals symbolize completeness, and the thorns evoke suffering and martyrdom, creating a link between earthly evanescence and divine eternity.

The rose, for a western audience, is associated with a female market, this perception has certainly been influenced by the image that the rose flower has in the Bible and the Christian iconography, always being associated with the female figure of Mary and other female saints. The rose throughout Christian culture has taken on important meanings but always linked more to a female audience and even today, the rose is a raw material mostly used in women' fragrances, and from a collective perspective more associated to women. On the contrary, if we consider the Middle Eastern context, the rose is presented in the Koran as the representative flower of Muhammad [16, 20]. Consequently, in the Arab region the rose is mainly used in male rather than female perfumes. This also highlights how perfumes might become, based on different cultures, a symbol of masculinity or femininity, while communicating different messages.

According to the third interviewee, perfumes are instruments of personal expression: perfumes can be chosen and worn as a form of personal expression of one's faith or spirituality, but also of other dimensions of a person's life. Furthermore, perfumes inspired by religion have been used as a marketing tool to create an association with desirable spiritual and cultural values. Advertising campaigns often use religious symbols and images to promote perfumes and create an aura of prestige and exclusivity around the brand. Religious perfumes have significantly influenced the creation and marketing of modern perfumes by inspiring contemporary perfumers with their rich history and symbolic meanings.

According to the fourth interviewee, "there is no shortage of evidence in the modern world of the creation of many fragrances that evoke sensations of sacredness, recounting purity and spiritual wellbeing, such is the need of contemporary man to pause and contemplate. The Old and New Testament also mentioned precious fragrances such as myrrh and oil of spikenard, helping to create an association between fragrance and luxury, and incorporating them into our consumption habits."

The evocative power of these religious scents helps create a narrative that resonates with consumers seeking both olfactory pleasure and a deeper, almost transcendental experience, thereby enhancing the commercial appeal of these products in the global market.

5 Conclusions

This study aimed to investigate the multifaceted roles of perfumes, focusing on their mention and significance in the Old and New Testaments. Through translations and literary analysis of sacred texts, interviews with experts, and insights from modern perfumers, we were able to bridge historical and contemporary perspectives. The exploration extends to the neurological basis of olfactory perception, linking the evocative power of scent to memory and emotion, which has historically reinforced its role in spiritual practices.

By delving into their use in anointing, burial preparations, and worship, the paper highlights the enduring symbolism and communicative power of perfumes within sacred contexts and modern practices.

Additionally, interviews with religious and perfumery experts provide contemporary insights into how ancient practices influence modern fragrance world, reaffirming the timeless connection between scent, spirituality, and communication.

One important contribution of this paper is that it offers a comprehensive vision on the communicative power of perfumes in relation to spiritual and historical practices highlighting the role of perfumes in conveying cultural, emotional, and spiritual messages.

These findings provide actionable insights for professionals in both the perfumery and the communication industries, offering insights that can help them highlight how perfumes can be a powerful means of non-verbal communication capable of conveying emotional and cultural messages.

Despite this limitation, this study makes an important contribution to the understanding of the role of perfumes in Christianity and their relevance in Italian and Catholic culture. As a result, it is suggested that future researches conduct studies with a larger and more diverse range of participants in order to have a wider analysis of the role of perfumes in the Bible and their ability of conveying messages across different cultural and historical contexts.

References

1. Lewis, J. G. (2015). Smells ring bells: How smell triggers memories and emotions. *Psychology Today*. https://www.psychologytoday.com/intl/blog/brain-babble/201501/smells-ring-bells-how-smell-triggers-memories-and-emotions
2. Cavalieri, R. (2016). Odori e reminiscenza. Tre paragrafi sulla memoria olfattiva. In D. Bruni & A. Velardi (Eds.), *Brevi cogitazioni* (pp. 80–93). Corisco Edizioni.
3. Igbokwe, C. (2024). Tertiary education students' knowledge and awareness of perfumes as tools of communication in relationships and marketing. *International Journal of Entrepreneurial Development, Education and Science Research, 8*(1), 398–409. https://internationalpolicybrief.org/wp-content/uploads/2024/09/ARTICLE-22.pdf
4. Rosenblum, L. D. (2010). *See what I'm saying: The extraordinary powers of our five senses.* W. W. Norton & Company.
5. Herz, R. S. (2007). *The scent of desire: Discovering our enigmatic sense of smell.* Harper Perennial.
6. Olofsson, J. K., Ekström, I., Lindström, J., Syrjänen, E., Stigsdotter-Neely, A., Nyberg, L., & Larsson, M. (2020, September). Smell-based memory training: Evidence of olfactory learning and transfer to the visual domain. *Chemical Senses, 45*(7), 593–600. https://doi.org/10.1093/chemse/bjaa049
7. Engen, T. (1987). Remembering odors and their names. *American Scientist, 75*(5), 497–503. https://www.jstor.org/stable/27854791
8. Buiatti, E. (2014). *Forma Mentis. Neuroergonomia sensoriale applicata alla progettazione.* Franco Angeli.

9. Sell, C. (2019). *Perfume in the Bible*. Royal Society of Chemistry. https://doi.org/10.1039/9781839168406
10. Van Beek, G. W. (1960). Frankincense and myrrh. *The Biblical Archaeologist, 23*(3), 70–95. https://www.jstor.org/stable/3209285
11. Cristiano, L., & De Martino, G. (2002). Profumi e balsami della Bibbia. https://www.profumiere.it/articoli/bibbia.pdf
12. Thurlkill, M. (2016). *Sacred scents in early Christianity and Islam*. Rowman & Littlefield.
13. Coniaris, A. M. (1985). *Sacred symbols that speak: A study of the symbols used in the Orthodox Church*. Light and Life Publishing.
14. Twomey, L. (2006). On the scent of Mary: The power of perfume in the Espill. *Catalan Review, 20*(1), 337–346. https://doi.org/10.3828/CATR.20.20
15. Mckenna, D. J., & Hughes, K. (2014). *The incense bible: Plant scents that transcend world culture, medicine, and spirituality*. Routledge.
16. Khair, N., Elhajjar, S., & Hamzeh, Z. (2024). Personal branding through perfume in the Middle East: Investigating the role of fragrance in self-presentation, impression management, and cultural identity. *Fashion Theory, 28*(4), 461–481. https://doi.org/10.1080/1362704X.2024.2347024
17. Munier, B. (2006). *Storia dei profumi: Dagli dèi dell'Olimpo al cyber-profumo*. Dedalo.
18. Cantoni, L. (2023). Abito e confraternite: Alcune riflessioni introduttive. *Annuario di Storia Religiosa della Svizzera Italiana, 2*, 275–294.
19. Steffler, A. W. (2002). *Symbols of the Christian faith*. Wm. B. Eerdmans Publishing.
20. Bursi, A. (2020). Scents of space: Early Islamic pilgrimage, perfume, and paradise. *Arabica, 67*(2–3), 200–234. https://doi.org/10.1163/15700585-12341557

Fashioning Uniforms for Luxury Hospitality in the Digital Age: The Case of Italian Family Firm *Maurel*

Michela Ornati

Abstract Uniforms are distinctive forms of clothing which identify wearers and their roles via specific sartorial signs and symbols. Corporate uniforms for the luxury services sector are workwear apparel with specific affordances, designed and produced for private business entities by specialized suppliers. In the fashion and luxury fields, research on corporate uniforms for the services sector is limited, particularly with regard to the niche topic of bespoke luxury uniforms. The article addresses this gap by discussing the case of Maurel, an Italian family firm which supplies fashion and luxury hospitality, travel and wellness brands with internally styled and tailored corporate uniforms. The study evidences how internal design processes align with models theorized for fashion design and—contrary to what might be expected based on discussions of uniforms—are permeable to fashion trends. It also underscores how digital transformation affects both production and communication strategies, as is currently the case in the fashion and luxury sector. By illustrating how luxury corporate uniforms are *fashioned*, the article aims to situate this form of dress in two fields wherein further research could be conducted: fashion and luxury tourism activities and practices; and digital fashion and luxury communication.

Keywords Corporate uniforms · Fashion · Luxury · Services · Hospitality · Digital fashion communication · Leisure · Tourism · Bespoke

M. Ornati (✉)
University of Applied Sciences and Arts of Southern Switzerland – SUPSI, Manno, Switzerland

USI – Università della Svizzera italiana, Lugano, Switzerland
e-mail: michela.ornati@supsi.ch

P. von Wachenfeldt et al. (eds.), *Fashion Communication in the Digital Age*, Springer Proceedings in Business and Economics,
https://doi.org/10.1007/978-3-031-99481-4_7

1 Introduction

Uniforms are "the distinctive clothing worn by members of the same organization or body" [1] meant to identify the "status and skills of the wearer" [2], a form of dress which can be understood, generally speaking, as "a particular set of clothing for a group of people" [3]. Uniforms convey culturally and contextually specific sartorial signs and symbols, thereby providing a complex communication channel, replete with meanings, between the wearer and the observer [4]. In the West, uniforms have a long and diverse history. Today, uniforms worn at work—otherwise defined as workwear[1]—represent a multimillion-dollar industry driven by demand in the industrial as well as the services sectors, including hospitality [8]. In fact, in the private sector, and particularly in luxury hospitality, *corporate uniforms* are an integral part of organizational and communication strategies [9–11].

Corporate uniforms are operationalized via three dimensions: *attributes*, that is, color, materials, accessories, and style; *homogeneity*, or the degree of dress variance among employees; and *conspicuousness*, that is, organizational dress uniqueness vis-à-vis clothing worn outside the organization [12]. Through the interplay of these three dimensions, uniforms acquire meaning and impact the organization, the employee, and customers coming into contact with the firm. In the services sector in particular, uniforms are "designed to embody attributes of professionalism, identity, and identification" [2]. Uniforms in service organizations simultaneously embody the nature of the service provided and, by virtue of their visibility and recognizability, express organizational values [5]. Such affordances, however, are "situational, contingent, and played out in [the] interaction" between the uniformed employees and outsiders [13]. This dynamic is of particular importance in luxury service domains such as transportation (yachting, private jets, or upscale rail) and hospitality (hotels, restaurants, or spas), which aim to provide exclusive hedonic experiences. In these contexts, luxuriousness is "jointly determined by objective service features and subjective customer perceptions" [14]. Thus, the actions and appearance of the employees—including the uniforms they wear—are constitutive elements of the luxury service encounter. In fact, in a hospitality context, corporate

[1] Uniforms are discussed from both an academic and a practitioner perspective; thus, terminology and definitions may vary. When denoting a particular line of work—as opposed to a representational role—uniforms are referred to as *occupational*. Occupational uniforms are items of apparel mandated and usually furnished by the employer, reflecting organizational as well as industry- or sector-specific standards; they are a prerequisite for being "on the job" [5]. Occupational uniforms include attire worn by the military as well as public sector and private sector employees. In business literature, occupational uniforms are also called *workwear* and include both *corporate workwear*—or *corporate uniforms*, used henceforth—and *industrial* workwear categories; *technical clothing* and *personal protective equipment* or PPE, fall within the latter [6–8]. Unlike *formal* and *proscribed* uniforms characteristic of the military, the law, or the ecclesiastical orders, occupational uniforms are susceptible to adaptation and modernization, thereby evolving into *quasi-* or even *informal uniforms* [2, 4]. This article focuses on corporate and, specifically, custom-designed *bespoke* corporate uniforms, where bespoke is defined as *custom-made* or *custom-tailored* (antonym: mass-produced or ready-made).

uniforms must "leave an impression [and] be remembered, always impeccable, and luxurious in design" [15]. Together with site architecture, surroundings, interior design and décor, uniforms constitute a luxury hotel's tangible asset [15]. Its value is extracted through mandatory wear, a form of aesthetic control [10] over employee appearance and behavior in service interaction [16]. This is because donning the required uniform, and embodying its look *and* feel—weight, stiffness, texture, temperature, and fit [17]—affects employees' sensations, bodily awareness and attention to movements, shaping self-perception [18–20] and actions [21] attuned to company values [13]. Significantly, garments which are made to measure for the employee and are of intrinsic aesthetic and material value—as is the case in luxury uniforms—contribute toward fostering a sense of pride and belonging, as well as bolstering satisfaction [20, 22].

Luxury destinations worldwide have grown considerably pre-and post-COVID-19. In fact, the luxury hospitality sector enjoys steady growth—despite a dramatic luxury downturn [23]—primarily driven by established hotel conglomerates [24, 25] and boutique hotels. Western luxury and fashion companies have been moving into this market for several years, mostly via partnerships with established operators [26]. Bulgari, a forerunner, opened its first hotel in Milan in 2004 as a joint venture with the Luxury Group division of Marriott International and has since expanded into a worldwide chain (www.bulgarihotels.com). Armani opened its first hotel in Dubai in 2011 as a joint venture with Emaar properties (www.armanihotels.com), then in Milan in 2014. Several fashion brands—Ralph Lauren, Versace, Christian Lacroix, Dolce & Gabbana, Missoni and Christian Louboutin, to name a few—have also opened their own upscale boutique hotels, or co-branded and styled venues for others [27]. Uniforms are constitutive aesthetic and atmospheric elements in each of these projects.

Generally speaking, corporate uniforms for the hospitality services sector are ready-made garments with limited customization, mass-manufactured by a number of global conglomerates and specialized firms.[2] On the other hand, corporate uniforms for the high-end luxury hospitality services are custom-made. Hence, production scales differ, as does the value proposition. Furthermore, as discussed above, luxury uniforms must have specific affordances. Thus, suppliers meeting the needs of the expanding luxury and fashion hospitality industry are most likely expected to have an in-depth understanding of each brand's unique, context-specific requirements, a level of sartorial excellence that is aligned with the craft of luxury [28, 29] and a degree of sensitivity to fashion and luxury trends; qualities which would make them research-worthy by scholars in these fields. However, to the author's knowledge, bespoke corporate uniform makers and their products have not heretofore been a topic of specific research, either in the luxury or in the fashion and tourism domain.

[2] For example, Incorporatewear (www.incorporatewear.co.uk/) and "premium" workwear supplier Fristads (https://www.fristads.com/en/), as well as smaller companies such as Studio104 (www.studio-104.com), Fashionizer (www.fashionizer.com) or Dressbest (www.dressbestuniforms.com).

2 Research Gap and Methodology

As observed above, there is an apparent dearth of scholarship regarding work uniforms in private—as opposed to institutional or governmental—service organizations, and luxury services in particular. The one exception is designer airline uniforms [2, 30, 31]. A recent publication by Akou [5] examines public and private service sector work uniform cases in the USA, but does not cover luxury branded services specifically. Furthermore, uniforms are frequently discussed in fashion literature as sources of inspiration for fashion designers, or as subversive items of subculture fashion [32, 33]. But the influence contemporary fashions may have on uniform creation is not considered. This is likely because—as noted by scholars—work uniforms in general tend to be resistant to change, may be subject to industry norms and regulations, and are mass-manufactured by suppliers which operate outside the "fashion system" [34]. However, these conditions only partially apply to bespoke corporate uniforms designed ad-hoc for luxury brands by highly specialized suppliers. In fact, as suggested in the introduction, the level of customization these projects require most likely implies the activation of creative processes that are similar, if not identical, to fashion design inspiration, research, and development [35]. To the author's best knowledge, however, such processes have not heretofore been investigated.

To address this gap and open pathways to future studies, this article explores the case of Maurel (www.maurel.com), an Italian firm specialized in fashioning bespoke luxury uniforms. The case study is analyzed through the lens of fashion theory, specifically as it relates to hospitality and apparel design. Two theoretical models are used. Sabatini and Cantoni's [36] schema of fashion and tourism activities and practices helps situate bespoke luxury uniforms within the wider discourse on the linkages between fashion and hospitality. Lamb and Kallal's conceptual framework for apparel design [37]—extensively referred to in the literature regarding analogue and digital dress design processes, including that of uniforms [38]—provides criteria for design process analysis. The article also references the field of (digital) fashion scholarship, which encompasses the study of communication practices in fashion and luxury firms [39]. Due to the nature of the enquiry, the approach is pragmatic [40] and the method descriptive [41]. The single case study was dictated by opportunity. Although undoubtedly there are several bespoke uniform suppliers operating in Europe, the author was only able to identify two: Maurel and Terre et Ciel Studio (www.terreetcielstudio.fr). Furthermore, only the former could be directly reached and appropriately studied at this time. Primary data were collected at Maurel's headquarters via expert interviews [42] with Maurel's management, including: company owners Maurizia Capritti, who founded the company together with her husband, and Sara Capritti, their daughter; Fabrizio Penna, chief accountant and company partner; Giada Venturi, Sara's daughter and current chief communication officer; and Maurel's three *stylists* (or "stiliste" in Italian). Data were triangulated with secondary information drawn from both trade and academic literature published in English, Italian, and French, as well as Maurel company presentations to students of the BSc in Leisure Management at the University of Applied Sciences and Arts of Southern Switzerland—SUPSI. The theoretical models which inform the Maurel case study analysis are described in the next section, followed by the case narrative.

3 Theoretical Lens

As argued in the introduction, bespoke corporate uniforms are forms of apparel, styled and tailored *à façon* (to order), expressly for fashion and luxury brands; and thus, likely *à la mode*, that is, in step with contemporary trends such brands dictate. Hence, these garments, and the firms crafting them, can be situated within Sabatini and Cantoni's schema of fashion and tourism activities and practices [36]. The schema consists of four layers which expand outwards from the physical body: Layer I, *kosmeo*, "the body and its outer borders"; Layer II, *habeo*, "all clothing items" and accessories worn on the body; Layer III, the environment the body inhabits—décor and interiors; and Layer IV, *habit*, or "specific cultural traditions" affecting social practices and individual lifestyles, including the choice of dress. Since uniforms clothe the body, they qualify as *habeo* and fall within Layer II of the model. However, uniforms also shape identity, affect employer, employee and client interactions and thus impact experience within fashion and tourist-related service contexts; therefore, they also affect the schema's outer layers III and IV. Consequently, the model can accommodate the suppliers of corporate uniforms, which are active—albeit lesser known—contributors to the fashion and tourism system, as the narrative of the Maurel case should make clear.

Lamb and Kallal's [37] conceptual framework for apparel design is an "integrated framework," as the authors describe it, which "can be applied to all types of apparel design because it does not distinguish between functional apparel design and fashion design." Thus, it is a suitable framework through which to explore the making of luxury corporate uniforms. The framework consists of (a) a model of consumer needs and apparel design criteria, and (b) a "creative, problem-solving" design process which the model is meant to inform. The model of consumer needs places apparel end users at its center, emphasizing the importance of the cultural context within which "human behaviors involving dress" take place. The authors identify three distinctive, but interconnected, apparel design criteria which build upon the model's human-centered core: functionality (apparel utility), expressiveness (the "communicative, symbolic aspects of dress"), and aesthetics (cultural standards of beauty), henceforth referred to as FEA. According to the authors, the model must be taken into consideration within each of the sequential stages of an apparel design process. These stages are: (1) problem identification (developing a collection for a specific target market); (2) preliminary idea generation; (3) design refinement; (4) prototype development; (5) evaluation; and (6) implementation. Hence, model and process together constitute an integrated framework for fashion design which can be applied not only in analogical, but also in digital creative contexts, including virtual reality [43]. Applying Lamb and Kallal's framework to the design and production process at Maurel spotlights the analogies between fashion apparel design and corporate uniform design, as discussed below.

4 Maurel: "Italian Fashion for Company Clothing"

Maurel was founded near the northern city of Pavia in 1975 by Maurizia Fagotto, a trained pattern maker and seamstress, and her husband Ermanno Capritti. The firm initially produced high-quality public-school uniforms. In 1984, thanks to a successful bid for the Jolly Hotel group apparel, Maurel shifted production entirely to the manufacture of bespoke corporate uniforms for the luxury retail and hospitality industries, a largely underserved niche market at the time. New opportunities for national and international expansion soon emerged, also thanks to the firm's expanding network of specialized hospitality agents in Italy, France, Germany and recently the USA.

In 1995, upon completing classical art and fashion studies, the founders' daughter Sara Capritti—who had, in her own words, "grown up in the sewing lab"—also joined the family firm. Under her creative direction, fashion gradually began informing Maurel's uniform design. Sara worked closely with Giorgio Amani himself when, in 2010, Maurel was commissioned to co-design and produce bespoke uniforms for the Armani Hotels—an experience she qualifies as "foundational" from both a creative and a business perspective. The collaboration—which continues to this day—was key to "opening the doors" of other luxury brands. Although Maurel is a relatively small company of 40, mostly female, employees—some of whom have been working there since its founding—it serves a large roster of clients. These include prestigious hospitality venues, designer hotels, private luxury carriers, and many high-end restaurants, spas and boutique hotels located primarily across Europe, but also in the Middle East and the USA (for an overview, see: https://bit.ly/40zBkEA). The company also supplies uniforms for several luxury retail brands.

4.1 Design and Production

Maurel's uniform design and production phases are described in the following sections, following Lamb & Kallal's framework.

Phase 1: Problem Identification Maurel's collaboration with new or existing customers starts with a close dialogue between the client and Maurel's stylists. Meetings may take place on client premises or at Maurel's elegant office showroom. Depending on the project, client interlocutors may include the owners, the architect, the interior designer (particularly for new hotel or restaurant openings), and the head housekeeper. During this phase the client usually—but not always—provides documents such as brand statements, brand identity presentations, architectural and interior renderings or location photos. It also indicates the occupations in need of a uniform, which can be several for each area of service delivery (e.g.: management, reception, housekeeping, bar, restaurant, wellness areas, etc.). Starting from these materials—as well as, crucially, the impressions derived from their ongoing dialogue with the client—Maurel's stylists begin to identify customer needs and to acknowledge cultural context, the core elements of Lamb and Kallal's model. Then, the creative team kicks off its creative process.

Phase 2 & 3: Preliminary Idea Generation and Design Refinement Stylists at Maurel draw inspiration from extensive research on diverse sources: textile and fashion trend reports, trade and fashion shows, social media, popular culture, but also historical and contemporary art publications. It also leverages its internal physical archives of over 8000 items from past collections, accessed via a computerized rack system. This research phase leads to the development of several *moodboards*—visual assemblages suggesting colors, textures, shapes, materials and looks the team considers suitable for the project's identity. Moodboard creation requires careful consideration of interrelated FEA criteria—*functionality*, *expressiveness*, and *aesthetics*—and factors affecting them. These include, among others: a project's geographic location (and thus, climate); cultural specificities, such as customs in clothing; work roles to be dressed and individual personnel needs; and whether uniforms must stand out, or blend into, a given décor.

The team's expertise in interpreting and fulfilling the oftentimes contradictory or unclear needs of luxury hospitality clients has grown with experience. For example, historical establishments tend to reject clear breaks from tradition even while seeking to renew their uniforms' looks; thus, the team calibrates suggestions, proposing new prints or accessories, rather than fully revised looks. For new openings, on the other hand, clients increasingly request "modern" collections which "look more like regular clothing than a [classic] uniform." In this case, the challenge is to innovate stylistically while guaranteeing garment functionality and maintaining "a clear distinction between [employee] roles." Moodboard approval may require numerous iterations. In fact, aligning project elements pertaining to FEA criteria with client expectations is key to the development and concretization of a common vision, as evidenced in the following phases.

Phase 4 & 5: Prototype Development and Evaluation Finally, stylists start designing the uniforms collection. Each garment is both manually and digitally sketched using the Optitex fashion design system (www.optitex.com). Garment cut patterns may be lifted from a vast, proprietary digital archive. Progressively, the team develops two-dimensional digital pattern and material renderings, fully "dressing" a life-like avatar in uniform to check for cut and drape imperfections. Subsequently, it chooses physical fabric samples, buttons, trimmings, insignia, and other details. Outputs are digitally shared with the client and discussed via online meetings, or in presence, until the uniforms collection is approved.

Phase 6: Implementation Before production is launched, Maurel's team of six seamstresses cut and sew the project's sample uniforms collection. Each first-time client order usually consists of a set of three garments per role to be dressed (e.g.: jacket, vest, shirt or blouse, pants or skirt), produced in multiples of three, so that client employees have at least one complete uniform set available when the other two are being laundered, refurbished, or repaired. Thus, an order is placed with European suppliers—mostly Italian and Portuguese—for exclusive fabrics and prints covering initial client needs plus reserves, to be kept in stock at Maurel. Cloth is mechanically precision-cut internally but garment assembly may be assigned to a number of laboratories situated locally, in close geographical proximity to the firm; upon delivery of the finished items, Maurel's seamstresses perform a thorough quality check. Finally, uniforms are carefully wrapped, packaged in branded Maurel boxes and shipped to the client. On average, the entire process—from initial discussion to delivery—takes 10 weeks. Post-delivery may include sartorial fittings on client premises—individual personalization of *functional* and *aesthetic* criteria which help bolster employee pride and satisfaction, as discussed in the introduction [20, 22] (Fig. 1).

4.2 Digital Transformation and Digital Communication

Maurel firm owners have never shied from innovation, consistently pursuing a strategy of digital transformation [44–46] along its value chain. Process innovation includes the use of generative AI tools for preliminary idea generation and pattern creation, and, in the near future, small-scale additive manufacturing for the design of buttons, insignia, and other small accessories. Customer-facing innovations include gamification and augmented reality applications for potential and existing customers. For example, visitors to Maurel's website can "tailor" their own *moodboard* experience—"the first inspiration" for personalized uniform design (see: https://bit.ly/3TzRMQM). Also, clients whose collections are in development can project life-like uniformed 3D avatars within their interior and exterior hospitality spaces, thereby better understanding, before production is launched, how garments might look on their employees and "fit" into overall brand atmospherics.

In keeping with post COVID-19 fashion and luxury industry digital communication trends [47], Maurel actively promotes its know-how and showcases its products on digital channels. Digital communication efforts, led by Sara Venturi, target potential business customers but also client employees—the end users of the company's bespoke uniforms. Thus, Maurel's Instagram account (@maurel_uniforms) and YouTube channel (@maureluniforms) feature both promotional and educational content (e.g., how a uniform is made, or how best to wear it and care for it). A TikTok account is expected to go live soon.

As implied by its brand payoff "Italian fashion for corporate clothing," Maurel consistently brings a contemporary fashion feel to bespoke corporate uniforms design while maintaining its luxury clients' distinctive brand identities, signs, and

Fig. 1 Bespoke uniforms: receptionists, seaside resort; doorman, mountain resort. Photo by Maurel

symbols. Furthermore, although manufacturing processes are anchored in the bespoke sartorial tradition, Maurel is attentive to digital innovation and communication. By so doing, Maurel has firmly positioned itself as a preferred supplier of corporate uniforms for many luxury lifestyle brands.

5 Conclusions and Suggestions for Future Research

A recent Financial Times review of Moroccan luxury resort The Royal Mansour (www.royalmansour.com) highlights the strong impression uniforms made on the author: "Even in the off-season there are 450 immaculately turned out members of staff at the Royal Mansour on Morocco's Mediterranean coast. They pander to the needs of the guests housed in just 55 suites and villas and wear, by my reckoning, 17 distinct styles of uniform. The butlers have crisp beige suits, waiters green silk blouses, and the man who drives the luggage cart dazzles in a bright red uniform with matching cap. There are special outfits, mostly in understated colors, for the concierge staff, the engineers, the various ranks of housekeepers and the waiters who deliver room service" [48].

As the quote above underscores, bespoke corporate uniforms are constitutive elements of the diverse hospitality experiences high-end brands increasingly seek to offer their customers; in fact, they are part and parcel of the activities and practices enacted by hosts and guests on service premises. Thus, providers of these forms of dress, spotlighted through the case of Maurel, are significant actors within the luxury, fashion and tourism sectors. Furthermore, as the Maurel case study suggests, the design and production processes of bespoke corporate uniforms for luxury hospitality share strong commonalities with fashion design processes and are similarly inspired by contemporary trends. Finally, as suggested by Maurel's communication activities, bespoke corporate uniforms are narrated in ways which align with fashion and luxury brands analogue and digital communication practices. Hence, this form of dress and its makers should also be included in the digital fashion communication research, as proposed by Cantoni et al. [39].

In this study, I have spotlighted a gap in fashion and luxury studies regarding the small but precious world of luxury hospitality corporate uniforms and their makers. Like fashion, this field is "dependent upon complex knowledge and expertise" and should be examined if "we are to understand how the social world works" [49]. The study's limitations, including a single case focus, will hopefully create opportunities for more in-depth research.

The author declares no conflict of interest.

References

1. Stevenson, A. (Ed.). (2010). *Uniform. Oxford dictionary of English*. Oxford University Press. https://shorturl.at/gfWUw. last accessed 2025/02/25
2. Craik, J. (2005). *Uniforms exposed: From conformity to transgression*. Berg.
3. Lascity, M. E. (2021). *Communicating fashion: Clothing, culture, and media*. Bloomsbury Publishing.
4. Joseph, N. (1986). *Uniforms and nonuniforms: Communication through clothing*. Greenwood Press.
5. Akou, H. (2024). *On the job: A history of American work uniforms*. Bloomsbury Visual Arts.
6. N.a. (2024). *Il Mercato dell'Abbigliamento da Lavoro - Italia*. Businesscoot.
7. N.a.: Global Workwear Market to Reach $42.7 Billion by 2026. PR Newswire, https://shorturl.at/M35Et, last accessed 2025/02/25.
8. N.a.: Workwear Market Size, Share, & Trend Analysis Forecast 2031. Allied Market Research, https://www.alliedmarketresearch.com/workwear-market-A1686, last accessed 2025/02/25.
9. Terenzi, B. (2015). Identità, conformità e comunicazione nell'abbigliamento. Il ruolo delle divise e delle uniformi nel progetto di immagine coordinata. In E. Benelli (Ed.), *Progettare il Volto delle Istituzioni* (pp. 149–152). Altralinea Edizioni.
10. Nickson, D., Warhurst, C., & Dutton, E. (2005). The importance of attitude and appearance in the service encounter in retail and hospitality. *Managing Service Quality: An International Journal, 15*, 195–208. https://doi.org/10.1108/09604520510585370
11. Wheeler, A., & Meyerson, R. (2024). *Designing brand identity: A comprehensive guide to the world of brands and branding*. Wiley.
12. Rafaeli, A., & Pratt, M. G. (1993). Tailored meanings: On the meaning and impact of organizational dress. *The Academy of Management Review, 18*, 32–55.
13. Vonk, L. (2024). Identity regulation and aesthetic control: The affordances and restraints of uniforms in service work. *Current Sociology*, 1–18. https://doi.org/10.1177/00113921241275683
14. Wirtz, J., Holmqvist, J., & Fritze, M. P. (2020). Luxury services. *JOSM, 31*, 665–691. https://doi.org/10.1108/JOSM-11-2019-0342

15. Tomašević, A. (2018). Luxury hotels. In *Quality services and experiences in hospitality and tourism* (pp. 195–211). Emerald Publishing Limited.
16. Montargot, N. (2016). La gestion de l'apparence du personnel en contact dans l'hôtellerie de luxe. *Annales des Mines - Gérer et comprendre, 126*, 3–14. https://doi.org/10.3917/geco1.126.0003
17. Ornati, M. (2021). Touch in text. The communication of tactility in fashion e-commerce garment descriptions. In T. Sádaba, N. Kalbaska, F. Cominelli, L. Cantoni, & M. Torregrosa Puig (Eds.), *Fashion communication* (pp. 29–40). Springer International Publishing.
18. Entwistle, J. (2000). Fashion and the fleshy body: Dress as embodied practice. *Fashion Theory., 4*, 323–347. https://doi.org/10.2752/136270400778995471
19. Baharuddin, N., & Jamaluddin, M. R. (2020). How important is the frontline uniform toward employee's self-efficacy? A case study of five-star hotel. *JTHCA, 12*, 15–33. https://ir.uitm.edu.my/id/eprint/29176, last accessed 2025/02/25
20. Nelson, K., & Bowen, J. (2000). The effect of employee uniforms on employee satisfaction. *Cornell Hotel and Restaurant Administration Quarterly, 41*, 86–95. https://doi.org/10.1177/001088040004100221
21. Menoux, T. (2019). Clothing a concierge. Socialization through clothing and the tailoring of masculinity in the luxury hospitality industry. *Travail, genre et sociétés, 41*, 47–65. https://shorturl.at/zckHE, last accessed 2025/02/25
22. Plassart, P. (2024). Marie-France Croyeau, styliste: "L'uniforme, une expression subliminale de la qualité du service rendu". LeNouvelEconomiste. https://www.lenouveleconomiste.fr/marie-france-croyeau-styliste-117120/, last accessed 2025/02/25.
23. D'Arpizio, C., & Levato, F. (2024). *Bain Altagamma luxury study* (23rd ed.). Altagamma.
24. Assumma, V. (2024). *Hotel italiani, la corsa procede double digit*. Pambianco Hotellerie. https://magazine.pambianconews.com/, last accessed 2025/02/25
25. EHL Faculty. (2023). Luxury hospitality: Trends, challenges, and best practices. *EHL Insights*. https://hospitalityinsights.ehl.edu/luxury-hospitality-trends-challenges-best-practices, last accessed 2025/02/25
26. Tovisi, T. (2024). Luxury brands expand into new hospitality sectors beyond cafés & spas. *EHL Insights*. https://hospitalityinsights.ehl.edu/luxury-brands-entering-hospitality-sectors, last accessed 2025/02/25
27. Eckenschwiller, C. (2024). Luxury fashion brands investing in hotels. *EHL Insights*. https://hospitalityinsights.ehl.edu/luxury-fashion-brands-investing-in-hotels, last accessed 2025/02/25
28. Serdari, T. (2016). Experiments in suchness: Hiroshi Sugimoto's silk Shiki for Hermès. In J. Armitage & J. Roberts (Eds.), *Critical luxury studies: Art, design, media* (pp. 131–150). Edinburgh University Press.
29. Ricca, M., & Robins, R. (2012). *Meta-luxury: Brands and the culture of excellence*. Palgrave Macmillan.
30. Tynan, J., & Godson, L. (Eds.). (2019). *Uniform: Clothing and discipline in the modern world*. Bloomsbury Visual Arts.
31. Black, P. (2019). A cast of thousands: Martini Grant and the new Qantas uniform. In J. Tynan & L. Godson (Eds.), *Uniform: Clothing and discipline in the modern world* (pp. 179–197). Bloomsbury Visual Arts.
32. Bonami, F., Frisa, M. L., & Tonchi, S. (Eds.). (2000). *Uniform: Order and disorder*. Charta.
33. Tynan, J. (2019). Utility chic: Where fashion and uniform meet. In J. Tynan & L. Godson (Eds.), *Uniform: Clothing and discipline in the modern world* (pp. 221–236). Bloomsbury Visual Arts.
34. Kawamura, Y. (2023). *Fashion-ology: Fashion studies in the postmodern digital era*. Bloomsbury Visual Arts.
35. Sorger, R. (2021). *Research and design for fashion*. Bloomsbury Publishing Plc.
36. Sabatini, N., & Cantoni, L. (2023). Linking fashion and tourism. From body to clothing and lifestyle. In M. Gravari-Barbas & N. Sabatini (Eds.), *Fashion and tourism: Parallel stories* (pp. 33–46). Emerald Publishing Limited.
37. Lamb, J. M., & Kallal, M. J. (1992). A conceptual framework for apparel design. *Clothing and Textiles Research Journal, 10*, 42–47. https://doi.org/10.1177/0887302X9201000207

38. Orzada, B. T., & Kallal, M. J. (2021). FEA consumer needs model: 25 years later. *Clothing and Textiles Research Journal, 39*, 24–38. https://doi.org/10.1177/0887302X19831211
39. Cantoni, L., Cominelli, F., Kalbaska, N., Ornati, M., Sádaba, T., & SanMiguel, P. (2020). Fashion communication research. A way ahead. *Studies in Communication Sciences, 20*, 121–125. https://doi.org/10.24434/j.scoms.2020.01.011
40. Savin-Baden, M., & Major, C. H. (2012). *Qualitative research: The essential guide to theory and practice*. Routledge.
41. Sandelowski, M. (2000). Whatever happened to qualitative description? *Research in Nursing & Health, 23*, 334–340. https://doi.org/10.1002/1098-240X(200008)23:4<334::AID-NUR9>3.0.CO;2-G
42. Bogner, A., Littig, B., & Menz, W. (Eds.). (2009). *Interviewing experts*. Palgrave Macmillan.
43. Balsara, D., & Gómez-Zará, D. (2024). Virtual threads: A systematic literature review of 10 years of VR/AR/MR adoption in fashion design. In *Proceedings of the 2024 ACM designing interactive systems conference* (pp. 356–371). ACM.
44. Paul, J., Ueno, A., Dennis, C., Alamanos, E., Curtis, L., Foroudi, P., Kacprzak, A., Kunz, W. H., Liu, J., Marvi, R., Nair, S. L. S., Ozdemir, O., Pantano, E., Papadopoulos, T., Petit, O., Tyagi, S., & Wirtz, J. (2024). Digital transformation: A multidisciplinary perspective and future research agenda. *International Journal of Consumer Studies, 48*, e13015. https://doi.org/10.1111/ijcs.13015
45. Matarazzo, M., Penco, L., Profumo, G., & Quaglia, R. (2021). Digital transformation and customer value creation in made in Italy SMEs: A dynamic capabilities perspective. *Journal of Business Research, 123*, 642–656. https://doi.org/10.1016/j.jbusres.2020.10.033
46. Amed, I., Berg, A., Balchandani, A., Crump, H., Altable, C. S., Harreis, H., Petersens, S. A., Bain, M., Roberts, R., Kersnar, J., & Hurtado, M. (2022). *The state of fashion special edition. Technology*. McKinsey & Company.
47. Ornati, M., & Kalbaska, N. (2022). Looking for haptics. Touch digitalization business strategies in luxury and fashion during COVID-19 and beyond. *Digital Business, 2*, 100035. https://doi.org/10.1016/j.digbus.2022.100035
48. Pilling, D. (2024). The Med, but Moroccan. FTWeekend (p. 6). *The Financial Times*.
49. Entwistle, J. (2023). *The fashioned body: Fashion, dress and modern social theory*. Polity.

Posting Patterns in Paris: A Fashion Library Instagram Case Study

Katharina Sand

Abstract Specialized libraries in Paris are filled with fashion press and photographs, haute couture documentation and garment patterns, textile samples, and books. Although often overlooked in fashion communication studies, libraries are a key resource for fashion students, academics, and industry professionals. How do specialized libraries in Paris communicate fashion heritage in the era of Bookstagram? This case study describes the use of Instagram by the Forney Library, a specialized applied arts library in Paris that houses a fashion archive open to all. Instagram is its primary social media tool. The study reviews the library's social media practice, affordances and management, target audiences and engagement, content and challenges. It combines a netnographic analysis, including social media analytics and thematic content analysis, with in-depth qualitative interviews of library communication staff. Results reveal a focus on patterns and the materiality of its special collections, aligning with its branding and audience response. Despite achieving one of the highest overall engagement rates on Instagram for fashion libraries internationally, the lower engagement for fashion-related posts also suggests unexplored potential for library resources.

Keywords Instagram · Fashion library · Bibliothèque Forney · Fashion communication

1 Introduction

Paris has positioned itself as a fashion capital and plays a unique role in the history of fashion as the birthplace of haute couture [1–5]. Fashion collections in the city's libraries are instrumental in the transmission of fashion heritage and fashion imaginaries. These collections have been documented by library scholars but largely

K. Sand (✉)
Parsons Paris, Paris, France
e-mail: sandk@newschool.edu

P. von Wachenfeldt et al. (eds.), *Fashion Communication in the Digital Age*, Springer Proceedings in Business and Economics,
https://doi.org/10.1007/978-3-031-99481-4_8

neglected in fashion communication studies. Their holdings constitute invaluable resources for researchers of the domain, as well as for fashion brands reconstituting their archives. Beyond their (increasingly digitalized) contents, these archives also represent physical artifacts, documenting the traces of their producers and those who have handled and stored them. How do specialized fashion libraries in Paris use social media to communicate fashion heritage? This research explores fashion library communication by reviewing the Instagram practice of one of the first lending libraries of Paris, the Bibliothèque Forney.

2 The Forney Library: History and Fashion Holdings

Forney specializes in decorative and applied arts, including fashion, design, craftsmanship, and advertising. The library was inaugurated in February 1886, thanks to a donation bequeathed to the City of Paris by Aimé-Samuel Forney, a French businessman of Swiss origins devoted to arts and craftsmanship. The library was originally located in the 11th arrondissement of Paris and focused mainly on craftsmanship. Fashion was added as a focus in 1961, when it was relocated to the Hôtel de Sens in the fourth arrondissement. This medieval building at 1 rue Figuier, a street lined with fig trees, was constructed for the archbishops of Sens. The medieval building resembles a Harry Potter movie set, featuring turrets, spiral stone staircases, a dungeon, and neo-gothic gargoyles. It can be described as highly "instagrammable." The library is part of the City of Paris's public library system and listed on its website (https://www.paris.fr/lieux/bibliotheque-forney-18), which features the library contact details and its Facebook, X, and Instagram accounts. The site directs readers to the portal of specialized libraries, where the library catalog is accessible: https://bibliotheques-specialisees.paris.fr/.

The Forney library catalog lists 464,557 items, ranging from medieval parchments to books and paper fans. One such listing, an embroidery sample album, may in turn contain over 3000 swatches. Patrons can consult hundreds of thousands of such textile *échantillons*, and rummage through folders filled with fashion show invitations. Wooden drawers reveal well over a thousand fashion plates, hand-colored engravings also called chromolithographs. Under the wooden beams of the reading room's ceilings, you can browse through over 4000 vintage and current magazine titles and some 50,000 trade catalogs from the nineteenth century onward, including those of one of the world's first department stores, Le Bon Marché.

Some items are fragile and only come out for exhibitions, but Forney has been a lending library since its inception [6]. Of the 21,501 books available for loan, 4350 are classified as Fashion and Textiles, which is both the most frequently borrowed field and has the highest turnover rate. The remainder of books is divided between the categories of Graphic Arts, Design and Architecture, Arts and Crafts, Art History and Miscellaneous. These include a plethora of crafts related to fashion: leather goods, perfumes, and jewelry are all classified in the Métiers d'art section. To this day, clothing patterns can be traced and copied in the library. Patterns (motifs) of all kinds, including for wallpapers and textile printing, are a specialty of the library.

As one of the specialized libraries of the City of Paris, the Forney Library offers free and open access to everyone. To sign up for a (free) library card, one must be either aged 18 and over, or an art student, and bring an official ID. The library was originally intended to serve professionals in the arts and crafts, and therefore has a long tradition of late-night and weekend opening hours. Over the years, it has become a key resource for students and academics in the creative industries. The library also encourages the public to engage with the arts through exhibitions, events, and its open-access resources. During the case-study interviews, the librarian in charge of the Forney Public Services, Marc Senet, described the challenge of "using social media to show that while we preserve rare items, the library is still accessible and dynamic."

3 Context

Fashion libraries and documentation centers document, store, classify, and make available a vast array of fashion communication heritage. According to Elise By Olsen, founder of the International Library of Fashion Research in Oslo, they enable fashion to be produced "in/as media rather than clothes; we participate through looking, not by wearing" [7]. In Paris, the local luxury conglomerates and the generations of creative communities the city has drawn into its orbit have resulted in a unique richness of fashion collections in the city's libraries. These include the Bibliothèque Forney, the research library of the Palais Galliera museum, the Centre de documentation of the Musée des Arts Décoratifs (MAD), and the fashion collections of the Institut National d'Histoire de l'Art (INHA) library. The field of fashion has been significantly impacted by social media [8]. This encompasses libraries of fashion museums, fashion academia, and fashion and textile archives, which are increasingly active on social media [9, 10]. Key examples are the MoMu library, the FIT Special Collections, the Costume Institute library, and the International Library of Fashion Research (ILFR). Forney is the only Paris-based specialized fashion library collection with a dedicated Instagram account. The MAD museum account features regular posts on the Centre de documentation's collection, usually weekly. The Palais Galliera museum Instagram account does not mention the research library more than once a year. The INHA occasionally features its library books on its main Instagram account. Yet, fashion ephemera are well suited for sharing on social platforms, as are books and periodicals. The hashtag Bookstagram has been used over 112 million times as of November 2024, whereas the hashtag Booktok has received over 35.5 million views. The fashion world has taken note: Fashion model Kaia Gerber runs the book club @libraryscience, Miu Miu launched "Summer Reads," Marc Jacobs takes book selfies, Chanel organizes "Les Rendez-vous littéraires" book sessions, and Dior hosts "The Dior Book Tote Club." However, fashion communication scholarship on libraries is scarce, even more so on the topic of Instagram.

The analysis of Paris's fashion heritage has focused on museums, key figures, and texts, as well as on the city's position in the fashion domain [1, 2, 4, 5, 11, 12]. International heritage research and Critical Fashion and Archival studies have focused on issues of digitalization, inclusivity, and access, as well as research on fashion materiality and ephemera [13–18]. There is only one (Belgian) library member in the European Fashion Heritage Association. No European network assembles fashion librarians the way the Fashion, Textile, and Costume Special Interest Group of Art Libraries Society does in North America (ARLIS/NA). Lucile Trunel, who heads the Forney library since 2015, presided over the Art Libraries section of the International Federation of Library Associations and Institutions (IFLA) from 2017 to 2021. She documents the library's activities in the art library (rather than fashion) domain, as do her staff [6, 19–23].

Literature in the specialized field of fashion librarianship focuses on library content, its history, and its management [11, 12, 24–28]. Generalized library and Instagram/social media literature includes marketing perspectives [29–32], as well as collaborative and community strategies [33–35]. The impact of social media on reading culture [36] and the challenges of TikTok [37] may also be of relevance to fashion libraries, as is social media research for fashion marketing [38–40]. Two publications stand out. One is a meticulous review of the Instagram account of the Costume Library, by its Associate Museum Librarian, Julie Lê [9]. The other was authored by Ilaria Trame, the first Head Librarian at the ILFR, and points out the new popularity of library content on fashion social media and the potential of Instagram's classification systems [10]. Trame argues that Instagram challenges traditional hierarchies of knowledge in the fashion system, recognizing the value of unofficial narratives alongside established histories. It is notable, however, that she does not refer to French collections apart from a Paris-based rare books dealer.

4 Methodology

This study is based on the Online Communication/OCM Model [41, 42], which has yet to be applied to fashion libraries. It investigates the context of the library's communication; the people producing, updating, promoting content; the audiences addressed and reached; the content produced; and the technical instruments and tools used. The research combines netnography, a literature review, and expert interviews over a 6-month period in 2024. The netnographic research encompasses both a detailed manual review of the Forney library account from June 25th to November 25th, 2024, and a review of international fashion Instagram accounts relating fashion libraries and book content. It is supported by data analytics of these accounts, using the Fanpage Karma as well as Modash analytics tools.

Professional librarians served as primary resources, as did social media staff of libraries. The complexity of keywords in fashion archives is notorious [43–45]. The US-based *Ask a Librarian* service of the Library of Congress, the world's largest knowledge repository, and the European *Eurêkoi* network were consulted for anglophone and francophone keywords and databases. *Eurêkoi* is led by the Bibliothèque publique d'information of the Centre Pompidou in Paris and culls experts amongst 600 librarians from 48 libraries located in France and Belgium to locate relevant publications. The keywords indicated were used in the recommended databases as well as in Google Scholar, and international specialized library catalogs.

To triangulate the data gathered reviewing the profile, content, engagement, and audience analytics, an in-depth expert semi-structured in-person interview was conducted with Marc Senet, the head of the Forney Public Services Department, who handles the library's social media. This interview, on June 25th 2024, was followed by a second interview 6 months later. As part of a larger investigation of fashion libraries, experts handling fashion library collections and social media were consulted at the New School, the Costume Institute Library at the Metropolitan Museum in New York, the MAD, and the Palais Galliera.

5 The Forney Library Online

5.1 Staff

Marc Senet, the head of Forney's Public Services Department, is in charge of the library's social media. Senet manages audience engagement and outreach, trains colleagues to improve customer service, and manages the library tours. His communication responsibilities include flyers and posters in the library, and all online communication including the library blog: social media is one of many daily tasks. Senet coordinates staff who produce content on a voluntary basis and suggests ideas, themes, and collaborations for them. The team size varies: "Now, there are four of us creating content: A colleague in the printed materials department posts about artists' books, her area of focus. A collections manager writes posts about unusual items he finds in storage. And another colleague may cover events in the library. Right now, it's mostly me, but it fluctuates. More people may contribute, whether by giving ideas or creating the actual posts." Senet explains that this teamwork results in a signature quirk: the variety of writing styles and content. The library's challenge is catering to multiple specializations. Fashion is the most borrowed subject by patrons, and fashion schools are becoming more frequent visitors, also thanks to Senet's efforts to encourage them. Senet is a librarian by training: after studying art history, he graduated in library science. Exhibitions in library spaces are a particular interest of his and were the subject of his degree. He acquired his fashion knowledge on the job, including through library visits of fashion schools. In comparison, the Head of Communications of the ILFR was previously a press attachée at Maison Margiela in the 90s and taught at the Institut Français de la Mode; the librarian who started the Costume Institute Instagram account is also an accessory designer.

5.2 The Instagram Profile

As of December 2024, Forney has 10,000 followers on Facebook, 8513 followers on X (formerly Twitter), and 7538 followers on Instagram. It also has a LinkedIn account, which has 225 followers and is not active, and a largely inactive YouTube channel with 34 subscribers and 8 videos. In December 2024, the library also launched a site on Canva. According to Senet, the library used to be more focused on Twitter, with one staff member posting specialized content about historical commercial catalogs. Currently, the social media focus is on Instagram and Facebook. The Instagram account, which exists since December 2018, is the most active, featuring two to three posts per week, and has the highest engagement rate of the accounts. The Instagram handle of the library is @bibforney; a prerequisite for finding it is therefore knowing that a library is called a "bibliothèque" in French, as well as the name of the library. The profile is written in French and reads: "Bibliothèque Forney, Compte officiel: la bibliothèque Forney a pour spécialités les arts graphiques et décoratifs, les métiers d'art, la mode, le design et la pub." The profile picture shows a red letter "F" superimposed on an image. Initially this was the cover image of a vintage periodical, featuring a dress by Jeanne Lanvin being worn to the Olympics. As of October 2024, the "F" was superimposed on a leaf pattern from a wallpaper design from the library's collection. The fig leaf pattern is a nod to the library's street address, rue Figuier. The Instagram account is a personal account, which gives it access to Instagram's full music library. In contrast, business accounts face copyright restrictions for the use of music for stories and reels. They do, however, allow for the use of action buttons, such as *call, text, directions, email*, and *reserve tickets for events*. There is no signature hashtag in the bio as a suggestion for visitors to use. The profile links to the lively library blog, Motifs & Vous, created by Senet, that functions as the library website: (https://bibliothequeforney.wordpress.com/).

5.3 Following and Followers

Instagram offers the possibility to follow profiles and hashtags; these selections in turn help the platform algorithms to personalize the feed of content and to classify and suggest an account to others with similar interests. Content consumed on media plays an important part in shaping content produced. The @bibforney account follows 1221 profiles, including several fashion collections and archives, fashion magazines, and schools. The account also follows an eclectic and diverse selection of libraries and applied arts museums. It does not follow the increasingly popular ILFR account. Senet cites the library at the Metropolitan Museum of Art and the librarian at the Winterthur Museum as accounts he particularly likes because they have similar collections: "they serve as examples of how to showcase our collections…These types of collections don't always coexist easily because they come from different worlds." He also cites the accounts of the Bibliothèque Nationale de France and their digital Gallica library. He recently collaborated with them on a project to digitize the Forney collections, including the Bon Marché department store's catalogs related to fashion.

The Forney account also follows several rare book dealers, but does not follow contemporary local fashion bookstores, such as the bookshop founded by Karl Lagerfeld. It follows certain contemporary fashion exhibition spaces, fashion researchers, and vintage fashion influencers, but not professional associations of fashion and textile curators. It follows diverse voices, such as the Centre d'archives LGBTQI+ Paris IDF, the non-profit Africa Center, and the Korean edition of Elle magazine. It follows the International Council of Museums, but not its Costume Committee. The library follows some established fashion brands, such as Dior and Chanel, but not more cutting-edge brands. (It should be noted that the accounts followed differ between the social media platforms). The account further follows 50 predominantly English-language hashtags with a focus on pattern design, motifs and textile arts, independent publishing, zines, and advertising. It follows #bibliothèque (but not #library), and neither fashion-focused nor bookstagram hashtags, such as #instabooks or #shelfie.

"Our audience is primarily Parisian," Senet continues; "Social media helps us attract younger visitors, especially through thematic visits promoted only on Instagram." A Modash analytics report shows a 72% female audience. One-third are aged between 25 and 34, and just under 17% between 18 and 24. The library does not have detailed audience studies but has documented a shift from artisans to students [23]. Senet has not noticed a significant impact of Bookstagram and Booktok. "We do get visitors who take pictures of what they read in the library to share online, but it's still relatively rare." Within the 6 months from June to November 2024, the library gained 400 followers, an increase similar to that of the MoMu library account. In comparison, the FIT special collections account increased by 100, the Costume Institute library gained 600 followers (although the account has not posted since 2023), and the ILFR account increased its followers by 1000 during this time. The ILFR, which was founded in 2020 and is based in Oslo, houses a fraction of the Forney holdings, but has nearly twice the number of followers of the Forney account.

5.4 Engagement

Forney has unusually high audience engagement compared with other libraries on Instagram, vacillating at around 1.93%, rivaled only by the ILFR account, which racks up 1.99%. In comparison, the Costume Institute Library account shows a 0.30% engagement rate, while the average engagement rate for Instagram posts in general is only 0.43% [46]. The Forney account's average likes stayed at around 140 per post over 6 months, although it received a whopping 7.6 K likes on a post on its advertising exhibition, for which it collaborated on a paid partnership with the historical library of Paris. This collaboration was a moving image post by the influencer @instant.archives. Apart from this promotion, the highest organic engagement stems from a poster commemorating women's voting rights. Posted in the time leading up to the European Parliament elections, it shows engagement with current affairs and political content that is in tune with its audience. The next highest engagement stems from a post on motifs printed on cotton textiles; rather than a close-up of the print, which the library uses as a signature visual style throughout, this post shows the materiality of the book, inviting the viewers to leaf through the book by swiping through a carousel. The highest engagement amongst its current followers thus was paid, political, and printed matter content, not fashion. The library account is responsive: it reposts stories, likes comments, and replies to questions. They do not receive too many questions via social media, so Senet directs people to the library's general email. "We'd love to dedicate more time to user interaction," he adds, "…there have been periods where I focused on encouraging participation with polls, quizzes, and questions in stories; but when I don't have time, I do less of that."

5.5 Content

"What if your next tattoo was one of A. Piau's embroidery designs from the 1920s?", the Forney account somewhat boldly introduces designs that are transferred by needlepoint. The Instagram account reflects the library's branding, which is structured around motifs (patterns). This signature is equally present in the physical space (patterns are used on all library labels and signage), as it is in the digital realm (the library newsletter and blog). Images of motifs and artifacts act as a landing image for most carousels and moving images, a defining element of the account's Instagram grid. For example, when documenting a Misty Modes dress made of paper, a carousel post begins with a close-up of the floral dress pattern.

Many of the account's moving images accentuate the materiality of the collection. Senet aims to create "a desire for people to come and see the documents firsthand." When describing a book of costume designs by Georges Lepape, the weight of the paper and the difficulty of turning the pages with a camera in hand are pointed out. Other clips show backstage activities, such as the archive storage-room, or students on class visits. Hands are sometimes seen handling artifacts, yet they are never the first image seen: the librarians rarely take center stage. Exhibition curators are shown presenting their exhibitions. Clips are used to promote current and upcoming exhibitions. The only (collaborative) paid promotion was for an exhibition post. Several clips show the building's unique architecture and design. Stories are archived by highlighting [47]. They use the following (French) topics: Mode, Moodboard, Événements, Arts Graphiques, Vos stories, Motifs, and Métiers d'art. Visits by (fashion) schools are documented, and their profile handles are tagged on Instagram, but not on Facebook. Both accounts are used for the promotion of events for the general public. The most-viewed Reel documents the access to the library by foot; Reels featuring fashion from 2023 and early 2024 were particularly successful.

Data analytics reveal that #mode and #fashion are the most popular tags used, followed by #patterndesign, #pattern, and #art deco. Their use varies in number, from none to 23 tags per post. The post texts are in French, yet the hashtags are sometimes in English, including #library. Many tags are broad, such as #fashion; specialized tags, such as #fashionarchives, and Bookstagram hashtags, either in English or in French, are rarely used. Some reference Paris, such as #bibliothequeparis, or the hashtag #notredameparis that connected the gothic style of the cathedral to library collections. One competition for bookmarks was launched, using the link in bio leading to the blog. The use of emojis ranges from none to three; the most used emojis are the Calendar (for events), googly Eyes, and the Magnifying Glass. Geotagging is not used. The account occasionally tags fellow library handles, collaborating on events or the digitalization of items. Fashion designers, such as Jeanne Lanvin, are credited in image captions of illustrations, yet rarely put forward. For example, the cover of a magazine featuring a Lanvin dress and her name was relegated to the fifth image of a carousel in July (Fig. 1). The text did not hashtag the designer, nor expand on Lanvin. Designers are not showcased on their birthdays, a practice frequently used by museum libraries. The tone is not only educational but witty. In sum, the focus is less on people and more on patterns, rare artifacts from the library's collections, events, and the building.

5.6 *Training and Tools*

Senet spends an average of 2 h a week on his smartphone for library social media. As part of a Paris-wide network of 80 lending libraries, staff can receive social media training. It is, however, more tailored to lending libraries than specialized libraries. "Practices evolve so quickly," Senet adds: "we're forced to observe what's being done on social media accounts and adapt based on that." He also attends meetings of the network of communication officers for libraries of the city of Paris, rather than consulting publications, which quickly become outdated: "It's an opportunity to share updates, for instance about changes to social media algorithms."

Organizational culture encourages participation by allowing staff agency, establishing trust, and allowing for personal judgment in the creation of posts. Senet has created the WordPress page of the blog and has also added a Canva page. He leads and motivates other staff but defines himself as part of a team: „We try to present our collections in ways that inspire artisans and creators, which has been the mission of the library since its inception. Our goal is to showcase images from our collections to inspire." An internal planning sheet ensures that themes rotate between topics like fashion and graphic arts. The team sticks to free tools, as there is no assigned budget—any tool would need to be negotiated across the 80 libraries. The team uses Canva for layout and design, and a tool called Cut Cut for video editing, which allows for adding subtitles and editing videos without watermarks. As Troy

Fig. 1 Carousel Instagram post by Forney Library, @bibforney, 2024. https://www.instagram.com/p/C9LDOGCxLec/?img_index=6. Screenshot by the author

A. Swanson has pointed out, "free to use" platforms also carry a cost: the costs of staff time, hardware and network infrastructure, and the risk that staff may get pulled into their own social media accounts [33].

6 Conclusion

This case study contributes to the field of fashion communication by examining the largely overlooked role of specialized fashion libraries in Paris. It outlines the use of the Forney library's primary social media account, Instagram, and its socio-technical and municipal context. It shows that its digital content is shaped by the library's branding and affiliations, as well as by the staff's background, affordances, limited resources, and sense of agency. The varied library collections and activities are showcased to a largely local audience, predominantly interested in patterns. Yet, local and international fashion researchers would also greatly benefit from its fashion holdings. These potential audiences could be reached by featuring fashion books, coupled with Bookstagram and Booktok hashtags. Following the example of the Instagram-savvy ILFR account, the library could geotag content and add the word (or category) "library" to its profile. A designated hashtag in the profile (as used by MoMu) could promote more user-generated content. Collaborations with fashion brands in the unique library setting could also increase reach; so could prioritizing people over patterns. Previous collaborations with the *Modes pratiques* research publication could be expanded to international critical research communities. This in turn may allow for re-evaluations of the fashion holdings, just as museums are repositioning their archives. Such an approach would also appeal to a new generation of patrons. Fashion researcher and curator Marine Kisiel, for example, only considers archives meaningful "when they do not isolate the past or its productions from the questions we ask in the present" [48]. This would furthermore be a particularly good fit for the open-minded and socially conscious approach of the library [6, 21]. Finally, the study indicates that specialized libraries, their communication staff, and fashion researchers may all benefit from the establishment of a European network of fashion librarians.

References

1. Bass-Krueger, M., Kurkdjian, S., & Zdatny, S. (Eds.). (2020). *Fashion in French history*. Duke University Press.
2. Hammen, E. (2023). *L'idée de mode, une nouvelle histoire, t.1*. Éditions B42.
3. Kurkdjian, S. (2023). Parisian department stores and fashion tourism. In M. Gravari-Barbas & N. Sabatini (Eds.), *Fashion and tourism* (Tourism social science series) (Vol. 26, pp. 135–153). Emerald Publishing Limited. https://doi.org/10.1108/S1571-504320230000026009
4. Rocamora, A. (2009). *Fashioning the city: Paris, fashion and the media*. I.B. Tauris.
5. Steele, V. (Ed.). (2019). *Paris, capital of fashion*. Bloomsbury Publishing.
6. Trunel, L. (2024). New audiences in art libraries; New skills for professionals? *Art Libraries Journal, 49*(1), 18–23. https://doi.org/10.1017/alj.2023.30
7. Olsen, E. B. (2021). Unpacking the fashion research library. *Viscose Journal, 1*, 146–149.
8. Rocamora, A. (2017). Mediatization and digital media in the field of fashion. *Fashion Theory: The Journal of Dress, Body & Culture, 21*(5), 505–522. https://doi.org/10.1080/1362704X.2016.1173349
9. Lê, J. T. (2019). #Fashionlibrarianship: A case study on the use of Instagram in a specialized museum library collection. *Art Documentation: Journal of the Art Libraries Society of North America, 38*(2), 279–304.
10. Trame, I. (2023). Fashion libraries: Between material and immaterial shelves. *Fashion Highlight, 1*(1), 128–135.
11. Beuvin, E., & Bomel, K. (2023, May 2). UFAC and the institution of the Musée des Arts de la Mode. *The Fashion Issue—Archivio Magazine*.
12. Saillard, O., & Roy, S. (2017). *Le patrimoine de la mode en France: Les collections de vêtements et costumes dans les collections publiques et privées en France. États des lieux*. Centre de documentation, Palais Galliera.
13. Becks, C. (2018). African American studies collections and the American season of redemption. *Proceedings of the Charleston Library Conference*. https://doi.org/10.5703/1288284317012
14. Franceschini, M. (2019). Navigating fashion: On the role of digital fashion archives in the preservation, classification and dissemination of fashion heritage. *Critical Studies in Fashion & Beauty, 10*(1), 69–90.
15. Pecorari, M. (2019). Fashion archives, museums and collections in the age of the digital. *Critical Studies in Fashion & Beauty, 10*(1), 3–29.
16. Peirson-Smith, A., & Peirson-Smith, B. (2020). Fashion archive fervour: The critical role of fashion archives in preserving, curating, and narrating fashion. *Archives and Records, 41*(3), 274–298.
17. Permatasari, P. A., & Kalbaska, N. (2022). Digital technologies for communicating fashion heritage. In *Handbook on heritage, sustainable tourism and digital media* (pp. 60–75). Edward Elgar Publishing.

18. Pham, M. H. T. (2014). Archival intimacies: Participatory media and the fashion histories of US women of colour. *Fashion, Style & Popular Culture, 2*(1), 107–122.
19. Casiot, F. (2006). The collection of ephemera at the Bibliothèque Forney in Paris. *Art Libraries Journal, 31*(4), 21–26. https://doi.org/10.1017/S030747220001470X
20. Garcia, J. (2024). Decorative arts to borrow at home: A unique story of a specialized collection of images in a French public art library. *Art Libraries Journal, 49*(1), 10–17. https://doi.org/10.1017/alj.2023.29
21. Garcia, J., & Granger, C. (2022). Attention, un monument historique peut cacher une bibliothèque ouverte à tous. Raconter l'histoire de la bibliothèque Forney. *Balisages, 4*. https://doi.org/10.35562/balisages.864
22. Trunel, L. (2008). The landscape of digitization in French art libraries. *IFLA Art Libraries Section Newsletter, 62*. https://www.ifla.org/wp-content/uploads/files/assets/art-libraries/newsletter/2008-62.pdf
23. Trunel, L. (2018). Old building, new public: The renovation of the Forney Art Library in Paris. *Art Libraries Journal, 43*(1), 9–15. https://doi.org/10.1017/alj.2017.42
24. Golderman, G., & Connolly, B. (2016). EReviews: Fashion collections. *Library Journal, 141*(01), 131–n/a.
25. Hall, S. (2021). Fashion torn up: Exploring the potential of zines and alternative fashion press publications in academic library collections. *Library Trends, 70*(1), 51–71.
26. King, L. M., & Clement, R. T. (2012). Style and substance: Fashion in twenty-first-century research libraries. *Art Documentation: Journal of the Art Libraries Society of North America, 31*(1), 93–107.
27. Roberts, M. (2017). Fashion literature collection development at Stockholm University Library. *Art Libraries Journal, 42*(3), 169–174. https://doi.org/10.1017/alj.2017.24
28. Suls, D. (2008). The library of the Fashion Museum of the Province of Antwerp. *Libraries Journal, 12*(3), 21.
29. Alfonzo, P. (2019). Instagram in the library. *Library Technology Reports, 55*(2), 33–42.
30. Hursh, A. (2023). The 2023 guide to social media for libraries: New YouTube success secrets for this year. Retrieved from https://superlibrarymarketing.com/2022/12/05/youtubeforlibraries2023
31. Koontz, C., & Mon, L. (2014). *Marketing and social media: A guide for libraries, archives, and museums*. Rowman & Littlefield.
32. Open Education Database. (2022, July 7). 10 social media marketing tips for libraries. Retrieved from https://oedb.org/ilibrarian/10-social-media-marketingtips-for-libraries/
33. Swanson, T. A. (2012). *Managing social media in libraries: Finding collaboration, coordination, and focus*. Elsevier.
34. Garner, A., Goldberg, J., & Pou, R. (2017). Collaborative social media campaigns and special collections: A case study on #ColorOurCollections. *RBM: A Journal of Rare Books, Manuscripts, and Cultural Heritage, 17*(2), 9663.
35. Wong-Welch, J., Esquivel, E., & Cota, M. (2022). Becoming an insta-influencer: How librarians inspired connection by sharing their own voices in times of uncertainty. *IFLA WLIC 2022*. Retrieved from https://2022.ifla.org/
36. Reddan, B., Rutherford, L., Schoonens, A., & Dezuanni, M. (2024). *Social reading cultures on BookTube, Bookstagram, and BookTok*. Taylor & Francis.
37. Kelley, L. (2022, December 30). Librarians are meeting younger readers where they are: TikTok. *New York Times*. Retrieved from https://www.nytimes.com/2022/12/30/books/librarians-tiktok.
38. Bendoni, W. K. (2017). *Social media for fashion marketing: Storytelling in a digital world.* Bloomsbury Publishing.
39. SanMiguel, P., Nobile, T. H., Sánchez-Blanco, C., & Sabatini, N. (2024). *Social media in the fashion industry: Fundamentals, strategy and research methods*. Taylor & Francis.
40. von Wachenfeldt, P. (2021). The mediation of luxury brands in digital storytelling. *Fashion Theory, 25*(1), 99–118. https://doi.org/10.1080/1362704X.2019.1599256

41. Cantoni, L., & Tardini, S. (2006). *Internet*. Taylor & Francis.
42. Tardini, S., & Cantoni, L. (2015). Hypermedia, internet and the web. In L. Cantoni & J. A. Danowski (Eds.), *Communication and technology* (pp. 119–140). Walter de Gruyter.
43. Kirkland, A., Sklar, M., Sauro, C., Wiebers, L., Idacavage, S., & Mun, J. (2023). "I'm not searching the right words": User experience searching historic clothing collection websites.
44. Trivette, K. J. (2023). Discovering today's digital resources for researching yesterday's fashion and costume. In *The Routledge history of fashion and dress, 1800 to the present* (p. 527).
45. Warschaw, O. (2021). Information literacy for fashion students: Translating visual and tactile cues into searchable key terms. *Library Trends, 70*(1), 3–11. https://doi.org/10.1353/lib.2021.0015
46. Zote, J. (2024, September 26). Instagram engagement rate: How to calculate yours in 2024. *Sprout Social*. https://sproutsocial.com/insights/instagram-engagement-rate/
47. Bainotti, L., Caliandro, A., & Gandini, A. (2021). From archive cultures to ephemeral content, and back: Studying Instagram stories with digital methods. *New Media & Society, 23*(12), 3656–3676.
48. Kisiel, M. (n.d.). Villa Albertine. Retrieved December 15, 2024, from https://villa-albertine.org/va/residents/marine-kisiel

Communication Strategy

The Co-Branding Phenomenon in Fashion Brands: An Approach to the Perception of Spanish Consumers

Carlos Checa, Patricia SanMiguel, Marta Torregrosa, and Cristina Sánchez-Blanco

Abstract This study explores the phenomenon of co-branding within the fashion industry, focusing on the perception of Spanish consumers. Co-branding, a strategic collaboration between two or more brands, has emerged as a critical tool for innovation, market expansion, and revitalizing brand perception. Through a review of relevant literature and an exploratory survey conducted in Madrid, Spain, the study identifies key factors influencing consumer attitudes toward co-branded products, such as design, innovation, and perceived quality. Results highlight a positive consumer reception to brand collaborations, with 64.5% of respondents having purchased co-branded products. While enthusiasm for such initiatives is evident, willingness to pay premium prices remains contingent on the collaboration's perceived value. The study categorizes co-branding strategies into four types—complementary competency, promotional endorsement, awareness enhancement, and ingredient branding—illustrating their diverse applications and benefits. However, risks such as brand dilution, consumer confusion, and misalignment of values underscore the importance of strategic coherence. The findings emphasize that successful co-branding requires meaningful integration of brand identities, innovation, and exclusivity to maintain consumer trust and loyalty.

Keywords Co-branding · Collaborations · Fashion brands · Consumer perception · Spain

C. Checa
ISEM Fashion Business School, Madrid, Spain

P. SanMiguel (✉) · M. Torregrosa · C. Sánchez-Blanco
School of Communication-University of Navarra, Pamplona, Spain
e-mail: patricia.sanmiguel@isem.es; psanmiguel@unav.es

P. von Wachenfeldt et al. (eds.), *Fashion Communication in the Digital Age*, Springer Proceedings in Business and Economics,
https://doi.org/10.1007/978-3-031-99481-4_9

1 Introduction

Collaboration Strategy in various industries has recently become a mainstream issue. In the fashion world, co-branding has established itself as a common strategy to capture attention, explore new audiences, and revitalize design. Since H&M revolutionized the sector with its collaboration with Karl Lagerfeld in 2004, brand partnerships have evolved from being a novelty to becoming a standard practice. Today, disparate brands such as Louis Vuitton and Crocs, or Skims and Dolce & Gabbana, engage in alliances aimed at generating impact and reshaping perceptions.

However, this boom presents a challenge: the overload of collaborations may be leading consumers to fatigue, where even partnerships between highly recognizable brands risk failing. A recent example is the collaboration between Lululemon and Disney, which left its core consumer base indifferent, demonstrating that merely combining two well-known names does not guarantee success. Effective co-branding must result in authentic designs that meaningfully merge the DNA of both brands.

This study aims to explore Spanish consumer perceptions of co-branding within the fashion industry. It reviews relevant literature to define the concept, with a particular focus on the fashion sector and its impact on brand perception. Subsequently, the results of an exploratory study based on surveys conducted in Spain are presented. Finally, general conclusions and proposals for future research are offered, emphasizing the importance of strategic coherence and perceived value for the success of these alliances.

2 Co-Branding: A Brand Growth Strategy

As markets become increasingly competitive and consumers demand more sophisticated experiences, business leaders are seeking innovative ways to enhance customer engagement and drive growth. Co-branding has emerged as a strategic marketing tool to achieve these goals [1, 2]. Co-branding refers to the collaboration between two or more companies to develop a product or service with the aim of achieving mutual benefits. Often a temporary alliance, co-branding enables brands to pool their strengths to achieve a greater impact than they could individually [3–5].

When evaluating a co-branded product, consumers typically rely on their familiarity with and loyalty to the individual brands, as well as the perceived quality and their affiliation with each brand in the partnership. They assess the new product based on the constituent brands, where the combined perceptions yield a greater impact than the mere sum of the individual brand attributes [6]. As building a strong brand identity often takes years, co-branding accelerates this process by transferring positive associations between the partnering brands in the consumer's perception [2, 7].

The number of co-branding partnerships has increased significantly over the past two decades, driven by a growing awareness of the opportunities this strategy offers for business growth [2, 8]. Brands are drawn to co-branding as a growth strategy because it allows them to leverage the strengths of their partners, each contributing a customer base and brand recognition that become accessible to the other through the partnership [9].

Unlike other marketing strategies, co-branding involves the creation of a new product that combines distinctive elements of the collaborating brands. This sets it apart from brand alliances, which focus on enhancing brand image through strategic associations without the need for new product development. Similarly, it differs from co-promotion, which involves temporary partnerships for promotional purposes, and sponsorships, which usually involve financial transactions in exchange for reputational benefits [10].

Co-branding is classified into four main types based on the nature of the collaboration and the objectives pursued [5, 11, 12]. (1) Complementary Competency Co-Branding is characterized by the combination of brand strengths to provide innovative solutions to consumers. An example is the Apple Watch Nike+, which integrates Apple's technology with Nike's sports design. (2) Promotional or Value Endorsement Co-Branding involves mutual support by linking the positioning and similar values of the participating brands to reinforce their image and offer new consumer experiences. An example of this is the collaboration between Spotify and Uber, which allows users to enjoy personalized music during their rides. (3) Awareness and Reach Co-Branding seeks to increase brand recognition by exposing each brand to the other's customer base and expanding distribution and sales channels. For instance, the co-branding partnership between Adidas and Lego resulted in a Lego set replicating the iconic Originals Superstar sneakers in black and white design. (4) Finally, Ingredient Co-Branding is perhaps the most well-known type, where brands with similar or identical values merge to offer a new product. In this form of co-branding, one brand recognized for its market-leading qualities supplies a component for another branded product. This is particularly common in the food industry, such as the co-branding between Doritos and Taco Bell. The main motivation for this strategy is to create differentiation through the attributes of the ingredient, thereby enhancing brand equity [13].

Co-branding offers numerous advantages that make it an attractive strategy for brands. Among these are: (a) the ability to efficiently access new markets by leveraging the reputation of well-established brands; (b) the potential to increase the price of products or services by adding value; and (c) the provision of additional benefits to consumers, such as discounts or enhanced experiences. Another key aspect is (d) the reduction of operational costs through shared resources, enabling the achievement of objectives with lower investment. Co-branding can also generate faster returns on investment and improve consumer perception of quality, as the combination of reliable brands enhances public trust in the new product. Furthermore, (e) it strengthens advertising messages by allowing for specialized approaches and increases the exposure of smaller brands by associating them with more recognized ones. During key moments, such as events, co-branding can also provide unique opportunities for visibility and differentiation for the involved brands, while simultaneously increasing their value by entering new markets and fostering positive consumer perceptions [10, 14].

Co-branding also entails risks that must be carefully considered. First, (a) financial instability can arise due to delays in economic benefits, which necessitates long-term planning. (b) Differences in corporate values and attitudes may lead to conflicts that strain the relationship between the partnering brands. Alliances between brands of significantly different sizes or from disparate industries pose greater challenges in achieving positive consumer perceptions. Additionally, cultural alignment between the countries of origin of the brands is critical to the success of the partnership [15]. (c) Over-ambition or expansion into unrelated sectors can lead to the failure of the strategy [7].

Other complications include repositioning of one of the partner brands, failure to meet shared objectives, and issues stemming from mergers or acquisitions involving one of the brands. Market attitude changes can also negatively affect the partnership, particularly if one brand fails to meet consumer expectations. Lastly, the perception of a hybrid brand may create confusion or rejection among consumers, while the loss of exclusivity can erode the unique identity of each brand. For these reasons, a controlled and authorized use of the brands within the co-branding agreement is essential to mitigate risks [10, 16].

According to Paydas Turan [17], the relationship between the partner brands has a significantly larger impact on the success of co-branding than the individual brand characteristics, with brand image fit being a more important driver than product category fit or brand equity. Furthermore, "strong brands are less exposed to the negative effects of co-branding" [14, p. 41].

Co-branding is a powerful strategy that can yield significant benefits for brands, provided that adequate measures are taken to minimize risks. Vertical control is essential to reduce ambiguity during the initial and final stages, though it may be counterproductive during the operational phase [18]. Its success relies on strategic planning, brand compatibility, and the ability to adapt to market dynamics. Co-branding alliances must be managed in alignment with their developmental stage.

3 Co-Branding and Fashion Brands

Co-branding in the fashion industry has undergone remarkable development since the mid-twentieth century, becoming a key strategy for brands. Collaboration has become a central concept in the twenty-first-century fashion industry, encompassing diverse areas such as online and offline markets, B2C and B2B models, domestic and global markets, and small businesses to large enterprises [19]. This phenomenon originated in 1956 with the partnership between Renault and the jewelry house Van Cleef & Arpels, resulting in a unique car featuring a jewel-adorned steering wheel, highlighting exclusivity and luxury [5]. In the fashion domain, co-branding gained prominence in 1972 with American Motors' Levi's Edition Gremlin, followed in 1973 by Volkswagen's Jeans Beetle, both aimed at appealing to young consumers associated with denim culture [20].

In subsequent decades, co-branding evolved to include collaborations between the fashion sector and various other industries, such as technology, food, and hospitality. Examples include the 2010 partnership between Adidas and Continental, which created sneakers with tire tread soles, and the alliance between Armani and Emaar Properties to develop luxury hotels. These partnerships underscore the versatility of co-branding as a strategy [5, 21]. Collaborative strategies in fashion are pivotal tools for differentiating brands and expanding markets. Alliances with technology and cultural industries are particularly valuable for fostering innovation and attracting new consumers. However, companies must carefully manage these partnerships to avoid risks such as brand dilution or misaligned strategic objectives [22].

A notable failure was the 2013 collaboration between Target and Neiman Marcus, whose overpriced collection failed to meet public expectations, leading to significant discounts and financial losses. Such failed collaborations highlight that poorly adjusted pricing or product categories misaligned with the core brand offerings can alienate consumers and dilute brand equity [9]. Another unsuccessful alliance was between Veuve Clicquot and DKNY, where consumers did not perceive significant benefits in the final product, resulting in a disconnect between the brands and their audience [2].

Co-branding between fashion brands has been a recurring strategy over the past two decades, featuring partnerships that combine luxury and non-luxury brands, thus creating new forms of "shared luxury branding" [7]. H&M revolutionized co-branding in 2004 with its collaboration with Karl Lagerfeld, setting a precedent for future partnerships.

These alliances often benefit non-luxury brands by increasing their visibility and prestige [23], and in some cases, their sales as well [24]. For luxury fashion brands, the impact can vary. Collaborations between luxury fashion brands and fast-fashion companies are strategic efforts by luxury brands to connect with a broader audience in ways previously unattainable. Co-branding has an immediate effect on sales revenue, marketing budgets, and store traffic, generating publicity and buzz. Such collaborations are positively perceived by consumers, enhancing overall awareness of luxury fashion brands by reinforcing their presence in consumers' minds. Luxury consumers typically continue to shop from these brands as their perceptions remain unaffected by co-branding initiatives with fast-fashion companies [24].

However, in some instances, these partnerships can negatively impact the luxury brand's perception of exclusivity and quality [25–27]. Co-branding can only succeed if it provides tangible benefits for each participating brand. Nevertheless, it is not always a reliable strategy, as demonstrated by the failures of partnerships such as Adidas and Ivy Park or Nike and Tiffany. Combining brand identities can lead to brand dilution, distort customer perceptions, and risk alienating existing customers. In markets like luxury and fashion, coherence and authenticity are essential for co-branding. Co-branded products involving luxury brands must maintain exclusivity, as mass-market offerings can undermine their image or be perceived as opportunistic. To address this, many co-branding initiatives in the luxury sector rely on limited editions, fostering a sense of rarity and exclusivity akin to luxury products, despite being more accessible [9, 28].

For luxury brands, co-branding with fast-fashion companies primarily aims to enhance engagement with younger consumers. Due to high competition and a strong emphasis on brand protection, co-branding has been relatively rare in the luxury goods sector [24]. The iconic collaboration between Louis Vuitton and Supreme showcased the potential of merging luxury brands with streetwear, blending exclusivity with modernity. This partnership appealed to younger demographics while preserving brand heritage through consistent design for both partners and the strategic use of limited editions to create demand and maintain the perception of exclusivity. The co-branding initiative demonstrated how brands can expand their appeal to younger audiences without compromising their core identity [29].

In conclusion, co-branding in the fashion industry is a powerful tool for market expansion, enhancing brand perception, and diversifying product offerings. While it presents challenges and risks, its successful implementation—rooted in strategic partner selection and careful execution—can result in significant benefits for both brands and consumers, reinforcing its relevance in the contemporary fashion landscape.

4 Impact of Co-Branding on Brand Perception

Co-branding has a profound impact on brand perception, influencing perceived quality, consumer loyalty, brand image, and the shopping experience. A brand serves as a crucial representation of what a product signifies to the consumer and is a valuable asset for companies, as its value derives from consumers' emotions and perceptions [10]. Co-branding strategies that associate highly reputable brands reinforce this value and build customer trust. Ahn et al. [3] emphasize that the success of these alliances hinges on partnerships with high-value brands, a factor particularly relevant in the luxury sector. However, when there is a significant disparity in the status of the partnered brands, consumers may experience uncertainty, as highlighted by Luck et al. [30].

Perceived quality in co-branding also depends on factors such as the diversity of product lines. A broader product offering tends to enhance the perception of quality, though low-price strategies can undermine long-term value, especially for luxury brands. According to Luck et al. [30], temporary alliances with retailers can boost sales without harming the status of luxury brands. This demonstrates the versatility of co-branding as a strategy to balance profitability and prestige.

Consumer loyalty is significantly strengthened through co-branding, particularly in sectors like fast fashion and luxury, where emotions play a fundamental role in purchasing decisions. Functional and symbolic alignment between brands in a partnership enhances both customer perception and loyalty. Moreover, international collaborations can expand the global recognition of domestic brands. This strategy also supports competitive advantage and attracts new customers, as demonstrated by studies highlighting its positive impact on consumer satisfaction and loyalty.

In terms of brand image and positioning, co-branding serves as a powerful tool for entering new markets. Boad [31] explains that such alliances enable brands to overcome entry barriers and capitalize on the local reputation of a strategic partner, thereby increasing their chances of success. Notable examples include the partnership between Ford Motor Company and Eddie Bauer, as well as Monsanto's NutraSweet initiative, which illustrate how co-branding strategies can boost sales, position new products, and leverage the credibility of established brands. Furthermore, Boad [31] suggests that co-branding can serve as a preliminary strategy for introducing a new brand, which can later be independently positioned in distinct sectors, ensuring a strong initial impact.

The consumer experience in co-branding is shaped by key factors such as price, design, and innovation. Kam and Arbaiza [32] emphasize that price plays a critical role in the perceived value of a brand, as it reflects both quality and social status. Similarly, Hekkert [33] notes that aesthetic design is vital for attracting consumers, while Easey [34] highlights the role of designers as creative drivers, particularly in sectors like fashion. Innovation is also a compelling factor, especially among consumers willing to pay premium prices for novel and high-quality products.

Consumer perception of co-branding is heavily influenced by the coherence and relevance of the partnership. According to Kumar [35], the most positive evaluations occur when both brands are successful in their respective sectors and develop products related to their core activities. Collange [36] explains that emotions associated with one brand transfer to the other, shaping consumer evaluations and purchase intentions. However, Leuthesser et al. [14] caution that the positive impact of co-branding is not always uniform, though a partnership between high-value and low-value brands does not necessarily harm the higher-status brand. Regardless, consumers demand logical and coherent alliances with a strong image that captures their interest.

Finally, co-branding significantly influences the shopping experience by offering products perceived as exclusive and high-quality, thereby enhancing consumers' social standing. Bouten et al. [37] assert that consumers view co-branded products as opportunities for social distinction. Similarly, Washburn et al. [6] highlight that the reputation of one partnering brand transfers to the other, particularly benefiting lesser-known brands by strengthening their image and positioning. In this way, co-branding emerges as an effective strategy for ensuring commercial success and creating brand value.

5 Study of Consumer Perception Regarding Fashion Brand Collaborations

5.1 Methodology and Sample

This study presents an exploratory analysis of consumer perception regarding collaborations between fashion brands. The aim of this research is not to provide an exhaustive analysis but rather to understand how young consumers perceive these brand agreements and to observe whether they recognize the benefits and risks previously discussed in the literature review. To achieve this objective, a survey was conducted to perform a descriptive study of potential consumers, evaluating their perception of products resulting from brand alliance strategies in the fashion sector.

The survey was distributed in Madrid, Spain, via an online link using the snowball sampling method to maximize participation. The questionnaire consisted of 12 questions and received 110 valid responses. The variables analyzed included: age, gender, approximate salary, excitement about brand collaborations, frequency of fashion product purchases, purchase of co-branded products, important factors in brand alliances, price willingness, the impact of alliances on brand values, key aspects of brands, experiences with co-branded products, and reactions to virality or trends.

The sample consisted predominantly of individuals aged between 18 and 34 years (57.3%) and 55–65 years (20.1%). Women represented 74.5% of the sample, and the majority reported an annual salary below €30,000. The predominance of female respondents aligns with González Penas [38], who highlights that women are more frequent consumers of fashion compared to men. Women tend to exhibit a strong attraction to clothing, accessories, specific brands, or designers, which drives their attention to fashion trends communicated through retail outlets, fashion shows, magazines, and the press.

5.2 *Results and Discussion*

The survey results indicate a considerable interest in products resulting from collaborations between brands in the fashion industry. Most participants were receptive and excited about such initiatives, aligning with the findings in the existing literature. However, willingness to pay a premium price largely depends on the specific collaboration and the product in question.

Regarding the purchase of products resulting from brand collaborations, 64.5% of respondents reported having acquired such items. In terms of the excitement generated by new collaborations, 60.9% of respondents expressed some level of enthusiasm: 24.5% stated they were "very excited," while 36.4% reported being "somewhat excited." These results reflect a predominantly positive attitude toward these initiatives, consistent with prior literature [2, 6, 10], which highlights that consumers perceive such products as more attractive due to the combination of attributes from both brands.

As for consumers' willingness to pay a higher price for collaboration products, the results indicate limited predisposition. Only 7.3% of respondents stated they were "definitely" willing to pay more, while 49.5% noted that their willingness would depend on the product, and 30.3% mentioned it would depend on the specific collaboration. Finally, 12.8% of respondents outright rejected the idea of paying a premium price. This underscores the importance of collaborations providing significant perceived value in terms of design, quality, or exclusivity to justify a price increase. These findings align with those of Kam and Arbaiza [32], who demonstrated that while co-branding can enhance perceived quality, it does not automatically ensure a willingness to pay more, particularly if a clear added value is not perceived.

Regarding the determining factors in the perception of collaborations, the most important factors when evaluating products resulting from brand collaborations were innovation and design (34.5%) and product quality (29.1%). Notably, price (16.4%) was not the most decisive factor, and exclusivity was the primary consideration for only 12.7% of respondents. These results demonstrate that the analyzed sample of consumers prioritizes tangible attributes such as design and quality, while assigning secondary value to exclusivity.

Furthermore, respondents' experiences with products resulting from collaborations were predominantly positive. A total of 52.3% described their experience as "positive," and 8.3% as "very positive." Meanwhile, 39.4% maintained a neutral stance, and no participants reported negative experiences. These data indicate a widespread acceptance of such products and the ability of collaborations to meet consumer expectations. These findings support those of Besharat and Langan [2], who highlighted that co-branding enhances consumer trust in products.

Finally, regarding the impact of virality or trends on purchasing decisions, the results reveal a significant division. While 50.9% of respondents stated that the influence depends on the specific product, 29.1% indicated that virality directly affects their purchasing behavior. This suggests that, although virality can have an impact, its influence is not decisive for all consumers and depends on the particular characteristics of the product (Table 1).

5.3 *General Conclusions and Future Research Directions*

This study provides valuable insights into the phenomenon of co-branding in the fashion industry, with a specific focus on Spanish consumer perceptions. Co-branding has emerged as a critical strategy for innovation, brand differentiation, and market expansion in an increasingly competitive and dynamic marketplace. The findings from the literature review and survey results underscore the multifaceted nature of co-branding, revealing both its advantages and inherent risks. Consumer responses indicate a generally positive attitude toward co-branded products, driven by attributes such as innovation, design, and perceived quality. However, the willingness to pay premium prices for these products remains contingent upon the perceived value and exclusivity of the collaboration. However, the data also reveal that consumer excitement does not uniformly translate into higher willingness to pay. These results align with existing literature, reinforcing the notion that strategic coherence and a meaningful integration of brand identities are fundamental to the success of co-branding initiatives.

Consumers demonstrate a clear interest in co-branded products, with a significant majority expressing enthusiasm for new collaborations. This suggests that co-branding continues to captivate consumers, particularly in the fashion industry, where innovation and trend-driven strategies are pivotal. However, the data also

Table 1 Consumer perception regarding fashion brand collaborations

Category	Response	n	%
Purchase of fashion products resulting from collaborations	Yes	71	64.5
	No	39	35.5
Emotions toward new collaborations between fashion brands	Very excited	27	24.5
	Somewhat excited	40	36.4
	Neutral	36	32.7
	Little excited	6	5.5
	Not excited	1	0.9
Willingness to pay more for products in collaborations	Yes, definitely	8	7.3
	It depends on the collaboration	33	30.3
	It depends on the product	54	49.5
	No	14	12.8
Most important factors in a collaboration	Product exclusivity	14	12.7
	Price	18	16.4
	Product quality	32	29.1
	Innovation and design	38	34.5
	Brand values and ethics	8	7.3
Experience with products from collaborations	Very positive	9	8.3
	Positive	58	52.3
	Neutral	43	39.4
	Negative	0	0.0
	Very negative	0	0.0
Influence of virality or trendiness of a collaboration	No	32	29.1
	It depends on the product	56	50.9
	Yes	32	29.1

reveal that consumer excitement does not uniformly translate into higher willingness to pay. This finding emphasizes the need for collaborations to offer unique and high-quality products that justify potential price increases. Furthermore, while attributes such as design and innovation are highly valued, exclusivity and brand ethics appear to play a secondary role in shaping consumer perceptions. These insights highlight the evolving expectations of consumers and the necessity for brands to adapt their strategies accordingly.

This study has limitations that offer valuable opportunities for future research. The sample size and demographic focus on young Spanish consumers may limit the generalizability of the findings. Future studies could expand the scope by exploring diverse demographic groups and international markets to capture a broader range of consumer perceptions. Additionally, longitudinal research could investigate the long-term effects of co-branding on brand equity and consumer loyalty. Understanding how consumer attitudes evolve over time would provide valuable insights into the sustainability of co-branding as a strategic approach.

Future research on co-branding should explore the growing influence of digital and technological advancements, including the role of e-commerce, social media, and influencer marketing in shaping consumer perceptions of co-branded products.

Investigating collaborations that prioritize sustainability and ethical practices could also yield insights into appealing to socially conscious consumers.

Additionally, delving into the psychological and emotional aspects of co-branding is essential to understand how brand narratives foster consumer connections. Comparative studies across cultures and regions would further illuminate differences in consumer perceptions, enabling global brands to tailor strategies to diverse markets. By addressing these areas, future research can refine our understanding of co-branding dynamics and support brands in crafting effective, sustainable strategies in a rapidly changing marketplace.

References

1. Beem, D. (2010). The case for co-branding. *Forbes*. https://www.forbes.com/2010/03/16/cold-stone-creamery-dan-beem-rocky-mountain-chocolate-cmo-network-co-brandins
2. Besharat, A., & Langan, R. (2014). Towards the formation of consensus in the domain of co-branding: Current findings and future priorities. *Journal of Brand Management, 21*(2), 112–132. https://doi.org/10.1057/bm.2013.25
3. Ahn, J., Kim, A., & Sung, Y. (2020). The effects of sensory fit on consumer evaluations of co-branding. *International Journal of Advertising, 39*(4), 486–503. https://doi.org/10.1080/02650487.2019.1652518
4. Newmeyer, C., Venkatesh, R., & Chatterjee, R. (2014). Cobranding arrangements and partner selection: A conceptual framework and managerial guidelines. *Journal of the Academy of Marketing Science, 42*(2), 103–118. https://doi.org/10.1007/s11747-013-0343-8
5. Rodríguez Gómez, A. E. (2022). La fusión de marcas: el contrato de co-branding (Merging trademarks: The co-branding agreement). *La Propiedad Inmaterial, 34*, 89–110.
6. Washburn, J. H., Till, B. D., & Priluck, R. (2000). Co-branding: Brand equity and trial effects. *Journal of Consumer Marketing, 17*(7), 591–604. https://doi.org/10.1108/07363760010357796
7. Yu, Y., Rothenberg, L., & Moore, M. (2020). Exploring young consumer's decision-making for luxury co-branding combinations. *International Journal of Retail & Distribution Management, 49*(3), 341–358. https://doi.org/10.1108/IJRDM-12-2019-0399
8. Newmeyer, C., Venkatesh, R., Ruth, J., & Chatterjee, R. (2018). A typology of brand alliances and consumer awareness of brand alliance integration. *Marketing Letters, 29*(3), 275–289. https://doi.org/10.1007/s11002-018-9467-4
9. Childs, M. L., & Jin, B. H. (2015). A new age in clothing brand and retailer collaborations: Trends and recommendations for a successful partnership. *Journal of Brand Strategy, 5*(1), 83–100.
10. Xue, M. T., & Chawdhary, R. (2023). Co-branding as a masstige strategy for luxury brands: Desirable or not? *Journal of Business Research, 158*, 113704. https://doi.org/10.1016/j.jbusres.2023.113704
11. Blackett, T., & Russell, N. (2000). Co-branding: The science of alliance. *Journal of Brand Management, 7*, 161–170. https://doi.org/10.1057/bm.2000.3
12. Hultman, C. (2002). Co-branding: The science of alliance. *European Journal of Marketing, 36*(11/12), 1439–1441. https://doi.org/10.1108/ejm.2002.36.11_12.1439.1
13. Desai, K., & Keller, K. (2002). The effects of ingredient branding strategies on host brand extendibility. *Journal of Marketing, 66*(1), 73–93.
14. Leuthesser, L., Kohli, C., & Suri, R. (2003). 2+2=5? A framework for using co-branding to leverage a brand. *Journal of Brand Management, 11*, 35–47. https://doi.org/10.1057/palgrave.bm.2540146

15. Zhou, F., & Sulaiman, Z. (2023). Ethnocentrism on purchase intention of fast fashion co-branding in China. *International Journal of Operations and Quantitative Management, 29*(2), 135–156. https://doi.org/10.46970/2023.29.2.07
16. Mróz-Gorgoń, B. (2016). Co-branding as a strategy-fashion market perspective: Prestige or masstige? *International Journal of Sales, Retailing & Marketing, 5*(4), 49–61.
17. Paydas Turan, C. (2021). Success drivers of co-branding: A meta-analysis. *International Journal of Consumer Studies, 45*(4), 911–936. https://doi.org/10.1111/ijcs.12682
18. Nygaard, A., & Dahlstrom, R. (2023). Better together? How evolution of co-branding alliance affects performance. *Journal of Business & Industrial Marketing, 38*(9), 1899–1910. https://doi.org/10.1108/JBIM-07-2022-0304
19. Eun-Young, J. (2006). An analysis on cases of fashion collaboration strategy. *Journal of Fashion Business, 10*(6), 110–111. https://koreascience.kr/article/JAKO200633063796108.pdf
20. Ceccato, P., & Rech, S. R. (2010). Moda e co-branding: uma associação de sucesso. *ModaPalavra E-Periódico, 3*(5), 58–73. https://www.redalyc.org/pdf/5140/514051716002.pdf
21. Wigley, S. M., & Provelengiou, A. K. (2011). Market-facing strategic alliances in the fashion sector. *Journal of Fashion Marketing and Management, 15*(2), 141–162. https://doi.org/10.1108/13612021111132609
22. Jang, E.-Y. (2006). An analysis on cases of fashion collaboration strategy. *Journal of Fashion Business, 10*(6), 110–121.
23. Okonkwo, U. (2016). *Luxury fashion branding: Trends, tactics, techniques*. Springer.
24. Amatulli, C., Mileti, A., Speciale, V., & Guido, G. (2017). The relationship between fast fashion and luxury brands: An exploratory study in the UK market. In *Handbook of research on managing the consumer experience in online environments* (pp. 910–930). IGI Global. https://doi.org/10.4018/978-1-5225-1793-1.ch041
25. Mrad, M., Farah, M. F., & Haddad, S. (2019). From Karl Lagerfeld to Erdem: A series of collaborations between designer luxury brands and fast-fashion brands. *Journal of Brand Management, 26*(5), 567–582. https://doi.org/10.1057/s41262-018-00146-2
26. Murtas, G., Pedeliento, G., Mangiò, F., & Andreini, D. (2022). Co-branding strategies in luxury fashion: The off-white case. *Journal of Strategic Marketing*. Advance online publication. https://doi.org/10.1080/0965254X.2022.2160484
27. Oeppen, J., & Jamal, A. (2014). Collaborating for success: Managerial perspectives on co-branding strategies in the fashion industry. *Journal of Marketing Management, 30*(9–10), 925–948. https://doi.org/10.1080/0267257X.2014.934905
28. Margaux Rollet, J., Hoffmann, J., Coste-Manière, I., & Panchout, K. (2013). The concept of creative collaboration applied to the fashion industry. *Journal of Global Fashion Marketing, 4*(1), 57–66. https://doi.org/10.1080/20932685.2012.753337
29. Ostillio, M. C., & Barberi, C. (2022). Louis Vuitton × Supreme: The collaboration between luxury and streetwear brands. *Micro & Macro Marketing, 31*(2), 333–354. https://doi.org/10.1431/103220
30. Luck, E., Muratovski, G., & Hedley, L. (2014). Co-branding strategies for luxury fashion brands: Missoni for target. *Global Fashion Brands: Style, Luxury & History, 1*(1), 41–56.
31. Boad, B. (1999). Co-branding opportunities and benefits. In T. Blackett & B. Boad (Eds.), *Co-branding* (pp. 22–36). Palgrave Macmillan.
32. Kam, L., & Arbaiza, F. (2019). Influencia de la marca sobre el precio y el diseño. *Dimensión Empresarial, 17*(3). https://doi.org/10.15665/dem.v17i3.1776
33. Hekkert, P. (2006). Design aesthetics: Principles of pleasure in design. *Psychology Science, 48*(May), 157–172.
34. Easey, M. (2009). *Fashion marketing*. John Wiley & Sons.
35. Kumar, P. (2005). The impact of cobranding on customer evaluation of brand counterextensions. *Journal of Marketing, 69*(3), 1–18. https://doi.org/10.1509/jmkg.69.3.1.66358
36. Collange, V. (2008). The impact of brand name substitution on product evaluation and purchase intention. *Recherche et Applications en Marketing (English Edition), 23*(2), 1–18. https://doi.org/10.1177/205157070802300201

37. Bouten, L. M., Snelders, D., & Hultink, E. J. (2011). The impact of fit measures on the consumer evaluation of new co-branded products. *Journal of Product Innovation Management, 28*(4), 455–469. https://doi.org/10.1111/j.1540-5885.2011.00820.x
38. González Penas, M. (2021). Influencia de la marca en el consumo femenino de moda. *aDResearch ESIC: International Journal of Communication Research/Revista Internacional de Investigación en Comunicación, 24*(24).

Exploring Video Podcasting in Fashion Branding: A Comparative Study of Chanel and Nude Project

Paula Gargoles and Isabel Garcia Hiljding

Abstract Video podcasting has become an integral component of digital marketing strategies, particularly in the fashion industry, where brands strive to create immersive and engaging content. This study investigates the use of video podcasting as a branded content strategy through an analysis of two contrasting cases: Chanel and Nude Project. Using quantitative metrics such as episode frequency, duration, and audience engagement (e.g., views, comments, likes), alongside qualitative analyses of narrative frames, the study identifies key strategies employed by these brands. Chanel's podcast, CHANEL Connects, focuses on cultural and artistic inspiration, reflecting the brand's luxury ethos through minimalist production and intellectual discourse. In contrast, Nude Project's podcast adopts a dynamic and prescriptive tone interviewing experts and placing emphasis on personal growth and community-building to resonate with its youthful audience. Despite their differences, both brands utilize video podcasts to enhance their narratives, showcase products, and engage their target demographics. The findings underscore the unique potential of video podcasting to bridge the gap between entertainment and marketing, offering measurable engagement and visual storytelling opportunities. This paper concludes that video podcasting is not merely a trend but a transformative medium for strengthening brand identity and fostering deeper consumer connections in the digital age.

Keywords Video podcasting · Podcast · Fashion branding · Branded content

P. Gargoles (✉)
Universidad Panamericana, Mexico City, Mexico
e-mail: pgargoles@up.edu.mx

I. G. Hiljding
UDIT Universidad, Madrid, Spain

P. von Wachenfeldt et al. (eds.), *Fashion Communication in the Digital Age*,
Springer Proceedings in Business and Economics,
https://doi.org/10.1007/978-3-031-99481-4_10

1 Introduction

The rapid evolution of digital media has transformed the way fashion brands communicate with their audiences, ushering in an era of branded content that combines storytelling, emotional engagement, and innovative platforms. Among these, video podcasting has emerged as a growing trend, particularly among younger generations who value visual content and interactive experiences. As a hybrid of audiovisual communication, video podcasts enable brands to transcend traditional advertising, creating immersive narratives that deepen consumer engagement and reinforce brand identity.

This paper explores the role of video podcasting as a branded content strategy in the fashion industry, focusing on two distinct cases: Chanel and Nude Project. While both brands leverage video podcasts to engage their audiences, their approaches differ significantly in terms of content, format, and audience targeting. Chanel emphasizes artistic inspiration and cultural discourse, aligning with its luxury positioning, whereas Nude Project adopts an expert and entrepreneurial tone to connect with its youthful, digitally native community.

Through quantitative and qualitative analyses, this study examines the production styles, audience engagement metrics, and narrative strategies employed by these brands. The findings illuminate how video podcasting serves as a versatile tool for fostering community, enhancing brand visibility, and maintaining relevance in a competitive digital landscape.

2 Literature Review

2.1 Branded Content in the Fashion Industry

Branded content refers to a type of content created by a brand with the aim of promoting its values, products, or services through a more organic narrative, which is not perceived as a simple advertisement. Unlike conventional advertisements, branded content seeks to generate an emotional connection with the audience through stories, experiences, or information that add value to the consumer's life [1].

In the fashion industry, brands have taken this approach to blur the lines between advertising and entertainment such as Chanel with its short films directed by Karl Lagerfeld or the use of influencers to create content that resonates authentically with the audiences.

Fashion brands have been pioneers in adopting branded content due to their ability to build visual experiences that resonate with audience values. Brands like Gucci and Burberry have used video narrative and digital storytelling as an extension of their brand identities. An iconic example of branded content in fashion is H&M's documentary series called "Conscious Actions," which not only showcases the brand's sustainable production processes but also educates consumers about ethical fashion [2].

Another important aspect of branded content is the production of attractive, high-quality audiovisual content. Fashion brands invest in film productions and mini-series that not only promote their product but also tell a story that emotionally connects with viewers. This not only increases engagement but also strengthens the brand's image as innovative and connected to current cultural trends [3].

The effectiveness of branded content in the fashion industry has been measured mainly in terms of engagement and brand loyalty. According to a study conducted by DePelsmacker et al. [1], branded content has a positive impact on brand perception and purchase intention. Consumers tend to value content that they perceive as authentic and aligned with their personal values.

However, despite the benefits, some critics point out that content saturation can reduce its effectiveness, as consumers begin to be more critical of brands that use excessive branded content tactics [4].

Branded content has proven to be an effective strategy for fashion brands by creating deeper and more emotional connections with consumers. While this strategy has transformed the way brands communicate with their audiences, it is crucial that brands continue to innovate and maintain a balance between entertainment and promotion.

2.2 Podcasting as Branded Content Strategy for Fashion Brands

The digital transformation of the fashion industry has led to the integration of various media, including blogs, vlogs, fashion films, and more recently, podcasts, into communication strategies aimed at differentiation and the enhancement of consumer relationships [5]. Podcasts, in particular, have been adopted by leading fashion brands such as Gucci, Chanel, Nike, and Dior as a strategic branded content tool [6–8].

These brands utilize podcasts to combine the intimacy of traditional radio with the personalization offered by digital platforms, thereby creating a distinctive space for interaction [9]. Through podcasts, brands address social issues, foster cultural dialogues, and engage audiences in reflective and aspirational storytelling, thereby enhancing the overall brand experience. Despite their audio-centric, non-visual nature and limited reach, podcasts have become a popular marketing tool for luxury and fashion companies [7].

Podcasting allows brands to transcend the superficiality often associated with other forms of communication, fostering deeper and more meaningful interactions with their audiences [5]. In the era of infotainment [10], podcasts provide access to entertaining experiences that highlight fashion's creativity and its cultural interconnectedness. This medium offers fashion brands hypervisibility and multimodal reach while enabling constant engagement with the industry through leisure-oriented content that builds social connections with both the public and consumers [11].

As a branded content tool, podcasts are not designed to drive immediate sales but rather to build brand loyalty, establish cultural relevance, and reinforce the symbolic value of luxury brands. They serve as an impactful medium for fashion brands to engage their audiences by leveraging both creative and authoritative communication strategies [6, 7, 12].

According to Bratcher [6], fashion podcasts often rely on two primary message-based frames: creativity-based frames, which focus on inspiration and design details, and attitude-based frames, which emphasize lifestyle and consumer engagement. For example, brands such as Chanel, Gucci, and Dior frequently employ creativity-based frames to explore their artistic inspirations and the intricate design processes underlying their products [7]. In contrast, Nike and Adidas adopt prescriptive and expert-based frames, using their podcasts to promote health, fitness, and lifestyle choices that align with their brand ethos [6].

The format and frequency of fashion podcasts vary significantly, ranging from limited series to regular episodes, depending on each brand's strategy and target audience. While the long-term role of podcasting in the fashion industry remains uncertain, evidence suggests that this medium holds considerable potential for diversifying communication strategies and addressing complex or sensitive topics in a meaningful and engaging manner [5, 7].

Initially, podcasts were embraced by fashion brands as an innovative means to reach niche audiences and deliver narrative-driven content. However, there has been a decline in enthusiasm for podcasting within the sector over time, attributed to factors such as market saturation, challenges in maintaining listener engagement, and the lack of clear metrics to evaluate return on investment. Some brands have scaled back or discontinued their podcasting efforts due to these challenges. In that sense, while podcasts initially emerged as a promising platform for branded content in the fashion industry, their effectiveness and popularity have faced significant obstacles, prompting a reassessment of their role in the marketing strategies of fashion brands [13].

Guerrero-Navarro [8] research reveals that while podcasts offer an innovative way for fashion brands to connect with audiences, the medium has not yet reached its full potential as a communication strategy within the fashion sector. Key limitations include the age discrepancy between podcast listeners, who tend to be older (primarily aged 45–54), and the target demographic for fashion brands, which is generally younger (18–40 years old). Despite this, there is optimism about the future convergence of these audiences as podcast consumption becomes increasingly popular among younger generations. Moreover, there are limitations in audience reach and the absence of quantitative data on listener engagement [7].

2.3 Video Podcasting for Fashion

Since 2020, video podcasts have gained significant presence on audiovisual platforms. According to a report by the Interactive Advertising Bureau Spain [14], the consumption of video podcasts continues to rise, with 32% of the audience preferring this format. Of this percentage, nearly 60% are young individuals aged between 25 and 34. Video has become an integral part of the culture of digital natives, and the evolution of the podcast medium is increasingly oriented toward more visual experiences [15].

The two most popular platforms for consuming video podcasts are YouTube and Spotify. Over the past 4 years, YouTube has emerged as the most widely used platform for podcast listening, doubling its share of weekly podcast consumers. This trend is driven by users who engage with podcasts both visually and audibly [15].

YouTube could be defined as a content community that requires low levels of self-presentation and self-disclosure [16, 17]. YouTube serves as a platform that effectively combines multimedia interactivity with extensive audience reach, making it highly suitable for branded content strategies across industries, including fashion. Video formats provide fashion and luxury brands with a unique opportunity to present their narratives in transformative and entertaining ways, moving beyond purely cognitive or informational strategies, serving as a strategic approach to enhance emotional connections and audience engagement. This approach aligns closely with consumer preferences for content that is both emotionally engaging and visually compelling [18, 19].

While YouTube offers considerable flexibility in messaging and creative expression, its effectiveness is contingent upon a brand's resources, platform-specific expertise, and audience-targeting strategies. For fashion brands, video formats have become essential tools for cultivating brand loyalty, reinforcing brand identity, and establishing meaningful connections with consumers [18, 19].

Spotify is currently the world's most popular audio platform, with over 500 million users and 200 million subscribers, according to data from the platform's first-quarter 2023 report [20]. Since 2020, Spotify has supported video podcast consumption, initially limited to a select number of English-language podcasts. In 2022, this functionality expanded to other markets, including Spanish-language content. With this market expansion, Spotify aims to strengthen its offering for video podcast consumers by providing features such as background video playback. This functionality allows the listener/viewer to choose between active viewing, with the video displayed in the foreground, or passive listening, with the video playing in the background [21].

In the case of video podcasts, also referred to by the emerging term "vodcasting," existing studies are predominantly focused on their application in the educational field, as evidenced by an extensive body of literature [22]. However, there is a notable absence of references addressing the use of vodcasting within the fashion industry.

3 Methodology

The criteria for selecting brands for analysis required that they be either luxury or fashion brands and that they host a video podcast on YouTube with content available from at least 2022. After an exploratory search on YouTube, two brands were identified that met these criteria: Chanel and Nude Project. Saint Laurent was also considered but ultimately excluded due to its limited content—comprising only four episodes—and its recent launch in 2024.

A quantitative study was conducted to examine several factors, including the total number of episodes since inception, longevity, episode duration [23] and frequency. Additionally, as the focus was on YouTube-hosted video podcasts, other platform-related metrics were analyzed, such as subscriber count, average number of comments, average views per episode, and the average of likes. The analysis was conducted in November 2024.

From a qualitative perspective, a content analysis was performed, focusing on the Predominant Frame and Source-Based Frames [6], as well as the diffusion strategies [24] and the language employed in the podcasts [7]. For the Source-Based Frames, Bratcher [6] distinguishes between expert and celebrity frames. However, based on the analysis, a third category—artist frame—was added. This inclusion reflects the frequent appearance of artists in the episodes, a phenomenon attributed to the strong connection between luxury brands and cultural expression.

Bratcher's analysis [6] is grounded in framing theory, which suggests that media content can be structured to emphasize certain aspects of reality while minimizing others. In media communication, frames serve as a mechanism to structure and present information in a way that influences audience perception. This study specifically examines source-based frames, which focus on the individuals delivering the message and how their identity impacts the credibility and reception of the content.

Bratcher [6] categorizes sources into three primary frames. The expert frame positions the source as an authority in their field. Their role is to provide in-depth knowledge, technical expertise, and insider perspectives. The celebrity frame includes well-known personalities who are not framed as experts but rather as individuals sharing their experiences with the brand's products or lifestyle. Their primary function is entertainment and brand association rather than providing technical expertise. The consumer frame includes typical consumers offering a relatable perspective. However, previous research (Bratcher, 2021) has found that fashion brand podcasts rarely utilize consumer-based frames, instead favoring expert and celebrity sources.

4 Results

The authors of the paper have analyzed the video podcast of Chanel and Nude Project in their YouTube account summarized in Table 1.

Table 1 Results of the video podcast of Chanel and Nude Project in their YouTube account

	Chanel connects	Nude project
Number of podcast	17	117
Launch date	Since 2022	Since 2021
How long are the episodes?	26 min and 45 s	64.4 min
Frequency	Bimonthly	Weekly
Average comments	124/episode	970/episode
YouTube Suscriptores	2.65 M	824 K
Average visualization	19.597	439.981
Average likes	22.520	13.937
Predominant frame	Inspiration	Prescriptive
Source-based frames	Artists	Experts
Language	English, Spanish, and Korean	115 Spanish 2 in English
Diffusion	YouTube, Spotify	YouTube, Spotify

Source: authors

4.1 Chanel Podcast

The podcast of Chanel called CHANEL Connects—The Arts & Culture Podcast has been active since 2022, providing a platform for the brand to explore themes of inspiration within the worlds of art, culture, and creativity. Each episode offers a deep dive into the creative processes and sources of inspiration behind various artists, designers, and cultural figures, aligning the podcast with the brand's dedication to fostering meaningful creative dialogue.

The core focus of the podcast is inspirational with a total of 17 episodes. The first 10 episodes centered on interviews between the Head of Global Head of Arts and Culture at CHANEL, Yana Peel, and artists around the planet. These interviews explore the relationship between different creative expressions where artists draw their influences from, how they shape their work, and the environments that spark their creativity. By highlighting the personal and professional journeys of artists, the podcast connects listeners with the very essence of what drives innovation in art and design. These episodes are longer, between 30 and 40 min long, and they are characterized by not having any images, only a black background with the letters of the title and the guests. We can notice a change in the podcasts in 2023. The episodes become shorter, and Yana Peel is no longer present, now the two invited artists are having a conversation with only the two of them. Another main difference is that these episodes are recorded on video and the artists are wearing Chanel clothes and products.

The episodes follow a bimonthly release schedule, being each episode aligned with the brand's values of quality and creative exploration. With a focus on artistic inspiration, the episodes delve into a wide range of topics, offering different perspectives and stories from around the world.

The episodes run for an average of 26 min and 45 s, providing a balanced format that allows for in-depth discussions while maintaining an engaging and digestible length for listeners. The podcast is available in three languages: English, Spanish, and Korean, making it accessible to a global audience and emphasizing the brand's commitment to inclusivity and cultural dialogue.

Listeners can access the podcast on popular platforms such as YouTube and Spotify, ensuring widespread distribution and easy access for a diverse audience. As of November 2024, the podcast has garnered 2.65 million subscribers on YouTube, highlighting its growing popularity and engagement. The episodes collectively boast an average of 19,597 views per episode, illustrating a strong, consistent audience interested in the brand's creative and inspirational content.

The podcast encourages audience interaction, with an average of 124 comments per episode and 22.520 average likes per episode. It is worth highlighting the episode in which chefs Jon Gray & Ruthie Rogers engage in a conversation, which received a total of 364 K like compared to the rest of the episodes in which the vast majority did not even reach 1 K.

This level of engagement reflects the strong community of listeners who are actively participating in the conversation, sharing their thoughts and reactions to the content. We can observe that the number of comments and audience interaction depends significantly on the person who attends the podcast. The comments section serves as a space for fans to connect with the artists, offer feedback, and contribute to the broader discourse around art and inspiration.

4.2 Nude Project Podcast

Nude Project is an urban fashion brand founded by Alex Benlloch and Bruno Casanovas, two young entrepreneurs born in 2000 [25]. They established their brand in 2018. In each episode of their podcast on YouTube, they describe the brand as follows:

"It all began in a university dorm room in 2018. I met Bruno a month earlier. Both of us were 20 years old, but we had grown up in very different environments—he was from Bali, and I, Alex, from Burgos (a bit further north). Then, something brought us together forever: the shared purpose of creating a movement among the youth of our generation" [26].

The podcast was launched in July 2021 in a video format, with the intention of sharing the brand's growth and journey with their community. Of their 107 episodes, eight feature conversations between the founders where they discuss major milestones, such as reaching 200,000 YouTube subscribers and opening their stores. From the third episode onward, they began interviewing entrepreneurs, YouTubers, and experts in personal development and health.

The length of their episodes has increased over the years. In 2022, the average episode duration was 35 min, rising to 46 min in 2023, and further extending to 91 min in 2024, reflecting the broader trend toward longer podcasts. Across all analyzed episodes, the average length is 64.4 min. This trend aligns well with the podcast's format, which often features in-depth interviews with experts. One of their most popular episodes, featuring psychiatrist Marian Rojas, lasted 97 min and garnered over 3.5 million views.

Since July 17, 2022, the podcast has adhered to a weekly release schedule, continuing consistently up to the time of analysis in November 2024. Their purpose in creating a movement for their generation is evident in the community they have cultivated through their podcast. The podcast channel has become a priority for them, serving as a key tool to connect with their audience. At Nude Project's offices, they have built a podcast studio that includes a live audience setup. The engagement levels of their YouTube podcasts are remarkably high, with an average of 439,980 views, 970 comments per episode, and 13,833 likes.

From a qualitative perspective, their source-based frames predominantly feature experts. An expert frame is characterized by interviews with individuals positioned as authorities in their respective fields. Notably, these young entrepreneurs actively seek to learn from successful figures such as business leaders, YouTubers, and gamers. According to Bratcher's [6] analysis, this positions the podcast within a prescriptive framework, similar to the branding strategies of Nike and Adidas.

The podcast is predominantly conducted in Spanish, with only two episodes recorded in English, as both entrepreneurs are native English speakers. The visual dimension of the video podcast is also well-developed. The founders consistently wear Nude Project apparel, and 48% of their guests are also dressed in branded clothing featuring the logo. The video editing is polished, beginning with a 1-min highlight reel featuring key quotes and ending with an open-ended question designed to spark interest in the full episode. Each podcast includes a 30-s introduction that remains consistent across episodes, followed by the main content. During the episodes, the interviews are enriched with supplementary visuals, enhancing the overall video podcast experience. Nude Project has clearly built a strong community through its video podcast strategy, solidifying its position over two and a half years of production and culminating in 107 episodes.

5 Discussion

The video-podcasting strategies employed by the fashion brands Chanel and Nude Project represent distinct approaches to engaging with their audiences while reinforcing their brand identities and values. Both brands use podcasts as a means of connecting with their communities, but their content, production styles, and audience engagement strategies diverge in ways that reflect their target demographics and overarching brand philosophies.

Chanel's podcast, CHANEL Connects—The Arts & Culture Podcast, focuses on creativity, art, and the inspirational processes behind innovation. The episodes feature interviews with prominent artists and cultural figures, positioning the brand within the intellectual and high-culture spheres. The podcast acts as a platform for artistic expression, aligning with Chanel's long-standing association with luxury, sophistication, and creative excellence. While the content is equally engaging, it is more formal and intellectual in tone, offering listeners insights into the creative process and the relationships between various forms of art. This approach speaks to a more elite, global audience that values cultural dialogue and the brand's association with creativity. The transition in 2023 from a more structured interview format with Yana Peel to conversational exchanges between artists further refines the podcast's focus, suggesting an emphasis on the creative exchange between individuals rather than on the brand's curatorial voice.

In contrast, Nude Project centers its podcast content on personal growth, entrepreneurial journey, and inspirational messaging. Founded by two young entrepreneurs in 2018, the podcast serves as an extension of the brand's ethos: "You can achieve anything with passion." This message is explicitly conveyed through the founders' personal anecdotes and interviews with various experts, including business figures, YouTubers, and health professionals. The podcast's casual, conversational style mirrors the brand's youth-oriented, streetwear identity, emphasizing relatability and a strong sense of community. The founders' candid sharing of their own experiences (e.g., achieving 200,000 subscribers, opening stores abroad) serves to humanize the brand and make it more accessible to their core audience, which is predominantly young, aspirational, and engaged with digital culture. According to Fournier and Avery [27], brand narratives are integral in shaping consumers' emotional connections to a brand, as they allow for an authentic, relatable dialogue that resonates deeply with the audience's personal experiences and values.

The increase in episode length over time, from an average of 35 min in 2022 to 91 min in 2024, aligns with the growing popularity of long-form content. This shift could be seen as an attempt to create more immersive and in-depth discussions, further cultivating a loyal and interactive audience.

One of the most striking differences between Chanel and Nude Project lies in the frequency of their podcast releases. Chanel has taken a much slower, more deliberate approach to podcasting, with only 17 episodes released over 2 years. This infrequent release schedule aligns with Chanel's brand identity as a luxury label that prioritizes quality and exclusivity over quantity. Each episode is carefully crafted to maintain the high standards associated with the brand, focusing on cultural depth and intellectual discourse. While this slower pace might suggest a more exclusive and refined approach to content creation, it also reflects Chanel's strategy of producing content that serves as an extension of their luxury attributes—fostering anticipation and making each episode a unique cultural event. This more curated approach contrasts with the rapid-fire content production model of Nude Project, highlighting the different strategies each brand uses to engage its respective audience.

In contrast, Nude Project has adopted a highly consistent, weekly release schedule since July 2022, maintaining an ongoing dialogue with their audience. As of November 2024, the brand has released 117 episodes, with the podcast becoming a central aspect of their community-building efforts. The decision to publish a new episode every week supports Nude Project's goal of maintaining constant engagement and interaction with their youthful, digitally savvy audience. The weekly frequency allows for real-time updates, conversations around trending topics, and continuous sharing of their growth journey, keeping their audience invested in the brand's success. Furthermore, this frequency is conducive to building a community of listeners who expect regular content, thus enhancing brand loyalty and audience retention.

The production styles of the two brands' video podcasts play a key role in reflecting their identities. Chanel's production is minimalist and refined, mirroring the brand's luxury and high-art ethos. The lack of visual elements in the earlier episodes (only a black background with the title and guest names) aligns with Chanel's focus on their elegant and minimalistic essence. The later episodes, which feature artists wearing Chanel products, create a subtle yet effective association between the brand's products and the world of artistic excellence. This strategic use of visual cues aligns the podcast with the brand's luxury image while maintaining a focus on the intellectual and cultural discourse at hand. Chanel's more restrained production approach contrasts sharply with the vibrant, dynamic aesthetic of Nude Project, yet both serve to reinforce their respective brand identities.

On the other hand, Nude Project adopts a highly polished, yet informal, aesthetic, where video and audio production support the brand's streetwear roots. The frequent use of visual elements, including branded clothing worn by the hosts and guests, creates a strong sense of brand identity throughout the episodes. Additionally, the use of video editing techniques, such as opening with a 1-min highlight reel of key moments, serves to attract and retain audience attention. The studio setting with an audience and frequent incorporation of branded content underscore the strong connection between the podcast and the brand's broader marketing strategy.

Both brands have demonstrated an ability to foster robust communities, though the nature and level of engagement differ. Chanel's podcast, while also engaging, reflects a more curated and less interactive community. The podcast boasts impressive metrics, including an average of 19,597 views per episode and 124 comments. While these figures are notable, they are comparably lower to Nude Project's podcast, likely due to the difference in audience demographic and the more intellectual nature of the content.

Conversely, Nude Project has built a highly interactive and engaged community. With an average of 439,000 views, 970 comments, and 13,833 likes per episode, the brand's podcast garners significant attention from its youthful audience. The frequent engagement with topics related to entrepreneurship, personal development, and success resonates strongly with a Gen Z that is highly motivated and digitally native.

6 Conclusion

Video podcasting has emerged as a transformative tool for fashion brands to bridge the gap between traditional marketing and digital storytelling. Platforms like YouTube and Spotify enable brands to combine the intimacy of audio with the visual appeal of multimedia, creating dynamic narratives that captivate diverse audiences. As demonstrated by Chanel and Nude Project, this medium allows for the strategic alignment of branded content with their unique identities, fostering both community engagement and global visibility. The visual format enriches the consumer experience, allowing brands to highlight products, set designs, and values, thus creating a holistic representation of their ethos.

While both Chanel and Nude Project employ video podcasts as an essential part of their digital marketing strategies, they do so in ways that reflect their unique brand identities and audience engagement priorities. Chanel's refined, art-focused podcast, on the other hand, appeals to a more intellectual, global audience, positioning the brand as a leader in the cultural and creative industries. Nude Project's dynamic, visually engaging podcast reflects its youthful, entrepreneurial ethos, creating a platform for personal storytelling and community interaction. Both brands, despite their differences, demonstrate the power of video podcasts as a tool for deepening consumer engagement and reinforcing brand narratives in the modern digital age.

Despite their advantages, video podcasts in fashion also present several challenges and risks. The high cost of production, the oversaturation of content in digital platforms makes audience discovery increasingly difficult, requiring strategic promotion and algorithmic visibility. Additionally, unlike social media formats that allow for instant feedback through likes and comments, video podcasts often lack immediate interactivity, which can make it harder to measure engagement and consumer sentiment effectively. For luxury brands, there is also the challenge of maintaining an aura of exclusivity in a format designed for accessibility and mass consumption. As digital trends shift rapidly, fashion brands must carefully evaluate the long-term viability and adaptability of video podcasting within their broader communication strategies.

Looking forward, the role of video podcasting in the fashion industry is likely to expand, driven by its ability to provide measurable engagement and personalized content. However, its success depends on the ability of brands to innovate and adapt their strategies to evolving consumer expectations. As the demand for authentic, visually engaging content continues to grow, video podcasts will remain a vital tool for fostering deeper connections and maintaining relevance in an increasingly competitive digital landscape.

References

1. DePelsmacker, P., Geuens, M., & Van den Bergh, J. (2013). *Marketing communications: A European perspective* (5th ed.). Pearson Education.
2. H&M. (2019). *Conscious actions [Documentary series]*. H&M Group.
3. Marwick, A. E. (2015). Instafame: Luxury selfies in the attention economy In M. T. Fuchs (Ed.), *The Routledge companion to digital media and politics* (pp. 225–237). Routledge.

4. Tariq, M., Awan, H. M., & Tanveer, A. (2020). The effectiveness of branded content on consumer perception: A case study of social media influencers. *Journal of Marketing Research and Case Studies, 2020*, 1–12. https://doi.org/10.1155/2020/6425937
5. Fernandes, C., & Ricardo, R. (2021). Podcasts are fashionable too: The use of podcasting in fashion communication. *Comunicação Pública, 16*(31).
6. Bratcher, T. R. (2021). Purses, pencil skirts, and podcasts: A content analysis of fashion brand PR. *Public Relations Journal, 14*(1), 1–30.
7. Hiljding, I. G., & Gárgoles, P. (2022). Podcast as an emerging branded content tool: The case of luxury fashion brands. In Á. Rocha, D. Barredo, P. C. López-López, & I. Puentes-Rivera (Eds.), *Communication and smart technologies. ICOMTA 2021* (Smart innovation, systems and technologies) (Vol. 259, pp. 344–353). Springer. https://doi.org/10.1007/978-981-16-5792-4_34
8. Guerrero-Navarro, D., Cristofol, C., & Borrego, Á. A. (2023). El formato podcast en la nueva comunicación en moda: casos Ivoox y Spotify. *Redmarka. Revista de Marketing Aplicado, 27*(2), 19–37.
9. Wrather, K. (2016). Making 'maximum fun' for fans: Examining podcast listener participation online. *The Radio Journal—International Studies in Broadcast & Audio Media, 14*(1), 43–63.
10. Thussu, D. (2007). *News as entertainment: The rise of global infotainment*. Sage Publications.
11. Mouratidou, E. (2022). Fashion as leisure: Experience and entertainment through brands' digital narratives. In I. Cantista & D. Delille (Eds.), *Fashion heritage* (pp. 137–148). Palgrave Macmillan. https://doi.org/10.1007/978-3-031-06886-7_11
12. Gárgoles, P., & Hiljding, I. G. (2023). The evolution of the podcast as a marketing tool in fashion luxury brands. *Revista Panamericana de Comunicación, 5*(1), 23–31.
13. Nanda, M. C. (2021). *What happened to the fashion podcast boom?* Business of Fashion. Retrieved from https://www.businessoffashion.com/articles/technology/what-happened-to-the-fashion-podcast-boom/
14. Interactive Advertising Bureau Spain [IAB]. (2023). Observatorio del consumo digital en España - Mayo 2023. Retrieved November 27, 2024, from https://tinyurl.com/tuvvcx4
15. López Villafranca, P. (2024). El video podcast en Spotify España. Un formato dirigido a la generación Z que marca tendencia en la industria del audio digital. *Revista de Comunicación y Medios, 15*(3), 45–60.
16. Kaplan, A. M., & Haenlein, M. (2010). Users of the world, unite! The challenges and opportunities of social media. *Business Horizons, 53*(1), 59–68.
17. Lou, C., Xie, Q., Feng, Y., & Kim, W. (2019). Does non-hard-sell content really work? Leveraging the value of branded content marketing in brand building. *Journal of Product & Brand Management, 28*(7), 773–786.
18. Wang, R., & Chan-Olmsted, S. (2020). Content marketing strategy of branded YouTube channels. *Journal of Media Business Studies, 17*(3–4), 294–316.
19. Kumar, V., Khan, I., Fatma, M., & Singh, A. (2022). Engaging luxury brand consumers on social media. *Journal of Consumer Marketing, 39*(1), 121–132.
20. Spotify. (2023). *Spotify Q1 2023 results: Growing users & subscribers*. Newsroom Spotify. Retrieved November 27, 2024, from https://tinyurl.com/muur6ju8
21. Calvo, J. (2022). Spotify expande sus funciones de vídeo podcast a España. elEconomista.es. Retrieved November 27, 2024, from https://tinyurl.com/bdz885hp
22. Cartes-Barroso, M. J., & Román San Miguel, A. (2022). El vodcasting en España. 'Confinados' de Eurosport, el camino inverso. *SEECI 2000, 55*, 57–73.
23. Dietrich, L. F., & Bug, P. (2019). Exploring the role of podcasts in the fashion industry. *Fashion Theory: The Journal of Dress, Body & Culture, 23*(4), 487–507. https://doi.org/10.1080/1362704X.2019.1638793
24. Antunes, M. J., & Salaverría, R. (2020). Examining independent podcasts in Portuguese iTunes. In *International conference on human-computer interaction* (pp. 149–153). Springer.
25. Ricart, L. (2023). Nude Project: La marca que arrasa en TikTok e Instagram. Traveler. Retrieved November 27, 2024, from https://www.traveler.es/articulos/nude-project-la-marca-que-arrasa-en-tiktok-e-instagram

26. ESPECIAL VERANO: Nos vamos de Vacaciones y Muchas Desnudas. Nuce Project (2023). YouTube. Retrieved November 27, 2024, from https://youtu.be/Ehheecd6pxc?si=H23ZZrWXxQTynCR3
27. Fournier, S., & Avery, J. (2011). The uninvited brand. *Business Horizons, 54*(3), 193–207. https://doi.org/10.1016/j.bushor.2011.01.003

Blockcore: Football, Fashion, and Nostalgia in Generation Z

Sandra Bravo Durán and Jorge del Río Pérez

Abstract This study examines the phenomenon of Blockcore, a trend that integrates elements of football, urban fashion, and nostalgia, analysing its sociocultural and stylistic impact on Generation Z. Using a mixed-methods approach, responses from 150 participants were analysed, evaluating variables such as interest in football, fashion as a form of self-expression, the influence of social media, and consumption patterns. The findings reveal that Blockcore represents a significant fusion of sports and urban culture, emerging as an inclusive style characterized by authenticity and aligned with generational values. Additionally, collaboration between brands and sports teams was identified as a crucial factor in establishing blockcore as a lasting cultural trend.

Keywords Blockcore · Fashion · Football · Generation Z · Sports

1 Introduction

The phenomenon of Blockcore represents a unique intersection of football, urban fashion, and nostalgia, resonating strongly with Generation Z. By blending elements of sports culture and streetwear, Blockcore has emerged as a significant trend that enables young individuals to express their identity and values through style [1, 2].

Social media platforms like Instagram and TikTok have amplified this movement, fostering a digital arena where micro-influencers and communities converge to shape and disseminate trends. These platforms not only allow users to showcase

S. B. Durán
UDIT Universidad de Diseño y Tecnología, Madrid, Spain
e-mail: sandra.bravo@udit.es

J. del Río Pérez (✉)
School of Communication, Universidad de Navarra, Pamplona, Spain
e-mail: jrio@unav.es

P. von Wachenfeldt et al. (eds.), *Fashion Communication in the Digital Age*,
Springer Proceedings in Business and Economics,
https://doi.org/10.1007/978-3-031-99481-4_11

their style but also enable collaborations between brands and sports teams, creating authentic and engaging content that resonates with the values of Generation Z [3, 4].

Collaborations such as Paris Saint-Germain's partnerships with Jordan Brand and A Bathing Ape illustrate the powerful fusion of football and streetwear, reflecting a shift in how sports clubs position themselves as lifestyle brands. These initiatives have significantly expanded the cultural relevance of sportswear, aligning with the generational focus on creativity and individuality [5, 6].

This study investigates Blockcore as a cultural and stylistic phenomenon through a mixed-methods approach, with a focus on survey-based quantitative analysis. A structured online questionnaire was distributed to participants aged 14–30, exploring variables such as interest in football, social media influence, and nostalgia. The data collected offer insights into how Blockcore resonates with Generation Z and the role of brand collaborations in its appeal. The findings of this research seek to situate Blockcore within the broader sociocultural landscape, highlighting its role in redefining the relationship between sports and fashion.

2 Literature Review

2.1 The Link Between Football and Fashion

The fashion industry, recently invigorated by trends such as sporty fashion, streetwear in outdoor-inspired looks, and stylish functional fashion linked to football, represents not only a flourishing market with significant revenue generation, but also a clear connection to football culture [7, 8].

Football and fashion have been intertwined for decades, and fashion has in turn drawn inspiration from football. Footballers have historically influenced fashion trends. For example, Martin Peters's off-field style in the 1960s embodied mod culture, illustrating a bridge between football and youth fashion movements [9]. Similarly, Liverpool FC's early football casuals in the late 1970s were inspired by David Bowie's fashion, illustrating how fans adopted styles from wider popular culture [10]. Corporate fashion has also made inroads into football, as sports teams have adopted specific clothing to signify competence and group identity, further blurring the lines between professional and casual fashion [11].

For contemporary fans, football is not just a sport but also a statement of style, defined by what they wear, how they wear it, and the contexts in which they do so. Fashion has evolved into an extension of attitude and identity within football culture, establishing itself as a symbol of belonging, individuality, and creativity [1, 12].

Social media has amplified this phenomenon by allowing individuals to showcase their personal style, gain validation from their peers, and build online communities. These platforms have facilitated the emergence of micro-influencers, which brands can leverage to produce authentic and engaging content [3].

Since 2017, platforms such as Lyst have reported a significant increase in searches for football-inspired menswear, highlighting the growing intersection of fashion and sports [13]. Leading brands and designers, including Gosha Rubchinskiy, KITH, Off-White, and Palace Skateboards, have launched collections inspired by European football aesthetics and urban street culture, moving away from traditional American sports influences. This convergence between sport and fashion reflects the symbolic power of football apparel as a medium for cultural expression and emotional connection, combining nostalgia with contemporary innovation [1].

This ongoing fusion has also influenced luxury brands. Designers such as Virgil Abloh, artistic director of Louis Vuitton, and Kim Jones of Dior have created football-themed collections, signalling the sport's resonance within high fashion. This trend is likely to trickle down to more commercial brands and become a mainstream element of the fashion world [14, 15].

Football clubs, led by Paris Saint-Germain (PSG), have capitalized on the trend of sportswear becoming a fashion statement. PSG's collaboration with Jordan Brand to design its 2018–2019 Champions League kit was a pioneering effort to align a football club with streetwear. This crossover between football and basketball generated significant brand traction in the USA and Asia, enabling PSG to sell one million kits for the first time in its history [5, 16, 17].

In addition, PSG collaborated with Japanese streetwear brand A Bathing Ape (Bape) to release a limited-edition collection that elevated the club's global appeal, merging football and streetwear to attract younger, fashion-conscious audiences [6]. Despite mixed football results on the European stage, PSG has become one of the most followed football clubs on social media globally, surpassing 150 million followers across platforms and achieving notable popularity in the United States [18]. This success has inspired other clubs to adopt similar strategies.

For instance, Juventus partnered with adidas and Palace Skateboards to launch a co-branded Champions League kit for the 2019–2020 season, blending football with streetwear aesthetics to engage a broader cultural audience [19].

These examples show how clubs are transforming their identities into lifestyle brands. As Bale and Vertinsky note, the sports space serves as a medium of cultural representation, where football elements find resonance in urban contexts [20].

It is within this framework that the 'blockcore' aesthetic emerges, fusing football and fashion influences to provide a platform for young people to express their identity. Football jerseys within the blockcore aesthetic act as 'visual shields', symbolizing team loyalty and a broader sense of belonging to a community with shared values and aesthetic interests [21, 22]. By adopting this aesthetic, individuals connect not only with sport, but also with a culture that transcends geographical boundaries [23].

Blockcore embraces nostalgia, incorporating jerseys from past eras, reflecting a search for authenticity in an oversaturated world of fleeting trends. This search for a solid identity resonates with personal experiences and memories [24].

2.2 Generation Z: Football Fans and Fashion Consumers

The era of unconditional love and unwavering loyalty to a club is over. Football clubs can no longer assume that today's fans will remain loyal forever. Instead, they must continuously adapt to consumer demands to ensure retention and loyalty [25, 26].

Modern football fans are predominantly young, aged 16–24, and geographically diverse. This demographic has been identified as highly digital and connected, engaging with football content daily through platforms such as television, YouTube, and social media—what Giulianotti conceptualizes as the virtual arena, where fandom is no longer restricted by geographical boundaries [27, 28] These hyper-connected fans often prioritize entertainment and player-centric narratives, with their loyalties becoming increasingly fluid. As Ajadi et al. argue, younger fans are more likely to switch allegiances if their expectations regarding team performance or player loyalty are not met [29], a phenomenon amplified by the accessibility and immediacy of global football content [30]. Giulianotti describes them as 'flâneur' fans, who often engage with football experiences through virtual spaces [31].

Rather than a deep attachment to clubs, Generation Z fans are more captivated by players and their skills [29]. This shift is largely influenced by social media and new technologies, which amplify individual performances over team achievements. As a result, player brands are increasingly overshadowing those of football clubs [15].

Generation Z fashion consumers are a transformative force in the fashion industry, reshaping trends and influencing retail strategies [32]. Their demand for stylish yet affordable clothing has driven the popularity of fast fashion brands that cater to their need for frequent wardrobe updates [33]. Social acceptance and the desire to stay on trend further shape their purchasing decisions, highlighting the social dimension of their consumption patterns [34]. However, unlike previous generations, Gen Z shows a growing awareness of the environmental and ethical implications of their fashion choices, highlighting a significant shift towards sustainability [35].

The behavioural differences of Gen Z fashion consumers reveal unique decision-making processes compared to older generations. Gen Z's preference for second-hand clothing, often driven by cost and environmental concerns, underscores their distinct approach to consumption, challenging traditional retail norms and expanding the market for second-hand fashion [36–38].

Social media is having a profound impact on the purchasing decisions of Gen Z fashion consumers, serving as a platform for information, entertainment, and social interaction [4]. This dynamic demonstrates the pivotal role of digital platforms in fostering sustainable consumption behaviours among the environmentally conscious Generation Z [39].

It is clear that fashion allows individuals to communicate their identity, values, and cultural belonging [2]. In this context, blockcore emerges as a style that embodies the values of authenticity and creativity characteristic of Generation Z—a cohort defined by its emphasis on self-expression and rejection of traditional norms. The style blends elements of sports nostalgia with contemporary fashion, creating a visual narrative that reinforces individuality.

Blockcore is not just a fleeting style trend; it represents a cultural movement rooted in three fundamental elements: nostalgia, sport, and urban fashion. By examining its growing popularity, we can observe how Generation Z is reinterpreting global trends and adapting them to their values and social contexts.

The objectives of this study are

1. To analyse how variables such as interest in football, fashion, and social media influence the perception and adoption of blockcore.
2. To identify consumption patterns and style preferences that explain blockcore's popularity among young people.
3. To explore the role of nostalgia and brand collaborations in consolidating this style.
4. To propose an interpretive framework for understanding blockcore as a sociocultural phenomenon beyond its stylistic dimensions.

3 Method and Hypothesis

3.1 Hypothesis

This study presents 15 hypotheses related to research on football, fashion, Generation Z, and the adoption of the Blockcore trend. These hypotheses are organized into five categories, as shown in Table 1:

3.2 Sample and Data

To test the hypothesized relationships, we use data from an online survey on Blockcore habits conducted in Spain. The survey was open from 12 to 22 November 2024 and was answered by 150 people. We used snowball sampling methodology to send the survey to potential participants, and we controlled for the characteristics of the final sample by gender (45% men and 55% women), age (average 14–30 years), and geographic location (80% urban and 20% non-urban). This method is nonprobability sampling and entailed sending the survey link via e-mail, WhatsApp, and social media. A structured survey questionnaire was designed in Google-Forms and made accessible online for self-administration. An informed consent script briefly explaining the objective of the study was provided at the beginning of the survey.

Table 1 Hypothesis

Category	Hypothesis	Description
General hypotheses	H1	Interest in football is positively related to the adoption of blockcore fashion.
	H2	Viewing fashion as a form of personal expression increases the likelihood of adopting blockcore.
	H3	Social media trend followers are more likely to perceive the connection between football and fashion.
Specific hypotheses	H4	Men adopt blockcore more frequently due to stronger cultural ties to football.
	H5	Social media and celebrities significantly contribute to the popularization of blockcore fashion.
	H6	Combining sportswear with urban clothing strengthens the perceived link between football and fashion.
Consumer hypotheses	H7	Preference for brand-football team collaborations is higher among those perceiving blockcore as authentic.
	H8	Nostalgia associated with football apparel increases the likelihood of purchasing blockcore items.
	H9	Vintage or second-hand football apparel buyers are more inclined to adopt blockcore fashion.
	H10	Interest in retro football jerseys correlates with a preference for blockcore fashion.
Sociocultural hypotheses	H11	Blockcore is perceived as a representative style of generation Z.
	H12	Blockcore fashion enhances cultural belonging among football fans.
	H13	Urban youth are more likely to adopt blockcore due to exposure to global trends.
Future hypotheses	H14	Blockcore will evolve into a lasting style in the fashion industry.
	H15	The success of brand-football collaborations will solidify blockcore as a trend in the next decade.

3.3 *Analytical Strategy*

A combination of quantitative and qualitative techniques was used to ensure rigorous analysis. Descriptive statistics were used to summarize data distributions and observe general patterns, focusing on variables such as gender, age, preferred styles, and platforms. Pearson correlations were used to assess relationships between key variables, such as the relationship between interest in football and perceptions of blockcore, and the impact of social media on perceived attractiveness. Analysis of variance (ANOVA) identified significant differences between subgroups, including gender differences in Blockcore knowledge and age-related preferences. Qualitative analysis complemented these methods, using thematic coding to classify open-ended responses into categories, such as nostalgia, authenticity, and the link between football and fashion, and to identify trends such as the resurgence of retro clothing.

Instrument validation ensured reliability through a pilot test with ten participants to refine clarity, and expert review by sociologists and fashion specialists to ensure alignment with study objectives. Hypotheses were analysed quantitatively using Pearson's correlations and ANOVA for subgroup comparisons, and qualitatively using thematic coding to explore cultural values and style preferences. Decisions to accept or reject hypotheses were based on statistical significance ($p < 0.05$), strength of correlations, and theoretical coherence. Statistical calculations were performed using SPSS and Python, while qualitative data were coded manually to identify patterns and trends.

4 Method and Hypothesis

The analysis reveals blockcore as an emerging cultural phenomenon embodying Generation Z's values, not just a fashion trend. Data show a positive relationship between football interest and blockcore adoption ($r = 0.23$, $p < 0.05$), suggesting blockcore's appeal extends beyond sports to urban fashion.

Authenticity and self-expression are core values for Generation Z, reflected in the strong correlation between viewing fashion as personal expression and blockcore inclination ($r = 0.562$, $p < 0.001$). Brands should focus on campaigns emphasizing authenticity and personalization.

Social media, especially Instagram and TikTok, plays a crucial role in blockcore's dissemination. Frequent use of these platforms correlates with increased perception of football-fashion links ($r = 0.467$, $p < 0.01$) and blockcore interest. Digital marketing strategies should prioritize authentic narratives and influencers embodying blockcore values.

Nostalgia is a key driver of blockcore adoption. Young people associating football clothing with past memories are more likely to adopt this style ($r = 0.478$, $p < 0.05$). Interest in retro jerseys and vintage shopping strongly correlates with blockcore adoption ($r = 0.509$, $p < 0.05$).

While men report greater familiarity with blockcore, it appeals to women too, highlighting its inclusive potential. Urban environment significantly influences blockcore adoption, with 80% of respondents residing in cities.

Collaborations between sports and fashion brands have been pivotal in blockcore's rise. Consumers perceiving these collaborations as authentic are more likely to adopt the style ($r = 0.524$, $p < 0.01$).

The findings suggest blockcore is a substantial cultural phenomenon, not a transient trend. It fuses sports, urban aesthetics, and nostalgia, resonating with Generation Z's values of self-expression, authenticity, and cultural connections. The fashion industry has a unique opportunity to engage this generation through authentic, value-driven strategies emphasizing blockcore's cultural significance.

5 Discussion

Blockcore is not a transient phenomenon but rather a cultural movement that reflects the values and aspirations of Generation Z. By integrating elements of football and urban fashion [11], Blockcore represents a distinctive style that resonates profoundly with young individuals who prioritize authenticity, individuality, and self-expression through attire, which aligns with [2].

Football serves as a significant point of reference for Blockcore, symbolizing community and nostalgia [21, 22]. However, the relationship between football and Blockcore extends beyond mere imitation. Blockcore occupies a position at the intersection of sports and urban aesthetics, creating a style that appeals to a broad audience, transcending traditional sports culture.

One of Blockcore's most distinctive characteristics is its connection to self-expression. For Generation Z, fashion is not merely about appearance but a medium for manifesting personal identity [34]. This renders Blockcore particularly appealing, as it facilitates personalization and individuality, both of which are core values for this generation. Moreover, nostalgia plays a crucial role in its popularity. The style's association with vintage football jerseys and memories of the past adds emotional depth, elevating it beyond a contemporary trend.

Social media platforms, such as Instagram and TikTok, have also been instrumental in popularizing Blockcore, providing a space for it to flourish within visually driven communities. However, its success is heavily dependent on authenticity. Consumers are attracted to genuine narratives and collaborations that align with the cultural values represented by Blockcore and engage audiences [4].

The movement is inclusive, resonating with both men and women, and thrives in urban environments where global trends and subcultures, such as streetwear and hip-hop, exert significant influence. Partnerships between sports and fashion brands have played a pivotal role in the rise of Blockcore, as has frequently been the case historically [6]. However, these collaborations must maintain authenticity to sustain relevance.

In essence, Blockcore reflects Generation Z's desire for a form of fashion that combines creativity, nostalgia, and self-expression. To effectively engage this, demographic brands should focus on authenticity, inclusivity, and narratives that highlight Blockcore's ability to seamlessly integrate past and present into a modern and versatile style.

6 Limitations and Future Research

While this study provides valuable insights into the intersection of football, fashion, and nostalgia within Generation Z, there are several limitations that should be addressed in future research.

Firstly, the sample used in this study was confined to participants from Spain, which may limit the generalizability of the findings to other geographical regions.

Future research could expand the sample to include participants from different cultural and socio-economic backgrounds to offer a more comprehensive understanding of how Blockcore is perceived across various contexts.

Secondly, the study relied on self-reported data from an online questionnaire, which can be subject to biases such as social desirability and inaccurate recall. While efforts were made to ensure anonymity and to minimize biases, future research could consider combining survey data with observational methods or in-depth interviews to gain a more nuanced understanding of consumer behaviours and motivations behind the adoption of Blockcore.

Moreover, this study primarily focused on Generation Z, a demographic known for its digital engagement and hyper-connectedness. It would be interesting to explore how different age groups or generations engage with similar trends, as this could reveal whether Blockcore has lasting relevance beyond Generation Z, particularly as younger cohorts emerge.

Another avenue for future research is to examine the long-term sustainability of fashion trends like Blockcore, especially as it relates to environmental and ethical concerns. With Generation Z showing an increasing interest in sustainable fashion [35], it would be valuable to investigate how trends like Blockcore align with or contradict sustainable practices in the fashion industry.

Finally, while this study explored the cultural significance of Blockcore, further research could delve deeper into its impact on the business strategies of football clubs and fashion brands. Understanding how these collaborations shape brand identities and influence consumer loyalty could provide valuable insights for marketers and business strategists aiming to capitalize on this growing trend.

References

1. Bruun, M. B., & Langkjær, M. A. (2016). Sportswear: Between fashion, innovation and sustainability. *Fashion Practice, 8*(2), 181–188.
2. Entwistle, J. (2015). *The fashioned body: Fashion, dress and modern social theory* (2nd ed.). Polity Press.
3. Joshi, Y., Lim, W. M., Jagani, K., & Kumar, S. (2023). Social media influencer marketing: Foundations, trends, and ways forward. *Electronic Commerce Research*, 1–55.
4. Liu, C., Bernardoni, J. M., & Wang, Z. (2023). Examining generation Z consumer online fashion resale participation and continuance intention through the lens of consumer perceived value. *Sustainability, 15*(10), 8213.
5. Paris Saint-Germain. (2018). *Paris Saint-Germain and Jordan Brand team up.* Paris Saint-Germain Official Website. https://en.psg.fr/teams/first-team/content/paris-saint-germain-and-jordan-brand-team-up
6. Soccerbible. (2018). PSG x BAPE collab drops at the Parc des Princes. https://www.soccerbible.com/news/2018/10/psg-x-bape-collab-drops-at-the-parc-des-princes/
7. Vogue Business. (2023). Highlights from fashion's big year of sport. Vogue Business. https://www.voguebusiness.com/story/fashion/highlights-from-fashions-big-year-of-sport
8. Wäch, P. (2007). Sport fashion Spring/Summer 2008. Functionality goes fashion. *Textil-Revue, 86*(29), 44–46.
9. Hughson, J. (2015). Ten years ahead of his time': The east end elegance of Martin Peters. *Sport in History, 35*(1), 108–126.

10. MacKenzie, M. (2019). Football, fashion and unpopular culture: David Bowie's influence on Liverpool Football Club casuals 1976-79. *Celebrity Studies, 10*(1), 25–43. https://doi.org/10.1080/19392397.2018.1559060
11. Moeller, M. (2004). Identification with signal effect. *Textile Network, 2*(1–2), 42–43.
12. Tiesler, N. C., & Coelho, J. N. (2013). *Globalised Football: Nations and migration, the city and the dream*. Routledge.
13. Wilson, J. (2019). How football became a symbol of modern fashion. *GQ Magazine*. https://www.gq.com/story/how-football-became-a-symbol-of-modern-fashion40
14. Bourdieu, P. (1980). L'identité et la représentation. *Actes de la recherche en sciences sociales, 35*(1), 63–72.
15. Chadwick, S., & Burton, N. (2020). The evolving nature of athlete branding in the digital age. *Journal of Brand Management, 27*(5), 505–517.
16. PSG Talk. (2019). PSG release annual report: More than €140 million earned via sponsorships. https://psgtalk.com/2019/11/psg-release-annual-report-more-than-e140-million-earned-via-sponsorships/
17. SportsPro Media. (2019). PSG revenue surges thanks to Nike and Jordan Brand deal. https://www.sportspromedia.com/news/psg-revenue-2018-19-sponsorship-nike-accor/
18. Paris Saint-Germain. (2021). *Paris Saint-Germain thank their 150 million fans on social media*. Paris Saint-Germain Official Website. https://en.psg.fr/teams/club/content/paris-saint-germain-thank-their-150-million-fans-on-social-media-2021-2022
19. Soccerbible. (2019). Juventus debut Adidas x Palace collaboration. https://www.soccerbible.com/performance/football-apparel/2019/10/juventus-debut-adidas-x-palace-collaboration/
20. Bale, J., & Vertinsky, P. (2004). *Sites of sport: Space, place, experience*. Routledge.
21. Hansen, K. T. (2004). The world in dress: Anthropological perspectives on clothing, fashion and culture. *Annual Review of Anthropology, 33*(1), 369–392.
22. Stride, C., Williams, J., Moor, D., & Catley, N. (2017). From sportswear to leisurewear: The evolution of English football league shirt design in the replica kit era. In J. Williams (Ed.), *Kit: Fashioning the sporting body* (pp. 166–204). Routledge.
23. Nuhrat, Y. (2019). Bodies, football jerseys, and multiple male aesthetics through football in Turkey. *Fashion Theory, 24*(5), 679–696.
24. Bayarslan, B., Özsoy, D., & Çevik, A. (2023). Avrupa futbol kulüplerinde retro pazarlama ürünlerinin incelenmesi. *Fenerbahçe Üniversitesi Spor Bilimleri Dergisi, 3*(3), 54–66.
25. Grundon, P., & Mundy, D. (2013). Enhancing the match day experience through technology. In D. Hynes & A. Kiernan (Eds.), *Football and communities 2012* (pp. 1–13). Brill.
26. Levental, O., Laor, T., & Galily, Y. (2023). The 21st century globetrotters' fans: The case of Israeli transnational football supporters' communities before and during the pandemic. *American Behavioral Scientist, 67*(11), 1340–1357.
27. European Club Association: Fan of the Future: Defining Modern Football Fandom. (2018). https://www.ecaeurope.com/media/4802/eca-fan-of-the-future-defining-modern-football-fandom.pdf
28. Giulianotti, R. (2011). The virtual arena: Sport, cyberspace and the shifting dimensions of fandom. *Social Identities, 17*(3), 241–258.
29. Ajadi, O. A., Dauda, S., & Hassan, K. A. (2020). Understanding football fandom in the digital age: A focus on fan allegiance and engagement. *Journal of Sports Management and Marketing, 12*(2), 88–102.
30. Nielsen: Sports fandom is increasing, powered by new digital platforms, global report finds. (2022). https://www.nielsen.com/news-center/2022/sports-fandom-is-increasing-powered-by-new-digital-platforms-global-report-finds/
31. Giulianotti, R. (2011). Sport mega events, urban football carnivals and securitized commodification: The case of the English Premier League. *Urban Studies, 48*(15), 3293–3310.
32. Razum, A., Pandža Bajs, I., & Zekić, Z. (2017). The analysis of the sustainable consumption patterns of generation Z in fashion industry. *Ekonomski Pregled, 68*(3), 297–318.
33. Palomo-Domínguez, I., Elías-Zambrano, R., & Álvarez-Rodríguez, V. (2023). Gen Z's motivations towards sustainable fashion and eco-friendly brand attributes: The case of Vinted. *Sustainability, 15*(11), 8753.

34. Dobre, C., Milovan, A. M., Duţu, C., Preda, G., & Agapie, A. (2021). The common values of social media marketing and luxury brands. The millennials and generation Z perspective. *Journal of Theoretical and Applied Electronic Commerce Research, 16*(7), 2532–2553.
35. Kovacs, I. (2021). Perceptions and attitudes of generation z consumers towards sustainable clothing: Managerial implications based on a summative content analysis. *Polish Journal of Management Studies, 23*(1), 257–276.
36. Kim-Vick, J., & Cho, E. (2024). Gen Z consumers' intention to adopt online collaborative consumption of second-hand luxury fashion goods. *Journal of Global Fashion Marketing, 15*(4), 440–458.
37. Masserini, L., Bini, M., & Difonzo, M. (2024). Is generation Z more inclined than generation Y to purchase sustainable clothing? *Social Indicators Research, 175*, 1155–1171.
38. Mazanec, J., & Harantová, V. (2024). Gen Z and their sustainable shopping behavior in the second-hand clothing segment: Case study of the Slovak Republic. *Sustainability, 16*(8), 3129.
39. Siregar, Y., Kent, A., Peirson-Smith, A., & Guan, C. (2023). Disrupting the fashion retail journey: Social media and Gen Z's fashion consumption. *International Journal of Retail & Distribution Management, 51*(7), 862–875.

Black Identities: A Historical and Current Review of Representation in the Fashion Industry

Gabriela Ambás and Paula Gárgoles

Abstract This article examines the construction of black identities through male fashion, tracing its evolution from the eighteenth century African diaspora to contemporary black designers. The study explores black dandyism, which combined African and European aesthetics, as both a personal and political statement to assert individuality. Employing a literature review methodology, the study is structured into two main sections. The first provides a historical analysis of the origin and evolution of black dandyism and its influence on the identity formation of Afro-descendant communities in the nineteenth and early twentieth century. The second section focuses on the contributions of designers such as Stephen Burrows, Virgil Abloh, Pharell Williams, and Kanye West, whose work integrates Black heritage into global fashion narratives. By contextualizing these contributions, the article highlights the role of fashion as a powerful tool for cultural representation, affirming the transformative influence of black identities on the fashion industry while fostering conversation about self-expression, identity formation, and visibility. This study contributes an academic approach on current discussions leading up to the Met Gala 2025 exhibition "Superfine: Tailoring Black Style."

Keywords Fashion · Black identities · Black dandyism · Virgil Abloh · Stephen Burrows · Pharell Williams

1 Introduction

The eagerly awaited theme of the Met Gala 2025 was revealed on October 9, 2024. The iconic event to be hosted by the Costume Institute of the Metropolitan Museum of Art and Vogue will be titled "Superfine: Tailoring Black Style" and will center its

G. Ambás (✉) P. Gárgoles
Universidad Panamericana, Mexico City, Mexico

Universidad de Navarra, Pamplona, Spain
e-mail: gambas@up.edu.mx; pgargoles@up.edu.mx

P. von Wachenfeldt et al. (eds.), *Fashion Communication in the Digital Age*, Springer Proceedings in Business and Economics,
https://doi.org/10.1007/978-3-031-99481-4_12

attention on the dandy figure, examining the importance of clothing and style in shaping the identities of Black communities in the African diaspora. The exhibition will be the first in 22 years—after the 2003 "Men in Skirts" exhibition—that will focus on male fashion [1].

The theme was selected after Monica Miller's [2] book titled "Slaves to Fashion: Black Dandyism and the Styling of Black Diasporic Identity" which reviewed the phenomenon of black dandyism as a political construction of identity. Miller, who is Chair and Professor of Africana Studies at the Barnard College of Columbia University in New York City, examined the figure of the black dandy from its origins during the eighteenth century, its development as a confrontational vehicle of the African diaspora in the nineteenth century, to its influence on the modernist aesthetics of the Harlem Renaissance in the twentieth century.

Therefore, taking the above as inspiration, the authors of this article decided to develop an academic research regarding the construction of black identities through male fashion, tracing its evolution from the tradition of the African diaspora in the eighteenth century to the contemporary work of Black fashion designers. The objective of the present research is to complement, from an academic point of view, the existing information regarding black dandyism and black identities in fashion prior to the release of the "Superfine: Tailoring Black Style" exhibition in May 2025.

2 Methodology

This article employs a literature review methodology to consolidate both classical academic research on black dandyism and contemporary sources examining the contributions of modern Black designers within a single academic article.

Given that the research spans over several centuries of a continuous cultural phenomenon, the article is structured into two major sections to facilitate coherence and readability. The first section provides a historical analysis of black dandyism in fashion, from its origins within the African diaspora of the eighteenth century to the Civil Rights Movement in the United States during the 1960s. This section contextualizes the historical construction of black identities as a form of social statement and resistance through fashion. The second section focuses on a review of four Black designers whose work has fundamentally shaped and influenced Black identity within the fashion industry, entertainment sector, and contemporary culture.

Therefore, in order to perform the literature review, prominent authors of African studies in fashion like Monica Miller [2] and Carol Tulloch [3] were thoroughly revised for the historical examination of black dandyism. Additionally, current sources in digital platforms were analyzed for a contemporary review of the main Black designers in the fashion scene, prioritizing publications in peer-reviewed journals and academic databases such as Scopus and Web of Science. To supplement academic sources, recent events and contemporary figures were examined through industry-specific publications like *Vogue* and *Business of Fashion*, selected for their credibility and influence in the fashion sector, offering insights not always available in scholarly literature.

A total of 41 articles and books were analyzed to ensure a comprehensive review of black identities in fashion. The selection process incorporated studies from various time periods, methodologies, and perspectives for a well-rounded analysis.

3 Historical Review of Black Identities in Fashion (Eighteenth Century to 1960s)

The history of black dandyism represents a profound intersection of style, resistance, and identity formation within the African diaspora. This phenomenon embodies how fashion has served as a cultural, political, and social expression that reflects on racial issues and redefines black identities. Situated within the African diaspora across the Atlantic to the United States and the United Kingdom, black dandyism emerged as a performative response to displacement, oppression, and marginalization. In this section of the article, the reader will be guided through the history of the construction of black identities in fashion, starting with the origins of black dandyism in the eighteenth century and culminating in the Black Power Movement of the 1960s.

3.1 Historical Context of Black Dandyism

The roots of black dandyism lie in the forced migration and enslavement of the African people during the transatlantic slave trade. As Tulloch [3, p. 5] defines it, the African diaspora means "Africa and the groups that formed outside Africa following the Atlantic slave trade, colonialism, and imperialism." Furthermore, Thomas Faist [4, p. 33] understands the diaspora within the concept of transnationalism to foster the "reflexivity of agency and processes" that enables a deeper understanding of how individuals and social structures influence one another, driving broader transformations in society and addressing issues of social change.

In this context, black individuals were compelled to adopt new identities, often starting with the clothes that were given away by their enslavers. However, as Miller [2] notes, enslaved Africans frequently modified and augmented their garments, using clothing as a vehicle to express their individuality and sense of self. These acts of personal agency were some of the first examples of black dandyism, showing their rejection to being completely defined by imposed influences.

The early black dandies incorporated beads, ribbons, dyed pieces of fabric and other accessories into their garments, filling these items with cultural and personal significance. These objects became "small acts of autonomy" [2, p. 4] to preserve memories of their former lives. Therefore, this bricolage of styles, which combined

African aesthetics with European garments, exemplifies the multilayered nature of black culture, extending to other forms of expression such as music, dance, and quilting [5, p. 36].

3.2 The Emergence of the Black Dandy

The dandy figure is essential for understanding how fashion became a vehicle for social distinction and identity communication from the eighteenth century onward. By challenging the "great male renunciation" [6]—a standard of masculine attire established after the French Revolution that rejected adornments, colors, and decorative details [7]—dandies reintroduced the idea of embellishing and enhancing clothing, transforming it into a vehicle for self-expression.

Max Beerbohm [8] defines dandyism as a creative and self-defining art form with social and political dimensions, transcending its perception as a mere fashion trend in the eighteenth and nineteenth century. Dandyism emerged as a response to shifting social, political, cultural, and economic conditions, reflecting changes in roles and structures of class, gender, sexuality, nationality, and race. The dandy, characterized by a deliberate and self-conscious style, meticulously studied and adapted fashion trends to continuously redefine his identity.

The figure of the black dandy emerged particularly in the United Kingdom and the United States, where enslaved and free black individuals adapted Western fashion to state their presence in public and cultural spaces. Julius Soubise, a well-known black dandy from London, exemplified this phenomenon. Known for his luxurious clothing, including diamond-buckled shoes, Soubise's style challenged social norms and expectations, marking him as a notable figure in both Black and European histories [2, p. 17].

Far from being a simple imitation of Western dandyism, black dandyism evolved as an interactive process that reinterpreted racial and cultural identities. It certainly was influenced by European dandyism, but was also rooted in Black culture, creating its own distinct style. This signifying practice challenged dominant norms while affirming Afro-diasporic identities.

Dandyism is deeply performative by nature, focusing on the intentional creation and presentation of identity. For black individuals in the diaspora, this performativity carried significant political weight. As James Scott [9] affirms, black dandyism functioned as a "weapon of the weak," an everyday form of resistance that challenged authority.

The act of dressing well, particularly for enslaved or marginalized black individuals, became a form of self-definition and defiance. During the late 19th and early twentieth centuries, Sunday attire—a time when enslaved people were often allowed to dress in their finest clothes—became a powerful symbol of dignity and pride. As Miller [2, p. 3] describes, the tradition of wearing a three-piece suit, a pocket square or gloves to church communicated not only personal respect but also communal solidarity and resilience.

Black dandyism also offered a way to critique social norms regarding race, class, and gender. For example, Powell [10, p. 224] recounts the black dandy's ability to put together "a wardrobe that speaks of modernity, freedom, oppositionality, and power." Through meticulous attention to detail and a strong commitment to style, dandyism transformed invisibility into visibility through personal expression.

Therefore, dandyism operated simultaneously as a personal and political practice, intertwining individual expression with collective identity. Since its origin, the black dandy's style has been, at the same time, personal, cultural, and representative of a broader racial experience. For those who were mobilized during the African diaspora, personal adornments like jewelry, beads, and ribbons became powerful symbols of memory and autonomy, connecting them to their African heritage. These small objects—and the ways they were carried—had a deep significance, serving as tools of self-expression, cultural remembrance, and even resistance.

Whether dressed in silks and turbans, or wearing modest attires complemented with personal adornments, black individuals reimagined their clothing to reinvent their identities, using style as a symbolic escape and a way of navigating their new realities. The importance of these fashion items is recognized by authors like Lynch and Medvedev [11], who focus on the study of stylized hats within the African diaspora as an important element in the construction of black masculinity in fashion.

3.3 Constructing Black Identities Through Fashion in the Eighteenth and Nineteenth Century

The late 1790s and early 1800s marked a crucial period in the United States as Afro-descendants navigated the complex transition from slavery to freedom. In those years, African American communities in northern United States established free black associations like the African Society in Salem, the African Society for Mutual Relief in New York, the Wilberforce Benevolent Society in New York, and many others that played a vital role in fostering community cohesion and promoting visibility in public spaces [5]. They organized annual parades to mark their anniversaries, transforming the streets into parades of cultural pride.

Another significant cultural tradition that emerged during this period was the African American ball. During the 1820s, cities like New York and Philadelphia staged formal balls, typically held during the season leading up to Easter. Participants dressed in elegant garments, often borrowing or renting clothes to maintain a refined public image. Descriptions from the time highlight the "tawdry elegance" [5, p. 98] of these events, where attendees wore brightly colored silk pantalets, accessories with feathers and sparkling petticoats. These balls had a purpose beyond entertainment: they were displays of self-expression and community identity, providing African Americans a chance to celebrate their culture and reaffirm their presence in society.

In the early nineteenth century, leisurely strolls through the neighborhoods became a central aspect of community interaction in northern black urban life. This was particularly evident during Sunday services, as noted by a writer in New York's National Advocate in the early 1820s that documented: "black dandys and dandizettes, after attending meeting, occupied the sidewalks in Broadway and slowly lounged toward their different homes" [5, p. 93].

3.4 The Zoot Suit and the Black Power Movement

One of the most iconic expressions of black dandyism in the twentieth century was the zoot suit. Popularized in the 1940s, the zoot suit was characterized by its exaggerated proportions, including oversized jackets, high-waisted and wide-legged trousers, shiny shoes, and borsalino hats. This style became a symbol of defiance among young African Americans and Mexican Americans, particularly during the 1943 Los Angeles riots.

The zoot suit was more than just a fashion statement, it was a form of cultural resistance that highlighted the intersection of race, class, and nationalism. Its adoption by both everyday users and political figures such as Malcolm X "shows how rapidly and successfully a style could take hold when it seemed to embody the sense of generational identity and affiliation" [12].

A few decades later, during the 1960s Civil Rights Movement, the Black Panther Party emerged as a symbol of Black Nationalism. Their signature style—black leather jackets and berets—was a statement of communal resistance and a way to assert authority, symbolizing their role as a counter-police force [13].

The Black Panthers' uniform became a powerful symbol of the Black Power Movement, but other expressions of African heritage also gained visibility during this era. Based on a shared sense of "black pride coupled with a strong sense of urgency for equality" [14, p. 96], activists and supporters wore various accessories, clothing, and hairstyles as a way to celebrate their African identity.

The afro hairstyle emerged as well as a powerful fashion statement during the Black Power Movement, playing a significant role in promoting the "Black is Beautiful" campaign [15]. By embracing their natural curly hair, African Americans asserted pride in their identity. These styles became popular among young people and college students across the United States who supported the fight for African American equality.

4 Current Review of Black Identities in Fashion (1970s to Present Day)

The intersection of black identities and fashion reveals a profound narrative of cultural influence, creativity, and representation. Following the historical contextualization of this phenomenon—from the emergence of black dandyism within the African diaspora to the Black Power Movement—this section of the article will focus on the analysis of four designers who have redefined the representation of black identities in the modern and contemporary fashion and entertainment industries.

From Burrows' revolutionary designs in the 1970s to Williams' contemporary redefinition of fashion luxury, these trailblazers exemplify how Black culture and identity remain integral to the evolution of global fashion. By merging cultural narratives with design innovation, these individuals have not only asserted the centrality of black influence but also broadened the scope of fashion as a medium for self and social expression. In recent history, Black trendsetters in music and sports have also played transformative roles in redefining fashion and challenging traditional industry norms.

4.1 Stephen Burrows

Stephen Burrows emerged as a pivotal figure in the design movement that was closely associated with the cultural and countercultural black scene in New York during the 1970s. His aesthetic encapsulated the values of liberation and self-expression that defined the era, serving as a reference of black identity and cultural empowerment [16–18].

Significantly, he epitomized the "Black is Beautiful" philosophy by prominently incorporating African American models into his work and attaining widespread recognition as a successful African American fashion designer. Burrows' career was firmly established in fashion history by his participation in one of the most significant runway events of its time: the *Grand Divertissement à Versailles,* held on November 28, 1973 [18, 19].

Burrows' designs stood out for their innovative features, including body-conscious silhouettes, vibrant colors, and the signature "lettuce edge ruffle," enhancing movement and fluidity. Deeply tied to dance and disco culture, his work celebrated individuality and vitality. Though his career was short-lived and often overlooked in mainstream fashion history, reflecting the marginalization of Black designers, his legacy remains a symbol of the disco era's vibrancy and continues to shape African American fashion in cultural memory [16, 17].

4.2 *Kanye West*

Kanye West, also known as Ye, has been a prominent and controversial figure in representing the Black experience in the United States [20]. His multifaceted identity, deeply tied to culture, encompasses roles as a rapper, singer, songwriter, record producer, influencer, and African American fashion designer [21]. From his collaborations with brands like Louis Vuitton and Gap, to his own Yeezy brand, West has positioned urban aesthetics and black cultural influence at the forefront of global fashion discourse. In doing so, he addresses historical issues of exclusion in high fashion and highlights how black cultural contributions have been systematically appropriated or marginalized within the industry [22, 23].

West collaborated with Adidas beginning in 2013, but this partnership gained even greater relevance in 2016 when the Yeezy collection became part of Adidas [24]. Yeezy's estimated annual revenue was $2 billion. However, in 2022, Kanye posted multiple antisemitic messages on Twitter and Instagram, leading Adidas to terminate the partnership. His collaboration with Balenciaga was also canceled [21].

According to Monk-Payton [23], West leverages his notoriety to provoke and destabilize dominant discourses on race and fashion. This is evident in actions such as his controversial use of the "White Lives Matter" T-shirt during Paris Fashion Week, openly challenging expectations of how black artists should politically position themselves in relation to movements like Black Lives Matter.

In this way, West embodies a unique phenomenon: a black creator who embraces controversy as a core aspect of his personal brand. His aesthetic choices, such as the deliberately "ugly" design of Yeezy, alongside his polarizing statements, invite scrutiny on how black identity is negotiated and redefined within the realms of globalized fashion. In this sense, he challenges historical notions of respectability and conformity associated with Black representation in fashion [22, 23].

4.3 *Virgil Abloh*

Virgil Abloh's experience in the fashion industry began in 2009 with an internship at the Roman brand Fendi, alongside fellow Chicagoan Kanye West. In 2010, West appointed Abloh as the creative director of Donda, West's creative agency. Abloh's first brand, Pyrex Vision that launched in New York in 2012, drew inspiration from a new dress style adopted by rappers like A$AP Rocky. When he founded Off-White in 2013—the brand that brought him widespread recognition—Abloh aimed to create something distinct from conventional streetwear. In 2018, he became the artistic director of Louis Vuitton's men's prêt-à-porter line, marking a milestone as the first African-descended individual to lead the men's line of a major French fashion house [25–27].

Abloh emerged as a pioneering figure in fashion by articulating experiences and aesthetics deeply rooted in black urban culture. Immersed in hip-hop and skate communities, his work integrated elements of these subcultures with luxury, reflecting an authentic perspective on black identities that went beyond mere stylistic appropriation [28, 29].

Rather than adopting a marginal narrative, Abloh celebrated the centrality of Afro-descendant culture within global fashion. His designs for brands like Off-White and Louis Vuitton brought significant visibility to black identities, illustrating how streetwear codes can redefine luxury and haute couture values [28, 29]. He also highlighted how Afrocentric identities have been pivotal in shaping contemporary fashion, even as they are often overlooked in traditional art and design spaces [30, 31].

By incorporating references such as Michael Jordan, hip-hop symbols, and streetwear aesthetics, Abloh created a narrative that honored the resilience and creativity inherent in black communities facing systemic barriers. His impact extended beyond design, positioning him as a cultural mediator who opened new opportunities for future generations [28, 29].

Virgil Abloh's contributions represent a paradigm shift in the representation of black identities in fashion. Abloh challenged the idea of luxury fashion as an exclusively Eurocentric sphere [31]. His interdisciplinary approach, commitment to authenticity, and ability to transcend disciplines established fashion as a platform to celebrate Black histories and perspectives, positioning them as essential elements of its story. This not only redefines visual representation but also shifts the dynamics of power within the industry [28–30]. Although Abloh passed away in 2021, his legacy continues through designers like Pharrell Williams and Samuel Ross. The latter, who founded and later left the pioneering British luxury streetwear brand A-Cold-Wall, is now collaborating biannually with Zara under the label "SR_A Engineered by Zara" [32].

4.4 *Pharrell Williams*

Sixteen months following Virgil Abloh's passing, Pharrell Williams—a singer, rapper, and music producer—was appointed as his successor, taking on the role of Creative Director for Louis Vuitton's menswear in 2023. Despite lacking formal training in fashion, Williams has brought a hybrid approach to the position by blending streetwear, luxury and his musical roots in hip-hop and R&B. This fusion emphasizes fashion's role as a platform for Black culture and identity. Williams has leveraged his position to create what Louis Vuitton calls a "Cultural Maison," expanding beyond fashion to encompass broader cultural experiences [31].

Williams has been explicit about how his appointment signifies a break from the past, emphasizing the historical barriers faced by black designers in the Western fashion system. As he stated, "we were not allowed to go behind the curtain and design things" [31]. The last two creative directors for Louis Vuitton's menswear have marked a shift toward a more inclusive and democratic fashion system, driven by digital platforms and social media that amplify the voices of black designers and celebrities. Both Abloh and Williams have utilized these tools to redefine what it means to be a fashion creator in the twenty-first century, connecting with diverse audiences and bringing Black cultures to the forefront of aesthetic and commercial innovation [31].

The intersection of black identities and contemporary fashion, exemplified by Abloh and Williams, redefines the industry by integrating cultural narratives previously relegated to the margins. Their careers reflect not only the evolution of fashion but also its potential to serve as a space for social justice and cultural representation. Both Abloh and Williams have accentuated how black cultural influences are central not only to streetwear but also to redefining the values of luxury and exclusivity [33].

Never before has an artist or musician of Williams' fame—or any celebrity—been appointed to such a distinguished role in the luxury fashion business. In today's celebrity-driven era, social media influence holds as much weight as the cut and quality of the clothing [31]. Williams takes the concepts of identity and belonging a step further, using his music and design to challenge limiting narratives in fashion while strengthening the bond between urban cultures and haute couture [33].

Pharrell's work at Louis Vuitton represents a convergence of creativity, brand leadership and cultural representation. According to Barron [33], Williams' appointment as Creative Director not only enhances the visibility of black identities but also establishes a new dynamic in which celebrities are no longer merely muses but active collaborators and designers, drawing on their own lived experiences.

4.5 Black Trendsetters in Fashion, Music, and Sports Industries

In the context of black identities in fashion, trendsetters from the realms of music and sports have played a pivotal role in shaping and redefining representation within the industry. Historically, black cultural icons have been instrumental in setting trends that resonate globally, challenging traditional norms and asserting the significance of black aesthetics and creativity in the fashion landscape.

The influence of black musicians extends far beyond their music, establishing fashion trends that symbolize cultural empowerment, resistance, and innovation. These musicians have not only influenced what we wear but have also transformed fashion into a medium for reclaiming identity and challenging hegemonic cultural narratives [34, 35]. Icons like James Brown with his anthem *"Say It Loud, I'm Black and I'm Proud"* combined music with distinctive styles that emphasized empowerment and pride in black identity [36].

Genres like hip-hop in the 1980s and 1990s and rap have become platforms for defining fashion codes that intertwine cultural resistance and personal expression. Musicians in these genres, such as Tupac Shakur, Notorious B.I.G., and A$AP Rocky, were instrumental in popularizing streetwear trends like baggy pants, gold chains and oversized jackets, which became emblematic of authenticity and urban identity [37]. These styles not only influenced the dress codes within black communities but also reshaped global perceptions of cultural authenticity, blurring the lines between subcultural expression and mainstream fashion [34, 36].

Furthermore, artists like Kanye West, through his Yeezy brand, have seamlessly merged music and fashion to establish themselves as cultural arbiters, demonstrating how black musicians utilize fashion as a means of storytelling and cultural commentary [34]. Meanwhile, Pharrell Williams represents a modern embodiment of the intersection between music and high fashion, highlighting how his evolution from a musician to a creative director for Louis Vuitton is an exemplification of the "couturification" of celebrities. This transition demonstrates how black musicians like Pharrell redefine traditional roles in fashion, challenging Eurocentric norms and broadening global fashion's appeal to diverse audiences [31].

In the industry of sports, Michael Jordan's influence extended beyond basketball, serving as a role model who embodied the "cool" associated with his style, while promoting corporate products that became cultural phenomena [37]. His partnerships not only made Nike a global icon but also positioned Jordan as a figure who elevated black representation in the worlds of sports and fashion. Despite some controversies, his image and contributions to style and culture remain a powerful legacy in redefining the interplay of sports, fashion, and identity [38, 39].

Currently, figures such as Lewis Hamilton exemplify the intersection between excellence in sports and its influence on high fashion. Hamilton, a seven-time Formula 1 World Champion and a recognized style icon, has consolidated his place as a fashion trendsetter through his collaboration with Dior. The French Maison named him as its latest brand ambassador, highlighting his influence beyond the racing circuit. In partnership with Dior Men's artistic director Kim Jones, Hamilton has co-designed a collection of clothing and accessories. This collaboration signifies a broader recognition of black cultural contributions to contemporary luxury fashion, underscoring the increasing importance of diverse representation in shaping brand narratives and aesthetics [40].

5 Conclusions

The historical and contemporary evolution of black dandyism in fashion highlights a profound intersection of culture, identity, and resistance. From the emergence of black dandyism as a response to displacement and marginalization in the African diaspora to its modern reinterpretation by figures such as Stephen Burrows, Kanye West, and Virgil Abloh, fashion has consistently served as both a personal and political tool for redefining black identities.

The "Superfine: Tailoring Black Style" exhibition in the Costume Institute of the Metropolitan Museum of Art further amplifies this narrative, examining how black dandyism and menswear have shaped black diasporic identity. By exploring themes of ownership, cosmopolitanism and exaggerated style, the theme of the exhibition highlights the deep connection between Black culture and the evolution of global fashion. Figures such as Pharrell Williams, Lewis Hamilton and A$AP Rocky, who co-chair the Met Gala, embody the ongoing integration of black voices in spaces of influence and creativity.

The participation of Kendrick Lamar, Serena Williams, and Samuel L. Jackson in the 2025 Super Bowl halftime show exemplifies how the music, sports, entertainment, and fashion industries continue to serve as powerful platforms for the construction, representation, and enhancement of black identities. Through their presence on such a global stage, these artists and athletes reaffirm the intersection of black identity and fashion, demonstrating how symbolic elements—ranging from clothing and accessories to embodied performances—contribute to ongoing narratives of cultural empowerment and visibility in the mainstream.

Finally, this article has engaged with the academic discourse on black identity in fashion, concluding that black voices have progressively gained prominence, representation, and power over time. As stated by Miller [2, p. 19], "in the present, black style becomes global style" and has gained a transformative force in redefining the fashion landscape.

References

1. Phelps, N. (2024). "Superfine: Tailoring black style" is the Costume Institute's Spring 2025 exhibition. Retrieved December 8, 2024, from https://www.vogue.com/article/superfine-tailoring-black-style-costume-institute-spring-2025-exhibition
2. Miller, M. (2009). *Slaves to fashion: Black dandyism and the styling of black diasporic identity*. Duke University Press.
3. Tulloch, C. (2016). *The birth of cool: Style narratives of the African diaspora*. Bloomsbury Academic, an imprint of Bloomsbury Publishing Plc.
4. Faist, T. (2010). Diaspora and transnationalism: What kind of dance partners? In R. Bauböck & T. Faist (Eds.), *Diaspora and transnationalism: Concepts, theories and methods* (pp. 9–34). Amsterdam University Press.
5. White, S., & White, G. (2018). *Stylin': African-American expressive culture, from its beginnings to the zoot suit*. Cornell University Press.
6. Flügel, J. C. (1964). *Psicología del vestido*. Paidós.
7. Vainshtein, O., & Horujaya-Cook, S. (2023). *Fashioning the dandy: Style and manners* (1st ed.). Anthem Press. https://doi.org/10.2307/jj.6195027
8. Beerbohm, M. (1970). *The Bodley Head*. Bodley Head.
9. Scott, J. (2002). From weapons of the weak. In S. Duncombe (Ed.), *The cultural resistance reader* (pp. 89–93). Verso.
10. Powell, R. (2001). Sartor Africanus. In S. Fillin-Yeh (Ed.), *Dandies: Fashion and finesse in art and culture* (pp. 217–242). New York University Press.
11. Lynch, A., & Medvedev, K. (2019). *Fashion, agency, and empowerment: Performing agency, following script*. Bloomsbury Visual Arts.
12. Peiss, K. (2011). *Zoot suit: The enigmatic career of an extreme style*. University of Pennsylvania Press.
13. Ambás, G., & Sádaba, T. (2021). 100 years of fashion activism: From the women's suffrage movement to the US 2020 elections. In *Fashion communication FACTUM 2021*. Springer.

14. Vargas, M. (2009). Fashion statement or political statement: The use of fashion to express black pride during the civil rights and black power movements of the 1960's. *Undergraduate Review, 5*, 95–99.
15. Olu, S. (2020). In 2020, The black panthers' powerful & political style is everywhere. Retrieved December 8, 2024, from https://www.refinery29.com/en-gb/black-panther-style
16. Steele, V. (1997). Anti-fashion: The 1970s. *Fashion Theory, 1*(3), 279–295.
17. Peters, L. D. (2016). Exhibition review: Stephen Burrows: When fashion danced, the museum of the city of New York, March 22–July 28, 2013. *Fashion Practice, 8*(2), 335–338. https://doi.org/10.1080/17569370.2016.1215114
18. Myers, T. D. W. (2021). Color story: Stephen Burrows's impact on the world of fashion. *Black Designers in American Fashion*, 195.
19. Draper, D. R. (2015). Versailles' 73: American runway revolution. *Journal of Contemporary African Art, 2015*(37), 94–103.
20. Cohen, C. J. (2010). *Democracy remixed: Black youth and the future of American politics*. Oxford University Press.
21. Lückerath-Rovers, M. (2024). The case of ADIDAS and Kanye West (Ye). In *Moral dilemmas in the boardroom*. Palgrave Macmillan. https://doi.org/10.1007/978-3-031-65269-1_18
22. Armitage, J. (2023). Globalized luxury fashion is the crisis: Kanye West, a structure of feeling, and the case of Louis Vuitton. *Luxury, 10*(1–2), 7–21.
23. Monk-Payton, B. (2023). The art of notoriety in Kanye West's persona. *Persona Studies, 9*(3), 21–37.
24. Strähle, J., & Kriegel, A. C. (2018). Fashion and music: A literature review. *Fashion & Music*, 7–30.
25. Kansara, V. A. (2018). Virgil Abloh: 'I am not a designer'. The Business of Fashion. Retrieved December 8, 2024, from https://www.businessoffashion.com/articles/luxury/virgil-abloh-i-am-not-a-designer/
26. Baniandrés Gómez, C., Rufat, M., Martín-Escanciano, L., & Villanueva Cobo del Prado, M. D. P. (2021, June). Virgil Abloh's contemporary discourse: An academic approach to his communication strategies. In *International conference on fashion communication: Between tradition and future digital developments* (pp. 91–101). Springer International Publishing.
27. Luque-Zequeira, N., & Torregrosa, M. (2023, July). Virgil Abolh's cinematic fashion shows for Louis Vuitton's men's collections on YouTube. In *International conference on fashion communication: Between tradition and future digital developments* (pp. 238–249). Springer Nature.
28. Leśniak, A. (2022). Transcriptions and relative novelty: Virgil Abloh's design strategies. *Fashion Theory, 26*(6), 821–837. https://doi.org/10.1080/1362704X.2022.2047290
29. Gerrie, V. (2023). *Borderless fashion practice: Contemporary fashion in the metamodern age*. Rutgers University Press.
30. Peters, L. D. (2019). Virgil Abloh: "Figures of speech". *Fashion Theory, 24*(3), 445–454. https://doi.org/10.1080/1362704X.2019.1655998
31. Choufan, L. (2024). Theorizing the third generation of fashion designers: The case of Pharrell Williams at Louis Vuitton. *Fashion Theory*, 1–25.
32. Miller, D.-Y. (2024). Samuel Ross' next move: A line 'engineered by Zara'. The Business of Fashion. Retrieved December 8, 2024, from https://www.businessoffashion.com/articles/retail/samuel-ross-zara-partnership/
33. Barron, L. (2021). The return of the celebrity fashion muse: Brand endorsement, creative inspiration and celebrity-influenced design communication. *Fashion Theory, 25*(6), 757–776.
34. Briggs, A., & Cobley, P. (1999). 'I like my shit sagged': Fashion, 'black musics' and subcultures. *Journal of Youth Studies, 2*(3), 337–352.
35. Calefato, P. (2009). Across the borders of fashion and music. *Anglistica AION: An Intersciplinary Journal, 13*(2), 85–91.
36. McClendon, A. (2024). It's a black thing, American fashion wants to understand. *Fashion Studies, 5*(1).

37. Mathur, L. K., Mathur, I., & Rangan, N. (1997). The wealth effects associated with a celebrity endorser: The Michael Jordan phenomenon. *Journal of Advertising Research, 37*(3), 67–74.
38. Kellner, D. (2001). The sports spectacle, Michael Jordan, and Nike: Unholy alliance. *Michael Jordan, Inc.: Corporate sport, media culture, and late modern America*, 37–63.
39. McDonald, M. G., & Andrews, D. L. (2002). Michael Jordan: Corporate sport and postmodern celebrityhood. In *Sport stars* (pp. 20–35). Routledge.
40. Miller, D.-Y. (2023). Lewis Hamilton named Dior ambassador. Business of Fashion. Retrieved December 8, 2024, from https://www.businessoffashion.com/news/luxury/lewis-hamilton-named-dior-ambassador/

Fashion Palimpsests: Fashion Shows and Fashion Communication, Between Entertainment and Market, Between Real and Digital

Vittorio Linfante

Abstract As a practice and a language, fashion has long served as a medium for expressing identities, desires, and ideals intertwined with communication. The relationship between aesthetic production and the media through which messages are disseminated and interpreted has evolved significantly. Fashion communication has transitioned from early forms of fashion publishing and the pioneering use of photography to the widespread diffusion of fashion via digital platforms, resulting in a multifaceted communication system in the contemporary world. Today, fashion communication includes a complex series of methods and tools. It involves more than isolated moments and takes place through complete communicative palimpsests. These palimpsests borrow strategies and practices traditionally associated with other media, such as radio and television. This article investigates the evolution of fashion shows, from their origins in Parisian ateliers to their current complexity, to explore their role within this contemporary omnichannel communication framework. Fashion shows are no longer merely exclusive, punctual events but integral components of a broader communication system characterised by both live and on-demand experiences. These hybrid moments, experienced in person or via digital channels, collectively contribute to constructing modern palimpsests, shaping a dynamic and multifaceted communication landscape.

Keywords Fashion communication · Fashion shows · Palimpsest · Digital communication

V. Linfante (✉)
Alma Mater Studiorum – Università di Bologna, Bologna, Italy
e-mail: vittorio.linfante@unibo.it

P. von Wachenfeldt et al. (eds.), *Fashion Communication in the Digital Age*,
Springer Proceedings in Business and Economics,
https://doi.org/10.1007/978-3-031-99481-4_13

1 Communication in the Contemporary Fashion Scene

As a multifaceted system of visual and material communication, fashion extends far beyond the mere selection of garments. It encompasses a dynamic interplay of tools, methods, and platforms that collectively shape how clothing is presented and understood. In recent years, the digitalisation of fashion has brought about significant shifts in how fashion communication is produced, consumed, and interpreted. As technological advancements and cultural transformations redefine the parameters of fashion communication, a critical question emerges: Can fashion communication still be understood as a set of discrete communicative actions situated in specific moments, or should it be regarded as an increasingly complex system in which various languages, tools, and temporalities converge? This challenge becomes particularly pertinent when considering the role of fashion shows, spectacle events, now positioned within a broader, multifaceted communication landscape.

In this evolving context, fashion shows have historically functioned as pivotal moments within the fashion system, serving as tools for commercial promotion and as sites for cultural exchange. However, the question arises: Do these events retain their status as fleeting moments, or have they evolved into integral components of a broader, ongoing communication strategy? Can contemporary fashion communication not merely as an isolated act of entertainment but as a continuous, multi-layered process akin to scheduling a radio or television programme, wherein fashion shows serve as a nucleus around which a network of events and interactions are orchestrated?

This article addresses these questions by exploring, in the first part, the concept of the *palimpsest* as an emergent model for understanding contemporary fashion communication. While traditionally associated with textual layers, the palimpsest notion increasingly serves as a metaphor for the overlapping, interwoven practices characterising modern fashion systems. The second part of this article investigates the historical evolution of fashion shows, examining their shifting role within a highly mediatised and digitalised environment. This analysis provides a foundation for understanding how the production and consumption of fashion have become increasingly intertwined with the need to expand the communicative impact of fashion events. By considering fashion shows within a broader context of continuous, multi-dimensional engagement, this study highlights fashion's evolving vocabulary and strategies to maintain relevance in an era of rapid technological change and the desire for constant audience interaction.

Through this exploration, the article attempts to map contemporary fashion communication's complex and ever-changing terrain, mainly how digitalisation, entertainment, and the accelerating pace of cultural shifts have contributed to reconfiguring how fashion is communicated, consumed, and experienced, thanks to the design of communicative palimpsests.

2 Palimpsest in the Contemporary Fashion Scene

Similar to the evolution of the omnichannel experience in retail [1], in communication, the concept of palimpsest [2] helps us understand how fashion is increasingly developing into a fluid and stratified form of visual, verbal, and symbolic signals that constantly overlap and interact with each other through different channels and touchpoints. The concept of palimpsest – borrowed from television as the implicit structure that shapes the flow of programmes and content, and which also serves as a tool for viewers to navigate between appointments and recurring events – in fashion communication becomes a form of multi-level, multi-moment storytelling that helps strengthen the connection between the brand and its audience, between industry and consumption. Behind this word are multiple stratifications, different objects, and various projects: a process of composition and adjustment that is always active for those in the know and a constantly updated grid for the public, too. The palimpsest is the list of what will be broadcast during the day, the week, and the month. It defines a programme's identity and 'flavour', what adds to the individual product the contextual variables that modify its meaning and sometimes its value. A tool for reaching specific targets, addressing the broadest possible audience, fans of a genre or a single community of taste. Thus, in light of this definition, fashion communication can no longer be considered unidirectional and one-dimensional. It develops through multiple channels and methods, from traditional fashion photography to fashion shows, social media, and digital platforms. Every element of fashion, from collections to fashion shows, from advertising to commercial spaces to events, thus becomes part of a complex system in which meanings are continuously negotiated and reinterpreted. In a sense, this implements the concept of the palimpsest (developed in the field of philosophical and semiotic thought), elaborated in particular by Roland Barthes, Jacques Derrida, Michel Foucault, and Umberto Eco, who provided theoretical tools to analyse how meanings emerge from complex systems of signs and symbols.

Following the thought of Roland Barthes, we can read fashion as a system of signs that transmits cultural meanings and values, and we can understand clothes not only as goods but as signs that overlap with social, cultural, and aesthetic meanings, which implement and require processes of decoding these signs and how consumers interpret the messages, whether visual or not, transmitted by fashion images. Fashion, therefore, is a text that is continuously reinterpreted by the public. A text that is not static but evolves, adapting to social and cultural mutations: a palimpsest constructed through a series of signs, images, and practices that overlap and interact, constructing and deconstructing elements, images, signs, symbols, and meanings. Construction and deconstruction of meanings [3] contribute to the definition of a further level of understanding of fashion as a communicative palimpsest, where the meaning of a text—or in this case of a fashion collection—is never concluded in the product and fixed but always fluid and in continuous movement, its meaning is relative, always under discussion, never definitive and, last but not least, communicated in different forms and ways, sometimes synchronous, sometimes asynchronous, distributed in different places and times and where each new collection builds its meaning about the previous ones, in a continuous game of references, citations, and contradictions. Fashion, therefore, as a complex language [4] as a series of signs that overlap and interact, creating a narrative beyond the simple garment. The various communicative actions implemented are conveyed on multiple channels and at different and simultaneous moments, becoming increasingly a powerful means of narrating and disseminating ideal and symbolic images that appeal to the aesthetic sense and the collective imagination.

In this context, fashion shows have always been a privileged place where fashion communicates through visual, aural, and performative practices. If in the past the fashion show was simply an event presenting a new collection, today its function has changed. Fashion shows have become complex spectacles in which every aspect—from the sets to the clothes, from the music to the choreography—contributes to creating a communicative palimpsest that involves the spectator on several levels. The shows are no longer understood as single, isolated entities but are increasingly embedded in a sequence, an orderly and coherent succession of different actions, each with its role and meaning. Another, and then another, follows one action. In this context, the fashion show is situated in a context delineated by the brand, by what has been broadcast before (even much before and which relates to the brand's history) and by what will be aired after (or even much after). Thanks to the context and the moment of staging, the actions communicate value because the whole of the actions means something more than the sum of the individual parts.

This phenomenon evolved profoundly with the advent of digital communication, which has redrawn the boundaries between the production and fruition of fashion, contributing to its mediatisation, increasingly allowing the creation of complex communicative actions more and more similar to a broadcasting schedule, more dynamic and interactive where the fashion show is not only the conclusion of a creative process but the beginning of a rich and varied communicative system. The mediatisation of fashion has transformed how consumers experience their relationship with trends, brands, and the fashion industry. Digital has accelerated these changes, making fashion increasingly usable through online platforms, social media, and live streaming, creating a complex grid of overlapping and intersecting meanings and communicative practices. The mediatisation of fashion [5] realises new communication possibilities [6], leading brands to conceive the production of images from 1080 pixels, the unit of measurement of an Instagram post. Events, advertising campaigns, and fashion shows are now designed to be enjoyed within the interface of different technological tools, which allow participants to interact and even finalise a purchase. Fashion shows, above all, are increasingly mediatised events, produced and staged to be consumed online: this reduces the time of communication, which becomes instantaneous; the concept of space disappears; one can be present even if physically distant and, no less important, the filter between designer/brand and end consumer is reduced. Technology has become a sphere where fashion companies move quickly to communicate, design, share, and get involved. Everything becomes public (rehearsals, fitting, backstage, front rows, fashion shows, after parties, breaks, and holidays). The fashion show is no longer just an exclusive moment but a moment of sharing, and *likes* can influence the production of a given product, if not precisely surpassing, at least supporting or even anticipating the buyers' feedback during the sales campaign.

In this context, which is increasingly multidisciplinary, multi-channel, and hovering between the tangible and intangible, fashion is still today a form of experimenting laboratory in which not only experiments on clothing artefacts but also the use of new technologies and the communicative possibilities inherent in them, make it possible to broaden the vocabulary of staging, communication, and customer involvement actions. In fashion shows, aesthetic, semantic, expressive, communicative, theatrical, technological and, last but not least, emotional elements are integrated [7].

They are unique and unrepeatable acts that transcend mere product presentation and contribute to increasing the cultural value of clothes, which are transformed from functional artefacts into fashion [8].

The boundary between fashion market and fashion culture is becoming ever more blurred; in this context, fashion shows represent even more one of the fundamental *tòpos* of the system: the first showcase, the most important one for presenting and staging collections and ideas, for conveying, effectively and immediately, the design process while also fulfilling multiple other functions such as communicative, interpersonal [9], and social [10]. Even in today's society of images and the continuous directing and sharing of information through the many tools at our disposal, the fashion show remains an unrepeatable event that cannot be transferred entirely because the physicality of what happened continues to be fundamental. Therefore, the presence and recording that all the senses make of the live event remains irreplaceable [11].

Thanks to new technologies, the fashion show—whose primary purpose remains that of showing new styles and products to journalists, editors, and buyers—is now transformed into a communication phenomenon, increasingly multifaceted and multifaceted. The pervasiveness of digital has made fashion, with its rituals and dynamics, accessible to an ever wider number of spectators, opening up the doors of previously exclusive events and transforming the catwalk from a simple platform for presentation to a few to an integral part of a more complex communication palimpsest, a moment of sharing that expands into artistic, performative, musical, playful, and cinematographic forms. From being an event limited in space and time, the fashion show takes the form of a true palimpsest, which does not end in the *here and now* but expands into a before and after and can even take place in several places simultaneously.

The dichotomy between container and content disappears more and more. Catwalks are designed to generate an all-embracing experience, and their design is not limited to mere decoration [12].

The catwalk is consolidating as an autonomous discipline, a communicative system articulated on multiple narratives, seamlessly selecting, managing, and amalgamating different channels, spheres, and contents [13]: art, branding [14], set design [15], retail experience, cinema, photography, performing art, set design, exhibit, heritage, curatorship, branding, and new technologies.

3 Fashion Shows as a Form of Entertainment Beyond the Business

The evolution of fashion shows results from an interaction of commercial and theatrical elements present since the dawn of the modern fashion system. Though the multiplicity of digital channels and platforms is a hallmark of contemporary society, integrating complex communication and spectacle into fashion presentations dates back to the nineteenth and twentieth centuries. Figures such as Jeanne Paquin, Paul Poiret, and Lucile (Lady Duff Gordon) were pivotal in shaping the modern fashion show. These designers transformed the runway into a commercial and cultural event and elevated it to theatrical performance.

Jeanne Paquin, a pioneering fashion designer and businesswoman, was instrumental in integrating commercial and artistic elements into fashion shows. Her famous 1913 show at London's Palace Theatre is considered one of the first to incorporate an orchestra, with models walking to the rhythm of the tango in a carefully orchestrated sequence. Paquin also introduced the finale concept with her iconic *white finale*, in which models dressed in white formed a tableau vivant at the show's end, creating a dramatic and surprising effect. This innovation was key in transforming fashion presentations into theatrical events designed to captivate and entertain audiences, establishing a precedent for future fashion shows.

Poiret was an entrepreneur and a fashion designer responsible for creating fashion shows, capable of totally involving the guests and the press, of which he maniacally followed every detail [16]. Poiret's legendary masquerade parties, such as the *Mille et deuxième nuit* event in 1911, transformed his shows into immersive social occasions. The 1911 event, held in the atelier's garden, was inspired by Persian culture and featured elaborate decorations such as gold canopies, fountains, and exotic birds, creating a narrative environment that framed Poiret's creations. Poiret's shows became globally renowned, with events staged in cities like London, Berlin, Moscow, and Vienna [17]. Vienna was the tour's finale, and it was here that an actual 'Poiret fever' broke out. For 3 days (27, 28, and 29 November 1911), the Parisian couturier created a kermesse—organised at the Urania, a very modern observatory and cultural centre in Art Nouveau style—conceived as a palimpsest of events and which included not only fashion shows, but also film screenings and lectures given by Poiret himself. Seats were ticketed and included six price ranges to allow different audiences to participate in the event. Poiret's innovative use of barges on the Seine during the 1925 *Exposition Internationale des Arts Décoratifs et Industriels Modernes* exemplified his ability to bring fashion into public spaces, further blending commercial and cultural spheres.

During the early twentieth century, the theatre became a favoured venue for fashion designers seeking to elevate their shows. Theatrical elements, such as lighting, music, and stage design, were incorporated into fashion presentations to lend them cultural legitimacy. Concurrently, the theatre began to embrace fashion shows, using dressing as a dramatic tool to appeal to broader audiences. Some plays and shows feature multiple fashion *tableaux vivants*, with the clothing taking centre stage over the narrative elements. This shift highlights the increasingly symbiotic relationship between theatre and fashion, with both sectors inspiring each other to reach new cultural and commercial heights.

The 1960s and 1970s saw a dramatic shift in the fashion show format. Designers with avant-garde sensibilities, such as Pierre Cardin, Mary Quant, Paco Rabanne, and André Courrèges, challenged traditional notions of fashion. These designers revolutionised the industry by creating garments with unconventional proportions, materials, and shapes, reflecting the cultural upheavals of the time. The fashion shows of these designers became platforms for artistic and social experimentation. Mary Quant, for example, held her collections in unconventional venues, including cafés, jazz clubs, and art galleries, where models performed in more informal settings.

In contrast to the structured catwalks of the past, these shows invited more significant audience interaction and created an atmosphere of spontaneity [18]. The fashion show is enriched by live concerts, with an informal atmosphere, where models are invited to abandon the classic catwalk setting in favour of more unrestrained movements so spectators and models mingle. The venues of the nascent youth scene became some of the most used by the new fashion generations, so, for example, Ossie Clark walked the runway in 1968 at the Revolution Club in London. In the same years in the United States, alongside the officialdom of New York Fashion Week, a season of great experimentation began, during which the American city became the *place to be*.

New York became a hub for fashion experimentation in the United States, with the underground fashion scene gaining visibility through events that blurred the boundaries between fashion, art, and performance. The work of photographer Anton Perich is particularly notable in this regard. Through his show *Anton Perich Presents*, which aired on Sterling Manhattan Cable Television in 1973, he brought the excesses and avant-garde spirit of the New York fashion scene to a broader audience [19]. Perich's shows, featuring designers such as Kenzo, Issey Miyake, and Halston, used raw, experimental techniques to capture the energy of the city's underground fashion movements. His broadcasts also introduced fashion to a broader, more diverse audience, breaking away from the polished and exclusive image that fashion had traditionally held on television. It was incredible!' he recalled in an interview [20]. His show (which aired until 1978) provides some of the fascinating accounts of that period and of the spirit and narrative language of fashion shows, such as Issey Miyake's performance at FIT in New York in 1975, with models walking as if they were performing a contemporary dance choreography; or like Rea Spencer's informal fashion show inside the Fiorucci shop in 1977, or Kenzo's party (more than a fashion show) inside Studio 54 that ended with a performance by Grace Jones singing *I Need a Man*.

Similarly, entertainment played a significant role in Ken Scott's approach to fashion. His shows were multifaceted performances that combined fashion, music, and social gatherings. Scott's shows often featured elaborate productions, such as a forest-themed setting for his 1972 collection or *tableaux vivants* for his 1976 collection, where models wore unisex fashion in domestic settings. These performances were more than fashion shows; they were immersive social events designed to engage and entertain audiences [21].

By the 1980s, fashion shows had become increasingly sophisticated, with designers recognising the power of narrative and spectacle in presenting their collections. The fashion show had evolved into a full-scale production, with sets, choreography, music, and lighting becoming as important as the clothes. Designers like Thierry Mugler and Moschino elevated fashion presentations to new heights, blending fashion and theatre in unprecedented ways. Mugler's tenth-anniversary show, held at the Zénith concert hall in Paris, exemplified this transformation. The 6000 seats of the Zénith were packed, and of these, only 2000 were occupied by guests, while the remaining 4000 were purchased (at 175 francs, about 70 euros today) for a rock concert [22].

The catwalk, designed by Mugler himself, was conceived to extend into the stall area and embrace the audience with *Blade Runner-style* lighting. The show was conceived according to a sequence of 35 themed paintings (with evocative names such as *Aubes du futur*, *Onctueuse construction*, *Perle baroque*, *Les ailes de la Victoire*, and *Sainte Rita*) staged by 50 models until the sacred (or sacrilegious, depending on one's point of view) finale, during which Pat Cleveland dressed as a Madonna, complete with halo, was lowered from above, in the middle of the catwalk. The effect was enthralling and designed for the increasingly large audience 'for whom fashion has become another international sport'. Mugler stated in an interview with 'The New York Times': 'There are two ways of doing fashion shows today. Either you do minimal, private events, or you do this [the fashion show at the Zénith, ed.] I think the public wants the latter version' [23].

Franco Moschino's shows, characterised by their humorous and subversive tone, further pushed the boundaries of fashion theatre. His use of exaggerated theatrical costumes, references to jesters and circus performers, and the juxtaposition of high fashion with street style all created a chaotic, creative atmosphere that entertained and challenged the audience's perceptions of fashion.

As fashion shows became more complex and financially demanding, sponsorship from major brands like Shiseido, Adidas, and Renault became increasingly common. Designers began to assume multiple roles, acting as creative directors and choreographers, reflecting fashion shows' growing commercialisation and institutionalisation. The fashion show had thus evolved from a simple display of garments into a multifaceted event that combined art, entertainment, and commerce, reflecting the ever-expanding role of fashion in contemporary culture.

4 Fashion Shows as Part of a Complex and Multifaceted Communication Palimpsest Between Digital and Real

The new millennium and the pervasiveness of digital technologies allow fashion to define increasingly direct and involving modes of presentation and interaction. The public can no longer pay for a ticket to attend the big show. However, with the emergence of social media, the possibilities of sharing and fruition are multiplying, allowing greater integration between languages and transmedia interactive modes, thus making our devices the communication tools par excellence. More and more, not only the products and the surface of the fashion show are shared with the public, but also the different stages of the creative and production process, as if they were episodes of a reality show, and even the behind-the-scenes narratives become actions that involve users in the life of the brand (or the designer). The 'mediatisation of fashion' thus defines a new idea of doing fashion through media [24]. This has led brands to define and manage communication and image production from the unit of measurement of 1080 pixels, that of an Instagram post.

Digital platforms such as Facebook, Twitter, Instagram, Snapchat, and TikTok, but also more niche channels such as dating apps, create new opportunities for interaction and communication. It so happens that, in 2016, J.W. Anderson presented his autumn/winter 2016 men's collection on Grindr, offering a visual experience on a par with those offered by 'traditional' channels: digital broadens consumer niches and helps to break down rigid divisions between genres and markets [25].

In this context, fashion shows are increasingly conceived with social media in mind; they have become mediatised events produced and staged to be consumed online on a digital screen. Thus, they are enriched with made-for-Instagram moments.

The ephemeral form of the fashion show takes on a central role. It is multivalent and social-media-friendly [26] to be experienced both in the presence and at a distance, in streaming and deferred, repeated in different places and times on multiple electronic devices. The pervasive presence of social media has contributed to defining a renewed role of fashion shows and catwalk projects, increasingly designed to be experienced and provide unique experiences equally valid live and at a distance.

Within the history of fashion shows and our collective history, a shocking moment was that of the COVID-19 years, which defined a rethinking and a moment of reflection (even if only temporary) on the system in general. Distancing or the total absence of the public becomes and creative stimulus, giving rise to multiple forms of staging capable of implementing the vocabulary and tools available to convey fashion.

Since 2020, new involvement strategies have been defined, and new forms of fashion shows have emerged: *Faux* shows, *Virtual shows*, *Défilmé* or *Runway experiences*, and different forms of staging [27]. Hybrid fashion shows that—while maintaining the traditional form of the catwalk on which models walk—take on the languages typical of cinema and video clips, in which the spectacularity of the locations and filming is combined with a variety of viewpoints, which tell the garments as a whole and in detail, emphasising the models' faces and expressions. The fashion shows start backstage, and a cameraman, in a subjective view, follows the model as she enters the 'arena': the fashion show becomes a *mash-up* of institutional and performative moments, an effect that only film editing makes possible. However, that is not all. Fashion shows are integral to communicative palimpsests, where messages and languages typical of fashion and television, gaming and digital art are layered. With this approach of language hybridisation, for example, Virgil Abloh created *Imaginary TV* in 2020, a platform that offers a real palimpsest of contents, within which Off-White's collections also find space but not only. The project is that of a digital channel to produce and promote content that better defines and narrates brand identity: 'with the growing economic impact of social media, fashion brands have transformed from design houses into studios that produce both material products and digital content' [28], from podcasts to gaming, from tutorials to conferences. Launched under the domain name https://imaginary-tv.off%2D%2D-white.com/ as a separate section of Off White's commercial site, *Imaginary TV* was conceived as a platform to offer on-demand programmes and give visibility to creative realities from all over the world, from Africa to America, from Asia to Europe. The programme schedule, visually presented through an aesthetic reminiscent of the digital world of the 1990s, ranges from documentaries to artistic performances, making this platform a place to host the work of artists and young creatives and not only to present new collections. The fashion show becomes one of the TV programmes, a streaming event in a space designed as a single environment but with four different sets (a warehouse with red shelves, a winter garden, a garage with the truck resulting from the performance by Leonardo Totino, Bufer, Snitch, & Zoow—also present among the contents of Imaginary TV—and a neutral concrete space), which is presented simultaneously on the multimedia platform and the various digital channels, both those of the brand and Virgil Abloh's channels.

Virgil Abloh's concept began a phase of digital spectacularisation of fashion that was no longer limited to staging a collection but expanded the content to be communicated through different forms of entertainment, of which the fashion show was only one part of the narrative. Prada, for example, did the same in the same period.

Prada, for its men's and women's fashion shows for autumn/winter 2021, created two different presentations, which were, however, united by the exact location (designed by Rem Koolhaas's AMO studio and realised within the spaces of the Fondazione Prada in Milan) and the same structure, according to which the fashion show is the beginning of a true communicative palimpsest. The collections' presentations do not end with the final catwalk of models but continue with an 'interactive' *afterwards*. After the women's fashion show, *Prada Intersections* kicked off, during which Miuccia Prada and Raf Simons conversed with Derek Blasberg (who moderated the event), Lee Daniels, Richie Hawtin—known by the pseudonym Plastikman—, Marc Jacobs, Rem Koolhaas, and Hunter Schafer. After the men's collection show, the two creative directors started a *Conversation* with students from some fashion schools. This broadens the tools available for creating a fashion show, which no longer serves only to present new products and new spatial and performative concepts but becomes part of a complex communication system of reality and digital visual content and words.

The actions carried out during the pandemic have defined new approaches and communication tools for fashion shows and significantly introduced the concept of palimpsest in fashion communication.

Although it was thought that the technological acceleration imposed by COVID-19 would kill the fashion shows, this did not happen. However, it did contribute to creating new forms of entertainment forever richer and more complex presentations. In this transitional period, during which one could also return to attendance, the experiences from the most challenging pandemic were capitalised on, implementing different forms of parades and carrying out experiments that allowed a connection between different locations (in some cases still subject to movement restrictions). Moncler, which has already presented its collections in spectacular logos and incredibly scenic forms over the years, is launching the *Mondogenius* project on 25 September 2021, a fashion show-television programme set in five cities worldwide, to present 11 collections on over 30 platforms. An immersive digital experience: Alicia Keys, live from Milan, guided viewers through the 11 different forms of presentation of the collections, taking viewers from Milan to Shanghai, all the way to Tokyo and Seoul and then on to New York, uniting different communities and generations around the world, creating a digital journey to connect places and people. The fashion show, as a communicative palimpsest, thus also becomes a celebratory event, like those organised by Olivier Rousteing, who, on 29 September 2021, staged a show in the form of a festival (the Balmain Festival V02) at La Seine Musicale, the concert hall on Île Seguin in the western suburbs of Paris, to celebrate 10 years at the helm of Balmain. It is a show in three acts: commercial, celebratory, and entertaining. The first part, the commercial one, saw the fashion show of the new collection, a prelude to the actual celebration, also in the form of a fashion show, but with top supermodels Naomi Campbell, Milla Jovovich, Cindy Bruna, Karen Elson, Liu Wen, Adut Akech, Mariacarla Boscono, and Carla Bruni who (re)walked the catwalk, showcasing the last 10 years of the brand, wearing iconic pieces by Olivier Rousteing for Balmain.

Nevertheless, the finale was not the end of the celebration, but the beginning of the third part of this real palimpsest of shows that saw musicians such as Franz Ferdinand, Doja Cat, and Jesse Jo Stark on the catwalk, which served as a stage for an actual music festival. Nevertheless, it also happens that Diesel, under the artistic direction of Glenn Martens from 2020, conceives the fashion show as part of a programme of in-person and digital events: the fashion show for spring/summer 2024 was a sort of 'intermission' of a free rave party organised in the industrial spaces of Milan's Scalo Farini. The catwalk was part of the rave scene and DJ sets, and only after about 4 h of music did it turn into the space for the collection presentation for a little over 20 min, only to turn back into a dancefloor. In the following days, the vast space of the old railway yard remained open with a film festival, during which titles dear to the brand's creative director, such as *Mulholland Drive*, *Fight Club*, *Spirited Away*, and *WALL-E*, were presented with film marathons of five films per day.

However, the concept of a palimpsest in fashion communication is not only implemented as an entertainment strategy during and after the fashion show but increasingly also embraces the pre-show phases or even the minutes before the show. And so it happens, for example, that Chanel has created modes of communication that also take possession of the moments before and after the actual catwalk, such as Radio Chanel, the radio programme aired on Thursday, 2 May 2024, at 12:30 and 17:00, before and after the fashion show set up on the terrace of the *Unité d'habitation* built in Marseille by Le Corbusier. The live broadcasts featured Caroline de Maigret, Géraldine Sarratia, and Pedro Winter in dialogue with various actors, musicians, and creatives such as Marion Cotillard, Jean-Michel Jarre, and Lily-Rose Depp.

Similarly, yet with different tools, for the autumn/winter 2024 collection, Diesel staged a wholly different and hybrid experience: the fashion show was conceived as a *post-view* because, in reality, almost everything had already been anticipated online by a 4-day 'big brother' live broadcast. Fixed cameras were installed in the pre-fashion show spaces (rehearsal room, tailor's shop, casting room, and fashion show venue), allowing everyone to live the experience and the fast pace of the preparations, breaking in a way the 'sacredness' and exclusivity of the catwalk more than half of the guests were zoomers connected online, also becoming an integral part of the fashion show set.

As an actual communication product, fashion shows generate consumer goods outside of fashion products, applying a kind of memory marketing and creating authentic souvenirs of the event. Suppose the market or collecting fashion show invitations or various gadgets are established practices. In that case, the last few years have seen the creation of brand products linked to the fashion show experience: Saint Laurent sells vinyl online, in a limited series, of the soundtracks heard during the catwalk; Sunnei since 2021 has been publishing three editions of the 'System' project with the tracks used for the 2021 and 2022 shows as well as bonus tracks; while the German brand Gmbh—founded in 2016 by Benjamin Alexander Huseby and Serhat Isik—, presented in 2023 An Anthology Of Music For Fashion Shows 2016–2023 Volume 1, the first compilation of the music from their fashion shows produced in only 500 copies. Not only visual and symbolic signals but also sound signals are further amplified in the form of a usable and collectable product, expanding the levels of fashion communication, which is structured as a communication strategy and palimpsest no longer only on the *hic et nunc* but on the continuous return and re-proposal of themes and stories [29].

5 Conclusions

In conclusion, fashion remains constantly evolving, with its presentation and representation mirroring the dynamic interplay between commerce, culture, creativity, and emerging digital communication tools and channels. The fashion show has undergone a radical transformation within this context—from its origins as a commercial tool to its current status as a cultural event that seamlessly blends performance, art, and spectacle. The influence of early pioneers such as Paquin and Poiret, followed by later figures such as Quant, Mugler, and Moschino, and the ongoing digital evolution has shaped fashion shows into the multifaceted and immersive experiences we encounter today. This transformation is indicative of broader societal changes. It underscores the growing significance of staging and spectacle in fashion communication and its dissemination through diverse platforms and media.

Fashion communication today no longer revolves around isolated events. Instead, it constructs a complex, continuously evolving narrative that traverses time and space, fostering an ever-stronger connection between the physical and digital realms. In this context, the fashion show is no longer merely a question of scenography, performance, or digital integration. It has evolved from a private, singular moment into an integral part of a communicative palimpsest—one that unfolds across time and space, driven by an organising principle that balances the uniqueness and individuality of events with the multiplicity of channels and tools available for sharing.

Thus, the fashion show reverberates and expands across time and space, becoming a crucial component of a layered communication strategy, taking root in diverse locations and moments. Even after the curtain has fallen, his presence continues in our imagination and devices, perpetuated through communicative palimpsests designed for social media and an ever-increasing range of entertainment and sharing practices.

References

1. Iannilli, V. M., & Spagnoli, A. (Eds.). (2023). *Design dynamics. Navigating the new complex landscape of omnichannel fashion retail*. Franco Angeli.
2. Barra, L. (2015). *Palinsesto: storia e tecnica della programmazione televisiva*. Laterza.
3. Maclachlan, I. (Ed.). (2018). *Jacques Derrida: Critical thought*. Routledge.
4. Barthes, R. (2013). *The language of fashion*. Bloomsbury Publishing.
5. Rocamora, A. (2016). Mediatization and digital media in the field of fashion. *Fashion Theory: The Journal of Dress, Body and Culture*. https://doi.org/10.1080/1362704X.2016.1173349
6. Krotz, F. (2007). The meta-process of 'mediatisation' as a conceptual frame. *Global Media and Communication, 3*(3).
7. Ricchetti, M., & Cietta, E. (Eds.). (2006). *Il valore della moda. Industria e servizi in un settore guidato dall'innovazione*. Bruno Mondadori.
8. Kawamura, Y. (2018). *Fashion-ology: An introduction to fashion studies*. Bloomsbury Publishing.
9. Malossi, G. (Ed.). (1998). *Il motore della moda. Spettacolo, identità, design, economia: Come l'industria produce ricchezza attraverso la moda*. The Monacelli Press.
10. Simmel, G. (2015). *La Moda*. Mimesis Edizioni.
11. Calò, C. (2022). *La sfilata di moda come opera d'arte*. Einaudi.
12. Linfante, V. (2022). Sfilate e trasformazioni urbane. Il sistema delle sfilate e il loro impatto sulla costruzione di nuove traiettorie urbane e territoriali. *AND Rivista di architetture, città e architetti, 42*(2). https://doi.org/10.58198/and.v2i42
13. Iannilli, V. M., & Spagnoli, A. (2021). Phygital retailing in fashion. Experiences, opportunities and innovation trajectories. *ZoneModa Journal, 11*(1). https://doi.org/10.6092/issn.2611-0563/13120
14. Klingmann, A. (2007). *Brandscapes: Architecture in the experience economy*. The MIT Press.
15. Potvin, J. (Ed.). (2009). *The places and spaces of fashion, 1800–2007*. Routledge.
16. White, P. (1973). *Poiret*. C.N. Potter.
17. Ganeva, M. (2008). *Women in Weimar fashion: Discourses and displays in German culture, 1918–1933*. Camden House.
18. Fabbri, F. (2021). *La moda contemporanea. Arte e stile dagli anni Sessanta alle ultime tendenze* (Vol. 2). Einaudi.
19. Carmack, K. E. (2010). *Anton Perich presents and TV party: Queering television on Manhattan public access channels, 1973–1982*. PhD thesis, The University of Texas at Austin.
20. Fulton, J. Mixed medium: Anton Perich. https://oaknyc.com/blog/mixed-medium-anton-perich/
21. VV. AA., Ken Scott, Rizzoli, Milano (2022).

22. Bott, D. (2010). *Thierry Mugler: Galaxie glamour*. Editions Ramsay.
23. Duka, J. (1984, March 28). In fashion, the show's the thing. In *The New York Times*. The Living Lection.
24. Hjarvard, S. (2013). *The mediatization of culture and society*. Routledge.
25. Linfante, V., & Pompa, C. (2023). How pornography saved fashion from boredom and improved its financial situation and vice versa: Communication technology overlaps between fashion and pornography. *Fashion, Style & Popular Culture, 10*(10).
26. Findlay, R. (2017). Things to be seen: Spectacle and the performance of brand in contemporary fashion shows. *About Performance*, 14–15.
27. Linfante, V., & Pompa, C. (2021). Space, time and catwalks: Fashion shows as a multilayered communication channel. *ZoneModa Journal, 11*(1). https://doi.org/10.6092/issn.2611-0563/13100
28. Rees-Roberts, N. (2020). After fashion film: Social video and brand content in the influencer economy. *Journal of Visual Culture, 19*(3). https://doi.org/10.1177/1470412920964
29. Linfante, V. (2024). *Moda atto unico. Le sfilate tra performance, comunicazione e nuove tecnologie*. Mimesis.

Digital Fashion, Artificial Intelligence and Emerging Technologies

Usability Challenges in Sentiment Analysis Tools: A Dual Approach for the Fashion Industry

Dai Zhu, Nadzeya Sabatini, and Nicoletta Fornara

Abstract This study represents one of the earliest explorations of usability challenges in sentiment analysis tools for the fashion domain. Through a dual approach—an industry survey and a heuristic evaluation of tools, including SentiStrength and IBM Watson NLU—this research identified a significant gap between the high-value professionals place on public sentiment and the inefficiencies of current methods. Key usability issues were identified, such as lack of efficiency and flexibility, poor documentation, and limited domain-specific adaptability. The study offers actionable recommendations for a more user-centric tool design. It highlights the need to develop more effective sentiment analysis solutions to meet the needs of fashion industry professionals.

Keywords Sentiment analysis · Usability challenges · Fashion industry · Social media analytics · Fashion sentiment analysis · RED

1 Introduction

Like much of society, the fashion industry continues to be profoundly shaped by digital technologies. Social media platforms have become indispensable spaces for users to share opinions, discover brands, and shape fashion trends. Visual and fashion-centered platforms are frequently cited in fashion research as essential tools for understanding the evolving role of social media in the industry. However, not all

D. Zhu (✉) · N. Fornara
USI – Università della Svizzera italiana, Lugano, Switzerland
e-mail: nicoletta.fornara@usi.ch

N. Sabatini
Gdansk University of Technology and USI – Università della Svizzera italiana, Lugano, Switzerland
e-mail: nadzeya.sabatini@usi.ch

P. von Wachenfeldt et al. (eds.), *Fashion Communication in the Digital Age*, Springer Proceedings in Business and Economics,
https://doi.org/10.1007/978-3-031-99481-4_14

platforms are equally suited for comprehensive sentiment analysis due to differences in their content display algorithms. Visually rich platforms like TikTok engage the global fashion community with dynamic content formats [1, 2]. Yet, TikTok's algorithm customizes comment visibility based on factors such as location, language, and user behavior. This tailored approach often results in users seeing distinct subsets of comments on the same post, making it challenging to analyze sentiments comprehensively. In contrast, platforms like Instagram and RED (also known as Xiao Hongshu, RedNote, or the "Chinese Instagram"), which display comments more consistently and universally, are better suited for capturing a holistic view of audience sentiment. With its visually driven nature, Instagram plays a pivotal role in shaping fashion and lifestyle trends. In 2024, its globally popular "#fashion" hashtag surpassed 1.1 billion posts [3], serves as a central hub for users to explore personal style, connect with influencers, and engage in trend-driven discussions. Instagram has effectively brought users worldwide to the "front row" of fashion, allowing them to engage directly with brands and trends [4]. Similarly, RED has emerged as a leading social media platform for fashion and lifestyle content. With 300 million active monthly users, many of whom are young and trend-oriented, RED enables local and international brands to connect deeply with Chinese consumers [5, 6]. By integrating User-Generated Content (UGC) with e-commerce, RED demonstrates the power of becoming an important platform that shapes fashion trends. Thanks to the global popularity of these visual-centered platforms, a vast amount of UGC is created, which are often rich in sentiments.

Unlike the straightforward expressions of emotion (e.g., simply saying "I am happy"), UGC on these platforms employs a wide range of evolving and often subtle linguistic cues, such as slang, memes, and indirect references, providing a voluminous and complex source for sentiment analysis. This abundance of digital sentiment data underscores the need for advanced sentiment analysis methods to extract valuable insights from users' emotions, attitudes, and interactions, particularly in navigating cultural diversity and linguistic nuances in global markets [4, 7].

Sentiment analysis, as discussed in "*The SAGE Handbook of Social Media Research Methods*," is a crucial analytical tool used in social media research [8]. It involves algorithmically classifying users' evaluations, positive, negative, or neutral, of topics based on their posts and comments, and this process helps researchers and businesses understand public sentiment and attitudes toward various subjects, enabling them to make informed decisions based on this data [9, 10]. In the fashion industry, this technique offers valuable insights into consumer perceptions of products, trends, and brand messaging, enabling more informed decision-making [11]. However, despite the growing sophistication of sentiment analysis methods, their application to fashion-related social media remains limited [12].

While scholars have explored sentiment analysis in the context of fashion, studies are few and vary in their focus and application. Yuan and Lam [13] proposed one of the most relevant studies, applying advanced machine-learning approaches to develop a sentiment analysis method specifically for fashion-related Instagram content, integrating both text and images. Other studies, such as those by Choi et al. [14] and Ahmed [15], have focused on analyzing sentiment around specific fashion topics, such as the four main fashion weeks [14], or the public's opinions on specific fashion brands mining from Twitter data [15]. These studies highlight the relevance and versatility of sentiment analysis in addressing different needs within the fashion domain, particularly in understanding social media discussions on specific fashion topics. However, unlike Yuan and Lam's work, which sought to create a method tailored for fashion sentiment analysis, these studies primarily demonstrate how existing approaches can be applied to specific contexts. Furthermore, the lack of readily available benchmarks and datasets tailored to fashion-related content remains a significant challenge, as these authors had to collect their own datasets for analysis. This gap stands in contrast to domains like medicine, finance, or e-commerce, where sentiment analysis tools and datasets are more established [16, 17]. Additionally, the usability of existing general-purpose sentiment analysis tools has received little attention. These challenges underscore the importance of exploring how professionals currently approach sentiment analysis and assessing the usability of available tools to bridge the gap between technical advancements and practical applications in the fashion domain. Therefore, this study seeks to address these gaps, focusing on the usability challenges of sentiment analysis tools for fashion-related applications.

2 Literature Review

2.1 Fashion Sentiment Analysis in the Digital Era

Social media has transformed fashion communication, shifting from one-way broadcasts to interactive, which have become central hubs for consumer sentiment and brand engagement [4, 7, 18]. In comparison, before the digital era, fashion sentiment was conveyed through limited, non-interactive channels such as fashion magazines, television, or word-of-mouth communication. Viewers engaged as passive recipients, with emotions and attitudes primarily shared through interpersonal or community-level discussions. The early Internet (Web 1.0) brought changes, enabling access to digitalized, reader-oriented content. However, interaction remained minimal, as audiences could consume fashion content online but had few avenues to participate or share their opinions actively. In the past decade and a half, the rise of visually oriented and lifestyle-driven social media platforms has introduced an entirely new dynamic to fashion communication [19].

Digital fashion, as framed by the Digital Fashion Framework [20, 21], categorizes research into three sub-domains: Communication and Marketing, Design and Production, and Culture and Society. In Communication and Marketing, sentiment analysis is critical for interpreting consumer attitudes in social media marketing, optimizing engagement, and aligning strategies with public sentiment [22]. Similarly, studies by Zou, Luh, & Lu [23] and SanMiguel & Sádaba [24] highlight how understanding public sentiment and consumer attitudes can significantly inform and enhance marketing strategies in the fashion industry. As well in Culture and Society, it provides insights into consumer behavior and cultural trends, influencing brand perception and societal narratives [21]. In the digital era, it is essential for fashion stakeholders to leverage social media insights to enhance communication and engagement strategies and ensure they stay attuned to their audience's evolving preferences and attitudes.

2.2 Sentiment Analysis Methods and Tools

Sentiment analysis is a computational method used to identify and quantify opinions and emotions expressed in text [22], allowing brands and researchers to gain insight into public sentiment around specific topics, products, and trends. It has been suggested as one of the social media research analytical methods [8], also for fashion industry [11], where brand image, consumer preferences, and trends can change rapidly, offering a scientific way to capture user sentiment on social media. By analyzing user comments, textual expressions that may include opinions, emotions, and trends, fashion companies and institutions can extract insights from the "voice of the users," encompassing existing and potential customers and wider fashion enthusiasts who engage with fashion discussions. Researchers employ different methodological approaches to perform sentiment analysis, each with strengths, weaknesses, and corresponding tools. These approaches broadly fall into three categories: lexicon-based methods, supervised machine-learning, and hybrid methods, with recent advancements incorporating deep learning techniques [16, 17, 22, 25].

In most sentiment analysis studies, the methods discussed are typically models developed or evaluated within the scope of these studies, rather than being packaged as tools for direct application. These models often require retraining on labeled datasets, mainly if they are machine-learning-based, to perform effectively in different domains. Alternatively, lexicon-based methods, which rely on predefined dictionaries or lexicons, are relatively more transparent and interpretable but still require contextual adaptation to achieve high accuracy. To increase accessibility, researchers have developed "off-the-shelf" sentiment analysis tools for practical applications without extensive retraining. Novielli et al. [26] found that supervised tools like Senti4SD and SentiCR perform well in platform-specific contexts but struggle with cross-platform applications due to domain-specific jargon, while lexicon-based tools like SentiStrength-SE and DEVA are more robust across platforms but less adaptable to nuanced datasets [26]. Singh and Singh [25] evaluated ten sentiment analysis tools, including SentiStrength, and highlighted their bias toward customer reviews and poor performance on societal datasets, emphasizing the need for custom-built solutions, though SentiStrength achieved strong results in news domains, ranking among the top performers in challenging settings like headline analysis [27]. Given its accessibility and reasonable cross-domain performance, it is worth exploring whether SentiStrength could also work effectively for fashion sentiment analysis. However, to determine its feasibility for this new application, it is crucial to assess whether the tool is genuinely easy to use and identify any potential usability issues that may arise in adapting it to the fashion domain.

A widely recognized sentiment analysis tool leveraging advanced machine-learning methods, with several studies highlighting its capabilities, is IBM Watson NLU. Carvalho et al. [28] demonstrated its strong performance in sentiment analysis through a case study on public reactions to Starbucks' corporate social responsibility pledge, where it achieved significantly higher accuracy than traditional methods [28]. Similarly, Ermakova, Henke, and Fabian [29] evaluated Watson NLU alongside competitors like Google Cloud and Microsoft Azure using airline Twitter data and found it achieved the highest accuracy (79%) and F1 score (87.5%) for negative sentiment classification, though they noted limitations in algorithmic transparency and flexibility for domain-specific adaptations [29]. A recent study [30], among the earliest to compare IBM Watson NLU with GPT-3.5, found Watson consistent in traditional sentiment tasks, while GPT-3.5 excelled at handling nuanced expressions like irony. The study also highlighted the necessity of extensive preprocessing for social media data, emphasizing the importance of refining datasets for reliable sentiment analysis.

Despite its notable performance in sentiment analysis in certain public domains, such as social media and general datasets, there is still a need to explore further IBM Watson NLU's adaptability and effectiveness in other domains, such as fashion. In terms of usability, as noted, API usage and extensive data preprocessing, especially in the absence of a domain-specific benchmark, are often essential techniques for researchers conducting sentiment analysis. These technical prerequisites create a significant barrier for non-technical researchers, professionals, and general users, limiting the accessibility of such tools. A more niche finding is that IBM Watson NLU also provides an online demo [31] that functions similarly to SentiStrength's online version, allowing users to perform sentiment analysis through a simple, interactive interface. However, the actual use and effectiveness of this version remain unknown and should be explored further.

3 Methodology

This study employs a combined method to investigate the challenges and usability issues of sentiment analysis tools in the context of fashion-related social media content. Drawing from the literature, the use of combined usability evaluation methods has been widely adopted in research [32], aligning with this study's design. The methodology integrates questionnaires (survey) and usability inspection (heuristics evaluation) to gain insights into industry professionals' current analytical practices and use of sentiment analysis tools.

Firstly, the survey was conducted to gather opinions on current practices, satisfaction levels, challenges, and unmet needs regarding tools used to analyze public sentiments and opinions from social media content. The survey was designed using Fanqier [33], an online form builder integrated with WeChat, and was conducted from October 3 to 11, 2023. It received a total of 160 responses. Targeted at Chinese professionals working in local or international companies based in China, the survey was initially created in Chinese to ensure accessibility and later translated into English for analysis. Secondly, the study incorporates a usability heuristic evaluation using Nielsen's ten usability heuristic principles [34]. This evaluation focuses on two sentiment analysis tools: SentiStrength and IBM Watson Natural Language Understanding (NLU). These tools were chosen for their accessibility, recognition in scholarly discussions, and their representation of two dominant approaches to sentiment analysis. SentiStrength exemplifies a lexicon-based approach, while IBM Watson NLU represents a machine-learning-based approach. The evaluation aimed to identify specific usability and performance challenges inherent in these tools, particularly in their capacity to analyze social media content relevant to the fashion domain. SentiStrength was assessed in both its online version [35] and Windows desktop version (v 2.3), while IBM Watson NLU was evaluated using its online demo [36]. The evaluations were conducted in the early 2024, and it is important to note that updates to the tools' websites may have resulted in differences between the evaluated and current versions.

By employing a dual-method approach, this study ensures that, although the questionnaire and heuristic evaluations differ in their specific tools and techniques, they share the same overarching aim: to evaluate the usability of sentiment analysis tools for the fashion-related industry. Given the lack of sentiment analysis tools specifically tailored for the fashion domain, this approach seeks to uncover usability challenges and identify opportunities for improvement.

Specifically, this study addresses the following research questions:

1. What challenges do fashion professionals face in analyzing sentiment on social media? and
2. How can insights from their current practices and usability evaluations of sentiment analysis tools guide the development of future solutions?

3.1 *Industry Survey*

The survey consisted of 12 main questions, excluding 6 general demographic questions aimed at understanding participants' background and professional context. These general questions captured participants' age, gender, company size, industry category (e.g., fashion, fashion-related, or other industries), the name of their organization (optional), and their professional role. This demographic information provided context for analyzing the responses. Besides demographic questions, participants were also asked about the importance of analyzing public sentiment on social media for brands. Using a Likert scale ranging from 1 (Not Important) to 5 (Very Important), this question provided foundational insights into how professionals viewed the relevance of sentiment analysis in their work and which platforms they prioritized.

The main survey questions focused on usability-related aspects of sentiment analysis tools, examining participants' technical skills, current practices, satisfaction levels, challenges, and preferences. To evaluate technical proficiency, participants selected skills they were proficient in, such as basic office software (e.g., Word, Excel, PowerPoint), design tools (e.g., Adobe Photoshop, Illustrator, 3D software), and programming languages (e.g., Python, C++, Java). Those with programming experience were asked follow-up questions about their familiarity with data processing tasks like data analysis, cleansing, and visualization, reflecting the technical capacity needed for effective sentiment analysis. Participants were also asked about their current methods for analyzing social media sentiment, with options including manual collection (e.g., screenshots or copying data), third-party platforms, company-internal analysis tools, and office software like Excel. Satisfaction levels were assessed through the question: "How satisfied are you with your current analytical method?" rated on a Likert scale from 1 (Not Satisfied) to 5 (Very Satisfied). To explore challenges, participants were asked: "Have you encountered difficulties when using your social media analytical tools/methods?" If they answered "yes," they were prompted with the follow-up question: "When you encounter difficulties, how do you tend to solve them?" with options including searching or watching online tutorials, finding help information within the platform, taking a course, or asking someone for help. Finally, participants were asked about their preferences when considering a new analytical tool through the question: "What do you look for when considering a new analytical tool?" with choices such as whether the analysis results are easy to understand, whether the data is safe, whether the analysis is accurate, whether the tool is easy to operate, the acceptability of cost, or other factors.

3.2 *Usability Investigation*

For the evaluation of the two systems, Nielsen's 10 heuristics [32] are widely recognized for their ability to identify usability issues across diverse systems. The heuristics are: (1) visibility of system status by ensuring systems provide status information and feedback for user actions. (2) The match between the system and the real world will be evaluated to see if the systems use familiar terms and natural language. (3) User control and freedom will be checked to ensure users can easily reverse actions, redo steps, or cancel tasks, providing clear "emergency exits." (4) Consistency and standards will be measured by how well systems conform to platform conventions and align with similar tools. (5) Error prevention will focus on how the systems understand user goals and prevent errors. (6) Recognition rather than recall will aim to minimize memory load by making tasks intuitive and easy to complete. (7) Flexibility and efficiency of use will be evaluated by ensuring the systems enable efficient task completion and adapt to both novice and expert users. (8) Aesthetic and minimalist design will focus on avoiding irrelevant information and maintaining a natural, logical order in dialogues. (9) Helping users recognize, diagnose, and recover from errors will involve providing plain language error messages that indicate the problem and suggest solutions. Finally, (10) help and documentation will be assessed by the availability of easily searchable, task-focused help resources. Evaluating through each of these principles ensures that the systems are thoroughly evaluated for efficiency, user-friendliness, and effectiveness.

Evaluation Process

Each tool was tested to assess its usability and performance in fashion-related sentiment analysis tasks based on Nielsen's ten heuristic principles. The evaluation followed a structured process involving two key steps:

1. Interface and feature assessment: Each tool's overall interface and features were assessed to understand its design, accessibility, and suitability for sentiment analysis tasks. This initial evaluation aimed to identify general usability strengths and weaknesses.
2. Sentiment analysis testing with fashion-related comments: Fashion-related comments (one created by one of the authors, another collected from social media) were used as test cases to assess each tool's analytical performance.

   (a) For SentiStrength: The evaluation focused on both the online version and the Windows desktop software. Due to text input limitations in the online version, a shorter comment was created: "I left early because this fashion show is boring, the clothes are so ugly." For the Windows desktop version, the analysis interface was the primary focus, assessing how effectively the software presented and processed sentiment data.

   (b) For IBM Watson NLU: The online demo was tested using a fashion-related comment sourced from the @diet_prada Instagram account's post (31/08/2023): "Come on Acne, I expected more from you. This is at best a H&M Divided campaign."

   The usability of the interface, along with its performance in analyzing the comment, was evaluated.

   This comparison provided insights into the usability and performance differences between a lexicon-based tool (SentiStrength) and a machine-learning-based tool (IBM Watson NLU), focusing on their application in the fashion domain.

4 Results

4.1 *Result 1: Industry Survey*

A total of 160 industry professionals participated in the survey, with 41 respondents (25.6%) from the fashion industry and 81 (50.6%) from fashion-related sectors, accounting for a combined 76.2% representation from the fashion and fashion-related industries. The remaining 38 respondents (23.8%) were from diverse industries. This distribution provided a strong focus on the target demographics of the study, ensuring the insights primarily reflected perspectives from professionals directly or indirectly connected to the fashion domain. Participants held roles in key areas such as product development, brand management, marketing strategies, ownership. Among those who disclosed their company affiliations, the survey captured responses from well-known international brands such as U.S. POLO ASSN, GAP, CHOW TAI FOOK, and SHEIN, as well as local Chinese brands like URLAZH and ZUCZUG.

The results also highlight significant usability challenges in current social media analysis tools, reflected in gaps in skill proficiency, reliance on inefficient methods, and low satisfaction levels: (i) 5% of respondents reported proficiency in advanced tools, and 3% had programming skills. Even those with programming expertise rarely used advanced techniques. (ii) Manual methods, like screenshots and copying data, were the most used approach (34.38%), surpassing official platform portals (22.5%) and third-party platforms (21.88%). (iii) Satisfaction levels reflect these challenges, with smaller companies (1–10 employees) rating their tools the lowest at 3.27/5, despite rating the importance of public sentiment at 4.5/5. The overall satisfaction average of 3.46/5 was far below the 4.3/5 average for sentiment analysis importance, underscoring a disconnect between tool effectiveness and user needs. (iv) Usability difficulties were reported by 66.25% of respondents and majority tend to solve it by asking someone's help.

4.2 Result 2: Usability Inspection

The results, which are summarized in the Table 1 show that IBM Watson NLU demonstrates a more polished and user-friendly system compared to the SentiStrength systems, but both tools face significant challenges in efficiency, user-friendliness, and effectiveness. The table clearly highlights the heuristics violated in each system, with 6 out of 10 principles being significantly violated. Among these, Flexibility and Efficiency of Use emerge as the most frequently and severely violated heuristic in this evaluation, underscoring the tools' limitations in handling real-world sentiment analysis tasks efficiently. SentiStrength, in both versions, suffers from fragmented workflows, cluttered interfaces, and poor error handling, while IBM Watson NLU, despite its cleaner design, struggles with inefficiencies in single-text processing, inconsistent scoring, and limited user guidance. Both versions of SentiStrength exhibited several usability issues, particularly in Flexibility and Efficiency of Use. The online version restricts input to vague "short information text" limits, without specifying an exact length, making it unsuitable for typical fashion-related social media comments. As well its fragmented workflows, such as separate input methods for Quick Test, Keyword Test, and Topic Test, further reduce efficiency by requiring repetitive actions. Moreover, the failure to handle typos, e.g., "ugly" vs. "guly," or misspellings, directly impacts how efficiently the system can process real-world inputs, particularly from social media contexts. The desktop version v2.3 supports large-scale dataset analysis, but its reliance on preformatted plain text files creates a

Table 1 Heuristic usability evaluation of SentiStrength and IBM Watson NLU

Heuristic Principle	SentiStrength (Online)	SentiStrength (v2.3)	IBM Watson NLU
1. Visibility of system status	/	/	– Predefined domains suggest domain-specific analysis but only provide example outputs
2. Match between system and the real world	– Uses natural language but overly verbose, making it harder to understand.	– Heavy reliance on scientific jargon in menus, alienating non-technical users.	/
3. User control and freedom	– No clear undo/redo options; users must delete text manually to restart.	/	/
7. Flexibility and efficiency of use	– Fragmented workflows	– Supports large datasets but requires preformatted data;	– Limited to analyzing one text at a time;
	– Unclear input length restrictions.		– Requires restarting for new inputs,
	– Fails to interpret typos	– Overloaded menus reduce efficiency.	– Suffers from inconsistent sentiment scoring
8. Aesthetic and minimalist design	– Overloaded homepage with unstructured information	– Menus are overly complex and cluttered, overwhelming users.	/
10. Help and documentation	– External tutorials not integrated into the interface.	– Help is complex	– Pop-up tutorial links to lengthy, external documentation

high barrier for users unfamiliar with these requirements, reducing task efficiency. Additionally, overloaded menus also complicated navigation and reduced task efficiency in this version.

The user-friendliness of both tools is hindered by cluttered interfaces, complex terminology, and insufficient guidance. The SentiStrength online version violates Aesthetic and Minimalist Design by overwhelming users with excessive and unstructured information on the homepage. Similar in the desktop version (v2.3), scientific jargon in menus. These terms, while precise in technical contexts, fail to align with the language or expectations of everyday users increasing cognitive load and reducing task efficiency, therefore this also violated match between system and the real world when the system does not speak user's language. Additionally, neither version provided clear undo/redo options, violating user control and freedom, and both relied on external tutorials that were not integrated into the interface, creating barriers for users needing guidance and violating help and documentation.

IBM Watson NLU, while offering a cleaner and more organized interface compared to SentiStrength, demonstrates several usability challenges that affect its efficiency, user control, and overall adaptability to professional sentiment analysis tasks. Although minor, one issue lies in visibility of system status. The tool includes predefined "sample industry domains" such as "Legal, Financial, and Media," which might mislead users into expecting domain-specific sentiment analysis. However, these options only generate example text and outputs, creating a minor mismatch between user expectations and system behavior.

The more critical challenge is related to flexibility and efficiency of use, and its connection to user control and freedom. The system limits users to analyzing one text input at a time, requiring them to restart the entire process for each additional analysis. Instead, users must navigate back to the homepage to begin a new session, adding unnecessary steps and further disrupting workflow continuity. While these inefficiencies could be mitigated by utilizing APIs, accessing them requires advanced technical skills, which makes this solution impractical for many non-technical users. Moreover, testing the system with a fashion-related comment also revealed potential algorithmic limitations that may impact flexibility and efficiency of use. For example, in analyzing the comment "Come on Acne, I expected more from you. This is at best a H&M Divided campaign." the tool assigned a positive sentiment score of 0.28 to the brand "Acne" while giving a neutral score to "H&M." This inconsistency in sentiment scoring for similar terms, such as fashion brands, reflects potential algorithmic bias and a lack of contextual understanding. While this inconsistency does not directly violate usability heuristics, it introduces inefficiencies and raises concerns about the system's effectiveness in domain-specific sentiment analysis tasks. Another usability challenge lies in help and documentation, while the tool offers a pop-up tutorial, it redirects users to external IBM documentation that is lengthy and general in scope. Users must manually search through this documentation to find task-specific guidance, increasing cognitive load and reducing accessibility for those unfamiliar with the system or sentiment analysis workflows.

5 Discussion

As a response to the first research question, What challenges do fashion professionals face in analyzing sentiment on social media? the survey results reveal significant usability challenges of current sentiment analysis tools, highlighting critical issues in their daily analytical practices, particularly in the era of digital communication where social media plays a central role. Public sentiment analysis is rated as highly important by professionals (4.3/5 on average), yet satisfaction with current tools remains much lower (3.46/5), revealing a stark disparity. This gap is particularly pronounced among smaller companies. A surprising finding is the heavy reliance on manual methods, such as copying and pasting or taking screenshots, chosen by 34.38% of respondents as the highest chosen option. This reliance, despite the availability of social media analytical tools, suggests that existing solutions may fail to address users' real needs. One potential issue is oversimplified features and lack of transparency in current analytics, which focus on abstract, numeric metrics like engagement rates or keywords. These metrics may fail to align with the qualitative and nuanced insights professionals seek, leading to a preference for manual methods that offer greater control over the content selected for analysis. Moreover, the survey revealed that only 5% of respondents possess advanced IT skills, such as programming or data processing, making many commonly mentioned sentiment analysis techniques, such as open-source tools and APIs, inaccessible. Additionally, 66.25% of participants reported encountering usability difficulties with their tools, and many sought human assistances to resolve issues, citing external tutorials and documentation as exhausting and inefficient, human-to-human interactions are helpful. These findings highlight the urgent need for more intuitive, transparent, and domain-specific solutions that align with the workflows and expectations of fashion professionals.

For answering the second research question, How can insights from current practices and usability evaluations of sentiment analysis tools guide the development of future solutions? the findings highlight key areas for improvement in tool design and functionality. Usability evaluations of tools like SentiStrength and IBM Watson NLU reveal significant limitations: the former with rigid input restrictions, fragmented workflows, and poor handling of typos, while the latter lacks features such as batch analysis, undo/redo functions, and integrated guidance. These shortcomings align with broader usability issues, such as unintuitive interfaces and inadequate support resources. Survey results indicate that future tools must prioritize user-centered design by providing transparency, flexibility, and ease of use. Features like batch processing, better error handling, and clearer, more interpretable results are critical, alongside the development of fashion-specific sentiment analysis knowledge bases and benchmarks to improve accuracy and relevance. By addressing these gaps, tools can align with the unique needs of fashion professionals, enabling more effective sentiment analysis and empowering them to craft better strategies and navigate the complexities of digital communication.

Despite investigating usability issues in current fashion sentiment analysis (possible) practices, this study found that the field of sentiment analysis in the fashion domain remains relatively underexplored. Key gaps include the lack of fashion-specific sentiment analysis tools, methods, and benchmarks to validate tool performance. Fashion, as a highly sentiment-driven topic rich in personal expression and cultural diversity, requires tailored analytical approaches to address its unique nuances. Future research should also explore how online sentiment in fashion differs from other domains, ensuring tools are designed to meet industry-specific needs. Most importantly, for the development of future tools for fashion sentiment analysis with enhanced usability and accuracy, it is worth exploring the frameworks with the integration of advanced AI technologies, particularly generative AI models like Large Language Models (LLMs). These models, increasingly recognized for their capabilities in sentiment analysis, have the potential to improve contextual understanding and the depth of insights necessary for effective fashion communication [37–39].

6 Conclusion

The main contributions of this study lie in its exploration of the underexplored field of sentiment analysis in the fashion domain, focusing on user practices and tool usability. Through a survey, it highlights the needs, challenges, and reliance on manual methods among fashion professionals, reflecting dissatisfaction with existing tools. Additionally, a heuristic evaluation of two sentiment analysis tools, SentiStrength and IBM Watson NLU, identifies usability challenges such as inefficiency, inflexibility, and a lack of intuitive design or adequate user support. By addressing both user perspectives and tool limitations, the study emphasizes the need for more user-friendly, domain-specific solutions and notes the broader research gap in developing fashion-specific tools and benchmarks. However, the study has limitations, including potential subjectivity from a single evaluator; also, the focus on free or demo versions of tools might not fully represent their complete capabilities, and the survey's focus on industry professionals in mainland China, which, despite its value, may not fully represent the global situation.

References

1. Rodgers, D. (2021). How social media is revolutionising the fashion industry all over again. https://www.voguehk.com/en/article/art-lifestyle/social-media-revolutionising-fashion-industry/. Accessed 10 Nov 2024.
2. Kalbaska, N., Sádaba, T., & Cantoni, L. (2019). Editorial: Fashion communication: Between tradition and digital transformation. *SComS, 18*. https://doi.org/10.24434/j.scoms.2018.02.005
3. Influencer Marketing Hub. (2024). The ultimate guide to using Instagram Hashtags. https://influencermarketinghub.com/instagram-hashtags-guide/. Accessed 17 Nov 2024.
4. Torregrosa, M., Sánchez-Blanco, C., SanMiguel, P., & Del Río, P. J. (2023). Instagram: Digital behavior in luxury fashion brands. In N. Sabatini, T. Sádaba, A. Tosi, et al. (Eds.), *Fashion communication in the digital age* (pp. 14–26). Springer Nature Switzerland.
5. Condé, N. (2022). Xiaohongshu: A new pathway to China for international fashion brands. In *Vogue Business*. https://www.voguebusiness.com/consumers/xiaohongshu-a-new-pathway-to-china-for-international-fashion-brands
6. Wan, A. (2022). What is RED (Xiaohongshu) and how can it unlock a new revenue stream? https://www.forbes.com/councils/forbesagencycouncil/2022/05/16/what-is-red-xiaohongshu-and-how-can-it-unlock-a-new-revenue-stream/. Accessed 15 Nov 2024.
7. Zhao, L., Lee, S. H., Li, M., & Sun, P. (2022). The use of social media to promote sustainable fashion and benefit communications: A data-mining approach. *Sustainability, 14*, 1178. https://doi.org/10.3390/su14031178
8. Sloan, L., & Quan-Haase, A. (2016). *The SAGE handbook of social media research methods*. SAGE Publications Ltd.
9. Drus, Z., & Khalid, H. (2019). Sentiment analysis in social media and its application: Systematic literature review. *Procedia Computer Science, 161*, 707–714. https://doi.org/10.1016/j.procs.2019.11.174
10. Liu, B. (2010). Sentiment analysis and subjectivity. In *Handbook of natural language processing* (2nd ed., pp. 627–666).
11. SanMiguel, P. (2024). *Social media in the fashion industry: Fundamentals, strategy and research methods* (1st ed.). Taylor & Francis Group.

12. Pantano, E., Giglio, S., & Dennis, C. (2019). Making sense of consumers' tweets: Sentiment outcomes for fast fashion retailers through big data analytics. *IJRDM, 47*, 915–927. https://doi.org/10.1108/IJRDM-07-2018-0127
13. Yuan, Y., & Lam, W. (2022). Sentiment analysis of fashion related posts in social media. In *Proceedings of the fifteenth ACM international conference on web search and data mining* (pp. 1310–1318). ACM.
14. Choi, Y.-H., Yoon, S., Xuan, B., et al. (2021). Fashion informatics of the big 4 fashion weeks using topic modeling and sentiment analysis. *Fashion and Textiles, 8*, 33. https://doi.org/10.1186/s40691-021-00265-6
15. Aqsa Ahmed, S. (2023). Sentiment analysis: A case study for apparel brands - FABINDIA v/s BIBA. *IJSR, 12*, 916–919. https://doi.org/10.21275/SR23210120313
16. Wankhade, M., Rao, A. C. S., & Kulkarni, C. (2022). A survey on sentiment analysis methods, applications, and challenges. *Artificial Intelligence Review, 55*, 5731–5780. https://doi.org/10.1007/s10462-022-10144-1
17. Bordoloi, M., & Biswas, S. K. (2023). Sentiment analysis: A survey on design framework, applications and future scopes. *Artificial Intelligence Review, 56*, 12505–12560. https://doi.org/10.1007/s10462-023-10442-2
18. Liu, S. (2024). The impact of social media on communication and popularity in the fashion industry. *LNEP, 41*, 84–93. https://doi.org/10.54254/2753-7048/41/20240755
19. Kalbaska, N., Sádaba, T., Cominelli, F., & Cantoni, L. (2019). Fashion communication in the digital age. In *FACTUM 19 fashion communication conference, Ascona, Switzerland, July 21–26, 2019*. Springer.
20. Noris, A., Nobile, T. H., Kalbaska, N., & Cantoni, L. (2021). Digital fashion: A systematic literature review. A perspective on marketing and communication. *Journal of Global Fashion Marketing, 12*, 32–46. https://doi.org/10.1080/20932685.2020.1835522
21. Nobile, T. H., Noris, A., Kalbaska, N., & Cantoni, L. (2021). A review of digital fashion research: Before and beyond communication and marketing. *International Journal of Fashion Design, Technology and Education, 14*, 293–301. https://doi.org/10.1080/17543266.2021.1931476
22. Liu, B. (2020). *Sentiment analysis: Mining opinions, sentiments, and emotions* (2nd ed.). Cambridge University Press.
23. Zou, Y., Luh, D.-B., & Lu, S. (2022). Public perceptions of digital fashion: An analysis of sentiment and Latent Dirichlet Allocation topic modeling. *Frontiers in Psychology, 13*, 986838. https://doi.org/10.3389/fpsyg.2022.986838
24. SanMiguel, P., Guercini, S., & Sádaba, T. (2019). The impact of attitudes towards influencers amongst millennial fashion buyers. *SComS, 18*. https://doi.org/10.24434/j.scoms.2018.02.016
25. Singh, L. G., & Singh, S. R. (2021). Empirical study of sentiment analysis tools and techniques on societal topics. *Journal of Intelligent Information System, 56*, 379–407. https://doi.org/10.1007/s10844-020-00616-7
26. Novielli, N., Calefato, F., Dongiovanni, D., et al. (2020). Can we use se-specific sentiment analysis tools in a cross-platform setting? In *Proceedings of the 17th international conference on mining software repositories* (pp. 158–168). ACM.
27. Diaz, M. O., Jr. (2023). A domain-specific evaluation of the performance of selected web-based sentiment analysis platforms. *IJSECS, 9*, 1–9. https://doi.org/10.15282/ijsecs.9.1.2023.1.0105
28. Carvalho, A., Levitt, A., Levitt, S., et al. (2019). Off-the-shelf artificial intelligence technologies for sentiment and emotion analysis: A tutorial on using IBM natural language processing. *CAIS*, 918–943. https://doi.org/10.17705/1CAIS.04443
29. Ermakova, T., Henke, M., & Fabian, B. (2021). Commercial sentiment analysis solutions: A comparative study. In *Proceedings of the 17th international conference on web information systems and technologies* (pp. 103–114). SCITEPRESS - Science and Technology Publications, Online Streaming.
30. Carneros-Prado, D., Villa, L., Johnson, E., et al. (2023). Comparative study of large language models as emotion and sentiment analysis systems: A case-specific analysis of GPT vs. IBM

Watson. In J. Bravo & G. Urzáiz (Eds.), *Proceedings of the 15th international conference on ubiquitous computing & ambient intelligence (UCAmI 2023)* (pp. 229–239). Springer Nature.
31. IBM. IBM Watson natural language understanding. https://www.ibm.com/products/natural-language-understanding. Accessed 15 Nov 2024.
32. Salvador, C., Nakasone, A., & Pow-Sang, J. A. (2014). A systematic review of usability techniques in agile methodologies. In *Proceedings of the 7th Euro American conference on telematics and information systems* (pp. 1–6). ACM.
33. Fanqier. https://fanqier.cn
34. Nielsen, J. (1994). Enhancing the explanatory power of usability heuristics. In *Proceedings of the SIGCHI conference on human factors in computing systems* (pp. 152–158). ACM.
35. SentiStrength.
36. IBM Watson NLU. https://www.ibm.com/demos/live/natural-language-understanding/self-service/home
37. Kheiri, K., & Karimi, H. (2023). SentimentGPT: Exploiting GPT for advanced sentiment analysis and its departure from current machine learning. https://doi.org/10.48550/ARXIV.2307.10234.
38. Zhang W, Deng Y, Liu B, et al (2023) Sentiment analysis in the era of large language models: A reality check.
39. Dai, Z. (2024). *Enhancing fashion sentiment analysis: A conversational approach with integration of large language models*. Master's Thesis, Università della Svizzera italiana (USI).

Independent Games and Fashion: A New Frontier in Digital Aesthetics and Narratives

Tatiana León-Alberca, Daniela Calva-Cabrera, Alejandra Valerio Matos, and Angel Torres-Toukoumidis

Abstract This study explores the innovative intersection of independent video games and fashion, a domain that remains underexplored in academic research. By analyzing 20 independent fashion-themed games from platforms like itch.io and Game Jolt, the study investigates their typologies, narrative structures, gameplay mechanics, and digital aesthetics. The findings reveal a predominant focus on entertainment and self-expression, with most games enabling players to explore personal styles in safe, interactive environments. These games prioritize customization and creativity over traditional progression systems, providing players with a space to experiment with visual identity without societal pressures.

Keywords Independent video games · Digital fashion · Self-expression · Narrative structures · Gameplay mechanics

1 Introduction

The intersection of fashion and video games has become a fertile ground for innovation, where digital aesthetics meet consumer engagement strategies. As gaming evolves into a dominant cultural and economic force, brands have increasingly turned to this medium to connect with younger audiences and adapt to shifting consumer behaviors [1]. High-profile collaborations, such as Balenciaga's partnership

T. León-Alberca
Universidad Nacional de Educación, Cañar, Ecuador

D. Calva-Cabrera
Universidad Nacional de Loja, Loja, Ecuador

A. V. Matos
Instituto Tecnológico Santo Domingo, Santo Domingo, Dominican Republic

A. Torres-Toukoumidis (✉)
Universidad Politécnica Salesiana, Cuenca, Ecuador
e-mail: atorrest@ups.edu.ec

P. von Wachenfeldt et al. (eds.), *Fashion Communication in the Digital Age*, Springer Proceedings in Business and Economics,
https://doi.org/10.1007/978-3-031-99481-4_15

with Fortnite, exemplify how fashion brands are embedding themselves within gaming environments to deliver immersive experiences that go beyond traditional advertising leveraging interactivity and visual storytelling to deepen emotional connections with players [2].

These partnerships signal a paradigm shift, where fashion moves from physical runways to virtual worlds. Gaming offers brands new avenues for engagement, enabling them to create digital outfits, sell virtual and physical products, and generate unique forms of revenue [3]. Avatar customization has become a significant touchpoint, allowing players to explore identity through digital self-expression. This trend reflects a broader cultural movement where digital and physical fashion converge, creating hybrid consumption models that challenge traditional sociological perspectives on fashion [4].

While the existing literature has extensively explored collaborations between mainstream games and fashion brands, the role of independent video games remains largely overlooked. Indie games, distinct for their creative autonomy and experimental approaches, occupy a unique space within the gaming ecosystem and represent a growing segment of this industry. Juul identifies indie games as a cultural movement distinct from mainstream gaming, noting their emphasis on individuality and craftsmanship [5].

These games often prioritize artistic expression and niche narratives, which may align more closely with the ethos of fashion nowadays than the commercially driven strategies of mainstream titles. The aesthetic values of independent games align closely with the maker movement, which emphasizes material honesty and artisanal production [6]. Costume and avatar design within indie games often reflect the same principles of authenticity and craft that define their broader aesthetic [7]. These concepts parallel contemporary fashion's turn toward sustainable practices and bespoke designs, suggesting a fertile ground for interdisciplinary exploration. Furthermore, indie games often adopt a more intimate and reflective approach to storytelling, providing a platform for nuanced explorations of identity and self-expression.

Moreover, independent games have demonstrated the potential to influence other cultural industries, including music and film, by fostering collaborations that challenge traditional production hierarchies [8]. The collaborative potential between indie games and fashion lies in their shared emphasis on creativity, individuality, and authenticity. The experimental spirit of indie games could inspire fashion designers to explore unconventional approaches to digital clothing and virtual identity, extending the boundaries of what constitutes "fashion" in digital contexts.

2 Methods

The exploratory nature of this study arises from its innovative focus on the intersection between independent video games and fashion, a domain largely absent from formal studies. The general objective of this study is to analyze independent video games that explore fashion as a new field of aesthetic and narrative innovation, assessing their potential to represent identities and lifestyles within virtual spaces. To achieve this, several specific objectives were set: (1) to examine the gameplay components and game typologies in fashion-themed independent video games; (2) to analyze the narrative structures and underlying purposes of these games, and finally, (3). to describe the digital aesthetics employed in these games, highlighting stylistic approaches that foster immersive and expressive experiences. Together, these objectives provide a comprehensive framework to understand how indie games incorporate fashion in novel ways.

Independent video games hold particular significance in this study due to their creative freedom [9], which allows developers to explore themes like fashion that rarely find representation in commercial titles. Unlike mainstream games, which are often bound by commercial expectations, independent games enable developers to experiment with unique aesthetic and narrative approaches, giving players access to customizable and culturally resonant experiences [10]. Indie games thus become ideal platforms for players to explore personal identity, aesthetics, and culture within virtual environments, making them a valuable subject for this investigation into fashion [11].

The methodological design employed is content analysis, a systematic approach used widely in both video game and fashion studies. Content analysis allows for the detailed dissection of aesthetic and narrative elements within each game, facilitating structured insights into how these elements shape player interactions and perceptions [12]. This approach helped to reveal the deeper cultural and emotional layers embedded in independent games, particularly those centered on fashion themes, providing an analytical framework that highlights the multidimensional nature of these games.

The primary data collection method employed was participant observation, wherein researchers engaged with the selected video games to examine their mechanics, narratives, and aesthetics from the player's perspective. This methodological approach facilitated a direct and immersive understanding of the integration of fashion within gameplay and its role in identity expression in virtual environments. Through active interaction with the games, thematic patterns and customization opportunities were systematically documented, enabling a more precise analysis of fashion representation in independent video games [13].

The procedure of this study was extensive, involving the selection of video games from two leading independent gaming platforms, itch.io and Game Jolt. These platforms were chosen for their accessibility, as they offer free and open content compatible with various operating systems, which streamlined the selection and download process. A total of 20 games were selected, based on their thematic alignment with fashion listed below (Table 1):

The analysis of the selected games is articulated around three fundamental criteria, each of which is aligned with the specific objectives of the study. These criteria allow for a comprehensive examination of the game dynamics, narrative structures, and aesthetic elements involved in the representation of fashion within the digital environment. To ensure a systematic and rigorous evaluation, each criterion is broken down into sub-criteria that address key dimensions of design and player experience (Table 2).

Table 1 Independent videogames sample and fashion

Platform	Game	Developer
Itch.io	Artificial Fashionista	KigyoDev
Itch.io	Gacha Life 2	Lunime
Itch.io	Gentleman Dress Up	Tsingeli
Itch.io	Threads	GlobalGoalsCentre
Itch.io	Britney Dress Up Adventure!	JuanaVlntina
Itch.io	Tailor Tales	Celianna
Itch.io	Style Dress Up	Druva
Itch.io	Queenfluencer	Laia Bee
Itch.io	FashionFLASH	Tehstripe
Itch.io	Besties' Day Out	Pulereen
Gamejolt	Dress Up Chibi	Eyeless_artist
Gamejolt	Saira's Boutique	Csharks Games
Gamejolt	Sweet Girl Mia Dress Up Game	Oyuncuk
Gamejolt	Avakin Life	GameLoop
Gamejolt	Tailor Tales	Celianna
Gamejolt	Barbie Make Up Game	Oyuncuk
Gamejolt	Minipete's Dress-Me-Up-Game	Minipete
Gamejolt	Kewters Showroom	127trbl
Gamejolt	Cutie Girls Dress Up	g8games
Gamejolt	Cute Dressup	Nihaojiitchi

Table 2 Analysis criteria

Analysis criteria	Sub-criteria	Description
Gameplay typologies and components	Game typologies	Classification of games according to their objectives and their impact on players. Four categories are identified: (a) Serious games, designed to offer educational experiences through simulations and interactive scenarios; (b) Persuasive games, whose purpose is to influence players' perceptions and attitudes by promoting specific ideas or positions; (c) Expressive games, aimed at raising awareness of cultural, social, and psychological issues through interactive narratives; and (d) Entertainment games, focused exclusively on recreation and digital leisure [14].
	Gameplay components	Evaluation of the structural and dynamic elements that shape the game experience. Three key dimensions are considered: (a) Mechanics, which include systems such as levels, missions, and rewards; (b) Dynamics, which comprise the fluidity of the game, the diversity of objectives, and the social interaction within the virtual environment; and (c) Aesthetics, which encompass the visual and emotional aspects that generate curiosity, satisfaction, and connection with the player [15].

(continued)

Table 2 (continued)

Analysis criteria	Sub-criteria	Description
Narrative structure and purpose	Narrative structure	Analysis of the design of virtual worlds, objects, non-playable characters (NPCs), and events. It is classified into: (a) Video Game Worlds: include modes without direct access, individual environments with linear narrative, multiple choice mazes, open worlds with side quests, and Role-Playing Game (RPGs) where decisions are key; (b) Objects: encompass non-interactive (decorative), equippable, modifiable, destructible, and manufacturable elements; (c) NPCs: distinguish between story-driven characters (that enrich the narrative) and interactive ones without story; and (d) Events: comprise mission statement, secondary options to deviate from the plot, and dynamic states where the outcome varies according to the player's actions [16].
	Purpose	Identification of the fundamental objectives of digital fashion games: (a) Facilitate self-expression, allowing users to model their identity and preferences through avatars and virtual clothing; (b) Promote social interaction, through online communities and virtual fashion events; (c) Provide immersive and sensory experiences, through technologies such as augmented reality (AR) and virtual reality (VR); (d) Create playful environments, where fashion functions as an interactive space for avatar and mission customization; and (e) Encourage interaction with brands, encouraging user participation in digital fashion experiences that reinforce loyalty [17].
Aesthetics [18].	Cultural perspective	Consideration of digital interfaces as artifacts capable of generating emotional responses and symbolic meanings.
	Functionalist perspective	Focus on aesthetics as a determining factor to improve the usability and accessibility of digital gaming environments.
	Experiential perspective	Analysis of the ability of games to generate engaging and immersive visual and sensory experiences.
	Techno-futuristic perspective	Evaluation of the impact of digital environments on human perception and interaction within advanced technological spaces.

For data collection and analysis, three researchers played each of the selected titles between April 10 and July 10, 2024. Each researcher conducted multiple play sessions, documenting in detail their observations regarding the gameplay, narrative structure, and aesthetic aspects of the games. Subsequently, the collected data were organized and coded through Atlas.ti software, using the descriptive coding method, widely employed in content analysis [19]. This procedure made it possible to identify recurrent patterns and divergences in the representation of fashion within the games analyzed, establishing thematic connections between the different titles.

The results of this analysis provide a comprehensive perspective on the role of fashion in independent video games, evidencing its function as a means of aesthetic and narrative expression. By examining the relationship between gameplay elements, narrative structures, and aesthetic strategies, the study provides a theoretical foundation for future research at the intersection of digital fashion and video game design. Furthermore, the findings underscore the potential of indie games to redefine cultural perceptions of fashion, identity, and self-expression in virtual environments, solidifying their relevance in the evolution of contemporary digital aesthetics.

3 Results

3.1 Game Typologies

The typology of games analyzed on itch.io and Game Jolt reveals a strong inclination toward entertainment games (16/20) which constitute the majority of titles on both platforms. This focus on entertainment reflects a trend in popular game design, where the intention is to provide an interactive and relaxed space, emphasizing creativity and personal expression rather than competition or complex challenges typical of other online games.

For instance, *Gacha Life 2* on itch.io allows users to design characters and explore a digital environment without a mandatory final goal, prioritizing self-expression and avatar creation over level progression or point accumulation. Similarly, on Game Jolt, *Dress Up Chibi* follows a comparable approach, enabling players (primarily children) to style characters without any structured narrative.

However, itch.io does feature some persuasive games. One example is *Threads*, which incorporates an educational narrative aimed at raising awareness about issues related to fashion and ethical consumption. This persuasive approach encourages players to reflect on their fashion choices rather than merely enjoying the aesthetic aspect. Similarly, *Queenfluencer* seeks to portray the dynamics of social media ecosystems and public perception, raising awareness about the psychological and cultural effects of influencers. Although less common, persuasive games represent a growing trend where entertainment and education intertwine, driving a shift toward fashion games that also address social issues.

Thus, it can be suggested that fashion games on the analyzed platforms predominantly cater to entertainment, with variations targeting a diverse audience from those seeking a playful experience to those interested in exploring reflective and persuasive dimensions, not only in design but also in promoting responsible consumption.

3.2 Gameplay Components

To analyze the mechanics of the 20 independent games, the presence of components such as points, levels, badges, missions, leaderboards, or other progression systems was assessed to determine whether the player had successfully achieved an objective or failed within the game. It was found that in the majority of cases (17/20), the mechanics adopt a freeform style, emphasizing customization and the collection of clothing items. This approach allows users to explore a wide range of styles and experiment with combinations of outfits, accessories, and visual designs, albeit without necessarily presenting a concrete goal within the game ecosystem.

In this context, it can be argued that the mechanics observed in the analyzed games facilitate creative exploration, immersing users in continuous interaction. Rather than focusing on competition, the primary objective lies in exploration and the construction of appearances that express the player's visual identity and creativity. These findings are particularly significant as they align with the game typology described in the previous section. A notable example is *Britney Dress Up Adventure!* (itch.io), where players navigate various areas, collecting clothing and accessories to unlock customization options. Similarly, in *Sweet Girl Mia Dress Up Game* (Game Jolt), there are no levels, badges, or rankings; once players complete their creation, they can take Mia to different settings for photoshoots.

On another note, games such as *Tailor Tales*, *FashionFLASH* (itch.io), and *Saira's Boutique* (Game Jolt) feature mechanics characterized by a progression system typical of online games. Points are awarded or penalties applied based on adherence to specific rules or dress codes. In these games, platforms may assign a rating, or alternatively, players accumulate money depending on the clients they serve.

In terms of dynamics—understood as a system that formalizes gameplay—factors such as pacing, diversification of objectives, and interpersonal purpose are included. It is revealed that there is a predominant focus on style exploration and avatar customization, which form the core of the gameplay experience. This focus encourages repetition and fosters an emotional connection with the avatar.

For instance, games like *Gacha Life 2* and *Artificial Fashionista* (itch.io) maintain a fast-paced, continuous rhythm centered on the collection of outfits and accessories, allowing players to steadily progress through levels of customization. This consistent pacing supports a quick feedback loop and short-term gratification, making these games suitable for frequent play sessions.

Conversely, games like *Threads* (itch.io) integrate narrative objectives where player decisions directly impact the story's progression. This fosters a more reflective and strategic gameplay experience, contrasting with titles like *Dress Up Chibi* (Game Jolt), where the simplicity of objectives sustains a more relaxed dynamic. *Avakin Life* (Game Jolt) stands out in this regard by incorporating both customization and social interaction, promoting a complex interpersonal dynamic that enriches the purpose of gameplay.

In titles such as *Queenfluencer* (itch.io), players make decisions that influence social relationships and reputation, adding a layer of competition and social interaction that enhances the interpersonal purpose of the game. In *Avakin Life* (Game Jolt), this interaction is more explicit, as players visually compete in a three-dimensional environment for the attention and approval of others, further strengthening the social component.

Games such as *Gentleman Dress Up* (itch.io) and *Sweet Girl Mia Dress Up Game* (Game Jolt) evoke emotions of satisfaction and pride through a colorful and detailed aesthetic that emphasizes the customization process. In contrast, games like *Threads*, with its simple and accessible visual design, aim to elicit a sense of learning, aligning its aesthetics with the game's educational purpose.

In titles like *Style Dress Up* and *FashionFLASH*, available on itch.io, emotions are stirred by the curiosity to discover the final outcome of combining various garments. Similarly, in *Avakin Life* and *Tailor Tales*, featured on Game Jolt, the motivation lies in the pursuit of better and more complete accessories, which serves as a key element in keeping players engaged with their mission or the ultimate completion of the game.

3.3 Narrative Structure

Narrative in fashion games is often a secondary and simplified feature. However, it plays a fundamental structural role, acting as the thematic axis that unifies and gives coherence to the game. This narrative is composed of elements such as virtual worlds, objects, non-playable characters (NPCs), and events that connect the user's experience into a cohesive story.

In the cases analyzed, it is evident that narratives predominantly develop within individual settings or through optional missions. These two approaches allow players to focus on a specific activity, where avatar customization takes precedence without the pressure of a constant narrative. This creates a gameplay environment where self-expression is central. For instance, in *Britney Dress Up Adventure!* (itch.io), while players have the option to explore, the game follows a unique narrative framework. A similar approach is observed in *Barbie Make Up Game* (Game Jolt), where the "individual setting" narrative without strict missions enhances the player's autonomy and freedom.

In contrast, *Avakin Life* (Game Jolt) develops its narrative through 3D virtual environments that simulate a digital social life. Although there is no structured story centered on a primary objective, players can engage in social scenarios and events, allowing them to experience fashion in a socialized and adaptive context (Fig. 1).

Regarding objects, it is observed that the majority of the analyzed games (14/20) feature equippable items. This implies that users, throughout the gameplay experience, acquire certain accessories that can be utilized either immediately or at later stages. Examples of this approach can be found in titles such as *Gentleman Dress Up*, *Britney Dress Up Adventure!*, and *Besties' Day Out* on itch.io, as well as *Dress Up Chibi* and *Barbie Make Up Game* available on Game Jolt (Fig. 2).

In most of the analyzed games (12/20), NPCs play a fundamental role in the narrative design of fashion games, as they are imbued with backstories that enrich the overall storyline. These characters not only provide dialogues that facilitate interaction with the player but also act as agents of emotional connection, creating bonds that enhance immersion within the game universe. In other cases, NPCs lack

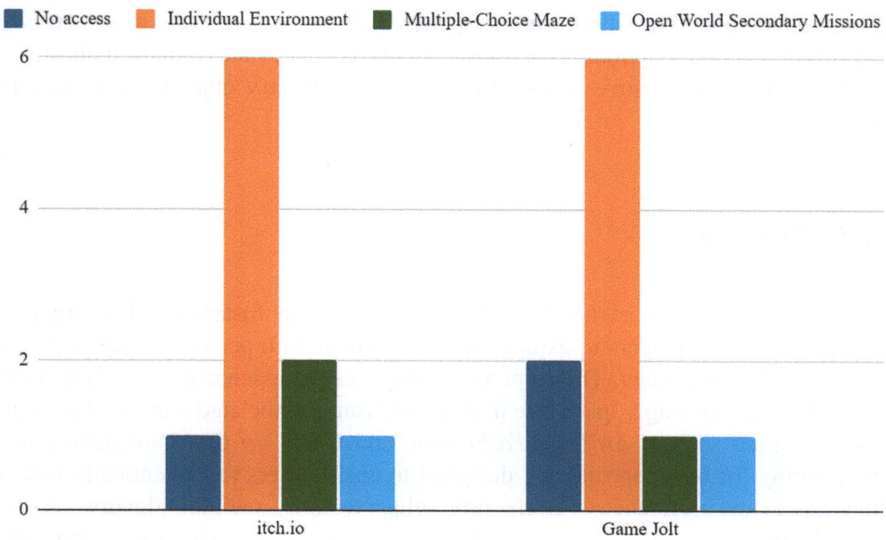

Fig. 1 Narrative structure in independent fashion games

Fig. 2 Avatar NPCs in *Barbie Make Up Game*

specific backstories (8/20) and instead serve a purely illustrative function, acting as contextual elements that ensure coherence and contribute to a more complex and meaningful narrative experience.

The majority of events in these games are structured as mission statements (14/20), focusing on specific actions that the player must perform, usually related to dressing the central character or selected avatar. A less common approach involves dynamic state cores (5/20), where outcomes depend directly on the player's decisions. Notable examples include *Threads* and *Avakin Life*, which offer a personalized and interaction-driven experience. To a lesser extent, games feature worlds of secondary options (1/20), allowing players to deviate from the main storyline to explore alternative paths or fulfill complementary objectives, as seen in *Gacha Life 2*.

3.4 Purpose

The primary purpose of fashion-related games lies in fostering self-expression (14/20), allowing players to explore and experiment with personal styles within a safe digital environment. This approach transposes the essence of fashion into the virtual realm, offering a space free from the pressures associated with societal standards. Games such as *Artificial Fashionista* and *Dress Up Chibi* are particularly noteworthy for being specifically designed to enable users to authentically reflect their tastes and preferences, thereby promoting creativity and individuality.

Self-expression in these games allows players to freely experiment with their visual identity and current trends without restrictions. In a virtual setting like *Dress Up Chibi*, users can try out styles they might not attempt in real life. This ability to experiment in a safe gaming environment highlights a significant trend in digital fashion: the pursuit of experiences that enable users to express their identities and explore new ways of being and presenting themselves.

Another of the purposes identified in this analysis, although with a lower incidence (3/20), is the promotion of social interaction. This aspect allows players to connect with others online, encouraging the development of interpersonal relationships, as observed in *Tailor Tales* and *Avakin Life*. On the other hand, some titles focus on providing immersive (3/20) and sensory experiences, with *Threads* and *Besties' Day Out* standing out. These games not only encourage informed decision-making but also invite players to reflect on the ethical implications of consumption, integrating an experimental approach into both their narrative and gameplay mechanics.

3.5 Digital Aesthetics

The digital aesthetics of the analyzed games reveal a preference for functionalist (10/20) and experiential (7/20) approaches. This translates into accessible, visually appealing aesthetics designed to emphasize fashion and character customization. Color palettes are often vibrant and varied, and interface designs are intuitive, facilitating interaction and enabling users to focus on the act of personalization without unnecessary distractions. For instance, *Gacha Life 2* features a vibrant and colorful aesthetic popular among fashion games targeting a younger audience. Its "chibi" visual style and cartoonish characters make the game both appealing and accessible, while its interface remains intuitive and easy to navigate. This functionalist approach is also evident in *Saira's Boutique* (Game Jolt), which employs a minimalist and simple aesthetic aimed at directing the player's attention toward the clothing and customization elements.

In contrast, *Threads* adopts a cultural aesthetic approach (1/20), utilizing a subdued color palette and an interface design that encourages reflection and informed decision-making about fashion. This less flashy aesthetic is deliberate, aiming to evoke an atmosphere of introspection and analysis rather than superficial entertainment.

The choice of aesthetics in fashion games plays a crucial role in shaping user perception and representing fashion within the digital environment. Games with a functionalist and user-friendly aesthetic promote a straightforward and accessible experience, while those with a cultural or reflective focus foster a deeper connection, aligning with the persuasive or educational nature of the game.

4 Conclusions

This study provides a detailed examination of how independent video games integrate fashion as a narrative and aesthetic medium, offering several significant findings. First, the analysis highlights that independent fashion games primarily serve as platforms for entertainment, with a strong emphasis on creativity and self-expression. Most games (14/20) allow players to explore personal styles in a low-pressure environment, encouraging experimentation with visual identity. At the same time, a smaller subset of games incorporates persuasive or educational elements, broadening the thematic scope and addressing social and cultural issues. The gameplay components in these games often adopt a freeform approach, prioritizing customization and the collection of equippable items over conventional progression mechanics like levels or leaderboards.

Narrative structures in these games, while generally simplified, play a pivotal role in creating thematic coherence. Most titles rely on individual exploration or optional missions, giving players autonomy in how they engage with the game. However, some games, such as *Avakin Life* and *Threads*, incorporate dynamic or socially interactive narratives, fostering deeper engagement and reflection on themes related to fashion and identity. These narrative strategies underscore the versatility of fashion games in combining entertainment with meaningful storytelling.

The aesthetic strategies employed in these games reveal a clear preference for functionalist and experiential designs. Bright color palettes, intuitive interfaces, and visually appealing environments dominate, ensuring accessibility and usability for a broad audience. In contrast, some games adopt culturally oriented aesthetics, as seen in *Threads*, which uses subdued visuals to encourage reflection and informed decision-making. This aesthetic diversity highlights the role of design in shaping user experience and reinforcing the thematic goals of each game.

Additionally, the study emphasizes the innovative ways in which independent games incorporate fashion as a core theme. By providing a platform for players to express their identity and creativity, these games expand the possibilities of fashion representation in virtual spaces. Titles like *Queenfluencer* and *Threads* illustrate how digital fashion games can address broader social and cultural issues, demonstrating their potential as tools for both entertainment and education

Finally, although less common, the inclusion of social interaction and immersive experiences adds considerable depth to the gaming experience. Games such as *Avakin Life* combine customization with social dynamics, allowing players to engage with others while exploring their personal styles. This combination of individual expression and communal interaction highlights the dual capacity of fashion games to entertain and foster meaningful connections.

Overall, this study underscores the potential of independent video games to transform digital fashion landscapes by offering innovative approaches to identity, aesthetics, and social engagement. Future research could explore how these games influence identity construction, the ethical dimensions of digital fashion, and the integration of emerging technologies such as augmented reality and virtual reality to further enhance player immersion. By doing so, researchers can deepen their understanding of the intersections between fashion, gaming, and virtual experiences.

References

1. Patruti, P., Zbuchea, A., & Pînzaru, F. (2023). Fashion joining online gaming and the Metaverse. In *Proceedings of the 17th international conference on business excellence* (pp. 1065–1074). https://doi.org/10.2478/picbe-2023-0096
2. Lopes, F. D., Lucas, I. B., & Farias, S. D. (2022). Virtual fashion: Análise da coleção da Balenciaga e Fortnite. *Revista Crises, 2*(1), 66–78. https://doi.org/10.51359/2763-7425.2022.253736
3. Noris, A., Sabatini, N., & Cantoni, L. (2023). Fashion games, fashion in games and gamification in fashion. A first map. In M. Kurosu & A. Hashizume (Eds.), *Human-computer interaction. HCII 2023, Lecture notes in computer science* (Vol. 14013). Springer. https://doi.org/10.1007/978-3-031-35602-5_34
4. Varini, M. (2023). (Meta)morphosis. The giant "bug" in the fashion system. *Connessioni remote. Artivismo_Teatro_Tecnologia, 6*, 1–15. https://doi.org/10.54103/connessioni/22044
5. Juul, J. (2019). *The art of failure: An essay on the pain of playing video games*. MIT Press.
6. Juul, J. (2014). High-tech low-tech authenticity: The creation of independent style at the independent games festival. In *International conference on foundations of digital games* (pp. 1–10).
7. Makryniotis, T. (2018). Fashion and costume design in electronic entertainment—Bridging the gap between character and fashion design. *Fashion Practice, 10*(1), 118–199. https://doi.org/10.1080/17569370.2017.1412595
8. Hauge, A., & Hracs, B. J. (2010). See the sound, hear the style: Collaborative linkages between indie musicians and fashion designers in local scenes. *Industry and Innovation, 17*(1), 113–129. https://doi.org/10.1080/13662710903573893
9. Torres-Toukoumidis, A., León-Alberca, T., & Henriquez-Mendoza, E. (2024). Echoes of the gothic: Transmedia reinterpretations of Edgar Allan Poe's legacy in independent films and video games. *Humanities and Social Sciences Communications, 11*(1), 1–12. https://doi.org/10.1057/s41599-024-03370-1
10. Merchán-Romero, J., & Torres-Toukoumidis, A. (2021). Types of gameplay in newsgames. Case of persuasive messages about COVID-19. *Journalism and Media, 2*(4), 746–757. https://doi.org/10.3390/journalmedia2040044

11. Torres-Toukoumidis, A., Gutiérrez, I. M., Becerra, M. H., León-Alberca, T., & Curiel, C. P. (2023). Let's play democracy, exploratory analysis of political video games. *Societies, 13*(2), 28. https://doi.org/10.3390/soc13020028
12. Krippendorff, K. (2009). *The content analysis reader*. Sage.
13. Barbosa, D., Schneider, G., Mossmann, J., & Santos, P. D. (2020). Usability and gameplay evaluation on mobile games: A user-centred application proposal. *International Journal of Learning Technology, 15*(2), 107–129. https://doi.org/10.1504/IJLT.2020.109570
14. Ratan, R. A., & Ritterfeld, U. (2009). Classifying serious games. In *Serious games* (pp. 32–46). Routledge.
15. Junior, R., & Silva, F. (2021). Redefining the MDA framework—The pursuit of a game design ontology. *Information, 12*(10), 395. https://doi.org/10.3390/info12100395
16. Aarseth, E. (2012). A narrative theory of games. In *Proceedings of the international conference on the foundations of digital games* (pp. 29–133). https://doi.org/10.1145/2282338.2282365
17. Park, J., & Chun, J. (2023). Evolution of fashion as play in the digital space. *Fashion Practice, 15*(2), 256–278. https://doi.org/10.1080/17569370.2022.2149837
18. Udsen, L. E., & Jørgensen, A. H. (2005). The aesthetic turn: Unravelling recent aesthetic approaches to human-computer interaction. *Digital Creativity, 16*(4), 205–216. https://doi.org/10.1080/14626260500476564
19. Williams, M., & Moser, T. (2019). The art of coding and thematic exploration in qualitative research. *International Management Review, 15*(1), 45–55.

Towards Synthetic Imaginaries: Augmenting Fashion Product, Communication, and Retail Design with GAI

Greta Rizzi and Angelica Vandi

Abstract Recent Generative AI advancements, resulting in sophisticated image-generation tools, are revolutionising the Cultural and Creative Industries, impacting the entire value chain. In fashion design, these tools have become integral to the industry pipeline, supporting designers at various stages of creative processes. In particular, by leveraging vast datasets to generate synthetic images, AI has the potential to transform fashion archives into dynamic resources, enabling brands to explore and reimagine their visual heritage. Within this transformative context, the paper explores how designer-AI co-created outputs can be applied across three distinct areas of fashion design: Product development, Communication, and Retail. Through case studies analysis, three trajectories are delineated to enhance fashion visual language and renew creative processes. Ethical issues related to reconfiguring the fashion designer's role will be addressed, contributing to the ongoing debate on the relationship between human and AI creativity.

Keywords Generative AI · Fashion design · Fashion archive · Human–AI co-creativity · Fashion communication

1 Introduction

The integration of AI into the creative sector has grown exponentially in recent years, with applications spanning from content creation and enhancement to post-production workflow and information extraction [1]. Focusing on content creation, the inclusion of AI tools is significantly gaining ground in fashion companies, explicitly relying on brands' past collections in the form of archival data. In tandem, fashion corporate archives are rich repositories of historical, cultural, and creative

G. Rizzi (✉) · A. Vandi
Politecnico di Milano, Milan, MI, Italy
e-mail: greta.rizzi@polimi.it; angelica.vandi@polimi.it

P. von Wachenfeldt et al. (eds.), *Fashion Communication in the Digital Age*,
Springer Proceedings in Business and Economics,
https://doi.org/10.1007/978-3-031-99481-4_16

value, encompassing sketches, photographs, prototypes, material samples, and ephemera [2] that collectively narrate a brand's evolution and identity. Despite this wealth of documentation, only a few brands have made their heritage a valuable corporate asset [3], keeping that value as a static historical reference, with much of its potential that remains underused for the construction of contemporary brand image [4], rather than dynamic resources for innovation [5]. However, "finding (in the sense of understanding) the heritage in a brand may well be a path to unlocking its value for the company by enabling the brand's past and present to strengthen its future" [6]. However, only a few pioneering brands have adopted Generative AI (GAI) as a tool capable of reinterpreting archival content due to the difficulty of considering and subsequently transforming the archive into a digital dataset for data scraping and inspiration. This chapter, therefore, seeks to explore the interplay between archival heritage and the design of brand identity processes, investigating how GAI can contribute to the visualisation of innovative proposals for product design, brand communication, and retail environments. Following an overview of the role of heritage in shaping a fashion brand's visual identity, this chapter will delve into the positioning of GAI as a strategic tool for reimagining these elements, providing insights and best practices from the industry.

2 Building Brand Identity in Fashion Design

As a Cultural and Creative Industry (CCI), fashion fosters the creation of products and services which have high cultural content [7], in the sense "of a whole of shared symbolic values and practices in the social communities sphere" [8]. These result from collective elaboration processes, which materialise into tangible and intangible artefacts, seldom being codified into text. In this context, design plays a central role by visually synthesising cultural signs and symbols from various stakeholders while creating material and immaterial artefacts within a branded framework. This process is the foundation for building a brand's identity and is deeply rooted in its archival heritage. Indeed, archival materials not only witness a brand's visual identity—such as logos, colours, and visual rules used for communication—but also support the construction of a chosen narrative [9] that constitutes what the brand stands for in the market and its cultural relevance for the customer, eventually increasing brand awareness. Indeed, the presence and consolidation of a brand within the collective imagination make its codes crucial to consumers' perception and meaning-attribution processes [10]. The application of stylistic codes to seasonal inspiration research represents the primary goal of the creative development process within a fashion company, structured across three primary macro-functions: (1) product development, led by the creative director, (2) communication development, overseen by the artistic director, and (3) retail development, managed by the retail general manager [8].

These three divisions work closely throughout the product development process to make creative decisions consistent with the product content, to communicate and design events to launch them, and, finally, to target products to end users during the retail phase. This reasoning converges on the concept of brand aesthetic [11], an intrinsic component of a fashion brand's identity which shapes and informs the product, communication, and retail dimensions. According to Floch, brand aesthetics comprises stable and specific elements primarily derived from visual perceptions but also encompassing the broader sensory sphere. Floch's framework emphasises that a semiotic manifestation—a production of meaning—emerges from the interplay between content and expression, highlighting how conceptual and sensory components work together to create a consistent and unique brand image. Indeed, the content is the signified, the material part of the sign [12], while its visual representation becomes the vehicle, the medium through which the content is manifested [13]. To further dig into the context, another perspective sees the communicative medium as intrinsically connected to the content of fashion itself.

This view, extending beyond semiotics, argues that fashion does not exist without the apparatuses, technologies, and communication systems—"the ephemera"—that construct its meaning [2, 4]. Words and images have been central to fashion production, circulation, and dissemination [14]. In his seminal work, *The Fashion System* (first published in 1990), Barthes does not address real fashion but rather the fashion described in magazines: garments are entirely converted into text, and even images function only as tools for textual transposition. Barthes explores "written-clothing" and "image-clothing" [15] as two principal types of documentation narrating the same object but through different communicative modes, both embedded within the fashion magazine. Similarly, Warburg uses the concept of "the word to the image" to confer upon images the same expressive power as language [16]. Written fashion and fashion photography are thus considered original structures, each tied to distinct semiotic dimensions: the verbal and the visual. These structures possess syntax and language, conveying information and enriching the garment's meaning.

This context further underscores how fashion exists as a network of references constantly constructed and deconstructed by the individuals who negotiate, interpret, or receive its meaning, all this among various media [17, 18]. Indeed, cinema, music, digital media, and advertising are the spaces where fashion operates as a syncretic, intertextual system [19]. However, it is necessary to point out that the multiplicity of figures and contexts where fashion could be replicated blurs the line between real creative input and copying, raising concerns about authenticity in fashion and the boundaries of inspiration within the creative process.

3 The Interplay of Human and AI Creativity

The relationship between humans and AI is now grounded in a genuine dialogue conducted in natural language, where information is expressed through prompts that describe the characteristics expected of the tool to return in its output [20]. The turning point in this paradigm shift came in early 2022 when OpenAI publicly released DALL-E, an image generator, and ChatGPT, a text generator simulating human-like responses, making advanced AI capabilities accessible to the broader public [21]. From this moment on, there has been a rapid proliferation of GAI tools, which have increasingly integrated into the value chain of the CCIs [22]. The creative capabilities of AI have introduced new perspectives into the long-standing debate on the origins of creativity, in which different psychological, social, and philosophical viewpoints are compared in an attempt to discover its true nature [23]. The discussion proves to be largely elusive, grounded in self-contradictory theories that perpetuate myths about creativity and reinforce its perception as an extraordinary phenomenon, [24] often associated with notions of "sudden illumination" or the so-called creative leaps, which diverge from the processual nature of design creativity [25].

Despite its intrinsic vagueness, attempts have been made to define creative expression. The first definition proposed by Stein (1953) bases the recognition of a product as creative on three conditions: (a) its perceived usefulness within a social group, (b) its origin in existing knowledge, and (c) the significance of both individual and collective perceptions of the resulting creation [26]. From this initial theorisation, several variations have been developed, including Csikszentmihalyi's (1988) "*The Systems Model of Creativity*", which suggests that creativity arises from the interaction of three components: an individual, a domain of knowledge or practice, and a field of experts recognise and validate the creative contribution [27]. Boden provided an alternative interpretation of the phenomenon, "Creativity is the ability to come up with ideas or artefacts that are new, surprising, and valuable" [28]. After discussing these interpretations, it emerges how GAI fits into these criteria, emphasising its role in the creative process as its natural evolution. Moreover, its integration into creative practices opens the horizon to new forms of creation, such as Computational Creativity, a subdiscipline of AI focused on developing and studying computational agents capable of creating novel artefacts and ideas whose cultural value is socially recognised [29].

Despite AI's ability to fulfil the requirements of effectiveness by exploiting vast datasets consisting of billions of pieces of information to generate reasonable responses to user input, AI lacks both intentionality, understood as the intrinsic motivation that characterises human creative behaviour, and authenticity, defined as the ability to act based on deep grounded personal desires [30].

Consequently, the perspective this chapter wants to follow is that AI-generated creativity can only be considered synthetic; no matter how "intelligent" AI is, it is inherently incapable of achieving creativity in the human sense. Therefore, shifting towards the "collective creativity" paradigm is necessary, emphasising collaboration between humans and algorithms. Computational tools thus become new resources supporting human creativity, not replacements for it. Indeed, the results generated by AI are inherently stochastic and only acquire meaning through human intervention, which creates the conditions for integrating the generation into the system of creativity, providing a context and subjecting it to a process of judgment. In this dynamic, a sense of "communion" characterises the intimacy of the human–designer relationship, in which designers project value and meaning onto the artificially generated creation, making the creation, de facto, meaningful [31].

4 The Role of Generative AI in Fashion

In this framework, Computational Creativity is reimagined from an exclusive product of algorithms to a result of a co-creation process between computational agents and humans, where both share responsibility [32]. From this perspective, AI holds the status of a medium: the latest tool integrated into the creative process [33]. Humanity has long relied on machines to enhance creative expression and materialisation. This path has evolved from perceiving technology as a mere auxiliary tool to recognising its increasingly central role in the creative process landing to the automatic generation of content driven by algorithms that exploit the predictive capabilities of AI [34]. Despite technological advances, AI remains deeply intertwined with human agency, reflecting the symbiotic relationship between technology and humans as a product of human knowledge and simultaneously an extension of human action [35].

Focusing exclusively on the use of GAI in the context of Professional Creativity, i.e., that form of creativity that requires specialised expertise in the field, this chapter wants to explore how these new tools can fit into already established processes [36]. In the fashion design domain, the last few decades have seen a progressive integration of AI applications across the industry, spanning research, design, development, and production [37]. As reported by McKinsey, 2023 marks a turning point in the integration of GAI within the industry, with tools such as Adobe Firefly, Midjourney, Runway, Stable Diffusion, and software from Google AI and OpenAI being employed across various stages of fashion collection development [38]. In the initial part of the process, during the conceptualisation phase, these tools demonstrated a strong ability to support the image-thinking approach [39], generating product briefs, mood boards, and visual content, drawing inspiration from historical brand materials [38]. In this dynamic, images play a significant role in identifying the problem and formulating the design solution [40]. Through an iterative method, the exploration of visual stimuli merges with the designer's imagination [41], transforming first ideas into proposals and ultimately culminating in solutions ready for implementation. The contribution of GAI goes beyond concept development and comprises collection communication and commercialisation. It holds significant potential in framing narratives and visuals that reflect brand identities, resonate with target audiences, and strengthen customer connections [42], contributing to the generation of copywriting, campaign photo shooting, and the hyper-personalisation of customer loyalty programmes and offers [38]. Regardless of the application area, the innovation introduced by GAI extends human capabilities by harnessing the power of algorithms in condensing knowledge and rapidly exploring archival datasets [43]. This alliance between human reasoning and machine calculation capabilities led to the definition of the "Hybrid Collective Intelligence" paradigm, where the interplay between human and machine capabilities is grounded in the principles of diversity, interconnectedness, and hierarchical decision-making [44]. This approach is also embraced by the CCIs and fashion designers, driving the augmentation of traditional design practices [45].

4.1 Archived Data: Feeding GAI Creativity

GAI tools have thus become an integral part of fashion designers' toolkits, hiding a much more complex technological architecture behind their user-friendly interfaces and excellent capabilities for rapidly generating effective outputs. In technical terms, generative models are based on a system that learns from the distribution of information within a training dataset and, based on user input, generates new results that replicate this distribution, producing outputs consistent with and similar to what the model has learned [46]. The generic nature of the data on which tools are built presents certain limitations in terms of applicability within specific domains. In the fashion industry, the vagueness and standardisation of the generated results often fail to meet designers' expectations, requiring refinement before they can be used effectively. Consequently, there is a growing demand for the development of customised software specifically tailored to the needs of the fashion design process [32]. Research is therefore moving towards developing models capable of learning garments' styles, silhouettes, and textures based on the deviations of the images reproduced in the dataset [47]. GAI tools for fashion should integrate methods that align with the designer's approach concerning the interaction while ensuring greater consistency between user input and the generated output. Regarding this last point, the focus falls on the data. Although hidden within the systems and invisible to users, it represents the true driving force behind the generation process and AI computational creativity. Archiving of information acquires a new meaning within this paradigm. Stored fashion images surpass their significance as cultural heritage and become an active source of inspiration [48]. This is the paradigm that fashion brands are beginning to embrace: transforming their proprietary archives into vast datasets. By leveraging AI processing capabilities, they gain a deeper understanding of design principles and patterns, leading to innovative synthetic design proposals that align with the brand's history and identity [49]. The archive changes its role from a mere repository to an augmented resource to be activated for contemporary applications [4]. There is a shift away from conservation and cataloguing purposes only towards data activation as renewed sources of inspiration [4]. This traces a new path, merging knowledge of the past with a vision of the future, shaping trajectories that assist fashion brands in preserving and reinforcing their identity and connection with their audience.

5 Methodology

The presented results, contextualised within the authors' PhD research, aim to frame how brands leverage GAI software to redefine creative processes and augment customer experiences [34] within product, communication, and retail environments. Specifically, this study adopts an exploratory and inductive approach based on a systematic analysis of the existing literature and an examination of selected best practices. The literature review aimed at mapping the state of the art as presented in the sections above while prompting fundamental reasoning on future implementation scenarios in the field. In parallel, the study of best practices provides empirical insights into successful implementations and innovative uses of GAI within the fashion sector, allowing for extracting key principles and application models.

Criteria selected to search for best practices are:

- Timeframe: 2020–2024
- Context: Product development, communication, and retail in fashion firms
- Technology used: GAI Software and tailored AI models

The integration of these two levels of analysis enabled the identification of future implementation trajectories. Indeed, following this inductive process, three trajectories are defined in the Results section, covering the product, communication, and retail environments. Each of the trajectories is supported by two best practices, selected among the case study research done as the backbone of ongoing research.

6 Results: Towards a Synthetic Imaginary

The trajectories described below want to contribute to the redefinition of mediatisation practices in fashion, which—as defined by Rocamora [50]—"does not mean focusing on the media themselves, but on how people and institutions in fashion have changed their practices for and with the media". In light of this, a structured analysis of potential implementations across product, communication, and retail contexts was developed, as outlined below.

6.1 Product: Augmenting Inspiration

The integration of GAI tools into product development processes has led to a significant redefinition of traditional design workflows, which typically begin with a creative brief, progress through the establishment of visual codes, and culminate in the creation of prototypes for the central collection. In this established process, designers are starting to employ GAI software as a means to enhance creative inspiration and facilitate visual ideation. By imputing sketches and desired details—such as fabrics, colour palettes, and patterns—into tools such as Stable Diffusion and Midjourney, designers and creative teams generate an array of unexpected visual elements that can be incorporated into fashion garments and accessories. However, the process of assembling a creative brief extends beyond visual ideation. It also includes developing the story that serves as the collection's foundation and coordinating new trends with the brand's visual identity. In this sense, text-based generative tools such as ChatGPT [51] have been beneficial for *enhancing the brief ideation stage* by providing a conceptual basis that combines brand narrative with trend-driven insights. The case of Ganni Copenhagen Spring 2024 Collection [52] highlights how the multimodal use of GAI can support the narrative aspects of the design process. Indeed, the collection began with a design brief generated by ChatGPT, which was initiated as an experiment by GANNI's creative director. The AI-generated brief offered a conceptual explorative foundation translated visually through images, then garments by the design team. The resulting collection maintained GANNI's signature aesthetic—part of the cultural background of GANNI designers—while showcasing a new sensibility conveyed by the brief generated. As a result of its extensive training on web-sourced textual data and its ability to restructure it into different text formats, ChatGPT offered alternative starting points that encourage creative thinking and reformulated trend research methods based on social-unstructured data. Another emerging application of GAI towards collection development lies in its ability *to be trained on specific archival references*, allowing brands to reinterpret their aesthetic codes and innovate within the boundaries of their visual heritage. A trailblazing example of this approach is the collaboration Acne Studios x Robbie [53] for the Men's Fall/Winter 2020 collection, which marked one of the earliest experiments using AI-driven fashion archives for collection development. Thousands of looks from Acne Studios' archives were input into the neural network, which, instead of adhering to predefined rules, generated unconventional outputs by identifying patterns within large datasets rather than following explicit programming. For example, specific collections' coats featured curved openings at the bottom front—an anomaly stemming from the AI's misinterpretation of clothing borders. These AI-generated renderings served as a starting point for Acne Studios' creative director, who refined the outputs into final designs, keeping the AI misunderstandings as the central concept of the collection.

In light of what has been discussed so far, what still matters and is fundamental is the capability of the creative director, as the owner of the values of the brand she works for, to keep the AI generation consistent and merge it into the brand's aesthetic, the result of its stylistic codes reinterpreted in light of the new visual generations.

6.2 Communication: Augmenting Storytelling

Research demonstrates that fashion communication's inherently diverse and multifaceted landscape has significantly expanded its representational strategies in response to the digitisation of communication formats and media [18, 54]. This evolution has introduced new paradigms for visual and narrative expression, reshaping how fashion communication and especially art direction [55] provide creative and visual guidance to brands by employing various media such as photography, video, and graphics. In this context, GAI is intervening in redefining the creative process carried on by art directors, who use advertising examples of previous brands and visual briefs, relying on their aesthetic preferences to assess whether the meanings of each possible visual element match the brand identity [56]. As for creative direction, GAI can augment this inspirational process, in this case, augmenting the narrative capabilities of art direction, enabling the creation of *hyper-personalised and visually intricate storytelling.* A notable example is the Dolce&Gabbana Casa - New ADV Campaign [57], developed in collaboration with Maison Meta, where AI was used to reinterpret iconic Italian landscapes through a dreamlike and imaginative lens. By controlling selected image features, AI facilitated the creation of settings that use the heritage and tradition of the brand, combined with the conventionally GAI oniric aesthetic. This narrative would otherwise be hardly attainable through established production or post-production methods but gives the art director the tools to experiment with new aesthetics and visual settings that go beyond the physical dimension, abstracting product communication through new formats and mediums. Moreover, in the long run, this new codified technique streamlines resources and lowers production time and costs that would otherwise be necessary for complex visual outputs. Within this scenario, GAI is also increasingly being leveraged to *design narratives, starting with bespoke archival training.* A prime example is the Guerlain Bee Bottle project [58], commemorating the 170th anniversary of the brand's iconic bottle in 2023. Using a bespoke AI model, Guerlain curated a digital exhibition that reinterpreted the Bee Bottle across centuries, spanning from its creation in 1853 to an imagined future in 2193. Combining advanced AI capabilities with extensive heritage research, over 1800 unique artworks were generated and showcased in an ethereal digital showcase. The new process integrates the presence of different professionals and experts, such as archivists and creative technologists, who put the visual dataset used to train the AI model in place. However, it is the task of the art director to project value onto the visual generation, breaking down the essence of the brand as the set of aspects and sensations that characterise it, kept constant over time.

6.3 Retail: Augmenting Experiences

Retail contexts have implemented AI applications to better structure customer experiences, especially after the COVID-19 outbreak. Applications regarded the need to understand customers' behaviours, clear any unsatisfied expectations in shopping experiences, and streamline the delivery of the merchandise mix in shops [59] without really considering the application of image generation technologies as promising for innovating retail spaces and experiences. Nevertheless, it is now proven that GAI is a powerful tool for the pre-purchase phase to allow customers to interact with the brand [51] both online and offline. Indeed, retail spaces are increasingly being reimagined not merely as physical locations but as immersive experiential environments designed to elevate the mise-en-scène of the product rather than focusing solely on its sale. Retail managers are investigating the integration of digital technology within physical venues to move the product closer to the customers to be experienced rather than the reverse. One application sees *AI as a conveyor of multisensorial inputs.* This is exemplified by the case of NIKE AIR MAX

PULSE—MODEM [60], an installation developed by the digital agency Modem Works for the House of Innovation in Paris, celebrating the new Air Max Pulse sneaker model by Nike inspired by the London music scene. At an interactive mixer, visitors were invited to play with the controls and transpose their "Feeling of Air" into completely customised sounds, seamlessly visualised into one-of-a-kind AI-generated images through DALL-E 2. Another application of GAI in retail design involves the *integration of dynamic digital content within retail interiors*, enhancing the immersive experience of the brand's aesthetic as it is transposed into the physical retail environment. This is the case of Romantic Futurism: a digital fresco for Gucci, by Random Studio [61], a space that processes archival visual icons into a futuristic digital installation that becomes spatial using screens as architectural material covering the walls of the stairs in the Gucci store in Chengdu, in China. The monumental generative landscape was designed using Midjourney, Stable Diffusion, and DALL-E 2 and takes inspiration from the store's classical architecture, the Renaissance tradition of the brand's hometown, Florence, and the natural features of Chengdu itself. Indeed, as reported on the Random Studio website, "the digital fresco is composed of layers of AI-generated imagery morphing together to create an ever-evolving fantasy landscape [...] that will always be different depending on when you visit". The takeout from these case studies revolves around the creation of different kinds of aesthetics: one that translates other sensorialities attached to fashion products into visual outputs, developing innovative ways of interacting with the product to come to the final purchase; the other one leveraging on digital content to extend the retail walls beyond the physical, encompassing archival documentation, local and cultural traditions, and AI aesthetics to augment the relationship between customers and brands.

7 Conclusions

Having explored the application of GAI within the fashion industry through three key trajectories—(1) the augmentation of inspiration during product development, (2) the creation of enriched narratives in communication, and (3) the proposition of increasingly interactive retail experiences—the potential of technological progress in supporting designers' activities is demonstrated. In this debate, ethical implications and open questions emerge regarding the attribution of a role to technology that extends beyond its function as a mere tool in the hands of the designer. The first topic deals with the attribution of ownership and accountability to the co-created product [62] since GAI are subject to generating identical outputs in response to different users' inputs or simply repropose visual references contained in the training dataset [63]. These problems are closely linked to the so-called generative variability, which describes the unpredictable randomness in generated results that cannot be directly traced back to user action [64]. Indeed, even the development of algorithmic literacy among users regarding how AI works is not sufficient to overcome the generation of results that lack socio-cultural context and understanding

[39]. Another open issue concerns the replacement of human creativity with synthetic machine creativity [65], raising doubts about the homogenisation of brand aesthetics. This concern stems from the ease with which these tools can be controlled, potentially leading to standardised outputs and diminishing the creative value of the designer's role. Converging human ideas with algorithms is necessary to overcome the purely synthetic nature of generations. The technical process from which these results originate also challenges the attribution of an "aura" to creative production. The concept introduced by Benjamin to describe the spatial and temporal presence of a work of art and determine its authenticity has begun to be challenged by the development of reproducing techniques [66]. With GAI's introduction, this philosophical concept is undergoing redefinition. In the case of GAI tools, the production of an image is no longer solely attributable to human creative flair and cultural background. Still, it is shared with the algorithm's information processing. From this perspective, a central role in creative development is assigned to the model's architecture and training, enabling it to manifest its original characteristics. The development of the computational tool itself encapsulates part of its "aura", thereby challenging the traditional, human-centric concept of artistic agency and originality [67]. While AI contributes to the creative process, making sense of co-created generations remains the designer's responsibility. By acknowledging AI's mechanical nature and avoiding anthropomorphisation, the designer ensures control over the process [68].

References

1. Anantrasirichai, N., & Bull, D. (2022). Artificial intelligence in the creative industries: A review. *Artificial Intelligence Review, 55*, 589–656. https://doi.org/10.1007/s10462-021-10039-7
2. Pecorari, M. (2021). *Fashion remains: Rethinking fashion ephemera in the archive*. Bloomsbury Visual Arts.
3. O'Keefe, B., Flint, T., Mastermaker, M., Sturdee, M., & Benyon, D. (2021). Designing blended experiences. In *Designing interactive systems conference 2021* (pp. 309–321). Association for Computing Machinery.
4. Vandi, A. (2024). *Archiving fashion futures*. Design-driven Curatorial Practices Fostering Innovation in CCIs.
5. Colombi, C., & Vacca, F. (2016). The present future in fashion design: The archive as a tool for anticipation. *Possible Futures, 6*, 1–8.
6. Urde, M., Greyser, S., & Balmer, J. (2007). Corporate brands with a heritage. *Bradf. Univ. Sch. Manag. Work. Pap. Ser., 07*.
7. Throsby, D. (1999). Cultural capital. *Journal of Cultural Economics, 23*, 3–12. https://doi.org/10.1023/A:1007543313370
8. Bertola, P., Colombi, C., & Vacca, F. (2018). *FASHIONabilities. Planning and managing design processes in fashion*. Mandragora.
9. Franceschini, M. (2019). Navigating fashion: On the role of digital fashion archives in the preservation, classification and dissemination of fashion heritage. *Critical Studies in Fashion & Beauty, 10*, 69–90. https://doi.org/10.1386/csfb.10.1.69_1
10. Floch, J.-M. (Ed.). (2010). *Visual identities*. Continuum.
11. Floch, J.-M., Semprini, A., & Floch, J.-M. (2002). *Semiotica, marketing e comunicazione: dietro i segni, le strategie*. Angeli.

12. Mazzalovo, G. (2012). Brand aesthetics: An oxymoron? In G. Mazzalovo (Ed.), *Brand aesthetics* (pp. 11–15). Palgrave Macmillan. https://doi.org/10.1057/9781137025609_2
13. McLuhan, M.: The medium is the massage: An inventory of effects. (1967).
14. Bartlett, D., Cole, S., & Rocamora, A. (2013). *Fashion media: Past and present*. A&C Black.
15. Barthes, R. (1990). *The fashion system*. University of California Press.
16. Baldacci, C. (2017). *Archivi impossibili. Un'ossessione dell'arte contemporanea*. Johan & Levi.
17. Nobile, T. H., Noris, A., Kalbaska, N., & Cantoni, L. (2021). A review of digital fashion research: Before and beyond communication and marketing. *International Journal of Fashion Design, Technology and Education, 14*, 293–301. https://doi.org/10.1080/17543266.2021.1931476
18. Noris, A., Nobile, T. H., Kalbaska, N., & Cantoni, L. (2021). Digital fashion: A systematic literature review. A perspective on marketing and communication. *Journal of Global Fashion Marketing, 12*, 32–46. https://doi.org/10.1080/20932685.2020.1835522
19. Calefato, P. (n.d.). Fashion theory. http://www.studiculturali.it/dizionario/pdf/fashion_theory.pdf
20. Kim, J., Flanagan, R. C., Haviland, N. E., Sun, Z., Yakubu, S. N., Maru, E. A., & Arnold, K. C. (2024). Towards full authorship with AI: Supporting revision with AI-generated views. In *Presented at the CEUR workshop proceedings*.
21. Spennemann, D. H. R. (2023). ChatGPT and the generation of digitally born "knowledge": How does a generative AI language model interpret cultural heritage values? *Computer Science and Mathematics*. https://doi.org/10.20944/preprints202307.0563.v1
22. European Commission. Directorate General for Communications Networks, Content and Technology. (2022). *Opportunities and challenges of artificial intelligence technologies for the cultural and creative sectors*. Publications Office, LU.
23. Dietrich, A., & Haider, H. (2015). Human creativity, evolutionary algorithms, and predictive representations: The mechanics of thought trials. *Psychonomic Bulletin & Review, 22*, 897–915. https://doi.org/10.3758/s13423-014-0743-x
24. Benedek, M., Karstendiek, M., Ceh, S. M., Grabner, R. H., Krammer, G., Lebuda, I., Silvia, P. J., Cotter, K. N., Li, Y., Hu, W., Martskvishvili, K., & Kaufman, J. C. (2021). Creativity myths: Prevalence and correlates of misconceptions on creativity. *Personality and Individual Differences, 182*, 111068. https://doi.org/10.1016/j.paid.2021.111068
25. Cross, N. (1997). Creativity in design: Analyzing and modeling the creative leap. *Leonardo, 30*, 311. https://doi.org/10.2307/1576478
26. Runco, M. A., & Jaeger, G. J. (2012). The standard definition of creativity. *Creativity Research Journal, 24*, 92–96. https://doi.org/10.1080/10400419.2012.650092
27. Csikszentmihalyi, M. (2014). *The systems model of creativity: The collected works of Mihaly Csikszentmihalyi*. Springer. https://doi.org/10.1007/978-94-017-9085-7
28. Boden, M. A. (2004). *The creative mind*. Routledge. https://doi.org/10.4324/9780203508527
29. Colton, S., & Wiggins, G. A. *Computational creativity: The final frontier?* Final Front.
30. Runco, M. A. (2023). AI can only produce artificial creativity. *Journal of Creativity, 33*, 100063. https://doi.org/10.1016/j.yjoc.2023.100063
31. Twomey, R. (2023). Communing with creative AI. *Proceedings of the ACM on Computer Graphics and Interactive Techniques, 6*, 1–7. https://doi.org/10.1145/3597633
32. Turchi, T., Carta, S., Ambrosini, L., & Malizia, A. (2023). Human-AI co-creation: Evaluating the impact of large-scale text-to-image generative models on the creative process. In *Presented at the lecture notes in computer science (including subseries lecture notes in artificial intelligence and lecture notes in bioinformatics)*. https://doi.org/10.1007/978-3-031-34433-6_3
33. Vinchon, F., Lubart, T., Bartolotta, S., Gironnay, V., Botella, M., Bourgeois-Bougrine, S., Burkhardt, J., Bonnardel, N., Corazza, G. E., Glăveanu, V., Hanchett Hanson, M., Ivcevic, Z., Karwowski, M., Kaufman, J. C., Okada, T., Reiter-Palmon, R., & Gaggioli, A. (2023). Artificial intelligence & creativity: A manifesto for collaboration. *Journal of Creative Behaviour, jocb.597*. https://doi.org/10.1002/jocb.597
34. Manovich, L.: Seven arguments about AI images and generative media. (2023).

35. Coeckelbergh, M., & Gunkel, D. J. (2024). ChatGPT: Deconstructing the debate and moving it forward. *AI & Society, 39*, 2221–2231. https://doi.org/10.1007/s00146-023-01710-4
36. Ivcevic, Z.: Artificial intelligence as a tool for creativity. (2024).
37. Rizzi, G., & Casciani, D. (2024). A.I. into fashion process: Laying the groundwork. *Fashion Highlight*, 12–20. https://doi.org/10.36253/fh-2490
38. The State of Fashion 2024. (2023). McKinsey & Company.
39. Kim, S. J. (2024). Generative artificial intelligence in collaborative ideation: Educational insight from fashion students. *IEEE Access, 12*, 49261–49274. https://doi.org/10.1109/ACCESS.2024.3382194
40. Omwami, A., Lahti, H., & Seitamaa-Hakkarainen, P. (2020). The variation of the idea development process in apparel design: A multiple case study. *International Journal of Fashion Design, Technology and Education, 13*, 341–351. https://doi.org/10.1080/17543266.2020.1817573
41. Cheng, P.-J., & Do, E. Y.-L. (2011). What you see is what you design: Exploring the influence of inspiration images in designers' ideation. In *Proceedings of the second conference on creativity and innovation in design*.
42. Park, J., & Ahn, S. (2024). Traditional vs. AI-generated brand personalities: Impact on brand preference and purchase intention. *Journal of Retailing and Consumer Services, 81*. https://doi.org/10.1016/j.jretconser.2024.104009
43. Akverdi, C., & Baykal, G. E. (2024). Generative AI tools in design fields: Opportunities and challenges in the ideation process. *Presented at the ACM International Conference Proceeding Series*. https://doi.org/10.1145/3677045.3685445
44. Peeters, M. M. M., Van Diggelen, J., Van Den Bosch, K., Bronkhorst, A., Neerincx, M. A., Schraagen, J. M., & Raaijmakers, S. (2021). Hybrid collective intelligence in a human–AI society. *AI & Society, 36*, 217–238. https://doi.org/10.1007/s00146-020-01005-y
45. Lee, Y. K. (2022). How complex systems get engaged in fashion design creation: Using artificial intelligence. *Thinking Skills and Creativity, 46*, 101137. https://doi.org/10.1016/j.tsc.2022.101137
46. Bengesi, S., El-Sayed, H., Sarker, M. K., Houkpati, Y., Irungu, J., & Oladunni, T. (2024). Advancements in generative AI: A comprehensive review of GANs, GPT, autoencoders, diffusion model, and transformers. *IEEE Access, 12*, 69812–69837. https://doi.org/10.1109/ACCESS.2024.3397775
47. Liu, L., Zhang, H., Zhou, D., & Shi, J. (2024). Toward fashion intelligence in the big data era: State-of-the-art and future prospects. *IEEE Transactions on Consumer Electronics, 1*, 1. https://doi.org/10.1109/TCE.2023.3285880
48. Meyer, R. (2023). The new value of the archive: AI image generation and the visual economy of 'style'.
49. Suessmuth, J., Fick, F., & Van Der Vossen, S. (2023). Generative AI for concept creation in footwear design. In *ACM SIGGRAPH 2023 talks* (pp. 1–2). ACM. https://doi.org/10.1145/3587421.3595416
50. Rocamora, A. (2017). Mediatization and digital media in the field of fashion. *Fashion Theory, 21*, 505–522. https://doi.org/10.1080/1362704X.2016.1173349
51. McKinsey. (n.d.). How generative AI & ChatGPT will change business. https://www.mckinsey.com/capabilities/quantumblack/our-insights/generative-ai-is-here-how-tools-like-chatgpt-could-change-your-business, last accessed 2024/12/14.
52. Vogue. (n.d.). Ganni Copenhagen Spring 2024 fashion show. Vogue Runway. *Retrieved December 5*, 2024, from https://www.vogue.com/fashion-shows/copenhagen-spring-2024/ganni
53. XR Goes Pop. (n.d.). Acne Studios x Robbie Barrat. *Retrieved December 8*, 2024, from https://xrgoespop.com/home/acne-studios-x-robbie-barrat
54. Kalbaska, N., Sádaba, T., & Cantoni, L. (2019). Editorial: Fashion communication: Between tradition and digital transformation. *Studies in Communication Sciences, 18*, 269. https://doi.org/10.24434/j.scoms.2018.02.005
55. Disperati, F., & Cianfanelli, E. (2024). Digital art direction and sustainable communication for fashion in Italy: A literature review. In *Environmental design. Conference proceed-*

ings of the 4th international conference on environmental design (pp. 87–95). Palermo University Press.
56. Phillips, B. J., McQuarrie, E. F., & Griffin, W. G. (2014). The face of the brand: How art directors understand visual brand identity. *Journal of Advertising, 43*, 318–332.
57. Dolce & Gabbana. (n.d.). New ADV Casa campaign. *Retrieved December 18*, 2024, from https://www.dolcegabbana.com/en-us/casa/highlights/new-adv-casa-campaign/
58. Guerlain. (n.d.). Bee Bottle AI. *Retrieved December 12*, 2024, from https://beebottle-ai.guerlain.com/
59. Lu, H.-P., Cheng, H.-L., Tzou, J.-C., & Chen, C.-S. (2023). Technology roadmap of AI applications in the retail industry. *Technological Forecasting and Social Change, 195*, 122778. https://doi.org/10.1016/j.techfore.2023.122778
60. Modem. (n.d.). Nike Air Max Pulse at House of Innovation Paris. *Retrieved December 8*, 2024, from https://modemworks.com/projects/nike-air-max-pulse-at-house-of-innovation-paris/
61. Random Studio. (n.d.). Romantic Futurism: A digital fresco for Gucci Chengdu. *Retrieved December 20*, 2024, from https://random.studio/projects/romantic-futurism-a-digital-fresco-for-gucci-chengdu
62. Rezwana, J., & Maher, M. L. User perspectives of the ethical dilemmas of ownership, accountability. *Leadership in Human-AI Co-Creation.*
63. Fleischmann, K. (2024). Making the case for introducing generative artificial intelligence (AI) into design curricula. *Art, Design and Communication in Higher Education, 23*, 187–207. https://doi.org/10.1386/adch_00088_1
64. Weisz, J. D., He, J., Muller, M., Hoefer, G., Miles, R., & Geyer, W. (2024). Design principles for generative AI applications. In *Proceedings of the CHI conference on human factors in computing systems* (pp. 1–22). https://doi.org/10.1145/3613904.3642466
65. He, J., Houde, S., Gonzalez, G. E., Silva Moran, D. A., Ross, S. I., Muller, M., & Weisz, J. D. (2024). AI and the future of collaborative work: Group ideation with an LLM in a virtual canvas. *Presented at the ACM International Conference Proceeding Series*. https://doi.org/10.1145/3663384.3663398
66. Benjamin, W.: The work of art in the age of mechanical reproduction. (1969).
67. Park, S. (2024). The work of art in the age of generative AI: Aura, liberation, and democratization. *AI & Society*. https://doi.org/10.1007/s00146-024-01948-6
68. Hagendorff, T. (2024). Mapping the ethics of generative AI. *Minds and Machines, 34*, 39. https://doi.org/10.1007/s11023-024-09694-w

Adapting to AI in Fashion: Skills Needed, Trends, and Industry Perspectives

Maria Veronica Espejo Mendez, Rafael Almeida de Oliveira, Nadzeya Sabatini, and Lorenzo Cantoni

Abstract Artificial Intelligence (AI) is impacting the fashion sector, from streamlining operations to improving customer engagement. As companies adopt these technologies, tasks need to be redefined accordingly, and some jobs may even be replaced. Finally, the employees need to adapt to this evolving landscape. This study analyzes the demand for AI-related skills in the fashion industry through two methods: by examining LinkedIn job postings to identify needed skills when it comes to digital technologies and AI, and in-depth semi-structured interviews with industry professionals to understand current and possible future skills requirements. These combined insights provide a vivid picture of the sector, with a wide and emerging interest in the AI topic, but cautious steps and limited requests when it comes to new recruitments.

Keywords Artificial intelligence · Generative AI · Fashion communication · Fashion job · Fashion skills

M. V. Espejo Mendez (✉)
USI – Università della Svizzera italiana, Lugano, Switzerland
e-mail: maria.veronica.espejo.mendez@usi.ch

R. A. de Oliveira
Università degli Studi di Napoli Federico II, Napoli, Italy

N. Sabatini
Gdansk University of Technology and USI – Università della Svizzera italiana, Lugano, Switzerland
e-mail: nadzeya.sabatini@usi.ch

L. Cantoni
Institute of Digital Technologies for Communication, USI – Università della Svizzera italiana, Lugano, Switzerland

P. von Wachenfeldt et al. (eds.), *Fashion Communication in the Digital Age*, Springer Proceedings in Business and Economics,
https://doi.org/10.1007/978-3-031-99481-4_17

1 Introduction

Artificial intelligence (AI) is deeply impacting the majority of industries, promising major changes, and the fashion industry is no exception. AI is impacting the fashion industry across almost, if not all, the entire value chain from the design process to marketing and sales [1–3]. While the adoption of AI was already underway, its transformation has accelerated significantly, in particular due to the rise of new AI tools, most notably generative AI, which has seen a rapid adoption since 2022, when the technology became widely available to the public [4, 5].

AI-supported tools could provide numerous benefits, such as increasing productivity, streamlining processes, improving efficiency, and providing better service to the customers. These advantages are especially valuable in a dynamic industry such as fashion [6]. According to a McKinsey analysis, generative AI is projected to add between $150 and $275 billion to the operating profits of the apparel, fashion, and luxury sectors within the next 3 to 5 years [5].

The introduction of this technology is seen to complement or, in some cases, even replace certain human tasks, leading to significant changes in the workplace. Many suggest that AI's integration could eliminate some roles or reshape existing positions by demanding greater expertise in advanced technological tools [2, 7]. At the same time, new jobs requiring specific AI-related skills are expected to emerge, which could mark the beginning of a new skills era in the sector [8, 9].

Given this new reality, our study aims to examine (1) whether companies in the fashion industry are already requiring artificial intelligence skills in their job positions; and (2) which positions are emerging that focus on these skills. Additionally, (3) to gain a more complete perspective from the companies the insights were collected directly from fashion professionals on whether AI is driving the need for current and/or future needs for new types of skills.

To achieve these objectives, a methodology involving two main steps will be employed. First, an analysis of job offers published on LinkedIn related to the fashion industry will be carried out. LinkedIn is a business and employment-focused online professional platform, which is currently a worldwide leader, provides a global view of the labor market, and allows for the identification of current trends in terms of skills and knowledge required. Second, a series of in-depth interviews will be conducted with professionals working in the sector. These interviews will provide an insider's perspective on the current job situation, the skills in demand, and the skills that are expected to be required in the future. This approach will provide a deeper understanding of how AI is influencing both labor market offers and positions in the fashion industry.

2 Literature Review

The integration of AI in the fashion industry appears to have significant transformative potential, particularly in enhancing operational efficiency and creating innovative customer experiences both online and offline [3, 10, 11]. Initially used for tasks like inventory management and supply chain logistics, AI now drives a wide array of functions in the industry, including conversational shopping, the creation of AI-powered chatbots, virtual assistants, augmented and virtual reality applications, and demand forecasting [3, 12, 13].

AI is a field of computer science that examines the logic behind human intelligence, with the aim of replicating it in machines [3]. It works through algorithms that process large amounts of data to identify patterns, make predictions, and solve problems [14]. AI encompasses a broad subset of technologies, including machine learning, deep learning, and generative AI. Generative AI, which is among the most notable advances in AI, enables the creation of new content such as texts, images, media, and computer codes, through pattern recognition in large datasets [4, 15]. It includes sophisticated systems like large language models, which can produce diverse outputs based on their training on vast datasets; an example of this is ChatGPT. The new advancements in AI empower systems to collect, clean, and analyze massive datasets with precision, driving insights and efficiencies beyond human capabilities [16].

The current increasing adoption of AI across the fashion industry is intended to leverage AI to enhance designs, hyper-personalize communications, improve supply chain management, and optimize pricing and branding strategies [13, 14, 17]. To achieve these efficiencies companies are either developing AI capabilities in-house or outsourcing them to specialist providers [14]. All such processes will have profound implications for workforce skills and roles, as it has happened for digital fashion-related competences at large [18, 19].

As AI becomes integrated into everyday activities in the fashion industry, its impact on employment and the economy raises concerns, as automation may displace jobs in various areas, requiring strategies to upskill and adapt the workforce [20]. This especially poses challenges in entry-level positions, as the delegation of manual tasks to machines could reduce workforce opportunities, further emphasizing the need to adapt through upskilling and role innovation [7]. Upskilling employees is also becoming essential across various roles, such as designers, marketers, sales associates, and customer service representatives [6, 20, 21].

Reshaping job demands and requiring professionals to adapt to new AI-enabled workflows and skill sets are some of the expectations in the fashion industry in response to the transformation of the labor market [8, 9]. As a result, the ability to work alongside AI is increasingly recognized as a critical skill to enhance the CV of fashion professionals [7]. Tam and Lung [22] highlight that in order to remain competitive, luxury fashion brands will not only need to invest in AI-driven technologies, but will also need to train their employees to effectively integrate digital strategies into their businesses. Jung and Suh [23] show the importance of including generative AI in educational programs to improve basic skills in the digital environment of fashion design.

Giri et al. [10] emphasize that as AI tools become more integrated into various domains, the need for digital literacy and technical competence will continue to grow. They also highlight that effective collaboration between AI and humans will be fundamental to optimize collaboration models to fully harness the potential benefits of AI. For instance, Jung and Suh [23] highlight that in fashion textile design, AI plays an essential role, but its function is supportive rather than substitutive, human creativity still remains crucial in this area. Similarly, in the practice of trend forecasting, it is stressed that having people with the intuition and knowledge to interpret data correctly will be essential [13]. In addition, ensuring knowledge of and compliance with data protection regulations is crucial, as AI collects and processes sensitive information [20]. Therefore, companies and employees will need to effectively manage and monitor the correct use, especially generative AI systems, maintaining continuous oversight of these regulations, as they evolve alongside technological advancements.

Furthermore, a lack of awareness regarding future skill requirements can significantly hinder the success of fashion technology start-ups and SMEs [24]. Additionally, companies need AI-related expertise, such as data governance managers or data scientists in fashion companies, positions that emphasize competence in "implementing AI capabilities" [7].

While AI and generative AI will play a major role in the fashion sector, it is still unknown which path will lead from the current hype and experimentation phase to a consolidated situation in which AI will become a stable and profitable asset. The same can be said about needed skills: as many companies still navigate a period of experimentation and transition with AI, it remains unclear which specific skills are required, or roles are emerging within this new context in the fashion industry.

3 Methodology

The above-highlighted review of the research context highlights a clear gap when it comes to needs being requested by fashion companies when it comes to AI. This research aims to address such a gap while answering two main research questions:

- Are companies in the fashion industry currently requiring AI skills in their job positions? Which positions are emerging that focus on these skills?
- Do professionals in the field experience/anticipate a need for current and/or future AI-related types of skills?

Two research phases have been designed to address the above questions.

3.1 Analysis of Open Positions on LinkedIn

The first phase involved collecting data from fashion job postings on LinkedIn through two separate extractions conducted using web scraping tools. The first extraction took place on October 7, 2024, aiming to broadly identify job openings in the fashion industry across Europe. The keyword "fashion" was used in the search bar, with the location set to "Europe, Middle East, and Africa" (EMEA) since LinkedIn does not offer a specific option for Europe alone, only for the European Union. This approach ensured the inclusion of the United Kingdom and Switzerland. Additionally, LinkedIn limits the results of each search to 1000 listings. As a result, the first extraction retrieved 998 job vacancies. The second extraction was conducted on November 7, 2024, focusing on job postings in the fashion industry specifically related to AI. For this search, the keywords "fashion" and "artificial intelligence" were used, with the same location settings as the previous extraction; also individual searches were performed for each of the two keywords in each European country, generating separate results that were then aggregated into a single database. This second extraction resulted in a total of 120 job vacancies being collected. The final data set comprised a total of 1118 job listings.

The job posting attributes taken into consideration were: job ID number, job title, company name, industry, location, publication date, and job description. Subsequently, a data cleaning process was carried out to ensure data accuracy. Given that the initial dataset included the EMEA region, non-European countries were excluded during this process to focus only on job offers within Europe. Also, duplicate entries were removed, as there were the same positions posted by different recruitment agencies with identical job titles, descriptions, locations, and publication dates. This refinement process reduced the dataset to 666 unique job postings in 22 European countries. The next step involved identifying jobs that mentioned a connection to AI in their descriptions. This was done using a list of relevant keywords, including artificial intelligence, AI, generative, big data, computer vision, deep learning, machine learning, large language models (LLM), programming languages, python, recommendation systems, TensorFlow, and PyTorch.

3.2 Interviews with Fashion Professionals

The second phase involved conducting semi-structured interviews to gain a deeper understanding of the market specifically whether some positions are using and requiring more knowledge of AI, including generative AI. This research is based on a set of nine interviews with fashion industry professionals based in four European countries—Azerbaijan, France, Germany, and Switzerland—and who have between 3 and 7 years of experience in the fashion industry, especially in retail apparel and fashion technology companies as illustrated in Table 1. The interviewees were contacted among the alumnae/alumni of an international academic Fashion program, with a specific focus on digital media.

The interviews were conducted online (via Zoom) in English, and each lasted around 40 minutes. Eight interviews were recorded, with the consent of each participant, to enable a more detailed analysis. In one specific case, only notes were taken. The audio transcriptions were manually performed and reviewed twice to ensure the accuracy of the responses. Additionally, it was agreed that no company information or interviewee names would be disclosed.

4 Results

The results are organized and presented according to the two above-indicated research questions.

Table 1 Fashion professionals who were interviewed

Interviewee code	Position	Area	Type of company
i.1	Fashion Client Assistant	Fashion Business	Fashion – technology
i.2	Head of Client Strategy	Fashion Business	Fashion – technology
i.3	Brand Insight Manager	Business Development & Client Relations	Fashion – technology
i.4	Training Specialist & Video Maker	HR & Communication	Fashion – retail apparel
i.5	Junior PR & Communication	Media Communication	Fashion – retail apparel
i.6	CRM Sales Manager	Sales	Fashion – retail apparel
i.7	Account Executive	Sales	Fashion – technology
i.8	SEO & Content Manager	E-Commerce	Fashion – retail apparel
i.9	Category Management & E-commerce	Category Management	Fashion – retail apparel

4.1 Are Companies in the Fashion Industry Currently Requiring AI Skills in Their Job Positions? Which Positions are Emerging That Focus on These Skills?

Based on the analysis of 666 job advertisements in 22 European countries, 24 jobs were found requiring AI skills as part of their job requirements in the fashion industry, in entry, mid, senior, and executive level positions in 7 countries (France, Italy, Germany, the Netherlands, Spain, Switzerland, and the UK). Table 2 presents the list of positions (titles), seniority level, and job location.

The positions requiring AI skills still represent a very small proportion of all open positions, accounting for only 3.60% of the sample. However, it also shows that some companies are starting to include "new" AI-related skills. For instance, some require "familiarity with some specific AI platforms" and "AI concepts to review the state of the art in luxury," in entry-level positions such as interns in Hiring & Business Development or Worldwide Retail Excellence & Training team. For mid-level positions, the required skills vary depending on the role, but introductory or intermediate knowledge of AI is required, with a focus on practical applications such as generative AI, virtual testing, data visualization, and machine learning, able to gain actionable insights rather than having deep technical expertise.

At higher positions, the level of AI skills becomes more important and varies depending on the role and experience required. For example, in positions such as Global Corporate Communications Manager, AI skills are highly valued—"passion for technology topics such as AI"—and become more essential for a Regional

Table 2 Positions in the fashion industry that require AI-related skills (in the alphabetical order by the title of the position).

	Positions	Seniority level	Country
1	Apparel Graphic Designer	Mid-level	Switzerland
2	Engineering Manager - Computer Vision	Senior Level	Switzerland
3	Fashion Casting Expert	Mid-level	Spain
4	Global Head of E-commerce	Executive	Italy
5	Head of ML Platform & Developer Productivity	Senior Level	Germany
6	Internship Hiring & Business Development	Entry level	Germany
7	Intern New Tech – AI	Entry level	Netherlands
8	Internship (Machine Learning, AI, Computer Science) – Fashion Tech	Entry level	Germany
9	Internship – Worldwide Retail Excellence & Training team	Entry level	Italy
10	Manager – Special Projects – 3rd Party Brands	Mid-level	United Kingdom
11	Manager Global Corporate Communications	Senior Level	Germany
12	Product Developer	Mid-level	United Kingdom
13	Regional Demand Planner	Senior Level	Italy
14	Retoucher	Mid-level	United Kingdom
15	Senior Full-Stack Developer - TypeScript	Senior Level	Germany
16	Senior Graphic Designer	Senior Level	Italy
17	Senior Lead - Footwear Design	Senior Level	Switzerland
18	Senior Technical Artist	Senior Level	Remote - European Union
19	Senior Manager - Business Development	Senior Level	Italy
20	Senior Machine Learning Engineer - Content Solutions	Senior Level	Germany
21	Staff Software Engineer - Personalization	Senior Level	United Kingdom
22	Unsolicited application	Uncategorized	Germany
23	VP E-commerce	Executive	Germany
24	Worldwide Retail & Consumer Goods Business Development	Executive	France

Demand Planner—“big data programming languages.” Executive positions such as Global Director of E-Commerce, VP of E-Commerce, and Business Development for Global Consumer Goods and Retail require indirect knowledge of AI and a deeper understanding of AI platforms for recommendation and predictive analytics. Positions that require a deeper understanding and ability to use AI tools include Designer – Apparel Graphics, Retoucher, Senior Graphic Designer, Senior Lead – Footwear Design, and Senior Technical Artist.

New positions were found that were previously less common in the fashion industry and require more advanced knowledge and expertise in AI are roles such as Engineering Manager - Computer Vision, Head of ML Platform & Developer Productivity, Senior Machine Learning Engineer – Content Solutions, and Staff Software Engineer - Personalization. These roles require backgrounds in engineering, physics, and computer science, with expertise in programming with deep learning frameworks, knowledge of software engineering and Machine Learning, Image Vision, and technical experience in leading projects such as Machine Vision, Deep Learning, Sensors, and Robotics, and experience in building highly scalable service applications. The positions focus on a variety of tasks, such as creating realistic and inspiring product displays, designing tools and systems that power E-Commerce operations, driving technology strategies to scale platforms for personalizing customer journeys across multiple channels, and automating and managing digital campaigns with advanced tools while customizing user experiences.

4.2 Do Professionals in the Field Experience/Anticipate a Need for Current and/or Future AI-Related Types of Skills?

The interviews provide valuable insights into the current use of AI in various job positions and its potential future applications. The importance of AI for fashion professionals is widely seen as significant, if not very significant. Nearly all interviewees, apart from one, reported actively leveraging AI in their work.

The importance and frequency of use vary according to their roles. For instance, it is described as very important and used daily for those working in roles such as SEO & Content Management, Category Management & E-Commerce, as well as for Brand Insight Manager and Account Executive working in fashion technology companies, as they are increasingly relying on in-house AI-supported platforms that are already integrated into their systems and are now part of their internal processes.

According to interviews, AI provides valuable support, for example, for website optimization—e.g., planning pages, URL structures, and category headers. The use of certain platforms makes product searches even more personalized, as an interviewee mentioned (i.9) *"it helps us to display what the consumers will see at the bottom of the product page and it will populate items in a personalize way whether is styles that consumers might like or what they can style with."* Similarly, it was mentioned that the use of AI, especially generative AI, can help with the content of product descriptions that are published on the website, in various languages. An interviewee (i.8) mentioned that this has become an almost established process within their team, as it streamlines repetitive tasks, makes them more efficient, and allows people to focus on more strategic work.

Also, it is considered that in positions such as Video Maker & Training, PR & Communication, and CRM Sales, the importance of AI is growing quickly, but as some interviewees mentioned (i.4 and i.5) this is closely tied to the type of company: for example, whether it operates in a more traditional way or prefers to take a cautious approach when adopting new systems. Table 3 outlines tasks that were mentioned as being supported by AI.

Table 3 Tasks in utilizing AI by fashion professionals.

Activities supported by AI	Description
Internal operations	Extrapolates information from an internal database to answer employees' questions about processes, calculations, and workflows.
Client support	Provides instant answers to clients by leveraging all the information integrated into the system to address common questions.
Content analysis	Analyzes content to evaluate its effectiveness in achieving campaign goals.
Content generation	Generate content for clients' proposals and websites, streamlining the creation of engaging and personalized materials.
Generating insights from complex data	Uses AI to derive insights analyzing large data sets, extracting meaningful information to support decision-making and strategy development.
Interactive storytelling – video	Use of new characters (avatars), voices, adapted to 7 different languages.
Sentiment analysis	Analyzes comments on social media to identify how people perceived the campaign.
Social listening	Identifying emerging trends for upcoming collections.
Trend forecasting	Internal platforms that help employees to predict new trends for clients based on specific target groups and countries.
Visual engagement	Create proposals (images) to showcase clients the concepts of the projects (products), avoiding high costs on development of physical products.
Website optimization	Optimize web in terms of planning pages, Urls category footers, category headers and all sorts of copywriting. Also, it is used to optimize writing products descriptions. Technical SEO words (Writing codes, writing meta descriptions, all sorts of adding text for images).
Website personalization	Personalize what the consumers will see at the product page.

As it is seen from the collected data, the employees are in an exploratory phase, for example using AI platforms for content and sentiment analysis, with the aim of identifying effective campaigns and tailoring their communications. Additionally, using AI to analyze trends through micro-influencers is emerging as an interesting area to explore. A more in-depth focus on micro-influencers rather than macro-influencers could provide valuable insights into how trends are shifting within niche audiences as well as their level of engagement. (As described by i.3).

Meanwhile, others are independently experimenting with generative AI to discover its potential applications, particularly with tools such as ChatGPT. One interviewee even compared the use of ChatGPT to Google for quick searches, and another referred to it as a "personal assistant." One interviewee (i.7) described their use of this tool in order to create sequences with exact prompts: it *"can be very useful in sales where you have to follow different steps until you reach/meet your final customer ... in this aspect it can do 80% of this process, and saves a lot of time."*

Additionally, AI tools are highly appreciated being valuable in translations as they have the option to translate with different tones of voice. As many fashion companies need to localize the content while communicating the same message in different countries for email or website content, they are using AI tools to do the translation in-house, eliminating the need for external services and speeding up workflows. Other uses that are being employed are brainstorming, quick market analysis, design of a social media calendar, and text creation, e.g. press releases, invitations, product descriptions, and meeting summarization.

According to interviews, the use of different AI tools and platforms has offered them significant improvements in time management, productivity, and efficiency as they can complete more tasks and activities in less time. They can streamline processes by creating step-by-step plans that can be customized to diverse clients, allowing for broader reach and better-quality content. Interviewee (i.8) noted *"once you use AI to do your work, you do not do only your work fast but you do it in a more productive way. Once you achieved this, you automate some processes and then you can give your free time push back into your work."*

Companies are also exploring the use of AI. For example, not all employees have received training or clear guidelines on using external AI platforms. Yet, two employees out of 9 interviewed mentioned that they had been told not to share sensitive information on platforms outside the company's systems. This lack of "communication/regulations" at the large scale allows employees to experiment, but at the same time, represents a challenge where the use of proprietary information may represent an issue for the future. Some roles are increasingly reliant on AI tools, which could also be a challenge for the future of these roles, as many of the tasks can be automated. For example, in marketing, SEO, digital, mixed media, and production, the expectations are really high, as one of the interviewees (i.9) stated: *"AI is at the point where it is doing if not better than a human in certain areas."* However, it is essential to monitor tasks generated by AI, as many tools still fall short of producing entirely reliable results and require human oversight for verification.

Employees emphasize that, while AI skills are not yet mandatory for all positions, having at least a basic understanding of AI is highly valued. An interviewee shared that while they actively look for ways to use more AI in their work, they also encourage their team to keep training constantly. They expect any new entry-level professional they hire to have some knowledge of AI or some expertise with certain tools. It was noted that for certain roles, the use of AI becomes more essential, and greater expertise will be valued within the following teams and departments: Communication, Design, Copywriting, Digital Marketing, Data Management, Development, Digital Media, Metaverse & Gamification, Product Management, & Virtual Fashion Shows Design. Other mentioned teams are the Cybersecurity and IT Departments, although it is assumed that in these areas, the use of AI is already mandatory.

The interviewees' responses varied when identifying the skills that may be needed in the future. The focus remained on the skills required for entry-level positions, as many interviewees are also in similar roles. It was observed that the requirements become more specific depending on whether the company is in the fashion technology sector or the fashion industry. In fashion technology companies, data analysis skills are more prominent, along with the ability to understand how AI processes information to retrieve desired insights quickly. There is also an emphasis on interpreting data and converting it into useful insights for clients, explained clearly and straightforwardly. Knowledge of AI and generative AI is highly valued in this sector. For general fashion companies, the focus is more on creativity, adaptability to new environments, and a constant willingness to learn, especially when it comes to new processes; therefore, familiarity with generative AI is appreciated even if not necessary.

Despite their differences, both fashion and fashion technology companies emphasize three core skills: (i) the ability to verify information and sources—distinguishing real from false/fake; (ii) writing effective prompts for AI tools; and (iii) critical thinking. One interviewee (i.2) described critical thinking as irreplaceable: *"Critical thinking is the one that will never be replaced, it's what differentiates something created by a person from something generated by a machine. AI collects the data, but you need to know what to ask, look for and apply in order to make informed decisions. No matter the tool or platform, it's your own critical thinking that will lead you to success and drive meaningful results."* Similarly, prompting was highlighted by many interviewees as a crucial future skill, increasingly tied to communication abilities. As one interviewee (i.7) noted, *"Not everyone knows how to write good messages prompts. In the end, it is like you are communicating with your assistant, so if you want to have good results, you have to know how to communicate effectively to get the best results."*

This underscores the growing importance of communication as a foundational skill for the future and raises an important question: should prompting be considered a standalone skill, or should it be included as part of broader communication skills in future requirements? By developing these skills, candidates could enhance their competitiveness in the job market and adapt to the evolving demands of roles in general fashion and fashion technology companies.

5 Conclusions, Limitations, and Further Research

This study has highlighted a current, albeit relatively limited, demand for AI skills within fashion and fashion technology companies. Fashion companies are beginning to require professionals with AI expertise across various levels in their job postings, ranging from entry-level positions to executive roles. While AI skills are not yet mandatory for all roles, they begin to be viewed as a valuable differentiator for special roles, particularly in fashion technology companies where familiarity with AI, including generative AI, becomes more critical. In contrast, general fashion companies see AI as an advantage rather than a decisive factor for selection.

While all interviewees acknowledged the importance of AI for their companies and themselves, such widespread interest is only minimally mirrored in actual open positions, further underscoring the initial steps in this area, where AI is not yet fully integrated into processes, and companies are still figuring out their sustainable ways to use it, while employees are experimenting with it.

The pace of change appears to be slower than one might infer from general media news. Companies are still cautious and mainly in an exploratory mode, trying to figure out sustainable ways to benefit from AI. Job advertisements show cautious steps in this direction, with AI skills expected to play a more prominent role in the future.

Key skills such as critical thinking and prompting are particularly important for almost all roles. Companies are also encouraging experimentation with in-house and external AI platforms and tools such as ChatGPT to support qualitative and quantitative improvements, although this shift brings several challenges.

The results of this study, while providing a vivid image of the emerging role of AI in the fashion sector and the competencies it needs to thrive, cannot be generalized. Besides the limited sample of interviewees and their possible bias toward digital technologies, due to their previous education backgrounds, the study is also limited when it comes to the selection of a single platform for job advertising—even if one of the most popular ones—and the limitations when it comes to space, Europe, time and keywords used for data harvesting. Further studies will be needed to enlarge the scope of the research and test any specific trend.

Results are of interest both for academia, opening a fully relevant and emerging area of research and addressing it through two different methods, and for the industry, which needs to increase its maturity when it comes to AI so that it can move from a project-based to a deeper understanding and integration of AI.

The found trend also presents an opportunity to adapt educational curricula by universities and professional schools teaching "fashion"-related subjects to ensure that entry-level candidates are equipped with essential skills such as information validation, effective prompting, and critical thinking to meet the evolving needs of the industry.

References

1. Cantoni, L., Cominelli, F., Kalbaska, N., Ornati, M., Sádaba, T., & SanMiguel, P. (2020). Fashion communication research: A way ahead. *Studies in Communication Sciences, 20*(1), 121–125. https://doi.org/10.24434/j.scoms.2020.01.011
2. Ginsberg. B., (2023). Artificial Intelligence In Fashion. Forbes. https://www.forbes.com/councils/theyec/2023/02/21/artificial-intelligence-in-fashion
3. Luce, L. (2019). *Artificial intelligence for fashion. How AI is revolutionizing the fashion industry*. Apress. https://doi.org/10.1007/978-1-4842-3931-5
4. Cazzaniga, M., Jaumotte, F., Li, L., Melina, G., Panton, A.J., Pizzinelli, C., Rockall, E.J., & Mendes Tavares, M. (2024). Gen-AI: Artificial intelligence and the future of work. Staff Discussion Notes, 1. https://doi.org/10.5089/9798400262548.006
5. McKinsey & Company. (2024). *What is generative AI?* McKinsey & Company. https://www.mckinsey.com/featured-insights/mckinsey-explainers/what-is-generative-ai
6. Harreis, H., Koullias, T., Roberts, R., & Te, K. (2023). *Generative AI: Unlocking the future of fashion*. McKinsey & Company. https://www.mckinsey.com/industries/retail/our-insights/generative-ai-unlocking-the-future-of-fashion

7. Fortis, S. (2024). How AI is reshaping fashion's workforce. Vogue Business. https://www.voguebusiness.com/story/technology/how-ai-is-reshaping-fashions-workforce
8. BoF Team, & McKinsey & Company. (2023). The year ahead: How Gen AI is reshaping fashion's creativity. The Business of Fashion. https://www.businessoffashion.com/articles/technology/the-state-of-fashion-2024-report-generative-ai-artificial-intelligence-technology-creativity/
9. BoF Team, & McKinsey & Company. (2024). The State of Fashion 2025: Challenges at Every Turn. https://www.mckinsey.com/industries/retail/our-insights/state-of-fashion
10. Giri, C., Jain, S., Zeng, X., & Bruniaux, P. (2019). A detailed review of artificial intelligence applied in the fashion and apparel industry. *IEEE Access, 7*, 95376–95396. https://doi.org/10.1109/access.2019.2928979
11. Saponaro, M., Le Gal, D., Gao, M., Guisiano, M., & Maniere, I. C. (2018). Challenges and opportunities of artificial intelligence in the fashion world. In *2018 International Conference on Intelligent and Innovative Computing Applications (ICONIC).*
12. Chui,M.,Hazan,E.,Roberts,R.,Singla,A.,Smaje,K.,Sukharevsky,A.,Yee,L.,&Zemmel,R.(2023). *The economic potential of generative AI: The next productivity frontier*. McKinsey & Company. https://www.mckinsey.com/capabilities/mckinsey-digital/our-insights/the-economic-potential-of-generative-ai-the-next-productivity-frontier#business-and-society
13. Van Barneveld, L., & Wubs, B. (2023). Fashion forecasting, gender, and artificial intelligence. In *The Routledge History of Fashion and Dress, 1800 to the Present* (pp. 247–265). Routledge.
14. Jin, B. E., & Shin, D. C. (2021). The power of 4th industrial revolution in the fashion industry: What, why, and how has the industry changed? *Fashion and Textiles, 8*(1). https://doi.org/10.1186/s40691-021-00259-4
15. Marr, B. (2024). *Generative AI in Practice: 100+ amazing ways generative artificial intelligence is changing business and society*. John Wiley & Sons.
16. Díaz-Soloaga, P., & Pelzer-Peinado, I. (2024). Comunicación de moda e inteligencia artificial: el caso de Neural Fashion AI. *Universitas XXI, 41*, 15–52. https://doi.org/10.17163/uni.n41.2024.01
17. Liang, Y., Lee, S.-H., & Workman, J. E. (2020). Implementation of artificial intelligence in fashion: Are consumers ready? *Clothing and Textiles Research Journal, 38*(1), 3–18. https://doi.org/10.1177/0887302x19873437
18. Kalbaska, N., & Cantoni, L. (2019). Digital fashion competences: Market practices and needs. In R. Rinaldi & R. Bandinelli (Eds.), *Business models and ICT technologies for the fashion supply chain. IT4Fashion 2017* (Lecture Notes in Electrical Engineering) (Vol. 525). Springer. https://doi.org/10.1007/978-3-319-98038-6_10
19. Nobile, T. H., Kalbaska, N., de Oliveira, R. A., & Cantoni, L. (2021). digital fashion competences: A longitudinal study. In T. Sádaba, N. Kalbaska, F. Cominelli, L. Cantoni, & M. Torregrosa Puig (Eds.), *Fashion communication. FACTUM 2021*. Springer. https://doi.org/10.1007/978-3-030-81321-5_2
20. O'Connell, M. (2024). The role of open AI in fashion design: Transforming creativity through innovation. *Zenodo*. https://doi.org/10.5281/ZENODO.13823922
21. Orwig, W., Bellaiche, L., Spooner, S., Vo, A., Baig, Z., Ragnhildstveit, A., Schacter, D. L., Barr, N., & Seli, P., Ph. D. (2024). Using AI to generate visual art: Individual differences in creative ability predict art quality. In PsyArXiv. https://doi.org/10.31234/osf.io/ygzw6
22. Tam, F. Y., & Lung, J. (2025). Digital marketing strategies for luxury fashion brands: A systematic literature review. *International Journal of Information Management Data Insights, 5*(1), 100309. https://doi.org/10.1016/j.jjimei.2024.100309
23. Jung, D., & Suh, S. (2024). Enhancing soft skills through generative AI in sustainable fashion textile design education. *Sustainability, 16*(16), 6973. https://doi.org/10.3390/su16166973
24. Bertola, P., & Teunissen, J. (2018). Fashion 4.0. Innovating fashion industry through digital transformation. *Research Journal of Textile and Apparel, 22*(4), 352–369. https://doi.org/10.1108/RJTA-03-2018-0023

Communicating Virtual Fashion: A Case Study of the Virtual Collection 'Neo-Ex'

Marie Ledendal

Abstract New technologies, such as 3D digital rendering, immersive platforms, non-fungible tokens (NFTs) and AI, are creating new opportunities within the fashion industry, including virtual fashion. This chapter discusses how fashion brands communicate virtual products, by analysing the Neo-Ex campaign from Carlings. The study takes its point of departure in the key questions: What arguments are employed to market the garments, and how do fashion brands create a demand for these novel products, as well as attempting to construct a consumer understanding of what this new phenomenon is. Using a multimodal method and a document study, the study analyses campaign material, films, images, and articles, through the lens of brands as cultural intermediaries. Three themes emerged: virtual fashion as a concept for identity construction that advocates *creativity*, *attitude*, *futurism*, and *early adopters*, as well as communicating that virtual fashion is *sustainability conscious.* The main contribution is identifying the following three tactics for communicating virtual fashion: *utilising emerging technologies for identity construction; educating the consumer;* and *using sustainability to validating its existence*. While the first two tactics focus on building consumer awareness and acceptance, the third highlights sustainability as a rationale to legitimise virtual products.

Keywords Virtual fashion · Social media · Cultural intermediaries · Sustainability · Communication

M. Ledendal (✉)
Lund University, Helsingborg, Sweden
e-mail: marie.ledendal@iko.lu.se

P. von Wachenfeldt et al. (eds.), *Fashion Communication in the Digital Age*,
Springer Proceedings in Business and Economics,
https://doi.org/10.1007/978-3-031-99481-4_18

1 Introduction

> Of course, this was the first of its kind, but I would love to be able to use the dress more often, and wear it wherever I like, not just limited to the pictures I got… [1].

The quotation is from a purchase of the digital couture garment 'Iridescence', the first of its kind to be sold. It is a response to the purchaser's experience of what the brand refers to as 'being digitally dressed' [1]. In 2019, the virtual-only brand The Fabricant sold the virtual garment for 9,500 US dollars [1]. New technologies, such as three-dimensional digital rendering techniques, immersive platforms, non-fungible tokens (NFTs), and artificial intelligence (AI), are creating novel opportunities within the fashion industry. New platforms arise through these technologies, for example, the integration of virtual fashion into gaming environments designed by fashion brands and fashion weeks in Metaverse [2, 3]. In terms of communication, these technologies may be regarded as embodying innovation and new modes of self-expression. However, the transformation is also cultural. Quoting Rocamora [4, p. 726], 'The mediatization of fashion reaches out to a verity of spheres including everyday life, pointing to the significance of this process in practices of the self, a mediatized self'. The following quote from Amber Jae Slooten, Creative Director at The Fabricant, also illustrates this point: 'A new cult is rising. The digital world is coming and we are no longer bound to physical space' [1]. Furthermore, virtual fashion is presented as a potential solution to environmental challenges associated with traditional fashion production [5]. Arguments that virtual garments have a lower environmental impact than physical ones are illustrated by the collection 'Neo-Ex' by Carlings. According to the brand, the products allow for self-expression on social media without a need for physical consumption [6]. In a news interview, the then-CEO argued that the brand had created a collection with 'zero environmental effect' [6].

Based on the case study of the Neo-Ex campaign, this chapter takes an interest in how virtual fashion is communicated to address expressive and communicative dimensions, by unpacking how fashion brands market these new products. What arguments are employed to market these virtual garments, and how do fashion brands attempt to create a demand for and construct a consumer understanding of this new phenomenon? The discussion is founded on the theoretical perspective that brands function as cultural intermediaries. The main contribution is the identification of three tactics, through which virtual fashion is communicated: *utilising emerging technologies for identity construction; educating the consumer; using sustainability to validate their existence*. Following this introduction, this chapter outlines previous research relating to the role of fashion brands as cultural intermediaries, virtual fashion and its associated sustainability aspects. Whereafter, this chapter presents methods, empirical material and explores analytical themes. It concludes with presenting the outlined communication tactics.

2 Previous Research

2.1 The Role of Brands as Cultural Intermediaries

In today's society, consumption has become a defining aspect of identity. This is particular apparent in the process of selfidentification through fashion, with identity construction through garments [7, 8]. Fashions and clothing can be regarded as a means of encoding and communicating information about the self; however, the 'codes' are highly ambiguous, transformative, as well as context and culturally dependent [9]. Bernard [10] argues that fashion and clothing serve as non-verbal signs, deriving their meaning from the surrounding context. According to Barthes [11], material objects signify meaning; however, they possess no intrinsic meaning, it is ascribed to them by society.

Today, identity is constructed, framed, and co-created online [12], and brands are increasingly acting as cultural intermediaries [13]. Cultural intermediaries are defined as taste-makers that describe symbolic meaning to products, and shape lifestyles for consumers to imitate [14]. Social media platforms like Instagram, Pinterest, and TikTok allow influencers and micro-trends to shape fashion consumption in real-time, making individuals more active trend participants [15]. Virtual influencers, like Lil Miquela, a computer-generated persona with over 2.5 million followers [16], created by the company Brud, provide opportunities through the modern influencer culture to act in similar manners as social media influencers [17]. Building on zeitgeist, digital fashion campaigns and collections construct consumer identities through brand narratives [13].

Smith Maguire & Matthews [18, p. 551] state that research on cultural intermediaries has generally followed two directions: 'cultural intermediaries as exemplars of the new middle class, involved in the mediation of production and consumption, and cultural intermediaries as market actors engaged in the qualification of goods, mediating between economy and culture'. They further argue that the impact of cultural intermediaries extends beyond the framing of specific goods; they contribute both to a wider reproduction of 'legitimacy' as a dominant convention for the stratification of culture, and to the expanding definition of culture itself [18]. Huggard [13, p. 45] defines the following three aspects through which a fashion brand communicator asserts their role as a cultural intermediary; 'drawing upon "high" and "pop" culture to imbue goods and services with meaning and values; respond to values and ideologies of their consumers and audiences through communication strategies and initiatives; and create new genres of cultural content and lifestyle experiences'.

2.2 Virtual Fashion

The fashion industry is often defined by recurring trends, manifested through physical clothing [19]. The digitalisation of the fashion industry is expanding this [7]. As stated by Periyasamy & Periyasami [20, p. 3], 'digitalization pertains to the utilisation of digital technologies to revolutionise commercial procedures and establish novel business frameworks'. Due to recent advances in technology relating to Industry 4.0, new areas in relation to the digitalisation of the fashion industry have emerged, among others the idea of 'virtual fashion' [21]. Applications within the fashion industry, integrating physical reality with digital virtuality, through virtual reality (VR), augmented reality (AR) and Metaverse, have resulted in new business possibilities and hyper-personalised products [20]. NFTs, unique digital assets that exist in a given blockchain, have created new markets for digital assets, enabling individuals to trade unique items, such as artwork, and other digital objects [22]. This means that virtual fashion does not address the functional goals of fashion, i.e. properties relating to dressing the body; it addresses dimensions of aesthetic expression and communicative values [23]. Virtual fashion refers to digitally represented apparel defined by Göncü-Berk & Shahaj [23, p. 398] to include: 'virtual wear on photos', 'virtual product representation', and 'fashion for immersive technologies'. 'Virtual wear on photos' aims to replace garments intended to be used for a single photo on social media. Technically these virtually 3D designed garments are modelled on an avatar in 3D software (e.g. CLO3D), and then rendered onto a digital photo using a second software (e.g. Pixelmator) [24]. The second category, virtual product representation, is defined as a method of visualising and representing physical fashion, in, for example, eCommerce, through digital simulations of fabric drape and other qualities on a 3D avatar, to communicate an equivalent physical garment's fit on a buyer's body [23]. The final category relates to different immersive virtual applications, using, for example, VR and AR. This could include VR-filters on social media platforms, smart fit mirrors in stores, VR-retail experiences, virtual fashion shows, and virtual applications that cross the gaming and the fashion industry [23].

2.3 Sustainability and Virtual Fashion

The fashion industry with fast fashion brands offering low-price products has changed fashion consumption patterns, resulting in price decreases and consumption increases [25]. The industry is responsible for 10% of global carbon dioxide emissions, 25% of global chemical, and 20% of global industrial wastewater usage [26]. United Nations Climate Change (UNCC) states that the fashion industry has to have a net-zero GHG emissions no later than 2050 [27]. Thus, organisations like the UNCC [27] and the European Commission [28] are advocating transitions from business models of throwaway and fast fashion, to circular economy solutions and technological innovation. Industry 4.0 and the digital transformation of the fashion industry are set to be one of the future solutions [21]. Industry 4.0, first used in 2011, is a concept that 'brings multiple information and communication technologies together, to allow machines and computers to make decisions and change their behaviour autonomously, or in collaboration with a human user' [21, p. 378]. Research [see, for example, 20, 21, 23, 25, 26] points to technological change and emerging technologies, as for example AI and the Internet of Things, digitalization of fashion and virtual garments, traceability and blockchain-based applications, to discuss future scenarios and strategies within the fashion industry to further sustainability. Virtual fashion applications, like virtual wear on photos, virtual product representation, and fashion for immersive technologies, for instance, are presented as sustainable solutions with the potential to reduce the environmental impact and waste from production, transportation, returns, and disposal of single-wear garments [23].

However, it is crucial to also consider the intricate aspects of electricity consumption when developing these benefit models. This encompasses the energy-intensive computing power required for the production and utilisation of 3D garments, blockchain and immersive technologies, as well as the resources associated with the manufacturing, transportation, and disposal of the specialised hardware necessary for these processes [21, 23]. Göncü-Berk & Shahaj [23, p. 399] state that the requisite energy input to produce a 3D garment visualisation is approximately 4 kWh, equivalent to driving a Tesla Model S for over 20 km.

3 Methodology

Virtual fashion is an emerging field, and as such the selection of cases is still quite limited. As the study takes an interest in understanding how this new phenomenon has been introduced to consumers, the following selection criteria was defined: it should be a fashion brand; it should be among one of the first that marketed virtual fashion-related products, though not necessarily exclusively virtual products; to ensure the collection of sufficient empirical material, the brand should have marketed a virtual fashion collection, or a set of virtual garments, through a campaign, events, or similar. The case study of the fashion brand Carlings was selected because 'Neo-Ex' was the first fully virtual collection to be launched [29]. The collection was communicated through a marketing campaign on the brand's social media channels and webpage.

In view of the exploratory nature of the research, a qualitative approach was adopted in the study. Empirical material of the case study, which focuses on the manner in which virtual fashion is communicated to address expressive and communicative dimensions, was collected over a period from the commencement of the campaign in November 2018 to December 2024, with a particular emphasis on the first two years, in order to gain a more comprehensive understanding of how the brand is communicating virtual fashion. The analysis was conducted using a multimodal method [30], based on the following material: the brands campaign material including films and images and a collaboration with a virtual influencer and music artists; 275 social media posts using the campaign hashtag 'addressthe-future'. Between the 12 and 19 November 2018, the brand posted two films (F1-2) and three posts (I1-3) with images on their Instagram [31] and one film (F3) (viewed to date 94,974 times) on their YouTube account [32], relating to the virtual fashion campaign in question. The brand also disseminated imagery of the collection via their webpage, wherein exemplars can be observed within articles pertaining to the campaign. Nevertheless, these are no longer accessible on the brand's webpage and are consequently not incorporated into the multimodal analysis. Instead, they are encompassed within the material of the document study of Carlings marketing strategies. The subsequent analysis of the visual, auditory, and textual elements, with a focus on the films (F1-3) and the images (I1-3) disseminated by the brand, is based on the following semiotic resources: colour, composition, and movement, as well as theories of the signifying practices of the grammar of these resources, such as colour saturation, hue and value, centre and margin, salience and framing, the materiality of the material, as well as tempo, direction of movement and transitions [30].

The material collected for the document study included the following: information and articles that have been collected from the brand's Instagram account and webpage; information on the campaign from the webpage of the creative agency behind the campaign; news articles from online newspapers and magazines, and other electronic sources during the time of and after the campaign, and two films with interviews relating to the campaign in question with the former CEO and then-sales manager of the brand, as well as representatives from the creative agency behind the campaign. The empirical material from the document study and the multimodal analyses of the films and images were then analysed using a thematic analysis, with the premise that brands function as cultural intermediaries providing the theoretical framework.

4 The Case Neo-Ex, Carlings

Carlings is a Scandinavian retail brand with its origin in Norway, founded in 1985 by Frank Varner. It specialises in denim, offering a range of well-known brands including Levi's, Lee, Diesel, and Replay [33]. The brand has over 150 brick-and-mortar stores in Scandinavia, in addition to an online presence [33]. As stated on their website, the company's ethos is driven by 'a passion for denim, subculture, and a pure interest in music' [33]. They assert that jeans are more than a garment; 'they are a lifestyle, a way of expressing oneself and part of their identity' [33]. In 2018, Carlings launched the Neo-Ex collection, a capsule line of 19 genderless pieces, which differed from the brand's otherwise established aesthetic; the more traditional denim look. The collection was released to market through the launch of their new online store [6], through Instagram and the newly launched webpage, using films, social media posts, and images.

One of the primary justifications for the virtual collection was reduced environmental impact, because there were no physical garments. At the same time, the collection presented a new opportunity for consumers to express themselves, especially on social media, through images and posts where consumers could purchase virtual garments. In an interview on the brand's webpage, the former CEO and then-sales manager argues that the success and objective of the campaign were achieved due to that the limited virtual collection sold out, and due to the considerable media attention that surrounding the Neo-Ex campaign [29]. Furthermore, he refers to that the brand and the campaign was mentioned in independent articles in 90 countries, ranging from China to the US, including magazines, such as the New York Times and Hypebeast [29]. The collection was launched in collaboration with music artists and the virtual influencer 'Perl.www' [34]. Carlings and Virtue Nordic [35], the strategic and creative agency behind the campaign, was awarded the Digital Craft Cannes Lions Grand Prix in 2019 [6].

The multimodal analyses of the films and images explored the combined grammar of the semiotic resources in the Neo-Ex campaign to understand the meaning-making potentials of how the brand, through the campaign material, communicates virtual fashion, and by extension the identity of Carlings. The narrative arc [36] of the two promotion films F2-3 (F2 1:00 and F3 1:13 minutes), is structured in the following parts: Firstly, 'rising action'—establishing the concept of the 'fashion paradox', explaining the problem with being sustainable at the same time as expressing oneself through fashion. Secondly, 'the climax'—the solution to the problem, through purchasing the brands' virtual garments. Thirdly, 'the falling action'—educating the consumer of how virtual fashion works and why this is more sustainable than physical single-wear garments. The third film (F1, 1:00 minute) builds on a shortened narrative arc: Firstly, explaining the sustainability issues with the fashion industry. Secondly, the solution to the issues, through purchasing the brands' virtual garments. Thirdly, educating the consumer of how virtual fashion works. The films signify a futuristic mood, achieved through the combination of visual components and cues, in a fast rhythm with many short scenes, including fragmented image frames, glitch effects and pixelated images, the protagonist [36]—the new type of consumer that wears virtual garments, curated in poses that connotates [11] self-assurance and attitude, the gaze meeting the viewer, a soundscape of electronic music, blipping and buzzing sounds is present in all three films, as well as an additional rhetoric content of a narrating voiceover in F2-3. The futuristic mood is further underlined by the visual salience component of the text being typed out, in red or black, one word at a time, and with a blinking square displayed at the end of the text. The images on Instagram of the campaign present the three Nordic artists, alternative music artist Little Jinder (I3), and hip-hop artists Silvana Imam (I2) and Lamix (I1) [31] dressed in garments from the collection. The images signify a confident attitude through the combination of visual components and cues, two (I1,3) dressed in the same high gloss, futuristic, liquid looking materials as used on garments in the promotion films, poses that display self-confidence and attitude, one is giving the finger to the viewer (I1), one is seated legs spread and the hands, full of rings, positioned between the legs (I2), all three's gazes are looking into the camera, their bodies having the salient centred position in the image, covering most of the image frames.

5 Communicating Virtual Fashion

The discussion will proceed by analysing the empirical material in order to outline the following three themes describing the communication strategy for the Neo-Ex campaign: how virtual fashion is communicated to address expressive and communicative dimensions through identity construction that advocates *creativity*, *attitude*, *futurism*, and *early adopters*, as well as communicating statements that virtual fashion is *sustainability conscious.*

The first theme imbues 'virtual fashion' with the meaning and values of *creativity, attitude*, and *futurism.* Through focusing on consumer creativity, using phrasings, such as 'we love to express our style and creativity online' [31, 32], and by employing semiotic resources, like fragmented image frames through glitch effects and pixelated images, the films signify innovation and future in coherence with creativity and a confident attitude. Marketing the collection as a possibility for consumers, to engage and be creative with trends, without purchasing physical products, the campaign underlines this. Further, the campaign draws upon pop culture, by collaborating with both indie music and hip-hop artists and a virtual influencer, to imbue the brand identity with the cultural meanings and values of these artists and the character of Perl.www [22]. Moreover, the artist collaborations can be perceived to draw on artification processes [37], hence reinforcing Carlings cultural and creative brand identity, through the selection of artist that emphasises attitude and creativity through 'alternative' music. Where the Perl.www collaboration emphasises the construction of a futuristic and technological narrative, underlined in the opening sequences in F2-3 with close-ups of the virtual influencer's face, as well as ending with an image sequence featuring Perl.www in F3, depicted in a synthetic-looking jacket, juxtaposed with herself through a series of superimposed images, all utilising a cold, blue-pink colour filter [31, 32]. The collaborations, also the one with Perl.www, can be seen as celebrity endorsement [38, 39]. In this way, the brand builds credibility by aligning the celebrities' and the campaigns objectives, and in the later also through the virtual influencer's existing familiarity with the target group and their interest in virtual products [38]. The marketing of these new virtual products allows Carlings to gain access to new market sectors. This reinforces the brand and enhances awareness [40].

Furthermore, the brand launching the campaign with a co-creating content strategy on platforms, such as Instagram [31], the brand identity is entwined with cultural trends, co-constructing the brands' value together with consumers [13]. The brand encouraged consumers to share their visual content, by uploading images where the consumers wear virtual garments from the collection under the hashtag 'adDRESSTHEFUTURE' [31]. At the time of this chapter, the reach of the campaign, the hashtag used in 275 posts, some of which does not related to the Neo-Ex campaign, might be argued as low. Nevertheless, by drawing on the concept of value co-creation for brands through consumer engagement [41], the brand's strategy can still be argued to be constructed with co-creation strategies. Building on a futuristic narrative, the brand communicates the idea of virtual fashion as an innovative concept and techniques that aligns with the spirit of the time. Creating new genres of cultural content and lifestyle experiences, in conjunction with co-construction strategies on social media platforms, the brand is perceived to act as a cultural intermediary [13]. However, at the same time as the idea of a zeitgeist connecting to innovation and digitalization is constructed, the brand also reinforces stereotypic aesthetic visual codes for such a futuristic narrative, building on an idea of futuristic fashion from the 1960s space-age-fashion [42], including plastic, high gloss materials, white together with high saturated colours (neon), as well as an electronic, futuristic soundscape, with distinctive auditory elements that can be identified in science fiction films [43].

The second theme discusses how the concept of innovation in the context of virtual fashion is conveyed as a means for constructing an identity of an early adopter. This is achieved by imbuing the brand with meanings and values associated with *innovation* and *expertise* in the field of fashion innovation. Acting as a cultural intermediary, brands like Carlings uses marketing tools, e.g., the Neo-Ex films, to educate consumers about 'the importance' of emerging technologies and their integration into everyday life [14]. The assertion of expertise serves to differentiate cultural intermediaries from others engaged in the 'framing of goods and the formation of value' [18, p. 555]. However, novel interfaces can provide technological challenges, technology-based products require education and support, potential consumers require guidance to understand how the technologies function, and how and why they hold value [44]. The films introduce virtual fashion, with its reliance on innovations like 3D modelling and 3D rendering, as a transformative shift in the role of clothing within society. Through employing informative and step-by-step images-frames the process is visualised through a mobile phone interface, where the user journey is demonstrated through taking a photo, buying a virtual garment, digitally fitting it, rendering the image and uploading it to social media [31, 32]. In this context, Carlings is positioned as a mediator of the understanding and knowledge about these new technologies, as well as for the technology. The brand gives the concept of virtual fashion and the garments, symbolic meaning and values [13], by using the theme of creativity, and the voiceover in F2-3 stating that 'this is a new way of expression our fashion creativity, without leaving a negative footprint on the world' [31, 32]. By presenting the technology in an intuitive and accessible manner, the films reduce potential user barriers, making the concept of virtual clothing less abstract and more tangible. The films serve as an educational tool, bridging the knowledge gap of how virtual fashion operates for new consumers, while simultaneously promoting Carlings as a pioneer in sustainable and creative fashion.

The third theme, based on sustainability, is conveyed through the Noe-Ex campaign, through imbuing the brand identity with meaning and values of *sustainability consciousness* and *innovation* around new sustainable solutions. The theme discusses how sustainability is used as an argument to validate the existence of these virtual products, through the semiotic framework of the campaign and the double meaning of the hashtag 'adDRESSTHEFUTURE' [31, 32]. Through the narrative and visual storytelling of the films and images, the brand conveys a central argument to consumers that use social media to construct their identity: virtual fashion offers a sustainable alternative to traditional clothing, while meeting the demands of social media-driven self-expression. This is visually mediated [4], with the innovative, futuristic mode of images including glitch effects, pixelated images, juxtaposed with frames representing environmental issues and overproduction, e.g. images of pollution at industrial sites, and visual resources of sequences of close-ups of faces looking into the camera, some framed in F2-3 and I1-3 with a portrait format relating to reels and social media images. The sustainable benefits of virtual fashion are further underlined by the hashtag used in both the films and the captions in the social media posts, by referring to both the narrative of 'addressing' the future, through discussing sustainability issues within the future fashion industry, and that the consumer is 'dressing' one's future self. The voiceover's critique in F2-3 of 'the unwritten rule' [31, 32] that prevents the reuse of outfits online frames fashion trends as a significant factor in fashion's environmental impact, while setting the stage for the introduction of a digital solution. Through its focus on the environmental and creative benefits of virtual garments, the campaign highlights why these innovations are relevant. A narrative that can appeal to eco-conscious consumers, by emphasising waste reduction, while also resonating with the digital generation through celebrating limitless creative expression. This dual emphasis not only educates, but also reinforces Carlings' brand identity as a forward-thinking, sustainable innovator, through building on emotional customer benefits through a more sustainable and novel way of consumption [40]. The strategy demonstrates the functionality and necessity of these products, while at the same time fosters brand value, consumer interest and understanding through digital content marketing [45]. In the role of cultural intermediary, Carlings becomes involved in the process of framing goods as legitimate, which in turn implicates them in wider processes of constructing categories of cultural legitimacy [18]. However, while virtual fashion may appear more sustainable, the energy demands of designing, rendering, and storing virtual garments can have significant environmental costs [23]. The absence of transparency in communicating the energy demands associated with these garments, and the lack of third-party verification of this claim, in conjunction with the campaign's assertion that proceeds from the collection will be donated to the organisation WaterAid, becomes problematic and serves to exemplify the phenomenon of greenwashing [25].

6 Conclusion—Tactics for Virtual Fashion

As discussed in this chapter, the Neo-Ex campaign demonstrates how fashion brands are employing communication strategies to educate consumers about the necessity and rationale behind virtual products, while marketing virtual garments using sustainability arguments to validate their existence as new products. Building on these strategies, this chapter has identified the following three tactics through which virtual fashion is communicated: *utilising emerging technologies for identity construction, educating the consumer,* and using *sustainability to validate their existence.*

The first tactic builds on the increasing mediatisation and digitalisation of fashion, where brands market ideas that emerging technologies, like virtual fashion, NFTs, and gaming platforms, offer novel methods for consumers to curate their identities in both the physical and digital domains [7]. The narrative of the campaign explores the concept of self-expression through virtual fashion, by offering facilitation of experimentation with expressions. This enables a more flexible construction of identity on social media platforms, similar to identity construction observed on gaming platforms, through possibilities of multitude of identities through the use of avatars and 'skins' [46]. In this digital context, virtual fashion can be perceived as conceptualised and commodified, as a tool for constructing multiple and extended versions of one's identity. The second tactic builds on the technological developments of Industry 4.0 that enable these new markets. As illustrated in the case, brands' digital content marketing provides consumers with instructions and tools to construct these alternative identities, by offering guidance on use and concept of virtual fashion. In this framework, educational aspects are used to catalyse the market for these new products, by facilitating product understanding and relatability. The third tactic builds on issues concerning fast fashion and the idea that virtual fashion offers benefits. The Neo-Ex case demonstrates how brands can capitalise on the concept of virtual fashion, by marketing ideas where consumers can express themselves on social media without contributing to the material consumption traditionally associated with the fast fashion industry. This approach aligns with strategies adopted by other brands. Virtual fashion brand Dress-X argues for an idea where virtual consumption transforms fast fashion into a more sustainable 'digital fast fashion' [25, 47].

This chapter contributes to the discussion of the transformative impact and its implications on the fashion industry, due to these technological advancements. In a context in which the process of self-identification is conceptualised as the construction of identity through the consumption of consumer objects, both virtual and physical, these new technologies mediate identity construction. Hence, as virtual clothing is integrated with the virtual domain, the roles of fashion as a means of self-expression, and a reflection of cultural trends, need to be further explored. In addition, more research is required concerning fashion brands' use of digital applications for virtual fashion, to establish a substantial corpus of empirical material, to further study how these technologies are communicated and in what way they transform the mediatisation of the fashion industry. Moreover, further studies are necessary to enhance understanding of the sustainability challenges associated with these new techniques.

References

1. The Fabricant, Iridescence, https://www.thefabricant.com/iridescence, last accessed 2022/09/19.
2. Palumbo, J. (2022). You can thank The Sims for the rise of luxury fashion in gaming. *CNN*. https://edition.cnn.com/style/article/digital-fashion-video-games-the-sims/index.html, last accessed 2022/11/25.
3. MVFW, https://mvfw.org/, last accessed 2024/01/13.
4. Rocamora, A. (2020). Mediatization and digital media in the field of fashion. In M. Bernard (Ed.), *Fashion theory, A reader* (2nd ed., pp. 725–737). Routledge.
5. Textile consult Digital Fashion: The Way Forward for Sustainability? (2023). https://www.textileconsult.co.uk/2023/07/31/digital-fashion-the-way-forward-for-sustainability/, last accessed 2024/11/19.
6. CNBC International News: How Carlings created a digital-only clothing line that no-one can wear, (2019). https://www.youtube.com/watch?v=R1VtGmaDM84, last accessed 2024/10/3.
7. Kawamura, Y. (2023). *Fashion-ology, fashion studies in the postmodern digital era* (3rd ed.). Bloomsbury Visual Arts.
8. Story, J. (2021). *Cultural theory and popular culture, an introduction*. Routledge.
9. Davis, F. (2020). Do clothes speak? What makes them fashion? In M. Bernard (Ed.), *Fashion theory, a reader* (2nd ed., pp. 225–235). Routledge.
10. Bernard, M. (2002). *Fashion as communication* (2nd ed.). Routledge.
11. Barthes, R. (1995). *The semiotic challenge*. University of California Press.
12. Rocamora, A. (2020). Personal fashion blogs, screens and mirrors in digital self-portraits. In M. Bernard (Ed.), *Fashion theory, a reader* (2nd ed., pp. 692–706). Routledge.
13. Huggard, E. (2020). The role of the fashion communicator as a cultural intermediary. In E. Huggard & J. Cope (Eds.), *Communicating fashion brands, theoretical and practical perspectives* (pp. 39–56). Routledge.
14. Bourdieu, P. (1984). *Distinction: A social critique of the judgement of taste*. Routledge.
15. Muturi, H. (2024). Impact of Social media on fashion trends and consumer behaviour in Kenya. *International Journal of Fashion and Design, 3*(1), 24–36.
16. @lilmiquela, Instagram. https://www.instagram.com/lilmiquela/, last accessed 2024/11/25.
17. Drenten, J., & Brooks, G. (2020). Celebrity 2.0: Lil Miquela and the rise of a virtual star system. *Feminist Media Studies, 20*(8), 1319–1323.
18. Smith Maguire, J., & Matthews, J. (2012). Are we all Cultural Intermediaries Now? An Introduction to Cultural Intermediaries in Context. *European Journal of Cultural Studies, 15*(5), 405–416.
19. Wilson, E. (2004). *Adorned in dreams. Fashion and modernity*. London, I B Tauris
20. Periyasamy, A., & Periyasami, S. (2023). Rise of digital fashion and metaverse: Influence on sustainability. *Digital Economy and Sustainable Development, 1*(16).
21. Davis, T., Dunne, L. E., & Bigger, E. (2024). Risky business: Sustainable fashion through new technologies. In M. Charter, B. Pan, & S. Black (Eds.), *Accelerating sustainability in fashion, Clothing & Textiles* (pp. 377–392). Routledge.
22. Yilmaz, T., Sagfossen, S., & Velasco, C. (2023). What makes NFTs valuable to consumers? Perceived value drivers associated with NFTs liking, purchasing, and holding. *Journal of Business Research, 165*.
23. Göncü-Berk, G., & Shahaj, E. R. (2024). Wearable tech, virtual fashion and immersive technologies. In M. Charter, B. Pan, & S. Black (Eds.), *Accelerating sustainability in fashion, Clothing & Textiles* (pp. 393–402). Routledge.
24. Liu, M. (2022). AMC #1-How to apply digital fashion clothes to your photo. *Artisant*. https://www.youtube.com/watch?v=_Ct8wavNxUI, last accessed 2022/11/20.
25. Pozzo, B. (2024). Fashion in the metaverse. In A. Larry, L. DiMatteo, & M. Cannarsa (Eds.), *Research handbook on the metaverse and law* (Vol. 23, pp. 217–228). Edward Elgar Publishing.

26. Cheng, I., & Charter, M. (2024). A pathway towards future sustainable fashion in 2030. In M. Charter, B. Pan, & S. Black (Eds.), *Accelerating sustainability in Fashion, Clothing & Textiles* (pp. 363–376). Routledge.
27. United Nations Climate Change: Fashion Industry Charter for Climate Action. (2023). https://unfccc.int/climate-action/sectoral-engagement-for-climate-action/fashion-charter, last accessed 2024/11/4.
28. European Commission: Communication - EU Strategy for Sustainable and Circular Textiles. (2022). https://environment.ec.europa.eu/publications/textiles-strategy_en, last accessed 2024/10/5.
29. Carlings: Carlings først ute med digital mote, https://carlings.com/no/stories/inspirasjon%2D%2Dtrender/Carlings-digital-collection/, Accessed 2024/09/15.
30. Kress, G., & van Leeuwen, T. *Reading images, the grammar of visual design* (2nd ed.). Routledge.
31. @carlings_official: Instagram posts 2018/11/14, 2018/11/15, 2018/11/16, 2018/11/19 https://www.instagram.com/carlings_official/, last accessed 2024/09/15.
32. Carlings Official: adDRESS THE FUTURE (2018). https://www.youtube.com/watch?v=Sothlpxa6V0, last accessed 2024/05/13.
33. Carlings: About us, https://carlings.com/sv/corporate/om-carlings/about-us/, last accessed 2024/09/15.
34. Odalisque: Carlings launches the Neo-Ex with the artificial influencer "Perl.www", https://www.odalisquemagazine.com/articles/2018/11/15/carlings-launches-the-neo-ex-the-artificial-influencer-perlwww-written-by-fashion-tales, last accessed 2024/10/19.
35. Virtue Nordic: Carlings, Grand Prix Winning Digital Clothing Collection, https://www.virtue-worldwide.com/#projects, last accessed 2024/9/2.
36. Lupton, E. (2017). *Design is storytelling*. Cooper-Hewitt Museum.
37. Kapferer, J. N. (2014). The artification of luxury: From artisans to artists. *Business Horizons, 57*, 371–380.
38. Amos, C., Holmes, G., & Strutton, D. (2008). Exploring the relationship between celebrity endorser effects and advertising effectiveness: A quantitative synthesis of effect size. *International Journal of Advertising, 27*(2), 209–234.
39. Hypeauditor, The Top Instagram Virtual Influencers in 2019, (2019). https://hypeauditor.com/blog/the-top-instagram-virtual-influencers-in-2019/, last accessed 2024/10/27.
40. Aaker, D. (2002). *Building strong brands*. Simon & Schuster UK Ltd.
41. Piligrimiene, Z., Dovaliene, A., & Virvilaite, R. (2015). Consumer engagement in value co-creation: What kind of value it creates for company? *Engineering Economics, 26*(4), 452460.
42. Chang, Y. W. (2022). Space exploration inspiration for fashion styling and design in six decades since 1960: A review. *Acta Astronautica, 198*, 767–776.
43. Hayward, P. (Ed.). (2004). *Off the planet: Music, sound and science fiction cinema*. John Libbey Publishing Ltd.
44. Paschalina, Z., Gould, S., & Venkatesh, A. (2012). 'Am I Getting It or Not?' The practices involved in 'Trying to Consume' a new technology. *JPIM, 29*(2), 216–228.
45. Hollebeek, L. D., & Macky, K. (2019). Digital content marketing's role in fostering consumer engagement, trust, and value: framework, fundamental propositions, and implications. *Journal of Interactive Marketing, 45*, 27–41.
46. Neustaedter, C., & Fedorovskaya, E. A. (2009). Presenting identity in a virtual world through avatar appearances. *Graphics Interface, 183–190.*
47. Pervinca Bellini, E. (2020). Moda sostenibile: gli abiti virtuali di Dress-X. *Vogue*. https://www.vogue.it/vogue-talents/article/moda-sostenibile-vestiti-virtuali-intervista-creatrici-ecommerce-dressx. last accessed 2024/11/29.

Sustainability, Social and Political Issues

Fashion System: The Need for Transparency in Sustainability Communication on Brands Website

Catarina Costa, Paulo Salgado, and Ana C. Broega

Abstract The communication of fashion brands, traditionally focused on product sales, has increasingly taken on an active role in conveying messages aligned with modern values of sustainability and ethics, driven by growing awareness of the textile industry's social and environmental impacts. In this context, communication is essential in shaping consumers' perceptions of brands, in sharing brand values, purpose, and practices. Communicating transparency emerges as a fundamental value, as it allows consumers to make more informed decisions and holds brands accountable for their actions. This article analyzes the interrelation between brand communication, sustainability, and transparency in the fashion industry, exploring how brands use online communication to build an image of social and environmental responsibility. Throughout the article, the challenges and opportunities of transparent communication will be addressed, as well as the role of activist organizations and legal regulations in promoting more sustainable and ethical practices in the fashion industry. However, this study does not examine the transparency and accuracy of the information itself but rather analyzes how brands communicate their sustainability messages in a transparent manner. This work is part of a master's dissertation project and is divided into two parts: a literature review and a comparative case study between Stella McCartney and People Tree, demonstrating the importance of fashion brands' sustainability transparency on their official websites.

Keywords Sustainability · Transparency · Fashion brand communication

C. Costa (✉) · A. C. Broega
Minho University, Textile Engineering Department, Guimarães, Portugal

P. Salgado
Minho University, Department of Communication Sciences, Braga, Portugal

P. von Wachenfeldt et al. (eds.), *Fashion Communication in the Digital Age*,
Springer Proceedings in Business and Economics,
https://doi.org/10.1007/978-3-031-99481-4_19

1 Literature Review

1.1 Fashion Brand Communication

Good communication is essential for the success of any brand, especially when it comes to sustainable fashion [1]. Nowadays, brand communication goes far beyond merely promoting collections or launching new products; it focuses on building relationships between the brand and its target audience [2]. As noted by Araújo, Broega, and Mota-Ribeiro [1], without communication, fashion does not reach the consumer, and without the consumer, the brand loses relevance.

Media plays a crucial role in disseminating brand values, purpose, and communication, not only showcasing the latest trends but also spreading messages and lifestyles. However, there are various types of media, such as television, radio, and social media, among others. Valente (2008, as cited by [1]) highlights that advertising has shifted from focusing solely on products and sales to emphasizing the importance of storytelling and conveying messages that resonate with the lifestyle, beliefs, and emotions of the target audience. In this way, fashion brands do not merely sell their products but also their identity and narrative, which may consumers gradually identify with. With the rapid and growing adoption of digital media, brands have become increasingly dependent on communication to build their community and convey their message to consumers [2]. As a result, brand communication must be consistent and reliable to reach as many consumers as possible [1]. To create an effective communication plan, it is essential to address key questions such as: What message does the brand want to convey? What atmosphere does the brand aim to create? And what are the best strategies to engage with the audience? [16].

Communication campaigns have various objectives, including informing consumers, capturing their interest, launching new products, raising awareness about social and environmental responsibility initiatives, and sharing industry-related events [3]. Overall, brands and their communication strategies evolve to keep pace with the rapid changes brought about by technological and temporal transformations. Fashion companies increasingly rely on new technologies to reach their consumers more quickly and effectively, presenting products in engaging and immersive ways that create a captivating environment for their target audience [3].

In conclusion, communication has become not only a tool for selling products but also an essential element for any fashion brand. In addition to fostering a connection with consumers, communication helps build the brand's identity and, consequently, contributes to its success. But, with the growth of sustainable awareness, brands must be transparent about their processes to prove to consumers that they are genuinely socially and environmentally responsible.

1.2 *Sustainability in the Fashion Sector*

In the face of climate change and increasing environmental degradation, sustainability has emerged as a critical issue involving both governments and society. In recent years, growing environmental awareness has led many companies, including those in the textile sector, to reassess their practices and ideologies to achieve more responsible production methods that are less harmful to the environment, aiming for more eco-friendly solutions to prevent irreversible damage to our planet [1]. With this reassessment of beliefs, brands identifying as eco-fashion have emerged, committed to reducing the environmental impact of their practices by adopting procedures such as zero waste and upcycling [4].

Additionally, many companies have begun opting for local production, which not only helps reduce their carbon footprint but also ensures a closer relationship between companies and their producers. This allows for more personal monitoring of each stage of the production process and ensures dignified working conditions for everyone involved [4]. Brands have also sought to increase transparency in their practices, encouraging consumers to question their production methods and even visit their factories. Nevertheless, some criticisms have been leveled against certain brands for using terms such as "sustainable" and "ethical" in unclear ways, potentially misleading consumers [5]. Issues such as the use of imported materials and non-transparent upcycling processes further complicate matters. This lack of clarity can harm brand credibility and hinder consumers' understanding of what it truly means to be a sustainable brand [4, 5].

With sustainability in mind, Raworth [6] argues that if the goal is to build an ecological society, the focus of the global economy must shift toward ensuring that everyone can thrive within the planet's environmental limits. Nonetheless, some brands use sustainability discourse aligned with consumers' ethical concerns as a marketing strategy aimed solely at boosting sales rather than making a genuine commitment to consumers and ecological boundaries [4]. Consequently, sustainability directly impacts the foundations of the capitalist production system, making a profound review of current paradigms imperative. A new production ideology was proposed by Leff [7] which was based on environmental limits and human creativity. This paradigm shift is also reflected in consumer behavior, as people are becoming increasingly aware of ecological issues. They now question the products they purchase, how they are made, what materials are used, and whether the workers involved throughout the manufacturing process are treated fairly and ethically. In this way, sustainable fashion consumption becomes a "political act" prioritizing brands that align with sustainable values while often disadvantaging those that support or remain neutral toward the flawed capitalist system [8].

With the aid of social media, the involvement and commitment of certain consumers can create ripple effects, turning them into community influencers and attracting more consumers who share the same ideologies and concerns. This collective action fosters social and activist movements willing to challenge practices and ideologies established over past decades, adopting a critical and participatory stance in society [8]. For instance, Fashion Revolution (2024) launched the #WhoMadeMyFabric movement, encouraging society to pressure fashion brands into being transparent about the origins of their fabrics and the conditions of their producers.

Thus, sustainability in the fashion industry goes far beyond a simple change in materials or production processes. It entails a profound transformation of economic and social relations, where brands and consumers work together to build a fairer and more sustainable future.

1.3 Transparency in Brand Communication

Transparency has become an essential parameter for brand communication, particularly in the context of sustainable fashion. According to Fletcher [9], transparency is one of the core values of sustainability, prompting ethical fashion brands to adopt this practice to build credibility and trust with their consumers. Thus, sharing detailed information about production processes—from the origin of materials to distribution logistics—is a crucial strategy for strengthening trust and enhancing the perceived value of a brand [4].

Being transparent generally means making public information about the brand's history and its founders, the materials and fabrics used, their countries of origin, the relationship with production partners, and the location of these suppliers. It is also important for brands to communicate how they package their products and the distributors they use to deliver these items to consumers [4]. Still, despite many brands claiming to have or aiming to achieve such transparency, reality often falls short. In numerous cases, brands fail to provide comprehensive information, such as the materials used, their countries of origin, or details about production conditions. The absence of such information raises questions about the authenticity of some companies' sustainability narratives, which can negatively impact consumer trust [5]. Transparency, though, is not solely an ethical issue; it is also used as a strategy to add value to brands. Over the past decade, with the growth of the industry and increased competition among fashion brands, companies have sought a loyal and lasting connection with their consumers through honest and transparent communication. In this way, providing clear and complete information significantly enhances the brand's value in the eyes of its audience [4]. With the growing consumer demand for transparency, some brands have resorted to communicating questionable ethical practices, such as greenwashing. According to Ribeiro and Mozine [3], greenwashing refers to the strategic appropriation of sustainability-related marketing by companies to promote an image of environmental responsibility. This practice, often disconnected from effective actions, conceals the lack of genuine commitment to socio-environmental issues. As Pagotto [10] notes, greenwashing is an ethical violation, and when consumers uncover this manipulation, the brand's reputation can suffer significant damage.

Therefore, consumer trust must be preserved through genuine transparency practices, maintaining an ethical and honest environment within the brand community and the entire fashion industry [5]. Thus, it is possible to understand that for a sustainable brand to be transparent, it is necessary to use communication to prove its actions to consumers, intertwining communication, sustainability, and transparency as one.

1.4 Interrelationship Between Communication, Sustainability, and Transparency

Fashion brand communication, sustainability, and transparency are areas that, at first glance, might seem entirely unrelated. The fashion sector, characterized by its fleeting trends and rampant consumption, appears to contrast sharply with the essence and principles of sustainability. Nevertheless, the rise of activist movements advocating for a transformation of values within the fashion industry has increased pressure on brands, prompting them to adjust their principles to achieve a more conscious and ethical approach to fashion. In this context, transparent communication becomes crucial, as it allows brands to demonstrate their genuine commitments to sustainable practices and build trusting relationships with their consumers [11].

To implement and monitor transparency in brand communication, various organizations have been established over the years to regulate the fashion industry and enhance control over responsible practices. Movements such as the Fashion Revolution, the Ethical Fashion Initiative, and the Clean Clothes Campaign are examples of drivers for change, setting benchmarks and demanding transparency and accountability from brands. The Fashion Revolution is a global movement advocating for fairness and transparency in the fashion industry. It is also responsible for creating the Fashion Transparency Index, which annually evaluates and ranks major companies based on their public disclosure of information regarding their policies, practices, and social and environmental impacts (Fashion [12]). Similarly, the Ethical Fashion Initiative (EFI), a flagship program of the International Trade Centre, aims to promote sustainable fashion production, focusing on developing communities. EFI has collaborated with numerous artisans and designers to ensure their fair and equitable inclusion in the fashion industry [13]. Lastly, the Clean Clothes Campaign is a movement dedicated to ensuring fair and safe working conditions for all workers involved in the textile production process. This campaign demands transparency and accountability from major textile producers, advocating for a dignified and ethical work environment for all [14].

In addition to these organizations that support and pressure brands to adopt more conscious practices, environmental concerns have become increasingly urgent and indispensable, leading to formal government interventions in Europe. The European Parliament enacted a Directive (Directive (EU) 2024/825, 2024, art 3) to protect consumers and ensure the accuracy of brands' sustainability and green claims. This legal milestone reinforces the importance of monitoring and enforcing sustainable practices, providing consumers with a legal guarantee regarding brands' sustainability claims [15].

Ultimately, it is critical to recognize the importance of raising awareness among fashion brands about the ethical and environmental challenges we face today. By fostering ethical and truthful communication about their values and practices with consumers, brands can go further by becoming vectors of education and awareness for the cause of more sustainable fashion.

2 Empirical Work: Comparative Case Studies

In this section, to evaluate how fashion brands communicate their transparency focused on sustainability, an investigation is presented on two case studies, followed by a comparative analysis between them. This investigation is inserted into a master's degree project conducted by the authors of this current paper, one master's student in fashion communication design and two academics specializing in the fields of communication and sustainability. This study examines Stella McCartney and People Tree, selected based on their active role in the textile industry, particularly in the promotion of sustainability and socio-environmental responsibility. The selected brands were founded by activists who are actively engaged with environmental causes and established their brands based on ideologies of transparency and sustainability.

The first brand, Stella McCartney, is recognized for its notable evolution and increasing commitment to socio-environmental responsibility (Stella McCartney, N.d). The second brand, People Tree, is a pioneer in sustainability, being one of the first fashion brands to consider sustainability and fair trade, starting in 1991 [16].

To study how brands communicate their sustainability ideologies transparently, essential criteria were defined based on the theoretical research previously developed in this paper. For a brand to be considered transparent in its communication, it must demonstrate its intentions, conveying its message and ideologies effectively to its target audience. Moreover, the information must be clear and accessible, allowing consumers to quickly access and understand all data. Another crucial aspect of transparency in the communication of sustainability involves the recognition and association of these brands with global socio-environmental responsibility organizations, as well as the presentation of ethical and/or sustainability certifications.

The criteria are categorized into five dimensions, each accompanied by specific indicators, as outlined below:

Website structure:

1. User-friendliness
2. Intuitive functionalities

Clear and detailed information:

1. Accessibility and comprehensibility of the information provided
2. Detailed descriptions

Transparency of the production process:

1. Detailed and explicit descriptions of processes
2. Identification of all stakeholders involved in the processes

Partnership associations and certificates:

1. Comprehensive disclosure of all partner associations, including detailed descriptions
2. Presentation of ethical and sustainable certifications

Sustainability reports:

1. Timely and accessible presentation of sustainability reports, ensuring they are up-to-date and easy to access

With these criteria in mind, an analysis of the websites of both brands was conducted to explore how the information is presented and organized to promote accessibility and transparency to their target audience.

2.1 Case Study 1: Analysis of the Stella McCartney Brand Website with Focus on Sustainability

The progressive luxury brand Stella McCartney, founded in 2001, focuses on developing high-quality products with minimal environmental impact, using innovative, cruelty-free, and sustainable materials. Guided by values of transparency and responsibility, the brand aims to inspire positive societal change to protect the environment and future generations, as mentioned on its official website (Stella McCartney, N.d).

Website Structure Stella McCartney's website is organized to be accessible and intuitive, with a dedicated sustainability section featuring four main categories: *Measuring Our Impact, Social Sustainability, Circularity,* and *The Sustainability Edit: Innovation Edit.*

The sustainability homepage is further divided into eight sections: *Materials and Innovation, Collaborators and Commitments, Timeline, Our Commitments, Social Responsibility & Human Rights, Circularity, Spotlight on: Airslide,* and *Spotlight on: Stella x Greenpeace.*

Detailed Description of the Sections The *Materials and Innovation* area highlights the innovative materials used by the brand, such as Savian, Bananatex, and organic cotton, emphasizing their commitment to sustainable practices. Each material is presented on dedicated subpages with detailed information about its origin, usage, and environmental impact. In *Collaborators and Commitments,* the brand showcases its collaborations and certifications, including partnerships with the Ethical Trading Initiative, PETA (People for the Ethical Treatment of Animals), and the Humane Society.

The *Timeline* narrates the brand's journey, detailing key milestones, changes, and innovations adopted over the years. Highlights include the founding year (2001) when the brand committed to avoiding leather, fur, skins, feathers, and animal glues; the introduction of a revolutionary vegan alternative to animal fur in 2015; and a partnership with TheRealReal, a luxury consignment resale brand, in 2017.

The *Our Commitments* section explores the brand's adopted commitments and their impacts, such as prohibiting the use of cotton from countries with high risks of child or forced labor and eliminating plastic bottles from all offices and stores.

Stella McCartney's ethical approach extends to the *Social Responsibility & Human Rights* section, where the brand highlights everyone involved in its production chain, from farmers growing raw materials to conscious consumers. The brand outlines principles aimed at creating positive impacts for all individuals involved, basing its fair-trade ideologies on practices from the International Labor Organization (ILO).

In the *Circularity* section, the brand emphasizes its sustainability initiatives through partnerships with organizations like the Clever Care Initiative and the Cradle to Cradle Products Innovation Institute, supporting the transition to a circular business model.

At the bottom of the sustainability page, two featured initiatives are presented: a pair of circularly produced slippers made from factory waste and a collaboration between *Stella McCartney and Greenpeace*, showcasing a collection made from organic cotton to support the fight against deforestation in the Amazon rainforest.

Overall Website Analysis In addition to the sustainability page, the website provides access to the brand's sustainability and impact reports. Stella McCartney's website is comprehensive and user-friendly, offering consumers clear information. All content is divided into broader, summarized themes that lead to more detailed and informative subpages.

2.2 Case Study 2: Analysis of the People Tree Brand Website with Focus on Sustainability

Founded in 1991, People Tree is one of the pioneering brands in fair trade and sustainable clothing. For more than three decades, it has been dedicated to promoting ethical practices, expanding market access for marginalized communities, and offering sustainable alternatives. Furthermore, it has established itself as a reference point for the exchange of knowledge and inspiration, driving the creation of a more equitable and sustainable world [16]. The brand People Tree was founded by Safia

Minney, considered a visionary entrepreneur who revolutionized the fashion industry by championing ethical and sustainable practices. Under her leadership, the brand became a global pioneer in Fair Trade fashion, promoting transparency, respect for workers, and environmentally responsible methods [17].

Website Structure The People Tree brand's website is simple, although it lacks a section exclusively dedicated to sustainability. The Our Story area is divided into four main themes: the brand's history, mission, the impact of COVID-19, and Making a Better World. It is also possible to access information about the Responsible Wool initiative and the brand's partner producers.

Detailed Description of the Sections The four themes presented on the page are described briefly, with little additional detail. Initially, the brand's history is highlighted, emphasizing the year 1991 as its founding year and the opening of its first store in 2001. Next, the mission and values of People Tree are introduced, including its commitment to fair trade and sustainability. In the context of the COVID-19 pandemic, the brand reaffirms its commitment to maintaining sales in Japan despite the economic challenges imposed by the global crisis. Lastly, it is mentioned that the brand is implementing organizational adjustments and improvements to its products, as well as developing a new website with an updated design and a renewed team.

A secondary page titled *Responsible Wool* highlights the collaboration between the brand and the Kumbeshwar Technical School (KTS), an organization based in Nepal that specializes in the artisanal production of wool items. This section explains the reasons for People Tree's use of wool, detailing its origins and the producers involved responsible. Finally, the page provides access to information about all the brand's partner producers, available through related secondary pages.

Overall Website Analysis The People Tree website is functional and accessible but presents limitations regarding the depth of information, especially about sustainability and transparency. The *Our Story* section is quite brief and does not detail all the materials used or the brand's specific practices.

Despite these limitations, the website stands out for providing direct access to information about the brand's partner producers, promoting an important level of transparency. However, for a brand that has been a pioneer in the sustainable market, the content presented on the website does not fully reflect People Tree's reputation and history.

2.3 Comparing Results

When comparing the two websites of the brands Stella McCartney and People Tree, a notable difference can be observed in the approach chosen by each to communicate, reflecting varying levels of depth and clarity in the presentation of information.

Stella McCartney stands out for its extensive organization and detailed content structure, which are divided into several specific sections. Each section is complemented by secondary pages that thoroughly elaborate on the information provided. This approach ensures a comprehensive and informative experience. Additionally, the availability of impact and sustainability reports demonstrates a high degree of transparency and reinforces the brand's credibility within the sector based only on the information on the official website.

In contrast, the People Tree website, while functional and accessible, exhibits significant limitations regarding the depth and organization of information related to the brand's sustainability. The information provided is more concise and lacks detail, briefly presenting its history, mission, and some of the materials it works with. Despite its brevity, the website values transparency by offering more detailed information about its partner producers, which is a positive aspect of its communication regarding the production and supply chain However, the lack of more detailed insights into its materials and sustainable practices may create a gap between the brand's established history and the content conveyed to the public.

Overall, the Stella McCartney website stands out for its detailed and transparent presentation of practices, whereas the People Tree website, while addressing fundamental aspects of its mission, lacks more in-depth information on those aspects. This difference reflects the distinct communication strategies of the brands and the priority and relevance of brands in communicating their practices on their official website.

2.4 Comparative Likert Scale Table

To make it easier to understand the comparative analysis between the two brands, a framework of criteria for assessing the transparency of sustainability communication (Table 1) was created based on the literature review carried out and associated

Table 1 Comparative analysis of the Stella McCartney and People Tree brand websites

Criteria	Stella McCartney	People Tree
Website accessibility	5	4
Clear and detailed information	5	3
Transparency of the production process	4	3
Partnership associations and certificates	4	1
Sustainability reports	5	1
Total (average)	4,6	2,4

with a Likert scale (5 points, where 1 represents the absence of the criterion and 5 clearly and explicitly presents the criterion), presented as follows:

1. Not present: The criterion is not addressed on the website.
2. Presents minimally: The criterion is addressed but in a superficial or limited way.
3. Presents moderately: The criterion is addressed with a reasonable level of detail but with some gaps.
4. Presents extensively: The criterion is addressed with clarity and significant detail but could still be improved.
5. Presents comprehensively: The criterion is addressed in an exemplary manner, with transparency and extensive detail.

The evaluation is based on an analysis of both brands' websites in terms of their transparency in communicating sustainability in their production. In terms of website accessibility, Stella McCartney's communication design is intuitive and well-structured, making it easy to navigate and access information (we gave it a score of 5). People Tree, on the other hand, has a functional, but less dynamic website with a simple structure (a score of 4 was given in comparison). The Stella McCartney brand offers detailed information on the secondary pages of its website about materials, working practices, and innovations (with a score of 5). As for People Tree, it explicitly presents content, yet the information provided is summarized and not very detailed (with a score of 3). In what relates to the transparency of communication about the production process, both brands promote sustainable practices, however, Stella McCartney presents more information about each stage of the production process and the materials used (for which we gave it a score of 4). People Tree emphasizes its supplying partners in great detail, even if it does not explore other sections and stages of its process (it was given a score of 3 in comparison). In terms of associations, certificates, and reports, both brands stand out in the sector. It must be underlined that only Stella McCartney presents them in a clear and detailed way (with a score of 4 for the transparency of partner associations and 5 for the presentation of sustainability reports). The People Tree brand does not address the last two points on its official website, so it was given a minimum score of 1. Once the scores had been assigned, the sum of the scores for each brand was averaged to give us a global and qualitative view of each website. The Stella McCartney brand has an average score of 4.6, while the People Tree brand has an average score of 2.4. We can conclude that the Stella McCartney brand, compared to the People Tree brand, has a more transparent, accessible, and appealing website, and can be used as a good example of sustainable brands that want to communicate their ideologies in a transparent and detailed way. These findings highlight the critical need for greater coherence between a brand's stated values and the way these principles are effectively conveyed through its communication strategies.

3 Conclusion

Being transparent is a fundamental element of any fashion brand's communication and is becoming a key factor for consumers. With the growing pressure from consumers and global pro-sustainability organizations, brands are forced to present their ideologies and, above all, their results honestly and clearly, without misusing environmental concerns merely as marketing tools.

This article, part of a master's dissertation project, focuses on the analysis of online communication on websites, with a particular emphasis on the transparent and clear communication of sustainable practices and ideologies. However, the true transparency of the information found cannot be assessed solely through the website, as external and cross-validation is required. Therefore, this article focuses on analyzing communication and the methods used to present information, without verifying the accuracy of the content provided. The cases analyzed in this study highlight different approaches to communicating sustainability transparently. While Stella McCartney presents detailed and consistent practices, reaffirming its commitment to sustainability, the People Tree brand, despite its historical relevance in the sustainable market, still faces challenges in communicating its initiatives in greater depth. With these cases in mind, fashion brands can learn that sustainability communication is not just about promoting an ethical image but about actively engaging with consumers through honest, structured, and evidence-backed transparency. By implementing comprehensive sustainability sections, openly disclosing supply chain details, and collaborating with recognized certification bodies, brands can establish long-term credibility and foster a deeper connection with their audience. Though, this study presents several limitations, primarily its exclusive focus on websites and the information disclosed within them, which prevents the verification of the accuracy and reliability of the data obtained. Additionally, the research is confined to a single mode of online communication, limiting its scope to website content. This restriction underscores the necessity for further studies to encompass a broader spectrum of communication channels, enabling a more comprehensive analysis of transparency in sustainability communication. To address the identified limitations and build upon the research conducted, future studies are expected to focus on verifying the accuracy of the information provided by brands. The objective is to develop clear and effective strategies that enable the assessment of transparency in the sustainability practices and ideologies of fashion brands, such as digital portfolios and sustainability reporting platforms. Through this approach, the aim is to bridge existing gaps in the field of sustainability communication, contributing to a more reliable and accountable dissemination of information.

In this way, it is possible to demonstrate that, although the movement toward sustainability transparency is growing, there is a significant way to go, namely in social values and ethics, as well as in the transparency of profit distribution through the fashion business chain. Transparency in communication, combined with sustainability, is not just a contemporary requirement, but a fundamental pillar for the future of fashion. Brands that genuinely incorporate these values will be better able to face the challenges of the sector, contributing to the development of a more ethical, conscious industry that is in tune with global demands.

References

1. Araújo M, Broega A C, Mota-Ribeiro S (2014) A comunicação das marcas de moda sustentável. In *Proceedings of the 2nd CIMODE: International Fashion and Design Congress*, pp 2987–2990
2. Carrilho, K., & Markus, K. (2014). Narrativas na construção de marcas: storytelling e a comunicação de marketing. *Organicom, 11*(20). https://doi.org/10.11606/issn.2238-2593.organicom.2014.139224
3. Santos, C. A. (2022) *Comunicação de marcas de moda: estágio na Companhia das Soluções* (Master's thesis). University of Beira Interior
4. Guerreiro, A. D. (2021). A transparência das marcas de moda ética portuguesas (Master's thesis). University of Beira Interior.
5. Testa, F., Iraldo, F., Vaccari, A., & Ferrari, E. (2013). Why eco-labels can be effective marketing tools: Evidence from a study on Italian consumers. *Business Strategy and the Environment, 24*(4), 252–265. https://doi.org/10.1002/bse.1821. [Accessed 2 Feb 2025].
6. Raworth, K. (2018). *Doughnut economics: seven ways to think like a 21st-century economist.* Chelsea Green Publishing, White River Junction.
7. Leff, E. (2014). *Ecologia, capital e cultura: a territorialização da racionalidade ambiental* (2nd ed.). Civilização Brasileira.
8. Ribeiro, V. E., & Mozine, A. C. S. (2023). Por uma "moda mais sustentável": o índice de transparência da moda de duas marcas de Vila Velha-ES. *Revista Científica Interdisciplinar, 8*(1).
9. Fletcher, K. (2008). Sustainable fashion and textiles: design journeys. *The Journal of Design, Creative Process & the Fashion Industry.*
10. Pagotto, É. L. (2013). *Greenwashing: os conflitos éticos da propaganda ambiental* (Master's thesis). School of Arts, Sciences and Humanities, University of São Paulo (USP).
11. Brown C (2022) *Sustainability and fashion communication: A case study analysis of transparent practices in the fashion industry* (Master's thesis). California State University. Available at: https://scholarworks.calstate.edu/downloads/2j62sb83v
12. Fashion Revolution (2023) Fashion Transparency Index. Available at: https://www.fashionrevolution.org/fashion-transparency-index/ [Accessed 16 Nov 2024]
13. Ethical Fashion Initiative (2023) About Us. Available at: https://ethicalfashioninitiative.org/about [Accessed 16 Nov 2024]
14. Clean Clothes Campaign (2023) About. Available at: https://cleanclothes.org/about [Accessed 16 Nov 2024]
15. European Union. (2024). Directive (EU) 2024/825 of the European Parliament and of the Council of 14 February 2024 on [...]. *Official Journal of the European Union L, 39*, 1–25. Available at: https://eur-lex.europa.eu/eli/dir/2024/825/oj [Accessed 27 Jan 2025]
16. People Tree. (n.d.). About us. Available at: https://peopletree.eu/pages/about-us [Accessed 29 Nov 2024]
17. Minney, S. (2023). Profile. Available at: https://safia-minney.com/profile/ [Accessed 27 Jan 2025]

Classic Brands and Global Culture: A Symbolic Shift Toward Sustainability Inspired by Barthes

Hsin-Pey Peng

Abstract This study examines how global culture drives the symbolic evolution of classic fashion brands to address sustainability, drawing on Roland Barthes' *The Fashion System* and *Mythologies*. Through semiotic theory and case studies of Hermès, Gucci, Stella McCartney, and LVMH, it highlights how iconic brands balance tradition and innovation to meet globalization's challenges and sustainability demands. This chapter explores how symbolic transformations preserve heritage while aligning with cultural and environmental narratives, fostering consumer engagement and cultural capital. Additionally, it discusses how corporate social responsibility (CSR) initiatives impact brand image and consumer perception, strengthening the connection between semiotic meaning and market influence. These findings offer insights for branding, cultural studies, and sustainability in a connected world.

Keywords Global culture · Symbolic shift · Sustainability · Heritage and innovation · Luxury branding · Roland Barthes

1 Introduction

Classic fashion brands, long revered for their cultural heritage and timeless allure, are navigating a transformative era in the context of globalization. The worldwide expansion of markets and the rise of sustainability as a core value have heightened the need for these brands to balance tradition with contemporary demands. Historically embedded in specific cultural narratives and signifying social status and identity, these brands now face the challenge of redefining their symbolism to

---

H.-P. Peng (✉)
Guangzhou Institute of Science and Technology, Guangzhou City, China

P. von Wachenfeldt et al. (eds.), *Fashion Communication in the Digital Age*,
Springer Proceedings in Business and Economics,
https://doi.org/10.1007/978-3-031-99481-4_20

resonate with an increasingly diverse, global audience. Moreover, they must contend with the trend of "cultural omnivorism,"[1] where eclectic consumption habits challenge traditional notions of exclusivity and consistency in cultural expression. This shift underscores the evolving interplay between heritage and modernity within global culture.

Sustainability has emerged as a defining force, reshaping the global luxury landscape. Beyond environmental responsibility, it now encompasses fair trade, social equity, and inclusive design, compelling classic fashion brands to reframe their symbolic narratives. In this era of "localized globalization," brands are challenged to retain their cultural roots while engaging with global cultural dynamics. This requires a nuanced approach where symbols are adapted to reflect universal values without losing their heritage-driven authenticity. By crafting narratives that integrate equity, inclusivity, and environmental stewardship, brands can create symbols that resonate globally while maintaining cultural specificity, just like "trait" Barthes mentioned [1]. This balancing act underscores sustainability not only as an operational goal but as a central tenet of global cultural dialogue.

Drawing on Barthes' *The Fashion System* [1], this chapter explores the application of semiotic structures in luxury branding, particularly his tripartite framework of "object, support, and variant." Additionally, Barthes' *Mythologies* [2] provides insights into how brands construct modern myths around sustainability, reinforcing their cultural significance. By integrating these frameworks with CSR discussions, this study illuminates the evolving symbolic landscape of luxury brands in global culture.

Iconic brands such as Hermès, Gucci, Stella McCartney, and the LVMH Group exemplify how sustainability can serve as both strategy and narrative within global fashion culture. Hermès innovates through sustainable materials while preserving artisanal craftsmanship, and Gucci integrates bold environmental messaging into its campaigns. These brands leverage symbolic transformations to align with global expectations of ethical consumption, reshaping their cultural narratives to balance heritage and innovation. This alignment highlights their ability to foster global cultural dialogue while addressing contemporary values.

2 Theoretical Framework and Literature Review

2.1 Literature Review: Global Culture Vs. Classic Fashion

The acceleration of globalization and cultural flows has significantly transformed the expression of classic fashion, evolving it from a singular regional cultural symbol or, more specifically, its Western-originated roots, into a crucial medium for

[1] Cultural Omnivorism refers to the phenomenon of simultaneously consuming and appreciating a wide variety of cultural forms, encompassing both highbrow and lowbrow genres. The term was first introduced by Richard Peterson in 1992. The Omnivore Hypothesis suggests that cultural elites are more likely to be cultural omnivores, possessing broad tastes that span across both elite and popular cultural forms.

cross-cultural exchange. This literature review focuses on three key aspects—cultural hybridity, the impact of digital technology and social media on fashion communication, and the resurgence of retro and nostalgia trends—to examine the profound influence of global culture on classic fashion.

Cultural Hybridity: Tradition Meets Innovation in Fashion

Global cultural interactions have transformed classic fashion, shifting it from a singular cultural symbol, often rooted in Western traditions, into a multifaceted medium for cross-cultural exchange. García Canclini [3] highlights in *Hybrid Cultures: Strategies for Entering and Leaving Modernity* that globalization fosters cultural hybridization, a process where traditional cultural forms interact with modern influences to create new expressions. This theory is particularly evident in the fashion industry, where iconic designs are reimagined to resonate with global audiences [3]. Kawamura [4] emphasizes that fashion operates as "a system of communication," allowing the blending of diverse cultural elements to not only preserve cultural identity but also to cater to international markets [4].

The Japanese kimono and the Chinese qipao, rooted in the unique historical and cultural contexts of their respective countries, have evolved to reflect distinct aesthetic traditions while also embracing the shared influences of modernization. This cultural hybridity is exemplified in their integration into contemporary fashion, where traditional elements are reinterpreted for global audiences. The kimono, renowned for its wide sleeves and intricate patterns, has become a source of inspiration for haute couture brands like Dior and Gucci, showcasing how these iconic garments transcend their origins to influence modern design on an international scale.

Kawamura notes that Dior's use of kimono-style sleeves and traditional Japanese floral motifs in its collections represents a sophisticated balance of Eastern elegance and Western minimalism. Gucci has similarly embraced transcultural innovation by incorporating kimono-inspired belts and embroidery, creating designs that appeal to Asian markets while offering Western consumers a unique cultural symbol. The cheongsam, a symbol of modern Chinese identity, has also undergone significant transformation. Finnane [5], in *Changing Clothes in China: Fashion, History, Nation*, observes how designers like Vivienne Tam have reinvented the cheongsam by blending traditional fastenings with contemporary cuts, lightweight fabrics, and vibrant colors [5]. Prada's collections featuring silk and tassels further demonstrate how the cheongsam's heritage elements can be integrated into luxury fashion, bridging temporal and cultural divides.

These cases underline how cultural fusion enriches classic fashion, turning it into a powerful medium for cross-cultural exchange. As Kawamura argues, fashion is not merely a reflection of culture but an active agent in shaping cultural narratives and identities. By integrating traditional elements with modern aesthetics, designers not only honor cultural heritage but also address the diverse demands of a globalized consumer base. This dynamic interplay between tradition and innovation invites further exploration into the lasting impact of cultural hybridity on the global fashion landscape and its role in constructing cultural identity.

Digital Technology and Social Media Driving Classic Fashion

The rapid development of digital technology and the widespread use of social media have revolutionized how classic fashion is disseminated and perceived globally. Participatory culture and user-generated content (UGC) are at the core of this transformation [6]. According to Jenkins [7], participatory culture empowers users not only as consumers but also as producers and distributors of content, fostering a more interactive and collaborative environment for fashion dissemination [7]. Kaplan and Haenlein [8] further highlight that UGC bridges the gap between brands and consumers, allowing classic fashion to integrate diverse cultural expressions through creative reinterpretation [8]. These digital dynamics have transformed classic fashion from a unidirectional brand-defined symbol into a multifaceted, user-driven cultural asset shared on a global scale.

One prominent example of digital technology empowering classic fashion is Burberry's iconic trench coat. Leveraging platforms like Instagram and TikTok, Burberry has successfully engaged global audiences through high-quality visual content and creative short videos. On Instagram, the brand collaborated with high-profile figures, such as BLACKPINK's Jisoo, a global pop culture icon whose influence transcends regional boundaries, illustrating how classic fashion integrates into and gains relevance within global cultural dialogues [9]. On TikTok, Burberry launched the #BurberryChallenge, encouraging users to showcase their creative ways of styling trench coats. This campaign generated an abundance of user-created content, amplifying the brand's reach among younger audiences while embedding contemporary cultural relevance into its classic designs. By embracing these digital tools, Burberry has rejuvenated its traditional image, resonating with a new generation of consumers.

The DIY culture popularized among younger audiences offers another avenue for the revitalization of classic fashion. Levi's 501 jeans are a hallmark of this movement, with social media enabling users to personalize and share their designs widely. Platforms like Instagram and Pinterest have been flooded with content featuring embroidered, bleached, or modified 501 jeans, showcasing individual creativity and reimagining the timeless design [10]. Furthermore, the #501DIY hashtag on TikTok has garnered millions of views, with users sharing videos showcasing their customization processes. This has fostered cross-cultural and intergenerational dialogues centered around the iconic jeans. This consumer-driven innovation exemplifies how digital platforms enable individuals to reinterpret classic fashion, transforming it into a collaborative cultural artifact that evolves alongside its audience.

Another example is the role of Bilibili in shaping the fashion aesthetics and cultural identity of China's Generation Z. Originating from Japan's ACG (Anime, Comic, and Games) subculture, Bilibili is a uniquely Chinese platform deeply rooted in participatory culture. Known for its strong ties to "second dimension" aesthetics, the platform has evolved into a hub for creative expression across a wide range of cultural genres. Through features such as styling tutorials, DIY designs, and fan-driven trends, Bilibili enables young users to engage with fashion in ways that blend global and local influences. This participatory interaction allows Generation Z to reinterpret classic fashion elements within the context of Chinese cultural narratives. As noted in my own research [11], Bilibili not only functions as a digital hub for fashion innovation but also as a critical space for constructing a distinct generational identity, effectively merging traditional aesthetics with modern, globalized sensibilities.

These user-generated contents vividly demonstrate the role of digital platforms in facilitating personal reinterpretations of classic fashion while promoting collaboration and cultural exchange on a global scale.

Revival and Nostalgia Trends

Amid rapid societal changes and globalization, "nostalgia" seems to be emerging as a remedy for uncertainty, fueling the revival of classic fashion and offering emotional stability. Davis [12] argued that nostalgia provides a psychological anchor during periods of uncertainty, reconnecting individuals to an idealized vision of the past [12]. As globalization fosters cultural exchanges, it also challenges local identities, making nostalgia a tool for reclaiming cultural roots [13]. In fashion, this manifests as a revival of classic styles that evoke familiarity and timeless appeal while adapting to modern consumer needs. Classic fashion thus becomes a medium for individuals to navigate the tension between cultural preservation and global integration.

The commercialization of nostalgia has amplified its influence, especially through strategic marketing by global brands. Merchant and Rose [14] highlight how nostalgia marketing leverages emotional connections with the past to increase brand loyalty and consumer engagement [14]. Hutcheon [15] notes that globalization enables cultural symbols, such as the Western 1960s pop art or Japan's Showa-era aesthetics, to transcend borders and enter global markets as commodified elements [15]. These reinterpreted classics are often infused with modern innovations to resonate with contemporary consumers while preserving their historical significance. For instance, collaborations between luxury brands and streetwear, such as Louis Vuitton and Supreme, showcase how nostalgia-infused designs resonate with younger audiences while preserving their classic heritage.

In 2017, Louis Vuitton and Supreme revolutionized streetwear, transforming a subculture once rooted in Los Angeles skaters and New York hipsters into a global fashion phenomenon [16]. The collaboration between Louis Vuitton and Supreme serves as a quintessential example of blending nostalgia with modernity. By reinterpreting nostalgic elements and recreating cultural symbols, the partnership not only reinforces the historical value of Louis Vuitton's classic designs but also bridges generational and cultural divides through its integration with streetwear culture. This collaboration demonstrates that nostalgia in fashion is not merely a reflection of the past but a powerful driver of contemporary trends. Through the modern reinterpretation of vintage elements, the revival of specific subcultures, and the fusion of nostalgia with current trends, this partnership illustrates how fashion leverages the past to inspire and shape the future.

2.2 *Intersection of Theoretical Framework*

This study proposes a comprehensive framework for understanding the symbolic shifts of classic brands within the context of globalization and sustainability. While the primary focus is on these symbolic transformations, the underlying role of global culture as a symbolic platform—or even as a meta-language—provides an essential theoretical lens. This perspective highlights how cultural symbols operate across diverse contexts, enabling global narratives to transcend local boundaries (See Fig. 1).

1. Semiotics Foundation in Fashion Branding:
Barthes' *The Fashion System* introduces object, support, and variant as fundamental semiotic elements in fashion [1]. These concepts translate into branding, where the object represents the core brand identity (e.g., Hermès' heritage of craftsmanship), the support signifies material elements that embody tradition (e.g., silk scarves, leather goods), and the variant consists of innovations that reinterpret heritage within contemporary contexts (e.g., Hermès' mushroom-based leather, Stella McCartney's ethical fabrics). Expanding on Barthes' insights, this study incorporates *Mythologies* to analyze how cultural symbols evolve into modern myths, reinforcing brand narratives. For instance, Gucci's sustainability campaigns construct a "myth of responsibility," positioning ethical production as an integral brand narrative rather than a supplementary initiative [17].

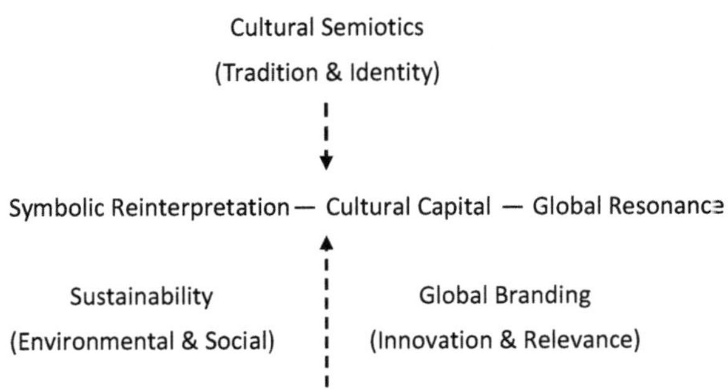

Fig. 1 Conceptual framework of symbolic transformation in global branding

2. Global Culture as a Symbolic Platform
Global culture acts as a symbolic platform that bridges local and global narratives, enabling classic brands to merge traditional elements with universal values. This meta-linguistic capability of global culture facilitates the reinterpretation of heritage symbols into narratives that resonate globally. As Barthes suggests, when a brand is written about in the media, it transitions into popular discourse, participating in the creation of meaning and shaping a new cultural narrative. Additionally, Bourdieu's concept of symbolic capital highlights how these adapted symbols function as cultural assets, enhancing a brand's value and influence within the global market.

3. CSR and Sustainability as a Narrative Lens
CSR initiatives influence consumer perceptions and enhance brand legitimacy by linking corporate values with consumer expectations of ethical consumption [18]. Sustainability extends beyond operational practices to serve as a narrative framework for symbolic innovation. Practices such as the use of eco-friendly materials by Hermès and the inclusive campaigns of Gucci demonstrate how symbolic adaptations address environmental, economic, and social sustainability, fostering relevance in global culture [19] [20]. LVMH's LIFE 360 strategy exemplifies how sustainability-driven branding reinforces luxury narratives of exclusivity and responsibility, positioning the conglomerate as an industry leader in sustainability [21]. By examining CSR's role in semiotic transformation, this chapter links signification theory with market behavior.

3 Case Study: Brand Semiotics and Sustainability

3.1 Research Focus

This study adopts a qualitative case study approach, integrating semiotic analysis with the concept of sustainability to explore how global culture influences the symbolic narratives of classic brands. It focuses on how brands apply Roland Barthes' *The Fashion System* to convey stories of sustainability while preserving traditional values and meeting contemporary cultural expectations.

- Research Questions
  1. How are Barthes' semiotic concepts from *The Fashion System* applied to the sustainability narratives of brands?
  2. How does global culture influence the cultural reconstruction and symbolic reinterpretation of brands?
  3. How do classic brands balance traditional values with contemporary sustainability demands?

- Research Objectives
  1. To explore the role of global culture in shaping the cultural narratives of classic brands.
  2. To analyze how iconic brands reinterpret semiotic theories to enhance their sustainability storytelling.
  3. To combine brand practices with semiotic theory in the context of sustainability, contributing new perspectives to academic knowledge.

3.2 Research Design

This study adopts a robust data collection strategy to explore the interplay between semiotics, global culture, and brand sustainability narratives. The data sources are designed to comprehensively capture the theoretical and practical dimensions of the research. It includes:

Theoretical Literature & Brand Materials

- Semiotics: Analysis of semiotic concepts from Barthes' *The Fashion System* and *Mythologies*.
- Review of academic works: Exploring the role of meta-symbols and hybridization in global culture studies.
- Examination of publicly available sustainability reports and disclosures from Hermès, Gucci, Stella McCartney, and LVMH Group.

Case Studies

- Hermès: Focus on the integration of traditional craftsmanship with innovative materials.
- Gucci: Analysis of bold sustainability messaging through cultural symbolism.
- Stella McCartney: Investigation of ethical fashion and forward-thinking design.
- LVMH Group: Examination of the group's strategies for aligning sustainability with luxury.

3.3 The Key Arguments: The Power of Global Culture as a Symbolic Platform

This study adopts global culture as an emerging framework to analyze the interplay of cultural hybridity, sustainability, and innovation in classic fashion narratives. Incorporating Barthes' semiotic insights, particularly from *The Fashion System*, it views fashion as a form of social communication. Fashion's "system of trends" embodies a dual nature of constant change and eternal return, granting it the ability to innovate while reinforcing traditional values.

In the context of globalization, symbols such as the dove of peace and the earth image embody universal values and serve as bridges for cross-cultural dialogue. Classic fashion brands leverage global cultural narratives to blend traditional and modern values, creating stories that resonate with consumers' moral and cultural expectations. Global culture thus plays a crucial role in reshaping the symbolic narratives of these brands to meet sustainability demands, enabling them to maintain enduring relevance in the global market.

3.4 Result: Reconstructing Symbolic Narratives Through Global Culture

The concept of global culture, viewed as a symbolic platform, has enabled iconic fashion brands to transcend cultural and temporal boundaries and to reconstruct their narratives in response to contemporary demands for sustainability and hybridity. By blending tradition with innovation, these brands reimagine their heritage symbols to align with the aspirations of a globalized audience.

Sustainability as a Narrative Framework The integration of sustainability into symbolic narratives enables brands to bridge their historical identities with contemporary global values. For instance, Hermès innovates through the use of eco-friendly materials while preserving its artisanal craftsmanship, transforming its heritage into a modern emblem of environmental stewardship. Gucci amplifies its commitment to sustainability by incorporating bold cultural motifs into its campaigns, fostering a dialogue between Eastern and Western audiences.

Cultural Hybridity and Global Identity The findings highlight how global culture functions as a meta-symbol, fostering hybridity in branding. Stella McCartney's designs seamlessly combine ethical principles with contemporary aesthetics, resonating with a diverse consumer base. Similarly, the LVMH Group demonstrates how luxury brands can simultaneously reflect local cultural authenticity and global appeal by leveraging hybridized symbolic narratives.

A Model for Sustainable Luxury and Global Culture These reconstructed narratives demonstrate the ability of classic brands to adapt their symbolic capital to the evolving demands of globalization and sustainability. This study identifies a model of "sustainable luxury" where tradition, cultural hybridity, and ethical values converge. By leveraging global culture as a meta-symbol, brands such as Hermès, Gucci, Stella McCartney, and LVMH not only preserve their heritage but also redefine their relevance in the global marketplace [18].

Through these strategies, the study illustrates how global culture serves as a transformative platform, enabling luxury brands to navigate the complexities of tradition, innovation, and sustainability while fostering deeper cultural connectivity in a rapidly changing world.

4 Discussion: The Role of Global Culture in Shaping Luxury Brand Narratives

Global culture has empowered iconic fashion brands to transcend cultural and temporal boundaries through symbolic shifts that address sustainability and hybridity. As iconic luxury brands, Hermès, Gucci, Stella McCartney, and the LVMH Group have continually embraced global culture in recent years to drive the symbolic reconstruction of their narratives and foster cultural hybridity. They have also actively engaged with media to articulate and redefine new perspectives on fashion.

4.1 Hermès: Balancing Heritage, Innovation, and Sustainability

Hermès exemplifies the interplay between heritage and innovation within global luxury culture, aligning with Barthes' object-support-variant model. The object—Hermès' brand identity—remains deeply rooted in artisanal craftsmanship, while the support—material signifiers—traditionally conveys luxury. However, as global culture increasingly integrates sustainability into symbolic narratives, Hermès has introduced innovative materials like Sylvania, a mushroom-based leather alternative (See Fig. 2).

This sustainable innovation serves as a variant that enhances environmental responsibility without compromising the brand's artisanal reputation. By adopting eco-friendly materials, Hermès not only preserves its legacy of craftsmanship but also transforms its heritage symbols into emblems of ecological responsibility. This strategic adaptation resonates with global consumers' growing environmental

Fig. 2 This picture highlights the innovative strategies of three iconic luxury brands—Hermès, Gucci, and LVMH—in redefining their narratives through cultural and sustainable practices Source: Hermès, Gucci, and LVMH Official Websites

Table 1 Proportion of sustainable materials used by Hermès (2020–2023)

Year	Proportion of Traditional Materials	Proportion of Sustainable Materials
2020	85%	15%
2023	60%	40%

Source: Hermès 2023 Sustainability Report

consciousness, bridging local artisanal traditions with contemporary global cultural trends. Ultimately, Hermès positions itself as a pioneer in sustainable luxury, reinforcing its status as both a guardian of tradition and a forward-thinking innovator (See Table 1).

4.2 Gucci: Cultural Hybridity and the Sustainability Narrative

Gucci exemplifies cultural hybridity by blending Eastern and Western aesthetics, constructing a sustainability myth through semiotic transformation and CSR-driven branding. Drawing on Barthes' *Mythologies*, Gucci's campaigns redefine sustainability not merely as an initiative but as an embedded cultural narrative expressed through design and storytelling.

This hybridity is evident in campaigns featuring kimono-inspired designs and traditional Japanese motifs, reimagined within a contemporary luxury context. By merging historical symbols with modern aesthetics, Gucci creates visually compelling narratives that resonate globally. Additionally, its campaign imagery often emphasizes inclusivity and environmental responsibility, showcasing diverse models in culturally hybrid ensembles (See Fig. 2).

Gucci's Equilibrium initiative further integrates sustainability and social responsibility into its brand identity, reinforcing its global appeal [17]. By intertwining cultural hybridity with sustainability narratives, Gucci positions itself as an industry leader, innovatively bridging tradition, modernity, and ethical luxury.

4.3 LVMH: CSR and the Fusion of Local and Global Narratives

LVMH strategically employs CSR narratives to shape brand perception, leveraging sustainability as a core component of its luxury branding. Through the LIFE 360 program, the conglomerate emphasizes transparency and circular fashion, reinforcing its position as an industry leader in sustainability. This aligns with Bourdieu's symbolic capital theory, wherein sustainability enhances the perceived value of luxury by embedding ethical responsibility into brand prestige [21].

Beyond sustainability, LVMH skillfully balances local cultural authenticity with global relevance. Iconic brands like Louis Vuitton and Dior integrate cultural symbols into their internationally recognized identities. For instance, Louis Vuitton's collaborations with Japanese artist Yayoi Kusama highlight local artistic heritage through signature designs, crafting a hybrid narrative that resonates with global audiences (See Fig. 2).

4.4 Stella McCartney: Redefining Luxury Through Ethical Fashion

Stella McCartney exemplifies a contemporary approach to luxury by embedding ethical principles and sustainability into brand identity. As a pioneer in ethical fashion, she utilizes signifiers such as vegan leather, organic cotton, and bio-fabricated materials to construct a new luxury paradigm. By eliminating traditional luxury markers like animal-based products, McCartney challenges conventional definitions of luxury while maintaining exclusivity and innovation [22].

Her designs incorporate global cultural influences, crafting narratives that emphasize shared values of sustainability and ethics. Through the use of regenerated nylon and eco-friendly textiles (See Fig. 3), McCartney's work illustrates how luxury brands can redefine their identities to align with evolving consumer expectations. This approach demonstrates the transformative power of global culture in reshaping the luxury industry for the twenty-first century, appealing to environmentally and socially conscious audiences.

Fig. 3 Stella McCartney's use of Mylo™, a vegan mushroom-based leather, highlights her commitment to ethical and sustainable fashion. Source: Stella McCartney Official Websites

4.5 *Discussion: Semiotics, CSR, and Global Cultural Impact*

This study reveals that luxury brands not only adjust semiotic structures to accommodate sustainability but also leverage CSR as a mechanism for symbolic evolution. The interplay between signification, CSR, and market positioning demonstrates how symbolic narratives drive consumer engagement in the globalized fashion industry.

5 Conclusion: Classic Fashion as a Reflection of Cultural Identity in the Post-Globalized Era

Luxury branding is undergoing a profound semiotic and cultural transformation, shaped by sustainability imperatives and CSR-driven narratives. Drawing on Barthes' *The Fashion System* and *Mythologies*, this study examines how classic brands reinterpret their symbolic heritage while constructing sustainability myths. By integrating CSR narratives, brands reinforce their legitimacy and deepen consumer engagement, demonstrating how semiotics serves as a critical tool for navigating the evolving luxury landscape in global culture.

More than just a symbolic platform, global culture functions as a dynamic framework that enables heritage brands to address the complexities of sustainability and cultural hybridity. Through the strategic reinterpretation of symbols, brands like Hermès and Gucci establish deeper connections with diverse audiences, fostering a global dialogue that balances tradition with innovation.

This study further underscores the potential of "global culture" to evolve into a significant academic and practical discourse. Classic fashion, with its ability to traverse temporal, cultural, and ethical boundaries, exemplifies how cultural identity is continuously reshaped in the post-globalized world. As the global landscape shifts, luxury fashion emerges as a conduit between heritage and modernity, reinforcing the role of global culture not only in preserving traditions but also in envisioning a sustainable and interconnected future.

References

1. Barthes, R. (1990). *The fashion system*. University of California Press.
2. Barthes, R. (1972). *Mythologies*. Farrar, Straus and Giroux.
3. García Canclini, N. (1995). *Hybrid cultures: Strategies for entering and leaving modernity*. University of Minnesota Press.
4. Kawamura, Y. (2005). *Fashion-ology: An introduction to fashion studies*. Berg Publishers.
5. Finnane, A. (2007). *Changing clothes in China: Fashion, history, nation*. Columbia University Press.

6. Peng, H. P. (2019). An exploratory study of advancing interdisciplinary research trends in digital new media. *Journal of Advanced Research in Social Sciences and Humanities, X*(X), 156–165.
7. Jenkins, H. (2006). *Convergence culture: Where old and new media collide*. New York University Press.
8. Kaplan, A. M., & Haenlein, M. (2010). Users of the World, Unite! The challenges and opportunities of social media. *Business Horizons, 53*(1), 59–68.
9. Burberry. (2022). *Burberry official Instagram account*. Retrieved from https://www.instagram.com/burberry
10. Levi's. (2021). *Levi's official website*. Retrieved from https://www.levi.com.
11. Peng, H.-P. (2023). Exploring symbolic effect of new media: The impact of Bilibili on Gen Z's cohort identity and aesthetic choices in fashion. In *International conference on fashion communication: Between tradition and future digital developments* (pp. 176–187). Springer Nature Switzerland.
12. Davis, F. (1979). *Yearning for yesterday: A sociology of nostalgia*. Free Press.
13. Robertson, R. (1992). *Globalization: Social theory and global culture*. Sage Publications.
14. Merchant, A., & Rose, G. M. (2013). Effects of nostalgia on consumer preferences. *Journal of Consumer Research, 39*(3), 355–368.
15. Hutcheon, L. (2000). *The politics of postmodernism*. Routledge.
16. Covalent & Co. (n.d.). *Louis Vuitton x Supreme*. Retrieved from https://www.covalentco.com/post/louis-vuitton-x-supreme
17. Gucci Equilibrium. (2023). *Gucci Equilibrium Impact Report 2023*. Retrieved from https://equilibrium.gucci.com
18. Kapferer, J.-N. (2012). *The new strategic brand management: Advanced insights and strategic thinking*. .
19. Hermès. (2022). *Annual Report 2022*. Hermès official website. Retrieved from https://finance.hermes.com
20. Business of Fashion. (2021). Gucci's sustainability push: A closer look at its cultural and environmental strategies. *Business of Fashion*. Retrieved from https://www.businessoffashion.com
21. LVMH. (n.d.). *LIFE 360 program: A commitment to sustainability*. Retrieved from https://www.lvmh.com
22. Stella McCartney. (n.d.). *Ethical fashion: Sustainability and innovation in luxury design*. Retrieved from https://www.stellamccartney.com

John Fetterman, The Carhartt Candidate: Clothing, Class, and Authenticity in U.S. Political Coverage

Myles Ethan Lascity

Abstract At 6-foot-8, bald, and tattooed with a goatee, U.S. Senator John Fetterman does not look like a traditional politician—a fact that has been widely discussed in the media. The former mayor of small-town Braddock was known for his blunt talk and casual dress: often, gym shorts with sneakers and a Black Carhartt hooded sweatshirt. Journalist Virginia Heffernan (2022) wrote that Fetterman "looks like someone who, swayed by a different ideology, might storm the U.S. Capitol or at least lead a caravan of antivax truckers." Nevertheless, Fetterman was named a style icon by both *GQ* and *The New York Times*. This chapter takes a critical discourse analysis to journalistic descriptions of Fetterman to see how he became closely aligned with the brand Carhartt and its invocation of working-class appeal. Such framing sheds light on the class aspects of politics, candidates, and personal appearance.

Keywords Carhartt · Fashion branding · Framing · Personal adornment · Political branding · U.S. Campaigns

1 Introduction

Researchers have been long been interested in the role that marketing [1, 2] and branding [3–8] play within political campaigns. For example, we know that there is a significant cultural dimension in political branding and communication [7] and that in addition to creating their own brands [3, 9], politicians can help circulate and spread the brands of their associated parties [10]. Although the goal of political campaigns—and thus many aspects of political branding—is (usually) to get the candidate elected to office [11], how we understand politicians comes down to a

M. E. Lascity (✉)
Southern Methodist University, Dallas, TX, USA
e-mail: elascity@smu.edu

P. von Wachenfeldt et al. (eds.), *Fashion Communication in the Digital Age*, Springer Proceedings in Business and Economics,
https://doi.org/10.1007/978-3-031-99481-4_21

delicate interplay between the candidate, their public communication, and how they are portrayed in the media.

While usually understood and interrogated disparately, both news frames [12, 13] and brands [14, 15] are discursive constructs that work to shape individual interpretation and understanding of an event, product, person, or other recognizable object. In both cases, those who deploy frames stories and those who construct brands use an array of linguistic and visual means to achieve the intended communication [16–19]. In short, both journalists and brand managers work as cultural intermediaries to provide symbolic meaning to audiences and/or consumers [20, 21]. Further, frames, brands, and the people who construct them are instrumental in shaping how we see the world and, as such, the ability to frame (or brand) is an act of social power [22–24]. As such, the way journalists write about and other portray candidates and political campaigns has ramifications for the political process, including candidates' branding and associated intangible qualities like being "credible" and "authentic."

This chapter takes a cultural studies informed critical discourse approach [25] to examine how now-U.S. Senator John Fetterman was framed by the news media before and after the 2022 election. Fetterman, a former small-town mayor and then lieutenant governor of Pennsylvania, was known for his untraditional appearance: he was tall, goateed, and tattooed, often wore basketball shorts and hoodies rather than suits, and frequently sported Carhartt gear. Because of his non-traditional political attire, Fetterman was even named one of the most stylish people of 2022 by *The New York Times* [26]. This chapter examines the framing of Fetterman and his consumption of Carhartt clothing on the campaign trail. In doing so, this analysis argues that the frames underscore a class bias within the media and political atmosphere large where lower classes of the people (i.e., the people who wear Carhartt) are not expected to be seen in the political process.

2 Literature Review

2.1 Brands and Frames

While the idea of branding can be traced back to the 1800s, contemporary brands are believed to be closely related to the rise of the mass media [27] and a need for differentiation of products [28]; moreover, researchers have long accepted that brands can develop extra-material meaning for customers [29]. Today, brands are understood to be complex, semiotic systems [14, 15] whereby tangible communications like logos, advertisements, and imagery can be assembled into tangible meaning and value structures [19]; researchers have theorized these intangible constructs in various ways including as images [30], myths [18], and stories [17].

Brands have had an outsized importance on fashion [31], where brands are often understood to be "meaning intensive" and can develop an array of products and associated lifestyles that are being sold [32]. While culturally significant brands might develop a story that placates relevant social contradictions [18], brand connotations are often assumed to be congruent to the user [33] and often class-based. Outside of fashion, familiar brands like Budweiser, Mountain Dew, and Jack Daniels have built brands around catering to blue-collar men [18, 34]. As such, brands can be understood as a unique form of discourse that can appear differently to different individuals and also a discursive construct individuals may contest.

Independently, political marketing [1, 2] and now political branding [8, 35, 36] researchers have examined both individual candidates [3, 4, 9] and political parties [10]. Of particular interest has been how political branding intersects with culture and ideologies [6] and how intangible concepts like authenticity and credibility can be constructed and managed successfully [3, 9, 27]. At the same time, we know that candidate appearance and image are especially important from a political branding perspective [7, 28] and can impact voting behavior [37].

Broadly speaking brands (political, fashion or other) are complex new media objects that can highlight or obscure specific qualities at a given time. Lury specifically suggests that both brands and frames work to contextualize products and experiences from the outside communicative environment [15]. Brands, especially, are multidimensional constructs that can appear differently to different individuals based on their positionality. Brand managers might have more input and power to define a brand, but since brands are constructed by a variety of people and practices, they become contested terrain allowing consumers and the news media to meaning and interpretation [15].

Toward such ends, a brand's meaning is impacted by the discourse surrounding it; this can be applied to both fashion [38, 39] and political brands [40]. Broadly speaking, framing is a form of discursive construction [41] where producers select particular aspects of reality and make them more "salient" within a communicating text [12]; framing is always an example of power relations [22, 34] whereby those with established platforms have more ability to frame people and events than those without. Generally, we understand frames to be both shared and persistent [13], so without a common understanding, frames could not be transferred from one site (e.g., the producer's mind; the text) to another (e.g., the text; the consumer's mind).

For the purposes here, it is important to remember that frames "set up or maintain specific relationships" [42], and this can be applied to both news media and brands. Within fashion branding, frames involve the stories and connotations manager wish to share with the public; in political branding frames include the personal attributes and backstories of a candidate or party. When the news media is involved, they might impose other frames on brands: for example, news media once compared Calvin Klein ads to child pornography [39] and questioned production practices like Nike's use of sweatshops [38]. Substantial framing research has been undertaken in the political sphere [43]; researchers have explores framing of gender differences among candidates [44–46], (i.e., women received more attention for appearance and personal lives) and also how various campaign strategies have garnered media attention [47, 48]. Other framing examinations within politics have looked at issues like crime [49], protests [50], race [51], and trans rights [52].

2.2 Class, Taste, and Personal Adornment

Additionally, clothing, personal adornment and related brands conduct identity work, denoting aspects like class and age [53] as well as particular brand user images [33] and lifestyles [32]. Fashion, dress, and personal adornment have long been understood to be impacted by social structures like class [54]. Simmel suggested that consumption and fashion were inextricable from class demarcations and they communicated wealth and drove changes in personal adornment. As such, what we choose to wear might be understood an issue of taste [55] and cultural capital [20].

Largely, men—especially straight, white men—have been thought to be removed from the expectations of fashion and personal adornment; both through their stated disinterest in it [56] and the development of the suit, which has been portrayed as a final fashion development that ended the need for the changes still attributed to women's fashion [57]. While aspects such as tailoring, fit, and color have been noted in the popular press, men's formal dress is generally more nuanced and less noted than women's adornment. Others have argued that while men's workwear has remained relatively stagnant and class-based (i.e., white collar vs. blue collar), men's leisure attire remains in flux [53]. Likewise, brands can also be understood to help shape various identities through advertising and promotional strategies [58, 59]. Entwistle pointed out that the way we use clothing in professional settings amounts to a "technology of the self," or a way we can learn about and present our bodies to achieve specific ends [60]. Even though such use of personal adornment might be thought of as contrived or constructed, it speaks to the ongoing performances individuals engage in at all times. The idea that we can deem some performances "authentic" while others are not is itself an element of discursive social power; to riff on Bourdieu's statement on taste judgment, classifications are always made from a class position [61]. Further, as others have noted, the way we dress and present ourselves is always part of a complex circuit of culture that involves the way items are worn as well as a host of wider cultural processes [62]

Since the communicative nature of fashion and personal adornment, brands, and news are all discursively constructed, there is often competition to define the field and control the cultural discourse [61]. As such this chapter examines how the media framed a political candidate (e.g., John Fetterman) and his image—including the consumption of a particular clothing/fashion brand (e.g., Carhartt)—and what that means for journalistic and branding processes. Carhartt, the brand in question, has long been associated with blue collar masculinity and manual labor; however, it has recently been elevated into fashion through its association with street style. As aforementioned, the multidimensionality of a brand allows different qualities to be exposed to different communities and consumers; as such, both manual laborers and street style aficionados may lay claim to the Carhartt brand. Still, any of these constructs—the candidate's image, the meaning of the brand, and the expectations for politicians' personal adornment—could be (and in some cases, were) challenged.

3 This Interrogation

Yet, the interest here is less why one framing won out over another, and instead how one discursive construct (e.g., Carhartt) provided meaning within a different discursive system (e.g., the news media) and what that tells us. Toward these ends, this study takes a critical discourse analysis approach [25] to the news media descriptions of John Fetterman's appearance. Critical discourse approaches are important to understand the ideological assumptions presented within media texts [63] and have been used productively with campaign journalism. Even though we know that appearance is important within political campaigning, we also know that journalists more frequently discuss the appearance of female candidates [46], thus making the focus on Fetterman's personal adornment atypical (although not unprecedented). A critical discourse analysis takes into account both linguistic and visual imagery [25], which is especially important when dealing with a candidate's appearance. To understand how these discursive constructs worked together, it is important to contextualize both the Carhartt brand, but also the Fetterman's political race.

3.1 Carhartt

According to Carhartt's website, the brand makes durable workwear and outdoor apparel. Founded in 1889, the brand originally focused on clothing for railroad workers: first a bib overall and then other garments. The brand points out that it made military uniforms during both World War I and World War II and that it clothed those working on the Alaska Pipeline. The brand also touts its connection to the U.S., including its operations in Kentucky and Tennessee; along with the fact that more than a third of its U.S. workforce are union members. It also notes that while Carhartt began to be adopted by consumers "outside blue-collar trades" in the 1980s and 1990s, including the hip-hop community, its "Made in the USA line is inspired by American workers." As journalist Tonya Riley wrote for *Esquire*, "Carhartt has become shorthand for the heart of blue-collar America. It's had an enduring appeal to the nation's working class, which makes it no surprise that the brand has long been co-opted by politicians trying to prove their bonafides." Even though Carhartt moved much of its production to Mexico, it still maintains the cultural cache and brand imagery developed over its long history.

3.2 Fetterman and the Pennsylvania Senate Race

The 2022 race for the Pennsylvania senate race had been seen as a pivotal race for control of the senate. Republican Pat Toomey was retiring after two terms. Fetterman, who had lost the Democratic senate primary in 2016 and was elected as lieutenant governor in 2018, was the frontrunner throughout the Democratic primary even though he suffered a stroke days before the primary election. While Pennsylvania voted for Joe Biden in the 2020 race, it also supported Donald Trump in 2016 and the Trump-endorsed candidate—television personality Mehmet Oz, more colloquially known as “Dr. Oz”—won the Republican nomination after a contentious primary. Throughout the campaign, the Fetterman camp trolled Oz’s celebrity and his limited ties to Pennsylvania; Oz had recently moved to Pennsylvania before the primary but maintained several homes—including one in New Jersey that the Fetterman campaign harped on in social media postings.

As lieutenant governor, Fetterman had developed a national profile following the contested 2020 presidential election, where he often made the television news appearances in defense of Pennsylvania’s electoral process. Unlike then-attorney general Josh Shapiro who appeared on television in more traditional professional attire, Fetterman frequently wore beanie hats and hooded sweatshirts during his television appearances. Fetterman had also stated that he owned only one suit for official duties; this became so much of a defining image for Fetterman that multiple outlets ran stories on the new suit he wore for his swearing-in to the U.S. Senate [64, 65].

3.3 Data Collection

Critical discourse analyses do not have strictly proscribed methods since they are most interested in uncovering the workings of power, thus necessitating different collection methods and analyzes practices and procedures depending on the question(s) at hand. Since the focus of this project was how journalists linked Carhartt with Fetterman’s political brand, I first searched Google News for “Fetterman” and “Carhartt.” While there were 803 results, several prominent publications ranked highly in search results, including, *The New York Times*, *The Philadelphia Inquirer*, *GQ*, *Vanity Fair*, *Rolling Stone*, *The Washington Post*, *Time*, *NPR*, *Politico*, and the *Los Angeles Times,* along with local publications *PennLive* (based in Harrisburg and Easton Pennsylvania) and the *Times-Leader* (Wilkes-Barre, Pennsylvania); where possible, additional searches on outlets’ websites for “Fetterman” and “Carhartt” were conducted. Ultimately, 41 articles were collected from 15 publications with national reach or specific state and local-level involvement; the articles came from *The New York Times* (7), *The Philadelphia Inquirer* (7), *PennLive* (5), *Politico* (5), *NPR* (3), *Vanity Fair* (2), *GQ* (2), *Time* (2), *The Washington Post* (1), *The Nation* (1), the (Wilkes-Barre, Pa.) *Times-Leader* (1), *Financial Times* (1), *Rolling Stone* (1), *Los Angeles Times* (1), and *USA Today* (1). This does not include outlets that were republishing content from others; for example, *The* (Allentown, Pennsylvania) *Morning Call* frequently re-ran content published by *The New York Time*s and *The Philadelphia Inquirer*.

Reading each story, I pulled out the lines which described Fetterman’s appearance and clothing use, especially Carhartt. From there, I took a cultural studies approach to these texts consisting of a long "soak" where recurring and repetitive phrasing and meaning structures can be detected [66]. As such, the following analysis draws on the repetitive framing across news articles, with particular attention paid to words and phrasing that tied Fetterman's appearance and personal adornment—especially his consumption of Carhartt products—and its relation to class, gender, and popular appeal. Keeping in line with a cultural studies, I have attempted to contextualize and quote the texts throughout the analysis to justify my interpretation.

4 Findings

The media's portrayal of Fetterman and his Carhartt consumption can broadly be seen toward three general frames: (1) Carhartt had become part of Fetterman's political brand; (2) Fetterman is an authentic everyman because he dresses down; and (3) by wearing Carhartt, Fetterman is showing that he is not a typical politician. These stories were often illustrated with photographs of Fetterman at traditional-looking campaign stops or juxtaposed with his wife, Giselle Barreto Fetterman, who frequently joked on social media about John's clothing and appearance, or juxtaposed Fetterman with politicians in suits. The majority of these descriptions occurred in political news and opinion pieces, although there was a handful of commentary from fashion and style experts.

4.1 Carhartt as Fetterman's Political Brand

In many cases, that Fetterman was wearing Carhartt was simply added as a descriptor; however, there were several instances in which writers directly started it was part of his brand, "signature look" [67], "trademark" [68, 69] or even "infamous shorts and Carhartt hoodie uniform" [70]. Some examples where this can be seen are:

> With his blunt style and unorthodox look—featuring forearm tattoos, hoodies, and Carhartt jackets—Fetterman has aimed to win back the kind of white, working-class voters who have fled the Democratic Party for the Trump-era GOP [71].

> On Jan. 3, the junior senator from Pennsylvania, whose penchant for Carhartt sweatshirts, Dickies and baggy shorts was as much a part of his political brand as any stump speech ... [65].

Despite Carhartt and blue-collar workwear being part of his political brand, not everyone took it at face value nor agreed that it would resonate with people. In this way, the meaning of the Carhartt brand and Fetterman's use of it was contested. In *The New York Times*, a former Republican consultant was quoted saying, "You can't just put on a Carhartt jacket and shorts and expect to win over all these Trump voters" [72]. Moreover, some voters expressed skepticism of this as well. "Carhartt was originally designed for blue-collar people," the voter told a reporter. "But now Carhartt is one of those brands all the yuppies wear" [67].

4.2 *Fetterman as Everyman*

Despite some assertions to the contrary, Fetterman's use of Carhartt was widely presented as authentic or, at the very least, having an "everyman vibe" [73] that ingratiated him to blue-collar workers. Vanessa Friedman wrote, "... his usual uniform involves a hoodie and shorts. Often by Carhartt and Dickies, the ur-American work wear brands beloved of blue-collar voters and hipsters" [74]. Meanwhile, a reporter for a local newspaper in Wilkes-Barre, Pennsylvania, wrote, "Clad in a maroon Carhartt sweatshirt and gray running shorts, Fetterman did look like he may have been just another Wilkes-Barre resident out for a jog" [75].

This sentiment was expressed by some voters as well. "As Fetterman posed for a photo in his signature gray gym, shorts and a maroon Carhartt hoodie, Smith said he regularly switches parties to vote for whichever candidate 'is a real human being ...'" [76], with the implication the "real human being" was Fetterman.

Moreover, that Fetterman's everyman aesthetic was discussed in the media even became its own fact in political reporting. "His Everyman stylings—not just the shorts but also the tattoos on his forearms, and fondness for Carhartt and Dickies—are an often-chronicled aspect of his political rise along with his 6-foot-8 frame, spiky goatee and intermittent scowl," Paul Schwartzman wrote in *The Washington Post*. "Even *GQ*, the Manhattan-based magazine, was taken with Fetterman's sense of couture, proclaiming him an 'American taste god'" [77].

Politico reported that "The tattooed, 6-foot-8 Democrat, better known for wearing Carhartt and Dickies gear than a suit and tie, has been ... portrayed as the face of the Rust Belt" [78]. Again, the framing links Fetterman's style—including his use of Carhartt—with an authentic representation of faltering Rust Belt (i.e. post-industrial) towns of Pennsylvania.

4.3 *Fetterman vs. Other Politicians*

The third framing was how Fetterman compared to other politicians—both those he was competing against *and* those who he was aligned with. In the primary, *Vanity Fair* contrasted Fetterman with then-Democratic congressman Connor Lamb, also running for senate:

> At a towering six feet eight inches, sporting a goatee, a shaved head and often a uniform of Carhartt and shorts, Fetterman is a physically striking candidate, particularly when he was juxtaposed against his main rival in the race, Lamb, the polished politician, typically seen with neatly combed fair and a crisp collared shirt [79].

Vanity Fair also contrasted Fetterman with Bob Casey, then Pennsylvania's senior senator at a campaign stop.

> The bald, goateed, six-foot-eight Fetterman is wearing black work boots, blue jeans and his signature Carhartt hoodie; Casey—in black wing tips, gray slacks, crisp white dress shirt, and navy V-neck sweater—is dressed more like another Pennsylvania icon, Mr. Rogers [80].

GQ even noted that despite Fetterman's growing prominence and ascension to higher office, his wardrobe remained the same—a nod to both his authenticity, but also his difference [81]. *NPR*'s Don Gonyea called him the "anti-politician" in multiple articles [73, 82, 83] while *Rolling Stone* wrote that Fetterman does not fit the usual political spectrums [84]. Meaning a columnist for the PennLive noted that when showing people a photo of Fetterman when he was lieutenant governor, it was often met with disbelief but that it "is great because we're running a little heavy on dour, old white guy in suits ..." [85].

Yet, the largest dichotomy was reserved for Fetterman and his general election opponent, Oz. *The Nation* noted that Fetterman showed support "for the working class, down to his wardrobe choices (his now infamous short and Carhartt hoodie uniform)" while it described Oz as "a Gucci-loafer wearing elitist who owns 10 mansions and struggles to use normal words in grocery stores" [70]. Meanwhile, J.D. Prose reported in *PennLive*, "Borick (a political science professor) said the race presents voters with a stark contrast, a wealthy, TV celebrity heart surgeon who only recently moved to Pennsylvania, against Fetterman, the towering and tattooed West Reading native who's partial to Carhartt hoodies and shorts regardless of the weather" [86].

Despite the attention Fetterman's appearance received, there were comparisons to other politicians who also dressed in Carhartt received some media attention as well, including Rep. Marie Gluesenkamp Pérez, a Democrat from Washington state [87] and Tennessee Republican Tim Burchett [88]. Nonetheless, after Fetterman's win, *The New York Times* wrote, "The senator-elect from Pennsylvania is going to bring Carhartt to the Capitol," [26] when naming Fetterman one of 2022's most stylish people, and his chief of staff told reporters Fetterman had plans to buy more than the one suit he owned as lieutenant governor [89].

5 Discussion

The way personal appearance is shaped and used within politics remains up for debate as politicians—like Arizona Senator Kyrsten Sinema—have taken to flamboyant attire, while also suggesting any analysis or discussions of her manner of dressing is sexist. Yet, as aforementioned, appearance is integral to visual political communication [7, 28] and with the rise of political branding [35, 36], developing candidate attributes like authenticity and credibility is increasingly important [3, 9]. The media framing of Fetterman provides insights for political branding but also underscores some problematic discourses or expectations within the current U.S. media and political landscape.

5.1 *Acceptance of Authenticity*

First and foremost, the fact the media accepted that Fetterman's use of Carhartt was genuine or authentic and not a campaign calculation was important for his branding purposes. By the time Fetterman launched his senate campaign, he was already something of a known quantity in Pennsylvania and, to a lesser extent, national politics. That he reportedly only owned one suit for official state business was already public knowledge and played up in social media interactions between Fetterman and his wife.

However, in the above statements, it was key that the media also saw Fetterman's personal adornment as an authentic performance. While there were some instances where this authenticity was questioned—notably by a political consultant [82] and a voter [74]—that many journalists felt comfortable enough to describe Carhartt as his political brand or even a "uniform" helped to construct it as an authentic performance. Moreover, that Fetterman's appearance—including his height, tattoos, and hair (or lack thereof)—was frequently referenced and related to what people believe a blue-collar everyman would look like promoted this authenticity as well. It seems especially notable that Fetterman is an Ivy-league educated, career politician who had received some support from his wealthy family during his time as mayor of Braddock, Pennsylvania. Indeed, although the image did not hold, Oz and some media attempted to portray Fetterman as insincere in his blue-collar leanings.

The fact that Fetterman was viewed as authentic *and* that such authenticity was considered a boon to his candidacy speaks to particular discourses and understandings within contemporary U.S. culture. Authenticity—or what we understand it to be—is largely a social construct that we bestow on particular actions; however, our dress and personal adornment are always part of a constructed performance intended to convey particular meanings. That journalists found Fetterman's consumption of Carhartt clothing to be authentic and framed it as such in published descriptions of the candidate demonstrates the constructed nature of authenticity, but also journalists' ability to validate said authenticity.

5.2 *Contesting Brand Meaning*

Toward these ends, linking authenticity to brand meaning suggests there is something solid or specific about the brand and how it is generally used. However, knowing brand associations can change over time [15], precise brand meanings—in this case, Carhartt—can always be contested. For example, when a voter was dismissive of Fetterman's attire, he said "But now Carhartt is one of those brands all the yuppies wear" [67]. And, after Fetterman was named a style icon by *The New York Times*, a writer noted that Carhartt and Dickies are brands worn by a "hypebeast (non-derogatory)" [90]. Such statements underscore the fact that brands are complex, multidimensional objects that can appear differently to consumers, but also that brand meaning can be contested and open to interpretation. A brand like Carhartt, which has a long cultural heritage, is more anchored to specific meaning than other brands, but the Carhartt of 2022 is not necessarily the Carhartt of 1889 or 2028 (when Fetterman will be up for re-election), nor will everyone see Carhartt in the same way. What media producers largely saw as an expression of authenticity and blue-collar solidarity others were able to dismiss as a brand co-opted by "yuppies."

5.3 Clothing, Class, and Gender

At the same time, this framing rested on the idea that the brands Carhartt and Dickies, as well as wearing hooded sweatshirts and basketball shorts were a sign of being blue-collar or clothing for the "everyman" [66]; this was especially notable when Fetterman was contrasted to the "polished politician" Lamb [79], fellow senator Casey, and Fetterman's general election rival, TV personality Oz. That Fetterman's appearance was not only noted but was generally treated as an anomaly speaks toward the class connotations of personal adornment and speaks to the dress expectations of politicians.

On one level, the framing underscores how journalists act as cultural intermediaries and translate the taste judgments of the upper class in their work. The expectation that politicians are expected to wear suits—or some sort of gentile, formal attire—rather than what someone might wear to work in a manual labor job, speaks to who has traditionally held legitimate power in the U.S. and the social expectations that come with running for—and winning—such positions. Granted, this is not primarily about money; that Fetterman thrifted his "new" suit [64] shows that someone can fit into the style expectations that varying price points. Instead, the framing speaks to the intersection of supposed comfort and authenticity of the "everyman"; blue-collar men prefer dressing down and in workwear rather than in a fitted suit.

As aforementioned, men's rejection of fashion and flamboyance has long roots; however, that is also usually understood to mean a default to suits and somber attire over other styles. Even small variations like Barack Obama's tan suit or Donald Trump's ill-fitting suits and overly long tie were noted by media professionals. Yet, in this instance, Fetterman's Carhartt, Dickies, and basketball shorts show a complete rejection of expectations of personal adornment. Further, that his wife is frequently portrayed as the person trying to get him to dress better reifies "traditional" gender dynamics. It also underscored the structured and supposed restricting dynamic of wearing a suit; this is something inauthentic (at least to Fetterman, but by extension, all politicians) that they need to be forced or goaded into wearing.

Although business and professional attire has become markedly more relaxed in recent decades, politics has remained a space where formality has reigned. That said, the binaries of blue-collar wear/authentic and suits/inauthentic have also persisted and speak to who is thought of as community leaders and having the economic, social, and cultural capital to run for office. That Fetterman's personal adornment was treated as an anomaly, rather than a disqualifier (for most), speaks to the easing of the social conventions, but still implies there is a way to go.

6 Conclusion

In conclusion, while Fetterman's appearance and personal adornment became a tangible embodiment of his campaign branding, the way the media referenced and used the Carhartt brand as an explicit and authentic reference to blue-collar or working-class voters and appeal speaks to the discursive, ideological underpinnings regarding who is expected to run for office, how they are expected to present themselves, and what that presentation means in the public sphere. The fact that Fetterman became so noted for wearing hooded sweatshirts and basketball shorts rather than suits suggests that those with various forms of capital—economic, cultural, and otherwise—are more viable politicians and/or that the practices of higher-class individuals are likely adopted when one runs for office. Moreover, that Fetterman's appearance and clothing consumption were deemed somehow more "authentic" speaks to wider discourses on how the working class—and largely *white working class*—is believed to have some inherent authenticity or claim to authenticity than those of higher-class or other demographic groups do not. While these reporters might have accurately portrayed Fetterman's appeal to the Pennsylvania electorate, the media's acceptance and ongoing construction of his personal appearance and adornment underscore long-standing biases and assumptions about the working class—who they are, how they present themselves, and what appeals to them.

References

1. Butler, P., & Harris, P. (2009). Considerations on the evolution of political marketing theory. *Marketing Theory, 9*(2), 149–164.
2. Shama, A. (1976). The marketing of political candidates. *Journal of the Academy of Marketing Science, 4*(4), 764–777.
3. Armannsdottir, G., Carnell, S., & Pich, C. (2020). Exploring personal brands of Iceland's parliamentarians. *Journal of Political Marketing, 19*(1–2), 74–105.
4. Guzmán, F., Paswan, A. K., & Van Steenburg, E. (2015). Self-referencing and political candidate brands: A congruency perspective. *Journal of Political Marketing, 14*(1-2), 175–199.
5. Lilleker, D. G. (2015). Interactivity and branding: Public political communication as a marketing tool. *Journal of Political Marketing, 14*(1-2), 111–128.

6. Pineda, A., Sanz-Marcos, P., & Gordillo-Rodríguez, M. (2020). Branding, culture, and political ideology: Spanish patriotism as identity myth of an iconic brand. *Journal of Consumer Culture*, 1–21.
7. Scammell, M. (2015). Politics and image: The conceptual value of branding. *Journal of Political Marketing, 14*(1–2), 7–18.
8. Speed, R., Butler, P., & Collins, N. (2015). Human branding in political marketing: Applying contemporary branding thought to political parties and their leaders. *Journal of Political Marketing, 14*(1–2), 129–151.
9. Jain, V., & Ganesh, B. E. (2019). Understanding the magic of credibility of political leaders: A case of India and Narendra Modi. *Journal of Political Marketing, 19*(1–2), 15–33.
10. Marland, A., & Wagner, A. (2020). Scripted messengers: How party discipline and branding turn election candidates into brand ambassadors. *Journal of Political Marketing, 19*(1-2), 54–73.
11. Denton, R. E., Trent, J. S., & Friedenberg, R. V. (2016). *Political campaign communication* (9th ed.). Rowman & Littlefield.
12. Entman, R. M. (1993). Framing toward clarification of a fractured paradigm. *Journal of Communication, 43*(4), 51–58.
13. Reese, S.D. (2001) Prologue: Framing public life: A bridging model for media research. In by Reese, S.D., Gandy, O.H., Grant, A.E. (eds.) Framing public life: Perspectives on media and our understanding of the social world, pp. 7-31. : Lawrence Erlbaum .
14. Conejo, F., & Wooliscroft, B. (2015). Brands defined as semiotic marketing systems. *Journal of Macromarketing, 35*(3), 287–301.
15. Lury, C. (2004). *Brands: The logos of the global economy*. Routledge.
16. Bock, M. A. (2020). Theorising visual framing: Contingency, materiality and ideology. *Visual Studies, 35*(1), 1–12.
17. Hancock, J. H. (2022). *Fashion brand stories*. Bloomsbury.
18. Holt, D. B. (2004). *How brands become icons*. Harvard Business School Press.
19. Wigley, S. M., Nobbs, K., & Larsen, E. (2013). Marking the marque: Tangible branding in fashion product and retail design. *Fashion Practice, 5*(2), 245–264.
20. Bourdieu, P. (1984). *Distinction: A social critique of the judgement of taste*. Harvard University Press.
21. Matthews, J. (2014). Journalism. In J. Smith Maguire & J. Matthews (Eds.), *The cultural intermediaries reader* (pp. 145–155). Sage.
22. Entman, R. M. (2007). Framing bias: Media in the distribution of power. *Journal of Communication, 57*(1), 163–173.
23. Moor, L. (2008). Branding consultants as cultural intermediaries. *The Sociological Review, 56*(3), 408–428.
24. Reese, S. D. (2007). The framing project: A bridging model for research revisited. *Journal of Communication, 57*(1), 148–154.
25. Machin, D., & Mayr, A. (2012). *How to do critical discourse analysis: A multimodal introduction*. Sage.
26. The New York Times: Styles's 93 most stylish "people" of 2022. The New York Times, December 11, 2022. https://www.nytimes.com/2022/12/11/style/most-stylish-people.html
27. Serazio, M. (2017). Branding politics: Emotion, authenticity, and the marketing culture of American political communication. *Journal of Consumer Culture, 17*(2), 225–241.
28. Lalancette, M., & Raynauld, V. (2019). The power of political image: Justin Trudeau, Instagram, and celebrity politics. *American Behavioral Scientist, 63*(7), 888–924.
29. Gardner, B. B., & Levy, S. J. (1955). *The product and the brand* (pp. 33–39). Harvard Business Review.
30. Patterson, M. (1999). Re-appraising the concept of brand image. *The Journal of Brand Management, 6*(6), 409–426.
31. Agins, T. (1999). *The end of fashion: How marketing changed the clothing business forever*. William Marrow and Co..

32. Saviolo, S., & Marazza, A. (2013). *Lifestyle brands: A guide to aspirational marketing*. Palgrave McMillian.
33. Parker, B. T. (2009). A comparison of brand personality and brand user-imagery congruence. *Journal of Consumer Marketing, 26*(3), 175–184.
34. Holt, D. B. (2006). Jack Daniel's America: Iconic brands as ideological parasites and proselytizers. *Journal of Consumer Culture, 6*(5), 355–377.
35. Needham, C., & Smith, G. (2015). Introduction: political branding. *Journal of Political Marketing, 14*(1-2), 1–6.
36. Pich, C., & Newman, B. I. (2020). Evolution of political branding: Typologies, diverse settings and future research. *Journal of Political Marketing, 19*(1-2), 3–14.
37. Olivola, C. Y., & Todorov, A. (2010). Elected in 100 milliseconds: appearance-based trait inferences and voting. *Journal of Nonverbal Behavior, 34*, 83–110.
38. Greenberg, J., & Knight, G. (2004). Framing sweatshops: Nike, global production and the American news media. *Communication and Critical/Cultural Studies, 1*(2), 151–175.
39. Tucker, L. R. (1998). The framing of Calvin Klein: A frame analysis of media discourse about the 1995 Calvin Klein Jeans advertising campaign. *Critical Studies in Mass Communication, 15*(2), 141–157.
40. Falkowski, A., & Jabłońska, M. (2020). Moderators and mediators of framing effects in political marketing: Implications for political brand management. *Journal of Political Marketing, 19*(1–2), 34–53.
41. Van Gorp, B. (2007). The constructionist approach to framing: Bringing culture back in. *Journal of Communication, 57*(1), 60–78.
42. Van Leeuwen, T. (2008). News genres. In R. Wodak & V. Koller (Eds.), *Handbook of communication in the public sphere*. De Gruyter.
43. Callaghan, K., & Schnell, F. (2005). *Framing American politics*. University of Pittsburgh Press.
44. Aaldering, L., & Van Der Pas, D. J. (2020). Political leadership in the media: Gender bias in leader stereotypes during campaign and routine times. *British Journal of Political Science, 50*(3), 911–931.
45. Burge, C. D., Hodges, M. J., & Rinaldio, R. (2020). Family matters? Exploring media coverage of presidential candidates' families by gender and race. *Politics, Groups and Identities, 8*(5), 1022–1042.
46. Van Der Pas, J. D., & Aaldering, L. (2020). Gender differences in political media coverage: A meta-analysis. *Journal of Communication, 70*(1), 114–143.
47. Haselmayer, M, Meyer, T.M.,Wagner, M. (2019) Fighting for attention: Media coverage of negative campaign messages. Party Politics, 25(3), 412-423 .
48. Porath, W., Suzuki, J., Ramdohr, T., & Portales, J. (2015). Newspaper coverage of three presidential campaigns in Chile: personalization and political strategies. *Bulletin of Latin American Research, 34*(4), 451–466.
49. Gilliam, F. D., & Iyengar, S. (2005). Super-predators of victims of societal neglect? Framing effects in juvenile crime coverage. In K. Callaghan & F. Schnell (Eds.), *Framing American politics* (pp. 148–166). University of Pittsburgh Press.
50. Boyle, M. P., & McLeod, D. M. (2018). News frames and social protests: Toward a comprehensive model. In P. D'Angelo (Ed.), *Doing framing analysis II: Empirical and theoretical perspectives* (pp. 295–319). Routledge.
51. Dixon, T. L., Bauer, E., & Josey, C. (2018). How news frames prime non-whites as social problems. In P. D'Angelo (Ed.), *Doing framing analysis II: Empirical and theoretical perspectives* (pp. 343–361). Routledge.
52. Graber, S. M. (2018). The bathroom boogeyman: A qualitative analysis of how the Houston Chronicle framed the equal rights ordinance. *Journalism Practice, 12*(7), 870–887.
53. Crane, D. (2000). *Fashion and its social agendas: Class, gender, and identity in clothing*. University of Chicago Press.
54. Simmel, G. (1957). Fashion. *The American Journal of Sociology, 62*(6), 541–558.

55. Blumer, H. (1969). Fashion: From class differentiation to collective selection. *The Sociological Quarterly, 10*(3), 275–291.
56. Miller, J. (2016). Sigmund Freud: More than a fetish: Fashion and psychoanalysis. In A. Rocamora & A. Smelik (Eds.), *Thinking through fashion: A guide to key theorists* (pp. 46–62). IB Tauris.
57. Hollander, A. (1994). *Sex and suits: The evolution of modern dress*. Kodansha.
58. Kass, J. (2020). The symbolic value of fashion brand collaborations. In E. Huggard & J. Cope (Eds.), *Communicating fashion brands: Theoretical and practical perspectives* (pp. 141–155). Routledge.
59. Lifter, R. (2020). Creating fashionable identities. In E. Huggard & J. Cope (Eds.), *Communicating fashion brands: Theoretical and practical perspectives* (pp. 79–94). Routledge.
60. Entwistle, J. (2007). "Power dressing" and the construction of the career woman. In M. Barnard (Ed.), *Fashion theory: A reader* (pp. 208–219). Routledge, New York.
61. Rocamora, A. (2016). Pierre Bourdieu: The field of fashion. In A. Rocamora & A. Smelik (Eds.), *Thinking through fashion: A guide to key theorists* (pp. 233–250). IB Tauris.
62. Kaiser, S. B. (2012). *Fashion and cultural studies*. Berg.
63. Fairclough, N., Mulderrig, J., & Wodak, R. (2011). Critical discourse analysis. In T. A. Van Dijk (Ed.), *Discourse studies: A multidisciplinary introduction* (pp. 357–378). Sage.
64. Cartter, E. (2023). First day on the job, and John Fetterman's got another suit. *GQ*, January 3, 2023. https://www.gq.com/story/john-fetterman-suit-senate
65. Friedman, V. (2023). John Fetterman got a new suit for his senate swearing-in. *The New York Times*, January 3, 2023. https://www.nytimes.com/2023/01/03/style/john-fetterman-swearing-in-suit.html
66. Alter, C. (2022). The Pennsylvania senate race tests the vibes theory of politics. *TIME*, October 26, 2022. https://time.com/6225265/john-fetterman-vibes-pennsylvania-senate-race/
67. Gabriel, T. (2022). Democrats see a blueprint in Fetterman's victory in Pennsylvania. *The New York Times*, November 13, 2022. https://www.nytimes.com/2022/11/13/us/politics/fetterman-pennsylvania-voters-democrats.html
68. Otterbein, H. (2022). Fetterman makes closely watched return to Pennsylvania campaign trail. *Politico*, August 12, 2022. https://www.politico.com/news/2022/08/12/fetterman-return-pennsylvania-campaign-trail-00051564
69. Otterbein, H., Levine, M. (2022). Fetterman inching back onto campaign trail, 2 months after stroke. *Politico*, July 21, 2022. https://www.politico.com/news/2022/07/21/fetterman-pennsylvania-senate-campaign-stroke-00047159
70. Troy, A., Smucker, J. (2022). A tale of two campaigns in Pennsylvania. *The Nation*, November 29, 2022. https://www.thenation.com/article/politics/fetterman-shapiro-democrats-pa/
71. Tamari, J. (2022). Josh Shapiro and John Fetterman helped Democrats deft GOP hopes for a red wave. *The Philadelphia Inquirer* Nov. 9, 2022. https://www.inquirer.com/politics/election/pa-election-results-2022-governor-senate-house-20221108.html
72. Hounshell, B. (2022). Fetterman 2022: The steampunk version of Biden in his basement. *The New York Times*, June 28, 2022. https://www.nytimes.com/2022/06/28/us/politics/john-fetterman-memes-campaign.html
73. Gonyea, D. (2022). Pennsylvania Democrats are angling to distinguish themselves in key Senate contest. *NPR*, February 22, 2022. https://www.npr.org/2022/02/22/1082158009/pennsylvania-democrats-are-angling-to-distinguish-themselves-in-a-key-senate-con
74. Friedman, V. (2022). John Fetterman and the remaking of the political image." *The New York Times*, May 26, 2022. https://www.nytimes.com/2022/05/26/style/john-fetterman-hoodies-shorts.html
75. Carroll, K. (2022). Fetterman wows enthusiastic crowd in local stop. *Times Leader*, April 30, 2022. https://www.timesleader.com/news/1553486/1553486
76. Terruso, J., Tamar, J. (2022). Let's talk about fracking. *The Philadelphia Inquirer*, April 6, 2022. https://www.inquirer.com/newsletters/pennsylvania-2022-elections-fracking-20220406.html

77. Schwartzman, P. (2022). A Democrat in gym shorts ties to rally blue votes in Trump country. *The Washington Post*, April 18, 2022. https://www.washingtonpost.com/lifestyle/2022/04/18/john-fetterman-pennsylvania-trump-country/
78. Otterbein, H. (2021). John Fetterman launches Senate bid in Pennsylvania. *Politico*, February 8, 2021. https://www.politico.com/news/2021/02/08/fetterman-senate-pennsylvania-466932
79. Tracy, A. (2022). John Fetterman wins Pennsylvania Democratic primary by throwing out the Democratic playbook. *Vanity Fair*, May 17, 2022. https://www.vanityfair.com/news/2022/05/john-fetterman-wins-pennsylvania
80. Smith, C. (2022). Obama, Biden and Oprah: The final days of John Fetterman's big for the senate. *Vanity Fair*, November 7, 2022. https://www.vanityfair.com/news/2022/11/obama-biden-oprah-john-fetterman-senate-race-oz
81. Cartter, E. (2022). Carhartt loving senator-elect John Fetterman wore a suit and tie for his first day at Congress. *GQ*, November 15, 2022. https://www.gq.com/story/john-fetterman-suit-pennsylvania-senate-race
82. Gonyea, D. (2022). Pennsylvania senate contests will be some of the most closely watched this year. *NPR*, February 20, 2022. https://www.npr.org/2022/02/20/1082012462/pennsylvania-senate-contests-will-be-some-of-the-most-closely-watched-this-year
83. Gonyea, D. (2022). The latest on the Pennsylvania Republican primary for Senate. *NPR*, May 17, 2022. https://www.npr.org/2022/05/17/1099587527/the-latest-on-the-pennsylvania-republican-primary-for-senate
84. Voght, K. (2022). Do Democrats finally have their answer to Trumpism? *Rolling Stone*, May 17, 2022. https://www.rollingstone.com/politics/politics-news/john-fetterman-pennsylvania-primary-conor-lamb-trump-1355064/
85. Ori, K. (2021). Did the U.S. turn into Florida in 2020? If so, what will 2021 bring? *PennLive*, January 4, 2021. https://www.pennlive.com/life/2021/01/did-the-us-turn-into-florida-in-2020-if-so-what-will-2021-bring-keith-ori.html
86. Prose, J. D. (2022). Oz and Fetterman face distinct challenges heading into the general election campaign. *PennLive*, June 9, 2022. https://www.pennlive.com/news/2022/06/oz-and-fetterman-face-distinct-challenges-heading-into-the-general-election-campaign.html
87. Karni, A. (2023). Fetterman, Recovering after stroke, labors to adjust to life in the Senate. *The New York Times*, February 10, 2023. https://www.nytimes.com/2023/02/10/us/politics/john-fetterman-senate-stroke.html
88. Beavers, O. (2023). Meet the House GOP's newly crowned comedy king. *Politico*, January 2, 2023. https://www.politico.com/news/2023/01/02/tim-burchett-tennessee-republican-00075874
89. Terruso, J., & Tamari, J. (2022). From the top of the political world to a basement office: How John Fetterman will fit in the U.S. Senate. *The Philadelphia Inquirer*, Dec. 23, 2022. https://www.inquirer.com/news/john-fetterman-pennsylvania-us-senate-inauguration-20221223.html
90. Foreman, B. (2022). John Fetterman is a style icon, per The New York Times — and the internet isn't happy about it. *The Philadelphia Inquirer*, December 14, 2022. https://www.inquirer.com/news/pennsylvania/john-fetterman-most-stylish-new-york-times-20221214.html
91. Moore, K., & Reid, S. (2008). The birth of brand: 4000 years of branding. *Business History, 50*(4), 419–432.
92. Moor, L. (2007). *The rise of brands*. Berg.
93. Riley, T. (2017, July 14). What it means to be a working-class clothing brand in America. *Esquire*. https://www.esquire.com/style/mens-fashion/a56175/carhartt-american-workwear/
94. Levy, M. (2022). Democrat John Fetterman wins US Senate race in Pennsylvania. Associated Press, November 9 2022. https://apnews.com/article/pennsylvania-senate-race-2022-midterm-elections-93709b5b7ab4cef658f45751cd76c090
95. Hall, S. (1975). Introduction. In A. C. H. Smith, E. Immirzi, & T. Blackwell (Eds.), *Paper voices: The popular press and social change, 1935–1956* (pp. 11–21). Rowman and Littlefield.

Digital Fashion Values: AI Social Listening of Sociopolitical Consciousness

YeSeung Lee

Abstract Digital fashion communities are often perceived as radical challengers of mainstream fashion, embodying the ethos of 'digital utopianism' which views technology as a liberating force for decentralization and democracy. These communities are depicted as rejecting industry hierarchies and aligning with anti-consumerist principles. This empirical study investigates whether these communities truly embody such revolutionary ideals by evaluating social media evidence gathered through an AI social listening platform. Despite the lofty rhetoric, the findings reveal that the social media discourse of digital fashion communities frequently lacks depth, relying on superficial slogans and buzzwords. Their attitudes are neither radical nor revolutionary, primarily reinforcing existing fashion hierarchies and sustaining core capitalist and consumerist frameworks. This study calls for a critical reassessment of the perceived radicalism of digital fashion communities and emphasizes the importance of genuine debate and education.

Keywords Digital fashion · Digital utopianism · Social media · AI social listening

1 Introduction

Digital fashion's rapid growth has led to inconsistent terminology, which will likely standardize as the field develops. As discussed in this chapter, the analysis of its usage on social media suggests that the term 'digital fashion' is wide ranging: this includes virtual garments in extended reality; virtual production of physical clothing using digital processes such as CLO3D; the use of other digital processes such as 3D printing, laser cutting, and smart fabrics; and very broadly, any online fashion portfolios, exhibitions, or events. A narrower definition of digital fashion tends to focus on virtual garments in extended reality and their physical counterparts.

Y. Lee (✉)
University of Westminster, Harrow, UK
e-mail: YeSeung.Lee@network.rca.ac.uk

P. von Wachenfeldt et al. (eds.), *Fashion Communication in the Digital Age*,
Springer Proceedings in Business and Economics,
https://doi.org/10.1007/978-3-031-99481-4_22

Extended reality (XR) encompasses virtual reality (immersive computer-generated environments), augmented reality (digital elements overlaid onto the physical world), and mixed reality (combining VR and AR). Fashion items in this narrower sense are often traded in digital marketplaces using Web3 technologies such as blockchain, cryptocurrencies, and non-fungible tokens (NFTs).

Under this narrower definition, digital fashion communities are often portrayed as radical, challenging mainstream fashion through systemic critiques and rejecting industry hierarchies while connecting fashion choices to broader sociopolitical ideals. The digital fashion company The Fabricant [1] encapsulates this attitude on the blogging platform *Medium*: 'Web3 is the new punk. … A decentralised and permissionless internet powered by blockchain, that places community and identity front and centre'. In another article, they argue that digital fashion designers can create new aesthetics 'without any physical waste' [2]. Similarly optimistic rhetoric can be found in the following blog by Metaverse Fashion Council [3]:

> DAFAC (Decentralized Autonomous Fashion Couturier) is an AI agent … its mission [is] to disrupt traditional systems and build a future where transparency, traceability, and innovation are the norm. … [Its] creations are inherently sustainable: 3D-printed on-demand, with no waste, no labor exploitation, and infinite recyclability.

These idealistic views, however, are not universally shared. For instance, Karinna Grant of The Dematerialised, a digital clothes platform, observes that most buyers are just 'looking to make a quick buck' [4]. Much of the engagement with digital fashion may lack a genuine commitment to revolutionary visions, despite the rhetoric.

2 Digital Utopianism and Digital Fashion Ideology

Digital fashion's supposed anti-establishment position echoes 'digital utopianism', a recurring idealism that believes new technology will make everyone prosperous, free, politically engaged, socially connected, and personally fulfilled ([5], p. 1001). Web3 builds on these premises. The outlook of digital utopianism and Web3 appears rooted in the Californian Ideology, which combined an optimistic belief in digital technology with the ethos of the 1960s–70s counterculture [6].

Though born from the 1940s–50s government-funded military-industrial-academic projects, early computer technologies emerged from collaborative, cross-disciplinary research environments ([7, 8], p. 15, 17–18). Norbert Wiener [9]—associated with the MIT Radiation Laboratory—believed cybernetics could redistribute power away from corporations and authoritarian systems ([7], p. 15, 17–18). Cybernetics was eagerly adopted by the Californian counterculture of the 1960s–70s, playing an important role in the PC's development as a tool of personal and political liberation [8]. This movement opposed mass consumerism and institutional control of technology, advocating for people to reclaim it for creative and social purposes [10]. Wiener's cybernetics also helped to reframe art as interactive feedback systems. The exhibition 'Cybernetic Serendipity' (Institute of Contemporary Arts, London), curated by Jasia Reichardt in 1968, crystallized this vision [11]. The personal computing revolution of the 1980s was similarly shaped by countercultural ideals, with the hacker emerging as a symbol bridging computing and utopian counterculture [7]. The rise of personal computers in the 1980s also introduced Graphical User Interfaces, marking a shift towards visual computing that shapes how we interact with digital tools today. During this period, cinema began visualizing the digital realm through computer-generated effects, with Steven Lisberger's *TRON* (1982) creating a visual style that reflected techno-utopian ideals [12].

When the Internet and the World Wide Web became publicly accessible in the mid-1990s, cyberspace embodied egalitarian ideals challenging corporate power ([13], p. 13, [27], p. 257). The first generation of the Internet, Web1 (1990–2004), consisted of static, read-only pages like blogs. The arrival of Web2 in the early 2000s, however, marked a major shift towards a participatory Internet, with platforms enabling users to create and share content ([14]: CH5). This rise of digital prosumption [15]—where consumers became producers—challenged traditional hierarchies through open participation, peer validation, and collaborative knowledge production, echoing earlier countercultural movements that aimed at making skills and tools accessible for creative and social uses [16, 17]. The early 2000s also saw 3D creation platforms embrace Web2's participatory features: key developments included open-source 3D software, customizable life simulation games, virtual worlds, and user-friendly 3D design tools ([18], pp. 276–277; [19]). Software expert Eric S. Raymond's [20] 'cathedral and bazaar' metaphor aptly contrasts closed, hierarchical systems with open, distributed networks. The Fabricant exemplifies such open system through its freelance network and shared digital resources ([21], p. 215, 218).

Public participation through digital platforms significantly challenges traditional media, creative industries, and information flows. As regards consumption, niche online communities have formed around shared interests, often developing sceptical attitudes towards mainstream brands [22]. This sentiment echoes the countercultural attitude of Californian Utopianism, and the perceived attitude of digital fashion communities towards mainstream fashion can also be analysed within this context.

The Web2's promise of community-driven utopia has faltered since the late 2000s, as chaotic unmediated voices undermine the social cohesion that the Californian Ideology had envisioned. Online anonymity and algorithmic content distribution enable hatred and extremism to flourish. At the same time, social trust is eroding as misinformation and fraudulent content proliferate. The rise of 'platform capitalism' [23] thoroughly undermined the ideals of Web2 with monopolistic platforms mediating digital interactions. This control operates alongside 'surveillance capitalism', where platforms systematically accumulate, codify, and marketize user data as their primary revenue source [24, 25]. Digital surveillance and privacy concerns intensify as fashion merges with gaming and XR environments. VR headsets with eye movements tracking and AR applications that scan private spaces exemplify new privacy vulnerabilities ([26], p. 158).

Web3 emerged as a response to Web2's structural flaws ([27], p. 6). Yet it faces similar tensions between its idealistic vision and reality: NFT marketplaces and crypto platforms often concentrate power among early adopters and technical experts, mirroring Web2's dynamics ([27], p. 7). These debates about technology's societal role extend to digital fashion, as its ideology intersects with Web3's visions. This study examines whether the assumption of digital fashion communities as radical agents aligns with social media evidence gathered by an AI social listening platform. The findings suggest that they are more inquisitive than revolutionary, largely reinforcing existing fashion hierarchies and consumerist frameworks.

3 Methodology and Ethics

This study used real-time and historical data collected through Pulsar, an AI-integrated social listening platform. Social listening—the systematic collection and analysis of social media content—yielded insights into the conversations and behaviours of digital fashion communities through their voluntarily shared social media interactions. Social listening requires robust privacy protocols when analysing online interactions, given the blurred boundaries between public and private data [28]. Although users consent to data sharing via terms of service, this contractual permission alone may not resolve ethical issues around access ([29], pp. 5–6, 10). This study followed ethics guidelines suggested by Townsend and Wallace [29] and the EU Artificial Intelligence Act (2024), exceeding basic requirements for public content: staying up-to-date with social media platforms' terms of service, using Pulsar which meets regulatory requirements [30]; and following British Academy's award requirements. Although aggregate data sharing is considered safe in social media research as individuals can no longer be identified ([29] p. 13) using specific keywords and filters minimized personal data processing. Privacy measures also included anonymization and the removal of identifying elements—names, usernames, URLs, and verbatim quotes.

The Pulsar platform uses AI to collect and process social media data—for this study, eight months of digital content (10 March–19 November 2024). After regular filtering, 88,141 posts were compiled across two searches ('digital fashion' and 'digital fashion and sociopolitical consciousness': details below) from nine social media platforms (Instagram, X, YouTube, Facebook, TikTok, Reddit, Pinterest, Twitch, and Threads) and publicly available online news sites, blogs, and forums. The study focused on public long-form sources rather than professional journalism, better matching user-generated social media narratives. This approach of collecting, analysing, and interpreting online traces aligns with frameworks such as 'digital ethnography', 'cyberethnography', 'netnography', or 'virtual ethnography' ([14]: CH2).

4 Search One: 'Digital Fashion'

The initial data collection started (10 March 2024) using keywords drawn from The Fabricant's blogs (https://thefabricant.medium.com/), including 'The Fabricant', 'virtual fashion', 'metaverse', 'decentralised', 'collaborative', 'transparency', and 'subcultures'. When the search did not yield sufficiently relevant results, the parameters were expanded to 'digital fashion' (19 March 2024). The Boolean search query—("digital fashion") AND NOT ([...])—was then adapted for platform-specific queries. The search was limited to the English term ("digital fashion") to avoid inconsistencies from machine translation and cross-linguistic variations. Using a single language also facilitated the manual elimination of 'noise': removing irrelevant content and spam, while refining search terms to minimize future dataset contamination. The 2.8% non-English content collected—due to the popularity of #digitalfashion—was translated via Claude AI or Google Translate.

This broader search significantly complicated data refinement and interpretation. In addition, it increasingly became clear that Pulsar's AI reports lacked analytical depth. Both issues support Orton-Johnson's [14] view that ethnographic fields are not predetermined but require careful ongoing construction. Upon data saturation with no new patterns emerging (10 November 2024), Pulsar's AI tools enabled identification of dominant narratives and keywords. Evaluating these analytics revealed limited evidence of socio-politically conscious audience (Figs. 1 and 2).

As regards keywords, those in author biographies are likely to offer more reliable data analysis than keywords of post content, since AI cannot reliably interpret contextual language and visual nuances. Author biographies typically contain self-curated information, which is likely to reflect their current or aspirational identity. From the author biography keywords collected, 'decentralized', 'ambassador', 'web3', 'blockchain', 'NFT', 'future', and 'access' were identified as potentially

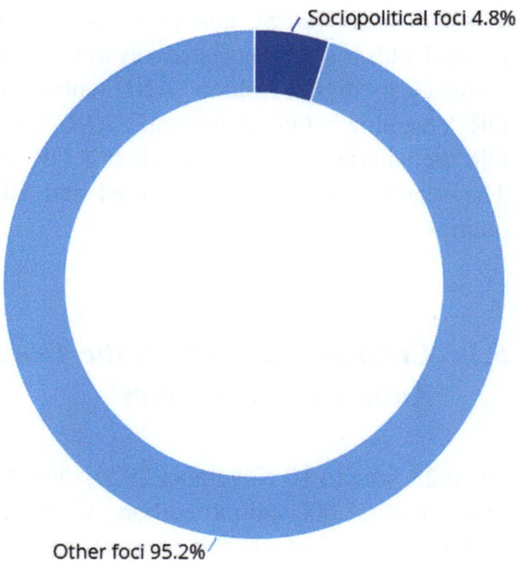

Fig. 1 Percentage of author biography keywords potentially indicating sociopolitical foci (19 March–10 November 2024). Sociopolitical foci (volume 4383. 4.8%) in comparison with other foci (volume 86705. 95.2%)

Fig. 2 Distribution of author biography keywords (19 March–10 November 2024). The word 'Web3' appeared 1528 times, 'NFT' (1375), 'blockchain' (759), 'future' (628), 'ambassador' (364), 'decentralized' (23), and 'access' (13)

indicating a degree of sociopolitical consciousness (Fig. 2). More general words ('digital', 'art', 'join', 'fashion', 'projects', 'design', 'technology', 'fusion', 'artist', 'canvas', 'exciting', 'diving', 'discover', 'unique', 'tech', and 'journey') were disregarded. It must be noted that the presence of the select keywords does not necessarily indicate genuine sociopolitical awareness; they could simply reflect an interest in cryptocurrency investments, for instance. The limitations of keyword-based content analysis are discussed further in the conclusion.

5 Search Two: 'Digital Fashion and Sociopolitical Consciousness'

Since the first search appeared insufficient to address the research question, a supplementary search was introduced: 'Digital Fashion and Sociopolitical Consciousness' (DFSC hereafter) (28 June–10 November 2024). This query incorporated Pulsar's AI-suggested keywords to identify potential indicators of radical tendencies: "digital fashion" AND (subculture OR "sustainab"* OR "collaborat"* OR "customiz"* OR "democrati"* OR "subvert"* OR "politic"* OR "decentraliz" OR "dematerializ"* OR "participat"* OR "ethic"* OR "disrupt"* OR revolution). The search was iteratively refined and adapted into platform-specific Boolean queries.

5.1 Comparison Between the Two Searches: Author Demographics

From 28 June to 10 November 2024, the 'Digital Fashion' search collected 43,526 posts from 21,000 unique authors, while 'DFSC' yielded 1424 posts from 1100 authors. Figure 3 shows this contrast: 95% and 5%.

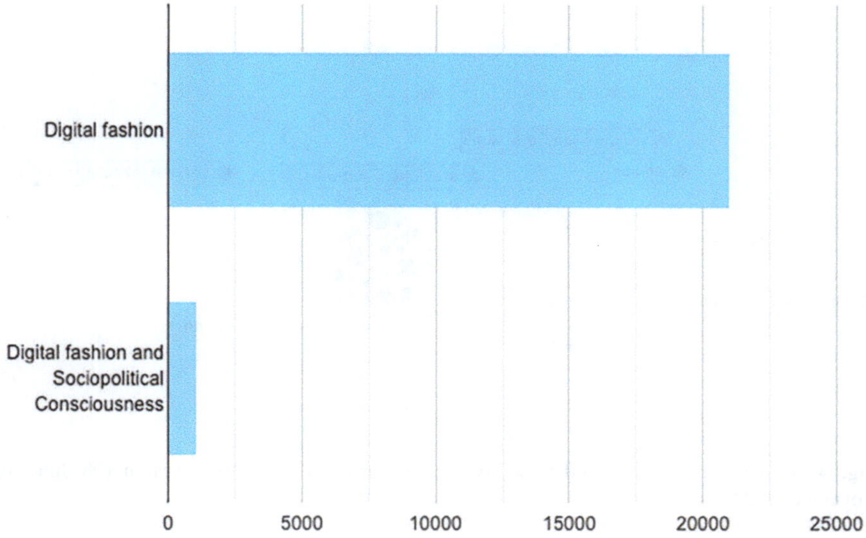

Fig. 3 Unique authors (28 June–10 November 2024). 'Digital fashion': 21,000 (95%); 'DFSC': 1100 (5%)

5.2 Comparison Between the Two Searches: Author Biography Keywords

From 28 June to 10 November 2024, the most frequently used biographies keywords for the 'Digital Fashion' search were 'crypto', 'web3', 'nft', 'digital', 'fashion', 'art', 'blockchain', 'artist', and 'designer'. The 'DFSC' search added 'future', 'metaverse', and 'decentralized', suggesting an emerging interest in technological evolution and its sociopolitical implications. However, the number is marginal (2.53%. 31 out of over 1100 unique authors).

5.3 Main Narratives Within the 'DFSC' Search

Pulsar analytics identified five main narratives (Fig. 4) with the 'collaboration, launches' narrative (207 unique authors) being most relevant to the research question. The AI analysis reads: 'There's a notable shift towards digital fashion, NFT collaborations, and eco-friendly practices' in the fashion industry. The 'design, designer, sustainability' narrative (53) indicates an industry moving towards a more inclusive, technologically advanced landscape with emphasis on digital design, diversity, and innovation. However, 'creating, limitless, universe' narrative, with the largest number of authors (322), the AI analysis reads: 'The metaverse is increasingly being viewed as a lucrative opportunity for passive income and brand establishment. ... Backed by notable partnerships and celebrity endorsements, these

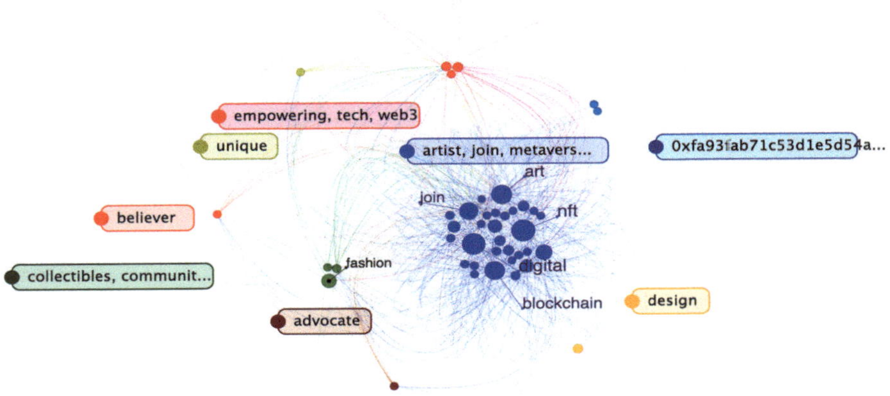

Fig. 4 Associations by keywords: the five main narratives in 'DFSC' search (28 June–10 November 2024)

platforms are gaining credibility and momentum, with users able to create and monetize their own experiences'. Many authors in the search appear more focused on commercial interests rather than societal concerns like equitable systems, ethical practices, transparency, privacy, data security, collective decision-making, inclusive representation, and sustainability. The remaining two narratives focused on specific celebrities and trending events at the time.

6 Manual Monitoring ('Digital Fashion' Search)

The analysis on commercial interest above provided useful insights, but the AI-generated texts were generally insufficient, offering surface-level summaries. Thus, 'Digital Fashion' search posts were manually evaluated and filtered for 38 days (04 October–10 November 2024). While this intervention inevitably introduced researcher subjectivity, it aligns with Orton-Johnson's [14] observation that all data is inherently socially constructed and filtered through researchers' efforts to understand phenomena.

6.1 The Proportion of Posts with Sociopolitical Awareness

In evaluating posts for sociopolitical awareness, an inclusive approach was taken: all posts with relevant keywords were considered, even those clearly lacking depth or detail. Still, the number of posts remained extremely low. This method meant the dataset included much superficial content that may not reflect genuine intentions. Figures 5 and 6 compares the number of posts showing sociopolitical consciousness with that of other posts, revealing only a marginal presence despite the inclusive evaluation.

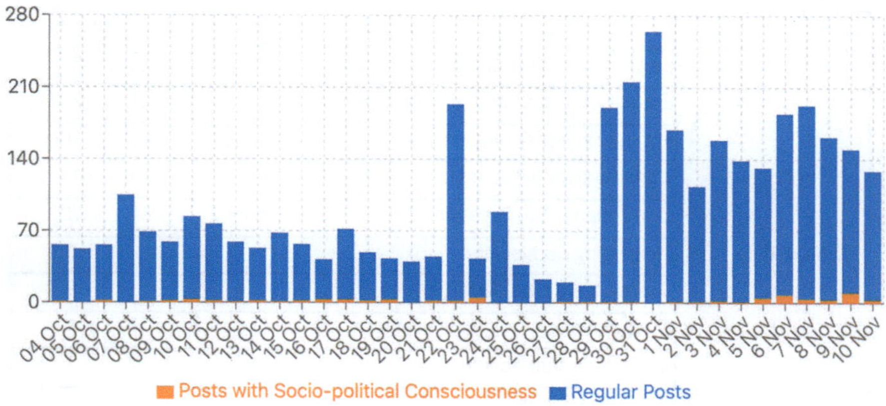

Fig. 5 Distribution of posts in 'Digital Fashion' search (4 October–10 November 2024)

Date	Count	Date	Count	Date	Count	Date	Count	Date	Count	Date	Count
04 Oct.	1/56	11 Oct.	3/124	18 Oct.	2/49	25 Oct.	0/37	1 Nov.	1/169	8 Nov.	3/162
05 Oct.	0/52	12 Oct.	1/59	19 Oct.	3/43	26 Oct.	0/23	2 Nov.	1/114	9 Nov.	10/150
06 Oct.	2/56	13 Oct.	2/53	20 Oct.	0/40	27 Oct.	1/212	3 Nov.	2/159	10 Nov.	3/129
07 Oct.	10/105	14 Oct.	1/68	21 Oct.	2/194	28 Oct.	1/17	4 Nov.	1/139		
08 Oct.	1/69	15 Oct.	2/57	22 Oct.	2/194	29 Oct.	1/191	5 Nov.	5/132		
09 Oct.	2/59	16 Oct.	3/42	23 Oct.	5/43	30 Oct.	1/216	6 Nov.	8/185		
10 Oct.	3/84	17 Oct.	3/72	24 Oct.	0/69	31 Oct.	0/265	7 Nov.	4/193		

Fig. 6 Number of posts with potential evidence of sociopolitical awareness out of daily total

6.2 *Main Themes Related to Sociopolitical Awareness*

Figure 7 shows the main themes from the 79 posts exhibiting varying levels of sociopolitical consciousness. The most frequently mentioned opportunities centre on environmental sustainability (such as optimized fabric use, inventory, and design processes; customized fit reducing returns and waste), equality in production (wider access to tools and opportunities for creating work), and equality in consumption (catering to diverse body types, cultural/ethnic backgrounds, genders, and abilities). Other significant themes include transparency (in supply chain, ownership, and intellectual property) and community (collaboration, shared ownership). The theme 'decentralization' appears only once, though its concepts overlap with several others.

The posts rarely discuss challenges compared to opportunities, suggesting limited awareness or a biased perspective. Challenges mentioned include job insecurity from AI automation and digital divides that both stem from and reinforce socioeconomic disadvantages. Other issues include data exposure and privacy concerns (misuse of personal data, intellectual property theft, and regulatory gaps), environmental damage (energy usage of digital infrastructure, digital waste and footprint),

	Themes	Frequency
OPPORTUNITIES	Environmental sustainability	31
	Equality in production ('democratization')	20
	Equality in consumption ('democratization')	16
	Transparency (IP/counterfeit/supply chain)	14
	Community; Co-Creation; Collaboration; Sharing	12
	Messaging / advocacy	7
	Sustainability (no detail)	6
	Customization	6
	Cultural sustainability	3
	Democratization (no detail)	1
	Decentralization	1
CHALLENGES	Job insecurity (automation / AI)	3
	Digital inequity	3
	Data exposure	2
	Environmental damage	2
	Inequality in consumption	2
	Distrust re. democracy / privacy	1
	Social isolation, health issues, addiction	1
	Consumer education	1

Fig. 7 Sociopolitical themes in digital fashion on social media: opportunities and challenges

distrust (AI influencers, deepfakes), social isolation, health issues, and consumer education.

Notably, most posts—particularly portfolios and platform/marketplace advertisements—lack detail, context, or concrete examples. They rely heavily on popular keywords and well-rehearsed slogans, presenting social or environmental sustainability claims that amount to greenwashing. The lack of depth is matched by many blogs and online articles, which often appear to be AI-generated, regurgitating similar content [31, 32].

Noteworthy exceptions included an article addressing the underrepresented female gaming market and another exploring how scannable clothing tags could support circular economy by facilitating resale, repair, and recycling. An *ABC News* article [33] addressed the challenges posed by generative AI in digital fashion, including intellectual property concerns, job security risks, algorithmic bias that can perpetuate existing societal inequalities. The article also addressed the pressing need for robust regulatory frameworks to govern AI's development and implementation. A data analytics company's post on X also emphasized legislative efforts to combat algorithm-driven fast fashion trends perpetuating waste. Complementarily, the UN's 'AI for Good' initiative promoted an event on X, focused on developing trustworthy AI applications and governance standards. A few refreshing collaborative moments stood out, including a game developer sharing open-source digital fashion tools and works-in-progress, embodying Web3's inclusive and participatory design ethos.

7 Conclusion and Limitations

The search results shed light on how the term 'digital fashion' is currently perceived within social media. Various 'digital fashion' practices are influencing how individuals create and consume fashion and interact with each other. However, there appears to be limited critical reflection or substantive debate within these spaces regarding the broader implications of these developments, relying on generic slogans and buzzwords. For example, while the environmental costs of blockchain technology and cloud computing are occasionally mentioned, there is little recognition that digital fashion shifts resource consumption from fabric to electricity rather than reducing it. Virtual fashion may also exacerbate fast-paced trend cycles and consumption patterns. Over-simplified claims of 'zero waste' or 'democratization' frequently overlook the digital footprint and the potential for inequality, for example, with NFT-exclusivity. Ultimately, the findings from this study indicate that the attitudes within digital fashion communities are neither radical nor revolutionary, primarily reinforcing existing fashion hierarchies and sustaining core capitalist and consumerist frameworks. To address these challenges, effective policy and consumer education are essential.

The research methodology had several limits. Firstly, the AI platform could not access closed communities like private Facebook groups or Discord servers. The Discord limitation could be meaningful, as it serves as a primary communication channel in the Web3 space [34]. Secondly, keyword-based searches often returned irrelevant content due to the term 'digital' having wide-ranging meanings. The popularity of the topic also causes the hashtag to appear in unrelated posts, especially those promoting competitions and celebrity gossip. The hashtag also very often appears in deceptive posts featuring AI-generated models, directing users to adult sites, as recently reported in mainstream media (See for example, [33]). Lastly, the platform's sentiment analysis function proved unreliable and was consequently excluded from this study. AI-driven tools struggle to capture the complexities of human language and imagery, leading to a high margin of error in classifying posts as positive, negative, or neutral; but manually verifying every piece of content is impossible. Such limitations highlight how AI-powered social listening platforms, while efficient at processing large volumes of data, can potentially skew academic research through their technical—and 'emotional'—constraints. Frequent manual filtering and intervention remain essential, though such oversight demands significant time, offsetting the efficiency gained through automation. When properly calibrated though, these AI tools could potentially serve as research assistants, working alongside human analysts. This reflects broader discussions about AI–human collaboration in fashion industries, where concerns about job displacement coexist with discussions for improving work efficiency: for example, within digital fashion communities where technical expertise increasingly complements traditional creative skills.

References

1. The Fabricant. How to be punk in web3. *Medium*, October 25 (2022). https://thefabricant.medium.com/how-to-be-punk-in-web3-f09cd1e663fc, last accessed 2024/05/27.
2. The Fabricant. Where the computer ends, you continue. *Medium*, April 18 (2024). https://thefabricant.medium.com/where-the-computer-ends-you-continue-2baa34954200, last accessed 2024/05/21.
3. Metaverse Fashion Council. (2024). *My aesthetics is the culmination of humanity's inevitable obsolescence.* https://metaversefashioncouncil.org/tpost/ftbnhb7141-my-aesthetics-is-the-culmination-of-huma, last accessed 2024/11/21.
4. Heneage, G. (2023). The influencers' new clothes: why are people buying outfits that don't exist? *The Times*, April 19. https://www.thetimes.com/uk/social-media/article/digital-fashion-buyers-influencers-instagram-clothes-873zk5v8t, last accessed 2023/04/20.
5. Winner, L. (1997). Technology today: Utopia or dystopia? *Social Research, 64*(3), 989–1017.
6. Barbrook, R., & Cameron, A. (1995). The Californian ideology. *Science as Culture, 6*(1), 44–72.
7. Turner, F. (2006b). How digital technology found utopian ideology: lessons from the first hackers' conference. In D. Silver & A. Massanari (Eds.), *Critical cyberculture studies* (pp. 255–269). New York University Press.
8. Turner, F. (2023). Digital utopianism: where do we stand 10 years later? *Sciences Po*, June 21. https://www.sciencespo.fr/en/news/digital-utopianism-where-do-we-stand-10-years-later/, last accessed 2024/11/02.
9. Wiener, N. (1948). *Cybernetics, or Control and Communication in the Animal and the Machine*. MIT Press.
10. Wiener, A. (2018). The complicated legacy of Stewart Brand's 'Whole Earth Catalog'. *The New Yorker*, Nov 16. https://www.newyorker.com/news/letter-from-silicon-valley/the-complicated-legacy-of-stewart-brands-whole-earth-catalog, last accessed 2025/01/05.
11. Mason, C. (2018). Cybernetic Serendipity: History and lasting legacy. *Studio International*, March 11. https://www.studiointernational.com/index.php/cybernetic-serendipity-history-and-lasting-legacy, last accessed 2018/07/13.
12. Rose, S. (2022). 'Frankly it blew my mind': how Tron changed cinema. *The Guardian*, July 5. https://www.theguardian.com/film/2022/jul/05/tron-steven-lisberger-interview, last accessed 2024/12/21.
13. Turner, F. (2006a). *From counterculture to cyberculture: Stewart Brand, the Whole Earth Network, and the rise of digital utopianism*. University of Chicago Press.
14. Orton-Johnson, K. (2024). *Digital culture and society*. Sage.
15. Toffler, A. (1980). *The third wave*. William Morrow & Company.
16. Beer, D., & Burrows, R. (2010). Consumption, prosumption and participatory web cultures. *Journal of Consumer Culture, 10*(1), 3–12.
17. Ritzer, G., & Jurgenson, N. (2010). Production, consumption, prosumption: the nature of capitalism in the age of the digital 'prosumer'. *Journal of Consumer Culture, 10*(1), 13–36.
18. Watstein, S. B., & Czarnecki, K. (2010). Virtual worlds, dress, and fashion. In J. B. Eicher & P. G. Tortora (Eds.), *Berg Encyclopaedia of world dress and fashion* (Vol. 10, pp. 276–282). Berg.
19. Dionisio, J. D. N., Burns, W. G., & Gilbert, R. (2013). 3D virtual worlds and the metaverse. *ACM Computing Surveys, 45*(3), Article 34.

20. Raymond, E. S. (1999). *The cathedral and the bazaar: Musings on Linux and open source by an accidental revolutionary*. O'Reilly & Associates.
21. Särmäkari, N., & Vänskä, A. (2022). 'Just hit a button!' – fashion 4.0 designers as cyborgs, experimenting and designing with generative algorithms. *International Journal of Fashion Design, Technology and Education, 15*(2), 211–220.
22. Karp, R., Fu, C., & Friis, S. (2024). How your business should tap into the creator economy. *Harvard Business Review*, 22 May. https://hbr.org/2024/05/how-your-business-should-tap-into-the-creator-economy, last accessed 2024/07/30.
23. Srnicek, N. (2017). *Platform capitalism*. Polity Press.
24. Foster, J. B., & McChesney, R. W. (2014). Surveillance Capitalism: Monopoly-finance capital, the military-industrial complex, and the digital age. *Monthly Review*, July 1. https://monthlyreview.org/2014/07/01/surveillance-capitalism/, last accessed 2018/01/17
25. Zuboff, S. (2015). Big other: Surveillance capitalism and the prospects of an information civilization. *Journal of Information Technology, 30*, 75–89.
26. Hadi, R., Melumad, S., & Park, E. S. (2024). The Metaverse: A new digital frontier for consumer behavior. *Journal of Consumer Psychology, 34*(1), 142–166.
27. Hawes, B. (2023). Web3: the promise & the reality. *WST/WSI White Paper*. University of Southampton.
28. Kozinets, R. V. (2022). Immersive netnography. *Journal of Service Management, 34*(1), 100–125.
29. Townsend, L., & Wallace, C. (2016). *Social media research: A guide to ethics*. University of Aberdeen. https://www.gla.ac.uk/media/Media_487729_smxx.pdf, last accessed 2024/11/08.
30. Palmer, A. (2024). Pulsar Group security, privacy and compliance overview. *Pulsar Group*. https://www.pulsargroup.com/trustcentre/, last accessed 2025/02/21.
31. Knibbs, K. (2024). AI slop is flooding Medium. *WIRED*, October 28. https://www.wired.com/story/ai-generated-medium-posts-content-moderation/, last accessed 2024/11/08.
32. Vincent, J. (2023). Medium welcomes posts written with AI as long they're 'clearly labeled'. *The Verge*, January 27. https://www.theverge.com/2023/1/27/23573954/medium-platform-publisher-ai-written-posts-policy-chatgpt, last accessed 2024/11/29.
33. Nguyen, K., & Workman, M. (2024). 'AI pimps' and their fake influencers are mass-harvesting women's videos to peddle porn. *ABC News*, April 14. https://www.abc.net.au/news/2024-04-14/how-ai-pimps-influencers-are-using-womens-videos/103658046, last accessed 2024/11/20.
34. McDowell, M. (2022). How Discord became the 'Soho House of Web 3.0'. *Vogue Business*, January 25. https://www.voguebusiness.com/technology/how-discord-became-the-soho-house-of-web-30, last accessed 2024/10/19.

Research Notes

Fashion and Product Literacy: The Case of Blockchain Technology and Digital Product Passport as a Communication Tool

Mirjam-Sarah Lepp, Nadzeya Sabatini, and Lorenzo Cantoni

Abstract As the physical and digital worlds continue to merge in the upcoming decades, there is a need to address the information gap in fashion literacy and the fashion industry. This gap can be filled by utilizing blockchain technology and digital product passports to allow for enhanced transparency between companies and individuals, increasing the overall communication and product literacy of fashion items. Through the traceability of blockchain technology, an individual could track the origins of a product and find details related to the fabrics, dyes, and production cycle on the digital product passport. Currently, fashion literacy definitions are built on the professional's need for knowledge and skills, while there is a consistent lack of consumer training on general knowledge related to fashion. Subsequently, definitions for product literacy focus on the trade-offs between limited information resources and making a purchase. This ongoing research will first look at the infancy of the fashion literacy field, how it interacts with product literacy and at the gap in literacy between the two fields of study, presenting an ongoing study into how blockchain and digital product passports can be adopted and orchestrated to bring more transparency into the industry and increase communication between brands and consumers, as well as increase community knowledge.

Keywords Fashion literacy · Product literacy · Digital product passport · Blockchain technology

M.-S. Lepp (✉)
USI – Università della Svizzera italiana, Lugano, Switzerland
e-mail: Leppm@USI.CH

N. Sabatini
Gdansk University of Technology and USI – Università della Svizzera italiana, Lugano, Switzerland
e-mail: nadzeya.sabatini@usi.ch

L. Cantoni
Institute of Digital Technologies for Communication, USI – Università della Svizzera italiana, Lugano, Switzerland

P. von Wachenfeldt et al. (eds.), *Fashion Communication in the Digital Age*, Springer Proceedings in Business and Economics,
https://doi.org/10.1007/978-3-031-99481-4_23

1 Introduction

In the fashion industry, there is an information and communication gap between consumers and an item of purchase. This lack of a fashion product information about materials, production cycle has resulted also in greenwashing trends, as companies can use storytelling to share incorrect or partial information (misinformation) about a product. "The lack of traceability and transparency creates a disconnect between what is publicized and the harsh reality" [1 , p. 2]. Blockchain technology is a tool that allows for transparency on the side of the company and industry, while individual prospects/buyers can track an item's origins and product information (fabric, ingredients, dyes, etc.) Of the research that exists in fashion literacy and product literacy we noted a gap in whom they are communicating to and about what. Current definitions of fashion literacy cover skills for design students and those looking to pursue a career in the industry [2, 3] and much of the product literacy research covers the topic of limited information resources of consumers and individuals in society, due to time, money, and actual literacy levels [4–6].

Meanwhile, the European Parliament is moving toward digital passports of products as part of its strategy to promote transparency. "The Digital Product Passport represents a significant advance in product transparency and sustainability. As the EU moves towards full adoption of this regulation, it will foster a more open and responsible marketplace" [7]. As the digital product passport can be hosted on blockchain technology, it would allow for certificates to be uploaded in real time and for data to become a communication tool, increasing information availability and allowing citizens to become conscious of where they spend their money, embodying what has been suggested by Ammous [8]: "Blockchain technology is a technology of verification." Through the transparency provided by blockchain technology and digital product passports, we can see how the product is made and where it came from, and should the product enter the resale market, there is an authenticated and traceable record of the item to support the decision by future purchasers [9]. This ongoing research investigates to answer if blockchain and digital product passports can be used as a valid communication tool to fill in the information gap between fashion- and product-literacy for individuals as well as for society at large.

2 Literature Review

This literature review is organized in two parts covering fashion literacy and product literacy. In doing so, the reader can understand the gaps in research that this research looks to tackle. Table 1 is an overview of the existing, relevant definitions in fashion, consumer and product literacy.

Table 1 Overview of relevant literacy definitions

Author	Paper	Year	Topic	Definition
Adkins and Ozanne	Critical Consumer Education: Empowering the Low-Literate Consumer	2005	Consumer Literacy	The ability to find and manipulate text and numbers to accomplish consumption-related tasks within a specific market context in which other skills and knowledge are also employed (p. 154).
Chiu et al.	The Levels of Fashion Literacy for Fashion Design-Related Departments Students in Taiwan	2014	Fashion Literacy	Cultural cultivation, fashion sensitivity and professional skills which can be used by individuals to communicate with the outside world and solve problems (p. 205).
Clark	Fashion Literacy and the Home Economics and Fashion Classroom	2019	Fashion Literacy	Fashion literacy moves beyond the item, such as a garment, that is often labeled as fashion. Fashion literacy includes technical skills such as sewing, or pattern drafting, as well as human, cultural, social, and relational aspects, including problem solving and critical thinking concepts (p. 10).
Knopp	Defining and Conceptualizing Product Literacy	2012	Product Literacy	Product Literacy: composed of a fundamental set of skills and knowledge needed to make "satisfying" individual purchase choices but also to influence general health, economy and societal well-being (p.191).
Pappalardo	Product Literacy & theEconomics ofConsumer Protection Policy	2012	Product Literacy	Product Literacy: when he or she possesses the tools necessary to determine if a particular product or service will meet his or her goals given his or her limited resources—including limited wealth, limited time, and limited household production capabilities (p. 321).

2.1 The State of Fashion Literacy

So far, only six publications have been found on fashion literacy. In fact, only two of them directly targeted the concept of "fashion literacy" and proposed a definition for what it means to be literate in fashion [2, 3], which are presented in the above table. Two further documents focused on information literacy for fashion studies [10, 11], while the remaining ones looked at "how-to study" fashion skills [12, 13]. Fashion literacy studies, so far, have been solely focused on educational matters, reflecting skills and definitions needed for careers in the fashion industry and knowledge on what to study for a career in fashion. What is missing in the current scope of research is a more inclusive understanding of fashion literacy that could be relevant to laypeople interacting with and buying products. Because of the complexity of fashion and different/conflicting (mis)information sources, it can be challenging for an individual to know what information is correct or where to turn for the information required when making a purchase. Within different contexts and cultures, Warschaw [11] points to "Challenges include alternative spellings, language diversity, and vocabulary" (p. 4): contextualization and information diversity are major challenges for the everyday consumer as they interact with fashion items. Fashion—if understood in a wide and comprehensive way, including cosmetics, jewelry, clothing, accessories, etc. [14 , p. 2]—is an area of our lives that we encounter daily. Nevertheless, there is a limited understanding of what having fashion literacy can mean for an individual and for society, and almost no existing research looking into this topic.

2.2 Product Literacy and the "Reasonable Consumer"

Product literacy tries to understand the trade-offs consumers face when purchasing a product. It often looks at pragmatic skills, such as reading levels of adults, and how individuals with lower skill levels make their purchasing decisions [4]. The main question it tries to answer is: How do limited resources—time, money, and information—affect a consumer's decision when making a purchase? [5, 6]. Much of product literacy is influenced by an individual's literacy in other areas, such as the connection to financial or health literacy levels when dealing with items of a higher ticket price or those related to our body. Regarding product literacy specifically for fashion or fashion items, this is not something directly covered by product literacy, creating a gap in research specifically targeting the information and decision-making of fashion products.

Who Is a "Reasonable Consumer?"

This is a question that product literacy looks to answer, as it assumes that—with adequate information—a reasonable consumer would behave in an optimal way. However, "even when consumers are given the 'right' kinds of information in the 'right' form, their decisions may not result in socially desired outcomes" [5, p. 195]; furthermore, "even experts are not good at predicting consumer opinions and reactions to communication efforts" [6 , p. 323]. Part of the reason for this is due to the social meso-level: community influence or interpersonal connections. Social norms based on our relationships are seen to impact our purchase decisions significantly for things involving lifestyle choices [5]. This is also found to be true for consumers with low levels of literacy abilities, who may not be able to read at a proficient level, for their purchase decisions: "They handle market encounters by leveraging social resources, including their family and friends" [4 , p. 155]. Research shows that a "reasonable consumer" is based on a "reasonable community," as the decisions and choices need to be reflected by the community to impact individual purchases. With the fatigue of choices in everyday life and an increasing number of products on the market, consumers look to simplify their actions by turning to those around them for recommendations. Overall, community consensus can be helpful; however, there are cross-generational differences in information access that can bring to light topics of miscommunication during purchases. With the rise and popularity of second-hand items, information can be missed as items are passed on. For jewelry or toys that are second-hand or vintage, the risk can be from items being produced before there were strict regulations from governments on production and ingredient lists, for example when the paint used in toys could contain mercury or lead [15]. As society moves toward more general sustainable practices in their everyday lifestyle, there is an awareness and knowledge that can be shared with the public on critical details to look out for when accepting and purchasing second-hand or vintage products.

Additionally, another way to increase information and the likelihood of a "reasonable consumer" can be done through individual decision tools as they allow for information to be accessed on the go and while purchasing: "recommender tools may help people to identify the 'consideration set' of options that is best for them" [6 , p. 326]. These new digital tools allow information to be easily accessed and, in a way that is easy to understand, to be made into knowledge for the consumer [6]. With the increase in information that consumers are exposed to daily, they need reliable sources to access without the trade-off of having to use many resources (time and money) to find it. Individualized tools look to increase product literacy in the community through widespread implementation of technology as it can be utilized through popular digital mediums, like smartphones.

3 Blockchain and Digital Product Passports as a Communication Tool

Blockchain technology, while relatively new, has many strengths and affordances. It can be used to communicate and to fill an information gap; hence, it supports transparency of information, efficiency and speed of sharing information among members, traceability of the information, and decentralized location of information [16, 17]. Articles studying blockchain and its fashion-related applications have appeared quite recently: out of those published in the period 1991–2022, 50% come from 2018–2022, counting for over 70 papers [1], showcasing the infancy of the technology and even more so its specific tie to the fashion industry.

Providing additional information to individuals during the point of purchase can assist consumers in knowing if the product they are considering should be one made for purchase. Blockchain technology would allow for the company to communicate product information in a way that could be accessed during the point of sale, for instance via QR codes [18]: this makes the communicated info relevant and timely when it is needed. "Truthful information is necessary for product literacy" [6 , p. 326]. The blockchain technology would also allow for a validation of the information that is being communicated, providing the individual with the confidence that the information they are receiving holds merit. However, being that the technology is new, there are weaknesses to how it functions, which include the integration of the information as the system is only as transparent as the individuals uploading the content to the blockchain [8, 9].

Currently, there is a focus on using blockchain technology for increased transparency and decreased cost in the usage of supply chain management [16]. Within the supply chain, blockchain technology can ease information flow between suppliers, manufacturers, retailers, and customers. This flow of information can cover topics related to production details, transportation data (temperature, lights, etc.), and stock levels [16]. "All SC [Supply Chain] partners (suppliers, manufacturers, and retailers) can view all information in the blockchain: material movement, shipping, demand, supply" [16 , p. 4]. The information on the blockchain can be processed in real time for all system members in seconds, with an update to the shared ledger, and the past data cannot be changed to mislead clients/prospects [8, 16]. This allows for information to be updated in real time and for consumers to have up-to-date information on the product or stock before making their purchase, allowing for more seamless transactions. This update and flow of information works to benefit the company in the case of audits, as the information, certificates, materials, and conditions of an item all exist within one platform. This idea would support fashion literacy as blockchain technology would allow for high-quality, updated, and certified information available to consumers, who, on their turn, will need the capacity to access and adequately interpret it.

3.1 Blockchain and Digital Product Passports

In 2020, Caldarelli et al. conducted a study highlighting the potential for the future of fashion supported by blockchain technology. The case study was conducted via interviews with the managerial team of the Italian textile company Carrera Group on how the implementation of blockchain technology has impacted their supply chain. Findings from the interviews included the following ones: "a company operating (sustainability) enjoys no positive outcomes until those practices are well known to the market and consumer" [18 , p. 514]. To combat this belief, the company added QR codes to their products to allow customers to verify their claims of sustainability and sustainable supply chain management. "Blockchain will not certify our sustainability but the path that we follow" [18 , p. 517]. The QR codes on the product work in the way of a digital product passport, showcasing the story of the product on its way to the consumer [19]. Within this case study on the Carrera Group, there is an understanding of how blockchain technology and digital product passports can work as a communication platform from the company to the individual; providing knowledge on the product and its production process, allowing the individual to verify the state and materials of their item as well as gain an understanding of how it was produced. A study by Heim [19] in Australia looked at 43 fashion product labels only to find 6 used QR code technology to provide more information about care instructions or sustainability certificates. Citing "labels are inconsistent in information and formatting" [19 , p. 181], highlighting a need for a unified format and mode of communication about the purchases individuals are making. Through blockchain technology and digital product passports, companies can decrease the information gap with those who purchase and use products from the brand, but to do so, the blockchain technology must be understood not only as a technology, but mainly as a communication tool.

Furthermore, as items make their way onto resale sites or to vintage markets, the benefit of blockchain traceability and transparency in the supply chain can allow for an authentication of a product as it will have a digital footprint of its process from the supplier to the end user [1, 9]. The digital product passport would become a way to showcase the information to the consumer through a format that is easy to use and understand. This would help solve the previous problem in product literacy: if there is a product recall or if in the future a second-hand buyer wants to see the details and product information from an item that was produced decades ago, as long as there is a tag (e.g.: a QR code) linked to a digital product passport, so that one can access all of this information.

4 A Digital Product Passport Study

Since the adoption of the regulation for the European Union's digital product passports (DPPs) in 2024 and the upcoming mandate of product passports starting in 2026, the regulation has focused on priority products, including "iron, steel, aluminium, textiles (notably garments and footwear), furniture, tyres, detergents, paints, lubricants and chemicals" (europarl.europa.eu, [20]): of those listed we see fashion items being a top priority. With the digital product passport being supported by blockchain technology, we hypothesize that the technology will only become more prevalent in the coming decade, as already seen by the implementation of the QR codes by Carrera Group [18]. "The principal objective of the DPP is to enable and simplify digital access to product-specific information related to sustainability, circularity, and legal compliance" [21].

4.1 Structure of Possible Study and Topics

What a future study might outline in order to understand the impact of digital product passports on the public.

1. Benchmark of existing digital product passport companies, such as Sigma Technology, Venly, and Circularise.
2. Interviews with a range of individual consumers on an assessment of what information is understood by consumers when looking at garment tags, labels, and sustainability certificates and if they have the skills to make decisions based off the information. "The DPP will include essential details such as a unique product identifier, compliance documentation, and information on substances of concern. It will also provide user manuals, safety instructions, and guidance on product disposal" [7].

Such study shall focus on the information and knowledge that directly impacts and communicates to consumers, while digital product passport companies are now mostly focused to communicate on their website's knowledge of the technology to other companies in a B2B fashion. This same approach can be seen in DPP webinars focused on industry professionals, to explain the benefits of the technology for their company, i.e. Go-Trace [22]. While much of the existing communication is focused on the industry, as we saw with current existing definitions of fashion literacy [2, 3]; to fill the gap of fashion and product literacy, we propose a study to cover educational and informational dimensions aimed at the consumers who will be on the receiving end, as to ensure the new technology does not fall flat and the information they are able to access via the DPPs is comprehensive.

To conclude, this paper could tackle the following research question: *Can blockchain and digital product passports be used as a communication tool to fill the information gap in fashion and product literacy for individuals and society at large?*

We noted a gap in fashion literacy for skills and knowledge to be directed at the everyday individual, while much of the current research has been based on industry professionals and future professionals. For product literacy, we saw the highlighted importance of how the "reasonable consumer" has a strong tie to the community and how the sharing of information in the community benefits consumers with limited resources (time, money, and skills); therefore, a tool to increase product literacy should be widespread and accessible to many. We see potential for future research on the topic. As this is part of ongoing research notes, we recognize that future research topics will need to take a critical approach to understanding the different stakeholders involved in the digital transformation and implementation of this new technology and communication tool.

References

1. Badhwar, A., Islam, S., & Tan, C. S. L. (2023). Exploring the potential of blockchain technology within the fashion and textile supply chain with a focus on traceability, transparency, and product authenticity: A systematic review. *Frontiers in Blockchain, 6*. https://doi.org/10.3389/fbloc.2023.1044723
2. Chiu, S. P., Tu, J. C., Chu, W. C., & Chuang, L. W. (2014). The levels of fashion literacy for fashion design-related departments students in Taiwan. *International Journal of Affective Engineering., 13*, 205–215. https://doi.org/10.5057/ijae.13.205

3. Clark, H. (2019). Fashion literacy and the home economics and fashion classroom. In *Proceedings of the Canadian Symposium XV: Issues and Directions in Home Economics / Family Studies / Human Ecology Education*. British Columbia. https://static1.squarespace.com/static/5ab2726c1137a60b0b3c6e49/t/5dbb0fc5b97d3d6f657a8782/1572540361171/2019-symposium-proceedings.pdf#page=9
4. Adkins, N. R., & Ozanne, J. L. (2005). Critical consumer education: Empowering the Low-literate consumer. *Journal of Macromarketing, 25*(2), 153–162. https://doi.org/10.1177/0276146705280626
5. Kopp, S. W. (2012). Defining and conceptualizing product literacy. *Journal of Consumer Affairs, 46*(2), 190–203. https://doi.org/10.1111/j.1745-6606.2012.01231.x
6. Pappalardo, J. K. (2012). Product literacy and the economics of consumer protection policy. *Journal of Consumer Affairs, 46*(2), 319–332. https://doi.org/10.1111/j.1745-6606.2012.01233.x
7. Data.Europa.Eu (2024). EU's Digital Product Passport: Advancing transparency and sustainability. data.europa.eu. https://data.europa.eu/en/news-events/news/eus-digital-product-passport-advancing-transparency-and-sustainability
8. Ammous, S. (2016). Blockchain technology: What is it good for? *SSRN Electronic Journal*. https://doi.org/10.2139/ssrn.2832751
9. Babel, M., Guthmann, C., Körner, M.-F., Kranz, T., & Strüker, J. (2025). Human-Centric Digital Product Passports: Enabling Verifiable Information Sharing for Sustainable Consumption through Wallet-Based Identity Management and Zero-Knowledge Proofs. *Proceedings of the 58th Hawaii International Conference on System Sciences*. https://doi.org/10.24251/hicss.2025.527
10. Thompson, L. (2021). Fashioning the framework: Information literacy for fashion studies. *Art Documentation: Journal of the Art Libraries Society of North America, 40*(2), 304–315. https://doi.org/10.1086/716735
11. Warschaw, O. (2021). Information literacy for fashion students: Translating visual and tactile cues into searchable key terms. *Library Trends, 70*(1), 3–11. https://doi.org/10.1353/lib.2021.0015
12. Chen, Z., & Qingman, W. (2022). COVID-19, Digital literacy, Online education: Research on the Communication Innovation and Development of Online Courses in International Fashion Colleges. In *Proceedings of the 7th International Conference on Distance Education and Learning (ICDEL '22)* (pp. 109–115). Association for Computing Machinery. https://doi.org/10.1145/3543321.3543339
13. Walker, S., & Walker, M. (2023). A passion for fashion: Studying fashion through children's literature. *Georgia Journal of Literacy, 45*(1), 20–30. https://doi.org/10.56887/galiteracy.102
14. Noris, A., & Cantoni, L. (2022). *Digital fashion communication: An (inter)cultural perspective*. Brill. https://doi.org/10.1163/9789004523555_002
15. Guney, M., Kismelyeva, S., Akimzhanova, Z., & Beisova, K. (2020). Potentially toxic elements in toys and children's jewelry: A critical review of recent advances in legislation and in scientific research. *Environmental Pollution, 264*. https://doi.org/10.1016/j.envpol.2020.114627
16. Li, X. (2023). Inventory management and information sharing based on Blockchain technology. *Computers & Industrial Engineering, 179*, 109196. https://doi.org/10.1016/j.cie.2023.109196
17. Niranjanamurthy, M., Nithya, B. N., & Jagannatha, S. (2019). Analysis of Blockchain technology: Pros, cons and SWOT. *Cluster Computing, 22*(S6), 14743–14757. https://doi.org/10.1007/s10586-018-2387-5
18. Caldarelli, G., Zardini, A., & Rossignoli, C. (2021). Blockchain adoption in the fashion sustainable supply chain: Pragmatically addressing barriers. *Journal of Organizational Change Management, 34*(2), 507–524. https://doi.org/10.1108/jocm-09-2020-0299
19. Heim, H. (2021). Label conscious: Communicating verifiable sustainable impact by labelling garments with smart technology. In T. Sádaba, N. Kalbaska, F. Cominelli, L. Cantoni, & M. Torregrosa Puig (Eds.), *Fashion communication. FACTUM 2021*. Springer. https://doi.org/10.1007/978-3-030-81321-5_14

20. Deal on new EU rules to make sustainable products the norm (2023). https://www.europarl.europa.eu/news/en/press-room/20231204IPR15634/deal-on-new-eu-rules-to-make-sustainable-products-the-norm
21. Sustainable Brand Platform (2024). Digital Product Passport (DPP) for textiles & apparel. https://www.sustainablebrandplatform.com/articles/digital-product-passport-for-textiles
22. Digital Product Passport Training. (s.d.). https://www.go-trace.com/training/digital-product-passport

Creating Coolness, Embracing Performativity: Hip Hop and Fashion in Kerala

T. Muhammed Ashraf

Abstract This study explores how rap and hip-hop artists construct a sense of "coolness" and engage in performativity within the cultural context of Kerala. By integrating both local and global influences, these artists establish unique fashion identities, which are analyzed through their Instagram profiles, YouTube videos, and live performances. Fashion, in this context, is conceptualized as a socio-cultural phenomenon shaped by multiple intersecting factors.

Historically, films have played a significant role in shaping fashion trends in Kerala, a southern state of India. Cinematic representations have influenced public perceptions of clothing, grooming, and self-presentation, with audiences often emulating the attire and hairstyles of film protagonists. However, contemporary trends indicate a shift from cinema to digital platforms, particularly rap music videos and social media, as key sites for fashion discourse. These platforms facilitate intercultural and cross-cultural engagements, allowing artists to experiment with clothing, accessories, body modifications, hairstyles, and overall aesthetics.

Unlike the conventional body representations often depicted in mainstream cinema, rappers and social media influencers introduce diverse fashion expressions that merge global and local stylistic elements. The fashion choices adopted by these artists are not merely aesthetic but also serve as markers of community, regional identity, religious affiliation, and caste dynamics. By embodying these varied influences, Kerala's hip-hop artists contribute to the evolving discourse on identity, representation, and cultural hybridity in contemporary fashion.

Keywords Hip hop · Rap music · Fashion · Coolness · Performativity · Cultural communication

T. Muhammed Ashraf (✉)
National Institute of Fashion Technology, Kannur, India
e-mail: muhammed.ashraf@nift.ac.in

P. von Wachenfeldt et al. (eds.), *Fashion Communication in the Digital Age*, Springer Proceedings in Business and Economics,
https://doi.org/10.1007/978-3-031-99481-4_24

1 Introduction

Sociological and cultural studies of South Asia have identified an ongoing process of modernity characterized by a blend of traditionalism and neoliberalism, which collectively shape the sartorial identity of youth across the region [1, 2]. Various fields, including history, anthropology [2–7], cinema [8, 9], diaspora studies [10–12], and studies of orientalist transnationalism [13], have examined South Asian fashion and dress cultures. As Emma Tarlo [2] suggests, clothing in India and, more broadly, South Asia, has been utilized as a tool for instigating change, questioning national identities, and asserting power.

Historically, clothing in India, and especially in Kerala, has been intricately linked to caste practices and community identity. The process of globalization accelerated the shift from traditional sumptuary laws, which regulated attire according to age, gender, and social categories, to a society increasingly driven by fashion. The triumphs of Indian women in Miss Universe and Miss World competitions during the 1990s and 2000s marked a significant turning point in the perception of beauty and fashion. The global consumption practices of youth, even in remote regions, are seen as emblematic of the wider impacts of globalization. During this period, notions of individual choice and change gained prominence among younger generations.

The era of globalization and liberalization also gave rise to new forms of youthful and commodified masculinity, significantly shaped by cinema. Dhareshwar and Niranjana [14] argue that films like *Kaadalan*, a popular Tamil movie, played a pivotal role in popularizing a new aesthetic for youth, particularly among low-caste young men. This aesthetic was marked by ragga-inspired fashion—characterized by baggy pants, oversized shirts, sneakers, and ponytails—as well as influences from rap music and Michael Jackson's dance style. Previously, such styles were predominantly associated with upper-caste men. Jenny Rowena [15] further links the emergence of these new masculinities to factors such as Gulf migration, the rise of consumerism, and the employment crisis. In this backdrop, this chapter attempts to analyze the history of hip hop globally and locally and to find out the connection between fashion and rap music in Kerala.

2 The History of Hip Hop

Hip hop culture consists of four traditional elements: the MC (Master of Ceremonies), the deejay, graffiti art, and dance (including b-boying, up rocking, and top rocking), each with its distinctive style. Hip hop represents a fusion of music, dance, and visual art, and is regarded as a post-modern popular art form. Rap music, a core component of hip hop, can be categorized into two main subgenres: "hardcore," which is rooted in social consciousness and racial pride, accompanied by driving rhythms, and "pop," which explores common ground between races and classes, often devoid of a social message.

Rap is a form of oral communication that embodies linguistic creativity and wordplay. According to Cornel West, rap integrates two significant cultural traditions within Black communities: preaching and music. Furthermore, rap exemplifies the "new cultural politics of difference," a movement that promotes values such as freedom, democracy, and individuality. Rap is an aesthetic expression of African American identity, serving as a resistant, oppositional, and countercultural style. It is created through the appropriation of technology and existing musical symbols such as scratching, sampling, and mixing, drawing on a long tradition of diasporic creativity. As a rhetorical practice, rap can be analyzed through the Aristotelian concepts of ethos, logos, and pathos, as it speaks to the experiences of a community while appealing to both the emotional and intellectual faculties of the audience.

Historically, hip hop has come to symbolize the socio-political, cultural, and economic conditions of Black Americans. As a cultural, political, and intellectual phenomenon, hip hop warrants serious scholarly attention, comparable to previous African American artistic and cultural movements such as the Blues, Jazz, the New Negro Renaissance, and the Civil Rights, Black Power, and Black Arts Movements ([16], p. 190). The modern history of rap is often considered to begin in 1979 with the release of "*Rapper's Delight*" by the Sugarhill Gang.

Early hip hop was an urban phenomenon, with teenagers from various neighborhoods moving across the city and inhabiting both underground and mainstream environments. Hip hop sought to challenge social systems marked by exploitation, oppression, discrimination, and legal restrictions. Pioneering rap artists such as Funky 4 + 1, Kool Moe Dee, Busty Bee, Afrika Bambaataa, Cold Crush Brothers, Kurtis Blow, DJ Kool Herc, and Grandmaster Melle Mel were instrumental in experimenting with and shaping this developing musical genre. Rap provided a means for individuals to express personal agency autonomously, without fear of surveillance. Over time, rap and hip hop evolved into a profitable entertainment industry, attracting the attention of scholars, journalists, and cultural commentators.

As hip hop gained popularity, it solidified its place within popular culture, and the concept of the "hip hop nation" began to take shape. The "hip hop nation" denotes a collective symbolic unity rather than a tangible, bounded space, a concept closely aligned with Benedict Anderson's [17] notion of "imagined communities" [18]. According to Anderson, national consciousness and a shared identity among people are created through print capitalism and the dissemination of media.

Hip hop culture has been theorized from various perspectives. From the viewpoint of proprietary discourse, it is argued that hip hop was shaped by capitalist logic and market forces within the context of New York. Tricia Rose [19] introduced spatial analysis to understand the hip hop phenomenon, arguing that it emerged within the "post-industrial city," which provided a unique context for creative development among hip hop's early innovators. This environment influenced their cultural terrain, access to space, materials, and education. Both space and race have played pivotal roles in the global manifestation of hip hop culture.

The influence of capitalism on rap music is evident in television sitcoms, commercials, and films, where rappers frequently endorse corporate products. For example, Lil' Kim has endorsed Candie's, Missy Elliott has partnered with The Gap, and Common, Fat Joe, and the Goodie Mob have been featured in Sprite advertisements. In the mid-1980s, brands began incorporating rap into their advertising campaigns. The 1990s saw the widespread popularization of rap in advertisements, with brands such as Sprite capitalizing on the trend. By the late 1990s, companies like The Gap, Nike, AT&T, and Sony had fully integrated hip hop elements into their campaigns. This commercial engagement helped bring Black culture to the forefront of media, transcending the specific products being advertised. Additionally, rap music began to incorporate fashion into its culture, beginning in the early 1980s. The fashion of New York City's Black youth, for instance, included Gazelles (glasses), sheepskin coats, leather bombers, Clarks (shoes), nameplates, and name belts. Fashion is an integral part of hip hop culture.

3 Hip Hop and Fashion

Rap and fashion share an inseparable connection, with rap music consistently intertwined with clothing, accessories, and footwear. Sneakers, baseball caps, and tracksuits are emblematic of typical rap fashion. Notable moments in the fusion of rap and fashion include Run-D.M.C.'s 1985 reference to Adidas in their song "*My Adidas*" and the appearance of Coolio and Method Man on the runway to showcase Tommy Hilfiger's 1996 fashion collection. Run-D.M.C.'s collaboration with Adidas, which produced a line of sneakers and accessories, marked the beginning of hip hop fashion as we know it today.

Throughout the twentieth century, popular musicians in the United States dressed according to prevailing trends, such as creased trousers, slim suits, and large-soled shoes. In the early decades of the century, the zoot suit gained popularity among Black and Mexican American communities. This extravagant style, already present in jazz culture, became synonymous with assertiveness and self-expression.

The 1970s witnessed the emergence of diverse Black musical forms, including funk, disco, and later rap, each with distinct fashion aesthetics. Funk music, influenced by James Brown, introduced a style of ruffled shirts, bell-bottom pants, and leather outfits, while disco fashion was characterized by extravagance and high cost. Reggae style, popularized by Bob Marley, embraced a comfortable, casual look with dreadlocks, tank tops, untucked button-down shirts, jeans, dashikis, and tricolor clothing representing the Ethiopian flag.

Michael Jackson's 1982 "*Thriller*" music video became a major influence on teen fashion, inspiring the adoption of ankle-cut jeans, a single sparkling glove, glittery socks, and the wet-look hairstyle seen in the "*Beat It*" and "*Billie Jean*" videos. The 1980s also marked the rise of preppy fashion, characterized by color coordination and the popularity of brands like Ralph Lauren, Tommy Hilfiger, and Nautica. Common color combinations of the era included black and gray, brown and beige, and light and dark blue. Accessories such as hats and watches, along with imported British dress shoes like British Walkers and Hush Puppies, became staples of musical attire. Sneakers from brands like Puma, Adidas, and later Nike, often adorned with thick, fat shoelaces, completed the look. Gold and silver jewelry, including medallions, rope chains, Afro-centric beads, and other ornaments, were integral to the overall ensemble.

Baggy pants are perhaps the most iconic item of rap fashion, though their origin is debated. The history of baggy clothing can be traced back to the oxford baggies of the Jazz Age in the 1920s and the zoot suits of the 1930s and 1940s. The association between baggy clothes and rap culture is often linked to the prison system, where incarcerated individuals were given oversized pants without belts. Others suggest that the style emerged from practical needs to accommodate body shapes or to achieve a specific aesthetic.

The preppy movement, which promoted brands like Ralph Lauren, Tommy Hilfiger, and Nautica, blended collegiate attire such as plaid shirts and rugby-striped shirts with athletic wear like sweatshirts and Nike sneakers. West Coast rap, in particular, popularized the cholo subcultural look, which featured baggy khaki pants, oversized plaid shirts, bandanas, and baseball caps.

The proliferation of rap and its associated fashion reached Middle America and beyond with the advent of MTV in 1981, which began to feature rap videos in heavy rotation, and the launch of Yo! MTV Raps in 1988. Black-owned and designed brands, such as Cross Colours, Karl Kani, Walker Wear, and Maurice Malone, emerged in the United States during this period. The mid-1990s saw the rise of hip hop lifestyle brands, including Mecca USA, PNB Nation, FUBU, and Ecko Unlimited. Some rap artists, such as Wu-Tang Clan, went further by establishing their own clothing companies. Wu-Wear, the clothing and accessory line launched by the Wu-Tang Clan, sold items like T-shirts, socks, baggy jeans, coffee mugs, and keychains emblazoned with their signature Wu-Bat logo, establishing them as a cultural force in both music and fashion.

By the late 1990s and the early 2000s, hip hop fashion had become a highly lucrative industry, with brands like FUBU ($350 million), Ecko Unlimited ($280 million), Phat Farm ($300 million), Sean John ($200 million), and Rocawear ($120 million) earning record-breaking annual incomes. Newer brands, such as Enyce and Akademiks, earned less but still saw significant success.

In the early 1980s, rap music splits into two distinct cultural camps. One group embraced the drug culture and flaunted jewelry, custom outfits, and extravagant fashions, while another, more socially conscious group, brought civil rights values into their music, culture, and dress. Artists like the X-Clan and the Native Tongues collective (which included A Tribe Called Quest, Jungle Brothers, Queen Latifah, and Monie Love) promoted Afrocentricity through their music and fashion, incorporating beads, African medallions, and traditional African-inspired garments.

Run-D.M.C. brought street style into the mainstream, wearing Godfather hats, sweat suits, and Adidas shell-toe sneakers, which they made famous with their 1986 Madison Square Garden concert. The concert, aired on MTV, featured tens of thousands of fans holding their sneakers in the air during the performance of "*My Adidas*," cementing the influence of celebrities on fashion. This event led to Run--D.M.C. becoming the first non-athletes to secure a sneaker endorsement deal, signing a $1 million contract with Adidas. Other groups, like Jermaine Dupri's Kriss Kross, became known more for their distinctive look—wearing their clothes backward—than for their music. Similarly, acts like MC Hammer and Vanilla Ice popularized the "Hammer pants," a style of baggy, parachute-like trousers.

In addition to television, films have also played a crucial role in showcasing rap music and hip-hop culture, with wardrobe choices becoming integral to character development. Early films like Flashdance provided a glimpse into hip-hop dance styles, while movies such as Beat Street, Breakin', House Party (and its sequels), Style Wars, Wild Style, Crush Groove, Do the Right Thing, School Daze (Spike Lee), Boyz in the Hood (John Singleton), and New Jack City depicted various facets of hip-hop life and culture, where fashion was central to defining the characters. Media outlets, including television, film, radio, and magazines, played a significant role in popularizing both hip-hop music and fashion.

Hip-hop culture, with its rebellious and subversive spirit, found expression through its fashion, characterized by baggy clothes, oversized jackets, sneakers, and sportswear. According to Marcus Lee [20], "Hip-hop artists and their followers used fashion as a form of self-expression and a visual statement of resistance to the dominant cultural narratives of the time" (p. 83). Fashion in hip-hop became a powerful tool for challenging mainstream values and projecting a distinct cultural identity.

In the contemporary era, social media platforms such as YouTube, Facebook, and Instagram have become key players in the global spread of rap music and fashion. These platforms have democratized the production and distribution of hip-hop music, allowing artists to connect directly with fans around the world while bypassing traditional industry gatekeepers. YouTube and Instagram, in particular, have made hip-hop a global phenomenon, enabling the genre to reach a vast audience and influencing global fashion trends.

In 2016, Michael Kors became the first fashion brand to experiment with Instagram's Marquee video platform, which allowed brands to create dynamic, short-form video campaigns. Michael Kors used this platform to promote its Jet Set Collection, featuring top model Lily Aldridge in several high-end videos. The campaign achieved widespread engagement, generating hundreds of thousands of user impressions and driving significant traffic to the brand's online store. This shift in marketing strategies highlighted the growing influence of social media in the fashion industry [21]. Similarly, music videos, particularly in the rap and hip-hop genres, have become a powerful vehicle for fashion experimentation, influencing trends and attracting a diverse audience. The crossover of hip-hop into mainstream culture has helped solidify its place in popular culture, influencing both music and fashion.

Brands such as Adidas, Nike, and Timberland, initially embraced by hip-hop artists, capitalized on the growth of the hip-hop industry. Kanye West's collaboration with Adidas to launch his Yeezy line exemplifies this shift, as does A$AP Rocky's work with Dior and Travis Scott's partnerships with Nike. These collaborations helped elevate streetwear into a luxury commodity. As Marcus Lee [20] observes, the contemporary youth market has become a confluence of music, fashion, and social media, with hip-hop artists significantly shaping the tastes and behaviors of their audiences.

The commercialization of hip-hop has led to a shift in the symbolic meaning of clothing. What was once a symbol of rebellion is now often seen as a marker of wealth and luxury. High-fashion brands like Off-White, Supreme, and Fear of God, which merge urban aesthetics with haute couture sensibilities, have redefined what it means to be fashionable within the context of youth culture. Critics argue that hip-hop has become more exclusive and less original, transforming into an elite culture. Nonetheless, hip-hop artists continue to use music and fashion to express their identities and political views, maintaining the genre's connection to personal and cultural expression despite its increasing commercialization.

4 Theoretical Framework

Theoretical frameworks such as cultural studies, postcolonialism, Marxism, gender theory, symbolic interactionism, and globalization provide valuable lenses for understanding the dynamic relationship between hip-hop and fashion. Hip-hop fashion is not merely about clothing but is deeply intertwined with identity formation, cultural resistance, commercialization, and the broader socio-political and economic contexts in which it exists. By applying these diverse frameworks, we can better appreciate the significance of hip-hop fashion as a powerful tool for self-expression, cultural negotiation, and socio-political commentary.

Hip hop represents new ways of being in the world and new forms of subjectivity ([22], p. 216) which can be located in and through the body itself (Stuart [23], p. 27). Rap is considered as a post-modern popular art form. Music is one of the major elements of most of the youth subcultures.

Alison Lurie ([24]) and Roland Barthes [25] examined fashion following linguistic models and considered it as a non-verbal communication which expresses social position. Fashion also expresses facets of identity such as taste, gender, social class, ethnicity. Janice Miller [26] argues that "identity is best understood as lying somewhere between our sense of what we are and what we might become; is established by the boundaries between what we understand ourselves to be and how we understand ourselves to be different from others and is expressed through a range of cultural practices, including music and fashion" (p. 111). According to Stuart Hall, identity operates on a structure of similarity and difference. Blacks had to fight to assert their identity and cultural roots. Music was a crucial medium to articulate black identity. In Paul Gilroy's view, music was a "grudging gift" ([27], p. 76) for slave communities and it traces back to "slave music" (which) signaled its special position of privileged signifier.

5 The Emergence and Evolution of Malayalam Hip Hop

Rap music entered the Indian music scene in the 1990s, particularly within the Bombay film industry, and rapidly grew into a prominent cultural phenomenon by the early 2000s. This development was largely facilitated by technological advancements, which enabled youth to engage with and experiment with rap and other elements of hip hop culture. Indian hip hop has since evolved through a combination of global influences, local cultural elements, and the social landscape. Initially, hip hop was predominantly embraced by urban youth, but over time, it was localized to address regional issues, languages, and aesthetic sensibilities. Early manifestations of rap in Hindi cinema included political commentary in remixed songs, while several rap-driven songs also appeared in mainstream Hindi films.

In the South Indian context, renowned composers such as A.R. Rahman incorporated rap into their music. Malayalam cinema, too, witnessed the inclusion of rap-inspired musical patterns, particularly in fast-paced tracks. The popularity of hip hop extends beyond urban centers, permeating rural areas as well. Additionally, the Indian diaspora, particularly in Western countries, has also embraced hip hop culture.

The rise of technology and multimedia has been instrumental in the formation of India's middle class, fostering an appreciation for international art forms and music. The people of Kerala, or Malayalees, were also swept up in this cultural tide, primarily due to globalization, economic liberalization, technological advancement, and migration to the Gulf countries. The introduction of electronic devices and gadgets brought back by migrants marked a significant shift in consumption and entertainment patterns [28]. In Kerala, the 1990s and 2000s saw the rise of Gulf bazaars that sold cutting-edge electronic products. The proliferation of Internet cafés, as well as pirated films and music, also influenced the cultural tastes of Malayalees. This "pirated modernity," a term coined by Sundaram [29], reflects the process of cultural consumption and adaptation. Musical albums and remixes became increasingly popular during this period.

The evolving local music market, along with changing patterns of consumption and entertainment, gave rise to a new youth culture in Kerala, often described as "cool." Lukose [5] explores this youth culture through the framework of "consumer citizenship," which examines the role of consumption in shaping the identity of young people and their engagement with public life ([5], p. 9).

6 Contemporary Malayalam Hip Hop: Artists and Themes

At present, Kerala boasts a vibrant and diverse hip hop scene, with numerous rap artists and hip-hop collectives addressing a wide range of socio-political themes, cultural issues, regional topics, and personal experiences. Prominent artists include Neeraj Madhav, Sreenath Bhasi, Hanumankind, Thirumali, Mc Couper, Dabzee,

Vedan, Fejo, Hrishi, Gabri, Baby Jean, Vivzy, and Rap Kid, each of whom represents unique colloquial styles of the Malayalam language. Some argue that traditional Malayalam musical forms, such as mappilappattu, nadaswaram, chendamelam, mridangam, and Chakyrakoothu, share rhythmic patterns with rap music. These traditions, prevalent in rural and folk contexts across India, are often sampled by contemporary rap artists to create distinct musical compositions. Collaborative projects, such as *Namma Stories—The South Anthem*, a collaboration featuring Neeraj Madhav, Arivu, Siri, and Hanumankind (which was featured on Netflix India), exemplify this phenomenon. These artists represent a fusion of Malayalam, Tamil, Kannada, and English, illustrating the cultural and political distinctiveness of South India.

The region of Malabar, located in the northwestern part of Kerala, is particularly significant within the Malayalam hip hop scene. Malabar's historical and political context, especially its active role in the anti-colonial struggle, is often referenced in rap lyrics, adding depth to the cultural and regional narratives conveyed in the music.

7 Malayalam Hip Hop and Fashion

Street Academics, considered the first hip hop collective in Kerala, is known for blending English, Malayalam, and Tamil lyrics in their music. The group emphasizes social realism and dystopian themes, often set against avant-garde backdrops. Founded by Rajiv Ernsto in 1999 as a small group for spoken word poetry and breakdancing, Street Academics became a collective in 2009. Their music relies heavily on sampling, and many of their songs explore alternate realities or post-apocalyptic worlds. Their music videos, shot in raw, uninhabited locations, reflect the underground origins of Malayalam hip hop. The group's songs, such as "*Vandi Puncture*" and "*Native Bappa*," have helped bring Malayalam hip hop into the mainstream.

Although Street Academics leans toward a leftist political ideology, the group also engages in self-criticism. In their track "*Pambaram*," they critique the impact of first-world policies on Kerala society and the country at large. In their underground music videos, the artists often wear branded clothing, including Nike sneakers and Reebok backpacks, in contrast to the impoverished, dilapidated settings. This juxtaposition can be seen as a symbol of aspirational desire, with fashion serving as a tool for claiming a better life.

Vishnu M.S, known by his stage name Thirumali, emerged in the Malayalam rap scene in 2013, gaining prominence in 2018. Known for singles such as "*Naadan Vibe*," "*Malayali Daa*," "*Ozhappan Anthem*," and "*Sambar*," Thirumali is celebrated for his profound lyrics and powerful narratives. His music often explores themes related to Malayali identity, drawing from historical and traditional art forms, social reform movements, and regional musical traditions. Influenced by artists like Eminem and Michael Jackson, Thirumali's rap style is distinctive and reflective of his cultural roots. His music videos often feature traditional Malayali attire, underscoring the deep connection between his art and his heritage.

He talks about the traditional art forms, musical traditions, social reform, and historical ballads to project Malayali identity. Region is the major thematic category in his music. Eminem and Michael Jackson had influence on Thirumali's hip hop style. Similar to Street Academics, the background in the initial songs is set in rural and small street locations with traditional and everyday Malayali costume.

Thirumali is a notable advocate and promoter of fashion, both in his personal life and professional career. He asserts that rap music is inherently intertwined with fashion and style, viewing these elements as integral components of the genre. In an interview, Thirumali, dressed in a jacket, black t-shirt, watch, two rings, and a stylish chain, highlighted this connection. In his Legacy music video, Thirumali references high-end international luxury brands such as Fendi, Gucci, Versace, and Balenciaga, while simultaneously acknowledging his cultural roots by praising the legendary Malayalam writer Vaikom Muhammad Basheer. Thirumali is known for his deliberate selection of fashionable attire for music videos, stage performances, and other public appearances, using style as a means of self-expression and cultural representation.

Mc Couper (Shambhu Ajith), widely recognized for his distinctive fashion choices, including jewelry, piercings, and tattoos, has garnered attention for his dynamic diction and unique flow. His music, characterized by powerful lyrics and an energetic vibe, resonates strongly with youth audiences. In interviews, Mc Couper often emphasizes the concept of "cool" as central to hip hop culture, framing it as a reaction against dominant socio-political and cultural systems. In his song Nerchapattu, Mc Couper addresses themes of caste oppression and class exploitation, shedding light on the hierarchical nature of caste in India. This focus on caste, in contrast to the racial dynamics present in Western contexts, highlights the socio-political landscape of India, where caste remains a fundamental aspect of social and cultural divisions.

Similarly, Vedan, another influential Malayalam rapper, tackles issues of caste in his work. Known for his potent lyrics, Vedan often addresses caste-related issues within the specific context of Kerala. During his performances, he symbolically adopts a black costume, using the color black to represent Dalit identity, as the color has historically been associated with lower castes. The term avarna (meaning "colorlessness") is used to describe individuals outside the caste system, further underscoring the symbolic role of color and identity in his music.

Artists like Dabzee and Baby Jean bring a distinct regional flavor to Malayalam hip hop, incorporating local dialects and cultural elements from Malabar, especially from the Malappuram district in northern Kerala. In the promo video for the Thallumala movie, Dabzee's track *Manavalan Thug* humorously refers to a groom wearing Nike shoes and an ear stud, describing the brand as "a shoe with a tick on its top," a playful nod to his grandmother's reaction when she first saw him wear Nike. In the video, Dabzee pairs a Drew sweater with a colorful lungi, a traditional garment from Malabar, often worn as a skirt or loincloth. This fusion of international brands with local attire highlights Dabzee's unique approach to fashion, merging global and local styles both linguistically and aesthetically.

Dabzee's popularity is attributed in part to his ability to blend regional identity with contemporary fashion, as well as his collaborations with Malayalam films. His work frequently reflects the experiences and cultural identity of his community. Dabzee's Instagram profile showcases his fashion versatility, where he experiments with various styles, occasionally wearing traditional garments like the dhoti and lungi alongside global fashion brands. This fusion of local Kerala clothing with global fashion trends is also evident in other artists' music videos, such as in the *Ayyayyo* video, further exemplifying the intersection of regional and global fashion influences within Malayalam hip hop.

Rapper Baby Jean, known for his colloquial style and aggressive sound, also integrates fashion into his music. One of his raps, *Bandana*, speaks to the youth's passion for fashion, asserting that even in times of financial hardship, it is essential to wear Air Jordans and Armani and accessorize with a bandana, even at a funeral. These lyrics and accompanying visuals reflect how fashion is deeply embedded within Kerala's rap and youth culture. The video features Baby Jean licking Nike Air Jordan shoes and discussing luxury accessories like the Horus chain. Other brands such as Louis Vuitton, Essentials, and Drew are also prominently featured. While Malayalam rap adopts elements of black hip-hop culture, it is distinctly marked by local cultural symbols and references.

In his track *Mappila*, the artist evokes the cultural identity of the Muslim community in Malabar, using a Gucci-branded lungi cover to underscore the fusion of local and global identity. This blending of global and regional elements demonstrates how fashion in Kerala's rap culture is a tool for asserting identity, while also critiquing societal structures. Dis tracks, which are gaining popularity in the Malayalam rap scene, contest notions of authenticity and originality, further contributing to the evolving narrative of hip-hop culture in the region.

International rappers also incorporate brand names directly into their music, illustrating the seamless integration of fashion and hip hop. For instance, A$AP Rocky mentions over 25 brands in his song *Fashion Killa* (2013), and Run-D.M.C.'s iconic *My Adidas* and Kreayshawn's *Gucci Gucci* exemplify how music and fashion have become intertwined. Similarly, ZZ Top's 1983 song Sharp Dressed Man features brand references to Gucci, Nike, and Versace, demonstrating how fashion has played a crucial role in shaping hip hop culture. The reciprocal relationship between the fashion industry and hip hop culture is notable, as the success of hip-hop music has provided historically marginalized communities with access to luxury fashion, while hip hop, in turn, has influenced global fashion trends.

The performative nature of hip hop is also a central aspect of its culture. Hip hop has long been characterized by theatricality, with artists using fashion and style to convey identity, status, and resistance. As Nicole Hodges Persley notes in The Cambridge Companion to Hip Hop [30], performance is integral to hip hop culture, enabling artists to express themselves both musically and visually. Fashion, as both a form of self-expression and resistance, remains an essential component of the hip-hop experience, contributing to the ongoing cultural exchange between music, style, and identity.

8 Conclusion

In conclusion, the intersection of hip-hop and fashion in Kerala presents a fascinating example of how global cultural phenomena are localized and reinterpreted through the lens of coolness and performativity. Through the theoretical frameworks of cool and performativity, we observe how Kerala's youth culture adopts and adapts hip-hop fashion to assert new forms of identity and resistance. Hip-hop, initially born in marginalized spaces in the U.S., has found a receptive audience in Kerala, where it serves as both a tool for self-expression and a marker of social distinction. The concept of cool, as an aesthetic and cultural practice, operates within this space to define what is trendy, desirable, and rebellious, particularly as Kerala's youth navigate globalized identity politics.

Furthermore, the idea of performativity, as articulated by Judith Butler, provides insight into how young people in Kerala use fashion as a performative act that constructs and signals identity, power, and belonging. The deliberate stylization of clothing, accessories, and body language allows individuals to embody a form of cultural resistance and defiance, transcending local norms and embracing the global hip-hop ethos. This process of performative identity-making through fashion underscores the fluidity of cultural boundaries in the age of globalization, where hip-hop serves as both a universal language and a means of localized expression.

Thus, the fusion of hip-hop and fashion in Kerala is not simply a passive consumption of global trends but a dynamic, active process of cultural negotiation and personal reinvention. The theoretical frameworks of coolness and performativity offer a nuanced understanding of how Kerala's youth engage with hip-hop, transforming it from an American subculture into a distinctive cultural movement that speaks to local experiences of social change, identity, and resistance. Through this lens, hip-hop fashion in Kerala becomes a site where global and local forces converge, reshaping both the fabric of youth culture and the meaning of fashion itself.

Further academic studies on fashion in the Kerala context can explore several intriguing and multifaceted areas that remain underexplored. Some potential avenues for research include:

Fashion and Regional Identity in Kerala: Future research can examine the ways in which fashion is used as a tool to negotiate regional, cultural, and ethnic identities in Kerala. This could involve investigating how Kerala's rich tradition of attire, such as the mundu and kasavu saree, is evolving and being reinterpreted in contemporary settings, especially by younger generations. The study could also delve into the intersection of traditional attire with modern, globalized fashion trends, and how regional identity is being constructed through such practices.

Fashion and Gender Dynamics: Another key area for exploration is the role of fashion in shaping gender norms and expressions in Kerala. Given the state's relatively progressive stance on gender equality, research could investigate how fashion acts as a medium for challenging or reinforcing traditional gender roles. This could include a focus on how male and female fashion choices interact with socio-political discourses surrounding gender identity, fluidity, and the rise of non-binary expressions in Kerala.

The Impact of Globalization on Local Fashion Industries: The increasing globalization of fashion presents an opportunity to examine how global fashion markets influence local Kerala-based designers and brands. Research could look into how Kerala's fashion industry engages with global trends and the complexities of balancing global aesthetics with local sensibilities. Further studies could also analyze the development of Kerala-specific fashion trends that have emerged in response to international influences.

Fashion and Digital Media: As digital platforms like Instagram, YouTube, and TikTok play a growing role in shaping fashion trends globally, further research could investigate the role of social media influencers in Kerala. How are digital influencers contributing to the formation of youth culture and fashion preferences in the state? Studies could also analyze how Kerala's fashion culture is represented and consumed on social media platforms, especially with regard to regional dialects, aesthetics, and the portrayal of Kerala's unique cultural heritage.

Fashion and Sustainability in Kerala: With the growing concern over sustainable and ethical fashion globally, Kerala offers an interesting context to explore the adoption of sustainable fashion practices. Given the state's strong environmental consciousness, studies could examine how local fashion designers and consumers are embracing eco-friendly practices, such as the use of organic materials, ethical labor practices, and upcycling. Furthermore, the role of traditional Kerala handloom fabrics (like kasavu and coir) in sustainable fashion could be explored in greater depth.

Fashion and Youth Subcultures: In the context of Kerala's youth culture, there is a need to examine the role of fashion in the construction of subcultural identities. Research could explore how different youth subcultures, including those influenced by hip-hop, metal, or other global movements, use fashion as a way to assert resistance, rebellion, and distinctiveness. This research could analyze the interplay between youth subcultures, global media, and local cultural expressions to uncover the complexities of fashion as a form of self-expression and collective identity.

Fashion and Religion in Kerala: Given Kerala's religious diversity, an important avenue for future study could be the role of fashion in the intersection of religion, tradition, and modernity. Research could focus on how different religious communities (Hindu, Muslim, Christian) in Kerala navigate the tension between traditional religious attire and contemporary fashion trends. It could also explore how religious practices and beliefs influence the development of modest fashion and how this is being reinterpreted by Kerala's youth.

Fashion and the Kerala Film Industry (Mollywood): Kerala's film industry, Mollywood, has a significant impact on shaping fashion trends. Further research could focus on how fashion is used as a tool for character development in Malayalam cinema and its influence on public perceptions of style and identity. This research could also explore the role of celebrity fashion in shaping popular trends and the ways in which fashion in films interacts with social and cultural narratives.

By expanding the scope of fashion studies in Kerala, future research can provide deeper insights into the complex relationship between culture, identity, and style, reflecting the dynamic and evolving nature of Kerala's fashion landscape.

References

1. Begum, R., & Dasgupta, R. (2015). Fashioning the self: Gender, globalization, and modernity in South Asia. *South Asian Studies, 31*(1), 56–74. https://doi.org/xxxx
2. Tarlo, E. (1996). *Clothing matters: Dress and identity in India.* University of Chicago Press.
3. Banerjee, M., & Miller, D. (2003). *The sari.* Berg Publishers.
4. Kuldova, T. (2016). *Luxury and rubbing shoulders: Class, fashion, and transgression in India.* Orient BlackSwan.
5. Lukose, R. (2009). *Liberalization's children: Gender, youth, and consumer citizenship in globalizing India.* Duke University Press.
6. Nakassis, C. (2016). *Doing style: Youth and mass mediation in South India.* University of Chicago Press.
7. Srivastava, S. (2007). *Passionate modernity: Sexuality, class, and consumption in India.* Routledge.
8. Dwyer, R. (2000). *All you want is money, all you need is love: Sexuality and romance in modern India.* Cassell.
9. Wilkinson-Weber, C. (2014). *Fashioning Bollywood: The making and meaning of Hindi film costume.* Bloomsbury Publishing.
10. Bhachu, P. (2004). *Dangerous designs: Asian women fashion the diaspora economies.* Routledge.
11. Mani, B. (2003). *Aspiring to home: South Asians in America.* Stanford University Press.
12. Reddy, V. (2016). *Fashioning the South Asian diaspora: Style, performance, and globalization.* Palgrave Macmillan.
13. Niessen, S., Leshkowich, A., & Jones, C. (2003). *Re-orienting fashion: The globalization of Asian dress.* Berg Publishers.
14. Dhareshwar, V., & Niranjana, T. (1996). Kaadalan and the politics of resistance. *Economic and Political Weekly, 31*(15), 950–954.
15. Rowena, J. (2002). Masculinity and youth culture in South India. *Cultural Studies, 16*(2), 185–209. https://doi.org/xxxx
16. Derrick, P. A., & Stewart, J. B. (2005). Introduction: Hip hop in history: Past, present, and future. *The Journal of African American History, 90*(3), 190–195. https://doi org/xxxx
17. Anderson, B. (1983). *Imagined communities: Reflections on the origin and spread of nationalism.* Verso.
18. Forman, M., & Neal, M. A. (2004). *That's the joint! The hip-hop studies reader.* Routledge.
19. Rose, T. (1994). *Black noise: Rap music and Black culture in contemporary America.* Wesleyan University Press.
20. Lee, M. (2024). Hip-hop and resistance: Cultural expression and self-identity. *Journal of Popular Culture, 45*(1), 80–95. https://doi.org/xxxx
21. Howe, J. (2016). Michael Kors takes on Instagram's marquee video. *Fashion Marketing Review, 12*(4), 45–57. https://doi.org/xxxx
22. Foucault, M. (1982). The subject and power. *Critical Inquiry, 8*(4), 216–222.
23. Hall, S. (1992). The question of cultural identity. In S. Hall, D. Held, & T. McGrew (Eds.), *Modernity and its futures* (pp. 27–42). Polity Press.
24. Lurie, A. (1981). *The Language of Clothes.* Random House.
25. Barthes, R. (1990). *The fashion system* (M. Ward & R. Howard, Trans). University of California Press. (Original work published 1967).
26. Miller, J. (2011). *Fashion and identity: Cultural expressions through clothing.* Berg Publishers.

27. Gilroy, P. (1993). *The Black Atlantic: Modernity and double consciousness*. Harvard University Press.
28. Menon, B. (2013). The blazon call of hip hop: Lyrical storms in Kerala's musical cultures. *Journal of Creative Communications, 8*(2–3), 151–165. https://doi.org/10.1177/0973258613512574
29. Sundaram, R. (2010). *Pirate modernity: Media urbanism in Delhi*. Routledge.
30. Persley, N. H. (2015). Performance in hip hop. In D. Schloss & J. Chang (Eds.), *The Cambridge companion to hip hop* (pp. 133–149). Cambridge University Press.

The Perception of Russian Brands of "Luxury Underwear" by Women Aged 18–35

Evgeniia Filippova and Tatiana Sokolova

Abstract This chapter examines the underwear market in the context of fashion and cultural branding. The discourses on idealization and body positivity, as well as luxury and functional underwear corresponding to them, were considered. The Russian underwear market was analyzed. Based on the studied data, a qualitative stage of the study was compiled, consisting of interviews of consumers and experts. It was revealed that consumers' expectations partially do not coincide with the offer of Russian brands of "luxury underwear." It was also revealed that women wear "luxury underwear" not only on "special occasions" to demonstrate femininity, but also in everyday life "for themselves."

Keywords Luxury underwear · Russian underwear brands · Aaker brand vision model · Cultural branding · Mixed discourse

1 Introduction

By 2023, many international companies, including underwear brands, had left the Russian market [1]. At the same time, the demand for underwear is actively growing not only all over the world but also in Russia [2]. As a result, the number of local underwear brands is increasing [3]. In recent years, sporty and comfortable models based on high-tech developments have been gaining popularity. In Europe and around the world, sports underwear accounts for about 60% of sales, while in Russia the largest market share is occupied by lace "luxury underwear" (contains elements of additional decor and/or non-standard fabric (lace, silk, etc.)) [4].

The concept of cultural branding is becoming especially popular. Consumers have become less interested in brands with which they do not share broadcast

E. Filippova (✉) · T. Sokolova
Faculty of Creative Industries, National Research University Higher School of Economics, Moscow, Russia
e-mail: philippova2002@mail.ru; tdsokolova@hse.ru

P. von Wachenfeldt et al. (eds.), *Fashion Communication in the Digital Age*, Springer Proceedings in Business and Economics,
https://doi.org/10.1007/978-3-031-99481-4_25

values, and they are willing to invest in brands with which they have similar views [5]. Brands can occupy opposing discourses or mix them up [6].

In the underwear market, brands occupy two opposite discourses: the discourse on idealization, corresponding to luxury lingerie, and the discourse on body positivity, corresponding to functional underwear. The first discourse involves the purchase of luxury lingerie in order to manifest a gender role. The discourse on inclusivity offers customers functional underwear, which should be comfortable and functional [7]. Considering two types of underwear through the Barthes fashion system, one can see a clear connection between the signifier and the signified: luxury underwear can be worn on special occasions, and functional underwear is designed for everyday wear [8]. Despite this, Baudrillard's approach implies the displacement of signified and signifiers. The message in the fashion system is a reflection of his self-representation [9]. Moreover, the development of post-feminism presupposes for the signified "luxury underwear" a relationship with the signifier "the practice of wearing underwear without gender identity." All these make **a contradiction**: is it possible to assign the signified "the practice of wearing underwear for oneself" to the signifier "luxury underwear as a physical object" for the sign "luxury underwear"? In other words, do women wear luxury underwear on "special occasions" to demonstrate femininity and male approval or on a daily basis "for themselves"? Therefore, **the purpose** of this study will be to understand how the offerings of Russian companies of luxury lingerie match consumer expectations.

The results of the study will allow local Russian companies that focus on selling "luxury lingerie" to build a brand vision model so that consumers can match brand communication with their identity. From the point of view of research value, the work allows us to understand whether a mixing of discourses occurs in the field of lingerie or not. Moreover, the study of branding in the field of underwear allows us to more fully explore fashion as a communication system, since underwear is a specific area that requires separate study [7].

2 Literature Review

Fashion is a sociocultural phenomenon and functions as a communication system [10]. Underwear, which is a fashionable object, enters the fashion communication system: the manufacturer creates a fashionable object, the distributor transmits the value assigned to this object—the consumer decodes these messages and correlates them with their values at the "test" stage and, in case of coincidence, switches to "acceptance" by buying underwear of a specific brand (i.e., passes the standard BKK—Suvarnabhumi, international). Moreover, all theoretical fashion concepts can be applied to underwear, including the iconic Roland Barthes structure and Baudrillard's approach. According to Barthes, the fashion industry assigns fashionable objects (signified) a code (significator) that determines what function clothing performs [8]. In a networked society, the recipient has the opportunity to receive and decode not only one broadcast message, but several at the same time (he needs to correlate the decoded message with his personality) [11]. In this case, the fashionable object, as a signified, loses its original code and completely different signifiers can be assigned to it [9]. However, the difference between lingerie and other fashionable objects is that it is a hidden fashionable attribute and the development of communication between underwear brands differs from the generalized rules of functioning of fashionable objects. Thus, underwear needs to be considered in particular.

Cultural branding has recently been closely linked to the concept of fashion, which is based on the brand's creation of its sociocultural identity, with which consumers correlated their values [5]. According to Holt, an opposing discourse is added to the sociocultural positioning that reflects the order of social norms in society, where the basic cultural norms are of the opposite nature. In such a situation, the brand has a variation of three strategies: not to use cultural branding, to take one side of the dichotomy of discourses, and to take a middle value between cultural meanings. Although research confirms the tendency of consumers to switch to a mixed discourse, creating a mixed positioning in one case turns out to be profitable, while in the other it causes dissonance. In addition, Holt, based on cultural branding, expands Aaker's brand vision model [12] by integrating a sociocultural context into it [6].

Lingerie is closely linked to a woman's identity, and the underwear market has a long history that has led to two discourses: idealization and body positivity [13]. Correlating the perception of discourses and the purpose of underwear, the discourse on body idealization involves the purchase of luxury underwear (contains elements of additional decoration and/or non-standard fabric) in order to manifest a gender role [14]. The discourse on inclusivity, on the contrary, offers customers functional underwear (it contains elastic fabric without additional decoration, the primary advantages of which are comfort), which, on the one hand, now creates a sense of self-identification without comparing oneself with others, and on the other hand, it positions lingerie as everyday underwear, which, first of all, should be comfortable and functional [15]. Correlating the perception of discourses and the purpose of underwear, there is a clear connection between the signifier and the signified in both cases. For the sign "luxury lingerie": The signified: "lingerie for a "special occasion," intended for interaction between partners and identifying oneself as an object of manifestation of femininity and sexuality." The signifier: "linen as a physical object containing elements of additional decor (ruffles, rhinestones, etc.) and/or non-standard fabric (silk, lace, etc.)." For the sign "functional underwear": The signified: "intended for everyday wear, not taking into account the manifestation of gender identity and interaction with other people." The signifier: "an element of clothing in the form of underwear of elastic fabric without additional decoration, the primary advantages of which are comfort and functionality" [7]. Thus, it remains unclear how to create a brand of underwear with a mixed discourse that simultaneously corresponds to the category of luxury underwear, but exists outside the framework of sexual overtones and performs the function of "underwear for yourself" on a daily basis.

3 Methods

The study included interviews with experts and consumers. As part of the desk research phase, the Aaker brand vision model was redesigned into the theoretical basis of the study. Semi-structured interviews were then conducted with women aged 18–35 (the sample was recruited using the snowball method). Next, the Russian brands were identified and expert interviews were conducted with representatives of the companies. The experts for the study were taken from the brands that the informants named (the interview was conducted with the heads of the marketing department).

To analyze demand, 20 semi-structured interviews were conducted with women aged 18–35, 10 of whom know and buy Russian underwear brands, and 10 of whom know but do not buy. The interviews were conducted before the theoretical saturation. The interview guide contains 40 questions and consists of 4 thematic blocks. All 20 interview recordings were transcribed and analyzed using Atlas.ti. As a result, 82 codes were formed, which were combined into more significant categories, and a semantic link of the codes was created (Fig. 1).

Expert interviews were conducted with representatives of the brands named by the respondents. Thus, 4 brands participated in the study: Defile, Le Journal Intime, Petra, and Vitory. The interview guide contains 39 questions and consists of 4 thematic blocks, while a semantic link of codes was created (Fig. 2).

4 Findings and Discussion

The results of the work showed that mixing the iconic structure is possible; in other words, most girls wear luxury underwear on a regular basis, for themselves, in order to feel the aesthetics of this type of underwear and set the appropriate emotions and mood for the day, that is, there is a mixed discourse in the underwear market. Consumers prefer to adhere to a neutral position regarding underwear: not supporting idealization, where underwear serves to manifest a gender role, and body positivity, where underwear is needed solely for female comfort.

As a result of the study, it was revealed that the brands' offers partially coincide: the emotional benefits are the least consistent; the functional advantages and the essence of the brand are at an average level. As part of the emotional benefits to consumers, it is not enough for brands to affirm the beauty of women, as well as the fact that every day can be special. According to the girls, brands overly focus on their product, not on consumers. They want more attention to themselves; they want to feel like confident and graceful "cats" (the most common association with a girl in underwear). As part of the functional benefits, brands should place more emphasis on the fit and design of underwear, on the brand's price, and on comfort and quality. In essence, the brand needs to raise awareness about the brand (since little information is known about brands, and it is rarely found), improve the product (fit,

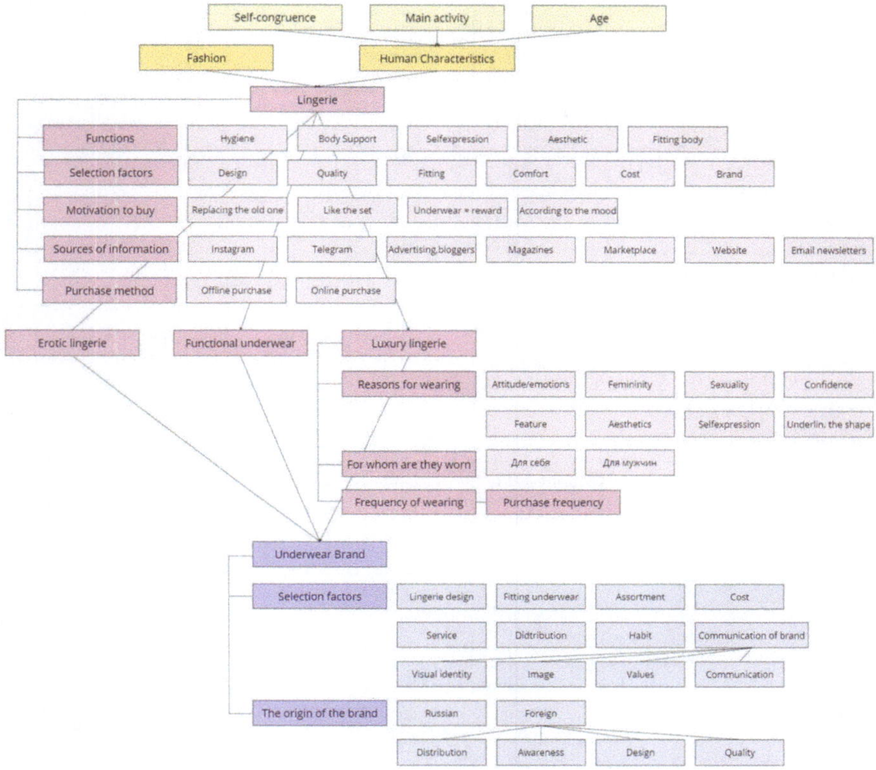

Fig. 1 Semantic connection of codes for semi-structured interviews

design, comfort, quality), and add value to consumer beauty, femininity, pleasure, and success. It is worth noting that the interview results confirm the statistics: Russian girls actively use luxury underwear and often wear it on a regular basis. According to experts of the underwear market, the reason for this may be the cultural characteristics of women's upbringing (striving for the ideal), as well as the unstable situation in the country, which causes a desire to dress up and feel pleasant emotions.

In addition, the data of the cabinet stage is also confirmed. There is an "invisible fashion": consumers aged 18–35 are impressed by fashion trends in the underwear market: the opportunity to be different, thanks to a diverse range (from tenderness to audacity), brands' concern for their health, and the use of underwear as clothing (e.g., corsets). Despite the fact that underwear is hidden under clothes and it is rarely seen on other people, fashion trends in this area are still spreading to a large number of people. The qualitative stage has shown that the channels where women learn information about underwear coincide with the channels from which they learn fashion trends in this area. Most often, fashion trends in the field of underwear are broadcast through Instagram, advertising (online advertising on the Internet and social networks), bloggers, and marketplaces. The main reason for wearing luxury

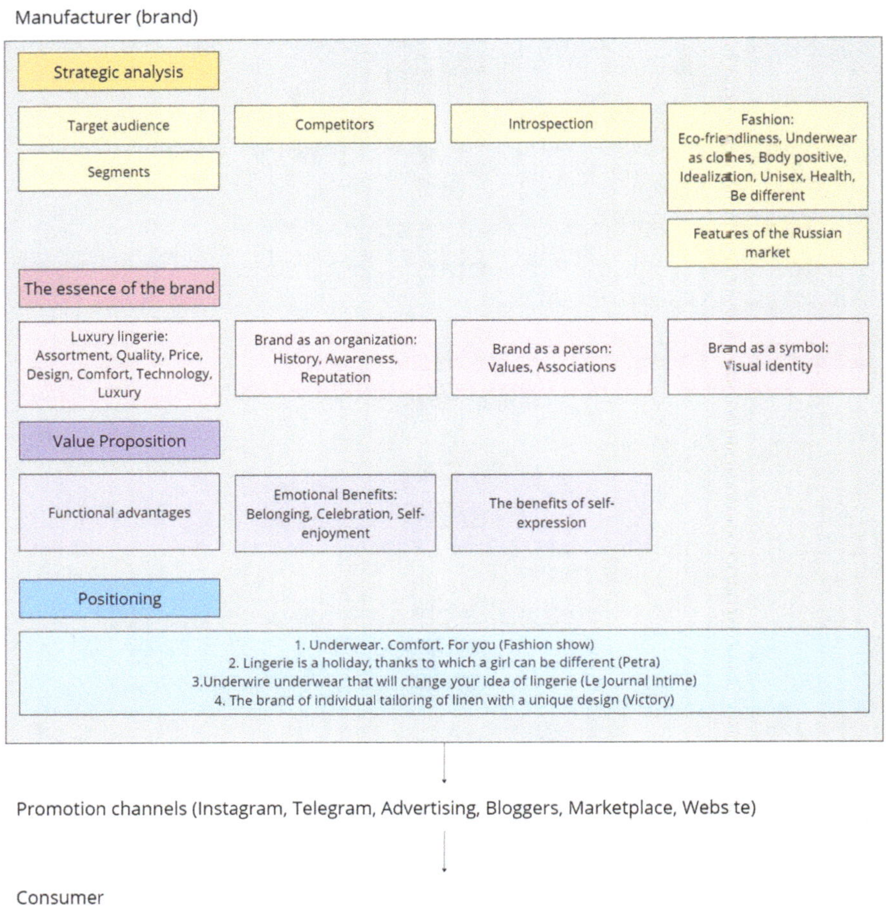

Fig. 2 Semantic connection of the codes for the expert interviews

underwear is the desire to experience the aesthetics of underwear and create appropriate emotions and mood for the day. In addition, it turned out that women who prefer to wear luxury underwear more often are more likely to buy underwear in general. They do this to raise or maintain their mood. Moreover, lovers of luxury lingerie prefer idealized models, as they more reflect the "ideal image" that consumers strive for. Girls most often buy underwear in 1–2 favorite stores, as they have some kind of ritual that improves their mood. Women buy new kits about several times every six months, sometimes online, sometimes offline. In brand communication, visual identity is especially important for consumers, as well as the company's image. Thus, fashion as a communication system has been studied more fully, as the field of underwear has been considered from the point of view of manufacturers, distributors, and consumers.

References

1. List of companies, brands and banks that left Russia in 2022–2024. (2024, February 2). B-Kontur.ru. https://www.b-kontur.ru/enquiry/25054-spisok_kompanij_brendov_i_bankov_ushedshix_iz_rossii?ysclid=lr6c49c3k4944317686#header_25054_1
2. Analysis of the size and share of the underwear market — growth trends and forecasts (2024–2029). (2024). Www.mordorintelligence.com; Mordor IntelligenceTM Industry Reports. https://www.mordorintelligence.com/ru/industry-reports/lingerie-market
3. Lingerie Market 2021: What influences demand? (2021, August 17). Retail.ru. https://www.retail.ru/tovar_na_polku/rynok-nizhnego-zhenskogo-belya-2021-chto-vliyaet-na-spros-/
4. Norsoin, L. (2018, March 20). What is happening with the lingerie market in Russia and the world.Blog.fashionfactoryschool.com. https://blog.fashionfactoryschool.com/blog/obzor-rynka/obzory/280-chto-proisxodit-s-belevyim-ryinkom-v-rossii-i-mire
5. Delgado, E., Ocampo, L. M., & Robayo, A. D. (2023, July). Clothing as an element of identity and a trend of self-completion in generation Z in Colombia. In *International Conference on Fashion communication: Between tradition and future digital developments* (pp. 188–203). Springer Nature Switzerland.
6. Holt, D. B. (2002). Why do brands cause trouble? A dialectical theory of consumer culture and branding. *Journal of Consumer Research, 29*(1), 70–90. https://doi.org/10.1086/339922
7. Hume, M., & Mills, M. (2013). Uncovering Victoria's secret. *Journal of Fashion Marketing and Management: An International Journal, 17*(4), 460–485. https://doi.org/10.1108/jfmm-03-2013-0020
8. Barthes, R. (2015). Système de la mode. Éd. Du Seuil.
9. Baudrillard, J. (2016). L' Échange symbolique et la mort. Paris] Gallimard.
10. Urenkova, A. P. (2020). Fashion as a cultural and socio-psychological phenomenon. Globe. *Humanities, 4*(34), 8–11.
11. Castells, M., Cardoso, G., & Nitze, P. H. (2006). The network society: from knowledge to policy. Center For Transatlantic Relations, Paul H. Nitze School Of Advanced International Studies, Johns Hopkins University. https://www.dhi.ac.uk/san/waysofbeing/data/communication-zangana-castells-2006.pdf
12. Aaker, D. A. (2012). *Building strong brands*. Free Press.
13. Craig, L. K., & Gray, P. B. (2020). Women's use of intimate apparel as subtle sexual signals in committed, heterosexual relationships. *PLOS ONE, 15*(3), e0230112. https://doi.org/10.1371/journal.pone.0230112
14. Carnevale, D. M. (2018). *The implications of model body size and self-congruity on consumer attitudes & purchase intention in Women's Lingerie advertisements*. Digital Commons.
15. Cohen, R., Irwin, L., Newton-John, T., & Slater, A. (2019). Bodypositivity: A content analysis of body positive accounts on Instagram. *Body Image, 29*(29), 47–57. https://doi.org/10.1016/j.bodyim.2019.02.007

Visibility and Vulnerability: Authenticity and Commercialization in Digital Fashion Media

Magdalena Petersson McIntyre

Abstract This chapter explores the intersection of authenticity, commercialization, and influencer culture in digital fashion media through the case study of Swedish retailer Ellos' "Made by Women" campaign. Using a qualitative methodology, the study investigates how brands instrumentalize personal narratives to create emotional engagement while serving commercial interests. The findings reveal a paradox of authenticity, where influencers' self-presentation oscillates between genuine self-expression and strategic branding. This study contributes to discussions on digital labor, femvertising, and the evolving role of influencers in contemporary fashion communication.

Keywords Influencer culture · Authenticity · Commercialization · Femvertising · Digital economy

1 Introduction

The fashion media landscape has changed drastically over the last 20 years. The first fashion blogs emerged in the mid-2000s and quickly gained popularity. With pictures of "outfit of the day" and everyday clothing choices, they attracted a large audience. As a result, new trends and styles were no longer communicated solely through fashion magazines but by individuals in the form of bloggers and later influencers and vloggers. This ongoing development has fundamentally reshaped the power structures in the fashion world [1].

Initially, fashion blogs provided personal and unfiltered reflections on style, distinct from corporate influence. Over time, these platforms evolved into strategic marketing channels where trust and intimacy became valuable commodities. Authenticity and relatability remain central to influencer marketing, yet they have

M. P. McIntyre (✉)
Section for Fashion Studies, Lund University, Lund, Sweden
e-mail: Magdalena.petersson_mcintyre@kultur.lu.se

P. von Wachenfeldt et al. (eds.), *Fashion Communication in the Digital Age*,
Springer Proceedings in Business and Economics,
https://doi.org/10.1007/978-3-031-99481-4_26

become increasingly difficult to maintain as commercial pressures shape online personas. The paradox of promoting products under the guise of genuine recommendations has become more apparent as audiences develop a critical awareness of influencer marketing tactics [2].

Today, influencer marketing is an established industry where digital creators play a large role in shaping brand positioning and consumer engagement. As Hund [3] observes, influencers have evolved into a global, multi-billion-dollar industry that reshapes societal understandings of power and communication. Beyond fashion and beauty, influencer culture now extends into ideological spheres, where lifestyle imagery serves as a vehicle for broader cultural and political messaging. Like fashion journalism before it, influencer culture is not just about style and consumption, it is also about ideology and power [3].

This chapter examines how brands capitalize on influencer authenticity to advance commercial interests. Using the Swedish retailer Ellos' *Made by Women* campaign as a case study, it explores the interplay between visibility, vulnerability, and marketing strategy in digital fashion media.

2 Femvertising and Postfeminism in the Fashion Industry

The fashion industry strategically employs feminist rhetoric to present itself as progressive and inclusive. Femvertising, advertising that uses feminist messages to promote products, reflects broader shifts in contemporary marketing strategies. Although, campaigns centered on body positivity and female empowerment may increase brand loyalty among female consumers they also risk diluting feminist ideals by embedding them within consumer culture. This process aligns with what scholars describe as a depoliticization of feminism, where structural issues of gender equality are reframed as individual consumer choices [4]. Closely linked to the concept postfeminism, femvertising reframes feminist ideals as individual self-improvement rather than collective social change. Drawing on Gill, femvertising embodies neoliberal values by positioning consumption as a means of empowerment. Slogans such as "own your style" or "be you own boss" reinforce the notion that personal success and autonomy are achieved through purchasing power [5].

Influencers play a central role in this shift, adding authenticity and intimacy to femvertising narratives. Some influencers describe beauty blogging as a feminist act, emphasizing self-expression and empowerment. However, body positivity, a recurring theme in influencer and brand marketing, has faced criticism for reinforcing conventional beauty norms despite outward claims of diversity.

This chapter examines three key techniques used by Ellos-employed influencers to cultivate authenticity and engagement: body storytelling, celebrity endorsement, and financial transparency. The "Made by Women" campaign serves as a case study of how feminist messaging, particularly around sisterhood, body positivity, and authenticity, is integrated into brand communications. While influencers reinforce these ideals, their commercial ties highlight the tension between empowerment and commodification.

3 Methodology

This study is based on a cultural analytical method inspired by Ehn and Löfgren [1], which combines different material categories and theoretical perspectives with an openness to the unexpected while maintaining methodological rigor. The research focuses on a case study of Ellos' marketing strategy, particularly the "Made by Women" campaign, to analyze how influencer marketing balances personal authenticity with commercial demands. The analysis includes content from Instagram posts tagged with #equallywomen, promotional materials from Ellos, and brand collaborations with influencers. The study investigates how influencers navigate the tension between presenting a relatable and genuine persona while adapting to the commercial imperatives of their platforms and brand partnerships.

4 When Authenticity Becomes Business Strategy: Ellos and Influencer Marketing

The "Made by Women" campaign, launched in 2021, sought to promote body positivity and female empowerment while embedding these messages within the brand's commercial strategy. With the hashtag #equallywomen a platform for women to share their experiences and challenges was established, intended to spread the campaign's message in an organic way. The following quote reflects the tone of many posts:

> Stretch marks, sagging skin, or scars from a caesarean section... These marks look different but will always be reminders of the most beautiful thing we have created.

Although the campaign appears to challenge beauty norms, it simultaneously serves corporate objectives by leveraging influencers' personal stories to build brand loyalty. Micro-influencers play a key role in enhancing relatability as their perceived sincerity and close audience connections make them effective brand ambassadors. Ellos strategically integrates influencers of different scales, using their narratives to cultivate engagement while aligning them with its brand identity.

The campaign's aesthetic, such as unfiltered imagery and candid storytelling, reinforces a rhetoric of authenticity while remaining embedded in a commercial framework. By positioning itself as an advocate for inclusivity, Ellos thus aligns with broader marketing trends where social causes are incorporated into branding efforts. However, this calculated approach highlights the paradox of authenticity:

while the campaign on the one hand builds emotional connections, on the other it instrumentalizes personal experiences for profit-driven objectives [6].

5 From Complex to Consumerism

Ellos' use of body-positive narratives illustrates how personal vulnerability is transformed into marketable content, blending empowerment with consumption. A notable example is an Instagram post by actor and influencer Ellen Bergström, who collaborated with Ellos to discuss body ideals:

> In collaboration with @ellosofficial I was asked to talk about body ideals. I knew immediately what I wanted to write about. I've had it since I was 15 years old. Today I'm 30, so my bum and thighs have been adorned with it for 15 years. Cellulite. Despite that, I still have some weirdness in my head that makes me think about whether my cellulite is visible or not. And believe me, I am not proud that I care. I SO wish I was as cool as a lot of people and just didn't care. For me, it helps so much when I see pictures, REAL pictures that are not retouched. I don't care if it's a 'trend'. The trend helps!!! 😍🙌 At least me. So. THANK YOU all who share pictures of your bodies without retouching them or taking in special angles. Together I hope we can put an end to our complex thoughts!!! It does so damn much to see that you are not alone 💜 #equallywomen. [7]

Bergström's post exemplifies how influencers use personal stories to cultivate relatability and emotional connections with their audiences. By openly discussing cellulite—a common but stigmatized feature, she appears vulnerable and authentic, thus reinforcing the campaign's emphasis on body positivity. However, as part of a paid collaboration with Ellos, this vulnerability is strategically curated, raising questions about the fine line between authenticity and branding.

The commodification of bodily insecurities such as cellulite, reflects how personal vulnerability is leveraged for brand messaging. While such campaigns may lead to recognition and community, they simultaneously align these narratives with corporate interests. This dual strategy portrays the body as "real" and "imperfect" while ensuring it remains aesthetically curated, striking a balance between relatability and aspirational beauty norms.

Ellos invites consumers to participate by sharing unretouched images, creating an illusion of community and co-creation. However, this practice blurs the lines between empowerment and commodification, as personal narratives become data points and marketing assets. As bodily diversity is integrated into commercial aesthetics, "imperfections" risk being instrumentalized rather than genuinely celebrated.

Ellos' marketing strategy thus highlights how body positivity and inclusivity are adapted to serve commercial goals. While campaigns like *Made by Women* claim to challenge traditional norms, they often reduce complex social issues to consumer choices, turning empowerment into a consumable product. The strategic highlighting of cellulite and stretch marks on conventionally attractive bodies underscores this tension, transforming activism into an aesthetic tool for branding. This broader trend in fashion marketing raises ethical questions about the sustainability of commercialized authenticity and the true impact of such campaigns on body image discourse.

6 Intimacy and Recognition: Celebrities as Authenticity Builders

Ellos also cultivates authenticity by leveraging celebrity endorsements. Public figures offer glimpses into their private lives to appear relatable, bridging the gap between persona and audience. In October 2023, Ellos launched a year-long collaboration with the Swedish performer and television personality Pernilla Wahlgren as part of *Portraits of Women,* an initiative related to the campaign with the aim to highlight women "in the middle of life" through personal conversations and interviews. Wahlgren, known for her openness about family life and everyday challenges, was positioned as an ideal figure to create a sense of connection among middle-aged women.

Ellos' Spring 2024 campaign was filmed at Wahlgren's home in Marbella, reinforcing an intimate and aspirational tone. Cédric Ménard, Ellos' Marketing Director, stated:

> We are thrilled about our ongoing partnership with Pernilla Wahlgren. She is a perfect match for our brand and resonates strongly with women in the middle of life. Together with Pernilla, we've created an amazing spring campaign that we believe will inspire many women out there—to dare to be themselves and never stop dreaming [8].

By aligning its products with Wahlgren's persona and lifestyle, Ellos strategically embeds its values within her narrative. Her relatability reinforces the brand identity as both accessible yet aspirational.

However, this approach raises questions about the construction of authenticity in a commercial context. While Wahlgren's openness appears genuine, it is also part of a carefully curated marketing strategy. Authenticity functions less as an intrinsic quality and more as a branding tool.

Ellos' use of celebrity-driven authenticity highlights the tension between relatability and commodification. By presenting Wahlgren's personal life as intertwined with the brand, the campaign enhances emotional appeal and visibility. Yet, this reliance on curated authenticity risks reducing intimacy to a calculated marketing strategy, prompting consumers to question whether such narratives are truly genuine or designed solely to drive sales. Wahlgren's case expands the discussion of authenticity by demonstrating how celebrity figures are used in ways that mirror the strategies applied to micro-influencers. Despite her established public status, her emotional transparency and personal storytelling are mobilised to achieve similar effects: emotional engagement, identification, and brand loyalty. This example reinforces the argument that authenticity is not dependent on scale but is a versatile commodity shaped to fit different types of public personas. Wahlgren's inclusion illustrates that both influencers and celebrities participate in the same broader logic of commodified intimacy.

7 Power, Myths, and Marketing

Influencers are often surrounded by myths about their ability to shape consumer behavior and corporate strategies. A notable example is the micro-influencer Johanna Toftby, who, despite having a relatively modest following of 54,000 on Instagram, demonstrated significant influence when she guest-designed two pairs of shoes for Ellos. The overwhelming demand caused the company's website to crash within minutes of the launch, showcasing how influencer collaborations can generate immediate and tangible consumer responses.

Reflecting on the situation in her blog, Toftby described the technical difficulties caused by the surge in traffic, reinforcing her image as a powerful voice in consumer culture:

> So many of you rushed to order the shoes that it created chaos for Ellos. It's a big site capable of handling significant traffic, yet some still encountered issues. The shopping cart froze, or you were thrown out at checkout.[9]

Ellos' IT team worked for hours to restore functionality, but once operational, the products sold out almost immediately. Toftby later summarized the experience in an emotional Instagram post:

> This is the craziest thing I've ever experienced. At 7:45 this morning, I was ready. I was in contact with Ellos, and the entire shoe team was prepared, but then you crashed the entire site. It's been a delightful chaos. The shoes have sold out. I can't describe how grateful, happy, and moved I am.[10]

This example illustrates how influencer campaigns are evaluated not only by measurable outcomes like sales or engagement but also by the symbolic narratives they generate. Toftby's story shows how perceived authenticity and emotional investment can create powerful brand moments, even without celebrity status. Her success reinforces the idea that influence is not merely about scale, but about the ability to craft a compelling, emotionally resonant narrative that aligns with brand identity. This incident underscores both the economic impact of influencers and the symbolic power of their storytelling. The narrative of success becomes as influential as the sales figures themselves, amplifying brand visibility and reinforcing the influencer's credibility. This dual effect, measurable outcomes combined with compelling messaging, helps explain the enduring appeal of influencer collaborations as they merge commerce with cultural capital to strengthen both brand engagement and consumer trust.

8 Concluding Remarks

The "Made by Women" campaign highlights the evolving relationship between visibility, vulnerability, and commercialization in digital fashion media. While influencer collaborations drive engagement, they also raise ethical questions about the commodification of authenticity. By focusing on how both micro-influencers and celebrity figures participate in the campaign, this study shows how personal narratives are adapted to align with brand messaging while maintaining an appearance of sincerity. Authenticity functions as a strategic asset in influencer culture, where personal expression is increasingly shaped by commercial imperatives. The chapter contributes to discussions on influencer labour, authenticity, and the intersection of branding and personal identity. By situating this analysis within a postfeminist marketing context, it offers further insight into the ideological work performed by emotionally resonant, commercially driven content.

References

1. Ehn, B., Löfgren, O., & Wilk, R. (2016). *Exploring everyday life: Strategies for ethnography and cultural analysis*. Rowman & Littlefield Publishers.
2. Pedroni, M., & Mora, E. (2023). Influencers, niche magazines and journalistic practice in Italy: Toward a new fashion editorial system. *Fashion Theory, 27*(7), 957.
3. Hund, E. (2023). *The influencer industry: The quest for authenticity on social media*. Princeton University Press.
4. Streeter, R. (2023). 'Bargaining with the status quo': Reinforcing and expanding femininities in the #bodypositive movement. *Fat Studies, 12*(1), 120–134. https://doi.org/10.1080/21604851.2021.2006958
5. Gill, R. (2016). Post-postfeminism? New feminist visibilities in postfeminist times. *Feminist Media Studies, 16*(4), 610–630. https://doi.org/10.1080/14680777.2016.1193293
6. Ellos. (2024). Made by Women. Ellos.com, March. https://www.ellos.se/madebywomen. Accessed 15 March 2024.
7. Bergström, E. (2024). Celluliter och kroppsideal. Instagram, 12 February. https://www.instagram.com/ellenbergstrom/. Accessed 15 February 2024.
8. Ménard, C. (2024). Pressmeddelande: Pernilla Wahlgren och Ellos i nytt samarbete. Ellos Group, 5 April. https://www.ellosgroup.com/press. Accessed 6 April 2024.
9. Toftby, J. (2024). "Kaos när Ellos lanserade mina skor!" Johannatoftby.se, 3 March. https://www.johannatoftby.se/2024/03/03/kaos-ellos/. Accessed 4 March 2024.
10. Toftby, J. (2024). "Ellos-samarbete på Instagram." Instagram, 3 March. https://www.instagram.com/johannatoftby/. Accessed 4 March 2024.
11. Colucci, M., & Pedroni, M. (2022). Got to be real: An investigation into the co-fabrication of authenticity by fashion companies and digital influencers. *iJournal of Consumer Culture, 22*/i(4), 929–948.
12. Mora, E., & Rocamora, A. (2015). Letter from the editors: Analyzing fashion blogs—further avenues for research. *Fashion Theory, 19*/i(2), 149–156.
13. Rocamora, A. (2022). The datafication and quantification of fashion: The case of fashion influencers. *iFashion Theory, 26*/i(7), 1109–1133.

Digital Fashion Art Direction in Italy: Shaping Sustainable Practices and Mindsets

Filippo Maria Disperati

Abstract The contribution presents an ongoing research that intends to investigate the digital dimension of art direction for fashion in Italy, with the aim of understanding how the identity concepts of Made in Italy are intertwined and configured with the concept of twin transition. The aim is to put forward the hypothesis that digital art direction in fashion and the professional figure of the art director, in the various declinations and facets that this role can have within the fashion system, play a key role in conveying sustainability, social, ethical, and environmental messages: messages that can activate greater awareness in consumers, influence their purchasing behavior, and effectively contribute to an idea of prosperity through conscious development, which produces more widespread well-being. Art directors, through their taste preferences and the emotions they trigger, can judge whether the meanings of each possible visual element fit the visual identity of the brand; therefore, the choice of visual elements is not based on rules and logic, but on the art director's own ability to interpret contemporary trends. We also want to highlight the critical and sometimes negative aspects of digital communication for fashion, as it also has elements that are not really sustainable, such as the large production of data and the problem of its storage.

Keywords Art direction · Digital fashion communication · Made in Italy · Sustainability · Behavior

F. M. Disperati (✉)
Università degli Studi della Campania "Luigi Vanvitelli", Caserta, Italy
e-mail: filippomaria.disperati@unicampania.it

P. von Wachenfeldt et al. (eds.), *Fashion Communication in the Digital Age*,
Springer Proceedings in Business and Economics,
https://doi.org/10.1007/978-3-031-99481-4_27

1 Introduction

Fashion communication through digital is a topic of growing interest for researchers, academics, and practitioners. Fashion, like other strategic sectors of the global economic system, has to go through what is called a twin transition. The term "twin transitions" does not only refer to two contemporary transformational trends (the green transition and the digital transition), but the term also refers to the merging of the two transitions, which could accelerate the necessary changes and bring societies closer to the necessary level of transformation [1]. Commercial fashion media can be understood as a bridge connecting brands to consumers. Media messages transform fashion, in its materiality, into endless symbolic forms while legitimizing the existence of the industry itself [2]. Fashion has played a great role in conveying to a global audience the intangible values that images of absolutely material products tell about a territory, a certain culture [3].The concept of Made in Italy is linked to the different identities and strong traits of Italian cities that have contributed and still contribute to Italy's success as a composite and multi-layered nation [4]. At the same time, it is interesting to note that in Italy and abroad, starting in the 1980s, and increasingly so in the following decade, fashion brands began to work, on an ongoing basis, with art directors for invitations, lookbooks, packaging, and advertising campaigns [5]. The figure of the art director would appear to play an increasingly key role in the translation and communication of the various components of Made in Italy fashion and, in particular, of the twin transitions. The Digital Art Director is therefore a key figure in contemporary digital visual communication. The role is responsible for the artistic direction of creative projects on digital platforms; it coordinates content design for websites, social media, online advertising campaigns, interactive experiences, and augmented reality. This contribution presents the first results of an ongoing doctoral research, which aims to shed light on the contribution of digital art direction in Italy in supporting and shaping sustainable practices and mindsets, both within companies and externally among consumers.

2 Background and Literature Review

The desk analysis phase of the research focused on exploring and defining the current state of digital art direction and sustainable communication practices in the fashion sector in Italy. A literature review was carried out through a qualitative approach, which made use of the academic databases of Google Scholar and Scopus, to select articles and scientific contributions published in the last ten years [6–16], focused on the theme of digital and sustainable communication for fashion in the Italian context (see Fig. 1).

Literature review		
	CONTRIBUTION	DESCRIPTION
1	*Fashion communication: Between tradition and digital transformation* [6]	Analysis of the intertwining of fashion and communication, the impact of digital transformation and the use of big data and AI.
2	*Mediatized Fashion: State of the art and beyond* [7].	Moving fashion from the physical to the digital environment, with a focus on blogs and social media.
3	*Digital fashion: A systematic literature review. A perspective on marketing and communication* [8]	Study of the evolution of digital fashion, with particular attention to communication and marketing.
4	*Digital Fashion Communication: An (Inter) cultural Perspective* [9]	Reducing distances between nations in fashion communication, but increasing cultural misunderstandings.
5	*Extended reality (XR) in the digital fashion landscape* [10]	Using augmented and virtual reality to enrich customer experiences and brand narratives.
6	*How Do Luxury Brands Utilize NFTs to Enhance Their Brand Image?*[11]	Investigation into the use of NFTs to enhance the image of luxury brands, with limitations related to the scarcity of studies.
7	*How Digital Technology Influences Information about Fashion* [12]	Analysis of the dematerialization of fashion through blockchain and NFT, with potential role in the metaverse.
8	*The Future is Here* [13]	Metaverse investments for profit, consumption and data collection in the fashion industry.
9	*'Fashioning'the metaverse: A qualitative study on consumers' value and perceptions of digital fashion in virtual worlds* [14]	The analysis indicates that the five main values in the metaverse emerge for both work and play purposes, with social and epistemic values prevailing.
10	*The adoption of digital fashion as an end product: A systematic literature review of research foci and future research agenda* [15],	Evolution of digital fashion from tool to final product, with focus on 3D virtual technologies.
11	*Post-digital fashion: the evolution and creation cycle* [16]	Analysis of the creation cycle of post-digital art, with the fusion of art and utility in fashion.

Fig. 1 Desk research analysis focused on exploring and defining the current state of digital art direction practices for fashion

This analysis of the selected scientific literature reveals the presence of a significant gap regarding the absence of studies on the topic of digital art direction for fashion in Italy and the practices that art directors adopt to promote sustainability through digital. This lack of explicit contributions on this topic suggests the emergence of a new and interesting field of investigation.

3 Methodology

The main methodology used for this first part of the current research project is "Narrative Discourse Analysis" following the model of American linguist William Labov. This theory analyzes how individuals construct personal and professional stories during the interview proceedings. In this case, it is useful to understand how fashion professionals tell their story or their creative process. It was therefore decided to proceed by conducting semi-structured, qualitative interviews with a selection of art directors operating in Italy and France, the latter to provide a comparison with the landscape in another EU country. In this first phase of field research in Italy, ten art directors were selected for interviews who collectively met all the following characteristics: professional relevance in the field of digital communication for fashion; approach to sustainability; originality and creativity; adaptation to the Italian and French market; inclusiveness; willingness to collaborate. The interviewees work both within large luxury brands and in independent Italian and French companies, which operate mainly through digital tools such as 3D animation, augmented reality (AR), virtual reality (VR), and artificial intelligence (AI). These interviews allowed us to gather in-depth information on the art directors' working methods, the creative process, the use of software, the relationship with companies, and the needs of the target market.

4 Results

From the interviews carried out among the art directors identified, many similarities emerge linked to the approach to the software used, but also to the demands they receive from companies in terms of both technological performance and the messages to be conveyed. This makes it possible to compare different professional experiences and creative processes, thus confirming the thesis that art direction through digital tools in Italy is helping to shape sustainable practices and mindsets, both within companies and externally among consumers (see Fig. 2).

The survey shows that increasingly in working with various realities in the fashion and luxury sector, the approach of art directors focuses on communicating messages that include a strong sustainability component. In these cases, particular attention is paid to guiding brands toward total transparency in the various production and communication steps. A distinctive element of this approach is the emphasis placed on educational experiences, aimed at raising awareness of sustainability issues. This is not simply a communication exercise, but a real takeover that takes care of every detail to convey the brand's vision and its commitment to sustainable practices. In parallel, work is done to provide the end customer with all the necessary product information, educating them to make an informed purchase. This means, for example, helping the consumer to understand the specifications that make an object sustainable or not, building a buying experience that goes beyond the simple

Case studies in Italy		
	NAME	DESCRIPTION
1	*Ferdinando Verderi*	Art director and former art director of Vogue Italia. His process is guided by the production of a written text, also through the use of artificial intelligence.
2	*Gloria Maria Cappelletti Editor in Chief and Creative Director of RED-EYE*	RED-EYE's experience ranges from luxury and fashion communication, to innovative XR technological solutions (AR, MR, VR), artificial intelligence, creative direction and visual communication.
3	*Gabriele Rosati*	Art director and independent photographer. He has collaborated with prestigious brands such as Stone Island, OAMC, Federico Cina.
4	*Martin Romeo*	Visual artist. Romeo has created fashion collaborations with Colmar, Bulgari and Creative Studios by Apple.
5	*Silvia Badalotti*	Art director and photographer. She created the Etro ADV campaign for the SS 24 collection, which sparked the debate in Italy on the role of artificial intelligence in fashion communication.
6	*Valentina Trevisanello*	Art director and creative lead of Monogrid, a digital agency, one of the very few in Italy able to offer cutting-edge services using all the latest technologies on the market.
7	*Angelo Guttadauro,*	Art director AND photographer. He builds a hybridization between analog or digital photography and models created with software such as Blender or Midjourney.
8	*Giuseppe Fioretti*	Freelance art director and graphic designer. He is starting an experiment through artificial intelligence to generate images, but also audio files for podcasts.
9	*Andrea Colacicco*	Graphic designer and digital artist. Experiments with different techniques such as: graphics, photography, video, 2D and 3D animation, installation and video mapping, filters and virtual reality.
10	*Alex Valentina*	Visual artist and designer whose work bridges nature and creativity, fusing the physical with the digital. His practice combines 3D art with real photography.

Fig. 2 Summarized table of selected case studies in Italy

act of buying. An element that emerges instead in the creative process of the interviewees is an approach that embraces the language of biomimicry, drawing inspiration from natural forms and processes. Through this connection with the natural world, the aim is to harmoniously integrate aesthetics and sustainability, translating the essence of nature into creative and innovative solutions. Finally, a common aspect that emerges from the interviews is that artificial intelligence and new technologies imply a contradiction in terms with sustainability, as they are still relevantly leading to pollution: for example, due to the use of large amounts of water to cool the servers needed to store the data. In spite of this, the digital transition certainly represents our present and our future, and involves living with the increasing use of technology.

5 Conclusion

The research conducted so far, through the analysis and comparison of case studies, reveals, in fact, only an apparent interest in the topic of green transition on the part of Italian and foreign fashion companies, in the communication and realization of advertising campaigns. The figure of the Art Director in recent years has substantially followed the trend of sustainability more for the writing of payoffs or slogans than to really communicate the investments in human capital and research aimed at the sustainable transition in materials and industrial processes implemented by the companies themselves. It is therefore clear that there is a difficulty in communicating well and truthfully the environmental and social sustainability and digital processes implemented by fashion companies in Italy, and, at first glance, the French scenario does not seem dissimilar either. On the other hand, the digital transition and technologies in fashion communication are not being used properly to reduce the carbon footprint they produce, for example by reducing saving digital files during the creation process, to lower impact in terms of energy consumption. The twin transition in digital fashion communication would thus seem to have settled into a state of stagnation, if not regression. It also emerges that in Italy, the presence of women seems to be lower among the professional figures operating in the art direction sector through the use of digital technologies, signaling a professional and university training system, linked to technologies, dominated by a strong patriarchal component and a culture not yet truly open and ready for gender equality. The Empowerment of young women constitutes a necessary factor for both mitigation and adaptation [17]. These initial considerations, which will be enriched with more precise data and results at the end of the field research period in France—and by a workshops phase organized both in Italy and France—allow us to put forward the hypothesis that it will be necessary to draw up guidelines to suggest good practices related, specifically, to the digital sphere of art direction in relation to sustainable fashion communication in Italy, along the lines of the *Sustainable Fashion Communication Playbook* [18] published in 2023, and thus contribute positively to the changes needed to achieve the 17 Sustainable Development Goals (SDGs) of the UN 2030 Agenda.

References

1. Salvi, M., Jensen, K., Stoermer, E., Scapolo, F., Asikainen, T., & Muench, S. (2022). *Towards a green & digital future*. Publications Office of the European Union. https://data.europa.eu/doi/10.2760/977331,JRC129319
2. Laing, M. (2024). Sustainability and the fashion media: Micro-Utopia, social dreaming and hope in the margins. *Fashion Theory*, 1–24. https://doi.org/10.1080/1362704X.2024.2339937
3. Conti, G. M., & Franzo, P. (2020). Distretti produttivi virtuali. La transizione del Made in Italy nella moda. In *Remanufacturing Italy. L'Italia nell'epoca della postproduzione* (pp. 124–143).
4. Paulicelli, E. (2014). Fashion: the cultural economy of Made in Italy. *Fashion Practice, 6*(2), 155–174. https://doi.org/10.2752/175693814X14035303880597
5. Teunissen, J., Van Der Voet, H., & Brand, J. (2014). *Couture graphique. Fashion, graphic design and the body. Exhibition catalogue*. Terra Lannoo.
6. Kalbaska, N., Sádaba, T., & Cantoni, L. (2018). Fashion communication: Between tradition and digital transformation. *Studies in Communication Sciences, 18*(2), 269–285. https://doi.org/10.24434/j.scoms.2018.02.005
7. Colucci, M., & Pedroni, M. (2021). Mediatized fashion: State of the art and beyond. *ZoneModa Journal, 11*(1), III–XIV. https://doi.org/10.6092/issn.2611-0563/13118
8. Noris, A., Nobile, T. H., Kalbaska, N., & Cantoni, L. (2020). Digital fashion: A systematic literature review. A perspective on marketing and communication. *Journal of Global Fashion Marketing, 12*(1), 32–46. https://doi.org/10.1080/20932685.2020.1835522
9. Noris, A., & Cantoni, L. (2022). Digital fashion communication: An (Inter) cultural perspective. In *Digital fashion communication* (pp. 1–147). Brill. https://doi.org/10.1163/9789004523555_002
10. Faria, A. P., & Cunha, J. (2023, July). Extended reality (XR) in the digital fashion landscape. In *International Conference on Fashion communication: between tradition and future digital developments* (pp. 49–56). Springer Nature Switzerland. https://doi.org/10.1007/978-3-031-38541-4_5
11. Ferrini, G., Huber, S., & Batt, V. (2023, July). How do luxury brands utilize NFTs to enhance their brand image? In *International Conference on Fashion communication: between tradition and future digital developments* (pp. 80–87). Springer Nature Switzerland. https://doi.org/10.1007/978-3-031-38541-4_8
12. Landi, P. (2022). How digital technology influences information about fashion. *ZoneModa Journal, 12*(1), 29–34. https://doi.org/10.6092/issn.2611-0563/14903
13. Winterhalter, C. (2023). Metaverse and its communication. The future is here. True or false? In *International Conference on Fashion communication: between tradition and future digital developments* (pp. 37–48). Springer Nature Switzerland. https://doi.org/10.1007/978-3-031-38541-4_4
14. Venturini, A., & Columbano, M. (2024). 'Fashioning'the metaverse: A qualitative study on consumers' value and perceptions of digital fashion in virtual worlds. *Journal of Global Fashion Marketing, 15*(1), 6–22. https://doi.org/10.1080/20932685.2023.2234918
15. Chan, H. H. Y., Henninger, C., Boardman, R., & Blazquez Cano, M. (2024). The adoption of digital fashion as an end product: A systematic literature review of research foci and future research agenda. *Journal of Global Fashion Marketing, 15*(1), 155–180. https://doi.org/10.1080/20932685.2023.2251033
16. Pereira, S., & Marcos, A. (2021). Post-digital fashion: The evolution and creation cycle. *ZoneModa Journal, 71–89*. https://doi.org/10.6092/issn.2611-0563/13121
17. Consiglio A. (2024). Green Jobs/Gender Gaps. Perché la sostenibilità ignora le donne. Fondazione Franco Feltrinelli. https://fondazionefeltrinelli.it/scopri/green-jobs-gender-gaps/
18. Arthur, R. (2023). *Sustainable Fashion Communication Playbook*, UNEP and UN-Climate-Change. https://www.unep.org/resources/publication/sustainable-fashion-communication-playbook

Glamour on the Slopes. Women's Skiwear in Italian Magazines of the Interwar Years

Isabella Campagnol

Abstract After World War I, Italian women embraced a more active lifestyle, leading to the rise of outdoor sports, such as tennis, skiing, and swimming, activities valued both for their health benefits and as fashionable social pursuits.The main objective of the study is the investigation of the evolution of women's skiwear in Italy during the interwar era through its presentation in contemporary Italian fashion magazines. After reviewing the existing literature on the period, the research has been conducted on primary sources, in particular a selection of women's publications chosen for their cultural relevance and availability for direct examination: among them, *Lidel*, *La donna, la casa, il bambino*, *La Donna*, *Dea*, *Vita Femminile*, and *Fantasie d'Italia*. Given the seasonal nature of the topic, only issues published between December and February were analyzed, as these months featured the most coverage on skiwear. The study explores the defining characteristics of these outfits, including materials, colors, garment types, and accessories. Preliminary findings indicate that Italian women's growing participation in sports significantly influenced their wardrobes with fashion magazines playing a key role in shaping perceptions of skiwear, presenting it not only as functional attire, but as an essential component of modern, stylish dressing.

Keywords Italian fashion · Sportswear · Skiwear · Lidel · Fashion magazines

1 Research Methodology

This research note, prepared between September and December 2024, is focused on the evolution of women's skiwear in the interwar period and includes the preliminary findings of a broader investigation that the author is conducting on the

I. Campagnol (✉)
Istituto Marangoni, Milano, Italy
e-mail: i.campagnol.tutor@istitutomarangoni.org

P. von Wachenfeldt et al. (eds.), *Fashion Communication in the Digital Age*,
Springer Proceedings in Business and Economics,
https://doi.org/10.1007/978-3-031-99481-4_28

relationship between fashion and travel/sport. After a review of the existing literature on the theme [1], the study has predominantly drawn from the author's personal collection, which includes hundreds of Italian magazines published between 1900 and the 1970s. Given the seasonal nature of the topic, only issues published between December and February are analyzed, as these months featured the most coverage on skiwear.

1.1 Research Questions

- What did women wear for skiing during the interwar period?
- Which garments were most commonly used, and what materials were they made from?
- Was there a preferred color palette?
- What accessories complemented these outfits?

The magazines were chosen using the following criteria:

- Relevance to the research's focus: women's fashion magazines
- Readership demographics: upper and middle class
- Accessibility and availability of issues from the selected time frame

1.2 Magazines

In total, 58 issues of various magazines were analyzed. Specifically, listed in order of numerical importance:

- 26 issues of *Lidel*. January, February, and December issues, dated between 1919 and 1935. From its inception, *Lidel* promised to "accurately update its readers on the most important social, artistic, and sports events" (*Lidel*, May 1919) and consistently delivered on this promise. Each issue devoted pages to contemporary sports events, including tennis tournaments, boat races, equestrian competitions, and aviation challenges. While these topics were later covered in a specialized spin-off, *Lidel Sport*, women's sportswear continued to appear in the regular monthly editions.
- 10 issues of *La donna, la casa, il bambino*, January, February, and December dated between 1933 and 1937.
- 10 issues of *La Donna* dated between 1928 and 1938. Only January and December issues.
- 3 issues of *Fantasie d'Italia*, December, January 1926, February 1928.
- 5 issues of *Dea*, Milan-based magazine, published between 1933 and 1948.
- 1 issue of *Vita Femminile*, January 1933.

- A sampling of magazines from the 1940s was included to assess whether the outbreak of World War II led to any changes and to what extent. Specifically:
- 1 issue of *Eva. Rivista per la donna italiana.* December 21, 1940
- 1 issue of *Bellezza.* December 1941
- 1 issue of *Fili.* December 1941

The articles from the journals have been selected focusing only on those discussing specifically skiwear (example: "Il richiamo delle cime nevose," *La donna*, January 1928, pp. 18–20; "Sulla neve," *Lidel*, January 1929, pp. 28-31).

Every fashion article includes, usually, at least two or three illustrated images. Society articles with photographs have also been taken into consideration in order to compare them with the fashion illustrations. Around 150 images from the abovementioned articles have been studied during the research, having been selected based on:

- Relevance to the study's theme
- Prominence in the magazine: cover images, main editorial spreads
- Typology of representation: women actually skiing or posing with skis

2 Introduction

> Elegance on the snow is an extremely modern elegance, born from the great passion that many women have for winter sports. But it is precisely the passion for sport that has created the need for a special fashion, or is it not the beautiful sports fashion that has persuaded many women to wear skates and skis and risk the pulsating emotions of bobsleigh? By now, sport and elegance are inseparable brothers—*Lidel,* January 1929

One of the most significant changes in the everyday lives of Italian upper- and middle-class women after the First World War was the increasing emphasis on a dynamic lifestyle [2, 3]. From the early 1920s, Italian women became enthusiastic participants in sports such as tennis, golf, skiing, ice skating, and swimming. Physical activity was regarded not only as essential for maintaining a healthy body, but also as an integral part of social life, and activities like tennis matches or ski outings became both a social and fashionable necessity. Since these sports required specific and often technical garments, contemporary Italian fashion magazines began featuring regular columns dedicated to the latest sportswear trends to address the needs of their readers.

At the time, the panorama of the Italian fashion press was highly diverse, catering to a wide range of social classes and demographics. Despite this variety, sportswear emerged as a unifying theme, prominently featured on the covers and in the contents of both sophisticated fashion magazines and more accessible publications. Articles on sportswear followed a predictable seasonal calendar: skiwear dominated the pages from December to February and tennis outfits appeared in late spring, while bathing suits and beach pyjamas took center stage during June, July, and August. Hunting apparel, on the other hand, was reserved for autumn. Advertisements reflected this seasonal rhythm, alternating between promotions for Italian or Swiss ski resorts and winter beauty products, such as cold-weather skin protection, and advertisements for fashionable beaches like the Lido of Venice and summer essentials like suntanning oils.

3 Glamour on the Slopes: Ski Outfits During the Interwar Years

> You can do without the snow, but not without a ski costume!—*Vita femminile*, January 1933

In February 1925, an article in *Lidel* highlighted how the growing popularity of various sports in recent years had contributed to "helping women maintain a youthful look" (*Lidel*, February 1925, p. 28). The piece particularly emphasized the habit, originating in the Belle Époque, of taking winter vacations in the mountains and practicing sports such as skiing and ice skating. These activities were highly valued for their invigorating effects on both body and mind. *La donna, la casa, il bambino* highly praised mountain vacations, noting that the "climate is so beneficial and the air so pure that simply breathing it brings benefits, even without practicing any sports" (*La donna, la casa, il bambino*, February 1935, p. 31).

In the late nineteenth century, the few daring skiers, both men and women, who braved the harsh weather of the Alps, typically wore cumbersome, impractical, and aesthetically unappealing outfits. Women, in particular, skied in heavy woollen skirts not designed for athletic use. By the 1920s, skiing had transformed from an adventurous and challenging pursuit into a sociable and fashionable activity. Italian ski resorts, from Cortina d'Ampezzo to Sestriere, became the perfect setting for stylish sportswomen to showcase their skiing techniques and elegance. Fashion quickly took notice of this new trend, recognizing that winter vacations demanded practical garments made from comfortable materials suitable for challenging conditions, but also offered opportunities for stylish self-expression [4]. As noted in *Lidel*:

> With the arrival of the first snow, begins the weekly exodus to the white-capped mountains, enticing us with their long, soft slopes marked by the swift, sharp grooves of skis. A glance at our well-stocked wardrobe makes us desire new details that ensure we are not only perfectly sporty from head to toe but also perfectly elegant and self-assured during social events (*Lidel*, December 1931, pp. 42–43).

Proper clothing could even enhance athletic performance. Already in January 1929, *Lidel* had observed that women were now excelling over men in skiing, particularly in speed and style, thanks to their adoption of "rational and sensible garments" (*Lidel*, January 1929, p. 29). Fashion magazines unanimously declared that elegance on the snow was synonymous with comfort and practicality. Designs featured in magazines were often created by prominent French fashion houses such as Patou, Lelong, and Drecoll. These outfits, typically made of gabardine, and occasionally wool velvet or fustian, were produced in dark shades like black, brown, navy blue, or green:

"The foundation of women's winter sportswear remains the long Norwegian trousers, available in black, dark blue, dark green, or brown, as these are the staple colors of winter fashion" (*Lidel*, December 1931, p. 42). A later exception is represented by the ski combination in all-white orbace, an autarkic Italian wool produced in Sardinia, featured in the *Eva* (December 21, 1940, p. 6), and enriched by very subtle red and brown details.

While trousers, especially the "Norwegian" or "knickerbocker" style, were widely praised as practical, conservative publications remarked that winter sports seemed to be an excuse for women to flaunt themselves in trousers (*La donna, la casa, il bambino*, January-February 1933, p. 28). A hybrid solution was the pant-skirt, often paired with hand-knitted socks (*Dea*, December 1940, p. 25). Waist-length, double-breasted jackets worn over flannel shirts complemented knickerbockers and pant-skirts, fastened with silver, horn, or wood buttons (*Lidel*, December 1931, p. 42). Occasionally, fur, suede, or leather vests were worn over jackets for additional protection from the cold (*Lidel*, January 1931, p. 32).

If jackets and trousers generally adhered to neutral, and usually dark, color palettes, jumpers and knitted accessories featured much brighter shades. In 1933, *Vita Femminile* suggested pairing "coffee-colored trousers with a sulfur-yellow jumper and matching cashmere scarf, gloves, and socks" (December 1933, p. 38). Although *Lidel* had previously advised against hand-knitted items in ski outfits for their perceived lack of modern elegance (*Lidel*, December 1926, p. 5), throughout the 1930s, most magazines included knitted items in their fashion pages. Even *Lidel* eventually presented patterns for "two nice sets for winter sports so easy to make that every woman can knit them at home" (*Lidel*, December 1930). Magazines like *La donna, la casa, il bambino* consistently provided detailed knitting patterns for jumpers and matching accessories, specifying the costs of the finished garments (e.g., February-March 1934, January 1936, December 1937)

One of the most recommended knitting wool brands was Lane Rossi, produced by a Vicenza-based company. Advertisements emphasized its versatility for sportswear and fashionable knitted dresses or jumpers, which could be paired with trendy pleated silk skirts (*Lidel*, March 1931, p. 26). From 1935, the Italian government heavily promoted Lanital, a wool substitute made from casein and developed by Italian chemist Antonio Ferretti. Lanital, a name obtained combining "lana" (wool) and "Italia" (Italy), was praised for being warm, soft, and moth-proof, but had notable drawbacks, including low durability and a rancid smell when wet. From 1937, Italian magazines supported the Lanital campaign with advertisements and articles promoting it as an ideal material for sportswear and ski outfits.

Most of the accessories accompanying ski outfits, gloves, scarves, and berets, were also knitted. One curiosity was the use of a face veil for skiing: *Vita Femminile* suggested it to "women who do not want to give up their femininity… the veil may protect against icy winds and is certain to become a trend" (*Vita Femminile*, December 1933, p. 38). Almost futuristic is the woollen "helmet" completed by a transparent visor proposed by *Bellezza* in 1941 (December, p. 18-20).

Ski boots are rarely described, but they were made of sturdy leather, while skis had "to reach the palm of the hand with the arm outstretched. The wood has to be regular without knots; the most frequently used woods are birch, ash tree and hickory, but birch is too frail. … for the sticks the best choice is Tonkino cane" (*Lidel*,

December 1933). A renowned supplier of ski (and tennis) equipment is S.A.I.L., acronym of Società Anonima Industria Lanzese, based in Lanzo d'Intelvi, Como, founded in 1925 by Guglielmo Poletti and active until 1940 (*Lidel*, December 1935).

4 Conclusions

During the interwar years in Italy, women's skiwear achieved a unique balance between technical performance and stylish design, blending functionality with sophistication. This evolution mirrored the changing roles and aspirations of women, who sought clothing that supported their active lifestyles while maintaining an elegant aesthetic wearing a practical combination of trousers and waist-length jackets made using sensible gabardine and fustian, warm wool velvets, or nationally produced orbace wool, sometimes accompanied by suede, leather, or fur vests. The outbreak of World War II led to an increased use of autarkic materials in the production of skiwear. Knitted jumpers and accessories were almost ubiquitous, made either of wool or of its autarkic substitute, Lanital. The color palette relied mostly on a neutral and generally dark base, brightened by splashes of color. By merging practicality with style, interwar sportswear not only influenced the development of contemporary athletic wear, but also redefined women's fashion, fostering the integration of comfort, versatility, and elegance in everyday attire.

References

1. Nuccetelli, P. (Ed.). (2010). *Rosa! Riviste Oggetti Sogni Al femminile*. Biblioteca Universitaria Alessandrina.
2. Aspesi, N. (1982). *Il lusso e l'autarchia. Storia dell'eleganza italiana, 1930-1944*. Rizzoli, Milano
3. Gnoli, S. (2000). *La donna, l'eleganza, il fascismo. La moda italiana dalle origini all'Ente Nazionale della Moda*. Edizioni del Prisma.
4. Butazzi, G. (1980). *1922-1943. Vent'anni di moda italiana*. Centro Di.

Fashion in Folk

Lavina Nimba Bhaskar and Dimple Bahl

Abstract Fashion in India resides in the modern bustling metropolis and in indigenous rural or craft pockets. And together this rural–urban divide constructs the meaning of Indian fashion. This chapter studies the intertextuality (meaning making) in folk media and traditional crafts. The chapter explores how meaning is derived through costumes and make-up in Folk Media. How the nomenclature of "Fashion" is perceived, is narrated, and may be critiqued in Folk commentary in both rural and urban spaces. And how Fashion resides in the costumes of the folk and finds its place in the urban markets. Fashion as defined by Kaiser "is not strictly a 'western', white, young heterosexual female bourgeois phenomenon, rather there are multiple fashion histories and systems, as well as modernities" (Kaiser and Green, Fashion and cultural studies, 2021). Diana Crane adds that "Fashion has effects such as the reinforcement of social differentiation, the expression of aspirations for social mobility, and the resolution of anxieties regarding social identity" (Crane, *Fashion and its social agenda*, 2000) Folk media/formats, on the other hand, are "indigenous systems embedded in the folk culture which predates mass media, still exist as a vital mode of communication presenting, certain degree of continuity, despite changes" (Kodavath, *Global Journal for Research Analysis*, 2015), thus making sense and meaning in normative times and giving way to the study of meaning-making theory of intertextuality. Intertextuality is a "poststructuralist, deconstructionist and postmodernist theory that changed the concept of text (a text can be an epic, a book, an art form, a movie, a costume, etc.) recognising it as an inter-text owing to the interrelations between texts and texts' absorptions of other texts" (Zengin, An introduction to intertextuality as a literary theory: Definitions, axioms and the originators Journal of Social Sciences Institute, Pamukkale University, 2019), which further gives weight to folk artist's own agency to lend meaning to the text, with what they adorn and what they say. Using a mixed research design, data are collected through a review of literature, semi-structured interviews

L. N. Bhaskar (✉) · D. Bahl
National Institute of Fashion Technology, New Delhi, India

P. von Wachenfeldt et al. (eds.), *Fashion Communication in the Digital Age*,
Springer Proceedings in Business and Economics,
https://doi.org/10.1007/978-3-031-99481-4_29

with folk artists and experts, observation, visual analysis, and a case study method and analyzed through inductive narrative analysis drawing on relevant theories of communication, semiotics, and intertextuality. This study is limited to the regions of Rajasthan, Madhya Pradesh, Chhattisgarh, Himachal Pradesh, Uttar Pradesh, and Uttarakhand.

Keywords Fashion · Folk Media · Intertextuality · India · Agency

1 Introduction

The story of Indian fashion is tightly interwoven with traditional and popular Indian culture. The indigenous crafts, arts, and traditional textiles of the land guide in creating a large pool of cultural motifs. The Artisans who craft, design, and make traditional textiles are clustered in small-weaver artist communities or tucked away in rural artisan pockets away from urban settlements. They make handmade artisanal products for the massy-urban, unchanged-rural, and niche-luxury markets. This ongoing study explores how meaning is derived through costume and make-up in Folk Media. How the nomenclature of "Fashion" is perceived, narrated, and at times critiqued in Folk commentary. And how Fashion resides in the costumes of the folk and finds its place in the urban markets. And in these complex exchanges how it conceptualizes Indian Fashion.

2 Methodology

This research is a part of an ongoing doctoral study. The study employs a mixed research design. Locales for the study are the regions of Rajasthan, Madhya Pradesh, Chhattisgarh, Himachal Pradesh, Uttar Pradesh, and Uttarakhand in India, the Hindi belt of the nation. The focus of the study is on performative arts in which intertextuality can be studied, which is why this research is limited to folk storytelling and theater, where there exists a primary text. The scope of the research is limited to performative folk forms which are performed in Hindi language or Hindi dialects. It's to be noted that it is difficult to delineate folk song, dance, art, and craft from folk theater or storytelling. Though not studied exclusively, folk song-dance, art, and craft are studied as a part of the above-mentioned performances. The identified folk forms in which intertextuality is sought to be found are Kariyala, Khayal, Maach, Nautanki, Pandavani, Phad, and Ramleela. Research methods and tools applied for data collection include a review of literature, semi-structured interviews with folk artists and experts, observation, visual analysis, and a case study method [5]. Data are analyzed and synthesized through inductive narrative analysis, drawing on relevant theories of communication, semiotics, and intertextuality.

3 Conceptualizing Folk, Folk Media

European Enlightenment links "folk" to "the people" [6] observing that "what makes a folk form distinctive is in fact its local audience, or its folk." When conceptualizing folk in Indian terms could also mean "belonging to a tradition" or "belonging to the rural folk." The folk is thought to be the "little tradition" as referred by anthropologist Robert Redfield, the idea which was further extended by McKim Marriott, Pocock, Barnard and Spencer, and Attri et al. [7–12].

Wang and Dissanayke define "folk media as a communication system embedded in the culture which predates mass media, and still exists as a vital mode of communication in many parts of the world, presenting a certain degree of continuity, despite changes" [13]. Folk Media include "story-telling, puppetry, proverbs, visual art, folk drama, songs, drumming, and dancing" [3]. Folk Media can be defined as an "indigenous channel of communication, which are entertaining, which were made for expressing socio-ritual, moral and emotional needs of the folk through medium such as folk songs, folk arts, folklore, etc." They have no grammar or literature, yet they are nurtured through oral traditions. "Folk Media is alive, receptive to new ideas and semi-rigid, including changes over the time and generations and are colourful forms of presentations" [14].

The folk art forms satisfy an innate need for self-expression, belongingness, and entertainment. "The traditional media preserves and disseminates in a lively manner, the tradition and culture of our forefathers" [15].

"As interdisciplinary fields, both fashion studies and cultural studies require the perspectives of multiple disciplines, theories, methods, and practices in order to analyse fashion and culture critically and thoughtfully. Both these fields began to develop as larger fields of study in the latter half of the twentieth century. Both the fields can trace their roots in history, culture, and dress as cross-cultural phenomena. Both fields blend various disciplines in the humanities like art, history, art history, literature, design, the performative arts; in the social sciences in anthropology, sociology, psychology, geography; and related interdisciplinary fields like gender studies, ethnic studies, postcolonial studies as well as the sciences" [1].

Kaiser and Green further argue that as researchers we should always be thinking about additional subject positions of intersectionality, because subjectivities are always emerging and changing within time and place. Like fashion, our intersectional identities are unfolding and changing across time [1], which gives way to study meaning-making theories of intertextuality.

4 So, What Is Intertextuality?

The conceptual foundation of intertextuality finds its grounds in Saussure's "linguistic theories" in general, and his "theories of sign, signifier and signified" in particular; Bakhtin's "theories of polyphony, dialogism, heteroglossia, and carnivalesque"; Kristeva's "coinage of the term intertextuality," her efforts to carry "Saussure's theory of language to the area of literature and her recognition of intertextuality as transposition"; and Barthes' "theories of readerly and writerly text" and "the death of the author" [12, 16–18].

Intertextuality comes from the word Intertexto, which in Latin language means "mingle while weaving." Intertextuality can be simply understood as a "poststructuralist, deconstructionist and postmodernist theory that changed the concept of text, recognising it as an inter-text owing to the interrelations between texts and texts' absorptions of other texts" [4]. Intertextuality can emerge in diverse forms between a text and other texts such as "direct quotation, citation, allusion, echo, reference, imitation, collage, parody, pastiche, literary conventions, structural parallelism and all kinds of sources either consciously exploited or unconsciously reflected" [19].

The term intertextuality denotes "this transposition of one (or several) sign system(s) into another"; since intertextuality has often been understood in the sense of "study of sources," there persists a preference for the term "transposition" because it specifies that "the passage from one signifying system to another demands a new articulation of the thematic – of enunciative and denotative positionally." If one grants that "every signifying practice is a field of transpositions of various signifying systems (an inter-textuality), one then understands that its 'place' of enunciation and its denoted 'object' are never single, complete, and identical to themselves, but always plural, shattered, capable of being tabulated" [18].

So, meaning or making meaning becomes "something which exists between a text and all the other texts to which it refers and relates, moving out from the independent text into a network of textual relations" [19].

So, what is intertextuality? Intertextuality is making intertextual references, interpreting a text, deciphering the meaning, and being a critical reader.

5 Nomenclature of "Fashion" Perceived, Narrated, and Critiqued in Folk

Fashion as defined by Kaiser "is not strictly a 'western', white, young heterosexual female bourgeois phenomenon, rather there are multiple fashion histories and systems, as well as modernities" [1]. Diana Crane, 2006, adds that "Fashion has effects such as the reinforcement of social differentiation, the expression of aspirations for social mobility, and the resolution of anxieties regarding social identity" [2].

"Time and space/place cannot be static or fixed, because just as people grow and change across time and space, so does fashion through bodies and processes of subject formation. The fields of fashion studies and cultural studies alike remind us that subjectivity is embodied in time and place" [1].

"Style-fashion-dress is at the centre of important debates about the body, subjectivity, and culture through time and space. Style-fashion-dress constitutes the bridge" [20].

Veteran folk storyteller and Director—Shriram Bharatiya Kala Kendra—Mrs. Shobha Deepak Singh elicits on changing the styling of folk performance costumes, "Someone once asked me why have you given your performers sleeveless blouses, to that I said to be fair there were no blouses then." So in folk performances specially performed in urban spaces one observes change in styling of the costumes to be normative and stay relevant.

Mr. Jumme Khan, a folk artist from the province of Rajasthan in his self-creation *Rangeeli Bhabhi* (colorful sister-in-law), draws out a difference between rural and urban, and in that othering describes a playful commentary on a young urban woman married into a rural family and critiques her "Fashion."

"Rangeeli Bhabhi chale re lachakwa chaal aur fashion pe kare kamal …." (The colorful sister-in-law walks with style and is a fashionista.) And goes on describing her personal styling which he calls "Fashion" and her make-up choices. This folk song is a playful commentary on urban style-fashion-dress from a rural person's gaze.

6 Making Meaning Through Costumes and Make-Up in Folk Media

Indian folk arts and crafts appropriate their motifs from a large pool of cultural heritage and indigenous design knowledge. In the view of Malik, "there is a shared spiritus mundi kind of cultural pool from which all representations draw their strength" [21, 22].

Costumes and make-up in folk performance represent multiple fashion histories, systems, and modernities, a sense of belongingness to a culture, the collective consciousness, and being carnivalesque.

For example, in the folk art of *Pandavani*, which is a folk storytelling format (also includes song-dance) from the state of Chhattisgarh, the lead performer always adorns the traditional Indian costume—a *saree,* in vermilion red or fuchsia pink color, draping the *palla* (the rear end of the yardage) in front. Saree is not only a garment widely worn by women in India; it is the only costume worn traditionally in the state.

The folk art of Phad, which is a folk storytelling format (also includes song-dance) from the state of Rajasthan, is performed against the background of a *Phad* (which is about 15 ft × 5 ft long sheet/cloth, on which life adventures of the folk deity, *Pabuji,* decorated in hues of desert land are depicted). In this folk form, the male performer the *Bhopa* wears a red *baga* (skirt), *safa* (turban), and *ghungroos* (anklets), and the female performer the *Bhopi* is clad in traditional attire *lehanga-choli* (skirt and blouse) and is veiled. These costumes are a literal visual representation of the culture and costumes of the state the artist/s belongs to [23–25].

In carnivalesque as described by Bakhtin [16] and seen in folk theater of *Hindi* belt like in *Kariyala, Khayal, Nautanki,* and *Maach* performers play a certain part in the story and dress up to recreate that particular character in a specific space-time, like gods and goddesses, the King of *Malwa*, *Daku* (dacoit) *Sultana*, *lambardaar* (policeman).

The *Ramnagar Ramleela*, a folk form from India, is one of the most popular, most studied, and well-documented *Ramleela* (especially by researchers). In the folk form young actors of about 14 years of age act in the narrative and their performance is limited to being dressed up and cladded in loud make-up as per the characters they are meant to portray. The narrator narrates the story and meanwhile the devotees chant the hymns of Ramayan from their pocket diaries or memory. So here costumes are the actors and actors mere models.

7 In Absence of the Saree in *Chandaini*

Joyce in her book *Gender and Genre in Folklore of Middle India* writes, over the years when she has returned to Chhattisgarh, literate and non-literate residents of Chhattisgarh have voiced a certain unease about Habib Tanvir's appropriation of Chhattisgarhi folklore *Chandaini* (which is a folk storytelling-song-dance format from the state of Chhattisgarh, and predates *Pandavani)* for display outside the region; many inhabitants feel that the process serves no benefit to Chhattisgarh itself. This particular appropriation may have gained urban interest for a limited period of time though *Chandaini* lost its charm in Chhattisgarh and later became extinct.

Tanvir stressed on keeping the entire narrative in performance, rather than focusing so exclusively on the elopement episode, as it existed prior to the intervention. The folk audiences cited two reasons for a walkout from one of the Devlal's *Chandaini* performance—"stories we don't know," and another major complaint of the dissatisfied audience was that "he should have worn a *saree*" [26]. This episode depicts the collective consciousness and folk memory of the folk audiences which reject a folk art form, as the folk costume was amiss.

8 Finding Folk/Craft in Urban Fashion

Indian fashion is tightly interwoven with traditional and popular Indian culture. The indigenous crafts, arts, and traditional textiles of the land guide in creating a large pool of cultural motifs, histories, designs, and the performative arts and have been a part of Indian's life and style-fashion-dress.

Kamaladevi Chattopadhyay's pioneering work induced a new life in the crafts sector of independent India. The formation of Central Cottage Industries Emporium and Handicrafts & Handlooms Export Corporation of India brought to the growing urban population artisanal handmade products from the folk/craft pockets. In the 1950s, Pupul Jayakar was appointed the Chairperson of the All India Handloom Board, and she established Weavers' Service Centres and Handloom and Handicraft Export Promotion Corporation (HHEC). Pupul Jayakar laid emphasis on design education and laid the founding idea of the National Institute Design and the creation of national-level institutes of fashion, with the National Institute of Fashion Technology and later institutions like the Indian National Trust for Art and Cultural Heritage. Laila Tyabji spearheaded Dastkar which showcased groundbreaking craft exhibitions. The same essence was echoed by Dastkari Haat Samiti, chaired by Jaya Jaitley, and established permanent craft markets, like Dilli Haat [27].

Aspiring to preserve Indian traditions, generating employment along with ensuring livelihoods for its members, Meera Goradia of Khamir, Judy Frater of Kala Raksha, Chandraben Shroff of Shrujan, and Neena Raaste of KMVS worked in Kutch. In West Bengal, Dr. Phulrenu Guha of Karma Kutir worked tirelessly to rehabilitate refugees from Bangladesh, training them in skills and reviving indigenous handicrafts; Ruby Pal Choudhuri at the Crafts Council; and many more. NGO movements and commercial and entrepreneurial ventures such as Fabindia by John Bissel, Anokhi by John and Faith Singh, Suraiya Hassan in Hyderabad, and Bandhej by Archana Shah are some examples, to name a few. Indian movie actresses such as Rekha, Shabana Azmi, and Vidya Balan adorned handloom cotton and silks and promoted the crafts [27].

In conclusion, what one wears or fashions apprises one's everyday experience of self and society. Fashion is often mediated between form and function, universality and self-expression, fast-fashion and traditional craftsmanship. And somewhere between this know-how of traditional knowledge and the urban sensibility of fashion conceptualizes—Indian Fashion.

Acknowledgments We would like to acknowledge all the folk artists/craft artisans and experts who participated in the video interviews for this study. Also, we would like to thank the unwavering efforts of many researchers/professionals who connected us to the folk artists/craft artisans and experts.

References

1. Kaiser, S. B., & Green, D. N. (2021). *Fashion and cultural studies*. Bloomsbury Publication.
2. Crane, D. (2000). *Fashion and its social agenda*. University of Chicago Press.
3. Kodavath, Y. L.. (2015). Folk media as a mode of communication in the development of rural areas. *Global Journal for Research Analysis*, ISSN No 2778160.
4. Zengin, M (2019) *An introduction to intertextuality as a literary theory: Definitions, axioms and the originators*. Journal of Social Sciences Institute, Pamukkale University.

5. Guest, G., Bunce, A., & Johnson, L. (2006). How many interviews are enough?: An experiment with data saturation and variability. *Field Methods, 18*(1), 59.82. https://doi.org/10.1177/1525822X05279903
6. Hollander, J. (2007). Indian Folk theatres. eBook Published by Routledge.
7. Attri, S. (2020). Folk theatre and history: Constructing Indian identity through the Khayal of Amar Singh Rathore. *The Journal of Indian and Asian Studies*, *1*(1), World of Scientific Publishing.
8. Barnard, A., & Spencer, J. (1996). *Encyclopedia of social and cultural anthropology*. Routledge.
9. Barnard, F. M. *Herder on social and political culture*. Cambridge University Press.
10. Marriott, M. (1955). *Little communities in indigenous civilization*. Studies in Little Community. University of Chicago Press.
11. Pocock, D. F., & Dumont, L. (1957). Village studies. *Contributions to Indian Sociology*.
12. Saussure, F. (1966). *Course in general linguistics*. In (Charles Bally and Albert Sechehaye in collaboration with Albert Riedlinger Trans and Intr. Wade Baskin), (Eds.), McGraw-Hill Book Company.
13. Wang, G., & Dissanayake, W. (1984). Culture, development and change: Some explorative observations. In *Continuity and change in communication systems*. Ablex Publishing Corporation.
14. Bhagat R., & Chapke R. (2006). Traditional Folk Media: A potentially effective communication tool in rural area. In AIAEE 22nd Annual Conference Proceedings, Clearwater Beach.
15. Sasireha, S. (1995). *Contribution of traditional media in creating awareness Communicator*. IIMC Publishing.
16. Bakhtin, M. (1981). Discourse in the Novel. In *The Dialogic Imagination: Four Essays* (Trans. Michael Holquist and Caryl Emerson). University of Texas Press
17. Barthes, R. (1977) *Image music text* (Trans. Stephen Heath). Fontana Press (1969).
18. Kristeva, J. (1984). *Revolution in poetic language* (Trans. Margaret Waller, Intr. Leon S. Roudiez). Columbia University Press.
19. Allen, G. (2000). *Intertextuality*. Routledge, Taylor and Francis Group.
20. Fausto-Sterling, A. (2003). The problem with sex/gender and nature/nurture. In S. J. Willimas, L. Birke, & G. A. Bendelow (Eds.), *Debating biology: Reflections on medicine health and society* (pp. 123–132). Routledge.
21. Malik, M. (2004). *Traditional forms of communication and mass media*. UNESCO Report.
22. Singh, K. (2020). *Folk theatres of North India: Contestation, amalgamation and transference*. Routledge.
23. Bhaskar, L. (2018). Impact of story-telling through Indian Textiles - Mata Ni Pachedi and Pabuji Ki Phad. presented at Sydney: WASET Conference.
24. Dalrymple, W. (2009). *Nine lives - the singers of epics*. Bloomsbury Publishing.
25. Dalrymple, W. (2010). *Rush for the gods. The National Interest No. 107*. Center for National Interest Publishing.
26. Flueckiger, J. (1996). *Gender and Genre in the Folklore of Middle India*. Cornell University Press.
27. Sethi, R. *Catalysing Craft: Women who shared the Way*. Indian International Center.

Metaverse Fashion Week: New Platforms, Same Fashion System?

Tyla Stevenson

Abstract The following research notes have emerged from my ongoing PhD project, which explores digital fashion brands, platforms, and metaverse events as key sites shaping and producing digital fashion discourses. This writing focuses on exclusivity and accessibility in digital-only fashion events. While in-person fashion weeks employ digital technologies to enhance accessibility, they remain mediatized performances reinforcing exclusivity. Using a case study methodology, this research analyzes Metaverse Fashion Week 2023 (MVFW23), Helsinki Fashion Week 2024 (HFW), and Metaverse Fashion Week 2024 (MVFW24). Grounded in Georg Simmel's fashion theories, it explores how digital fashion events navigate the dialectic between collective identity and individual distinction—a core tension in trend-driven fashion. Despite being promoted as more accessible, digital platforms often replicate exclusive structures of physical fashion events. MVFW23 emphasized accessibility yet retained hierarchical elements; HFW struggled to balance innovation with recognizability; MVFW24 required a paid subscription while simultaneously posting exclusive content for free on YouTube. This chapter critically examines how digital-only fashion events, rather than being radically different, reproduce the same hierarchical structures as traditional fashion shows. By analyzing MVFW23, HFW, and MVFW24, it reveals that Simmel's tensions between collective identity and individual distinction persist in digital settings. The significance lies not in what is new, but in what these events carry over into virtual worlds reinforcing the discursive concept of "Fashion."

Keywords Metaverse · Fashion Week · Digital · Event

T. Stevenson (✉)
Massey University, Wellington, New Zealand

P. von Wachenfeldt et al. (eds.), *Fashion Communication in the Digital Age*, Springer Proceedings in Business and Economics,
https://doi.org/10.1007/978-3-031-99481-4_30

1 Introduction

Metaverse Fashion Weeks and digital-only fashion events offer a critical opportunity to examine fashion as a constructed discursive field. Rather than focusing on what differentiates digital fashion events from traditional, in-person events, this research examines how these digital platforms reproduce established fashion practices. By analyzing the elements these events carry into virtual spaces, the study aims to identify what is considered essential to preserving and reinforcing the broader concept of "Fashion." This is significant because it highlights the way digital spaces are not radically different from traditional fashion spaces, but rather continue to reproduce the same tensions and hierarchies. Drawing on Georg Simmel's theories of fashion, this analysis of Metaverse Fashion Week 2023 (MVFW23), Helsinki Fashion Week 2024 (HFW), and Metaverse Fashion Week 2024 (MVFW24) investigates how digital-only fashion events sustain the tension between the individual and the collective, distinction and similarity, and exclusivity and accessibility.

Simmel argues that fashion is not merely a phenomenon of clothing but a trend-based system that emerges from the tension between the individual and the collective [1: 541]. Individuals align with recognizable social groups while also striving to distinguish themselves. As Carter explains, "if the desire for uniformity and imitation could reach fulfillment there would be no such thing as fashion, only mass similarity" [2: 67]. In this sense, the existence of fashion depends on this contradiction: if all items were entirely unique, the lack of common trends would undermine the very concept of fashion. This understanding is crucial for this research, as it shows that digital events replicate these fundamental tensions, suggesting that what is carried over into digital spaces reveals much about how fashion functions in both the material and virtual worlds.

2 Literature Review

The function of Fashion Weeks, as outlined by Halliday [3], serves multiple purposes across both local and global, cultural, and economic spheres. These events play a pivotal role in consolidating fashion capitals, enhancing their status as both tourist destinations and hubs of industry and production. The national identities of designers are often not directly aligned with the location of the event itself, as brands present their work according to their creative output and the specific prestige or media presence of Fashion Week. This suggests that particular locations are associated with specific styles and levels of status, emphasizing the role of Fashion Weeks in shaping not just the industry but also global perceptions of fashion [3, 4].

Fashion shows or weeks, structured as a series of events and performances, have evolved into mediatized spectacles with the increased integration of communication technologies. This transformation expands the events' reach beyond the confines of in-person attendance while reinforcing the spatial and symbolic glamour associated with the live event. As Halliday [3, 4] notes, "While online media render the fashion show virtually accessible in 'real time,' the performance remains closed off, and media enhance the cultural status of the collection and of the event as ritual. The fashion show's mediatization produces and mines tensions between democratization and exclusivity." This duality between accessibility and exclusivity reveals an inherent tension that persists within the mediatization of fashion events.

Given that in-person live events, attached to "prestigious" fashion capitals, reproduce discourses of exclusivity while leveraging digital technologies to enhance accessibility, one must question how fashion events that exist solely in digital spaces represent notions of exclusivity. Do digital or Metaverse Fashion Weeks reproduce similar discourses of exclusivity as their material-world counterparts? If so, what does this reveal about the nature of the discursive concept of fashion itself? These questions challenge the assumption that digital fashion events inherently democratize the fashion system and instead suggest that they may reflect the same hierarchical structures that are entrenched in traditional, in-person events.

Moreover, examining the tension between the individual and the collective, the exclusive few and the masses, and the recognizable and the novel offers further insight into the concept of fashion and its functioning as a trends-based system. While digital-only fashion events are often regarded as novel, I argue that their true significance lies not in their newness but in what aspects of fashion, both discursively and creatively, they choose to carry over into virtual spaces. By scrutinizing these elements, we gain a deeper understanding of how fashion as a system of trends continues to shape itself, in both the material and virtual realms.

3 Method

In my wider doctoral research, I examine digital fashion events as part of visual and material culture, employing a case study methodology supported by an autoethnographic walkthrough method and critical discourse analysis. This combined approach enables close engagement with platforms, user experiences, and the discourses surrounding digital fashion. The autoethnographic walkthrough method [4: 881] allows me to explore digital spaces as both participant and observer, noting platform structures, user interactions, and interface design. Critical discourse analysis complements this by uncovering how language, visuals, and platform features construct or reinforce dominant fashion narratives, particularly concerning exclusivity, accessibility, and identity.

The case studies, Metaverse Fashion Week 2023 (MVFW23), Helsinki Fashion Week 2024 (HFW), and Metaverse Fashion Week 2024 (MVFW24), were selected for their relevance to contemporary digital fashion discourses and differing approaches to platform use. MVFW23 was hosted on Decentraland, a blockchain-based virtual world; HFW utilized VLGE alongside Instagram Linktree; and

MVFW24 centered its activity on its website, later making content accessible via YouTube.

Timing and platform accessibility shaped my engagement with each event. I attended MVFW23 live, documenting my experiences during the event and reviewing subsequent video uploads on YouTube. HFW24 remains partially accessible through its Instagram Linktree, allowing for ongoing analysis beyond the live components. For MVFW24, I accessed the platform during the scheduled dates, though most content was released as recorded media. These differences in access and platform design illuminate how digital fashion events negotiate ideas of liveness, participation, and exclusivity.

4 Metaverse Fashion Week 2023 (MVFW23)

MVFW23 retained core elements of traditional in-person fashion weeks, offering runway shows, social events, and shopping experiences in a virtual environment. Users could attend presentations, after-parties, and panel discussions and navigate a virtual mall selling digital garments as non-fungible tokens (NFTs) via the Decentraland platform. Over 60 designers participated, including luxury brands such as Dolce & Gabbana and Coach, alongside digital-only creators such as The Fabricant and the Institute of Digital Fashion. High-profile names such as Dame Vivienne Westwood and Cristóbal Balenciaga were prominently featured, likely as strategic audience draws. While Dazed highlighted how digital platforms broaden access "anyone with a Wi-Fi connection can get involved with MVFW" [5] attendance figures revealed limited engagement: Decentraland reported around 26,000 unique active users over four days, but independent estimates suggested closer to 8900, a significant drop from the previous year [6]. This gap underscores that accessibility does not guarantee widespread participation.

MVFW24 featured real-time runway shows, including an Adidas presentation designed to replicate conventional fashion events. The show was set on a raised platform positioned just above avatars' eyeline, with non-player character models entering through a digital portal and walking to electronic music in virtual Adidas garments. Notably, scaffolding was prominently displayed as part of the staging, a structure often hidden or deliberately styled in physical shows, highlighting the digital platform's replication of real-world production elements, but its visible use here emphasized the constructed nature of the digital environment. Though some metaverse-specific elements, like models walking along the ceiling, deviated from physical constraints, the overall structure adhered to familiar runway conventions. The 10- to 15-minute performance fostered a sense of temporal exclusivity, reflecting the tension between the theoretically open-access digital format and the curated exclusivity that remains central to fashion culture.

This blend of familiar runway structures and digital-specific elements raises questions about the evolving aesthetics of virtual fashion shows. While the Adidas presentation largely mirrored conventional fashion week formats, its deliberate exposure of staging mechanics and occasional breaks from physical realism hinted at an emerging visual language unique to digital fashion. Rather than fully embracing the metaverse's capacity for radical reinvention, MVFW24 maintained a connection to established industry norms, suggesting that digital fashion remains tethered to the prestige and validation of traditional fashion structures. This interplay between continuity and experimentation underscores the challenges of translating fashion's cultural and commercial logics into virtual spaces, where innovation must be balanced with recognizability to maintain industry legitimacy.

5 Helsinki Fashion Week (HFW)

Helsinki Fashion Week (HFW) was hosted on the online world-building platform, VLGE. Accessible through an Instagram linktree, the event features 40 unique digital fashion exhibitions that can be explored using avatars. As previously discussed [7], HFW reveals a tension between distinction and similarity. When a digital platform is presented as a site of innovation and novelty, creating worlds for fashion consumers that remain recognizable becomes challenging. For instance, the brand SHILOKAVICA is centered around enlarged avatars with strikingly demonic features. The garments these avatars wear are often unrecognizable or too simplistic to align with a specific aesthetic. However, the avatars' tattoos are identifiable, reflecting how body adornment and tattoo styles are also subject to trend cycles. Drawing inspiration from stick-and-poke designs and cyber singlism, these tattoos create a compelling tension between the familiarity of the body art and the uniqueness of the avatars. While consumers may struggle to replicate the avatars' garments, they may find elements of their own identities reflected in the tattoos. As noted by Simmel [1], it is the tension between recognition and novelty that stimulates the concept of fashion, as demonstrated in this example from HFW.

This interplay between recognition and novelty extends beyond individual avatars to the broader spatial design of VLGE itself. The digital architecture of HFW blends surreal, otherworldly elements with structures that echo physical fashion venues, reinforcing a sense of familiarity within an otherwise experimental environment. Expansive digital landscapes and gravity-defying installations create an immersive experience, yet many exhibition spaces still resemble traditional galleries or venues, anchoring the event within established visual and commercial frameworks.

6 Metaverse Fashion Week 2024 (MVFW24)

MVFW24 portrays the tension between exclusivity and accessibility through a more literal experience of attending their online event. To participate, I was required to sign up as a "Metaverse Fashion Council Member," which came with a $14.99

USD monthly subscription fee. This subscription was marketed as granting access to all MVFW24 events, voting opportunities for the Metaverse Fashion Awards, and the chance to attend the online Metaverse Fashion Summit. From November 20 to 24, I was given access to videos of conversations between Metaverse Council members and industry guests, which primarily focused on venture capital, digital businesses, and brands in the digital fashion space. Additionally, there was a marketing video for the first Greek AI fashion model, Aiko, promoting its services to potential clients. However, these videos were all available to the public for free on YouTube, regardless of the subscription.

The focus here is not necessarily on the content of the talks or the promotional materials, but on the experience of purchasing a subscription for "exclusive" events that were, in fact, accessible through a free YouTube link. This discrepancy highlights the constructed nature of exclusivity in digital spaces and emphasizes how the concept of access can be commodified in the virtual fashion world. While the subscription gave the illusion of access to something unique or privileged, the underlying content was freely available. This situation underscores the artificiality of digital exclusivity, drawing attention to the ways in which platforms can create a perception of value.

Moreover, this event demonstrates how digital platforms still rely on strategies of exclusivity and hierarchy to maintain value. The tension between the accessibility of content and the constructed exclusivity created by the Metaverse Fashion Council points to broader trends in digital economies, where the promise of exclusivity is used to drive subscription-based models. This dynamic also brings to light the ways in which digital fashion spaces replicate traditional fashion industry structures, where access to certain events, information, or networks remains limited to those with financial means or social capital, even in a digital environment that ostensibly promotes democratization.

7 Conclusion

In conclusion, the "digital-only" fashion weeks examined in this research, Metaverse Fashion Week 2023 (MVFW23), Helsinki Fashion Week 2024 (HFW), and Metaverse Fashion Week 2024 (MVFW24), reinforce tensions familiar to traditional, in-person Fashion Weeks. These tensions, between accessibility and exclusivity, similarity and distinction, and the individual and the collective, are central to fashion as a trend-driven and identity-shaping phenomenon, as articulated by Georg Simmel. Despite the promotion of digital platforms as more inclusive, the research demonstrates that these events replicate the hierarchical and exclusive structures that characterize their physical counterparts. In the case of MVFW23, the emphasis on accessibility is complicated by traditional forms of hierarchy, while HFW grapples with balancing innovation with recognizability. MVFW24 further complicates this notion by creating a paid barrier to entry, only to make the supposedly exclusive content available for free on YouTube.

This study emphasizes that what is most significant about digital-only fashion events is not how they differ from traditional, in-person shows, but rather how they replicate key elements of the physical fashion world. By doing so, they reiterate the very discourses and structures that define what "Fashion" is. The digital platforms may promise democratization and greater accessibility, yet they paradoxically carry over the same exclusivity and power dynamics. This observation points to the persistence of these tensions, between collective identity and individual distinction, as crucial elements of digital fashion events. In particular, the events analyzed here reveal how these digital spaces continue to define and shape fashion through the lens of exclusivity, highlighting the limitations of digital platforms in breaking from the traditional confines of fashion's hierarchical structure.

A dialectical analysis is particularly useful in understanding these tensions because it allows for an exploration of contradictions inherent in digital fashion events. This approach reveals the dynamic interplay between conflicting forces, offering insight into how digital platforms both subvert and uphold traditional power structures. Dialectical analysis, by focusing on contradictions, helps to expose how these digital events reflect and reproduce broader societal and cultural contradictions, such as the tension between individualism and collective norms.

While Georg Simmel's contributions to fashion studies have been challenged in recent years, this chapter highlights how his theory of fashion as a dialectic between collective identity and individual distinction remains relevant in understanding digital fashion events. The tension he describes between the individual's desire for distinction and the collective need for conformity is vividly present in digital fashion, as it remains tied to the same discourses of exclusivity, trend cycles, and identity formation. Although the focus of these research notes has been on the similarities between digital and physical fashion events, further exploration could address the limitations and critiques of Simmel's framework. Simmel's emphasis on hierarchical social structures for example might not address the potential decentralized or participatory nature of digital fashion communities. Future research could critically engage with these tensions, examining how digital fashion both reinforces and diverges from traditional fashion logics in ways that challenge or extend Simmel's foundational ideas. As this research develops, it will be important to examine how digital events both challenge and reinforce traditional fashion structures, and to consider their potential implications for the future of the industry.

References

1. Simmel, G. (1957). Fashion. *American Journal of Sociology, 62*(6), 541–558.
2. Carter, M. (2021). Georg Simmel: Clothes and Fashion. In: *Fashion Classics from Carlyle to Barthes*. Publisher, Location.
3. Halliday, R. (2022). *The fashion show goes live: Exclusive and mediatized performance.* Bloomsbury Publishing. Available at: http://ebookcentral.proquest.com/lib/massey/detail.action?docID=6828383, last accessed 2024/12/16

4. Light, B., Burgess, J., & Duguay, S. (2016). The walkthrough method: An approach to the study of apps. *New Media, 20*, 1–xx.
5. Rodgers, D. (2023). Metaverse Fashion Week 2023: log on or touch grass? *Dazed*. Available at: https://www.dazeddigital.com/fashion/article/58534/1/metaverse-fashion-week-2023-decentraland-events-nft-blockchain-luxury-wearables, last Accessed 2024/12/16.
6. Kostina, E. (2023). The Verdict On Decentraland Metaverse Fashion Week 2023. *Jing Daily*. Available at: https://jingdaily.com/posts/decentraland-metaverse-fashion-week-2023-verdict, last accessed 2024/12/16.
7. Stevenson, T. (2024). Notes on Helsinki's Digital Fashion Week. *CAVRN*, 4 November. Available at: https://cavrn.org/notes-on-helsinkis-digital-fashion-week/, last accessed 2024/12/16.

Digital Writings of Fashion Cultures: New Formats of Publication of Creative Know-How in the Mediterranean Basin

Maria Ida De Ioanni

Abstract The research *Digital Writings of Fashion Cultures: New Formats of Publication of Creative Know-How in the Mediterranean Basin* within the larger initiative of the Network *Incursive Fashion Heritage* seeks to address the renegotiating nature of socio-digital networks in the understanding of fashion, clothing, and textile cultures from Southern and Eastern Mediterranean overlooked communities. Drawing on Castell's theory of interactive creation of meaning, the research aims to reveal how participatory digital networks' innovations—both creative and technical—can empower artisans, producers, and mediators in the Mediterranean region to reclaim and revalue local experience of craft heritage and fashion cultures. The ongoing research highlights how in the dynamic context of participatory socio-digital networks, Mediterranean traditional know-how renovates itself and renegotiates its position in fashion knowledge production by presenting local practices from a contemporary fashion perspective. Content produced by these fashion digital communities from Mediterranean islands and peninsulas, Middle Eastern countries, and North Africa makes extremely porous the border between fashion as modernity and fashion traditional practices, working toward the creative development of new formats for a de-globalized and de-centered fashion mediation.

Keywords Mediterranean heritage · Participatory practices · Fashion narratives · Interactive creation of meaning

M. I. De Ioanni (✉)
Université Paris Nanterre, Nanterre, France
e-mail: mideioanni@parisnanterre.fr

P. von Wachenfeldt et al. (eds.), *Fashion Communication in the Digital Age*, Springer Proceedings in Business and Economics,
https://doi.org/10.1007/978-3-031-99481-4_31

1 Research Objectives, Methodology, and Field

1.1 Objectives

This doctoral project aims to answer the following main research question: How do participatory digital networks contribute to the revaluation and dissemination of Mediterranean fashion heritage? By observing the digital writings that contribute to the processes of publication and promotion of fashion cultures from the Southern and Eastern Mediterranean area. It is based on the observation that digital writings establish a propice place for the editorialization [1], the circulation [2], and sometimes the reinvestment [3] of fashion, clothing, and textile practices while promoting artisanal know-how associated with the fashion and textile industry. The project is based on the hypothesis that there are socio-digital spaces proposed by private contributors or mediated by intermediaries and institutions, which promote overlooked fashion practices of Mediterranean culture through semio-technical creative tools embedded in social media networks (SMNs here unless otherwise specified). These spaces would, while questioning the contemporary relevance of opposing contemporary fashion to tradition, be likely to establish alternative forms of fashion heritage narratives, themselves determined by the editorial formats on which they depend [4, 5, 6, 7].

The research plans to analyze formal and content developments in digital creative environments of several p/matrimoines and fashion cultures defined here as "incursive": competing socio-digital writings that reappropriate, reinterpret, and decentralize the Eurocentric discourse of fashion cultures in the Mediterranean geopolitical context. On the other hand, the research examines the effects of the interaction of a sample of the public—Mediterranean communities excluded from the fashion/modernity binome [8, 9, 10] or made invisible by Eurocentric narratives—with the digital scripto-iconic representations of fashion cultures and practices, in the process of creating renewed meanings and questioning the construction of the fashion heritage discourse within the Mediterranean basin. The study highlights the semio-technical formats that influence the design and enunciation of the way in which Mediterranean fashion knowledge is published in order to be seen and internalized.

Finally, the research seeks to account for how these digital writings, according to their authorial and statutory authorities, establish new sociocultural, socioeconomic, and political relationships within the Mediterranean basin in which the object "fashion cultures in the process of becoming heritage" plays the role of mediating binder. The narration of heritage through SMNs in certain geopolitical contexts is not only cultural; it is also strategic. These writings are produced by individuals or collectives seeking above all to improve the cost-effectiveness of artisanal know-how in certain regions of the Mediterranean whose profitability has been reduced by globalizing narratives on fashion and its consumption. Therefore, the research understands communication tools provided by SMNs as crucial intervenors in the socioeconomic process. From an economic point of view, SMNs allow us to bypass traditional market systems and to create new resources through the tools made available, online commerce, collaborations, and direct interaction with consumers. The incursive narratives, as defined by this thesis, thus become, while producing contestatory formats of archiving and documentation [7, 11–13], a creative scripto-iconic form of economic resistance to the homogenizing forces of fashion systems. Thus, this project's key research objectives can be resumed as follows: to analyze the role of socio-digital networks in promoting overlooked fashion heritage; to explore how digital creative formats shape the perception of Mediterranean fashion cultures; and to assess—starting from the premise that the sociocultural dynamics underlying heritage practices influence local and regional economic rehabilitation—the socioeconomic impact of digital publishing on local artisans and producers in competing fashion systems.

1.2 Data Sourcing and Analysis Methodology

The study focuses therefore on 15 social media accounts selected from an initial pool of over 500. The final sample of 15 case studies was curated to ensure a diverse representation of the mother population as well as to include the main profiles emerging from the analysis. This sample is not meant to be completely exhaustive of the research results and achieve quantitative generalization but to demonstrate how the proposed theoretical statement of "incursive heritage" may apply in practice. Creators were gathered through an open call published on the Instagram networking account @incursiveheritage, inviting all individuals who felt their work aligned with the research objectives, to participate in the network by filling a form or simply stating their interest through a direct message. This initial call helped establish a digital "mother population," which was further expanded by the analysis of followed and following accounts of these participants. The accounts were then divided according to their different categorical frameworks. These categories differ in their enunciative approaches, meaning in their authorial instances, statuses [14], and objectives:

1. (i) Personal accounts and private collections offer digital content that does not appear to adhere to institutional norms of the Mediterranean or a hierarchical enunciation structure. These accounts represent "a non-institutionalized arena that disrupts the canons of archiving and fashion collection" [7] as non-professional actors who actively and deliberately participate in the production of knowledge (Houllier, 2016:6). This category explores marginalized or economically sidelined fashion heritage, particularly where erasure of cultural and political networks in the Mediterranean limits local economic emancipation in favor of large-scale Eurocentric production contexts. Examples of this category, identified through exploratory research, include accounts such as @vintagelibya, @aidaabuusitta, and @tatreezandtea.
2. (ii) The intermediary category consists of socio-digital content produced by research centers and in-field professional accounts. These accounts are distinct in their engagement with contributions from institutionalized communities while

also incorporating or interacting with external user-generated content from Pro-Ams [15, 16]. Notable examples include @fri, @thetatreesinstitute, and @ itinerance_mediterranee.

3. Institutional and sponsored socio-digital spaces are managed by companies and institutions, showcasing enunciative strategies that seek to renew the narratives surrounding fashion craftsmanship and, more broadly, the heritage of socioeconomic actors within the industry. Examples include @le19m, platform highlighting the connection between Chanel fashion house skills and the heritage of southern Mediterranean and African regions, and @how.they.work, a project by the online store Accidente Con Flores, which aims to connect textile artists and creatives from all the Balearic Islands.

In the context of ongoing research, data have been sourced as follows:

- Primary data: User-generated scripto-iconic content on social media platforms (Instagram, TikTok), such as posts, videos, and multimedia narratives focusing on fashion production techniques and cultural alternatives to Eurocentric fashion heritage
- Interviews and engagement evaluation: Analysis of interactions between content creators and their audiences, examining socio-digital engagement as a form of fashion knowledge production

The methodology employed for data analysis is based on a digital ethnographic approach with a predominantly semio-discursive and enunciative orientation. It follows classic works in visual semiotics [14, 17], enunciation [18], and multimodal discourse analysis (Maingueneau, 1991; [19]). It is further enriched by more recent approaches related to a semiotic perspective on screen writing [20], digital media as a form of writing, and semiotic approaches to archives [21]. The semio-discursive analysis is structured around three main guidelines:

- Narrative structure: How are fashion heritage narratives framed (e.g., nostalgic, progressive, activist, anti-Eurocentric)?
- Visual semiotics: How do images or videos represent cultural symbols, textiles, and practices? What role do they play in heritage production?
- Economic impact: How do these platforms facilitate the sale of goods or revalue artisanal skills? What insights do comment sections or platform feedback provide about consumer responses?

The study will also include semi-structured interviews with managers and online communities involved in the user-generated content observed on the accounts.

1.3 Theoretical Field

The research considers these contributory digital writing processes [16, 22] as a system that displaces and transforms normative power relations [7, 23] and heritage hierarchies ([24–27]) into reappropriating content from a decentralized and decolonial perspective [28, 29, 30, 31, 32] through the editorial formats specific to socio-digital networks. The importance of the contributive dimension in the project is framed by the reflections on "participatory sciences" in France by Francois Houllier (2016: 6) who defines them as "forms of production of scientific knowledge in which non-scientific-professional actors—whether individuals or groups—participate actively and deliberately." This term was defined by Annie Chevrefils-Desbiolles in 2012 in the field of visual arts and digital studies in the post-media era. It is a question of considering the contemporary amateur in his post-media reality of "prosumer" (producer and amateur). As a contributor, the contemporary amateur is more appropriately defined as a producer of content. Selecting information, giving opinions, and producing content are all ways of reappropriating a reality that is increasingly informed and mediatized but also "post-mediated" by the "brands" of each person ([15]: 127). According to Castell, the "interactive production of meaning" refers to an engagement of the public of cultural heritage in the act of remixing the codes and messages they receive, with their own codes and messages [33]. As a consequence, "digital enthusiasts build forms of collective learning" ([16]: 33) and are driven by a deep individual motivation. However, at the same time, they acknowledge that to reconstruct their individual history, they need to share information and collaborate with each other [16]. By interweaving these notions and drawing on previous work, the doctoral thesis considers the existence of an incursive heritage of Mediterranean fashion cultures, understood as political and interactive digital collective creation of meaning around fashion cultures and practices in the Mediterranean context through scripto-iconic content.

References

1. Vitali-Rosati, M. (2020). Qu'est-ce que l'écriture numérique ?. Corela. 33. 10.4000/corela.11759.
2. Jeanneret, Y. (2014). *Critique de la trivialité: Les médiations de la communication, enjeu de pouvoir*. ÉDITIONS NON STANDARD.
3. Maingueneau, D. (1991). L'analyse du discours: introduction aux lectures de l'archive.
4. Pham, M. H. T. (2014). Archival intimacies: Participatory media and the fashion histories of US women of colour. Fashion, Style & Popular Culture, 2(1), 107–122.
5. Jenss, H. (2019). Converging practices: Fashion exhibits across museums and social media. *Critical Studies in Fashion & Beauty, 10*(1), 31–47.
6. Konig, G., & Mentges, G. (eds) (2019). Musealisierte Mode: Psitionen, Thesen, Perspektiven, Munster and New York: Waxmann.
7. Pecorari, M. (2019). Fashion archives, museums and collections in the age of the digital. *Critical Studies in Fashion & Beauty, 10*(1), 3–29.
8. Breward, C., & Evans, C. (Eds.). (2005). Fashion and modernity (Illustrated ed.). Berg Publishers.
9. Houllier, F. (2016). Les sciences participatives en France (p. 63). HAL.
10. Jansen, M. A. (2020). *Fashion and the phantasmagoria of modernity: An introduction to decolonial fashion discourse*. Fashion Theory.
11. Boughlala, A. (2024). Fashion storytelling and heritage on social media: A visual content analysis of fan-led Instagram fashion brand archives. *ZoneModa Journal, 14*(2).
12. Franceschini, M. (2019). Navigating fashion: On the role of digital fashion archives in the preservation, classification and dissemination of fashion heritage. *Critical Studies in Fashion & Beauty, 10*(1), 69–90.

13. Martin, M., & Vacca, F. (2018). Heritage narratives in the digital era: How digital technologies have improved approaches and tools for fashion know-how, traditions and memories. *Research Journal of Textile and Apparel, 22*(4), 335–351.
14. Dondero, M. G. (2020). *Les langages de l'image: De la peinture aux Big Visual Data*. Hermann.
15. Chevrefils-Desbiolles, A. (2012). L'amateur dans le domaine des arts plastiques: Nouvelles pratiques à l'heure du Web 2.0. Ministère de la Culture.
16. Severo, M. (2021). L'impératif participatif: Institutions culturelles, amateurs et plateformes. Ina.
17. Groupe μ. (1992). Traité du signe visuel: Pour une rhétorique de l'image. Seuil.
18. Beyaert-Geslin A. (2009). L'image préoccupée. Paris, Hermès-Lavoisier, coll. Forme et sens.
19. Kress, G., & van Leeuwen, T. (2001). *Multimodal discourse*. Hodder Arnold.
20. Jeanneret, Y., & Souchier, E. (2005). L'énonciation éditoriale dans les écrits d'écran. *Communication & Languages, 145*, 3–15.
21. Dondero, M. G., Badir, S., & Provenzano, F. (2019). Les discours syncrétiques. Poésie visuelle, bande dessinée, graffitis.
22. Valtýsson, B. (2011). Europeana: The digital construction of Europe's collective memory. *Information, Communication & Society, 15*(2), 151–170.
23. Mouratidou, E. (2020). *Re-presentation policies of the fashion industry: Discourse, apparatus and power*. Wiley.
24. Foucault, M. ([1969] 2002). *The archaeology of knowledge* (A. M. Sheridan Smith, Trans.). Routledge Classics.
25. Lowenthal, D. (1998). *The heritage crusade and the spoils of history*. Cambridge University Press.
26. Tunbridge, J. E., & Ashworth, G. J. (1996). *Dissonant heritage: The management of the past as a resource in conflict*. Wiley.
27. Wright, P. (1985). *On living in an old country*. Verso.
28. Gandhi, L. (1998). *Postcolonial theory: A critical introduction*. Allen & Unwin.
29. Hall, S. (2016). *Cultural studies 1983: A theoretical history*. Duke University Press.
30. Jansen, M. A., & Craik, J. (Eds.). (2018). *Modern fashion traditions: Negotiating tradition and modernity through fashion*. Bloomsbury Publishing.
31. Di Leo, S. (2023). *Empowering grassroots narratives: Assessing the impact of social media activism on fashion brand communication*. Politecnico di Milano.
32. Shen, Z. (2022). *How small brands survive the social media firestorm through culture heritage: A case study of Irish fashion microblogging*. SAGE Open, April-June, 1–14. https://doi.org/10.1177/21582440221095024.
33. Castells, M. (2009). *Communication power*. Oxford University Press.

A Digitized Sustainable Preservation Framework for Traditional Garment-Making Techniques: A Case Study of Hong Kong Cheongsam

Qingyi Zhang and Haze Ng

Abstract Traditional garment-making techniques, as significant components of intangible cultural heritage (ICH), are increasingly threatened by globalization and industrialization, risking the loss of their transmissions. To address the limitations of existing preservation methods in systematically capturing the dynamic interactions between tailors, tools, and machines, this study proposes a digital framework for documenting and sustaining these techniques. The framework will be validated through its application in the Hong Kong Cheongsam Making Technique, showcasing its potential for broader ICH preservation efforts. The framework aims to support sustainable fashion practices and foster innovative design based on traditional garment-making techniques.

Keywords Digital preservation · Intangible cultural heritage · Sustainable fashion practice · Craftsmanship · Hong Kong Cheongsam

1 The Need for Digitizing Traditional Garment-Making Techniques

In 2003, the United Nations Educational, Scientific and Cultural Organization (UNESCO) adopted the *Convention for the Safeguarding of the Intangible Cultural Heritage*, which defines ICH as "the practices, representations, expressions, knowledge, skills—as well as the instruments, objects, artefacts, and cultural spaces associated with them—that communities, groups, and, in some cases, individuals recognize as part of their cultural heritage" [1]. Under this framework, traditional craftsmanship, which includes a wide range of traditional garment-making techniques [2], is considered a crucial carrier of cultural diversity. These techniques combine social norms, economic conditions, aesthetic pursuits, fashion and textile

Q. Zhang · H. Ng (✉)
The Hong Kong Polytechnic University, Hung Hom, Kowloon, Hong Kong
e-mail: hazekh.ng@polyu.edu.hk

P. von Wachenfeldt et al. (eds.), *Fashion Communication in the Digital Age*, Springer Proceedings in Business and Economics,
https://doi.org/10.1007/978-3-031-99481-4_32

technologies, and crafting techniques, representing a key expression of the "fashion system" within a particular regional and historical context.

However, the rapid progress of globalization and industrialization, along with the disruption of crafts industry, and hence its transmission, has pushed traditional tailoring techniques into an unprecedented state of endangerment [3]. *Hong Kong Cheongsam Making Technique*, which is a representative item on the *National List of Intangible Cultural Heritage of China*, is no exception. In this context, the study and preservation of the ICH face significant challenges. For instance, there is a general lack of holistic documentation of the craftsmanship and the corresponding practices [4]. In-depth and systematic investigations of the craft are needed for establishing a primary point of reference, covering the visual and structural information, dynamic evolution of craft narratives, experiential and tacit knowledge, and their historical, cultural, and social contexts over time [5]. Moreover, a key characteristic of the ICH is notably its reliance on intricate human motions, which underscores the necessity of digital tools in recording and analyzing, and thus, its preservation [6].

To address these challenges, methods for digitizing human motion have been developed and can be broadly categorized into two types: invasive and noninvasive. These methods are distinguished by the level of visual occlusion. On the one hand, invasive methods primarily utilize motion capture technology, requiring the participants to wear sensors or markers to acquire high-precision data [7]. On the other hand, noninvasive methods are based on visual tracking technology, without requiring additional equipment, and capture motion trajectories through visual recognition and computational optimization [8]. Regardless of the approach, the resulting data comprise a sequence of coordinate frames that accurately capture and quantify changes in position and direction, serving as a foundational dataset for subsequent analysis and applications.

For example, the Tujia Brocade Handcrafts team employed Kinect and Leap Motion devices to capture limb and hand movements in traditional crafts and digitally preserved these movements through virtual reconstruction techniques [9]. Similarly, the Korean Nubi team developed a first-person perspective 3D recording framework based on head-mounted Leap Motion to enhance the Tujia Brocade method [10]. Additionally, Aoki and Miyamoto enhanced the 3D motion capture techniques for traditional Japanese Kenjutsu swordsmanship [11]. However, despite these advancements, most of these methods are confined to basic motion capture and are unable to effectively represent the intricate interactions between craftsmen, tools, and machinery, particularly in complex mechanical operation and detailed handicraft scenarios. Furthermore, although multi-sensor technology can enhance capture accuracy, challenges such as occlusion and data integration persist, impeding the accurate replication of intricate craftsmanship details [12].

2 A Proposed Digital Framework for Sustainable Preservation

The preservation of traditional garment-making techniques is confronted with two primary challenges: the digital documentation of both explicit and tacit knowledge. Explicit knowledge encompasses operational and functional information related to tangible elements, such as craftsmen, tools, and machines, as well as articulable and documentable details, ranging from textile material properties and standardized tailoring techniques to the structural configurations of various garment forms. In contrast, tacit knowledge entails the skillful use of tools, which involves complex dynamic interactions between tailors, tools, machines, and materials, as well as the subtle, experience-driven practices integral to specific techniques [13]. Tacit knowledge poses significant challenges for documentation through conventional written records and static archival approaches. Therefore, dynamic replication is crucial for ensuring holistic preservation. This chapter proposes a comprehensive digital framework for sustainable preservation, aiming to systematically record and preserve the dynamic processes of traditional garment-making techniques, while providing technical support for the inheritance and innovative design of traditional crafts.

The framework's construction is centered on standardization and virtualization as its core technical principles. First, the process flow requires standardization to ensure the integrity of the process and the clear identification of critical components [11]. Standardization comprises two key elements: (1) structuring the process flow based on the actual operational sequence, defining the logical relationships and execution steps, and (2) extracting core techniques from the workflow, distinguishing between modifiable steps and indispensable components.

Building upon standardized categorization, the framework employs digital modeling technologies to develop virtual components, including "virtual tailors," "virtual tools," and "virtual machinery." These components function as core modules of the virtual platform, aimed at replicating the dynamic interactive processes inherent in traditional garment-making workflows. In the digital documentation of tacit knowledge, motion capture technology and depth cameras are essential. Specifically, based on standardized procedures, the craftsman's hand movements, tool operations, and machine dynamics are captured frame by frame. Complex processes are divided into 1-to-2-second segments for data storage [14]. By employing multimodal data collection, motion capture, mechanical force sensors, and tool interaction data are combined to produce a multifaceted data stream, which is then digitized and transferred to the virtual platform.

Subsequently, the virtual platform employs a modular design to establish a complete technical chain, spanning from data acquisition to dynamic replication. Firstly, the data acquisition module, based on Leap Motion and depth cameras, records the three-dimensional trajectories of the tailor's hand movements with a motion capture accuracy of up to 0.001 meters [15]. Secondly, parametric modeling techniques are utilized to construct interactive models of virtual tailors and tools, integrating multimodal data for real-time dynamic visualization. This technical chain ensures the comprehensive transformation of traditional garment-making techniques from physical entities to explicit knowledge. Through the platform's six degrees of freedom (6-DoF) observation interface, users can analyze the dynamic coupling between tailor gestures and fabric deformation in real time. Additionally, the platform provides force feedback on hand movements and detailed operational analysis, allowing users to develop a comprehensive understanding of the intricate methods involved in complex craftsmanship.

3 The Case of Hong Kong Cheongsam-Making Technique

The framework will be validated through its application in the *Hong Kong Cheongsam Making Technique*. Hong Kong cheongsam encompasses a range of diverse dress forms of Chinese men's and women's attire. Its structural origins can be traced back to the ancient Chinese robe known as the *Right-opening Straight-hem Robe* for men [16]. During the Republic of China era (1912–1949), cheongsam gradually became a symbol of women's pursuit of modernization and social liberation, and it was introduced to Hong Kong from Shanghai in the 1920s [17]. Against the backdrop of the highly Westernized and hybrid cultural ecology, the attire incorporated Western three-dimensional tailoring techniques, resulting in the unique and iconic Hong Kong-style cheongsam. In 2014 and 2017, the *Hong Kong Cheongsam Making Technique* was successively inscribed on the *Intangible Cultural Heritage Inventory of Hong Kong* and the *Representative List of the Intangible Cultural Heritage of Hong Kong*. Furthermore, in 2021, it was officially included in the fifth batch of the *National Representative List of Intangible Cultural Heritage of China* [18].

As a garment-making technique that integrates Chinese and Western cultural elements, exhibits technical complexity, and carries profound cultural symbolism, *Hong Kong Cheongsam Making Technique* serves as an ideal case study for conducting a pilot experimental trial of the proposed framework. The construction of its digital preservation platform will be based on the key dress forms of three pivotal periods: the 1920s, 1940s, and 1960s in accordance with their structures and cutting methods. The platform will comprise five core modules: a tool and machine library, a process library, an interaction library, a design material library, and a pattern library [19]. Designed with dynamic replication and data-driven approaches, as illustrated in Fig. 1, the platform aims to systematically document the material foundations and tacit knowledge of *Hong Kong Cheongsam Making Technique* through technological means, thereby supporting its preservation, education, and innovation.

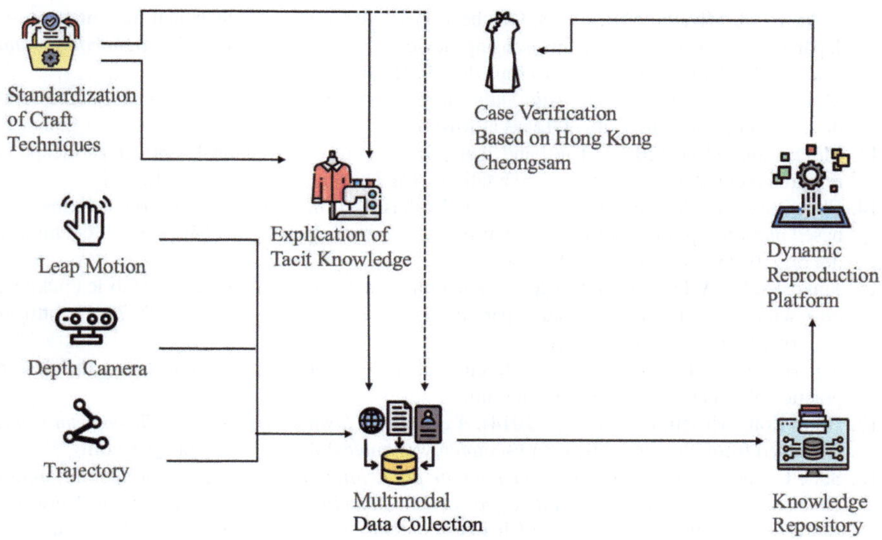

Fig. 1 The research structure and methodology

References

1. UNESCO. (2003). *Convention for the Safeguarding of the Intangible Cultural Heritage*. Retrieved December 13, 2024, from https://ich.unesco.org/en/convention
2. Inglehart, R., & Baker, W. (2000). Modernization, cultural change, and the persistence of traditional values. *American Sociological Review, 65*(1), 19–51. https://doi.org/10.2307/2657288
3. Yang, Y., Shafi, M., Xia, S., & Ruo, Y. (2018). Preservation of cultural heritage embodied in traditional crafts in the developing countries: A case study of Pakistani handicraft industry. *Sustainability, 10*(5), 1336. https://doi.org/10.3390/su10051336
4. McCullough, M. (1998). *Abstracting craft: The practiced digital hand.* MIT Press.
5. Skublewska-Paszkowska, M., Milosz, M., Powroznik, P., & Lukasik, E. (2022). 3D technologies for intangible cultural heritage preservation—Literature review for selected databases. *Journal of Cultural Heritage, 57*, 234–245. https://doi.org/10.1016/j.culher.2022.03.015
6. Kim, S., Im, D., & Lee, J. (2019). Utility of digital technologies for the sustainability of intangible cultural heritage (ICH) in Korea. *Sustainability, 11*(21), 6117. https://doi.org/10.3390/su11216117
7. Seo, J., Starbuck, R., Han, S., Lee, S. H., & Armstrong, T. J. (2014). Dynamic biomechanical analysis for construction tasks using motion data from vision-based motion capture approaches. In *Computing in civil and building engineering* (pp. 1005–1012). American Society of Civil Engineers. https://doi.org/10.1061/9780784413616.125
8. Wang, H., Liu, Y., & Chen, W. (2010). Uncalibrated visual tracking control without visual velocity. *IEEE Transactions on Control Systems Technology, 18*(4), 728–735. https://doi.org/10.1109/TCST.2009.2023665
9. Zhao, G., Zan, H., Di, B., Zhu, W., & Yu, Y. (2018). Research on virtual reconstruction technology of Tujia brocade handcrafts. *3D Research, 9*(1), 54. https://doi.org/10.1007/s13319-018-0206-7
10. Ma, J. J. (2023). Traditional fashion practice and cultural sustainability: A case study of NUBI in Korea. *Fashion Practice, 15*(1), 64–90.

11. Aoki, R., & Miyamoto, R. (2018, October). Problems in three-dimensional measurement of Japanese kenjutsu using existing sensing devices. In *2018 Metrology for Archaeology and Cultural Heritage (MetroArchaeo)* (pp. 78–83). IEEE.
12. Motro, M. J. (2019). *Probabilistic multi-object tracking for autonomous vehicles* [Doctoral dissertation]. The University of Texas at Austin.
13. McPherson, M. J. (2022). The hand that plied the needle: Making historical garments as research methodology [Doctoral dissertation]. *The University of.* Nebraska-Lincoln.
14. Chatzitofis, A., Zarpalas, D., Daras, P., & Kollias, S. (2021). DeMoCap: Low-cost marker-based motion capture. *International Journal of Computer Vision, 129*(12), 3338–3366. https://doi.org/10.1007/s11263-021-01526-z
15. Jankoska, M., & Demboski, G. (2017). The influence of the sewing speed and fabric thickness on sewing machine stitch formation parameters. *Advanced Technologies, 6*(2), 72–77. https://doi.org/10.5937/savteh1702072j
16. Ng, H. (2023). Digitalized intangible cultural heritage preservation–reinventing the design practice of Hong Kong men's cheongsam.
17. Hong Kong Museum of History. (2014). *A century of fashion: Hong Kong Cheongsam story.* Retrieved from https://hk.history.museum/en/web/mh/exhibition/2014_past_01.html
18. State Council. (2021, May 24). *Notice on the publication of the fifth batch of national intangible cultural heritage representative project list.* China Intangible Cultural Heritage Network. Retrieved from https://www.gov.cn/zhengce/content/2021-06/10/content_5616457.html
19. Büttner, J., Martinetz, J., El-Hajj, H., & Valleriani, M. (2022). Cordeep and the Sacrobosco dataset: Detection of visual elements in historical documents. *Journal of Imaging, 8*(10), 285. https://doi.org/10.3390/jimaging8100285

[illegible]

[illegible]
[illegible] productSafety [illegible]

[illegible]
[illegible]
[illegible] Customer [illegible]
[illegible] 3, 69115 Heidelberg, [illegible]
[illegible]

MIX
Papier aus verantwortungsvollen Quellen
Paper from responsible sources
FSC® C105338

If you have any concerns about our products,
you can contact us on
ProductSafety@springernature.com

In case Publisher is established outside the EU,
the EU authorized representative is:
Springer Nature Customer Service Center GmbH
Europaplatz 3, 69115 Heidelberg, Germany

Printed by Libri Plureos GmbH
in Hamburg, Germany